Unmasking Masculinities

Sara Miller McCune founded SAGE Publishing in 1965 to support the dissemination of usable knowledge and educate a global community. SAGE publishes more than 1000 journals and over 800 new books each year, spanning a wide range of subject areas. Our growing selection of library products includes archives, data, case studies and video. SAGE remains majority owned by our founder and after her lifetime will become owned by a charitable trust that secures the company's continued independence.

Los Angeles | London | New Delhi | Singapore | Washington DC | Melbourne

Unmasking Masculinities

Men and Society

Editors

Edward W. Morris
University of Kentucky

Freeden Blume Oeur
Tufts University

Los Angeles | London | New Delhi
Singapore | Washington DC | Melbourne

FOR INFORMATION:

SAGE Publications, Inc.
2455 Teller Road
Thousand Oaks, California 91320
E-mail: order@sagepub.com

SAGE Publications Ltd.
1 Oliver's Yard
55 City Road
London, EC1Y 1SP
United Kingdom

SAGE Publications India Pvt. Ltd.
B 1/I 1 Mohan Cooperative Industrial Area
Mathura Road, New Delhi 110 044
India

SAGE Publications Asia-Pacific Pte. Ltd.
3 Church Street
#10-04 Samsung Hub
Singapore 049483

Printed in the United States of America

ISBN 978-1-5063-2707-5

This book is printed on acid-free paper.

Acquisitions Editor: Joshua Perigo
Editorial Assistant: Alexandra Randall
Production Editor: Laureen Gleason
Typesetter: Hurix Digital
Proofreader: Talia Greenberg
Cover Designer: Michael Dubowe
Marketing Manager: Kara Kindstrom

SUSTAINABLE FORESTRY INITIATIVE
Certified Chain of Custody
Promoting Sustainable Forestry
www.sfiprogram.org
SFI-01268
SFI label applies to text stock

17 18 19 20 21 10 9 8 7 6 5 4 3 2 1

Contents

PART VII. VIOLENCE AND RESISTANCE   391

Introduction by Edward W. Morris and Freeden Blume Oeur

About the Editors

Edward W. Morris is an Associate Professor of Sociology at the University of Kentucky. He received his Ph.D. from the University of Texas at Austin. He teaches courses in Sociological Theory, Sociology of Education, Race and Ethnicity, and Masculinity. His research focuses on race, class, and gender inequality in education. He has served as a consultant for school districts and community organizations dedicated to social justice in education and the juvenile justice system. He is the author of *Learning the Hard Way: Masculinity, Place, and the Gender Gap in Education* (2012) and *An Unexpected Minority: White Kids in an Urban School* (2006).

Freeden Blume Oeur is an Assistant Professor of Sociology at Tufts University. He earned his Ph.D. from the University of California at Berkeley. His research examines the connections among neoliberalism, black politics, and masculine power. Blume Oeur is the author of the forthcoming book *Black Boys Apart: Racial Uplift and Respectability in All-Male Public Schools*.

Introduction

Power, Paradox, and Change

Edward W. Morris and Freeden Blume Oeur

Masculinity is everywhere, at the same time that it is nowhere.

What do we mean by this? Consider that men hold a firm grip on positions of power and influence. Every United States president has been a man. In 2016, the 10 wealthiest people in the United States were all men, and just 4% of Fortune 500 CEOs were women (Zarya 2016). Hollywood also remains a men's club. Coincidentally, only 4% of the top 1,000 grossing films between 2007 and 2016 were directed by women (Smith, Pieper, and Choueiti 2017). Men not only produce these cultural narratives behind the scenes, but do most of the talking on screen.[1] (Even in Disney blockbusters with female lead characters, such as *Mulan* and *Pocahontas*, male characters do the vast majority of the talking.) In other areas of popular entertainment, such as sports, men also dominate and wield enormous symbolic power. Millions of viewers tune in each year to watch the Super Bowl and the NCAA men's basketball tournament. But how many people do you know who host parties or follow tournament brackets for *women's* sporting events? Even fields with higher concentrations of women, such as education, reveal an uncanny male dominance in positions of authority. Men who enter women-dominated professions have the luxury of riding a "glass escalator" to better-paying and higher-ranking positions within those fields (Williams 2013). While 76% of public school teachers nationwide are women, over three-quarters of all district superintendents are men (Superville 2016).

Although there are exceptions, men worldwide continue to control the enactment and enforcement of national and international law; the structure of economic institutions and distribution of capital; and the production and dissemination of intellectual and cultural knowledge. Yet masculinity is also *nowhere*. That is because we rarely understand these facts in terms of *gender*. That is, we evaluate men as individuals and not as members of a gender category. This disassociation of gender from men has important implications. For one, it absolves men from confronting gender privilege and power. For example, the anti-violence activist Jackson Katz explains how the well-known phrase "violence against women" strangely erases men from violent relationships. Men in fact commit the overwhelming majority of gender-based violence; thus we should emphasize "*men's* violence against women."[2] Neglecting to name men implicitly frames gender issues as *women's* issues rather than men's issues. Yet violence against women is a problem perpetrated by men, which must be confronted by men. Bringing men into this discussion is a crucial step toward addressing the roots of violence against women (as well as against other men) and other features of gender inequality.

The detachment of men from gender also perpetuates the idea that men and masculinity are unmarked categories (Kimmel 1997). Take a moment to scan the "Pointlessly Gendered Products" page on the popular teaching website "Sociological Images." There you will find many pictures of amusingly gendered products that people have come across in stores. There are, for example, *women's* hand tools, *women's* ear plugs, and even *women's* pens.[3] "Normal" hand tools, ear plugs, and pens are for men and boys: the default gender category. This all may seem trivial, but oftentimes the detachment of men from gender has consequences for power relations. For example, children, both boys and girls, tend to sketch pictures of men when asked to draw a "scientist" or a "doctor" (Finson 2002). This reveals how doctors and scientists, like other high-status positions, behaviors, and institutions, are implicitly coded as masculine. What the children in that study assume, of course, is *male* scientist and *male* doctor, but those descriptors go unnamed. Sports fans may have also noticed that it is common for the sports media to explicitly mention *female* athletes and *women's* basketball.

Apart from elite positions, taken-for-granted norms of masculinity circulate throughout societal institutions and ideological systems, from who sits at the head of the table during family dinner, to characterizing god as male in monotheistic religions, to sexually aggressive "locker room" banter among men in workplaces. In order to promote more balanced, equal lives for everyone, it is necessary to expose and question the hidden power of masculine norms in our daily lives. Masculinity can be characterized as a mask, or a narrow set of expectations that harms young men and those around them. We therefore invite readers to *unmask masculinity*.[4]

The language that we use is important, too. While we emphasize the need to reveal what is "behind" masculinity, we recognize that the "mask" metaphor is limiting, despite its captivating imagery. Defining masculinity is a slippery proposition, but researchers have moved beyond the facile notion that gender is something that can be "worn" or taken on or off, to examine how gender is embedded in social relations, institutions, and historical trajectories.[5] With that in mind, this book is intended to be an accessible introduction to cutting-edge scholarship in critical masculinity studies. We begin with the proposition that it is impossible to understand gender and gender inequality without systematically questioning, researching, and confronting masculinity. We invite you to follow us in a journey through this engaging and vibrant field: to explore where masculinity comes from, how it is built, how it maintains power, how it is contradictory and paradoxical, and how it might be resisted and transformed for the better.

What Is Masculinity?

At first glance, this question seems straightforward. Masculinity is how men behave. But this explanation loses its simplicity upon closer inspection. A majority of famous visual artists are men, but people generally do not consider art a highly masculine pursuit. Girls now compete in equal numbers to boys in recreational sports, yet people continue to associate athletic power and skill with masculinity. Thus, masculinity cannot be defined simply by pointing to what men do, or what women do not do. Men and boys also vary in the degree to which they signify masculinity. Some men may be seen as effeminate "girly men" lacking in masculinity. Other men may be viewed as overly masculine brutes. The meanings behind these configurations of manhood are further shaped by racial and ethnic histories, as well as other forms of collective identity. Women can express qualities associated with masculinity, such as with female mixed martial arts fighters, or women who present as "butch" (Halberstam 1998). Moreover, what counts as masculinity is volatile and subject to change.

If we start with the basic idea that masculinity refers to a set expectations that guide behavior, it does not follow that all male-bodied people will practice that behavior. It does mean, however, that men and boys can be penalized (ostracized, ridiculed, or denied access to institutions) for failing to live up to expectations. Moreover, it does not mean that women cannot ascribe to masculine expectations. Women may occasionally (but not universally) adopt practices culturally associated with masculinity, but still be understood as women. In other instances, women may be held accountable or punished for not "doing gender" appropriately (West and Zimmerman 1987). And while masculine behaviors grant power and privilege, they also do great harm to men and women.

Masculinity can be distinguished from the male body and the category of men, although all concepts are closely entwined. Masculinity can be seen as the interactional "work" someone does in order to be interpreted as a man (West and Zimmerman 1987). As Douglas Schrock and Michael Schwalbe (2009) describe in Section I of this volume, a male body is neither necessary nor sufficient to claim status within the category of men (although it is an asset in this endeavor). Some men may possess a male body, but be seen as insufficiently or inappropriately manly. Some biological women may possess a female-sexed body, but present themselves as sufficiently and appropriately manly, such as transmen. Bodies are used as resources or strategies for the performance of masculinity, but masculinity is not itself reducible to the biological body.

Masculinity is, decisively, a *social construct*. This means that masculinity is determined not by biology or physiology, but by the structure of social relations and cultural norms. As leading neuroscientist Lise Eliot (2009) has shown, there are minute differences between male and female brains, but these alone cannot explain differences in power between men and women. Rather, manhood is socially patterned at multiple levels: at the level of face-to-face interactions (e.g., how people talk with one another, and people's quotidian routines), institutions (e.g., regulations, traditions, and cultural rituals), and the global (e.g., international politics and the relationships between nation-states). Or as Lynne Segal (1993:629) has written, masculinity "condenses, above all, the cultural reality of women's subordination," a reality visible in each "institution of social, economic, and political power."

The evidence shows that prevailing definitions of what it means to be a man have varied across time and across cultures. For example, it might surprise you that cheerleading was once considered a manly activity (Adams and Bettis 2003). At the turn of the 20th century, many college campuses were the exclusive domain of white male elites. In fact, women were barred from participating in many American college cheerleading squads until the 1930s. Cheerleading signified school solidarity and male camaraderie. It was only after World War II, as universities began to accept more women and more students from lower economic classes, that cheerleading began to evolve and include women. Cheerleading became more feminine as male sports grew in prominence, which reinforced a clear division of labor on the sports field. Male cheerleaders continue to populate college squads today, but cheerleading, especially at high school and professional levels, is now primarily associated with women.

As with cheerleading, fashions considered indisputably feminine today began as masculine. High-heeled shoes and long hair serve as one fascinating example. In 16th-century Europe, both represented paragons of masculinity.[6] High heels actually originated at this time as something to be worn by the French male aristocracy. Manly power here was tied strongly to social status. High heels, in their impracticality, announced that the wearer did not need to work (with the added benefit of enhancing physical stature). For male members of the elite, this signified their status as the most powerful men (Barber 2016). Women in aristocratic circles eventually took to wearing the shoes as well; but once they did men ceased to do so, and high heels carried status for women but not men. These examples demonstrate that what counts as masculine and feminine is arbitrary, or simply symbolic boundaries drawn to reproduce presumed gender differences. Thus, while there is nothing essential or natural about gender, social distinctions between masculinity and femininity, or among various configurations of manhood, these distinctions are real in their consequences. They become reproduced over time in laws, customs, popular discourses, and memories. When women begin to encroach on manly practices and spaces, this threatens the power of men, prompting reactionary measures against women or the redefinition of masculinity itself (Kimmel 2012; Schrock and Schwalbe 2009).

Masculinity also varies across cultural spaces. As you will see in this book, ideals of masculinity vary across nations, and across subgroups within nations. Being a man in rural Appalachia is very different than being a man in urban Japan. For this reason, this book emphasizes a cross-cultural and intersectional approach to masculinity. A cross-cultural lens reveals masculine variance, but also how relations of masculinity increasingly operate within the globalizing context of a world gender system (Connell 1998). An intersectional approach emphasizes how patterns of masculinity interact with other features of inequality and identity, such as race, class, gender, nation, age, and place (Cho, Williams, and McCall 2013). These approaches transform how masculinity is enacted and experienced. For example, while masculinity often serves as an advantage, for urban men of color the picture is more complex. Asserting gender and sexual power may win young men of color status among peers, but authorities punish them unduly for their presumed "hypermasculinity" and perceived criminality (Ferguson 2000; Rios 2011). In fact, police officers may humiliate and emasculate young men of color in a struggle for masculine domination.

Power, Paradox, and Change

Gendered patterns are woven into our social institutions and belief systems. People believe these patterns to be legitimate, or they appear like common sense and people do not think about them at all. Exposing the power and privilege that accompanies masculinity is a first step toward destabilizing it. Yet for men especially, this can feel threatening. As the masculinity scholar Raewyn Connell (2005:1808) has written, "men have a lot to lose from pursuing gender equality because men, collectively, continue to receive a patriarchal dividend," which refers to the various advantages men obtain from the overall subordination of women to men. Recent campaigns have brought attention to what might otherwise appear to be innocuous behaviors, including "mansplaining" and "manspreading," which refer, respectively, to how men speak to others (especially women) in a patronizing manner, and how men spread out their arms and legs to monopolize physical spaces. Men may scoff at such accusations and brush them off as no big deal, but they are examples of how men accumulate a patriarchal dividend without being aware of their privilege. At the same time, protecting privilege can have damaging consequences. White men in varied circumstances—from members of father's groups who are recently divorced, to teenage perpetrators of mass school shootings—express an "aggrieved entitlement" (Kimmel 2013) and lash out at women and feminists for having taken away what they feel is rightfully theirs.

But exposing masculinity can also be transformative for children, women, and entire communities. And for men, engaging in dialogue about masculinity can be liberating. It may require a refusal of privilege, but this refusal opens new windows into developing emotional intelligence, accepting vulnerability, and becoming part of a more egalitarian future. At the same time, a "hybrid masculinities" framework, which various contributors will touch on in this volume, cautions that claims of gender progress may hide the reproduction of deeper systems of oppression and power.

At the heart of masculinity lies a paradox: masculinity is powerful, yet fragile. Men are supposed to be leaders: physically strong, emotionally stoic, financially secure, and successful. Men are supposed to be the smartest, the fastest, the most visionary.

Virtually all qualities conventionally applied to masculinity symbolize power, control, and success. Yet, as several readings in this book demonstrate, this veneer of power masks a hidden insecurity. As Michael Kimmel (2012:5) states, "Throughout American history… men have been afraid of not measuring up to some vaguely defined notions of what it means to be a man." In fact, when men feel the least powerful and the least manly, they are the most likely to hurt themselves and others in attempts to reclaim power and manhood. A key task of this volume is to expose and break the assumptive ties between masculinity and power. Men are the gatekeepers of gender inequality, and thus can help unlock the unequal gender system that entraps so many. In what follows, we trace the social construction of masculinity and provide an overview of different ways scholars have conceptualized and studied masculinity. Ultimately, we hope to equip readers with the intellectual tools to expose and change the unequal and one-dimensional definitions of current masculinity.

Theorizing Men and Masculinity

Masculinity has only been a vibrant topic of study in the past three decades, but social scientists have tried to explain men and gender for much longer. Among the first explanations emerged from *functionalism*, a conceptual framework that dominated in the first half of the 20th century and should be familiar to most students who have taken an introductory Sociology or Anthropology course. Functionalist theorists such as Émile Durkheim, Robert Merton, and Bronislaw Malinoskwi sought in their work "to relate the parts of the society to the whole" and "to relate one part to another" (Davis 1959:738). Parts and people in society were endowed with just that—a function—and they together formed an integrated whole. The social theorist Talcott Parsons used this basic framework to explain differences between men and women within the nuclear family, in what became the basis for "sex role theory." According to this theory, women possess an "expressive role" that was needed to manage relations within the home, while men possess an "instrumental role" required for managing relations between the family and the rest of society (Parsons and Bale 1955). This theory provided a way of thinking about how families socialize children into their appropriate roles, which become so deeply internalized in individuals—so a part of who they are—that they become something akin to a gender personality.

Sex role research, with a focus on the "cultural contradictions" between women's "roles" in the workplace and the family, persisted through the 1970s, but by this point feminist scholars had grown skeptical of this framing (for a review, see Hochschild 1973). On the one hand, sex role theory was unable to account for the diversity of social life; it assumed "too much consistency to social expectations, too much homogeneity to social life" (Segal 1993:627). The roles were too neat and tidy, and inappropriately assumed a universal experience of gender. On the other hand, sex role theory fell flat when it came to issues of power. As Judith Stacey and Barrie Thorne (1985) observed, sex role theory focused on consensus among individuals at the expense of how social structures help to perpetuate forms of gender inequality. Or as Tim Carrigan and his colleagues argued in a groundbreaking 1985 article, sex role theory could not account for how roles created conflict: how most men, for example, *fail* to live up to their gendered role expectations, and the often destructive consequences that follow. Moreover, these scholars made clear that theories of masculinity should build on the core feminist observation of relations of domination between men and women.

Research on masculinity took a leap forward with the work of Raewyn Connell (1987; 2005). The Australian sociologist developed a sophisticated theoretical architecture that she and her colleagues have revised over the years, and continues to impact masculinities research far and wide (see Connell and Messerschmidt 2005). Connell provided a way of thinking about masculinity as a struggle for power. Building on the concept of *hegemony*, as it was theorized by the Marxist intellectual Antonio Gramsci, Connell argued that there is a hegemonic, or dominant form, of masculinity that rests atop a hierarchy of *multiple masculinities*. Or as Connell (2005:77) has written, hegemonic masculinity represents "[t]he configuration of gender practice which embodies the currently accepted answer to the problem of the legitimacy of patriarchy, which guarantees (or is taken to guarantee) the dominant position of men and the subordination of women." Few men ever achieve this cultural ideal or possess the institutional power that accompanies it, but hegemonic masculinity regulates other configurations of masculine practice that are marginalized by race, sexuality, ability, and other lines of difference. Connell's framework therefore helped to bridge the study of masculinity with intersectional research aimed at interrogating the interlocking nature of oppressions.

In 2009, the sociologists Douglas Schrock and Michael Schwalbe took stock of the first two decades of research on masculinities. As they saw it, the field had made important advances, but suffered from what they call a "men *and*" pattern. Wide-ranging research had examined topics such as men *and* sexuality, men *and* aging, and men *and* crime. But in doing so—in categorizing the seemingly endless groups of men, or what they call the "problems with plurality"—the field of masculinity research had lost sight of a key contribution of early studies: that masculinity is about securing and protecting power. Schrock and Schwalbe have asked scholars and students to focus again on what men and boys *do* (West and Zimmerman 1987). This "doing" they termed "manhood acts," which "are aimed at claiming privilege, eliciting deference, and resisting exploitation" (2009:281). A number of readings in this volume make use of this framework to show how men compensate for injured masculine selves with particular forms of manhood acts.

Just as Schrock and Schwalbe sought to re-orient the field with their concept of "manhood acts," a new way of understanding masculinity emerged. "Inclusive masculinity" posed a challenge to both hegemonic masculinity theory and manhood acts (Anderson 2009; McCormack 2013). According to this framework, more and more young men have demonstrated "inclusive" behaviors in the past several decades. For instance, they reject homophobic sentiments and are more accepting of gay classmates and teammates. In a period of declining "homohysteria," or strong anti-gay sentiments, young men also demonstrate more of a willingness to be emotionally and physically close (for example, hug and kiss) other young men. Researchers in this area of work have argued that team sports especially have come to reject "orthodox" forms of masculinity grounded in homophobia, aggression, and violence.

One final theoretical framework is important for this volume. Just as inclusive masculinity has challenged previous frameworks and asked readers to consider a more optimistic view of gender relations, a "hybrid masculinities" framework has been quite skeptical of inclusive masculinity (Bridges 2014; Bridges and Pascoe 2014). According to these researchers, transformations in men's opinions, attitudes, and appearances may not necessarily signal real change. Instead, men may draw on elements of marginalized and stigmatized others (e.g., a gay identity, femininity) and softer forms of expression (e.g., emotional expressiveness) in order to *maintain* gender inequality and (heterosexual) men's power over others. A hybrid masculinities perspective, therefore, asks readers to consider how masculine power does not operate as in a top-down and clearly authoritative fashion, but recruits many men to act in strategic and subtle ways that disguise the ongoing reproduction of hegemonic masculinity (Demetriou 2001).

What to Expect in This Book

The 35 readings in this volume include classic texts in the field; several innovative, cutting-edge readings; and a number of exciting original contributions. The readings are broken up into seven sections. Section I, "Theories of Masculinity," expands on our brief discussion above, and includes readings on several theoretical frameworks in the study of men and masculinity, including hegemonic masculinity, manhood acts, inclusive masculinity, and hybrid masculinities. The remaining six sections include readings that adopt, build on, and challenge these theories. Keep these general questions in mind as you read:

■ How does the author or authors use a particular conceptual framework to explain the case study at hand? How might another framework help to illuminate or even challenge the reading's data?

- How does the reading define masculinity?
- How does this study account or fail to account for power?
- How does the reading account for the strength of masculinity? And its fragility?
- How does the study theorize a change in gender relations? Or how might the reading cast doubt on improving gender relations?

The next section, "Representations and Media," includes a set of readings that examines how spaces such as films, commercials, and social media prop up dominant formations of masculinity and often aggravate gender inequalities. You'll read about how popular Pixar movies have pushed a "new man" discourse, and how an online leak of nude photos of female celebrities enabled a virtual community of anonymous Twitter users to engage in a particularly insidious form of masculine domination. The book then switches gears to the topic of "Politics and Nationhood" in Section III. This set of readings will show how presidents to gun-carrying men in Detroit view themselves as protectors of the nation. You'll also read about the unique case of Barack Obama, who faced specific challenges as a black man in the nation's highest office, and who the author provocatively suggests has performed a "unisex" identity.

In Section IV, "Masculine Strategies," you will consider how a diverse group of men use varied strategies to secure a masculine self. They include men in Japan who have seen the decline of a once-dominant "salaryman" masculinity, to self-identified "nerds" who participate in a live-action role-playing club. The next section, "Relationships and Intimacy," includes readings that cover topics such as why well-to-do young men engage in "hooking up" over having serious relationships, to how black men on college campuses navigate gender and racial stereotypes in their interracial relationships. Section VI, "Shifting Masculinities," asks whether gender transgressions constitute real, progressive change in gender relations. While one reading argues that male college players evince more inclusive and physical and emotionally close relationships, a second reading in this section considers how a similar population—young white men—identify with a gay discourse, but in a manner that does little to destabilize gender and sexual inequality. The last section, "Violence and Resistance," links to several other sections in the text, and considers how violence structures masculine identities and gendered relationships. They include a life-history analysis of feminist men who participate in anti-violence work, and a chapter on the work of fighting and preventing sexual assault on college campuses.

Each section begins with a brief introduction that should help guide you through the readings. These introductions also contain a series of "questions to ponder" that cover the readings in that section, and occasionally ask you to make connections across sections. As you move throughout the volume, also try and identify readings that draw on similar theoretical frameworks and define masculinity in similar ways. Each section also lists a number of key concepts that you can be on the lookout for as you read and unmask masculinity.

Notes

1. The success of the woman-directed *Wonder Woman* in 2017 is a notable exception that proves this rule. Among the top 100 films in 2015, only 32 featured a female lead or co-lead, and only 31% of the characters with speaking roles in these films were women (Smith, Choueiti, and Pieper 2016). The "Bechdel test" has been used to measure sexism and gender inequality in films. To pass, a film needs to fulfill three requirements. It has to feature (1) at least two women (2) who talk to each other about (3) something besides a man. According to a website dedicated to tracking and testing these films (http://bechdeltest.com), 40% of some 7,000 films fail the Bechdel test (Friedman, Daniels, and Blinderman 2017).

2. See Katz's Ted Talk at https://www.ted.com/talks/jackson_katz_violence_against_women_it_s_a_men_s_issue.

3. See https://www.pinterest.com/socimages/pointlessly-gendered-products. Of course, many products today are marketed to both men and women, and boys and girls. Often these products use stereotypical images and colors, and are intended to "toughen up" a product for men. Why drink sangria when you can drink mangria? Have a donut when you can eat a bronut? But there are, quite literally, important hidden costs to the consumption of gendered products. A product targeted to women (e.g., face moisturizer) often costs more than the equivalent product for men. This has been called a "woman tax" (Willett 2015).

4. See Jennifer Seibel Newsome's 2015 documentary *The Mask You Live In*. Seibel chose a title that sounds like "masculine." Michael Kimmel, the author of readings no. 14 and no. 21 in this volume, is interviewed in the film. Kimmel describes how the preeminent emotion associated with masculinity is anxiety. Never secure, boys and men feel constant pressure to prove their masculinity.

5. The idea that individuals wear masks in face-to-face interaction with others has its roots in the influential sociology of Erving Goffman (1970). A dramaturgical approach claims that people often attempt to conceal their authentic self behind masks.

6. See Lisa Wade's post "From Manly to Sexy: The History of the High Heel" (February 5, 2013) at https://thesocietypages.org/socimages/2013/02/05/from-manly-to-sexy-the-history-of-the-high-heel.

References

Adams, Natalie, and Pamela Bettis. 2003. "Commanding the Room in Short Skirts: Cheering as the Embodiment of Ideal Girlhood." *Gender and Society* 17:73–91.

Anderson, Eric. 2010. *Inclusive Masculinity: The Changing Nature of Masculinities*. London: Routledge.

Barber, Kristen. 2016. *Styling Masculinity: Gender, Class, and Inequality in the Men's Grooming Industry*. New Brunswick, NJ: Rutgers University Press.

Bridges, Tristan. 2014. "A Very 'Gay' Straight? Hybrid Masculinities, Sexual Aesthetics, and the Changing Relationship between Masculinity and Homophobia." *Gender & Society* 28(1):58–82.

Bridges, Tristan, and C. J. Pascoe. 2014. "Hybrid Masculinities: New Directions in the Sociology of Men and Masculinities." *Sociology Compass* 8(3):246–258.

Carrigan, Tim, Bob Connell, and John Lee. 1985. "Toward a New Sociology of Masculinity." *Theory and Society* 14(5):551–604.

Cho, Sumi, Kimberle Crenshaw, and Leslie McCall. 2013. "Toward a Field of Intersectionality Studies: Theory, Applications, and Praxis." *Signs* 38(4):785–810.

Connell, R. W. 1998. "Masculinities and Globalization." *Men and Masculinities* 1:3–23.

Connell, R. W. 2005. "Change among the Gatekeepers: Men, Masculinities, and Gender Equality in the Global Arena." *Signs: Journal of Women in Culture and Society* 30(3):1801–1825.

Connell, R. W. 2005. *Masculinities*. 2nd ed. Berkeley, CA: University of California Press.

Connell, R. W., and James W. Messerschmidt. 2005. "Hegemonic Masculinity: Rethinking the Concept." *Gender & Society* 19(6):829–859.

Davis, Kingsley. 1959. "The Myth of Functional Analysis as a Special Method in Sociology and Anthropology." *American Sociological Review* 24(6):757–772.

Demetriou, Demetrakis Z. 2001. "Connell's Concept of Hegemonic Masculinity: A Critique." *Theory and Society* 30(3):337–361.

Eliot, Lise. 2009. *Pink Brain, Blue Brain: How Small Differences Grow into Troublesome Gaps—and What We Can Do About It*. New York: Houghton Mifflin Harcourt.

Ferguson, Ann. 2000. *Bad Boys: Public Schools in the Making of Black Masculinity*. Ann Arbor: University of Michigan Press.

Finson, Kevin D. 2002. "Drawing a Scientist: What We Do and Do Not Know after Fifty Years of Drawings." *School Science and Mathematics* 102: 335–345.

Friedman, Lyle, Matt Daniels, and Ilia Blinderman. n.d. "Hollywood's Gender Divide and Its Effect on Films." The Pudding. Available at: https://pudding.cool/2017/03/bechdel.

Goffman, Erving. 1970. *Strategic Interaction*. Philadelphia: University of Pennsylvania Press.

Halberstam, J. Jack. 1998. *Female Masculinity*. Durham, N.C.: Duke University Press.

Hochschild, Arlie Russell. 1973. "A Review of Sex Role Research." *American Journal of Sociology* 78(4): 1011–1029.

Kimmel, Michael. 1997. "Integrating Men into the Curriculum." *Duke Journal of Law and Policy* 4:181–195.

Kimmel, Michael. 2012. *Manhood in America: A Cultural History*, 3rd edition. New York: Oxford University Press.

Kimmel, Michael. 2013. *Angry White Men: American Masculinity at the End of an Era*. New York: Nation Books.

McCormack, Mark. 2013. *The Declining Significance of Homophobia*. Oxford: Oxford University Press.

Parsons, Talcott, and Robert Bales. 1955. *Family Socialization and Interaction Process*. New York: Free Press.

Rios, Victor M. 2011. *Punished: Policing the Lives of Black and Latino Boys*. New York: New York University Press.

Schrock, Douglas, and Michael Schwalbe. 2009. "Men, Masculinity, and Manhood Acts." *Annual Review of Sociology* 35:277–295.

Segal, Lynne. 1993. "Changing Men: Masculinities in Context." *Theory and Society* 22 (5):625–641.

Smith, Stacey L., Marc Choueiti, and Katherine Pieper. 2016. "Inequality in 800 Popular Films: Examining Portrayals of Gender, Race/Ethnicity, LGBT, and Disability from 2007–2015." Los Angeles, CA: Media, Diversity, and Social Change Initiative, University of Southern California.

Smith, Stacey L., Katherine Pieper, and Marc Choueiti. 2017. "Inequality in the Director's Chair: Gender, Race, and Age of Film Directors across 1,000 Films, 2007–2016." Los Angeles, CA: Media, Diversity, and Social Change Initiative, University of Southern California.

Stacey, Judith, and Barrie Thorne. 1985. "The Missing Feminist Revolution in Sociology." *Social Problems* 32(4):301–316.

Superville, Denisa. 2016. "Few Women Run the Nation's School Districts. Why?" PBS News Hour. December 30. Available at: http://www.pbs.org/newshour/updates/women-run-nations-school-districts.

West, Candace, and Don H. Zimmerman. 1987. "Doing Gender." *Gender & Society* 1:125–151.

Willett, Megan. 2015. "Here's Proof Women Pay More for the Same Products Men Buy." *Business Insider*. April 14. Available at: http://www.businessinsider.com/womens-products-more-expensive-than-mens-2015-4.

Williams, Christine L. 2013. "The Glass Escalator, Revisited: Gender Inequality in Neoliberal Times." *Gender & Society*.

Zarya, Valentina. 2016. "The Percentage of Female CEOs in the Fortune 500 Drops to 4%." *Fortune.com*. June 6. Available at: http://fortune.com/2016/06/06/women-ceos-fortune-500-2016.

PART I

Theories of Masculinity

As we described in the Introduction to *Unmasking Masculinities*, the social scientific study of masculinity gained traction as research began to move beyond the limitations of sex role theory. Feminist scholars observed that this theory, associated with the sociologist Talcott Parsons, mistakenly assumed a universal experience of gender socialization and offered too-neat a picture of the sexual division of labor within families. Most important, however, was that sex role theory largely ignored issues of power. In a pioneering 1985 article, Tim Carrigan, Bob Connell, and John Lee wrote that "a strong radical analysis of masculinity" had become possible (552). What Carrigan and his colleagues meant was that, at a minimum, explanations had to move beyond mere discussions of *men* to feminist considerations of *masculinity* as a "political order" that structures relations of domination between men and women, as well as among groups of men. Therefore, theorizing masculinity entails exposing the specific character of relations of domination and of helping to pave the way to social change.

This section builds on our brief foray into theorizing masculinities in the Introduction. These readings will introduce you to four explanations of men, masculinity, and gendered power: hegemonic masculinity, manhood acts, inclusive masculinity, and hybrid masculinities. You will find that later chapters in this volume often draw on one or more of these frameworks to make sense of a wide range of gendered phenomena, groups of men and women, and institutional arrangements. As you continue on in this book, we think it is helpful to return often to the readings in this section: to see how researchers engage these frameworks and why they use certain theories, to draw your own connections between theories and case studies, and to develop your own repertoire of concepts to build on and critically evaluate the conclusions the authors reach.

The first reading, by Raewyn Connell, "The Social Organization of Masculinity," is an excerpt from the sociologist's groundbreaking text, *Masculinities*.[1] In this reading, Connell develops a comprehensive framework that is now ubiquitous in research on men and manhood. This framework posits a gender order with a multiplicity of masculinities. As Connell writes, a hegemonic masculinity is a "culturally exalted" manhood that defends the legitimacy of patriarchy. In specific contexts, a hegemonic masculinity assumes a dominant position over complicit, subordinate, and marginalized masculinities. Reading no. 2, by Sharon Bird, "Welcome to the Men's Club," explains how interactions among heterosexual men, or homosocial relations, help to maintain hegemonic masculinity. Drawing on interviews, Bird identifies three ways this maintenance occurs: emotional detachment, aggressive competition among men, and the sexual objectification of women.

Reading no. 3, "Men, Masculinity, and Manhood Acts," by Douglas Schrock and Michael Schwalbe, evaluates the widespread use in research of hegemonic masculinity and the multiple masculinities model. According to the authors, the focus on plurality—of different categories of men—has had the unfortunate consequence of flattening considerations of power. The authors argue that, rather than searching for abstract types of masculinities, scholars should concentrate on how masculinity reproduces dominance on the "micro" level of everyday life. As a corrective, Schrock and Schwalbe offer "manhood acts" to re-focus attention on what men *do* to maintain gender privilege over women and other men. The chapters in *Unmasking Masculinities* that draw on the notion of "manhood acts" include reading no. 18 by James Martin and colleagues, on men who participate in fantasy role-playing; and reading no. 20 by Kumiko Nemoto, on Japanese men who embrace compensatory forms of manhood during a period of economic decline. The next reading (no. 4) by Eric Anderson, "Inclusive Masculinity Theory," charts a different path than the previous three readings. Having observed a cheerleading team, a fraternity, and a rugby squad, Anderson found that hegemonic masculinity could not account for the inclusive and "softer" forms of male interactions that are more accepting of effeminate behaviors and that exhibit a lack of homophobic attitudes. Anderson asks readers to consider the possibility of more egalitarian forms of masculinity, and in doing so challenges the dominance of hegemonic masculinity theory (and even the concept of manhood acts). Adi Adams's chapter (reading no. 28) uses ethnographic data of a men's college soccer team to support the notion of an inclusive masculinity.

In the final reading (no. 5) in this section, Tristan Bridges and C. J. Pascoe outline a theory that casts skepticism on inclusive masculinity. Like Anderson, they acknowledge that there are important transformations in contemporary masculinities. However, they suggest instead that these are merely superficial and do not constitute meaningful change. There are three characteristics of "hybrid" forms of masculinity: young men attempt to "discursively distance" themselves from dominant or traditional features of masculinity, they culturally appropriate or "strategically borrow" from marginalized others, and their actions serve to reproduce deeper structural gender inequalities. Several readings lend support to hybrid masculinities, including Michael A. Messner's analysis of how California governor Arnold Schwarzenegger embodied what Messner calls a "Kindergarten Commando" (reading no. 13), Bridges's own study of several groups of young men who identify features of themselves as "gay" (reading no. 30), and Richard Mora and Mary Christianakis's chapter analyzing sexual violence and a college men's group (reading no. 35).

Questions to Ponder

1. How do the notions of manhood acts, inclusive masculinity, and hybrid masculinities respond to, reinforce, or challenge Connell's formulation of hegemonic masculinity?

2. In your own experiences, at your schools, and elsewhere, where have you observed performances of masculinity that appear inclusive? Or gender relations that instead point to the existence of hybrid masculinities? Can inclusive and hybrid forms of masculinity co-exist?

3. While inclusive masculinity theory and the notion of hybrid masculinities arrive at different conclusions about contemporary shifts in masculinity, they both largely focus on young heterosexual (and therefore privileged) white men. How might theories help to explain the actions of non-white and less privileged groups of men?

4. The four frameworks discussed in this section together provide robust, if occasionally competing, ways of making sense of men and masculinity. What about them do you find convincing? And where do they fall short in helping to explain what you have observed about contemporary masculinities?

5. Manhood acts are typically small-scale or face-to-face interactions that reinforce relations of gender domination. How might these micro-processes reinforce larger patterns of male domination? Or how might institutions, laws, and other large-scale structures facilitate manhood acts?

Key Concepts

Hegemonic masculinity and multiple masculinities	Homosociality Hybrid masculinities	Inclusive masculinity Manhood acts

Note

1. A transwoman, Connell published under the first name Robert (Bob) early in her career, including in her co-authored 1985 article with Tim Carrigan and John Lee. Connell now uses the first name Raewyn, but her chapter in this section was originally published using the initials R. W.

Reference

Carrigan, Tim, Bob Connell, and John Lee. 1985. "Toward a New Sociology of Masculinity." *Theory and Society* 14(5):551–604.

CHAPTER 1

The Social Organization of Masculinity

Raewyn Connell

The task of this chapter is to set out a framework based on contemporary analyses of gender relations. This framework will provide a way of distinguishing types of masculinity, and of understanding the dynamics of change.

Defining Masculinity

All societies have cultural accounts of gender, but not all have the concept 'masculinity'. In its modern usage the term assumes that one's behaviour results from the type of person one is. That is to say, an unmasculine person would behave differently: being peaceable rather than violent, conciliatory rather than dominating, hardly able to kick a football, uninterested in sexual conquest, and so forth.

This conception presupposes a belief in individual difference and personal agency. In that sense it is built on the conception of individuality that developed in early-modern Europe with the growth of colonial empires and capitalist economic relations.

But the concept is also inherently relational. 'Masculinity' does not exist except in contrast with 'femininity'. A culture which does not treat women and men as bearers of polarized character types, at least in principle, does not have a concept of masculinity in the sense of modern European/American culture.

Historical research suggests that this was true of European culture itself before the eighteenth century. Women were certainly regarded as different from men, but different in the sense of being incomplete or inferior examples of the same character (for instance, having less of the faculty of reason). Women and men were not seen as bearers of qualitatively different characters; this conception accompanied the bourgeois ideology of 'separate spheres' in the nineteenth century.

In both respects our concept of masculinity seems to be a fairly recent historical product, a few hundred years old at most. In speaking of masculinity at all, then, we are 'doing gender' in a culturally specific way. This should be borne in mind with any claim to have discovered transhistorical truths about manhood and the masculine.

Definitions of masculinity have mostly taken our cultural standpoint for granted, but have followed different strategies to characterize the type of person who is masculine. Four main strategies have been followed; they are easily distinguished in terms of their logic, though often combined in practice.

SOURCE: Connell, R. (2005). The Social Organization of Masculinity. In *Masculinities*, 2nd ed. Oakland, CA: University of California Press. Reproduced with permission from the University of California Press.

EDITORS' NOTE: Although the author originally published this piece under the name R. W. Connell, we have attributed it to the name that she now uses, Raewyn Connell.

Essentialist definitions usually pick a feature that defines the core of the masculine, and hang an account of men's lives on that. Freud flirted with an essentialist definition when he equated masculinity with activity in contrast to feminine passivity—though he came to see that equation as oversimplified. Later authors' attempts to capture an essence of masculinity have been colourfully varied: risk-taking, responsibility, irresponsibility, aggression, Zeus energy . . . Perhaps the finest is the sociobiologist Lionel Tiger's idea that true maleness, underlying male bonding and war, is elicited by 'hard and heavy phenomena'. Many heavy-metal rock fans would agree.

The weakness in the essentialist approach is obvious: the choice of the essence is quite arbitrary. Nothing obliges different essentialists to agree, and in fact they often do not. Claims about a universal basis of masculinity tell us more about the ethos of the claimant than about anything else.

Positivist social science, whose ethos emphasizes finding the facts, yields a simple definition of masculinity: what men actually are. This definition is the logical basis of masculinity/femininity (M/F) scales in psychology, whose items are validated by showing that they discriminate statistically between groups of men and women. It is also the basis of those ethnographic discussions of masculinity which describe the pattern of men's lives in a given culture and, whatever it is, call the pattern masculinity.

There are three difficulties here. First, as modern epistemology recognizes, there is no description without a standpoint. The apparently neutral descriptions on which these definitions rest are themselves underpinned by assumptions about gender. Obviously enough, to start compiling an M/F scale one must have some idea of what to count or list when making up the items.

Second, to list what men and women do requires that people be already sorted into the categories 'men' and 'women'. This is unavoidably a process of social attribution using common-sense typologies of gender. Positivist procedure thus rests on the very typifications that are supposedly under investigation in gender research.

Third, to define masculinity as what-men-empirically-are is to rule out the usage in which we call some women 'masculine' and some men 'feminine', or some actions or attitudes 'masculine' or 'feminine' regardless of who displays them.

Indeed, this usage is fundamental to gender analysis. If we spoke only of differences between men as a bloc and women as a bloc, we would not need the terms 'masculine' and 'feminine' at all. We could just speak of 'men's' and 'women's', or 'male' and 'female'. The terms 'masculine' and 'feminine' point beyond categorical sex difference to the ways men differ among themselves, and women differ among themselves, in matters of gender.

Normative definitions recognize these differences and offer a standard: masculinity is what men ought to be. Strict sex role theory treats masculinity precisely as a social norm for the behaviour of men. In practice, male sex role texts often blend normative with essentialist definitions, as in Robert Brannon's widely quoted account of 'our culture's blueprint of manhood': No Sissy Stuff, The Big Wheel, The Sturdy Oak and Give 'em Hell.

Normative definitions allow that different men approach the standards to different degrees. But this soon produces paradoxes, some of which were recognized in the early Men's Liberation writings. Few men actually match the 'blueprint' or display the toughness and independence acted by Wayne, Bogart or Eastwood. What is 'normative' about a norm hardly anyone meets? Are we to say the majority of men are unmasculine? How do we assay the toughness needed to resist the norm of toughness, or the heroism needed to come out as gay?

Semiotic approaches abandon the level of personality and define masculinity through a system of symbolic difference in which masculine and feminine places are contrasted. Masculinity is, in effect, defined as not-femininity.

This follows the formulae of structural linguistics, where elements of speech are defined by their differences from each other. In the semiotic opposition of masculinity and femininity, masculinity is the unmarked term, the place of symbolic authority. The phallus is master-signifier, and femininity is symbolically defined by lack.

This definition of masculinity has been very effective in cultural analysis. It escapes the arbitrariness of essentialism and the paradoxes of positivist and normative definitions. It is, however, limited in its scope—unless one assumes, as some postmodern theorists do, that discourse is all we can talk about in social analysis. To grapple with the full range of issues about masculinity we need ways of talking about relationships of other kinds too: about gendered places in production and consumption, places in institution and in natural environments, places in social and military struggles.

What can be generalized is the principle of connection. The idea that one symbol can only be understood within a connected system of symbols applies equally well in other spheres. No masculinity arises except in a system of gender relations.

Rather than attempting to define masculinity as an object (a natural character type, a behavioural average, a norm), we need to focus on the processes and relationships through which men and women conduct gendered lives. 'Masculinity', to the extent the term can be briefly defined at all, is simultaneously a place in gender relations, the practices through which men and women engage that place in gender, and the effects of these practices in bodily experience, personality and culture.

Gender as a Structure of Social Practice

Gender is a way in which social practice is ordered. In gender processes, the everyday conduct of life is organized in relation to a reproductive arena, defined by the bodily structures and processes of human reproduction. This arena includes sexual arousal and intercourse, childbirth and infant care, bodily sex difference and similarity.

I call this a 'reproductive arena' not a 'biological base' to emphasize that we are talking about a historical process involving the body, not a fixed set of biological determinants. Gender is social practice that constantly refers to bodies and what bodies do, it is not social practice reduced to the body. Indeed reductionism presents the exact reverse of the real situation. Gender exists precisely to the extent that biology does not determine the social. It marks one of those points of transition where historical process supersedes biological evolution as the form of change. Gender is a scandal, an outrage, from the point of view of essentialism. Sociobiologists are constantly trying to abolish it, by proving that human social arrangements are a reflex of evolutionary imperatives.

Social practice is creative and inventive, but not inchoate. It responds to particular situations and is generated within definite structures of social relations. Gender relations, the relations among people and groups organized through the reproductive arena, form one of the major structures of all documented societies.

Practice that relates to this structure, generated as people and groups grapple with their historical situations, does not consist of isolated acts. Actions are configured in larger units, and when we speak of masculinity and femininity we are naming configurations of gender practice.

'Configuration' is perhaps too static a term. The important thing is the process of configuring practice. Taking a dynamic view of the organization of practice, we arrive at an understanding of masculinity and femininity as gender projects. These are processes of configuring practice through time, which transform their starting-points in gender structures.

We find the gender configuring of practice however we slice the social world, whatever unit of analysis we choose. The most familiar is the individual life course, the basis of the commonsense notions of masculinity and femininity. The configuration of practice here is what psychologists have traditionally called 'personality' or 'character'.

Such a focus is liable to exaggerate the coherence of practice that can be achieved at any one site. It is thus not surprising that psychoanalysis, originally stressing contradiction, drifted towards the concept of 'identity'. Post-structuralist critics of psychology such as Wendy Hollway have emphasized that gender identities are fractured and shifting, because multiple discourses intersect in any individual life. This argument highlights another site, that of discourse, ideology or culture. Here gender is organized in symbolic practices that may continue much longer than the individual life (for instance: the construction of heroic masculinities in epics; the construction of 'gender dysphorias' or 'perversions' in medical theory).

Many find it difficult to accept that institutions are substantively, not just metaphorically, gendered. This is, nevertheless, a key point.

The state, for instance, is a masculine institution. To say this is not to imply that the personalities of top male office-holders somehow seep through and stain the institution. It is to say something much stronger: that state organizational practices are structured in relation to the reproductive arena. The overwhelming majority of top office-holders are men because there is a gender configuring of recruitment and promotion, a gender configuring of the internal division of labour and systems of control, a gender configuring of policymaking, practical routines, and ways of mobilizing pleasure and consent.

The gender structuring of practice need have nothing biologically to do with reproduction. The link with the reproductive arena is social. This becomes clear when it is challenged. An example is the recent struggle within the state over 'gays in the military', i.e., the rules excluding soldiers and sailors because of the gender of their sexual object-choice. In the United States, where this struggle was most severe, critics made the case for change in terms of civil liberties and military efficiency, arguing in effect that object-choice has little to do with the capacity to kill. The admirals and generals defended the status quo on a variety of spurious grounds. The unadmitted reason was the cultural importance of a particular definition of masculinity in maintaining the fragile cohesion of modern armed forces.

We need at least a three-fold model of the structure of gender, distinguishing relations of (a) power, (b) production and (c) cathexis (emotional attachment). This is a provisional model, but it gives some purchase on issues about masculinity.

(a) *Power relations.* The main axis of power in the contemporary European/American gender order is the overall subordination of women and dominance of men—the structure Women's Liberation named 'patriarchy'. This general structure exists despite many local reversals (e.g., woman-headed households, female teachers with male students). It persists despite resistance of many kinds, now articulated in feminism. These reversals and resistances mean continuing difficulties for patriarchal power. They define a problem of legitimacy which has great importance for the politics of masculinity.

(b) *Production relations.* Gender divisions of labour are familiar in the form of the allocation of tasks, sometimes reaching extraordinarily fine detail. Equal attention should be paid to the economic consequences of gender divisions of labour, the dividend accruing to men from unequal shares of the products of social labour. This is most often discussed in terms of unequal wage rates, but the gendered character of capital should also be noted. A capitalist economy working through a gender division of labour is, necessarily, a gendered accumulation process.

(c) *Cathexis.* Sexual desire is so often seen as natural that it is commonly excluded from social theory. Yet when we consider desire in Freudian terms, as emotional energy being attached to an object, its gendered character is clear. This is true both for heterosexual and homosexual desire. (It is striking that in our culture the non-gendered object choice, 'bisexual' desire, is ill-defined and unstable.) The practices that shape and realize desire are thus an aspect of the gender order. Accordingly we can ask political questions about the relationships involved: whether they are consensual or coercive, whether pleasure is equally given and received. In feminist analyses of sexuality these have become sharp questions about the connection of heterosexuality with men's position of social dominance.

Because gender is a way of structuring social practice in general, not a special type of practice, it is unavoidably involved with other social structures. It is now common to say that gender 'intersects'—better, interacts—with race and class. We might add that it constantly interacts with nationality or position in the world order.

This fact also has strong implications for the analysis of masculinity. White men's masculinities, for instance, are constructed not only in relation to white women but also in relation to black men. White fears of black men's violence have a long history in colonial and post-colonial situations. Black fears of white men's terrorism, founded in the history of colonialism, have a continuing basis in white men's control of police, courts arid prisons in metropolitan countries. African-American men are massively over-represented in American prisons, as Aboriginal men are in Australian prisons. This situation is strikingly condensed in the American black expression 'The Man', fusing white masculinity and institutional power. As the black rap singer Ice-T put it,

> It makes no difference whether you're in or out. The ghetto, the pen, it's all institutionalized. It's being controlled by the Man . . . Ever since 1976, they stop trying to rehabilitate Brothers. Now it's strictly punishment. The Man's answer to the problem is not more education—it's more prisons. They're saying let's not educate them, let's lock them the fuck up. So when you come outta there you're all braindead, so yeah it's a cycle.

To understand gender, then, we must constantly go beyond gender. The same applies in reverse. We cannot understand class, race or global inequality without constantly moving towards gender. Gender relations are a major component of social structure as a whole, and gender politics are among the main determinants of our collective fate.

Relations among Masculinities: Hegemony, Subordination, Complicity, Marginalization

With growing recognition of the interplay between gender, race and class it has become common to recognize multiple masculinities: black as well as white, working-class as well as middle-class. This is welcome, but it risks another kind of oversimplification. It is easy in this framework to think that there is *a* black masculinity or *a* working-class masculinity.

To recognize more than one kind of masculinity is only a first step. We have to examine the relations between them. Further, we have to unpack the milieux of class and race and scrutinize the gender relations operating within them. There are, after all, gay black men and effeminate factory hands, not to mention middle-class rapists and cross-dressing bourgeois.

A focus on the gender relations among men is necessary to keep the analysis dynamic, to prevent the acknowledgement of multiple masculinities collapsing into a character typology. 'Hegemonic masculinity' is not a fixed character type, always and everywhere the same. It is, rather, the masculinity that occupies the hegemonic position in a given pattern of gender relations, a position always contestable.

A focus on relations also offers a gain in realism. Recognizing multiple masculinities, especially in an individualist culture such as the United States, risks taking them for alternative lifestyles, a matter of consumer choice. A relational approach makes it easier to recognize the hard compulsions under which gender configurations are formed, the bitterness as well as the pleasure in gendered experience.

With these guidelines, let us consider the practices and relations that construct the main patterns of masculinity in the current Western gender order.

Hegemony

The concept of 'hegemony', deriving from Antonio Gramsci's analysis of class relations, refers to the cultural dynamic by which a group claims and sustains a leading position in social life. At any given time, one form of masculinity rather than others is culturally exalted. Hegemonic masculinity can be defined as the configuration of gender practice which embodies the currently accepted answer to the problem of the legitimacy of patriarchy, which guarantees (or is taken to guarantee) the dominant position of men and the subordination of women.

This is not to say that the most visible bearers of hegemonic masculinity are always the most powerful people. They may be exemplars, such as film actors, or even fantasy figures, such as film characters. Individual holders of institutional power or great wealth may be far from the hegemonic pattern in their personal lives.

Nevertheless, hegemony is likely to be established only if there is some correspondence between cultural ideal and institutional power, collective if not individual. So the top levels of business, the military and government provide a fairly convincing *corporate* display of masculinity, still very little shaken by feminist women or dissenting men. It is the successful claim to authority, more than direct violence, that is the mark of hegemony (though violence often underpins or supports authority).

I stress that hegemonic masculinity embodies a 'currently accepted' strategy. When conditions for the defence of patriarchy change, the bases for the dominance of a particular masculinity are eroded. New groups may challenge old solutions and construct a new hegemony. The dominance of *any* group of men may be challenged by women. Hegemony, then, is a historically mobile relation.

Subordination

Hegemony relates to cultural dominance in the society as a whole. Within that overall framework there are specific gender relations of dominance and subordination between groups of men.

The most important case in contemporary European/American society is the dominance of heterosexual men and the subordination of homosexual men. This is much more than a cultural stigmatization of homosexuality or gay identity. Gay men are subordinated to straight men by an array of quite material practices.

These practices are still a matter of everyday experience for homosexual men. They include political and cultural exclusion, cultural abuse (in the United States gay men have now become the main symbolic target of the religious right), legal violence (such as imprisonment under sodomy statutes), street violence (ranging from intimidation to murder), economic discrimination and personal boycotts.

Oppression positions homosexual masculinities at the bottom of a gender hierarchy among men. Gayness, in patriarchal ideology, is the repository of whatever is symbolically expelled from hegemonic masculinity, the items ranging from fastidious taste in home decoration to receptive anal pleasure. Hence, from the point of view of hegemonic masculinity, gayness is easily assimilated to femininity. And hence—in the view of some gay theorists—the ferocity of homophobic attacks.

Gay masculinity is the most conspicuous, but it is not the only subordinated masculinity. Some heterosexual men and boys too are expelled from the circle of legitimacy.

Complicity

Normative definitions of masculinity, as I have noted, face the problem that not many men actually meet the normative standards. This point applies to hegemonic masculinity. The number of men rigorously practising the hegemonic pattern in its entirety may be quite small. Yet the majority of men gain from its hegemony, since they benefit from the patriarchal dividend, the advantage men in general gain from the overall subordination of women.

Accounts of masculinity have generally concerned themselves with syndromes and types, not with numbers. Yet in thinking about the dynamics of society as a whole, numbers matter. Sexual politics is mass politics, and strategic thinking needs to be concerned with where the masses of people are. If a large number of men have some connection with the hegemonic project but do not embody hegemonic masculinity, we need a way of theorizing their specific situation.

This can be done by recognizing another relationship among groups of men, the relationship of complicity with the hegemonic project. Masculinities constructed in ways that realize the patriarchal dividend, without the tensions or risks of being the frontline troops of patriarchy, are complicit in this sense.

It is tempting to treat them simply as slacker versions of hegemonic masculinity—the difference between the men who cheer football matches on TV and those who run out into the mud and the tackles themselves. But there is often something more definite and carefully crafted than that. Marriage, fatherhood and community life often involve extensive compromises with women rather than naked domination or an uncontested display of authority. A great many men who draw the patriarchal dividend also respect their wives and mothers, are never violent towards women, do their accustomed share of the housework, bring home the family wage, and can easily convince themselves that feminists must be bra-burning extremists.

Marginalization

Hegemony, subordination and complicity, as just defined, are relations internal to the gender order. The interplay of gender with other structures such as class and race creates further relationships between masculinities.

Race relations may become an integral part of the dynamic between masculinities. In a white-supremacist context, black masculinities play symbolic roles for white gender construction. For instance, black sporting stars become exemplars of masculine toughness, while the fantasy figure of the black rapist plays an important role in sexual politics among whites, a role much exploited by right-wing politics in the United States. Conversely, hegemonic masculinity among whites sustains the institutional oppression and physical terror that have framed the making of masculinities in black communities.

Robert Staples's discussion of internal colonialism in *Black Masculinity* shows the effect of class and race relations at the same time. As he argues, the level of violence among black men in the United States can only be understood through the changing place of the black labour force in American capitalism and the violent means used to control it. Massive unemployment and urban poverty now powerfully interact with institutional racism in the shaping of black masculinity.

Though the term is not ideal, I cannot improve on 'marginalization' to refer to the relations between the masculinities in dominant and subordinated classes or ethnic groups. Marginalization is always relative to the *authorization* of the hegemonic masculinity of the dominant group. Thus, in the United States, particular black athletes may be exemplars for hegemonic masculinity. But the fame and wealth of individual stars has no trickledown effect; it does not yield social authority to black men generally.

These two types of relationship—hegemony, domination/subordination and complicity on the one hand, marginalization/authorization on the other—provide a framework in which we can analyse specific masculinities. (This is a sparse framework, but social theory should be hardworking.) I emphasize that terms such as 'hegemonic masculinity' and 'marginalized masculinities' name not fixed character types but configurations of practice generated in particular situations in a changing structure of relationships. Any theory of masculinity worth having must give an account of this process of change.

Historical Dynamics, Violence and Crisis Tendencies

To recognize gender as a social pattern requires us to see it as a product of history, and also as a producer of history. I defined gender practice as onto-formative, as constituting reality, and it is a crucial part of this idea that social reality is dynamic in time. We habitually think of the social as less real than the biological, what changes as less real than what stays the same. But there is a colossal reality to history. It is the modality of human life, precisely what defines us as human. No other species produces and lives in history, replacing organic evolution with radically new determinants of change.

To recognize masculinity and femininity as historical, then, is not to suggest they are flimsy or trivial. It is to locate them firmly in the world of social agency. And it raises a string of questions about their historicity.

The structures of gender relations are formed and transformed over time. It has been common in historical writing to see this change as coming from outside gender—from technology or class dynamics, most often. But change is also generated from within gender relations. The dynamic is as old as gender relations. It has, however, become more clearly defined in the last two centuries with the emergence of a public politics of gender and sexuality.

With the women's suffrage movement and the early homophile movement, the conflict of interests embedded in gender relations became visible. Interests are formed in any structure of inequality, which necessarily defines groups that will gain and lose differently by sustaining or by changing the structure. A gender order where men dominate women cannot avoid constituting men as an interest group concerned with defence, and women as an interest group concerned with change. This is a structural fact, independent of whether men as individuals love or hate women, or believe in equality or abjection, and independent of whether women are currently pursuing change.

To speak of a patriarchal dividend is to raise exactly this question of interest. 'Men gain a dividend from patriarchy in terms of honour, prestige and the right to command.' They also gain a material dividend. In the rich capitalist countries, men's average incomes are approximately *double* women's average incomes.

Given these facts, the 'battle of the sexes' is no joke. Social struggle must result from inequalities on such a scale. It follows that the politics of masculinity cannot concern only questions of personal life and identity. It must also concern questions of social justice.

A structure of inequality on this scale, involving a massive dispossession of social resources, is hard to imagine without violence. It is, overwhelmingly, the dominant gender who hold and use the means of violence. Men are armed far more often than women. Indeed under many gender regimes women have been forbidden to bear or use arms (a rule applied, astonishingly, even within armies). Patriarchal definition of femininity (dependence fearfulness) amount to a cultural disarmament that may be quite as effective as the physical kind.

Two patterns of violence follow from this situation. First, many members of the privileged group use violence to sustain their dominance. Intimidation of women ranges across the spectrum from wolf-whistling in the street, to office harassment, to rape and domestic assault, to murder by a woman's patriarchal 'owner', such as a separated husband. Physical attacks are commonly accompanied by verbal abuse of women (whores and bitches, in recent popular music that recommends beating women). Most men do not attack or harass women; but those who do are unlikely to think themselves deviant. On the contrary they usually feel they are entirely justified, that they are exercising a right. They are authorized by an ideology of supremacy.

Second, violence becomes important in gender politics among men. Most episodes of major violence (counting military combat, homicide and armed assault) are transactions among men. Terror is used as a means of drawing boundaries and making exclusions, for example, in heterosexual violence against gay men. Violence can become a way of claiming or asserting masculinity in group struggles. This is an explosive process when an oppressed group gains the means of violence—as witness the levels of violence among black men in contemporary South Africa and the United States. The youth gang violence of inner-city streets is a striking example of the assertion of marginalized masculinities against other men, continuous with the assertion of masculinity in sexual violence against women.

Violence can be used to enforce a reactionary gender politics, as in the recent firebombings and murders of abortion service providers in the United States. It must also be said that collective violence among men can open possibilities for progress in gender relations. The two global wars this century produced important transitions in women's employment, shook up gender ideology, and accelerated the making of homosexual communities.

Violence is part of a system of domination, but is at the same time a measure of its imperfection. A thoroughly legitimate hierarchy would have less need to intimidate. The scale of contemporary violence points to crisis tendencies (to borrow a term from Jürgen Habermas) in the modern gender order.

The concept of crisis tendencies needs to be distinguished from the colloquial sense in which people speak of a 'crisis of masculinity'. As a theoretical term 'crisis' presupposes a coherent system of some kind, which is destroyed or restored by the outcome of the crisis. Masculinity, as the argument so far has shown, is not a system in that sense. It is, rather, a configuration of practice *within* a system of gender relations. We cannot logically speak of the crisis of a configuration; rather we might speak of its disruption or its transformation. We can, however, logically speak of the crisis of a gender order as a whole, and of its tendencies towards crisis.

Such crisis tendencies will always implicate masculinities, though not necessarily by disrupting them. Crisis tendencies may, for instance, provoke attempts to restore a dominant masculinity. Michael Kimmel has pointed to this dynamic in turn-of-the-century United States society, where fear of the women's suffrage movement played into the cult of the outdoorsman. More recently, Women's Liberation and defeat in Vietnam have stirred new cults of true masculinity in the United States, from violent 'adventure' movies such as the *Rambo* series, to the expansion of the gun cult and what William Gibson has called 'paramilitary culture'.

References

Brannon, Robert. 1976. "The Male Sex Role: Our Culture's Blueprint of Manhood, and What It's Done for Us Lately." pp. 1–45 in *The Forty-Nine Percent Majority: The Male Sex Role,* eds. Deborah S. David and Robert Brannon. Reading, MA: Addison-Wesley.

Connell, R. W. 1987. *Gender and Power: Society, the Person and Sexual Politics.* Cambridge: Polity Press.

Franzway, Suzanne, Dianne Court, and R. W. Connell. 1989. *Staking a Claim: Feminism, Bureaucracy, and the State.* Sydney: Allen & Unwin.

Gibson, James William. 1994. *Warrior Dreams: Paramilitary Culture in Post-Vietnam America.* New York: Hill & Wang.

Grant, Judith and Pete Tancred. 1992. "A Feminist Perspective on State Bureaucracy." pp. 112–128 in *Gendering Organizational Analysis,* ed. Albert J. Mills and Peta Tancred. Newbury Park, CA: Sage.

Habermas, Jürgen. 1976. *Legitimation Crisis.* London: Heinemann.

Hollway, Wendy. 1984. "Gender Difference and the Production of Subjectivity." pp. 227–263 in *Changing the Subject,* ed. J. Henriques et al. London: Methuen.

Kessler, Suzanne J. and Wendy McKenna. 1978. *Gender: An Ethnomethodological Approach.* New York: Wiley.

Kimmel, Michael S. 1987. "'Rethinking Masculinity: New Directions in Research." pp. 9–24 in *Changing Men: New Directions in Research on Men and Masculinity,* ed. Michael S. Kimmel. Newbury Park, CA: Sage.

Messerschmidt, James W. 1993. *Masculinities and Crime: Critique and Reconceptualization of Theory.* Lanham, MD: Rowman & Littlefield.

Sartre, Jean Paul. 1968 [1960]. *Search for a Method.* New York: Vintage.

Staples, Robert. 1982. *Black Masculinity: The Black Man's Role in American Society.* San Francisco: Black Scholar Press.

Tiger, Lionel. 1969. *Men in Groups.* New York: Random House.

CHAPTER 2

Welcome to the Men's Club

Homosociality and the Maintenance of Hegemonic Masculinity

Sharon R. Bird

In this study, I focus on how meanings that correspond to hegemonic masculinity are maintained and how meanings that do not correspond to hegemonic masculinity are suppressed. Within the existing gender order, meanings associated with behaviors that challenge hegemonic masculinity are denied legitimation as *masculine*; such meanings are marginalized, if not suppressed entirely. Contradictions to hegemonic masculinity posed by male homosexuality, for example, are suppressed when homosexual masculinity is consistently rendered "effeminate" (Connell 1992).

The maintenance of hegemonic masculinity is explored here through investigation of male homosocial interactions. *Homosociality* refers specifically to the nonsexual attractions held by men (or women) for members of their own sex (Lipman-Blumen 1976). Homosociality, according to Lipman-Blumen, promotes clear distinctions between women and men through segregation in social institutions. I add, further, that homosociality promotes clear distinctions between hegemonic masculinities and nonhegemonic masculinities by the segregation of social groups. *Heterosociality*, a concept left untheorized by Lipman-Blumen, refers to nonsexual attractions held by men (or women) for members of the other sex.

Also critical to this analysis is an investigation of the relationship between sociality and the self-conceptualization of masculinity. As I argue here, homosocial interaction, among heterosexual men, contributes to the maintenance of hegemonic masculinity norms by supporting meanings associated with identities that fit hegemonic ideals while suppressing meanings associated with nonhegemonic masculinity identities. I focus specifically on the connection between individual masculinity and gender norms in small group interactions to capture subtle mechanisms of control. When personal conflicts with ideal masculinity are suppressed both in the homosocial group and by individual men, the cultural imposition of hegemonic masculinity goes uncontested (see Kaufman 1994).

The following meanings are crucial to our understanding of how homosociality contributes to the perpetuation of hegemonic masculinity: (1) *emotional detachment*, a meaning constructed through relationships within families whereby young men detach themselves from mothers and develop gender identities in relation to that which they are not (Chodorow 1978); (2) *competitiveness*, a meaning constructed and maintained through relationships with other men whereby simple individuality becomes competitive individuality (Gilligan 1982); and (3) *sexual objectification of women*, a meaning constructed and maintained through relationships with other men whereby male individuality is conceptualized not only as different from female but as *better than* female (Johnson 1988).

SOURCE: Bird, S. (1996). Welcome to the Men's Club: Homosociality and the Maintenance of Hegemonic Masculinity. *Gender & Society*, 10(2), 120–132. Reproduced with permission.

Conceptualizing Masculinities

Gender identity is distinguished from the heavily criticized concept of gender *role* in that the latter is used to refer to behavioral expectations associated with more or less static social positions, whereas the former refers to a continual *process* whereby meanings are attributed by and to individuals through social interaction. Gender, in other words, is relational. Gender identity originates in early interactions, becoming more stable through the accumulation of meanings attributed by and to the self over time (see Burke 1980; Burke and Reitzes 1981). Information received through interactions may be used either to reinforce existing self-notions of gender meanings or to weaken them. That is, mere socialization does not sufficiently explain how individuals conceptualize identity. Socialization provides the terms of social interaction but does not determine how individuals incorporate interactional meanings into their own conceptualizations of gender (Connell 1987).

The unique experiences of men, embedded within particular social institutions and subject to varying historical contexts, facilitate conceptualizations of masculinities that may differ considerably. Each male incorporates a variety of meanings into his gender identity, some of which are consistent with hegemonic masculinity and others of which are not (e.g., Connell 1992; Messner 1992b). The social ideal for masculinity, which in itself is a nonstatic notion, may be internalized (i.e., central to one's core self [see Chodorow 1980]) or simply interiorized (i.e., acknowledged by the self), enabling individuals to understand the gender norms to which they are held accountable. In either case, each male comes to understand both socially shared meanings of masculinity and the idiosyncratic meanings that comprise his unique gender identity. Internalization of hegemonic meanings provides a base of shared meanings for social interaction but also quells the expression of nonhegemonic meanings. The presumption that hegemonic masculinity meanings are the only mutually accepted and legitimate masculinity meanings helps to reify hegemonic norms while suppressing meanings that might otherwise create a foundation for the subversion of the existing hegemony. This presumption is especially prevalent in male homosocial interactions, which are critical to both the conceptualization of masculinity identity and the maintenance of gender norms.

Male Homosocial Interactions: Emotional Detachment, Competitiveness, and Sexual Objectification of Women

Three of the shared meanings that are perpetuated via male homosociality are emotional detachment, competition, and the sexual objectification of women. These meanings characterize hegemonic masculinity but are not always internalized as central to individual identity. First, emotional detachment (i.e., withholding expressions of intimacy) maintains both clear individual identity boundaries (Chodorow 1978) and the norms of hegemonic masculinity. To express feelings is to reveal vulnerabilities and weaknesses; to withhold such expressions is to maintain control (Cancian 1987). Second, competition in the male homosocial group supports an identity that depends not on likeness and cooperation but on separation and distinction (Gilligan 1982). Competition facilitates hierarchy in relationships, whereas cooperation suggests symmetry of relationships (Messner 1992a). Finally, the sexual objectification of women facilitates self-conceptualization as positively male by distancing the self from all that is associated with being female. The objectification of women provides a base on which male superiority is maintained (Johnson 1988), whereas identification with women (and what it means to be female) helps remove the symbolic distance that enables men to depersonalize the oppression of women.

Individual conceptualizations vary in the extent to which these meanings characterize one's masculinity. Masculinities that differ from the norm of hegemonic masculinity, however, are generally experienced as "private dissatisfactions" rather than foundations for questioning the social construction of gender (Thomas 1990; see also Kaufman 1994). Hegemonic masculinity persists, therefore, despite individual departures from the hegemonic form.

Method

The data collected for this study were gathered through personal interviews and field observations. Eight in-depth interviews were conducted in the fall of 1992 in a small northwestern city in the United States. Later, additional follow-up interviews were conducted with four new respondents to clarify how male homosocial and heterosexual interactions facilitate the perpetuation of hegemonic masculinity, on the one hand, but suppress nonhegemonic masculinity, on the other.

The men who participated in the interviews for this study were all selected from within the academic community of the city in which the study took place. Responses to questions, therefore, may reflect a level of education higher than that of the general population. The findings of this study, however, are consistent with findings of previous studies regarding the meanings associated with masculinity (e.g., Lehn 1992; Messner 1992a, 1992b; Phillips 1986). The men's educational level ranged from three years of undergraduate study to graduate level and post-Ph.D. The men ranged in age from 23 to 50 years. All but one of the interviewees were native-born Americans from various geographical regions of the country. The other male, a native of East Africa, had maintained residence in the United States for approximately two years before the time of the interview. Although the data received through the interview with this respondent were consistent with accounts offered by the respondents from the United States, this information was excluded from the analysis because of cultural differences that could contribute to misleading conclusions. Most of the men reported middle-class family origins, although three reported working-class backgrounds. Two of the men interviewed were Black, and the other nine were white. All of the men were raised primarily by female caretakers, and all were heterosexual.

The primary focus of the interviews was on the development of perceived consensual masculinity and the corresponding relationship between self-conceptualizations and hegemonic masculinity. Respondents were first asked questions about childhood. Each was asked to describe childhood memories of time spent with playmates, with siblings, and with parents. Responses to these questions provided general information from which more specific inquiries could be made regarding the meanings associated both with masculinity personally (i.e., identity) and with masculinity more generally (i.e., the beliefs, attitudes, and expectations of the group and of society).

To establish the parameters for the discussion during the interviews, each man was asked to consider the kinds of relationships he would find most desirable given non-work-related situations. Each was then prompted to elaborate on his experiences within groups, especially those experiences within the male homosocial group. Although the men varied in how much they desired male homosocial group interaction, each explained that such groups have had a significant impact on their beliefs, attitudes, and behaviors. The men were asked to elaborate on what exactly would be considered appropriate or inappropriate, desirable or undesirable, for conversation among men and what interests were commonly or not commonly shared within their homosocial groups. The topics of sports, women, business, politics, and drinking were most commonly specified as desirable for conversation, while the topics of feelings and gossip were most frequently mentioned as undesirable. Each man was then asked to explain his views on the degree to which his personal interests corresponded to interests more generally shared by the group.

Additional data were collected during the fall of 1992 through field observations of male homosocial interactions in small-group contexts. Observations and interviews were conducted within the same academic community, but the men *observed* were not the same as the men *interviewed*. Approximately 25 hours of observations were conducted. The majority of the observations were made at a single location: a deli/bar frequented by men associated with the university but also visited regularly by men not associated with academia. Remaining observations were conducted at two coffee shops and three taverns, all located in the same academic community. The focus of the observations was on the interactions among male customers, including their conversations. Field notes were taken in one- to two-hour time periods at various times of the day and/or night and on various days of the week. Because the locations in which observations were made are consistently patronized by students and university faculty, the recording of observations went unnoticed.

The meanings described in the interviews and that emerged from the observations have been organized under the following subtopics: (1) emotional detachment, (2) competition, and (3) sexual objectification of women. The remainder of this article focuses on the processes through which these meanings are sustained and the processes through which alternative meanings are suppressed in male homosocial interaction.

Emotional Detachment: "We Were Masculine Little Kids!"

The rules that apply to homosocial friendships and to masculinity are so familiar that they are typically taken for granted by men and women alike. Rarely does anyone (other than the social scientist) seriously question the expectations associated with gender identity or gender norms. Instead, it is assumed that "boys will be boys" and will just naturally do "boy things." By the same token, "men will be men" and will continue to do "men things." Doing men things or "doing Masculinity" is simply the commonplace activity of men's daily lives, recreated over and again, maintaining the norms of social behavior (West and Zimmerman 1987).

The men interviewed and those observed explained that being "one of the boys" is a key principle of symbolic and, in some cases, physical separation of "the boys" from "the girls." One man, for example, explained how, as a youngster, he and his pals "were rough and rugged . . . masculine little kids." He said,

> When you're a little boy, you hang out with other little boys and you do little boy things. You know, you burn ants and things like that. You just don't hang out with females because you don't want to be a wuss, you don't play with dolls, you don't whine, you don't cry . . . you do boy things, you know, guy stuff.

Being masculine, in other words, means being not-female. The masculinity ideal involves detachment and independence. The men interviewed indicated that emotions and behaviors typically associated with women were inappropriate within the male homosocial group. Among the emotions and behaviors considered most inappropriate, and most highly stigmatized, were those associated with feminine expressions of intimacy (e.g., talking "feelings"). As one of the men interviewed explained, "I usually talk about 'things' rather than getting into your head and asking, you know, that real intimate stuff."

This suppression of feminine emotions is more than merely a means of establishing individual masculinity. Emotional detachment is one way in which gender hierarchies are maintained. Expressing emotions signifies weakness and is devalued, whereas emotional detachment signifies strength and is valued (Cancian 1987).

In their discussions of feelings, the men hesitated; none of them made consistent use of the word *feelings*. Instead of feelings, they referred to "personal stuff," "those things," and "those matters," and when asked, many indicated that "ultimately you're doing it alone." The expectation is that "because you're going to be in situations where you're away from any support system . . . You're going to have to handle your stuff alone."

What these men explained was that within the male homosocial group, emotional detachment is viewed not only as desirable but as imperative. Those who do express their intimate emotions are excluded. On this point, the interviewees were quite clear: "If I was having a beer with a friend and they started crying, I would suspect that that person, if it were a male . . . I'd suspect that that person didn't have a very good definition of the social situation." If a guy did start crying, this interviewee was asked, where would that put him in relation to other guys? "Hmm, well, since . . . actually that would put him on the outs." The repercussion for violating the hegemonic meaning of emotional detachment, in other words, is to be "put on the outs," that is, to be ostracized from one's male homosocial group. Interviewees explained that violations of the norm of emotional detachment do not result in an alteration of the norm but instead result in the exclusion of the violator (see Schur 1984).

Data collected through observations clearly supported the pattern described by the men interviewed. Emotional detachment was exercised in even the most sensitive of topics. Two men observed, for example, appeared rather matter-of-fact as they discussed the marital problems that one of the men was experiencing: "Think of it this way, ya got a toothache. . . . You've got to have it taken out or you're gonna live with the bitch. Unless you bite the bullet and get the goddamn thing pulled out, you're gonna live with the pain." Feelings, as discussed by these two men, were something to "get over," not to experience—much less express. One man, when questioned about the possible repercussions for expressing feelings in the context of the male homosocial group, explained that feelings are "something for us all to joke about" because

> you certainly don't want to take things too seriously and have to deal with the heavy side, the heavy emotional side to it. . . . Tears are a very extreme thing in these male circles, partly because it's messy. . . . It has a lot to do with not looking soft and weak because if you do . . . it makes it difficult for men to have relationships with each other.

He explained that "developing emotional types of relationships with each other" is something men stereotypically do not do. Hegemonic masculinity is not expressed and maintained through excessive emotionality. This distinction separates the boys from the girls as well as the men who fit the hegemonic norm from those who do not. Through emotional detachment, the meanings formed in regard to masculinity are exaggerated so as to distinguish clearly that which all men are not, that is, female. The burden for demonstrating difference is on those trying to avoid the default meanings. Difference becomes an aspect of self in which men have a valued investment.

Departures from the norm of emotional detachment, however, do exist. Individual departures reflect an understanding of the dominant meanings but not necessarily an incorporation of them into one's self-concept. One man explained that although most men "do what the culture says and hide it" (i.e., hide their feelings), he had hoped to be able to express his feelings with other men: "A couple of times when I was hurting, uhm, I did kind of seek out a couple of male friends and I was really disappointed. . . . It was like they were embarrassed, you know, to talk about that shit, and so, uh, fuck it!" Five of the men who participated in the in-depth interviews and three of the four who participated in the follow-up interviews expressed discrepancies between hegemonic masculinity and their own masculinity. Each explained that although they knew they were *supposed* to separate themselves from things considered feminine, they did not assess their own identities to be as polarized as the hegemonic form would suggest.

> It was really unfortunate. As I grew older, I really wished that I wasn't so detached from my mom. I'm not that way now, though. After a while, I stopped caring about what everybody else thought. I mean, the intimate side got pushed aside for so long because that's not what "real" men are supposed to do. I got over it, though. . . . I guess I'm not what "real" men are supposed to be.

The degree to which the masculinity meanings individuals hold for themselves correspond to the meanings of hegemonic masculinity may vary over time and from person to person. The point, however, is that although individual conceptualizations of masculinity depart from the hegemonic norm, nonhegemonic meanings are suppressed due to perceptions of "appropriate" masculinity. Even in a community where notions of the "new man" are common and where antisexist attitudes are often expected, hegemonic patterns of masculinity prevail. One whose masculinity conceptualization is nonhegemonic still understands himself as "not what 'real' men are *supposed* to be" (emphasis added).

The men who made the distinction between self-masculinity and hegemonic masculinity made three things clear. First, they explained that hegemonic masculinity was the form that prevailed in their interactions with other men throughout childhood and adolescence. Second, they asserted that when they found themselves in homosocial situations in the present, the expectation of emotional detachment continued to prevail. Third, they described themselves in the present as more heterosocially than homosocially oriented. These men explained that they did not *prefer* exclusively male social interaction groups. In sum, homosocial and heterosocial masculinity meanings are clearly differentiated. For these men, homosocial masculinity was characterized by emotional detachment, whereas heterosocial masculinity downplayed these factors.

Competition: "It's a Pecking Order Between Males"

Competition with other men provides a stage for establishing self both as an individual and as appropriately masculine. Competition also contributes to the perpetuation of male dominance. When asked to explain what competition meant to him, one interviewee replied,

> By nature I'm terribly competitive. I suppose one's ego gets wrapped around the things that you do. It's pretty important for me to win because I do have my ego wrapped up in that [games] and so, uhm, you know when I play a game at a party or whatever I kind of expect to win and play pretty fiercely.

To establish self as not female, young men seek out other men with whom to display "non-femaleness" (Johnson 1988). Homosocial group interactions provide feedback and support for masculinity self-conceptualization. In this sense, masculinity conceptualization is itself a form of competition. Four men described competition as a critical part of their self-conceptualizations and stressed that the competitions they preferred were those with men. Men, they believed, could understand the intensity and importance of competition, whereas women seemed less accepting and less understanding. When asked about participating in athletics with women, one interviewee responded that "women start getting angry at you and it gets ugly" when "you start getting really intense." Another added that "women typically don't want to play [basketball] or sort of want to but feel they'll be intimidated or whatever."

The men who described themselves as less competitive (or noncompetitive), on the other hand, explained that they considered the intensity with which other men engaged in competitions (especially sports) as relatively unimportant for themselves. At the same time, however, these men recognized the *expectation*s of masculinity to be competitive. One man explained,

> Guys don't know what it means not to be competitive. Even those men who tell you that competition is silly know they have to [compete]. It's like otherwise you're gonna get walked on. Nobody appreciates that. I'm not as aggressive as most guys, but I can sure act it.

Again, the norms and expectations of hegemonic masculinity and individual conceptualizations do not necessarily fit; further, among the less competitive men, nonhegemonic masculinity and hegemonic masculinity meanings differ by sociality. Men whose conceptualizations of masculinity were nonhegemonic specified their lack of preference for homosocial interactions in both sporting and nonsporting activities. Men whose conceptualizations of masculinity were consistent with the hegemonic form specified a clear preference for homosocial interactions in sports. Homosociality corresponded with a focus on competitiveness, whereas heterosociality deemphasized competition. Homosocial and heterosocial meanings were clearly differentiated. In male homosocial groups, a man risks loss of status and self-esteem unless he competes. The meaning of competition is assumed under male homosocial circumstances, and violators of this norm are disadvantaged.

Sexual Objectification: "You Know, Women Were 'Othered' Early"

The competitions that support hegemonic masculinity continue throughout life in a variety of forms. Among the forms of competitions in which men engage are those that involve the objectification of women. Men often compete with one another in efforts to gain the attention and affections of women and in boasting about their sexual exploits. Observations revealed numerous stories about sexual objectification of women. In male homosocial conversations, references were made to women as "them," as clearly "other," as the nonthreatening "girl," and/or as objects to be used for sexual pleasure. While the use of these terms may or may not imply a conscious effort on the part of the speaker to objectify, they promote meanings that support hegemonic masculinity nonetheless.

The men not only explicated the objectification of women, they also explained and demonstrated the competition for objectified women. These competitions illustrate the interconnectedness of the meanings of emotional detachment, competition, and objectification. Conversations overheard at the deli/lounge, for example, shifted frequently from "shop talk" to competitive sex talk. Bantering sessions, in which one-upsmanship on stories of sexual exploits was the name of the game, were frequently overheard. For example, one man began,

> I've run across those kind. . . . I'll tell 'em, "I'll buy ya a beer." [And the hypothetical woman replies,] "Na, I'll buy you a beer." Then I'm thinkin' she's ready to get outta there with me. I just want one I can step out with, shoot up her, and get back in the bar in 5 or 10 minutes.

Another man then added his own story:

> Aw, shit, I had one down near Vegas. . . . Well, to make a long story short, when it was time to hit the rack we went back to her room. . . . We found a bucket of ice and a bottle of liquor at the door with a note from some other guy attached to it. . . . I just went ahead and drank the stuff and screwed her!

Not to be outdone, the remaining participant in the discussion followed with an account of his own:

> Yeah, one night I had a couple of beers, then went out to that country and western bar. . . . She was a bartender there. I'm tellin' ya, she was hanging all over me so much that the other bartender had to get on to her. Then later, she came knockin' on my trailer door. I thought, "What the hell, Judy won't find out, let's hop to it." She was a wicked thing.

Such conversations, according to the men interviewed, occur frequently but are less likely to be carried out with verbal explicitness when a woman or women actually join the interaction. In this case, the conversation will likely shift; but, as my interviewees explained, the competition will continue. The question, "What happens if a woman enters the scene where you are engaging in a conversation with another man or men?" prompted the following response: "Weird. Weird setup . . . because everybody is checking everybody else out . . . it's uncomfortable for everybody. You know, people are checking each other out. We'd see her as an issue of conquest." The men interviewed explained that men in homosocial groups both objectify and compete for women. When asked to describe the nature of interactions between men when an "available" woman is present among the group, one man explained, "It's competitive, you see, and it's a pecking order between men. If you do not peck, you get pecked. And so, one of the things over which there is a great deal of pecking is women."

To be "pecked" is an undesirable experience—one to be avoided if a man wishes to maintain status within the male homosocial group. Objectification of women and men's competitiveness over objectified women constitute the very essence of what hegemonic masculinity means in this society (Connell 1992). Not all men view themselves in accordance with hegemonic masculinity, however, when it comes to objectifying women. Even so, men often go along with hegemonic norms to avoid being pecked. All of the men interviewed, when asked how an individual man avoids being pecked by other members of the group, explained that, on the one hand, they knew what the rules of the game were because

> there's always an assessment going on in the group. Always. . . . Some guys will go along but wouldn't make a degrading comment about women themselves. But when some guy says something, because you want to be a member of the group, it becomes, "Yeah." You follow the lead.

Some men argued, however, that these hegemonic rules did not fit their own identities:

> That stuff [sexual objectification of women] doesn't interest me terribly much because for the most part I don't really talk about those things and I don't hang out with men who do. It's a very nasty type of chat, and the goal seems to be to hurt somebody anyway.

Although the rules of hegemonic masculinity included sexual objectification, some individual conceptualizations minimized and/or disregarded its importance. Even among those men who rejected hegemonic masculinity for themselves, however, the hegemonic norm for sexual objectification prevailed in male homosocial groups. In fact, none of the men in the study, for example, mentioned ever verbally rejecting these hegemonic meanings in their all-male groups. The meanings of emotional detachment, competitiveness, and sexual objectification all were understood and behaviorally followed. Hegemonic masculinity was maintained despite individual departures from the norm, as individual departures were suppressed in homosocial settings. Nonhegemonic masculinity was subordinated through relegation to heterosocial settings. Emotional detachment, competitiveness, and the sexual objectification of women remained as the criteria to which men are held accountable, especially in all-male interactions.

Conclusions: Hegemonic Masculinity and the Gender Order

Hegemonic masculinity is consistently and continually recreated despite individual conceptualizations that contradict hegemonic meanings. Violations of the norms of hegemonic masculinity typically fail to produce alterations in the gender order; instead, they result in penalties to violators. With particular attention to the meanings that help sustain a pecking order among men, I have outlined some of the processes that pose barriers to gender equality in the United States, that is, the devaluation of meanings considered feminine, the suppression of these meanings in male heterosexual homosocial settings, and the relegation of nonhegemonic masculinity to heterosocial settings. Hegemonic masculinity, as demonstrated here, prevailed even in an academic community where ideals of gender equality are generally promoted. Reification of existing gender arrangements continues despite individual conflicts with hegemonic masculinity. The contradictions that non-hegemonic masculinity meanings (e.g., expression of intimate emotions, cooperation, and identification with women) potentially pose to dominant masculinity patterns are suppressed in male homosocial heterosexual interactions, inhibiting change. When individual departures from dominant masculinity are experienced as private dissatisfactions rather than as reason for contesting the social construction of masculinity, hegemonic patterns persist.

Because the barriers that distinguish appropriate from inappropriate masculinity generally are not accomplished through reconceptualization of individual masculinity alone, recasting the gender order in more favorable terms must also involve changes instigated at levels of social organization beyond that of social interaction. Subversion of widely accepted gender beliefs, attitudes, and expectations requires special attention to the processes that facilitate their *institutionalization*. That which must be continually challenged and ultimately eradicated in terms of masculinity, therefore, is the taken-for-granted assumption that being male means being emotionally detached, competitive, and supportive of the sexual objectification of women as well as the assumption that men whose identities do not embody these meanings are not true men. These changes must take place not only within heterosocial contexts but also within homosocial contexts and throughout all social institutions. In even broader terms, the goal yet to be accomplished is the *degenderization* of meanings. In other words, emotional detachment, competitiveness, and the sexual objectification of women must cease to exist as criteria by which being a man is measured. Indeed, the beliefs, attitudes, and expectations that decree the valuation and/or devaluation of distinctive masculine and feminine meanings in the first place must be deconstructed.

References

Burke, Peter J. 1980. The self: Measurement requirements from an interactionist perspective. *Social Psychology Quarterly* 43:18–29.

Burke, Peter J., and Donald C. Reitzes. 1981. The link between identity and role performance. *Social Psychology Quarterly* 44:83–92.

Cancian, Francesca M. 1987. *Love in America: Gender and self-development.* Cambridge, UK: Cambridge University Press.

Chodorow, Nancy. 1978. *The reproduction of mothering.* Berkeley: University of California Press.

—. 1980. Gender, relation, and difference in psychoanalytic perspective. In *The future of difference*, edited by Hester Eisenstein and Alice Jardine. Boston: G. K. Hall.

Connell, R. W. 1987. *Gender and power: Society, the person, and sexual politics.* Stanford, CA: Stanford University Press.

—. 1992. A very straight gay: Masculinity, homosexual experience, and the dynamics of gender. *American Sociological Review* 57:735–51.

Gilligan, Carol. 1982. *In a different voice: Psychological theory and women's development.* Cambridge, MA: Harvard University Press.

Johnson, Miriam. 1988. *Strong mothers, weak wives.* Berkeley: University of California Press.

Kaufman, Michael. 1994. Men, feminism, and men's contradictory experiences of power. In *Theorizing masculinities*, edited by Harry Brod and Michael Kaufman. Thousand Oaks, CA: Sage.

Lehn, Gregory K. 1992. Homophobia among men: Supporting and defining the male role. In *Men's lives*, edited by Michael S. Kimmel and Michael A. Messner. New York: Macmillan.

Lipman-Bluman, Jean. 1976. Toward a homosocial theory of sex roles: An explanation of the sex segregation of social institutions. *Signs: Journal of Women and Culture and Society* 1:15–31.

Messner, Michael A. 1992a. Boyhood, organized sports, and the construction of masculinity. In *Men's lives*, edited by Michael S. Kimmel and Michael A. Messner. New York: Macmillan.

—. 1992b. *Power at play: Sports and the problem of masculinity.* Boston: Beacon.

Phillips, Gerald M. 1986. Men talking to men about their relationships. *American Behavioral Scientist* 29:321–41.

Schur, Edwin M. 1984. *Labeling women deviant: Gender, stigma, and social control.* New York: Random House.

Thomas, Alison. 1990. The significance of gender politics in men's accounts of their "gender identity." *In Men, masculinities, and social theory*, edited by Jeff Hearn and David Morgan. London: Unwin Hyman.

West, Candace, and Don H. Zimmerman. 1987. Doing gender. *Gender & Society* 1:125–51.

CHAPTER 3

Men, Masculinity, and Manhood Acts
Douglas Schrock and Michael Schwalbe

Introduction

It could be said that we know a great deal about men and every conventional category of social life. There are literatures on men and work, men and war, men and sports, men and race, men and health, men and aging, men and crime, men and sexuality, men and violence, men and family, and men and friendship. Viewed in these terms, the landscape of our knowledge appears vast. Yet the tendency for sociologists to embrace the men-and-(fill in the blank) pattern when studying men and masculinity has, in our view, become limiting. As we will argue, moving forward depends on reclaiming key insights from Carrigan et al. (1985) and from interactionist analyses of gender.

Our approach here is to avoid the *men and* pattern and instead look at what the literature tells us about what men do, individually and collectively, such that women as a group are subordinated to men as a group and such that some men are subordinated to others. This is meant to reassert the importance of studying practices and processes. Our approach accords with current sociological theory that sees gender not as an attribute of individuals but as the name we give to cultural practices that construct women and men as different and that advantage men at the expense of women (Lorber 1994, Martin 2003, West & Zimmerman 1987). We thus focus primarily on qualitative studies that provide insight into how males construct the category "men" and themselves as its members.

Definitions

Much of the contention and confusion in the field stems from vague definitions of key concepts, inconsistent use of key concepts, or both. Although it is impossible to impose, post hoc, a set of definitions on a body of literature, it is possible to offer a set of definitions that can be used to interpret the literature. Our definitions are anchored in a social constructionist perspective, and as such might not be congenial to all. Definitions are necessary, however, for any attempt at sense-making and for sorting out disagreements. So we begin with the basics: males, men, and masculinity.

Based on differences in reproductive anatomy, humans are sorted into the categories "male" and "female," reflecting a belief that males and females are or should become different kinds of people. Males are taught and expected to identify themselves not only as biological males, but, depending on age, as either boys or men. Females are taught and expected to identify themselves not only as biological females, but, depending on age, as either girls or women. This distinction between reproductive anatomy and gender identity is crucial for understanding what men are and how to study them.

SOURCE: Schrock, D. and Schwalbe, M. (2009). Men, Masculinity, and Manhood Acts. *Annual Review of Sociology*, 35, 277–295. Reproduced with permission from the Annual Review of Sociology.

In this view, the category "males" is not equivalent to the category "men." Men are (usually) bio-logical males claiming rights and privileges attendant to membership in the dominant gender group. For an individual male to enjoy the benefits that derive from membership in the dominant gender group, he must present himself to others as a particular kind of social being: a man. This is, as Goffman (1977) and West & Zimmerman (1987) remind us, a dramaturgical task. To be credited as a man, what an individual male must do, in other words, is put on a convincing manhood act (Schwalbe 2005). This requires mastering a set of conventional signifying practices through which the identity "man" is established and upheld in interaction.

The dramaturgical task of establishing creditability as a man and thus as a member of the domi-nant gender group is aided by having a male body. Because of the conventional association between maleness and manhood, a male body is a symbolic asset. It is normally taken as a sign of qualification for membership in the category "men." However, it is neither necessary (females can mask their sec-ondary sex characteristics, appear to be male, and attempt to put on a manhood act; see, e.g., Dozier 2005) nor sufficient (males can fail to muster the other signifiers necessary to establish themselves as creditable men worthy of full manhood status).

Distinguishing between sex and gender is conventional wisdom in sociology, yet the distinction is worth reiterating, as it remains common to mistake males for men. Even more trouble arises in defining masculinity. Carrigan et al. (1985; see also Connell 1995) define masculinity as a "configuration of practices"—practices that have the effect of subordinating women. Although this definition usefully highlights what men do to maintain dominance, it is not without problems. It is not clear, for instance, precisely which of men's practices constitute masculinity (Martin 1998). The definition also tends to take the category "men" for granted, rather than treating the category as con-structed by practices and the meanings given to those practices.

To avoid this problem, our definitional strategy is to say that males—if they are to do their part in maintaining men as the dominant gender group and if they wish to enjoy the privileges that come from membership in that group—must signify possession of a masculine self. This self is, however, only a virtual reality, a dramatic effect, or a consequence of how an actor's appearance and behavior are interpreted by others (Goffman 1959). In this view, as opposed to the commonsense view, a mas-culine self is not a psychological entity, nor a built-in feature of male bodies. It is, rather, a self imputa-tion to an individual based on information given and given off in interaction, but it is an imputation that matters greatly.

The qualities seen as constituting a masculine self can vary historically and culturally. The practices that are interpreted as signs of a masculine self can also vary depending on other features of the actor (age, race, ethnicity, class), the audience, and the situation. In Western cultures, and in the contempo-rary United States especially, the essential element is a capacity to exert control or to resist being controlled (Johnson 2005). To elicit the attribution of possessing a masculine self thus requires signifying—with or without conscious awareness—that one possesses the capacities to make things happen and to resist being dominated by others.

Two further notes may be helpful here. First, to observe that males strive to claim membership in the dominant gender category by signifying a masculine self is not a moral critique. All humans learn where they are supposed to fit in a set of preexisting cultural categories, some of which are hierarchi-cally arranged. So just as North Americans of European descent learn to think of and present them-selves as white, which is the dominant racial category in U.S. culture, males learn to think of and present themselves as men, which is the dominant gender category. The root of the problem, then, if one opposes racial or gender inequality, lies in a system of privilege, not in individuals. Examining how gender is interactionally constructed, as many scholars have done and as we do here, is a matter of trying to understand how the system is reproduced, not a matter of leveling moral judgment.

Second, we acknowledge that efforts to exert control over the environment—efforts that might be part of manhood acts—can yield positive results. Survival and the quality of human life indeed depend on controlling things in the world. Thus, it is not our claim that attempts to signify a masculine self through acts of control have nothing but oppressive consequences. Our claim is that, whatever other consequences they might have, and regardless of what individual males consciously intend, manhood acts have the effect of reproducing an unequal gender order.

Problems with Plurality

Current thinking in the field treats masculinity not as singular but as plural. There is not just one form of masculinity, it is said, but rather there are multiple masculinities. This notion grew out of the distinction between hegemonic masculinity—the kind of manhood act most revered in a culture (Connell 1987, 1995, 2000)—and lower-status ways that manhood is enacted by males with fewer resources. Thinking of masculinity as plural usefully sensitizes us to differences and inequalities among groups of men, but it can also make it hard to see what it is that masculinities have in common, other than enactment by male bodies. We propose that the common theme should be seen not as a type of body but as a type of act: one that signifies a masculine self.

The multiple masculinities concept reflects a laudable desire to value diversity. It is ironic, then, that this concept has fostered a kind of categorical essentialism in studies of men. To invoke, for example, the existence of Black masculinity, Latino masculinity, gay masculinity, Jewish masculinity, working-class masculinity, and so on is to imply that there is an overriding similarity in the gender enactments of males who are Black, Latino, gay, Jewish, or working class. The implicit claim is that all members of the category practice an identifiably unique form of masculinity. This strategy of using conventional categories of race, ethnicity, sexuality, religion, or class to define masculinities into existence is dubious. It can cause us to lose sight of what these allegedly diverse gender-signifying practices have in common (again, other than enactment by male bodies) that makes them masculinity. It can also obscure important within-group variations.

The discourse of multiple masculinities has also had the effect of detaching men from their actions. Despite the ritual defining of masculinities as forms of practice, it is not uncommon to see masculinity invoked to explain men's behavior, as if masculinity were an independent variable that caused men to behave in more or less oppressive ways. If the behavior in question—some form of practice being studied—is what constitutes masculinity, then masculinity cannot be used to explain that behavior. Attributing men's behavior to masculinity also tends to discount men's agency. Our preference for referring to manhood acts arises from a desire to discourage the reification of masculinity and to redirect analytic attention to what males actually do to achieve dominance.

All manhood acts, as we define them, are aimed at claiming privilege, eliciting deference, and resisting exploitation. As suggested earlier, body types are irrelevant, except inasmuch as a male body is a symbolic asset and a female body a liability, when trying to signify possession of a masculine self and put on a convincing manhood act. The view we take here also focuses attention on what males do to create, maintain, and claim membership in a dominant gender group.

Learning to Signify Masculine Selves

Children are born into a world in which males/boys/men are differentiated from females/girls/women. Children must learn to categorize themselves and others in these terms and learn to convey to others that they understand this system of categorization and their place within it. For young males, this means learning to identify themselves as boys and signify masculine selves. They must master, in other words, the "identity codes" (Schwalbe & Mason-Schrock 1996) that are symbolic constituents of the gender order. A great deal of research has examined how this aspect of symbolic culture is learned through childhood interaction and through exposure to media imagery.

Young males' initial adoption of the identity "boy" is micropolitical. Based on 18 months of fieldwork at a preschool, Cahill (1986) found that children and adults use the term "baby" to stigmatize children's socially immature behavior, whereas they reward more mature acts by bestowing the term "boy" or "girl." Such responses do not merely affirm that males are boys and females are girls. More than this, such responses link grown-up status and approval from others with doing gender properly.

Young males also learn that gender identities are signified by using appropriate props. Initially, much of this identity work is done by parents, as newborns and toddlers are equipped with gendered names, clothes, and toys (Pomerleau et al. 1990). Preschool boys who fail to grasp the pattern and wear dresses or pink ribbons are scolded by their peers for misbehavior (Cahill 1989). Based on 42 interviews with diverse parents of preschoolers, Kane (2006) shows that parents—especially heterosexual fathers—often censure preschool sons who play with Barbies or wear fingernail polish or pink clothing. Such policing leads young males to, as Cahill (1989, p. 290) put it, "reject and devalue . . . symbols of female identity" in order to "confirm their identities as boys."

Boys and girls are often sorted or, later, sort themselves into segregated groups. Lever's (1978) field study of 181 fifth graders revealed how girls tend to play in small groups that stress cooperation and intimacy, whereas boys play in larger groups that are more competitive, goal-directed, and rule-guided. Even when boys and girls play together, they often do so in ways that imply essential differences between boys and girls and, usually, the superiority of boys (Thorne 1993). Lever argues that this gender-segregated play can lead to differential skill development that may account for some gender inequality among adults. Our point is that participation in segregated activities comes to be understood as part of how gender identities are signified. Playing or watching sports—violent sports in particular (McBride 1995)—can thus be a way for boys and men to signify masculine selves (Messner 1992).

Another lesson for young males is that emotional display must be regulated, lest it undermine a manhood act. In their ethnographic study of a summer camp, McGuffey & Rich (1999) found that high-status boys ostracized boys who cried. Males involved in sports similarly police the expression of emotion, affirming the principle that boys should not express fear or pain (Curry 1993, Messner 1992). Parents are often complicit in this gendered training because they feel accountable—for their sons' behavior—to other adults (Kane 2006). Parents who believe that their son's masculinity is threatened may be especially inclined to encourage stoicism.

Boys also learn that they should feel, or at least express, sexual desire for girls. Among preadolescent and adolescent boys, this desire is signified mainly through talk about the sexual appeal of girls and women, through sharing pin-ups and pornography, and by presenting themselves as heterosexually active and knowledgeable (Fine 1987, Thorne 1993). As Pascoe (2007, p. 114) documented in her ethnography of a high school, boys use language and sometimes violence to turn girls and women into props for signifying heterosexuality. The boys she studied sexually harassed girls with unwanted comments and touching, and talked and joked about rape (see also Renold 2007).

One of the most important lessons about signifying manhood concerns aggression and violence. Young boys' play often reflects popular warrior narratives in which violence is "legitimate and justified when it occurs within a struggle between good and evil" (Jordan & Cowan 1995, p. 728). Fathers and older male relatives often encourage (subtly, if not overtly) boys to fight, and reward them for doing so (Athens 1992, Messerschmidt 2000). The importance of signifying manhood through displays of fighting spirit is reinforced in sports, as coaches and teammates celebrate aggressive play while demeaning nonaggressive play as feminine (Fine 1987, Messner 1992). The pervasiveness of bullying has been attributed to this valorization of aggression and violence (Phillips 2007).

Learning to signify a masculine self entails learning how to adjust to audiences and situations and learning how one's other identities bear on the acceptability of a performance. Males in marginalized social groups may face special challenges in this regard (Majors & Billson 1992, Staples 1982).

Research on schools shows that teachers and administrators often stereotype African American and Latino boys as unruly, prompting increased surveillance and discipline (Ferguson 2000, Morris 2005). Boys learn, however, that they can impress peers if they break rules, talk back to teachers, and disdain academics (Ferguson 2000, Fordham & Ogbu 1986, Mac and Ghaill 1994, Willis 1977). Boys socialized into urban gangs (Stretesky & Pogrebin 2007) or white supremacist groups (Kimmel 2007) learn that they can achieve manhood status through actual or symbolic acts of intimidation. The lesson—for boys who are marginalized because of class or race—is that a masculine self can be signified, and deference elicited, by evoking fear in others.

The process of learning how to signify a masculine self in situationally appropriate ways continues throughout life. Men in manual labor jobs may learn that signifying a masculine self requires displays of strength and endurance, as well as resistance to being bossed (Collinson 1992). Men training for professional jobs, such as students in traditional MBA programs (Sinclair 1995), learn to signify masculine selves by appearing to be instrumentally oriented, rational, and able to manage subordinates. Men in the military learn that toughness, in-group loyalty, and the sexual objectification of women are the marks of manhood (Higate 2007). Men entering new jobs must thus learn to signify masculine selves in ways that accord with the organization's culture and gender politics.

Media Imagery

Media imagery provides a repertoire of signifying practices that males can draw on to craft manhood acts. For example, in their fieldwork studies, Dyson (1994) shows how boys in elementary school enact superhero narratives, and Milkie (1994) shows how middle school boys discuss, identify with, exaggerate, and imitate the male heroes of Hollywood movies. More is learned, however, than simply which models to emulate or how to do so. Media imagery also provides a shared symbolic language for identifying certain practices as signs of masculine character.

Research on children's media reveals that it often glorifies men's power. Hamilton et al. (2006) analyzed 200 of the most popular children's books and found that male characters were typically portrayed as assertive and aggressive, rarely nurturing, and more likely than female characters to work outside the home. Research on educational software for preschool children (Sheldon 2004) and comic books (Pecora 1992) similarly finds that male characters are more likely than female characters to be athletic, aggressive, and heroic. Similarly, grade school texts still overwhelmingly depict males as argumentative and competitive (Evans & Davies 2000). And whereas video games depict female characters as "victims or sexual objects," they portray male characters as "heroes and violent perpetrators" (Dietz 1998, p. 438). A lesson conveyed by much of this children's media is thus that males naturally command the attention and deference of others by virtue of their greater strength, daring, and capacity for violence.

Media targeting adolescent and adult men also create signifiers of masculine selves. Popular low-brow men's magazines (e.g., *Stuff, Maxim*) root manhood in displays of heterosexual appetite and virtuosity (Ezzell 2008, Taylor 2005). As McCaughey (2008) shows, popular culture often frames men's sexual infidelity and violence against women as biologically determined and thus inevitable. In mainstream magazines aimed at male audiences, men are most often portrayed as at work (Vigorito & Curry 1998), thus affirming productivity and bread-winning as signs of a masculine self. Even television portrayals that depart from these stereotypes, such as news stories about "Mr. Moms," typically underscore heterosexuality as a sign of genuine manhood beneath a veneer of domesticity (Vavrus 2002). The theme of the peaceful, gentle male who turns into a death-dealing warrior after suffering an unbearable outrage has been recycled often in Hollywood films (Sparks 1996). Such imagery affirms the value of a male body as a baseline signifier of a masculine self.

Media imagery also shapes the value of other signifiers. Males in marginalized groups are often represented in derogatory ways. White working-class men are often portrayed on television as "dumb, immature, irresponsible, or lacking in common sense" (Butsch 2003, p. 576). Gay men, although less disparaged in recent years, are often shown as acceptable targets of others' disapproval (Linneman 2008). Black men are often portrayed as lazy, violent, criminal, hypersexual, or naturally athletic (Entman & Rojecki 2000). Latinos too are often depicted as criminal or as illegal immigrants who cause social problems (Dixon & Linz 2002). Arab men are often depicted as decadent sheiks, religious fanatics, or terrorists (Shaheen 2001). Such imagery implicitly affirms the hegemonic ideal as white, monied, and self-possessed. It also provides symbolic resources for crafting conformist and oppositional presentations of masculine selves.

Manhood Acts: Themes and Variations

All manhood acts imply a claim to membership in the privileged gender group. To present one's self as a man is to make this claim, whether the presentation emphasizes or deemphasizes the capacity to exert control. A concern that has guided much research in this genre is for showing how males compensate—that is, how they modify their manhood acts—when they are unable or unwilling to enact the hegemonic ideal.

Research on transsexuals is particularly instructive. These studies have shown how adults must relearn to use their bodies, clothing, speech, and gestures to signify alternate gender identities. Female-to-male transsexuals, or transmen, flatten their chests, take hormones to grow facial hair and muscle tissue, deepen their voices, and cultivate gestures (e.g., giving firm handshakes) to publicly claim their chosen identities as men (Dozier 2005, Johnson 2007). Transwomen likewise mask secondary sex characteristics through surgery, makeup, and vocal alteration and adopt submissive gestures and speech styles (Schrock et al. 2005). Being identified as a member of a gender category, these studies show, depends on mastering the requisite bodily, gestural, sartorial, and vocal signifiers.

Research on transsexuals also shows how the elicitation of deference depends on the type of man one is perceived to be. Based on in-depth interviews with 29 transmen, Schilt (2006) found that whereas white transmen beginning to work as men were taken more seriously, had their requests readily met, and were evaluated as more competent than they were as women, young, small Black, Latino, and Asian transmen did not gain similar advantages. Similarly, in her interview study of 18 transmen, Dozier (2005) found that, as men, white transmen reported being given more respect and more conversational space and being included in men's banter. They also experienced less public harassment. Transmen of color, on the other hand, reported being more frequently treated as criminals, and short and effeminate transmen reported being publicly harassed as gay.

The multiple masculinities concept, despite its problems, has been helpful for seeing how various groups of men, using the material and symbolic resources available to them, are able to emphasize different aspects of the hegemonic ideal as means to construct effective manhood acts. For men in heterosexual relationships, occupational status and income are particularly important for eliciting deference from their partners. Middle-and upper-middle-class men can invoke job demands to avoid childcare and housework (Hochschild 1989, Pyke 1996). Based on 70 in-depth interviews with divorced and remarried men and women, Pyke (1996) showed that middle-class women's deference stems from accepting the idea that men's careers are primary. Even when women earn more than men, women "often defer to their husbands in the decision-making process" to affirm the belief that men should be in control (Tichenor 2005, p. 200).

Men with fewer economic resources may use other strategies to maintain relationship control. Research shows a pattern of more frequent use of overtly coercive behavior, including verbal abuse and physical force, among poor and working-class men (Benson et al. 2004, Pyke 1996, Strauss et al. 1980). Based on in-depth interviews with 122 batterers, Cavanagh and associates (2001) show that males are more likely to be violent when they see their female partners as insufficiently submissive and not servicing their emotional and sexual desires. Men of all social classes may also use emotional withdrawal as a control strategy (Sattel 1976). The status of being the dominant partner can thus be achieved in different ways. Lacking one kind of resource for eliciting deference often leads to employing another kind of resource in exaggerated fashion. It is also worth noting that no control strategy is guaranteed to succeed.

Close attention to how manhood acts are actually performed shows variation in response to situations. Men in management positions, for example, can use institutional authority to elicit deference, but they must also demonstrate the qualities of rationality, resolve, and competitiveness (Collinson & Hearn 1994), and show loyalty to the male hierarchy (Jackall 1988, Martin 2001). They may sometimes adopt a paternalistic demeanor, playing the role of benevolent guide, and at other times use humiliation and threats (Kerfoot & Whitehead 1998). Professional men may also demonstrate capability by emphasizing their special knowledge (Haas & Shaffir 1977). And as Dellinger (2004) shows in her comparative ethnography of organizations that produce feminist and pornographic magazines, organizational culture influences how men present themselves at work. Manhood acts are thus strategically adapted to the realities of resource availability, individual skill, local culture, and audience expectations.

Manhood acts often entail the sexualization of women as a way to signify heterosexuality, to demarcate gender boundaries, and to challenge women's authority. A great deal of research has looked at how this occurs in workplaces (Prokos & Padavic 2002, Quinn 2002, Uggen & Blackstone 2004). Although the targets of gratuitous sexualization and harassment are often women of lower status, men also sexualize and harass women who are organizational superiors (Rospenda et al. 1998). The same phenomena can be found outside the workplace (Grazian 2007, Schacht 1996). Sexualizing women serves not only to signify heterosexuality and mark the boundary between gender groups, but it also protects males from homophobic abuse by their peers.

Men who publicly identify as gay reject heterosexuality as part of their manhood acts, yet the power of the hegemonic ideal is reflected in the creation of gay male subcultures that valorize large bodies and muscularity (Hennen 2005), sexual risk-taking and voracity (Green & Halkitis 2006), and macho fashion (Mosher et al. 2006). Feminist analysts have suggested that misogyny among some gay men is similarly related to a desire on the part of gay men to distance themselves from women and retain a grip on male privilege (Frye 1983).

Research on men in low-status jobs shows another form of compensation: Instead of trying to control others, these men try to show that they cannot be controlled. These manhood acts rely on joking, verbal jousting, sexist talk, and sometimes sabotage to assert autonomy vis-à-vis bosses (Collinson 1992). Resistance may be heightened when men are expected to perform tasks conventionally associated with women. As Henson & Rogers (2001, p. 233) found when conducting participation observation and in-depth interviews with 68 male temporary clerical workers in Chicago and Los Angeles, despite their relative powerlessness in the workplace, the men resisted "demands for deference [such as] smiling, waiting, taking orders, and tolerating the bad moods of their supervisors." And, as Leidner (1993) shows in her field study of insurance salesmen, when work requires interactional deference with customers, the interaction is redefined as a contest for control so that men will be willing to do it.

The hegemonic ideal pervades the culture and sets a standard against which all manhood acts are measured. Because it is impossible, however, for all men to meet the hegemonic ideal, adjustments must be made, not only individually, but also subculturally. We thus find some working-class men creating bar and music cultures in which they signify masculine selves through heavy drinking and aggressive posturing (Eastman & Schrock 2008, Tilki 2006); economically marginalized men of color relying on sports, fighting, and sexual conquests (Anderson 1999, Wacquant 2003); college men turning to binge drinking and high-risk behavior (Peralta 2007); and others using crime to show that they are fearless and indomitable (Messerschmidt 1993).

Research on male subcultures has documented both wide variation in what are defined as signifiers of a masculine self and consistency in what it means to possess such a self. For example, the politically liberal, middle-class white males who populated the mythopoetic men's movement of the 1990s drew on Jungian psychology to redefine qualities conventionally associated with women—emotional expressivity, nurturance, and gentleness—as evidence of the "deep masculine" residing within all men (Schwalbe 1996). Likewise, the politically conservative Promise Keepers drew on Christian theology to validate similar qualities as masculine (Newton 2005). In both cases, however, the claim was that whereas the masculine self might need cultivation, it is naturally present in males, and its other elements—strength, courage, fierceness, and willingness to sacrifice—suit males to being warriors, leaders, and benevolent fathers.

The Reproduction of Gender Inequality

The original impetus for studying masculinity was to better understand the reproduction of gender inequality. Carrigan et al. (1985) were expressly concerned with masculinity as configurations of practice that have the effect of subordinating women. More recently, however, some theorists have retreated from the idea that masculinity necessarily produces inequality (see Connell & Messerschmidt 2005, p. 853). Other gender theorists have questioned the detachment of masculinity from gender inequality (Hanmer 1990, Flood 2002, Hearn 2004), arguing that the study of masculinity must remain part of a feminist project aimed at ending men's domination of women.

One reason for the loss of connection to the issue of gender inequality may be the success of the multiple masculinities concept. Eager embrace of this concept led researchers to document the diverse ways males style themselves as men, but with a loss of attention to what these styles have in common. Partly in response to this development, more critically inclined gender scholars have urged a shift from the endless cataloging of masculinities to examining *how men's practices create inequality.*

Differentiation is, before all else, basic to the creation and reproduction of gender inequality (Lorber 1994). Manhood acts are how males distinguish themselves from females/women and thus establish their eligibility for gender-based privilege. Indeed, the existence of the category "men" depends on the collective performance and affirmation of manhood acts. And, as argued earlier, successful manhood acts elicit deference from others in concrete situations. In these ways, manhood acts are inherently about upholding patriarchy and reproducing gender inequality. We can, however, look at research that shows how specific elements of manhood acts operate to advantage men at women's expense.

In the workplace, occupational segregation depends, first, on the manhood acts that make it possible to identify and channel different kinds of people toward different kinds of jobs (Reskin 1988). Manhood acts also have the effect of legitimating occupational segregation by upholding the illusion that men are more fit for certain kinds of jobs, especially those that involve the exercise of command. As Jackall's (1988) field study of corporate managers shows, managers must cultivate images of themselves as winners, as able to "get the job done," and as morally flexible and emotionally tough. Among defense intellectuals, a manhood act that features cold rationality may be necessary to be taken seriously (Cohn 1987). Men in some female-dominated occupations are put on a "glass escalator" toward greater authority and reward (Cognard-Black 2004, Williams 1992), whereas others are segregated horizontally in more highly valued specialties (Snyder & Green 2008, Williams 1992). Putting on a manhood act is part of how one establishes similarity to those already at the top of the hierarchy and gets through what others experience as a glass ceiling (Kanter 1977). And to the extent that jobs are designed by those who imagine the ideal occupant to be a male who fits the hegemonic ideal, those whose manhood acts come closest to the ideal are likely to be advantaged (Acker 1990).

Striving to emulate the hegemonic ideal may serve one well when seeking managerial power, but even compensatory manhood acts can make a difference for obtaining economic rewards. If the hegemonic ideal is out of dramaturgical reach, it may be possible to craft a manhood act that emphasizes self-sacrificial endurance to achieve organizational goals. Cooper (2000) shows how this was the case for the 20 computer programmers she interviewed. Much like athletes who signify a masculine self through a willingness to suffer pain (Curry 1993), these programmers claimed manhood status by practicing "nerd masculinity" that involved suffering long hours of work to meet production goals and to establish a reputation for unique expertise.

In the political sphere, manhood acts approximating the hegemonic ideal may be crafted to achieve or consolidate power (Messner 2007). In the case of the presidency, the act must also serve an iconic function for the nation; that is, the act must represent the collectively imagined, idealized character of the nation (Hall 1979). George W. Bush, for example, refashioned his persona after the 2001 terrorist attacks to underscore his self-proclaimed role as a "war president" leading a great and powerful nation (Coe et al. 2007). Disrespecting the manhood acts of political opponents is also common. During the 2004 U.S. presidential election, the Bush campaign and much of the media framed the losing Democratic candidate, John Kerry, as feminine and French-like (Fahey 2007). Women who vie with men for such positions are often compelled to put on a compensatory manhood act or, as it is sometimes said, to "out-macho the boys."

Research on men in social movements, as noted in the previous section, shows that manhood acts often involve collaboration among men. This is true more generally. Even men who reject hegemonic ideals may feel compelled, when in all-male groups, to appear emotionally detached, competitive, and willing to objectify women (Bird 1996). In college fraternities, young men mutually affirm their manhood by collectively defining women as "servers" and as sexual "bait" or "prey" (Martin & Hummer 1989). In cases where men's oppressive behavior is challenged, such as batterer intervention programs (Schrock & Padavic 2007) or prison antiviolence groups (Fox 1999), men often collaborate to outwit social workers and assert a right to control women. Inequality is thus reproduced when males uncritically affirm oppressive elements of other males' manhood acts or conspire to resist challenges to those acts.

Individual Liabilities and Gender-Class Advantages

The consequences of manhood acts for the reproduction of gender inequality can be contradictory. Men as a gender class can benefit from the collective upholding of sexist ideology and of images of males as possessing essential qualities that suit them for the exercise of power. Yet compensatory manhood acts can sometimes reproduce inequalities in ways that disadvantage subgroups of men. For example, a number of studies (e.g., Willis 1977, MacLeod 1995, Anderson 1999) have shown how self-protective displays of toughness by poor and working-class young men lead to disinvestment in academic work and failure in school.

Young men may also distance themselves from intellectual work, which is defined as feminine, and embrace physical work, which is defined as masculine, and thus limit their chances for upward mobility via success in school (Fine et al. 1997).

Beyond school, compensatory manhood acts can undermine employment relationships. Young men who signify a capacity to resist control by others may find it difficult to get and hold jobs in the mainstream economy (Bourgois 1995). The use of crime to signify a masculine self carries the risk of getting caught and losing opportunities for conventional economic success (Messerschmidt 1993). Compensatory manhood acts that are adaptive in some contexts can thus be self-destructive in others. Much depends on who is presenting what kind of masculine self to whom and under what conditions. This suggests a need to examine how the consequences of manhood acts are shaped by racism and the class structure.

Whereas manhood acts that emphasize the defiance of authority can undermine the mobility prospects of individual men, men as a gender class may continue to enjoy privilege because of the collective image fostered by manhood acts that involve crime, violence, and interpersonal intimidation. (The use of state violence in manhood acts undertaken by elite males is also consequential in this regard.) To the extent that such acts imply the innate dangerousness of males, women may feel compelled to seek protection from males deemed safe—protection for which they exchange subservience (Schwalbe et al. 2000, pp. 426–27). Nonviolent males can thus derive privilege from the violent manhood acts of other males.

Males can also incur health damage as a consequence of manhood acts. Research has linked men's higher rates of morbidity and mortality to failure to seek help early (O'Brien et al. 2005); to higher levels of risk-taking behavior, including drinking, smoking, and reckless driving (Verbrugge 1985); and to poor social support networks (House et al. 1988). Men's sports injuries, death by violence, and suicide have also been linked to gender enactment (Sabo 2005). As with crime, much of this health-damaging behavior may be symbolic, intended to signify capacities to control one's own life, to be invulnerable and needless of help, and to be fearless and hence not easily intimidated by others. The effort to signify a masculine self, as some analysts have suggested (Courtenay 2000), can be toxic.

References

Acker J. 1990. Hierarchies, jobs, bodies: A theory of gendered organizations. *Gend. Soc.* 4:139–58.

Anderson E. 1999. *Code of the Street: Decency, Violence, and the Moral Life of the Inner City.* New York: W. W. Norton.

Athens L. 1992. *The Creation of Dangerous Violent Criminals.* Urbana: Univ. Ill. Press.

Benson ML, Wooldredge J, Thistlethwaite AB. 2004. The correlation between race and domestic violence is confounded with community context. *Soc. Probl.* 51:326–42.

Bird SR. 1996. Welcome to the men's club: Homosociality and the maintenance of hegemonic masculinity. *Gend. Soc.* 10:120–32.

Bourgois P. 1995. *In Search of Respect: Selling Crack in El Barrio.* Cambridge, UK: Cambridge Univ. Press.

Butsch R. 2003. Ralph, Fred, Archie and Homer: Why television keeps recreating the white male working class buffoon. In *Gender, Race, and Class in the Media,* ed. G Dines, JM Humez, pp. 575–88. Thousand Oaks, CA: Sage.

Cahill SE. 1986. Language practices and self definition: The case of gender identity acquisition. *Sociol. Q.* 27:295–311.

Cahill SE. 1989. Fashioning males and females: Appearance management and the social reproduction of gender. *Symb. Interact.* 12:281–98.

Carrigan T, Connell B, Lee J. 1985. Toward a new sociology of masculinity. *Theory Soc.* 14:551–604.

Cavanagh K, Dobash RE, Dobash RP, Lewis R. 2001. "Remedial work": Men's strategic responses to their violence against intimate female partners. *Sociology* 35:695–714.

Coe K, Domke D, Bagley MM, Cunningham S, Van Leuven N. 2007. Masculinity as political strategy: George W. Bush, the "war on terrorism," and an echoing press. *J. Women Polit. Policy* 29:31–55.

Cognard-Black AJ. 2004. Will they stay, or will they go? Sex-atypical work among token men who teach. *Sociol. Q.* 45:113–39.

Cohn C. 1987. Sex and death in the rational world of defense intellectuals. *Signs.* 12:687–718.

Collinson D, Hearn J. 1994. Naming men as men: Implications for work, organizations and management. *Gend. Work Organ.* 1:2–22.

Collinson DA. 1992. *Managing the Shopfloor: Subjectivity, Masculinity and Workplace Culture.* New York: Walter de Gruyter.

Connell RW. 1987. *Gender and Power: Society, the Person, and Sexual Politics.* Sydney: Allen & Unwin.

Connell RW. 1995. *Masculinities.* Sydney: Allen & Unwin.

Connell RW. 2000. *The Men and the Boys.* St Leonards, NSW: Allen & Unwin.

Connell RW, Messerschmidt JW. 2005. Hegemonic masculinity: Rethinking the concept. *Gend. Soc.* 19:829–59.

Cooper M. 2000. Being the "go-to guy": Fatherhood, masculinity, and the organization of work in Silicon Valley. *Qual. Sociol.* 23:379–405.

Courtenay WH. 2000. Constructions of masculinity and their influence on men's well-being: A theory of gender and health. *Soc. Sci. Med.* 50:1385–401.

Curry TJ. 1993. A little pain never hurt anyone: Athletic career socialization and the normalization of sports injury. *Symb. Interact.* 16:273–90.

Dellinger K. 2004. Masculinities in "safe" and "embattled" organizations: Accounting for pornographic and feminist magazines. *Gend. Soc.* 18:545–66.

Dietz TL. 1998. An examination of violence and gender role portrayals in video games: Implications for gender socialization and aggressive behavior. *Sex Roles* 38:425–42.

Dixon RL, Linz D. 2002. Overrepresentation and underrepresentation of African Americans and Latinos as lawbreakers on television news. *J. Commun.* 52:131–54.

Dozier R. 2005. Beards, breasts, and bodies: Doing sex in a gendered world. *Gend. Soc.* 19:297–316.

Dyson AH. 1994. The ninjas, the X-Men, and the ladies: Playing with power and identity in an urban primary school. *Teach. Coll. Rec.* 96:219–39.

Eastman J, Schrock DP. 2008. Southern rock musicians' construction of white trash. *Race Gend. Class.* 15:205–19.

Entman RM, Rojecki A. 2000. *The Black Image in the White Mind: Media and Race in America.* Chicago: Univ. Chicago Press.

Evans L, Davies K. 2000. No sissy boys here: A content analysis of the representation of masculinity in elementary school reading textbooks. *Sex Roles* 41:255–70.

Ezzell MB. 2008. Pornography, lad mags, video games, and boys: Reviving the canary in the cultural coal mine. In *The Sexualization of Childhood*, ed. S Olfman, pp. 7–32. Westport, CT: Praeger.

Fahey AC. 2007. French and feminine: Hegemonic masculinity and the emasculation of John Kerry in the 2004 presidential race. *Crit. Stud. Mass Commun.* 24:132–50.

Ferguson AA. 2000. *Bad Boys: Public Schools in the Making of Black Masculinity.* Ann Arbor: Univ. Mich. Press.

Fine GA. 1987. *With the Boys: Little League Baseball and Preadolescent Culture.* Chicago: Univ. Chicago Press.

Fine M, Weis L, Addelston J, Marusza J. 1997. (In)secure times: Constructing white working-class masculinities in the late 20th century. *Gend. Soc.* 11:52–68.

Flood M. 2002. Between men and masculinity: An assessment of the term "masculinity" in recent scholarship on men. In *Manning the Next Millennium: Studies in Masculinities*, ed. S Pearce, V Muller, pp. 203–13. Bentley, WA: Black Swan.

Fordham S, Ogbu JU. 1986. Black students' school success: Coping with the "burden of 'acting white.'" *Urban Rev.* 18:176–206.

Fox KJ. 1999. Changing violent minds: Discursive correction and resistance in the cognitive treatment of violent offenders in prison. *Soc. Probl.* 46:88–103.

Frye M. 1983. *The Politics of Reality: Essays in Feminist Theory.* Trumansburg, NY: Crossing.

Goffman E. 1959. *The Presentation of Self in Everyday Life.* New York: Doubleday.

Goffman E. 1977. The arrangement between the sexes. *Theory Soc.* 4:301–31.

Grazian D. 2007. The girl hunt: Urban nightlife and the performance of masculinity as collective activity. *Symb. Interact.* 30:221–43.

Green AI, Halkitis PN. 2006. Crystal methamphetamine and sexual sociality in an urban gay subculture: An elective affinity. *Cult. Health Sex.* 8:317–33.

Haas J, Shaffir W. 1977. The professionalization of medical students: Developing competence and a cloak of competence. *Symb. Interact.* 1:71–88.

Hall PM. 1979. The presidency and impression management. *Stud. Symb. Interact.* 2:283–305.

Hamilton MC, Anderson D, Broaddus M, Young K. 2006. Gender stereotyping and under-representation of female characters in 200 popular children's picture books: A twenty-first century update. *Sex Roles* 55:557–65.

Hanmer J. 1990. Men, power, and the exploitation of women. *Women's Stud. Int. Forum.* 13:443–56.

Hearn J. 2004. From hegemonic masculinity to the hegemony of men. *Fem. Theory.* 5:49–72.

Hennen P. 2005. Bear bodies, bear masculinity: Recuperation, resistance, or retreat? *Gend. Soc.* 19:25–43.

Henson KD, Rogers JK. 2001. "Why Marcia you've changed!" Male clerical temporary workers doing masculinity in a feminized occupation. *Gend. Soc.* 15:218–38.

Higate P. 2007. Peacekeepers, masculinities, and sexual exploitation. *Men Masc.* 10:99–119.

Hochschild A. 1989. *Second Shift: Working Parents and the Revolution at Home.* New York: Viking Penguin.

House JS, Landis KR, Umberson D. 1988. Social relationships and health. *Science.* 241:540–45.

Jackall R. 1988. *Moral Mazes: The World of Corporate Managers.* New York: Oxford Univ. Press.

Johnson AG. 2005. *The Gender Knot: Unraveling Our Patriarchal Legacy.* Philadelphia: Temple Univ. Press.

Johnson K. 2007. Changing sex, changing self: Theorizing transitions in embodied subjectivity. *Men Masc.* 10:54–70.

Jordan E, Cowan A. 1995. Warrior narratives in the kindergarten classroom: Renegotiating the social-contract. *Gend. Soc.* 9:727–43.

Kane EW. 2006. "No way my boys are going to be like that!" Parents' responses to children's gender noncomformity. *Gend. Soc.* 20:149–76.

Kanter RM. 1977. *Men and Women of the Corporation.* New York: Basic Books.

Kerfoot D, Whitehead S. 1998. "Boys own" stuff: Masculinity and the management of further education. *Sociol. Rev.* 46:436–57.

Kimmel M. 2007. Racism as adolescent male rite of passage: ex-Nazis in Scandinavia. *J. Contemp. Ethnogr.* 36:202–18.

Leidner R. 1993. *Fast Food, Fast Talk.* Berkeley: Univ. Calif. Press.

Lever J. 1978. Sex differences in the complexity of children's play and games. *Am. Sociol. Rev.* 43:471–83.

Linneman TJ. 2008. How do you solve a problem like Will Truman? The feminization of gay masculinities on Will & Grace. *Men Masc.* 10:583–603.

Lorber J. 1994. *Paradoxes of Gender.* New Haven, CT: Yale Univ. Press.

Mac an Ghaill M. 1994. *The Making of Men: Masculinities, Sexualities and Schooling.* Buckingham, UK: Open Univ. Press.

MacLeod J. 1995. *Ain't No Makin' It: Aspirations and Attainment in a Low-Income Neighborhood.* Boulder, CO: Westview.

Majors R, Billson JM. 1992. *Cool Pose: The Dilemmas of Black Manhood in America.* New York: Lexington

Martin PY. 1998. Why can't a man be more like a woman? Reflections on Robert Connell's Masculinities. *Gend. Soc.* 13:472–74.

Martin PY. 2001. "Mobilizing masculinities": Women's experiences of men at work. *Organization* 8:587–618

Martin PY. 2003. "Said and done" versus "saying and doing": Gendering practices, practicing gender at work. *Gend. Soc.* 17:342–66.

Martin PY, Hummer RA. 1989. Fraternities and rape on campus. *Gend. Soc.* 3:457–73.

McBride J. 1995. *War, Battering, and Other Sports: The Gulf Between American Men and Women.* New Jersey: Humanities Press.

McCaughey M. 2008. *The Caveman Mystique: Pop-Darwinism and the Debates Over Sex, Violence, and Science.* New York: Routledge.

McGuffey CS, Rich BL. 1999. Playing in the gender transgression zone: Race, class, and hegemonic masculinity in middle childhood. *Gend. Soc.* 13:608–27.

Messerschmidt JW. 1993. *Masculinities and Crime: Critique and Reconceptualization of Theory.* Lanham, MD: Rowman & Littlefield.

Messerschmidt JW. 2000. *Nine Lives: Adolescent Masculinities, the Body, and Violence.* Boulder, CO: Westview.

Messner MA. 1992. *Power at Play: Sports and the Problem of Masculinity.* Boston: Beacon.

Messner MA. 2007. The masculinity of the governator: Muscle and compassion in American politics. *Gend. Soc.* 21:461–80.

Milkie MA. 1994. Social world approach to cultural-studies: Mass-media and gender in the adolescent peer group. *J. Contemp. Ethnogr.* 23:354–80.

Morris EW. 2005. "Tuck in that shirt!" Race, class, gender and discipline in an urban school. *Sociol. Perspect.* 48:25–48.

Mosher CM, Levitt HM, Manley E. 2006. Layers of leather: The identity formation of leathermen as a process of transforming meanings of masculinity. *J. Homosex.* 51:93–123.

Newton J. 2005. *From Panthers to Promise Keepers: Rethinking the Men's Movement.* Lanham, MD: Rowman & Littlefield.

O'Brien R, Hunt K, Hart G. 2005. "It's caveman stuff, but that is to a certain extent how guys still operate": Men's accounts of masculinity and help seeking. *Soc. Sci. Med.* 61:503–16.

Pascoe CJ. 2007. *Dude, You're a Fag: Masculinity and Sexuality in High School.* Berkeley: Univ. Calif. Press.

Pecora N. 1992. Superman/superboys/supermen: The comic book hero as socializing agent. In *Men, Masculinity, and the Media*, ed. S Craig, pp. 61–77. Newbury Park, CA: Sage.

Peralta RL. 2007. College alcohol use and the embodiment of hegemonic masculinity among European American men. *Sex Roles* 56:741–56.

Phillips DA. 2007. Punking and bullying: Strategies in middle school, high school, and beyond. *J. Interpers. Violence.* 22:158–78.

Pomerleau A, Bloduc D, Cossette L, Malcuit G. 1990. Pink or blue: Environmental gender stereotypes in the first two years of life. *Sex Roles* 22:359–67.

Prokos A, Padavic I. 2002. 'There oughtta be a law against bitches': Masculinity lessons in police academy training. *Gend. Work Organ.* 9:439–59.

Pyke KD. 1996. Class-based masculinities: The interdependence of gender, class, and interpersonal power. *Gend. Soc.* 10:527–49.

Quinn BA. 2002. Sexual harassment and masculinity: The power and meaning of "girl watching." *Gend. Soc.* 16:386–402.

Renold E. 2007. Primary school "studs": (de)constructing young boys' heterosexual masculinities. *Men Masc.* 9:275–97.

Reskin BF. 1988. Bringing the men back in: Sex differentiation and the devaluation of women's work. *Gend. Soc.* 2:58–81.

Rospenda KM, Richman JA, Nawyn SJ. 1998. Doing power: The confluence of gender, race, and class in contrapower sexual harassment. *Gend. Soc.* 12:40–60.

Sabo D. 2005. The study of masculinities and men's health: An overview. In *Handbook of Studies on Men & Masculinities*, ed. MS Kimmel, J Hearn, RW Connell, pp. 326–52. Thousand Oaks, CA: Sage.

Sattel JW. 1976. The inexpressive male: Tragedy or sexual politics? *Soc. Probl.* 23:469–77.

Schacht SP. 1996. Misogyny on and off the "pitch": The gendered world of male rugby players. *Gender Soc.* 10:550–65.

Schilt K. 2006. Just one of the guys? How transmen make gender visible at work. *Gend. Soc.* 20:465–90

Schrock D, Padavic I. 2007. Negotiating hegemonic masculinity in a batterer intervention program. *Gend. Soc.* 21:625–49.

Schrock D, Reid L, Boyd EM. 2005. Transsexuals' embodiment of womanhood. *Gend. Soc.* 19:317–35.

Schwalbe ML. 1996. *Unlocking the Iron Cage: The Men's Movement, Gender Politics, and American Culture.* New York: Oxford Univ. Press.

Schwalbe ML. 2005. Identity stakes, manhood acts, and the dynamics of accountability. In *Studies in Symbolic Interaction*, ed. N Denzin, pp. 65–81. New York: Elsevier.

Schwalbe ML, Mason-Schrock D. 1996. Identity work as group process. In *Advances in Group Processes*, ed. B Markovsky, M Lovaglia, R Simon, pp. 113–47. Greenwich, CT: JAI.

Schwalbe ML, Godwin S, Holden D, Schrock D, Thompson S, Wolkomir M. 2000. Generic processes in the reproduction of inequality: An interactionist analysis. *Soc. Forces* 79:419–52.

Shaheen JG. 2001. *Reel Bad Arabs: How Hollywood Vilifies a People.* New York: Olive Branch.

Sheldon JP. 2004. Gender stereotypes in educational software for young children. *Sex Roles* 51:433–44.

Sinclair A. 1995. Sex and the MBA. *Organization* 2:295–317.

Snyder KA, Green AI. 2008. Revisiting the glass escalator: The case of gender segregation in a female dominated occupation. *Soc. Probl.* 55:271–99.

Sparks R. 1996. Masculinity and heroism in the Hollywood "blockbuster": The culture industry and contemporary images of crime and law enforcement. *Br. J. Criminol.* 36:348–60.

Staples R. 1982. *Black Masculinity: The Black Man's Blues in American Society.* San Francisco: Black Scholars.

Straus MA, Gelles RJ, Steinmetz SK. 1980. *Behind Closed Doors: Violence in the American Family*. Garden City, NY: Doubleday.

Stretesky PB, Pogrebin MR. 2007. Gang-related gun violence: Socialization, identity, and self. *J. Contemp. Ethnogr.* 36:85–114.

Taylor LD. 2005. All for him: Articles about sex in American lad magazines. *Sex Roles* 52:153–63.

Thorne B. 1993. *Gender Play: Girls and Boys in School*. New Brunswick, NJ: Rutgers Univ. Press.

Tichenor V. 2005. Maintaining men's dominance: negotiating identity and power when she earns more. *Sex Roles* 53:191–205.

Tilki M. 2006. The social contexts of drinking among Irish men in London. *Drugs* 13:247–61.

Uggen C, Blackstone A. 2004. Sexual harassment as a gendered expression of power. *Am. Sociol. Rev.* 69:64–92.

Vavrus MD. 2002. Domesticating patriarchy: Hegemonic masculinity and television's "Mr. Mom." *Crit. Stud. Mass Commun.* 19:352–75.

Verbrugge LM. 1985. Gender and health: An update on hypotheses and evidence. *J. Health Soc. Behav.* 26:156–82.

Vigorito AJ, Curry TJ. 1998. Marketing masculinity: Gender identity and popular magazines. *Sex Roles* 39:135–52.

Wacquant L. 2003. *Body and Soul: Notebooks of An Apprentice Boxer*. New York: Oxford.

West C, Zimmerman D. 1987. Doing gender. *Gend. Soc.* 1:125–51.

Williams CL. 1992. The glass escalator: Hidden advantages for men in the "female" professions. *Soc. Probl.* 39:253–67.

Willis P. 1977. *Learning to Labor: How Working Class Kids Get Working Class Jobs*. New York: Columbia Univ. Press.

CHAPTER 4

Inclusive Masculinity Theory

Eric Anderson

Social theorists frequently write about their theories in academically inaccessible language. This permits various people to interpret the theory differently, and perhaps contributes to the life and utility of a theory. As a public sociologist concerned with emancipatory research, however, my aim in describing inclusive masculinity theory is the opposite. I desire to explicate the theory in accessible language, so that the reader will understand exactly what I suggest, and what I do not.

The first thing to understand about inclusive masculinity theory is that it emerged from my data, and not the opposite way around. I approached my early research on masculinities using Connell's notion of hegemonic masculinity. This worked particularly well with my work on openly gay male athletes (Anderson 2002). However, in my subsequent research, I found hegemony theory incapable of explaining my data. I began the process of formulating inclusive masculinity theory to describe the emergence of an archetype of masculinity that undermines the principles of orthodox (read hegemonic) masculine values, yet one that is also esteemed among male peers.

For example, I found that the reduction of cultural homophobia in one cheerleading association challenged the dominance that hegemonic masculinity maintained over heterosexual university athletes. Here, openly gay athletes peacefully performed with their heterosexual counterparts, and heterosexual men celebrated men's femininity by dancing erotically and performing otherwise feminized behaviors. Conversely, in a rival association orthodox masculinity was esteemed, and these men did not perform as flamboyantly. And, although there were many gay men in this conservative cheerleading association, they largely remained closeted. Accordingly, I labeled one association as orthodox and the other inclusive, describing how institutional and organizational culture influenced masculine performances and values in each. However, two oppositional masculinities, each with equal influence, co-existing within one culture is not consistent with Connell's theorizing.

Connell suggests that multiple masculinities *do* exist within any organization, institution or culture, but she argues that there will be only one hegemonic archetype of masculinity. In other words, Connell describes hegemonic masculinity as a *hegemonic* process by which only *one* form of institutionalized masculinity is "culturally exalted" above all others (Connell 1995: 77). Then, according to Connell, men are culturally compelled to associate with this one dominant form (i.e. men looking up the hierarchy). This "looking up" is the *hegemony* in hegemonic masculinity. Again, this was not the case in cheerleading. Even *within* the orthodox institution there were a number of inclusive teams comprised of men who did not value most of the tenets of orthodox masculinity.

Some might be tempted to explain two equally subscribed to and competing forms of masculinity through Connell's notion of protest masculinity. This form of masculinity, she argues, contests the current hegemonic form for dominance. But again the resolution of this struggle is simply that a new,

SOURCE: Anderson, E. (2010). Inclusive Masculinity Theory. In *The Changing Nature of Masculinities*. Routledge. Reproduced with permission from Routledge.

singular, version of a (hegemonic) dominating masculinity emerges, even if it is a softer archetype. Protest masculinity is valuable for explaining individual men, or a group of men who opt out of an otherwise hegemonic system, but it fails to adequately capture what occurs with two dominate archetypes, in which neither hegemonically dominates. This is for two reasons.

First, hegemonic masculinity theory did not adequately frame the cheerleading results because neither group felt that they failed to model an ideal type of masculinity. Neither group thought that the version the other aspired to was right, natural, or desirable. The men who ascribed to inclusive masculinity did not aspire to or value orthodox masculinity and those aspiring to orthodox masculinity felt no cultural sway to become more inclusive. Thus, there is no evidence that men were influenced by hegemonic processes. This alone is enough to prove that hegemonic masculinity theory is incapable of capturing what occurred in this setting. In order to use hegemonic masculinity theory one must find examples of hegemony. However, neither group of men felt subordinated or marginalized by the other group. Men did not suffer for failing to meet the other group's mandates. Neither was hegemonic. Connell's theory does not account for this social matrix.

I continued to develop inclusive masculinity theory through the results of subsequent studies of university-attending men: in a fraternity, a rugby team and multiple soccer teams. In each setting, I found that a more inclusive version of masculinity dominated numerically, much more so than in the cheerleading research. But again this dominance did not seem hegemonic; it did not seem to dominate in the way Connell describes the operation of hegemonic masculinity. Furthermore, I am not the only one to describe such findings. Swain (2006a), for example, discusses a notion of personalized masculinity among the pre-adolescents he studies, suggesting that these young men are content to pursue identities not associated with orthodox masculinity.

The final piece to my theory came after conducting a semester-long ethnography with one of my graduate students, Mark McCormack, on a standard British high school. This school sits at the median of England's testing results, drawing students from two sides of a town divided by class. Nonetheless, all boys modeled an inclusive version of masculinity. We found various masculine archetypes co-existing without social struggle (jocks, emos, scholars, artists, etc.), and with no one group dominating. Boys are happy with their group affiliation, and none feel oppressed. Furthermore the public expression of homophobia or homophobic discourse is not acceptable within *any* group. While some elements of orthodox masculinity are valued in some groups (the athletes still value self-sacrifice), the outright expression of homophobia, misogyny, and masculine bravado associated with orthodox masculinity is not acceptable in any group.

Consequently, the temporal-shift in my sequential studies led to the completion of inclusive masculinity theory. I developed it to conceptualize what happens concerning masculinities in three cultural moments of homohysteria (Anderson 2005b, 2008c).

Key to these three phases is the degree of projection of homosexual suspicion and/or labeling of one as homosexual via homophobic discourse. In periods of high homohysteria, homophobia is used to stratify men in deference to a heteromasculine hegemonic mode of dominance (Connell 1987, 1995). The utility of homophobic discourse is made more salient through awareness that, in a homohysteric culture, heterosexual men are culturally incapable of permanently proving their heterosexuality. One's heterosexual capital waxes and wanes depending on the behaviors one exhibits, and the terrains one occupies. Thus heterosexual men (and gay men wishing to remain closeted) must continually attempt to prove and reprove their heteromasculinity through acquiescence to orthodox expectations and behaviors that are coded as heterosexual. As multiple masculinity scholars have shown (cf. Plummer 1999), in periods of high homohysteria, boys and men are compelled to act aggressively, to maintain homophobic attitudes, and they are socially encouraged to raise their masculine capital through sport and muscularity (cf. Pronger 1990).

In periods of high homohysteria, men must also remain emotionally and tactilely distant from one another (Allen 2007), because emotional intimacy and tactility are symbols of femininity and/or homosexuality. Thus, boys and men have traditionally been prohibited from holding hands, softly hugging, caressing, or kissing, in either public or private (Fine 1988; Kaplan 2006). Accordingly, in periods of high homohysteria, men's demonstrations of affection are generally relegated to the public sphere (such as playing sports), and physical intimacy often comes through symbolic acts of violence, such as mock punching and rancorous slapping. Also, unlike studies of today, which find various meanings associated with homophobic discourse (Pascoe 2005), in periods of high homohysteria, homophobic discourse maintains *specific* homosexual meaning.

It is in this zeitgeist that Kimmel suggests homophobia *is* masculinity (1994). The frenzied homo-hysteric masculine ethos that is esteemed in this cultural moment means that not only is physical femininity among men stigmatized, but anything associated with emotional or personal femininity is looked upon disparagingly, too. This, of course, has serious implications for femphobia, sexism, and the gender order.

It is in this cultural moment that Connell's hegemonic masculinity theory maintains particular utility. In a cultural zeitgeist of excessive homohysteria, homosexuality will be stigmatized, and boys and men will desire to distance themselves from it. Thus, in a highly homohysteric Anglo-American culture, a dominant form of masculinity will exist, and one can predict that it will be predicated in opposition to whatever cultural stereotypes are ascribed to gay men. Men who fail to meet the prescribed or achieved characteristic of whatever that archetype might be nonetheless pledge their allegiance to the dominant form because this association is in itself heterosexualizing and mascu-linizing. This means that the polarization of masculine and feminine will further separate, and, as Connell suggests, all men will gain in patriarchal privilege.

However, inclusive masculinity theory argues that as cultural homohysteria significantly declines, a hegemonic form of conservative masculinity will lose its dominance, and softer masculinities will exist without the use of social stigma to police them. Thus, two dominant (but not necessarily domi-nating) forms of masculinity will co-exist, one orthodox and one inclusive. Orthodox masculinity loses its hegemonic influence because there is a critical mass of men who publicly disavow it. Ortho-dox valuing men remain homophobic, femphobic, emotionally and physically distant from one another. These men necessarily fear transgressing feminized terrains. Conversely, those ascribing to more inclusive versions of masculinity demonstrate emotional and physically homosocial proximity. They begin to blur the lines between masculinity and femininity.

This is permitted because orthodox ascribing men lose the ability to question another's sexuality in order to force them to comply with orthodox masculinities' requisites. Homophobic discourse no longer maintains the homosexualizing effect that it once did, even if it remains the primary weapon of insult. This, I argue, is why some researchers (Burn 2000; Pascoe 2005) find that even though young men say 'that's gay' and 'fag' frequently, they do not unanimously intend for it to be inter-preted as homophobic. In this stage, the very meanings of the words and phrases are caught between dueling Zeitgeists. This does not mean that the use of homophobic discourse ceases to create frame-works of stigma around homosexuality, but the point remains that the *intent* of this discourse has, nonetheless, shifted.

In this moment, behaviors and terrains that once homosexualized men no longer have the same homosexualizing agency. And, once previously stigmatized terrains and behaviors become available to heterosexuals without the need for one to defend their heterosexuality, it opens up yet further social and emotional spaces for heterosexual men to occupy without threat to their publicly perceived het-erosexual identities.

In this phase, men ascribing to inclusive masculinity will also show improved social attitudes concerning women. This is a result of multiple processes, including the social permission men main-tain to bond with women in non-sexual ways. This is because the mandates of compulsory hetero-sexuality wane, and once men are permitted to befriend women in platonic ways, the stigma associated with women's narratives and worldly understandings begins to erode. This may have socio-positive implications for men's cultural dominance over women as well.

Finally, inclusive masculinity theory argues that in an Anglo-American culture with severely diminished homohysteria, homophobic discourse and/or its associated intent to degrade homosexuals, is no longer socially acceptable. In such a setting, the esteemed attributes of men will no longer rely on control and domination of other men; there is no predominance of masculine bullying or harassment and homophobic stigmatization will cease, even if individual men remain personally homophobic. Accordingly, inclusive masculinity theory maintains that, in such a zeitgeist multiple masculinities will proliferate without hierarchy or hegemony and men are permitted an expansion of acceptable heteromasculine behaviours. In such a zeitgeist, the gendered behaviors of boys and men will be less differentiated from girls, and the symbolic meaning of soft physical tactility and emotional intimacy between men is consumed within a heteromasculine identity (Ibson 2002).

When there is mass social inclusion of the form of masculinities once traditionally marginalized by hegemonic masculinity, some of the attitudes once esteemed by orthodox masculinity will no longer be valued: homophobia, misogyny, stoicism, and perhaps excessive risk taking. In a culture of diminished homohysteria, boys and men will be free to express emotional intimacy and physical expressions of that relationship with one another. Accordingly, this culture permits an even greater expansion of acceptable heteromasculine behaviors, which results in yet a further blurring of masculinity and feminine behaviors and terrains. The differences between masculinity and femininity, men and women, gay and straight, will be harder to distinguish, and masculinity will no longer serve as the primary method of stratifying men. Whereas gender expressions coded as feminine were edged to extinction among men in the 1980s, today they flourish.

Explicating this, my graduate student Mark McCormack and I show that in a British high school, multiple forms of equally esteemed inclusive masculinities exist, even if heterosexism persists. In this culture, there exists a collection of various archetypes, but no singular archetype dominates. Boys are not only free to associate with those of another group but they are esteemed for maintaining social fluidity. Accordingly, in an Anglo-American culture of diminished homohysteria, those traditionally excluded, dominated and marginalized should benefit from social inclusion. Mark also shows that individual boys are still socially ranked but that this occurs through popularity, which is largely determined by charisma.

I desire to be clear; a culture of diminished homohysteria does not necessarily lead to men's utopia. For example, heterosexual men will still maintain hegemonic dominance. Heterosexism is an independent and unrelated variable for the operation of inclusive masculinities. In other words, men can still assume one another heterosexual, while still being inclusive. Some individuals can still dislike homosexual men, but a culture need not be entirely free of homophobia in order to encourage a proliferation of inclusive masculinities. Rather, it is the social unacceptability of the expression of those beliefs that leads to the decreased policing of sexual and gendered boundaries: For inclusive masculinities, a culture must be free of men having to prove their heterosexuality. The driving tenet behind orthodox masculinity is homohysteria, not homophobia. Thus, while a culture of inclusive masculinity indicates a culture of diminishing or diminished homophobia, it does not necessarily mean that all men within that culture will cease to be heterosexist and/or homophobic.

Inclusive masculinities do not guarantee the erosion of patriarchy, either. The existence of hegemonic masculinity was but one of numerous understood cultural mechanisms in which men retain cultural dominance. Thus, a culture of inclusive masculinity is no guarantee for a realignment of the gender order. While decreased sexism is a characteristic of an inclusive culture of masculinities, it does not guarantee social parity for women. Nonetheless, when inclusive masculinities dominate, there should at least be *some* social benefit for women.

Also, categorizing men as ascribing to inclusive masculinities does not mean that these men are completely free from other forms of orthodox sentiment or behaviors. In some of my research, I describe men representing inclusive masculinities as rejecting the domineering, anti-feminine and homophobic behaviors and attitudes of orthodox masculinity, even *if* they maintain the risk-taking, bravado and violence of their sometimes violent sports. Conversely, in other studies I find men eschewing excessive risk. I do not provide a precise formula for determining whether a culture is to be considered inclusive or not. I am not suggesting that all university-attending heterosexual men in my studies have completely redeveloped orthodox masculinity, either. What they have done so far, however, is to make it more inclusive to those once traditionally marginalized, and severely less restrictive of their own gendered practices. Accordingly, the loose indication of a culture of inclusive masculinities is that men look disparagingly at homophobia, they value emotional intimacy and physical tactility, and they are *more* willing to engage in activities or display behaviors that were once stigmatized as feminine. One can assume there will be different versions of inclusive masculinity operating, but I make no claims as to the utility of inclusive masculinity theory in other than Anglo-American cultures. Other researchers will have to utilize the theory to make such determinations.

The implications of inclusive masculinity for the operation of heterosexuality are also varied. In some studies I find that heterosexual men are partaking in certain same-sex sexual behaviors (designed to illicit sexual pleasure) without fear of stigma within their peer culture. Here, these men use their culture of inclusivity to blur the lines between gay and straight. In other studies, I find men unwilling to do such. Nonetheless, I classify both as inclusive masculinities, because neither looks disparagingly at men who *do* engage in same-sex sexual behaviors. Ultimately, however, it seems plausible that as inclusive masculinities spread to groups of other men throughout Anglo-American cultures, it cannot help but influence the redefinition of various sexualities.

Finally, some scholars may find the relationship of inclusive masculinity theory to hegemonic masculinity theory perplexing. This is because inclusive masculinity theory serves as a social-constructionist theory that simultaneously incorporates and challenges Connell's (1987) hegemonic masculinity theory. Both hegemonic masculinity theory and inclusive masculinity theory emphasize the importance of homophobia in the social production of men; however, inclusive masculinity theory accounts for multiple masculinities existing within any one culture without necessarily having hierarchy or hegemony, something Connell's theory does not. Inclusive masculinity theory maintains that in periods of high homohysteria, one hegemonic form of masculinity will exist, and that it will be predicated in opposition to homosexuality. But as homohysteria lessens, other social processes occur that Connell's theory does not accurately account for. This is not an admonishment of Connell's theorizing, nor do I suggest that Connell's theory no longer maintains utility. It depends on the setting analyzed.

Metrosexuality and Inclusive Masculinities

The men in my studies do not refer to themselves as exhibiting inclusive masculinities. Instead, they sometimes either refer to themselves as metrosexual (particularly between 2001 and 2004), or they give no name to their gendered perspective. Mark Simpson coined the term *metrosexual* in 1994, but it became popular in 2003 when a global marketing research firm, RSCG, published findings that heterosexual men were more open to commoditization and sexualization. In his book *The Metrosexual: Gender, Sexuality and Sport*, David Coad (2008) provides an excellent genealogy of the term. Although the term originally referred to Manhattan heterosexual men who wore high-end clothing, it evolved into a definition for heterofemininity among men. For example, Cashmore and Parker (2003) referred to English soccer player David Beckham as metrosexual because:

> Beckham's complex and contradictory identity suggests that there is more room for more than one version of masculine construction (224). He possesses a kind of ambivalence that makes him beguiling to a wide audience. Beckham acknowledges this ambivalence, publicly confirming, for example, his awareness of the admiration of the gay community in the UK (222) . . .

To this end Beckham's inclusive popularity should be seen as a positive step in terms of the masculine norms which he clearly transcends and the subversive trends and behaviors he explicitly displays (225).

The broadening definition of the term is evident in my various research settings. Some use it to describe increased fluidity in gender. Others use it as a euphemism for bisexuality. Still others use it to describe a heterosexual male who dabbles in same-sex sex. When telling me about their differently gendered perspectives on sex, women, clothing, or just about anything else that varies from orthodox prescriptions, many of the men I interview ask me, 'So does that make me metrosexual?'

Defining the term metrosexual is not my intent. In fact, I like the indefinable nature of the label. This gives it 'queer' power. It provides men who contest orthodox masculinity a label with which to identify. So while I find that metrosexuality means very different things to differing people I hypothesize that it is this fluidity of the term that makes it so destabilizing to masculine orthodoxy. The label has given men a long-awaited justification for the ability to be associated with femininity, and it has been immensely helpful in decreasing homohysteria. The term metrosexuality permits men to say I am not gay, "I am metrosexual." It has therefore served as a mediating factor in the manner in which homophobia has traditionally policed gendered boundaries, and this reduces homohysteria.

I recognize the limitations of metrosexuality as an archetype or threat to the hegemonic position of orthodox masculinity. Edwards (2006: 4) has argued that just like the 'new man' literature, metrosexuality is a media invention that is more connected to patterns of consumption than gendered change. But in developing inclusive masculinity theory, I build upon the commoditized foundations of metrosexuality, and also suggest that inclusive masculinities operate in opposition to certain aspects of orthodox masculine values (Harris and Clayton 2007). Men who ascribe to inclusive masculinities might also be metrosexual, but one does not have to dress well to be inclusive. Conversely, it would be difficult to suggest that men who consider themselves metrosexual are also orthodox in their masculine performance. Of course, they are not. Thus, the emergence of metrosexuality compelled us to realize that an alternate masculine narrative existed at least for those privileged enough to afford it. A decade later, however, the muted definition of metrosexuality (real or imagined) has permitted men of all classes and backgrounds to more freely associate with femininity, with or without identifying as metrosexual.

Evidencing My Theory

In the next section, I show that inclusive masculinities are sometimes established with, and sometimes established without, the support of organizational and/or institutional cultures. I show that men who subscribe to inclusive masculinities behave in effeminate ways and that they are less defensive about their heterosexuality, all with less (or no) fear of social stigma. Men performing inclusive masculinities participate in tasks traditionally defined as feminine and support women who perform tasks traditionally defined as masculine.

Among the cheerleaders, for example, inclusive masculinities permit men to be tossed into the air (flying), to stand atop the shoulders of others, and even to wear clothing defined as feminine. For the rugby players, inclusive masculinities permit these men to show physical affection for one another, publicly kissing and embracing. For my university student-athletes, inclusive masculinities permit them to dance together, even in the same erotic fashion that they dance with women. And for men in all my studies, inclusive masculinities permit them to emotionally support each other in the face of loss or brutality.

Inclusive masculinities, and the reduction of cultural homohysteria that spawned it, also has a significant impact on the use and meanings associated with homophobic and femphobic discourse.

Similarly, the reduction in homophobia and the increased physicality between men has very serious implications for the categorization of what gay and straight behaviors are; and what gay and straight identities are, too. I show that many university men are now kissing each other (on the lips). Just a few years ago this behavior would have been labeled homosexual. But these men have stripped the sexual code from it, so that it is now just a form of affection between two ostensibly heterosexual men.

Finally, I show that the valuing of inclusive masculinities exists among athletes, but not necessarily among their coaches. Not only does this set the stage for strife, but it suggests that it is only a matter of time before the old guard is replaced by a new, more inclusive breed of gatekeepers. In fact, if social matters continue as they are, inclusive masculinities might soon be the normative standard by which we describe all sporting men.

References

Allen, L. (2007). Sensitive and real macho all at the same time: Young heterosexual men and romance. *Men and Masculinities,* 10(2): 137–152.

Anderson, E. (2002). Openly gay athletes: Contesting hegemonic masculinity in a homophobic environment. *Gender & Society,* 16(6), 860–877.

Anderson, E. (2005a). In the game: *Gay athletes and the cult of masculinity.* Albany, NY: State University of New York Press.

Anderson, E. (2005b). Orthodox and inclusive masculinities: Competing masculinities among heterosexual men in a feminized terrain. *Sociological Perspectives,* 48, 337–355.

Anderson, E. (2008a). Inclusive masculinities in a fraternal setting. *Men and Masculinities,* 10(5), 604–620.

Anderson, E. (2008b). "Being masculine is not about who you sleep with . . .": Heterosexual athletes contesting masculinity and the one-time rule of homosexuality *Sex Roles,* (1–2), 104–115.

Anderson, E. (2008c). "I used to think women were weak": Orthodox masculinity, gender segregation, and sport. *Sociological Forum,* 23(2), 257–280.

Burn, S. M. (2000). Heterosexuals' use of "fag" and "queer" to deride one another: A contributor to heterosexism and stigma. *Journal of Homosexuality,* 40, 1–11.

Cashmore, E., & Parker, A. (2003). One David Beckham: Celebrity, masculinity, and the soccerati. *Sociology of Sport Journal,* 20, 214–231.

Coad, D. (2008). *The metrosexual: Gender, sexuality and sport.* Albany: State University of New York Press.

Connell, R. W. (1987). *Gender and power.* Stanford, CA: Stanford University Press

Connell, R. W. (1995). *Masculinities.* Cambridge: Polity.

Edwards, T. (2006). *Cultures of masculinity.* London; New York: Routledge.

Fine, M. (1988). Sexuality, schooling, and adolescent females: The missing discourse of desire. *Harvard Educational Review,* 58(1), 29–52.

Harris, J. & Clayton, B. (2007). The first meterosexual rugby star: Rugby union, masculinity, and celebrity in contemporary Wales. *Sociology of Sport Journal,* 24, 145–164.

Ibson, J. (2002). *Picturing men: A century of male relationships in everyday life.* Washington, DC: Smithsonian Books.

Kaplan, D. (2006). Public intimacy: Dynamics of seduction in male homosocial interactions. *Symbolic Interaction,* 28(4), 571–595.

Kimmel, M. (1994). Masculinity as homophobia: Fear, shame, and silence in the construction of gender identity. In H. Brod & M. Kaufman (Eds.), *Theorizing masculinities.* London: Sage.

Pascoe, C. J. (2005). 'Dude, you're a fag': Adolescent masculinity and the fag discourse. *Sexualities,* 8, 329–346.

Plummer, D. (1999). *One of the boys: Masculinity, homophobia and modern manhood.* New York: Harrington Park Press.

Pronger, B. (1990). The arena of masculinity: *Sports, homosexuality, and the meaning of sex.* New York: St. Martin's Press.

Simpson, M. (1994*). Male impersonators: Men performing masculinity.* New York: Routledge.

Swain, J. (2006a). The role of sport in the construction of masculinities in an English independent junior school. *Sport, Education and Society,* 11, 317–335.

Swain, J. (2006b). Reflections on patterns of masculinity in school settings. *Men and Masculinities,* 8, 331–349.

CHAPTER 5

Hybrid Masculinities

New Directions in the Sociology of Men and Masculinities

Tristan Bridges and C. J. Pascoe

Introduction

A growing body of sociological theory and research on men and masculinities addresses recent trans-formations in men's behaviors, appearances, opinions, and more. While historical research has shown masculinities to be in a continuous state of change (e.g., Kimmel 1996; Segal 1990), the extent of contemporary transformations as well as their impact and meaning is the source of a great deal of theory, research, and debate. While not a term universally adopted among masculinities scholars, the concept of "hybrid masculinities" is a useful way to make sense of this growing body of scholarship. It critically highlights this body of work that seeks to account for the emergence and consequences of recent transformations in masculinities.

Today, scholars in the social sciences and humanities use "hybrid" to address cultural miscege-nation—processes and practices of cultural interpenetration (Burke 2009). "Hybrid masculinities" refer to the selective incorporation of elements of identity typically associated with various margin-alized and subordinated masculinities and—at times—femininities into privileged men's gender performances and identities (e.g., Arxer 2011; Demetriou 2001; Messerschmidt 2010; Messner 2007). Work on hybrid masculinities has primarily, though not universally, focused on young, White, heterosexual-identified men. This research is centrally concerned with the ways that men are increasingly incorporating elements of various "Others" into their identity projects. While it is true that gendered meanings change historically and geographically, research and theory addressing hybrid masculinities are beginning to ask whether recent transformations point in a new, more liberating direction.

The transformations addressed by this literature include men's assimilation of "bits and pieces" (Demetriou 2001: 350) of identity projects coded as "gay" (e.g., Bridges, 2014; Heasley 2005; Hennessy 1995), "Black"(e.g., Hughey 2012; Ward 2008), or "feminine" (e.g., Arxer 2011; Messerschmidt 2010; Schippers 2000; Wilkins 2009) among others. A central research question in this literature considers the extent and meaning of these practices in terms of gender, sexual, and racial inequality. More specifically, this field of inquiry asks: Are hybrid masculinities widespread and do they represent a significant change in gendered inequality?

In reviewing contemporary theorizing and empirical research on masculinity, we suggest that hybrid masculinities work in ways that not only reproduce contemporary systems of gendered, raced,

SOURCE: Bridges, T. and Pascoe, C. J. (2014). Hybrid Masculinities: New Directions in the Sociology of Men and Masculinities. *Sociology Compass*, 8(3), 246–258. Reproduced with permission from John Wiley & Sons.

and sexual inequalities but also obscure this process as it is happening. We argue that hybrid masculinities have at least three distinct consequences that shape, reflect, and mask inequalities. Hybrid masculinities may place discursive (though not meaningful) distance between certain groups of men and hegemonic masculinity, are often undertaken with an understanding of White, heterosexual masculinity as less meaningful than other (more marginalized or subordinated) forms of masculinity, and fortify social and symbolic boundaries and inequalities. As Coston and Kimmel write, "The idealized notion of masculinity operates as both an ideology and a set of normative constraints" (2012:98). We argue that the emergence of hybrid masculinities indicates that normative constraints are shifting but that these shifts have largely taken place in ways that have sustained existing ideologies and systems of power and inequality. Each of the consequences of contemporary hybrid masculinities we address here represent elaborations on the processes by which meanings and practices of hegemonic masculinity change over time in ways that nonetheless maintain the structure of institutionalized gender regimes to advantage men collectively over women and some men over other men. Indeed, hybrid masculinities may be best thought of as contemporary expressions of gender and sexual inequality.

Theorizing Changes in Masculinity

The question driving the bulk of the literature on hybrid masculinities is whether (and how) they are perpetuating and/or challenging systems of gender and sexual inequality. Scholars answer the question in three ways. (i) Some are skeptical of whether hybrid masculinities represent anything beyond local variation (e.g., Connell and Messerschmidt 2005). (ii) Others argue that hybrid masculinities are both culturally pervasive and indicate that inequality is lessening and possibly no longer structures men's identities and relationships (e.g., Anderson 2009; McCormack 2012). (iii) The majority of the research and theory supports the notion that hybrid masculinities are widespread. But, rather than suggesting that they are signs of increasing levels of gender and sexual equality, these scholars argue that hybrid masculine forms illustrate the flexibility of systems of inequality. Thus, they argue that hybrid masculinities represent significant changes in the expression of systems of power and inequality, though fall short of challenging them (e.g., Demetriou 2001; Messerschmidt 2010; Messner 1993, 2007).

While not necessarily challenging the notion that hybrid masculinities exist, Connell and Messerschmidt (2005)—in their analysis of "hegemonic masculinity"—question the extent of hybrid masculine practices, their meaning, and influence. "Clearly, specific masculine practices may be appropriated into other masculinities, creating a hybrid (such as the hip-hop style and language adopted by some working-class White teenage boys and the unique composite style of gay 'clones'). Yet we are not convinced that the hybridization . . . is hegemonic, at least beyond a local sense" (2005: 845). Here, Connell and Messerschmidt (2005) suggest that while hybrid masculine forms may exist and might promote inequality in new ways, they are unconvinced that hybrid masculinities are illustrative of a transformation in hegemonic masculinity beyond local subcultural variation. Thus, they argue that hybrid masculine forms have not significantly affected the meanings of masculinity at regional or global levels.[1] Significantly, while Connell and Messerschmidt (2005) are critical of the extent and reach of hybrid masculinities, they agree that, while these new identities and practices blur social and symbolic boundaries, they are not necessarily undermining systems of dominance or hegemonic masculinity in any fundamental way.

Anderson's (2009) theory of the rise of "inclusive masculinities" challenges Connell and Messerschmidt's (2005) perspective. He argues that contemporary transformations in men's behaviors and beliefs are widespread and are best understood as challenging systems of gender and sexual inequality. Studying a variety of young, primarily heterosexual-identified, White men, Anderson finds that masculinity among these groups is characterized by "inclusivity" rather than exclusivity (what

Anderson terms "orthodoxy"). In this model masculinities are organized horizontally, rather than hierarchically. As such, men are increasingly adopting practices characterized by acceptance of diverse masculinities, opening up the contemporary meanings of "masculinity" in ways that allow a more varied selection of performances to "count" as masculine. This "inclusivity"—like hybridity—is part of a process of incorporating performances that are culturally coded as "Other." Anderson argues that these practices indicate "decreased sexism" and "the erosion of patriarchy" (2009: 9). Thus, Anderson theorizes hybrid masculinities (which he calls "inclusive masculinities") as endemic and as a fundamental challenge to existing systems of power and inequality.

To account for this transformation, Anderson (2009) argues that what he calls "homohysteria" is decreasing (see also McCormack 2012). Broadly described as a "fear of being homosexualized" (2009: 7), the term considers three issues: popular awareness of gay identity, cultural disapproval of homosexuality, and the cultural association of masculinity with heterosexuality. While awareness of gay identity has increased, Anderson argues that disapproval of homosexuality is diminishing[2] as is the cultural association of masculinity with heterosexuality. Unyoked from compulsory heterosexuality, he argues that contemporary masculinities are characterized by increasing levels of equality and less hierarchy.

The majority of the research concerning hybrid masculinities supports Anderson's (2009) claim that hybrid masculinities are extensive but frames the meanings and consequences of hybrid masculine practices and identities differently. Rather than illustrating a decline in gender and sexual inequality, scholars suggest that hybrid masculinities work in ways that perpetuate existing systems of power and inequality in historically new ways (e.g., Demetriou 2001; Messner 1993, 2007). Thus, this body of research is at odds with Connell and Messerschmidt's (2005) analysis of the significance of hybrid masculinities and with Anderson's (2009) consideration of the consequences.

Messner (1993) analyzes transformations among American men toward more "emotionally expressive" performances of masculinity and critiques scholarly investigations of these transformations precisely because they tended to focus primarily on "styles of masculinity, rather than the institutional *position of power* that men still enjoy" (732). Messner examines the cultural impact of these shifts in men's behavior by analyzing the mythopoetic men's movement, men's increasing involvement as parents, and an increase in the number of high-status men crying in public.

Messner's framing of hybrid masculinities as "more style than substance" (1993: 724) represents a dominant approach in scholarship discussing the meanings and consequences of hybrid masculinities. This body of work discusses hybrid masculinities as

> represent[ing] highly significant (but exaggerated) shifts in the cultural and personal styles of hegemonic masculinity, but these changes do not necessarily contribute to the undermining of conventional structures of men's power over women. Although "softer" and more "sensitive" styles of masculinity are developing among some privileged groups of men, this does not necessarily contribute to the emancipation of women; in fact, quite the contrary may be true. (Messner 1993: 725)

This shift is complex and not unidirectional. In fact, new gendered practices and identities often work in ways that either produce new forms of inequality or conceal existing inequalities in new ways.

Messner's (2007) analysis of changes in the public image of Arnold Schwarzenegger, e.g., illustrates what he calls an "ascendant hybrid masculinity" combining toughness with tenderness in ways that work to obscure—rather than challenge—systems of power and inequality (Messner 2007). Similar phenomena have been documented within various "men's movements" like the Promise Keepers and the Ex-gay Movement (e.g., Donovan 1998; Gerber 2008; Heath 2003; Wolkomir 2001), new ways of performing heterosexuality while engaging in "gay" styles, practices, and sex (e.g., Bridges 2014; Pascoe 2007; Schippers 2000; Ward 2008; Wilkins 2009), the masculinization of concerns with hygiene and appearance (e.g., Barber 2008), presidential discourses surrounding militarism (Messerschmidt 2010), and throughout popular culture more generally (e.g., Carroll 2011; Jeffords 1994; Pfeil 1995; Savran 1998).

Contemporary transformations in masculinity have primarily been documented among groups of young, heterosexual-identified, White men. This fact evidences the flexibility of identity afforded privileged groups. Indeed, ignoring intersectional distinctions that inequitably distribute access to specific hybrid masculine forms risks presenting contemporary changes as indicative of transformations in systems of inequality that may still exist—albeit in new forms. Messner (1993) argues that, "framing shifts in styles of hegemonic masculinity as indicative of the arrival of a New Man [often situates] marginalized men (especially poor black men, in the United States) as Other" (1993: 733). Men of color, working-class men, immigrant men, among others, are often (in)directly cast as the possessors of regressive masculinities in the context of these emergent hybrid masculinities. That said, young, straight, White men are not the only ones with hybrid masculinities. Research also illustrates the ways that groups of marginalized and subordinated Others craft hybrid gender identities—though often with very different consequences and concerns.

Demetriou (2001) coins the term "dialectical pragmatism" to theorize the consequences of the changes Messner (1993) described. Dialectical pragmatism refers to the ability of hegemonic masculinities to appropriate elements of subordinated and marginalized "Others" in ways that work to recuperate existing systems of power and inequality. Dialectical pragmatism speaks to the transformative capacities of systems of power inequality. Demetriou suggests that what makes hegemonic masculinities so powerful is precisely their ability to adapt. He suggests that hegemonic masculinity is better understood as a "hegemonic masculine bloc" capable of appropriating "what appears pragmatically useful and constructive for the project of domination at a particular historical moment" (2001: 345). Demetriou argues that Connell's initial conceptualization of hegemonic masculinity fails to account for the ways that subordinated and marginalized masculinities affect the formation, style, look, and feel of hegemonic masculinity. Thus, Demetriou's framework illustrates how the meanings and consequences of hybrid masculinities are much more complicated than they might initially appear.

Demetriou focuses primarily on one example of hybridity: the assimilation of elements of "gay male culture" into heterosexual masculinities. He illustrates how this hybrid masculinity might be better understood as a contemporary expression of—rather than challenge to—existing forms of gender and sexual inequality. Demetriou shows how heterosexual men incorporate "bits and pieces [of gay male culture,] . . . [producing] new, hybrid configurations of gender practice that enable them to reproduce their dominance over women [and other men] in historically novel ways" (2001: 350–351). Like Messner (1993, 2007), Demetriou shows how hybrid masculinities blur gender differences and boundaries in ways that present no real challenge to existing systems of power and inequality.

The theorizing of hybrid masculinities as illustrated by Demetriou (2001) and Messner (1993, 2007) challenges the analyses set forth by Anderson (2009) and Connell and Messerschmidt (2005). Anderson's (2009) theory of "inclusive masculinity" argues that these new configurations of identity and practice are best understood as resistance to gender and sexual inequality, while Connell and Messerschmidt (2005) argue that these challenges to hegemonic masculinity have not been significant. The research in the following section, however, broadly supports Demetriou's (2001) conceptualization of "dialectical pragmatism" and Messner's (1993, 2007) analysis of transformations in masculine style but not substance of contemporary masculinities.

Research on Hybrid Masculinities

Research on hybrid masculinities highlights several consequences associated with these gender projects and performances. First, hybrid masculine practices often work in ways that create some discursive distance between young, White, straight men and hegemonic masculinity, enabling some to frame themselves as outside of existing systems of privilege and inequality. Second, hybrid masculinities are often premised on the notion that the masculinities available to young, White, straight men are somehow less meaningful than the masculinities of various marginalized and subordinated Others, whose identities were at least partially produced by collective struggles for rights and recognition. Third, hybrid masculinities work to fortify symbolic and social boundaries between (racial, gender, sexual) groups—further entrenching, and often concealing, inequality in new ways.

Discursive Distancing

Hybrid masculine practices often work in ways that create some discursive distance between White, straight men and "hegemonic masculinity." However, as men are distanced from hegemonic masculinity, they also (often more subtly) align themselves with it. Research on men's pro-feminist, political, and grooming activities illustrates how hybrid masculinities can work in ways that discursively distance men from hegemonic masculinity.

Bridges (2010) highlights this distancing in his documentation of men's participation in Walk a Mile in Her Shoes marches—an event to raise awareness about domestic violence. In it, men wear high-heeled shoes and walk one mile. This practice of standing with women and wearing women's clothing seemingly distances them from the sexism and gendered dominance that partially constitutes hegemonic masculinity. As Bridges points out, however, the men in this march can reproduce gender inequality even as they actively work against it. The way men interact during this march reiterates forms of gender inequality that undergird domestic violence. The male participants joke about wearing women's clothing, about their ability to walk in heels, and about same-sex sexual desire. These jokes discursively align participants with hegemonic masculinity even as their practices might seem to distance them from it.

The "My Strength is Not for Hurting" campaign—one of the few anti-rape campaigns directed at men—also acts to distance men from hegemonic masculinity by framing men "as a unitary group" made to look bad by rapists (Masters 2010). Non-rapist men are simultaneously aligned with hegemonic masculinity through framing "real" and "strong" men as fundamentally different from (presumably weak and unmanly) rapists. Campaigns like this discursively separate "good" from "bad" men and fail to account for the ways that presenting strength and power as natural resources for men perpetuates gender and sexual inequality even as they are called into question (see also Murphy 2009). Both Walk a Mile in Her Shoes marches and the My Strength is Not for Hurting campaign create some distance between these (good) men and (bad) hegemonic masculinity. Yet, in challenging men's violence against women, they simultaneously reaffirm many qualities that typify hegemonic masculine forms and dominance.

Similarly, men can embrace political stances that seem to distance them from hegemonic masculinity. Such stances allow public male figures to disguise toughness with tenderness. For instance, Arnold Schwarzenegger forged an identity that Messner (2007) refers to as the "kindergarten commando," representing a masculinity "foregrounding muscle, toughness and the threat of violence" followed with "situationally appropriate symbolic displays of compassion" (Messner 2007: 461). Schwarzenegger's "sexy, hybrid mix of hardness and compassion" is a "configuration of symbols that forge a masculinity that is useful for securing power among men who already have it" (Messner 2007: 473).

Messerschmidt (2010) illustrates a similar dynamic at work in international arenas. Analyzing speeches surrounding the "War on Terror" spanning the presidencies of George Bush and George W. Bush, he finds that both presidents mobilized discourses of rescue to justify military action. As Messerschmidt argues, "Bush Senior's and Bush Junior's inclusion of humane, sensitive, and empathic aspects in their masculine rhetoric shows how hegemonic masculinity at the regional and global levels is fluid and flexible . . . Such an appropriation of traditionally defined 'feminine' traits blurs gender difference but does not undermine gender dominance" (2010: 161). Messerschmidt illustrates the fluid properties of hegemonic masculinities and the ways in which masculinities are capable of incorporating elements of "femininity" to obscure gender boundaries, while reproducing existing systems of power and authority. These masculinized strategies allow trust to be gained "in times of fear and insecurity" and "[project] a veiled feminized stigma onto more liberal candidates" (Messner 2007: 461). Messerschmidt's findings also imply that hybrid masculinities have attained ideological power and influence on a global stage, suggesting—contrary to Connell and Messerschmidt's (2005) earlier assessment—that they are implicated in global-level processes and relations.

This kind of "feminization" has been documented in very different locations as well. For instance, Kristen Barber's (2008) study of White, middle-class, heterosexual men in professional men's hair salons illustrates one way that some men engage in beauty work formerly coded "feminine." Barber finds that these men rely on a rhetoric of expectations associated with professional-class masculinities to justify their participation in the beauty industry while simultaneously naturalizing distinctions between themselves and working-class men, framing the latter as misogynistic and reproducing gender inequality. While these men are engaging in a practice that might be labeled "feminine," Barber highlights the ways they avoid feminization and create some distance between themselves and masculinities they associate with reproducing gender and sexual inequality. Similarly, Wilkins (2009) addresses the ways that both goth and young Christian men engage in boundary-blurring gender projects that ultimately work to recuperate existing systems of power and privilege. Navigating "masculine" norms surrounding heterosexual interest and participation in different ways, Wilkins finds that both groups reiterate existing structures of gender power and authority much more than challenge them.

Strategic Borrowing

Hybrid masculinities are often premised on the notion that the masculinities available to young, White, straight men are meaningless when compared with various "Others," whose identities were forged in struggles for rights and recognition. Indeed, cultural appropriation is a defining characteristic of hybrid identities. Research on hybrid masculinities documents the way that men who occupy privileged social categories strategically borrow from Others in ways that work to reframe themselves as symbolically part of socially subordinated groups. Through this process, White men frame themselves as victims (Messner 1993: 77) and inequality becomes less easily identified. Like Waters' (1990) research documenting White people's relative ignorance of the ethnic flexibility they are afforded, the hybrid identities available to young, straight, White men may be very different from those available to marginalized and subordinated groups. As Patricia Hill Collins argues, "Authentic Black people must be contained—their authentic culture can enter White controlled spaces, but they cannot" (Collins 2004: 177). By strategically borrowing elements of the performative "styles" associated with various marginalized and subordinated "Others," research has documented the more pernicious consequences of these hybrid practices.

Demetriou (2001) charts this process by examining the incorporation of elements of gay culture by heterosexual-identified men. Rather than illustrating a fundamental challenge to systems of inequality, Demetriou theorizes the ways that culturally dominant models of masculinity assimilate elements from subordinated "Others" in ways that fundamentally alter the shape (but not structural position of power) of contemporary performances of gender and gender relations. Similarly, by theorizing the aesthetic elements of sexuality, Bridges (2014) analyzes the causes and consequences of heterosexual men subjectively identifying aspects of themselves as "gay" in ways that preserve their heterosexuality and simultaneously reinforce existing boundaries between gay and straight individuals and cultures.

Steven Arxer's (2011) study of interactions between heterosexual men at a college bar documents an analogous practice. Extremely different from the competitive, emotionally detached, sexually objectifying performances of masculinity that characterize straight men's interactions with each other in Bird's (1996) or Grazian's (2007) research, Arxer (2011) examines these men's assimilation of aspects of gay masculinity, but simultaneous maintenance of existing systems of power and dominance.

> These men seem to perceive a sense of intersectional deprivation wherein heterosexual masculinity (as defined traditionally to be aggressive and emotionally detached) is *devalued* relative to gay masculinities. In response to this "crisis" in hegemonic capital, the men agree to a hybridized model of masculinity that affords them a new framework to assess *who* ("gay people") has profited from being labeled as "sensitive" and *how* they can claim a slice of the dividend. (Arxer 2011: 408)

Yet, in the process of drawing on the emotionality presumably displayed by gay men, these men reassert gender inequality by using it to increase their chances of sexually "scoring" with women (Arxer 2011: 409). Thus, while a dramatically different collective performance of masculinity from "the girl hunt" that Grazian (2007) documents or Bird's (1996) "men's club," the consequences of these performances are strikingly similar in terms of sustaining existing systems of power and inequality.

Research has also analyzed racialized strategic borrowing—a process which works in similar ways. Similar to the research on men's appropriation of elements of gay culture, research on the cultural appropriation of and identification with hip-hop music among young White men finds that their incorporation of elements of "black culture" is often not associated with recognition of the consequences of this practice (e.g., Hess 2005; Hughey 2012; Rodriquez 2006). Rodriquez's (2006) research on young White hip-hop music fans documents these men justifying their interest in and identification with hip-hop utilizing "color-blind" discourses (e.g., Bonilla-Silva 2001) that enable them to conceal race (and racial inequality) as a significant element of this cultural form.

White appropriation of cultural forms is certainly not a new cultural phenomenon (e.g., Lott 1993; Deloria 1998), nor is the appropriation necessarily confined to boys and young men (e.g., Wilkins 2004, 2008) or the United States (Garner 2009). Yet, reasons behind and consequences of contemporary men's "borrowings" are historically novel. As Cutler points out with respect to White appropriation of African-American linguistic patterns and style, "Its origins are complex, its consequences can be serious, and although its representativeness can't be stated systematically, it is not an isolated instance" (1999:439).

Hughey's (2012) research with anti-racist and White nationalist groups composed primarily of men places these practices in a larger cultural perspective. Hughey refers to this appropriation as a reliance on what he terms "color capital" by Whites. He argues that Whites engage in these practices in an effort to assuage feelings of "culturelessness" associated with White identity (see also Perry 2001 and Wilkins 2004). In very different ways, the two groups in Hughey's study struggled to both relate to and distance themselves from color capital in ways that illustrated their cultural affiliation with racialized identities that they saw as bloated with meaning when situated alongside their own racial identities—which most understood as devoid of "culture." Yet, while working to alleviate feelings of meaninglessness associated with White identity, Hughey finds that these practices simultaneously promote more destructive racial consequences.

Messner (1993) argues that when we frame young, straight, White men's new performances of masculinity solely as indicators of a decline in gender and sexual inequality, already marginalized groups of men often end up situated as playing a greater role in perpetuating inequality. By framing middle-class, young, straight, White men as both the embodiment and harbinger of feminist change in masculinities, social scientists participate in further marginalizing poor men, working-class men, religious men, undereducated men, rural men, and men of color (among others) as the bearers of uneducated, backwards, toxic, patriarchal masculinities. Even as young White men borrow practices and identities from young, gay, Black, or urban men in order to boost their masculine capital, research shows that these practices often work simultaneously to reaffirm these subordinated groups as deviant, thus supporting existing systems of power and dominance.

Fortifying Boundaries

By co-opting elements of style and performance from less powerful masculinities, young, straight, White men's hybridizations often obscure the symbolic and social boundaries between groups upon which such practices rely. Through this process, systems of inequality are further entrenched and concealed in historically new ways, often along lines of race, gender, sexuality, and class.

Hybrid masculinities may, for instance, complicate claims about and understandings of relationships between normative masculinity and homophobia. In recent history, homophobia has been a hallmark of adolescent masculinity (Kehler 2007; Levy et al. 2012; Pascoe 2007; Poteat et al. 2010). However, research indicates that such sentiments are on the decline among young men (McCormack 2012). While fear or dislike of actual gay people may be declining, what Pascoe (2007) calls a "fag discourse" continues to structure the socialization practices of boys and young men. Simply put, boys socialize each other into normatively masculine behaviors, practices, attitudes, and dispositions in a way that has little relationship with boys' fear of actual gay men (Corbett 2001; Kimmel 1994). Indeed, many boys who would never insult a gay person by calling him "gay" do not hesitate to use these words to tease each other (McCormack 2012; Pascoe 2007). While McCormack argues that homophobic jokes—when not directed at gay boys—have been stripped of their discriminatory meanings, Pascoe's work illustrates that "fag discourse" is a potent form of gender policing for contemporary young men. Thus, while seemingly non-homophobic masculinities are proliferating (Anderson 2009, McCormack 2012), a closer look at the gendered meanings of homophobia complicates these claims (Bridges 2014; Pascoe 2007).

Even when men engage in sexual practices that challenge the relationship between normative masculinity and homophobia, they may reify inequality. Jane Ward's (2008) research on White straight-identifying men who have sex with men illustrates how their sexual practices may initially seem to transgress traditional notions of heterosexual masculinity but simultaneously work to reify gendered, sexual, and raced boundaries. Ward documents the ways that, in their search for sexual partners, these men objectify women, reject effeminacy among men, and hyper-eroticize men of color. They talk about hooking up with other men while watching "pussy porn," say they do not want to have sex with men who are feminine "sissy la las," and use exotic and stigmatizing language to describe their ideal men of color sex partners. Ward calls this particular configuration of practices "dude sex."

Ward's participants in some ways both reflect and invert Connell's (1992) and Levine's (1998) analysis of gay men's assimilation of elements of straight masculinities into some gay men's identity projects. Connell's discussion of gay Australian men who identify with elements of "straight" masculine performances and identities finds that the practices ultimately shore up gender and sexual boundaries. Connell (1992) argues that these performances are primarily undertaken out of an interest in gender identification (as "masculine" men) and concerns with safety (due to the threat of violence against men performing effeminate gay identities). Ward's participants take this a step further. Not only do they perform heterosexual masculinities—often relying on racialized performances associated with hip-hop and/or surfer culture—they also identify as "straight" because of their affiliation with straight culture, in spite of their participation in same-sex sexual behavior. In some ways, this research is also an example of "strategic borrowing," illustrating how, in practice, the three consequences of hybrid masculinities we address here often work in congress and overlap.

Men's practices that initially appear to be feminist can also reify gender inequality even as they obscure it. Recent changes in the ideologies and practices of fathering may seem progressive—such as increasing levels of emotionality and time spent with children. But upon closer investigation they also entrench gender inequality. Messner (1993) makes clear that the new fathering movement was not necessarily about challenging gender inequality in the family, but about a particular *style* of male parenting, that, as Stein (2005) indicates, may draw boundaries around male heterosexuality. In her study of the Promise Keeper movement, Melanie Heath (2003) examines the ways that men embody "new fathering" by playing larger roles in their children's lives and being more emotionally available while simultaneously enforcing gender inequality by espousing a "biblical" notion of "the family" in which women are instructed to submit to their husbands. Donovan (1998) refers to this process as "masculine rescripting," and also argues that such a process does not necessarily challenge existing systems of power and inequality. Schwalbe (1996) discusses similar ideological shifts as "loose essentialism"—a process that acknowledges and supports change in men and allows them to redefine traits formerly associated with femininity as "masculine."

Groups of evangelical Christian men may be the quintessential example of "loose essentialism" as research has documented their engagement in "masculine rescripting" practices when talking about sex in ways that are seemingly progressive, but simultaneously homophobic and working to reify gender inequality (Gerber 2008; Wilkins 2009). Gerber's (2008) analysis of the Ex-Gay Movement highlights some of the ways that ex-gay identities and performances of masculinity are often non-normative. In the interest of creating "a livable space" for Christian men grappling with same-sex desires, hybrid masculine options offer resources for alternative masculinities that illustrate a great transformation in styles of masculinity, but do little to challenge the boundaries between "gay" and "straight," or "masculine" and "feminine."

Conclusion

Connell (1995:84) argued that the gender order continually tends toward crisis, but also suggests that such "crisis tendencies" have intensified recently. "They have resulted, clearly enough, in a major loss of legitimacy for patriarchy, and different groups of men are now negotiating this loss in very different ways"(1995:202). Hybrid masculinities research has primarily examined this process of transformation among groups of men who hold concentrated constellations of power and authority in the current gender order (young, White, heterosexual, etc.).

Privilege works best when it goes unrecognized. Indeed, as Johnson notes, "Perhaps the most efficient way to keep patriarchy going is to promote the idea that it doesn't exist . . . Or, if it does exist, it's by reputation only, a shadow of its former self that no longer amounts to much in people's lives" (2005:154). Research on hybrid masculinities suggests that recent changes—sparked by feminist critique and reform—have shed light upon masculinity and masculine privilege in historically unprecedented ways. When privilege becomes visible, however, this research illustrates how it does not necessarily cease to exist. But, the experiences of privilege by privileged groups do change, as do the "legitimating stories" or justifications for existing systems of power and inequality. Hybrid masculinities are one illustration of what Johnson (2005) refers to as the "flexibility of patriarchy." This is not to say that men's awareness of privileges associated with masculinity causes their privileges to cease to exist. Rather, research on hybrid masculinities illustrates another possibility—experiences and justifications of privilege have transformed. And this transformation has led to a host of new identity projects as different groups of men negotiate this change in different ways.

Hybridization is a cultural process with incredible potential for change. Research on hybrid masculinities has primarily documented shifts in—rather than challenges to—systems of power and inequality. The question that remains concerns how we can recognize meaningful change in systems of gender inequality when we see it.

Notes

1. Importantly, Messerschmidt's (2010) more recent analysis of US presidential discourses mobilized during the "War on Terror" indicates that hybrid masculinities may increasingly exist on a global scale.

2. Indeed, public opinions in the United States concerning homosexuality have taken a marked turn in recent history—particularly those of younger men (Loftus 2001; Saad 2010). What these changes mean is more difficult to assess, as other data illustrates the continuance of harassment and bullying utilizing derogatory epithets for homosexuality and gender expression among US boys (Kosciw et al. 2012). Opinion polls are also at odds with a great deal of qualitative research among US boys and young men. So, there is some disagreement concerning how we can interpret the meanings of this change.

References

Anderson, Eric. 2009. *Inclusive Masculinity*. New York: Routledge.

Arxer, Steven. 2011. 'Hybrid Masculine Power.' *Humanity & Society* 35(4): 390–422.

Barber, Kristen. 2008. 'The Well-Coiffed Man.' *Gender & Society* 22(4): 455–76.

Bird, Sharon. 1996. 'Welcome to the Men's Club.' *Gender & Society* 10(2): 120–32.

Bonilla-Silva, Eduardo. 2001. *White Supremacy and Racism in the Post-Civil Rights Era*. Boulder: Lynne Rienner.

Bridges, Tristan. 2010. 'Men Just Weren't Made To Do This.' *Gender & Society* 24(1): 5–30.

Bridges, Tristan. forthcoming. 'A Very 'Gay' Straight?' *Gender & Society*.

Burke, Peter. 2009. *Cultural Hybridity*. New York: Polity.

Carroll, Hamilton. 2011. *Affirmative Reaction*. Durham: Duke University Press.

Collins, Patricia Hill. 2004. *Black Sexual Politics*. New York: Routledge.

Connell, R. W. 1992. 'A Very Straight Gay.' *American Sociological Review* 57(6): 735–51.

Connell, R. W. 1995. *Masculinities*. Stanford: Stanford University Press.

Connell, R. W. and James Messerschmidt. 2005. 'Hegemonic Masculinity: Rethinking the Concept.' *Gender & Society* 19(6): 829–59.

Corbett, Ken. 2001. 'Faggot = Loser.' *Studies in Gender and Sexuality* 2 (1): 3–28.

Coston, Bethany and Michael Kimmel. 2012. 'Seeing Privilege Where It Isn't.' *Journal of Social Issues* 68(1): 97–111.

Cutler, Cecilia. 1999. 'Yorkville Crossing: White Teens, Hip Hop and African American English.' *Journal of Sociolinguistics* 3(4): 428–42.

Demetriou, Demetrakis. 2001. 'Connell's Concept of Hegemonic Masculinity: A Critique.' *Theory and Society* 30(3): 337–61.

Donovan, Brian. 1998. 'Political Consequences of Private Authority.' *Theory and Society* 27(6): 817–43.

Garner, Steve. 2009. 'Empirical Research into White Racialized Identities in Britain.' *Sociology Compass* 3(5): 789–802.

Gerber, Lynne. 2008. 'The Opposite of Gay.' *Nova Religio* 11(4): 8–30.

Grazian, David. 2007. 'The Girl Hunt.' *Symbolic Interaction* 30(2): 221–43.

Heasley, Robert. 2005. 'Crossing the Borders of Gendered Sexuality.' Pp. 109–30 in *Thinking Straight*, edited by Chrys Ingraham. New York: Routledge.

Heath, Melanie. 2003. 'Soft-Boiled Masculinity.' *Gender & Society* 17(3): 423–44.

Hennessy, Rosemary. 1995. 'Queer Visibility in Commodity Culture.' Pp. 142–83 in *Social Postmodernism*, edited by Linda Nicholson and Steven Seidman. New York: Cambridge University Press.

Hess, Mickey. 2005. 'Hip-Hop Realness and the White Performer.' *Critical Studies in Media Communication* 22(5): 372–89.

Hughey, Matthew. 2012. *White Bound*. Stanford: Stanford University Press.

Jeffords, Susan. 1994. *Hard Bodies*. New Brunswick: Rutgers University Press.

Johnson, Allan. 2005. *The Gender Knot (revised and updated edition)*. Philadelphia: Temple University Press.

Kehler, Michael. 2007. 'Hallway Fears and High School Friendships.' *Discourse* 28(2): 259–77.

Kimmel, Michael. 1994. 'Masculinity as Homophobia.' Pp. 119–41 in *Theorizing Masculinities*, edited by Harry Brod and Michael Kaufman. Thousand Oaks, CA: Sage.

Kimmel, Michael. 1996. *Manhood in America*. New York: The Free Press.

Kosciw, Joseph G., Emily A. Greytak, Mark J. Bartkiewicz, Madelyn J. Boesen and Neal A. Palmer. 2012. The 2011 *National School Climate Survey: The Experiences of Lesbian, Gay, Bisexual and Transgender Youth in Our Nation's Schools*. New York: GLSEN.

Levy, Nathaniel, Sandra Cortesi, Urs Gasser, Edward Crowley, Meredith Beaton, June Casey and Caroline Nolan. 2012. *Bullying in a Networked Era*. Cambridge: Berkman Center for Internet & Society Research Publication Series.

Loftus, Jeni. 2001. 'America's Liberalization in Attitudes toward Homosexuality, 1973 to 1998.' *American Sociological Review* 66(5): 762–82.

Lott, Eric. 1993. *Love and Theft: Blackface Minstrelsy and the American Working Class*. New York: Oxford University Press.

Masters, N. Tatiana. 2010. "'My Strength Is Not for Hurting': Men's Anti-Rape Websites and Their Construction of Masculinity and Male Sexuality.' *Sexualities* 13(1): 33–46.

McCormack, Mark. 2012. *The Declining Significance of Homophobia*. New York: Oxford University Press.

Messerschmidt, James. 2010. *Hegemonic Masculinities and Camouflaged Politics*. Boulder: Paradigm Publishers.

Messner, Michael. 1993. "'Changing Men' and Feminist Politics in the United States.' *Theory and Society* 22(5): 723–37.

Messner, Michael. 2007. "The Masculinity of the Governator.' *Gender & Society* 21(4): 461–80.

Messner, Michael. 2011. 'Gender Ideologies, Youth Sports, and the Production of Soft Essentialism.' *Sociology of Sport Journal* 28(2): 151–70.

Murphy, Michael. 2009. 'Can 'Men' Stop Rape? Visualizing Gender in the "'My Strength Is Not for Hurting'" Rape Prevention Campaign.' *Men and Masculinities* 12(1): 113–30.

Pascoe, C. J. 2007. *Dude, You're a Fag*. Berkeley: University of California Press.

Perry, Amanda. 2001. 'White Means Never Having to Say You're Ethnic.' *Journal of Contemporary Ethnography* 30(1): 56–91.

Pfeil, Fred. 1995. *White Guys*. New York: Verso.

Poteat, V. Paul, Michael Kimmel and Riki Wilchins. 2010. 'The Moderating Effects of Support for Violence.' *Journal of Research on Adolescence* 21(2): 434–47.

Rodriquez, Jason. 2006. 'Color-Blind Ideology and the Cultural Appropriation of Hip-Hop.' *Contemporary Ethnography* 35(6): 645–68.

Saad, Lydia. 2010. Gallup Report: Americans' Acceptance of Gay Relations Crosses 50% Threshold. In *Gallup Politics*. Retrieved July 18, 2013, from http://www.gallup.com/poll/135764/americans-acceptance-gay-relations-crosses-threshold.aspx.

Savran, David. 1998. *Taking It Like a Man*. Princeton: Princeton University Press.

Schippers, Mimi. 2000. 'The Social Organization of Sexuality and Gender in Alternative Hard Rock.' *Gender & Society* 14(6): 747–64.

Schwalbe, Michael. 1996. *Unlocking the Iron Cage*. New York: Oxford University Press.

Segal, Lynne. 1990. *Slow Motion*. New Brunswick: Rutgers University Press.

Stein, Arlene. 2005. 'Make Room for Daddy.' *Gender & Society* 19(5): 601–20.

Ward, Jane. 2008. 'Dude-Sex: White Masculinities and 'Authentic' Heterosexuality among Dudes Who Have Sex with Dudes.' *Sexualities* 11(4): 414–34.

Waters, Mary. 1990. *Ethnic Options*. Berkeley: University of California Press.

Wilkins, Amy. 2004. 'Puerto Rican Wannabes.' *Gender & Society* 18(1): 103–21.

Wilkins, Amy. 2008. *Wannabes, Goths, and Christians*. Chicago: University of Chicago Press.

Wilkins, Amy. 2009. 'Masculinity Dilemmas: Sexuality and Intimacy Talk among Christians and Goths.' *Signs* 34(2): 343–68.

Wolkomir, Michelle. 2001. 'Wrestling with the Angels of Meaning: The Revisionist Ideological Work of Gay and Ex-Gay Christian Men.' *Symbolic Interaction* 24(4): 407–25.

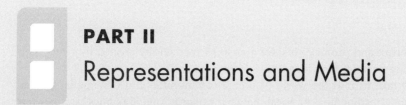

PART II
Representations and Media

How do people learn what it means to be a man? As we wrote in the Introduction to this book, cultural representations of masculinity fluctuate across time and space. These representations provide the parameters and standards that define masculine subjectivities and practices. They are the blueprints people use to assemble themselves (and others) as men. Cultural representations of masculinity often coalesce in what Raewyn Connell (see reading no. 1) calls "exemplars of hegemonic masculinity," or ideal types of manhood revered by men and women. Think about those guys who seem to possess a beguilingly manly aura: movie stars, athletes, business and political leaders.

Yet these carefully polished images of masculinity often disguise hidden tensions. Culture, especially popular culture, is awash with contradictory messages. Culture in (post)modern life is best understood not as a coherent and monolithic product of socialization, but as a site of struggle replete with incomplete and contested meanings. A consideration of various "exemplars of masculinity" in society quickly reveals these contradictions: chances are this list will consist of muscular sports stars, suave actors, techie innovators, forceful leaders, and even sensitive fathers. This is because masculinity is never predetermined, and thus multiple meanings appear simultaneously to compete for popular attention. This dialogue between different models of masculinity continues over time, influenced by political, economic, and technological shifts. The readings in this section capture such images along with the unstable social terrain they speak to and from. Before introducing these readings, however, a brief word about the importance of popular culture representations: the postmodern theorist Jean Baudrillard (1994) argued that mass media imagery does not merely represent real life—it *is* real life. We need to take advertising, films, television, and social media seriously, as more and more of our lives unfold within these platforms. The reality of masculinity is increasingly found in the "virtuality" of media representations and interactions.

Ken Gillam and Shannon Wooden begin this section with an interpretive analysis of Disney Pixar films (reading no. 6). You may remember many of these films, such as *Toy Story* and *Cars*. Although Disney is often criticized (correctly, in our estimation) for its gender stereotypical portrayals, the authors argue that Pixar productions actually communicate complex notions of masculinity. According to Gilliam and Wooden, male protagonists in Pixar films transform into a "New Man" by shunning older, alpha-male characteristics. (And in doing so, they develop certain "homosocial relationships"; recall also how Sharon Bird uses the concept of homosociality in reading no. 2.) Turning to programming aimed at a slightly older audience, Kristen Myers demonstrates how hegemonic representations of masculinity ultimately triumph over nonhegemonic representations. In "Cowboy Up," reading no. 7, Myers finds that most male characters in popular adolescent television shows are sensitive, vulnerable, and quiescent. However, these nonhegemonic representations merely serve as humorous foils to reinforce the dominance of hegemonic characters.

Reading no. 8 reveals the interplay between masculine imagery and social anxieties. Kyle Green and Madison Van Oort analyze television commercials that aired during the 2010 Super Bowl. During this deep economic recession, the authors explore how advertisements depict men as drifting aimlessly, beset by emasculation. Cleverly, the advertisers promise that their products can replenish this flagging masculine vitality and control, giving new meaning to the term *purchasing power*. The authors analyze how these commercials reflect and promise to solve a crisis of masculinity created by rising male unemployment and growing feminist consciousness.

Readings no. 9 and 10 take us into the world of online communities and new digital medias. In "Bitch, Slut, Skank, Cunt" (reading no. 19), Sarah Sobieraj explores "digital publics" as a new(er) space for the reproduction of gender inequality. In some ways, the anonymity and disembodiment of social media might appear to promote egalitarian interactions and a reassessment of gender norms. However, Sobieraj's research finds just the opposite. Drawing on data including interviews with women who have been targeted by online gender-based attacks, as well as interviews with professionals working to improve internet safety, the author describes how virtual networking platforms have become sites for disturbing expressions of misogyny, and have therefore limited women's participation in these online spaces. For their study, Mairead Eastin Moloney and Tony P. Love concentrate on one high-profile event to show how manhood acts are performed virtually; in this case, on the social media platform of Twitter. The researchers analyzed nearly 10,000 tweets in response to "#TheFappening" (reading no. 10), a public hacking of nude photos of female celebrities in 2014. They discovered that the tweets collectively affirmed Twitter as a heterosexist domain.

Questions to Ponder

1. Green and Van Oort identify how films and advertisements respond to (and potentially create) crises of masculinity in a perceived loss of men's social standing. Do you think such a crisis exists today? What films and advertisements can you think of that appear to replenish or stabilize masculinity? How might men now be trying to find a more "authentic" masculinity?

2. Have you observed or heard of online interactions similar to what is documented in readings no. 9 and 10? How is the enactment of masculinity in digital space different from, and similar to, face-to-face interactions?

3. What gender messages occur in children's media currently? Is there more awareness of gender flexibility and gender equality?

4. Can the concept of "hybrid masculinity" (see reading no. 5) be applied to media representations? In other words, how might the media misleadingly promote forms of gender egalitarianism? Think of some examples in advertising, television, and films.

5. Can media, including social media, be a tool of positive change in gender? If so, how can this be accomplished?

Key Concepts

Authentic masculinity   Digital publics/digital sexism   Postfeminism
Crisis of masculinity   Hyperheterosexuality

Reference

Baudrillard, Jean. 1994. *Simulacra and Simulation.* Ann Arbor: University of Michigan Press.

CHAPTER 6

Post-Princess Models of Gender

The New Man in Disney/Pixar

Ken Gillam and Shannon R. Wooden

Lisping over the Steve McQueen allusion in Pixar's *Cars* (2006), our two-year-old son, Oscar, inadvertently directed us to the definition(s) of masculinity that might be embedded in a children's animated film about NASCAR. The film overtly praises the "good woman" proverbially behind every successful man: the champion car, voiced by Richard Petty, tells his wife, "I wouldn't be nothin' without you, honey." But gender in this twenty-first-century bildungsroman is rather more complex, and Oscar's mispronunciation held the first clue. To him, a member of the film's target audience, the character closing in on the title long held by "The King" is not "Lightning McQueen" but "Lightning the queen"; his chief rival, the always-a-bridesmaid runner-up "Chick" Hicks.

Does this nominal feminizing of male also-rans (and the simultaneous gendering of success) constitute a meaningful pattern? Piqued, we began examining the construction of masculinity in major feature films released by Disney's Pixar studios over the past thirteen years. Indeed, as we argue here, Pixar consistently promotes a new model of masculinity, one that matures into acceptance of its more traditionally "feminine" aspects.

Cultural critics have long been interested in Disney's cinematic products, but the gender critics examining the texts most enthusiastically gobbled up by the under-six set have so far generally focused on their retrograde representations of women. As Elizabeth Bell argues, the animated Disney features through *Beauty and the Beast* feature a "teenaged heroine at the idealized height of puberty's graceful promenade [. . ., f]emale wickedness [. . .] rendered as middle-aged beauty at its peak of sexuality and authority [. . ., and] [f]eminine sacrifice and nurturing [. . .] drawn in pear-shaped, old women past menopause" (108). Some have noted the models of masculinity in the classic animated films, primarily the contrast between the ubermacho Gaston and the sensitive, misunderstood Beast in *Beauty and the Beast*,[1] but the male protagonist of the animated classics, at least through *The Little Mermaid*, remains largely uninterrogated.[2] For most of the early films, this critical omission seems generally appropriate, the various versions of Prince Charming being often too two-dimensional to do more than inadvertently shape the definition of the protagonists' femininity. But if the feminist thought that has shaped our cultural texts for three decades now has been somewhat disappointing in its ability to actually rewrite the princess trope (the spunkiest of the "princesses," Ariel, Belle, Jasmine, and, arguably, even Mulan, remain thin, beautiful, kind, obedient or punished for disobedience, and headed for the altar), it has been surprisingly effective in rewriting the type of masculine power promoted by Disney's products.[3]

Disney's new face, Pixar studios, has released nine films—*Toy Story* (1995) and *Toy Story 2* (1999); *A Bug's Life* (1998); *Finding Nemo* (2003); *Monsters, Inc.* (2001); *The Incredibles* (2004); *Cars* (2006);

SOURCE: Gillam, K., and Wooden, S. R. (2008). Post-Princess Models of Gender: The New Man in Disney/Pixar. *Journal of Popular Film and Television*, 36(1), 2–8. Reproduced with permission from the *Journal of Popular Film and Television*.

Ratatouille (2007); and now *WALL•E* (2008)—all of which feature interesting male figures in leading positions. Unlike many of the princesses, who remain relatively static even through their own adventures, these male leads are actual protagonists; their characters develop and change over the course of the film, rendering the plot. Ultimately these various developing characters—particularly Buzz and Woody from *Toy Story*, Mr. Incredible from *The Incredibles*, and Lightning McQueen from *Cars*—experience a common narrative trajectory, culminating in a common "New Man" model[4]: they all strive for an alpha-male identity; they face emasculating failures; they find themselves, in large part, through what Eve Sedgwick refers to as "homosocial desire" and a triangulation of this desire with a feminized object (and/or a set of "feminine" values); and, finally, they achieve (and teach) a kinder, gentler understanding of what it means to be a man.

Emasculation of the Alpha Male

A working definition of alpha male may be unnecessary; although more traditionally associated with the animal kingdom than the Magic Kingdom, it familiarly evokes ideas of dominance, leadership, and power in human social organizations as well. The phrase "alpha male" may stand for all things stereotypically patriarchal: unquestioned authority, physical power and social dominance, competitiveness for positions of status and leadership, lack of visible or shared emotion, social isolation. An alpha male, like Vann in *Cars*, does not ask for directions; like Doc Hudson in the same film, he does not talk about his feelings. The alpha male's stresses, like Buzz Lightyear's, come from his need to save the galaxy; his strength comes from faith in his ability to do so. These models have worked in Disney for decades. The worst storm at sea is no match for *The Little Mermaid*'s uncomplicated Prince Eric—indeed, any charming prince need only ride in on his steed to save his respective princess. But the postfeminist world is a different place for men, and the post-princess Pixar is a different place for male protagonists.

Newsweek recently described the alpha male's new cinematic and television rival, the "beta male": "The testosterone-pumped, muscle-bound Hollywood hero is rapidly deflating[. . . .] Taking his place is a new kind of leading man, the kind who's just as happy following as leading, or never getting off the sofa" (Yabroff 64). Indeed, as Susan Jeffords points out, at least since *Beauty and the Beast*, Disney has resisted (even ridiculed) the machismo once de rigueur for leading men (170). Disney cinema, one of the most effective teaching tools America offers its children, is not yet converting its model male protagonist all the way into a slacker, but the New Man model is quite clearly emerging.

Cars, *Toy Story*, and *The Incredibles* present their protagonists as unambiguously alpha in the opening moments of the films. Although Lightning McQueen may be an as-yet incompletely realized alpha when *Cars* begins, not having yet achieved the "King" status of his most successful rival, his ambition and fierce competitiveness still clearly valorize the alpha-male model: "Speed. I am speed . . . I eat losers for breakfast," he chants as a prerace mantra. He heroically comes from behind to tie the championship race, distinguishing himself by his physical power and ability, characteristics that catapult him toward the exclusively male culture of sports superstars. The fantasies of his life he indulges after winning the coveted Piston Cup even include flocks of female cars forming a worshipful harem around him. But the film soon diminishes the appeal of this alpha model. Within a few moments of the race's conclusion, we see some of Lightning's less positive macho traits; his inability to name any friends, for example, reveals both his isolation and attempts at emotional stoicism. Lightning McQueen is hardly an unemotional character, as can be seen when he prematurely jumps onto the stage to accept what he assumes to be his victory. For this happy emotional outburst, however, he is immediately disciplined by a snide comment from Chick. From this point until much later in the film, the only emotions he displays are those of frustration and anger.

Toy Story's Buzz Lightyear and Sheriff Woody similarly base their worth on a masculine model of competition and power, desiring not only to be the "favorite toy" of their owner, Andy, but to possess the admiration of and authority over the other toys in the playroom. Woody is a natural leader, and his position represents both paternalistic care and patriarchal dominance. In an opening scene, he calls and conducts a "staff meeting" that highlights his unambiguously dominant position in the toy community. Encouraging the toys to pair up so that no one will be lost in the family's impending move, he commands: "A moving buddy. If you don't have one, GET ONE." Buzz's alpha identity comes from a more exalted source than social governance—namely, his belief that he is the one "space ranger" with the power and knowledge needed to save the galaxy; it seems merely natural, then, that the other toys would look up to him, admire his strength, and follow his orders. But as with Lightning McQueen, these depictions of masculine power are soon undercut. Buzz's mere presence exposes Woody's strength as fragile, artificial, even arbitrary, and his "friends," apparently having been drawn to his authority rather than his character, are fair-weather at best. Buzz's authority rings hollow from the very beginning, and his refusal to believe in his own "toyness" is at best silly and at worst danger-ous. Like Lightning, Buzz's and Woody's most commonly expressed emotions are anger and frustra-tion, not sadness (Woody's, at having been "replaced") or fear (Buzz's, at having "crash-landed on a strange planet") or even wistful fondness (Woody's, at the loss of Slink's, Bo Peep's, and Rex's loyalty). Once again, the alpha-male position is depicted as fraudulent, precarious, lonely, and devoid of emo-tional depth.

An old-school superhero, Mr. Incredible opens *The Incredibles* by displaying the tremendous physical strength that enables him to stop speeding trains, crash through buildings, and keep the city safe from criminals. But he too suffers from the emotional isolation of the alpha male. Stopping on the way to his own wedding to interrupt a crime in progress, he is very nearly late to the service, show-ing up only to say the "I dos." Like his car and toy counterparts, he communicates primarily through verbal assertions of power—angrily dismissing Buddy, his meddlesome aspiring sidekick; bantering with Elastigirl over who gets the pickpocket—and limits to anger and frustration the emotions appar-ently available to men.

Fraught as it may seem, the alpha position is even more fleeting: in none of these Pixar films does the male protagonist's dominance last long. After Lightning ties, rather than wins, the race and ignores the King's friendly advice to find and trust a good team with which to work, he browbeats his faithful semi, Mack, and ends up lost in "hillbilly hell," a small town off the beaten path of the inter-state. His uncontrolled physical might destroys the road, and the resultant legal responsibility—community service—keeps him far from his Piston Cup goals. When Buzz appears as a gift for Andy's birthday, he easily unseats Woody both as Andy's favorite and as the toy community's leader. When Buzz becomes broken, failing to save himself from the clutches of the evil neighbor, Sid, he too must learn a hard lesson about his limited power, his diminished status, and his own relative insignificance in the universe. Mr. Incredible is perhaps most obviously disempowered: despite his superheroic feats, Mr. Incredible has been unable to keep the city safe from his own clumsy brute force. After a series of lawsuits against "the Supers," who accidentally leave various types of small-time mayhem in their wake, they are all driven underground, into a sort of witness protection program. To add insult to injury, Mr. Incredible's diminutive boss fires him from his job handling insurance claims, and his wife, the former Elastigirl, assumes the "pants" of the family.

Most of these events occur within the first few minutes of the characters' respective films. Only Buzz's downfall happens in the second half. The alpha-male model is thus not only present and chal-lenged in the films but also is, in fact, the very structure on which the plots unfold. Each of these films is about being a man, and they begin with an outdated, two-dimensional alpha prototype to expose its failings and to ridicule its logical extensions: the devastation and humiliation of being defeated in competition, the wrath generated by power unchecked, the paralyzing alienation and fear inherent in being lonely at the top. As these characters begin the film in (or seeking) the tenuous alpha position among fellow characters, each of them is also stripped of this identity—dramatically emasculated—so that he may learn, reform, and emerge again with a different, and arguably more feminine, self-concept.

"Emasculated" is not too strong a term for what happens to these male protagonists; the decline of the alpha-male model is gender coded in all the films. For his community service punishment, Lightning is chained to the giant, snorting, tar-spitting "Bessie" and ordered to repair the damage he has wrought. His own "horsepower" (as Sally cheerfully points out) is used against him when literally put in the service of a nominally feminized figure valued for the more "feminine" orientation of service to the community. If being under the thumb of this humongous "woman" is not emasculating enough, Mater, who sees such subordination to Bessie as a potentially pleasurable thing, names the price, saying, "I'd give my left two lug nuts for something like that!"

Mr. Incredible's downfall is most clearly marked as gendered by his responses to it. As his wife's domestic power and enthusiasm grow increasingly unbearable, and his children's behavior more and more out of his control, he surreptitiously turns to the mysterious, gorgeous "Mirage," who gives him what he needs to feel like a man: superhero work. Overtly depicting her as the "other woman," the film requires Elastigirl to intercept a suggestive-sounding phone call, and to trap her husband in a lie, to be able to work toward healing his decimated masculinity.

In *Toy Story*, the emasculation of the alpha male is the most overt, and arguably the most comic. From the beginning, power is constructed in terms conspicuously gender coded, at least for adult viewers: as they watch the incoming birthday presents, the toys agonize at their sheer size, the longest and most phallic-shaped one striking true fear (and admiration?) into the hearts of the spectators. When Buzz threatens Woody, one toy explains to another that he has "laser envy." Buzz's moment of truth, after seeing himself on Sid's father's television, is the most clearly gendered of all. Realizing for the first time that Woody is right, he is a "toy," he defiantly attempts to fly anyway, landing sprawled on the floor with a broken arm. Sid's little sister promptly finds him, dresses him in a pink apron and hat, and installs him as "Mrs. Nesbit" at her tea party. When Woody tries to wrest him from his despair, Buzz wails, "Don't you get it? I AM MRS. NESBIT. But does the hat look good? Oh, tell me the hat looks good!" Woody's "rock bottom" moment finds him trapped under an overturned milk crate, forcing him to ask Buzz for help and to admit that he "doesn't stand a chance" against Buzz in the contest for Andy's affection, which constitutes "everything that is important to me." He is not figured into a woman, like Buzz is, or subordinated to a woman, like Lightning is, or forced to seek a woman's affirmation of his macho self, like Mr. Incredible is, but he does have to acknowledge his own feminine values, from his need for communal support to his deep, abiding (and, later, maternal) love of a boy. This "feminine" stamp is characteristic of the New Man model toward which these characters narratively journey.

Homosociality, Intimacy, and Emotion

Regarding the "love of a boy," the "mistress" tempting Mr. Incredible away from his wife and family is not Mirage at all but Buddy, the boy he jilted in the opening scenes of the film (whose last name, Pine, further conveys the unrequited nature of their relationship). Privileging his alpha-male emotional isolation, but adored by his wannabe sidekick, Mr. Incredible vehemently protects his desire to "work alone." After spending the next years nursing his rejection and refining his arsenal, Buddy eventually retaliates against Mr. Incredible for rebuffing his advances. Such a model of homosocial tutelage as Buddy proposes at the beginning of the film certainly evokes an ancient (and homosexual) model of masculine identity; Mr. Incredible's rejection quickly and decisively replaces it with a heteronormative one, further supported by Elastigirl's marrying and

Mirage's attracting the macho superhero.[5] But it is equally true that the recovery of Mr. Incredible's masculine identity happens primarily through his (albeit antagonistic) relationship with Buddy, suggesting that Eve Sedgwick's notion of a homo-social continuum is more appropriate to an analysis of the film's gender attitudes than speculations about its reactionary heteronormativity, even homophobia.

Same-sex (male) bonds—to temporarily avoid the more loaded term desire—are obviously important to each of these films. In fact, in all three, male/male relationships emerge that move the fallen alphas forward in their journeys toward a new masculinity. In each case, the male lead's first and/or primary intimacy—his most immediate transformative relationship—is with one or more male characters. Even before discovering Buddy as his nemesis, Mr. Incredible secretly pairs up with his old pal Frozone, and the two step out on their wives to continue superheroing on the sly; Buddy and Frozone are each, in their ways, more influential on Mr. Incredible's sense of self than his wife or children are. Although Lightning falls in love with Sally and her future vision of Radiator Springs, his almost accidentally having befriended the hapless, warm Mater catalyzes more foundational lessons about the responsibilities of friendship—demanding honesty, sensitivity, and care—than the smell-the-roses lesson Sally represents. He also ends up being mentored and taught a comparable lesson about caring for others by Doc Hudson, who even more explicitly encourages him to resist the alpha path of the Piston Cup world by relating his experiences of being used and then rejected. Woody and Buzz, as rivals-cum-allies, discover the necessary truths about their masculine strength only as they discover how much they need one another. Sedgwick further describes the ways in which the homosocial bond is negotiated through a triangulation of desire; that is, the intimacy emerging "between men" is constructed through an overt and shared desire for a feminized object. Unlike homosocial relationships between women—that is, "the continuum between 'women loving women' and 'women promoting the interests of women'"—male homosocial identity is necessarily homophobic in patriarchal systems, which are structurally homophobic (3). This means the same-sex relationship demands social opportunities for a man to insist on, or prove, his heterosexuality. Citing Rene Girard's *Deceit, Desire, and the Novel,* Sedgwick argues that "in any erotic rivalry, the bond that links the two rivals is as intense and potent as the bond that links either of the rivals to the beloved" (21); women are ultimately symbolically exchangeable "for the primary purpose of cementing the bonds of men with men" (26).

This triangulation of male desire can be seen in *Cars* and *Toy Story* particularly, where the homosocial relationship rather obviously shares a desire for a feminized third. Buzz and Woody compete first, momentarily, for the affection of Bo Peep, who is surprisingly sexualized for a children's movie (purring to Woody an offer to "get someone else to watch the sheep tonight," then rapidly choosing Buzz as her "moving buddy" after his "flying" display). More importantly, they battle for the affection of Andy—a male child alternately depicted as maternal (it is his responsibility to get his baby sister out of her crib) and in need of male protection (Woody exhorts Buzz to "take care of Andy for me!").[6] *Cars* also features a sexualized romantic heroine; less coquettish than Bo Peep, Sally still fumbles over an invitation to spend the night "not with me, but . . ." in the motel she owns. One of Lightning and Mater's moments of "bonding" happens when Mater confronts Lightning, stating his affection for Sally and sharing a parallel story of heterosexual desire. The more principal objects of desire in *Cars,* however, are the (arguably) feminized "Piston Cup" and the Dinoco sponsorship. The sponsor itself is established in romantic terms: with Lightning stuck in Radiator Springs, his agent says Dinoco has had to "woo" Chick instead. Tia and Mia, Lightning's "biggest fans," who transfer their affection to Chick during his absence, offer viewers an even less subtly gendered goal, and Chick uses this to taunt Lightning. It is in the pursuit of these objects, and in competition with Chick and the King, that Lightning first defines himself as a man; the Piston Cup also becomes the object around which he and Doc discover their relationship to one another.

The New Man

With the strength afforded by these homosocial intimacies, the male characters triumph over their respective plots, demonstrating the desirable modifications that Pixar makes to the alpha-male model. To emerge victorious (and in one piece) over the tyrannical neighbor boy, Sid, Buzz, and Woody have to cooperate not only with each other but also with the cannibalized toys lurking in the dark places of Sid's bedroom. Incidentally learning a valuable lesson about discrimination based on physical difference (the toys are not monsters at all, despite their frightening appearance), they begin to show sympathy, rather than violence born of their fear, to the victims of Sid's experimentation. They learn how to humble themselves to ask for help from the community. Until Woody's grand plan to escape Sid unfolds, Sid could be an object lesson in the unredeemed alpha-male type: cruelly almighty over the toy community, he wins at arcade games, bullies his sister, and, with strategically placed fireworks, exerts militaristic might over any toys he can find. Woody's newfound ability to give and receive care empowers him to teach Sid a lesson of caring and sharing that might be microcosmic to the movie as a whole. Sid, of course, screams (like a girl) when confronted with the evidence of his past cruelties, and when viewers last see him, his younger sister is chasing him up the stairs with her doll.

Even with the unceremonious exit of Sid, the adventure is not quite over for Buzz and Woody. Unable to catch up to the moving van as Sid's dog chases him, Woody achieves the pinnacle of the New Man narrative: armed with a new masculine identity, one that expresses feelings and acknowledges community as a site of power, Woody is able to sacrifice the competition with Buzz for his object of desire. Letting go of the van strap, sacrificing himself (he thinks) to Sid's dog, he plainly expresses a caretaking, nurturing love, and a surrender to the good of the beloved: "Take care of Andy for me," he pleads. Buzz's own moment of truth comes from seizing his power as a toy: holding Woody, he glides into the family's car and back into Andy's care, correcting Woody by proudly repeating his earlier, critical words back to him: "This isn't flying; it's falling with style." Buzz has found the value of being a "toy," the self-fulfillment that comes from being owned and loved. "Being a toy is a lot better than being a space ranger," Woody explains. "You're his toy" (emphasis in original).

Mr. Incredible likewise must embrace his own dependence, both physical and emotional. Trapped on the island of Chronos, at the mercy of Syndrome (Buddy's new super-persona), Mr. Incredible needs women—his wife's superpowers and Mirage's guilty intervention—to escape. To overpower the monster Syndrome has unleashed on the city, and to achieve the pinnacle of the New Man model, he must also admit to his emotional dependence on his wife and children. Initially confining them to the safety of a bus, he confesses to Elastigirl that his need to fight the monster alone is not a typically alpha ("I work alone") sort of need but a loving one: "I can't lose you again," he tells her. The robot/monster is defeated, along with any vestiges of the alpha model, as the combined forces of the Incredible family locate a new model of postfeminist strength in the family as a whole. This communal strength is not simply physical but marked by cooperation, selflessness, and intelligence. The children learn that their best contributions protect the others; Mr. Incredible figures out the robot/monster's vulnerability and cleverly uses this against it.

In a parallel motif to Mr. Incredible's inability to control his strength, Buddy/Syndrome finally cannot control his robot/monster; in the defeat, he becomes the newly emasculated alpha male. But like his robot, he learns quickly. His last attempt to injure Mr. Incredible, kidnapping his baby Jack-Jack, strikes at Mr. Incredible's new source of strength and value, his family. The strength of the cooperative family unit is even more clearly displayed in this final rescue: for the shared, parental goal of saving Jack-Jack, Mr. Incredible uses his physical strength and, with her consent, the shape-shifting body of his super-wife. He throws Elastigirl into the air, where she catches their baby and, flattening her body into a parachute, sails gently back to her husband and older children.

Through Lightning McQueen's many relationships with men, as well as his burgeoning romance with Sally, he also learns how to care about others, to focus on the well-being of the community, and to privilege nurture and kindness. It is Doc, not Sally, who explicitly challenges the race car with his selfishness ("When was the last time you cared about something except yourself, hot rod?"). His reformed behavior begins with his generous contributions to the Radiator Springs community. Not only does he provide much-needed cash for the local economy, but he also listens to, praises, and values the residents for their unique offerings to Radiator Springs. He is the chosen auditor for Lizzy's reminiscing about her late husband, contrasting the comic relief typically offered by the senile and deaf Model T with poignancy, if not quite sadness. Repairing the town's neon, he creates a romantic dreamscape from the past, a setting for both courting Sally ("cruising") and, more importantly, winning her respect with his ability to share in her value system. For this role, he is even physically transformed: he hires the body shop proprietor, Ramone, to paint over his sponsors' stickers and his large race number, as if to remove himself almost completely from the Piston Cup world, even as he anticipates being released from his community service and thus being able to return to racing.

Perhaps even more than Buzz, Woody, and Mr. Incredible do, the New Man McQueen shuns the remaining trappings of the alpha role, actually refusing the Piston Cup. If the first three protagonists are ultimately qualified heroes—that is, they still retain their authority and accomplish their various tasks, but with new values and perspectives acquired along the way—Lightning completely and publicly refuses his former object of desire. Early in the final race, he seems to somewhat devalue racing; his daydreams of Sally distract him, tempting him to give up rather than to compete. The plot, however, needs him to dominate the race so his decision at the end will be entirely his own. His friends show up and encourage him to succeed. This is where the other films end: the values of caring, sharing, nurturing, and community being clearly present, the hero is at last able to achieve, improved by having embraced those values. But Lightning, seeing the wrecked King and remembering the words of Doc Hudson, screeches to a stop inches before the finish line. Reversing, he approaches the King, pushes him back on the track, and acknowledges the relative insignificance of the Piston Cup in comparison to his new and improved self. He then declines the Dinoco corporate offer in favor of remaining faithful to his loyal Rust-eze sponsors. Chick Hicks, the only unredeemed alpha male at the end, celebrates his ill-gotten victory and is publicly rejected at the end by both his fans, "the twins," and, in a sense, by the Piston Cup itself, which slides onto the stage and hits him rudely in the side.

Conclusion

The trend of the New Man seems neither insidious nor nefarious, nor is it out of step with the larger cultural movement. It is good, we believe, for our son to be aware of the many sides of human existence, regardless of traditional gender stereotypes. However, maintaining a critical consciousness of the many lessons taught by the cultural monolith of Disney remains imperative. These lessons—their pedagogical aims or results—become most immediately obvious to us as parents when we watch our son ingest and express them, when he misunderstands and makes his own sense of them, and when we can see ways in which his perception of reality is shaped by them, before our eyes. Without assuming that the values of the films are inherently evil or representative of an evil "conspiracy to undermine American youth" (Giroux 4), we are still compelled to critically examine the texts on which our son bases many of his attitudes, behaviors, and preferences.

Moreover, the impact of Disney, as Henry Giroux has effectively argued, is tremendously more widespread than our household. Citing Michael Eisner's 1995 "Planetized Entertainment," Giroux claims that 200 million people a year watch Disney videos or films, and in a week, 395 million watch a Disney TV show, 3.8 million subscribe to the Disney Channel, and 810,000 make a purchase at a Disney store (19). As Benjamin Barber argued in 1995, "[T]he true tutors of our children are not schoolteachers or university professors but filmmakers, advertising executives and pop culture purveyors" (qtd. in Giroux 63). Thus we perform our "pedagogical intervention[s]" of examining Disney's power to "shap[e] national identity, gender roles, and childhood values" (Giroux 10). It remains a necessary and ongoing task, not just for concerned parents, but for all conscientious cultural critics.

Notes

1. See Susan Jeffords, "The Curse of Masculinity: Disney's *Beauty and the Beast*," for an excellent analysis of that plot's developing the cruel Beast into a man who can love and be loved in return: "Will he be able to overcome his beastly temper and terrorizing attitude in order to learn to love?" (168). But even in this film, she argues, the Beast's development is dependent on "other people, especially women," whose job it is to tutor him into the new model of masculinity, the "New Man" (169, 170).

2. Two articles demand that we qualify this claim. Indirectly, they support the point of this essay by demonstrating a midcentury Disney model of what we call "alpha" masculinity. David Payne's "Bambi" parallels that film's coming-of-age plot, ostensibly representing a "natural" world, with the military mindset of the 1940s against which the film was drawn. Similarly, Claudia Card, in "Pinocchio," claims that the Disneyfied version of the nineteenth-century Carlo Collodi tale replaces the original's model of bravery and honesty with "a macho exercise in heroism [. . . and] avoid[ing] humiliation" (66–67).

3. Outside the animated classics, critics have noted a trend toward a postfeminist masculinity—one characterized by emotional wellness, sensitivity to family, and a conscious rejection of the most alpha-male values—in Disney-produced films of the 1980s and 1990s. Jeffords gives a sensible account of the changing male lead in films ranging from *Kindergarten Cop* to *Terminator 2*.

4. In Disney criticism, the phrase "New Man" seems to belong to Susan Jeffords's 1995 essay on *Beauty and the Beast*, but it is slowly coming into vogue for describing other postfeminist trends in masculine identity. In popular culture, see Richard Collier's "The New Man: Fact or Fad?" online in *Achilles Heel: The Radical Men's Magazine* 14 (Winter 1992/1993). http://www.achilles heel.freeuk.com/article14_9.html. For a literary-historical account, see *Writing Men: Literary Masculinities from Frankenstein to the New Man* by Berthold Schoene-Harwood (Columbia UP, 2000).

5. Critics have described the superhero within some framework of queer theory since the 1950s, when Dr. Fredric Wertham's *Seduction of the Innocent* claimed that Batman and Robin were gay (Ameron Ltd, 1954). See Rob Lendrum's "Queering Super-Manhood: Superhero Masculinity, Camp, and Public Relations as a Textual Framework" (*International Journal of Comic Art* 7.1 [2005]: 287–303) and Valerie Palmer-Mehtan and Kellie Hay's "A Superhero for Gays? Gay Masculinity and Green Lantern" (*Journal of American Culture* 28.4 [2005]: 390–404), among myriad nonscholarly pop-cultural sources.

6. Interestingly, Andy and *Toy Story* in general are apparently without (human) male role models. The only father present in the film at all is Sid's, sleeping in front of the television in the middle of the day. Andy's is absent at a dinner out, during a move, and on the following Christmas morning. Andy himself, at play, imagines splintering a nuclear family: when he makes Sheriff Woody catch One-Eyed Black Bart in a criminal act, he says, "Say goodbye to the wife and tater tots . . . you're going to jail."

References

Bell, Elizabeth. "Somatexts at the Disney Shop: Constructing the Pentimentos of Women's Animated Bodies." Bell, *From Mouse to Mermaid* 107–24.

Bell, Elizabeth, Lynda Haas, and Laura Sells, eds. *From Mouse to Mermaid: The Politics of Film, Gender, and Culture*. Bloomington: Indiana UP, 1995.

Card, Claudia. "Pinocchio." Bell, *From Mouse to Mermaid* 62–71.

Cars. Dir. John Lasseter. Walt Disney Pictures/Pixar Animation Studios, 2006.

Collier, Richard. "The New Man: Fact or Fad?" *Achilles Heel: The Radical Men's Magazine* 14 (1992–93). <http://www .achillesheel.freeuk.com/article14_ 9.html>.

Eisner, Michael. "Planetized Entertainment." *New Perspectives Quarterly* 12.4 (1995): 8.

Giroux, Henry. *The Mouse that Roared: Disney and the End of Innocence.* Oxford, Eng.: Rowman, 1999.

The Incredibles. Dir. Brad Bird. Walt Disney Pictures/Pixar Animation Studios, 2004.

Jeffords, Susan. "The Curse of Masculinity: Disney's Beauty and the Beast." Bell, *From Mouse to Mermaid* 161–72.

Lendrum, Rob. "Queering Super-Manhood: Superhero Masculinity, Camp, and Public Relations as a Textual Framework." *International Journal of Comic Art* 7.1 (2005): 287–303.

Palmer-Mehtan, Valerie, and Kellie Hay. "A Superhero for Gays? Gay Masculinity and Green Lantern." *Journal of American Culture* 28.4 (2005): 390–404.

Payne, David. "Bambi." Bell, *From Mouse to Mermaid* 137–47.

Schoene-Harwood, Berthold. *Writing Men: Literary Masculinities from Frankenstein to the New Man.* Columbia: Columbia UP, 2000.

Sedgwick, Eve Kosofsky. *Between Men: English Literature and Male Homosocial Desire.* New York: Columbia UP, 1985.

Toy Story. Dir. John Lasseter. Walt Disney Pictures/Pixar Animation Studios, 1995.

Wertham, Fredric. *Seduction of the Innocent.* New York: Reinhart, 1954.

Yabroff, Jennie. "Betas Rule." *Newsweek* 4 June 2007: 64–65.

CHAPTER 7

"Cowboy Up!"

Non-Hegemonic Representations of Masculinity in Children's Television Programming

Kristen Myers

From 2006–2011, Disney Channel featured a wildly popular show called *Hannah Montana*, aimed at an audience of pre-adolescent children. The show was about a teenaged girl named Miley (played by Miley Cyrus), who had a secret life as a pop-star named Hannah Montana. She lived with her father, a country singer named Robby Ray (played by Billy Ray Cyrus), and her brother Jackson (Jason Earles). On one episode (Season 2, Episode 22), a teenaged boy named Rico (Moises Arias) asked Robby Ray to teach him to line-dance so that he could impress a girl. When Rico danced, he moved his hips in big, fluid arcs, rather than stiffly shuffling about. He shimmied his shoulders. Robby Ray said, "A good ole boy ain't going to be wanting to do all that kind of stuff. I mean, your girl's wanting a championship line dancer, not the spin cycle on a washing machine!" Although Robby Ray didn't accuse Rico of being gay, he did problematize his feminine motion. To correct the problem, Robby Ray decided that Rico should "get in touch with his inner cowboy." He sat Rico on a deck railing, to pretend to be a cowboy riding a horse. After three hours of riding the deck railing, Rico was in so much pain that he walked bowlegged, like a real cowboy. He danced like one too—awkward, halting, and stiff. Rico was cured of his girly swishing moves—he had "cowboyed up."

Hannah and other television programs proffer complex messages about masculinity for young American children to consume and perhaps emulate (Baker-Sperry, 2007; Corsaro, 1997). In introducing young children to cultural conceptualizations of masculinity, television series help produce "regional masculinities" (Connell & Messerschmidt, 2005) that shape the ways that masculinity plays out in actual children's lives. Because they live in "media-rich worlds" (Martin & Kayzak, 2009, 317), children easily absorb these messages. Television has an especially great impact on children, who consume it while their identities are being formed (Kelley et al., 1999; McAllister & Giglio, 2005; Baker-Sperry, 2007; and Corsaro, 1997). Television helps construct a rhetorical "frame" (Goffman, 1974; Ridgeway, 2011) that shapes people's perceptions of the world (Kuypers, 2009), despite the fact that the characters are fictional and viewers may never actually meet the actors in the series (Ferris, 2001).

This article focuses on the contradictory versions of masculinity that were presented in four television series aimed at children. On the one hand, these shows featured protagonist boys who were soft-spoken, un-athletic, emotional, and thoughtful—antitheses to the hyper-masculine heroes of years past (Bereska, 2003). Popularizing images of non-traditional masculinity could help shift the patriarchal gender order in a feminist direction (Butler, 1999; Connell, 1987; Renold, 2004;

SOURCE: Myers, K. (2012). "Cowboy Up!" Non-Hegemonic Representations of Masculinity in Children's Television Programming. *Journal of Men's Studies*, 20, 125–143. Reproduced with permission from the *Journal of Men's Studies*.

Walsh et al., 2008). On the other hand, these boys were almost always the butt of jokes. They were consistently feminized, with femininity signifying weakness and failure. Traditionally masculine characters often lurked in the background, reminding viewers what a "real man" looked like. Here, I explore the extent to which these programs promote progressive masculinities, or if traditional gender orthodoxy prevails.

Masculinities: Theory and Practice

Connell has shown that societies construct multiple masculinities and multiple femininities, with one form of masculinity dominating all others: "hegemonic masculinity." All boys and men are measured by hegemonic masculinity, even though most boys and men will never accomplish it. Connell and Messerschmidt (2005, p. 844) have elaborated on the concept of hegemonic masculinity, explaining that "To sustain a given pattern of hegemony requires the policing of men as well as the exclusion or discrediting of women." Women, girls, men, and boys all engage in this policing. Masculinity is embodied and enacted through displays of strength, athleticism, risk-taking, and heterosexual prowess.

Boys recognize hegemonic masculinity at an early age. For example, Messner (1990) researched elementary-school boys as they learned that playing basketball was not just about having fun with your friends—it was about being evaluated by older, higher status boys and men. Renold's (2007) work on 10 and 11 year old boys showed that even elementary school–aged boys adopted hegemonically masculine personae—what she calls a "hyperheterosexual" identity (see also Haywood, 1996). Boys in her study distanced themselves from femininity by avoiding girls, but they knew that being desired by girls was a good thing. As one girl commented about a hyperheterosexual boy: "Todd likes having girlfriends, but he dislikes girls" (p. 286).

Because heterosexuality is a major component of successful masculinity, boys spend a lot of energy addressing it. As Korobov (2005, p. 228) writes, "adolescence is a time when young men in particular begin to routinely practice forms of heteronormative masculinity that may implicitly or explicitly sanction sexism, homophobia, and 'compulsory heterosexuality.'" Pascoe (2005) calls this discourse "fag talk." In Pascoe's study, adolescents used "fag" to mean weak and unmanly. "Fag talk" was central to boys' joking discourse. At the same time, however, "fag talk" was a potent threat—boys could be targeted at any time by anyone.

Ramlow (2003, p. 108) says that homophobic comments are effective because they ultimately demasculinize men: "Being called a 'faggot,' a 'pussy,' or 'gay,' then, is not always or overtly about the material fact of sexual difference or same-sex relations; it is about the failures of heteronormative masculinity." In name-calling, many boys use "gay" and "girl" interchangeably (Oranksy & Maracek, 2009). Indeed, Epstein (1997) argued that, in primary or elementary school, the worst thing a boy could be called is a girl. As Butler (1999) explains, the "heterosexual matrix" complexly interconnects masculinity and heterosexuality, rejecting femininity.

Taken together, this literature shows that the masculinity, femininity, heteronormativity, and homophobia are intertwined so that markers of one become imbricated as evidence of another. Boys reject femininity in order to establish their dominance, and they must continually degrade girls and feminize other boys so as to maintain their status—even as they pursue girls sexually.

Because of the harmful effects of hegemonic masculinity on boys and girls, some scholars have insisted that we begin to cultivate non-hegemonic masculinities (Pollack, 1998; Kimmel, 2006). Is being a non-hegemonic boy a panacea for patriarchy and its ill effects? Renold found that, instead of *subverting* the dominant gender order, "othered" boys' management strategies actually reinforced dominant masculinities by treating hegemonic boys as the standard. Rather than embracing their counter-hegemonic potential, these boys longed to be "normal." They adopted the misogynist practices of their bullying classmates, rejecting all things feminine, including girls. Renold says that, ironically, "they appeared not to make the connection between the devaluing of femininity more widely and the subordination of non-hegemonic masculinities" (p. 261). Rather than altering the gender regime, non-hegemonic boys actually helped reinforce the traditional order (see also Connell & Messerschmidt, 2005; Kimmel, 2006; Pascoe, 2003).

Culture and Media

Feminist television criticism argues that television has the potential to shift the gender order if it provides feminist messages and models for viewers (see Lotz & Ross, 2004; Walsh et al., 2008). However, rather than seizing its transformative potential, television programming often ". . . reinscribes patriarchal constellations and stifles the political aspects of feminism" (Walsh et al., 2008, p. 125). Rather than being feminist, most television programming is *postfeminist*, which McRobbie (2004) defines as such:

> My argument is that "postfeminism" actively draws on and invokes feminism as that which can be taken into account in order to suggest that equality is achieved, in order to install a whole repertoire of meanings which emphasize that it is no longer needed, a spent force. (p. 4)

McRobbie uses the term, "feminism taken into account" to indicate when feminism is simultaneously acknowledged and undermined. Ringrose (2007) conceptualizes post-feminism as "part backlash, part cultural diffusion, part repressed anxiety over shifting gender orders" (p. 473). Television media have been shown to impact children's early gendered behavior (Powell & Abels, 2002). Indeed, the media might have a greater impact on children today given the nearly ubiquitous nature of television programming directed at them (McAllister and Giglio 2005). McAllister and Giglio (2005) explain that cable television has produced entire networks—or "kidnets"—aimed at children. Recognized for their buying potential, and for their influence over parents' buying practices, children have become an important audience for advertisers. Children's programming is broadcast 24 hours a day, daily, and the number of adolescent and pre-adolescent' channels grows each year. The two largest kidnets are Disney and Nickelodeon. On March 14, 2011, Disney channel ranked as the number one network among tweens for the 16th week in a row, according to Tvbythenumbers.com. Even during the NBA playoffs in spring 2011, Disney ranked as the 3rd most watched network during prime-time, among all viewers. When rating all-day programming between November 2010 and May 2011, Nickelodeon consistently topped the charts at about 2.1 million viewers, with Disney coming in second at 1.6 million. *Hannah's* final episode garnered a monster 6+ million viewers. Adults and children watch these networks. They also buy t-shirts, dolls, CDs, and DVDs. These shows are an entire industry (McAllister & Giglio, 2005).

Even though children consume a great deal of television on a weekly basis, they do not passively absorb larger cultural messages. Children are actors in their own right, negotiating meanings among themselves (Myers & Raymond, 2010; Thorne, 1993; VanAusdale & Feagin, 2002), with adults (Baraldi, 2008; DeMol & Buysee, 2008; Ludvigsen & Scott, 2009), and with the media itself (Bragg & Buckingham, 2004; Fingerson, 1999). However, children are affected by and grapple with cultural frames (Myers & Raymond, 2010; Neitzel & Chafel, 2010). Martin and Kayzak (2009) have argued that it is therefore important to understand the messages that are available to the children who consume them.

In this paper, I analyze the content of four television programs on Disney and Nickelodeon that were aimed at young children. What real-life children do with these messages is not addressed in this project. Instead, I explore the contradictory messages about masculinity communicated to children, examining the implications of these messages for children's conceptualization of masculinity at the local level.

Methods and Analysis

To explore these issues, I conducted qualitative textual analysis of the content of four popular children's television programs: Disney's *Suite Life on Deck* (broadcast from 2008–2011)*; Hannah Montana* (2006–2011); and *Wizards of Waverly Place* (2007–2011); and Nickelodeon's *iCarly* (2007–2011). I chose these shows based on focus groups with elementary school girls, aged 5–11 ($N = 63$) (see Myers & Raymond, 2010). These were their most-watched programs: they quoted them, gushed over characters' exploits, gossiped about their sexual liaisons, and even wore clothes that featured the characters' likenesses. Because these shows informed most of the girls' cultural references, I decided to systematically study them so as to uncover patterns in their content.

Table 1 Description of Television Programs Analyzed

Program	Premise	Main characters	Gender	Race
Hannah Montana (Disney)	TN native, Miley, moves with her family to LA, where she lives a double life: she's secretly a pop-star (Hannah Montana).	Miley	Girl	White
		Robbie Ray	Man	White
		Jackson	Boy	White
		Oliver	Boy	White
		Lilly	Girl	White
		Rico*	Boy	Latino
Suite Life on Deck (Disney)	In this sequel to *The Suite Life of Zack and Cody,* twins Zack and Cody go to high school on a cruise ship.	Zack*	Boy	White
		Cody	Boy	White
		London Tipton	Girl	Asian
		Woody	Boy	White
		Bailey	Girl	White
		Marcus	Boy	Black
		Mr. Moseby	Man	Black
Wizards of Waverly Place (Disney)	A family of wizards live on Waverly Place, in NYC. The kids learn to be wizards from their father, and they interact with magical creatures from the wizarding world.	Alex	Girl	Latina
		Justin	Boy	Latino
		Max	Boy	Latino
		Theresa	Woman	Latina
		Jerry	Man	White
		Harper	Girl	White
iCarly (Nickelodeon)	Carly lives with her brother, Spencer, in an apartment in Seattle. Carly and her best friend, Sam, star in a weekly web show, *iCarly*, with friend, Freddy.	Carly	Girl	White
		Spencer	Man	White
		Sam	Girl	White
		Freddy	Boy	White
		Mrs. Benson	Woman	White
		Gibby	Boy	White

* indicates a hegemonically masculine character.

These children's shows were not made for girls only. They were watched by millions of viewers of all ages nationwide, as discussed above. *Hannah* and *iCarly* were hugely popular shows, rated in the top 10 most viewed cable shows week after week in the summer of 2010, during the period when I coded data. Each series was well-established, in at least its 3rd season, and each season had 25–30 half-hour episodes (about 22 minutes long without commercials).

Findings

I find that these television programs highlighted non-hegemonic masculinities routinely. However, rather than undermining hegemonic masculinity, non-hegemonic characters actually re-valorized hegemonic masculinity (Walsh et al., 2008).

Non-Hegemonic Masculinities

Almost all of the male characters on these shows embodied non-hegemonic masculinities: 14 out of 16 males (88%) listed in Table 1 were non-hegemonic. They were not domineering, competitive, or sexually predatory. Instead, these males were gentle and emotional. Rather than shunning femininity, they often marked themselves in feminine ways. Most were heterosexual failures, although none was overtly gay. I describe them here.

Suite Life's Cody (played by Cole Sprouse) was smart, polite, non-athletic, romantic, clean, goal-oriented, and cautious. Much of the show's humor centered on his being a nerd. Cody's roommate, Woody (Matthew Timmons), was overweight, wore braces, and had a head of bouncy, unkempt curly hair. Food-obsessed and gassy, Woody was the butt of many jokes. *Suite Life's* Mr. Moseby (Phill Lewis) was one of the few adults on the show. He directed the ship's activities and acted as the students' guardian. Moseby was short, black, and effeminate. His uniform consisted of a blazer with a pocket handkerchief, shorts, and knee socks. One day, Moseby was excited to receive a package: "It's here! My pocket hanky of the month!" He took it out of the box and exclaimed, "Oooo! *Stripes!*" (Season 1, Episode 19). The kids teased him about his diminutive size and his failure with women.

On *Hannah*, Miley's older brother, Jackson, was short, lazy, and an academic failure. He had trouble getting dates. Jackson and his father, Robby Ray—also a non-hegemonic character—had a close relationship. For example, Robby Ray insisted that Jackson register at the local community college (S3, E14). Jackson resisted, telling his father, "Just accept that I'm a slacker." Robby Ray said, "Son, it's totally natural to be scared to go to college." Jackson protested that he was not scared, but he quickly began sputtering, "I'm completely terrified." Robby Ray put his arm around him and said, "It's ok son."

Robby Ray was a widower, raising the children alone. Although he was a "good ole boy," he was also non-hegemonic: he wore pink and spent a lot of time on his hair. Robby Ray took great pride in his housework. In the same episode discussed above, Jackson pulled a towel from the laundry basket and held it to his face, saying "That [towel] smells great! Are you doing something different?" Robby Ray grinned and said, "I started adding fabric softener halfway through the rinse cycle. It's made all the difference in the world." Both men valued what is traditionally considered "women's work."

On *iCarly*, Carly's (played by Miranda Cosgrove) older brother, Spencer (Jerry Trainor), was her legal guardian. Spencer was a sculptor who worked at home. He was impulsive, playful, and clownish. For example, Spencer ordered a personalized credit card with a bunny hologram on it (S2, E12). He proudly showed the kids how the bunny changed when you moved it: "Happy bunny. Sad bunny. My bunny has conflicting emotions." *iCarly's* Freddy (Nathan Kress) was Carly's neighbor and the producer of the iCarly webshow. Freddy lived alone with his over-protective mother, who infantilized him. She followed him around with ointment and anti-bacterial spray, rubbing and spraying him whenever he stood still. Freddy had "Galaxy War" sheets on his bed, like a little boy. He was a "techy," unathletic, smart, and cautious. Their classmate, Gibby (Noah Munck), was doughy and quiet. He removed his shirt frequently, for no apparent reason—in the middle of the halls at school, at restaurants, parties, etc. His flabby body was a source of humor. Sam (Jennette McCurdy)—a girl—beat him up and stole his lunches regularly. Gibby vomited when he was scared or in trouble. The kids treated Gibby as a cute pet.

On *Wizards*, Alex's (played by Selena Gomez) older brother, Justin (David Henrie), was the most successful wizard in the family. He was studious, obedient, and risk-averse. For example, Justin refused to sing in the shower because he thought it was dangerous: "singing leads to dancing and dancing leads to slipping." A consummate "geek," he was a member of quiz bowl, the alien language club, chess club, and the Captain Jim Bob Sherwood Space Farmer fan club. He was openly emotional. On one episode, the "wizards" reunited their friend with his birth parents (S2, E18). Touched, Justin said, "I promised myself I wouldn't cry, I promised myself I wouldn't cry. . . . I'm not afraid of my emotions."

All of these males possessed at least some of the characteristics of non-hegemonic masculinity. In other words, all of them were feminized in some way. On the surface, one might assume that these masculinities could undermine gender orthodoxy, given the huge audience who consumes them. If so, the gender order could be transformed (Butler, 1999; Lotz & Ross, 2004). In the next section, however, we see that non-hegemonic masculinity was a comedic tool rather than a transformative archetype.

Hegemonic Masculinity

On these programs, characters co-constructed hegemonic masculinity at the expense of non-hegemonic characters. As Connell and Messerschmidt (2005) posited, the non-hegemonic characters served a larger purpose: reinforcing hegemonic masculinity and the traditional gendered order.

Hyperheterosexuality

Renold (2007) argued that hyperheterosexuality is an important marker of hegemonic masculinity, even among children. Some of the boys on these shows were hyper-heterosexual, and others aspired to be. For example, when the *Suite Life* ship docked in Greece, the students went to a museum (S1, E7). Cody watched helplessly while Bailey (played by Debby Ryan), his crush, flirted with their tour guide: "Look at her, drooling over him like he's some kind of Greek Adonis." The tour guide introduced himself to everyone: "Hello, my name is Adonis." Cody groaned, and said to his twin, Zack, "This guy might mess up my 6 month plan to win Bailey. This month, we have to get to at least hand-holding." Zack (Dylan Sprouse) told Cody, "Dude, while you're working on your 6 month plan, this guy is just *working it*." Sure enough, Bailey went to the roof with Adonis to "see the view," leaving Cody crushed. Cody wanted to be a smooth operator like Adonis, but he lacked hyperheterosexual seduction skills.

Zack—Cody's opposite—was a hyperheterosexual predator. Non-hegemonic boys studied Zack's techniques. Zack told Woody, "There is nothing, *nothing* better in this world than an unhappy hot girl." On one episode, he and Woody posed as janitors to scope out new girls as they arrived on the ship (S2, E13). Woody pointed out one girl he thought was pretty. Zack showed him that the girl had a lock on her luggage: "That means she's suspicious and cautious. I'm looking for naïve and vulnerable." Woody grinned, "There's so much to *learn* from you!" Zack said, "Now focus. These girls are only here for a week." Woody tried again: "How about that one: cute, blonde, *nice legs*, and carrying a text book—repressed book worm badly in need of a good time!" The "girl" whom Woody was talking about turned around, and Zack exclaimed, "That's *Cody*!" This scene secured Zack's superiority above both Woody—who failed his hyperheterosexual training—and Cody—who looked like a cute girl from the back.

Zack was surrounded by lesser boys, whom he mentored in the art of scoring. For example, Zack concocted a scheme to meet gullible girls, a fake beauty pageant:

Zack: "All the girls will fill out an application and send in a photo, which makes it easy to weed out the ones not worth pursuing. Then we just cancel the whole thing and they'll never know we were involved."

Woody: "Come on—no girl's stupid enough to fall for that."

London (played by Brenda Song) walked by, saw the sign, and exclaimed: "Ooo! A beauty contest! And I'm beauty-*ful*!"

The boys grinned at each other.

Zack wanted to "weed out" girls who were ugly and/or cautious. Dumb girls were easier to manipulate. For example, a pretty blonde girl named Capri (Brittany Ross) carried her pageant application to Zack and said, "Excuse me, I don't understand Question 4. What is your ick?" Zack said: "That's *IQ*." Capri said, "Ohhhhh!." Zack grinned at Woody: "This is gonna be *awesome*!"

Zack used the language of predator versus prey as he coached Woody in hyperheterosexuality. On another episode (S1, E19), Zack explained:

When the lions are out hunting gazelles, they don't attack the strong healthy ones. Oh no. They attack the weak ones. The ones crying and eating ice cream.

Woody grinned and said, "I worship this man." Hyperheterosexual bad-boy characters, like Zack, sat at the top of the hierarchy, reminding non-hegemonic boys how much they had to learn.

Cowboy-Up: "Fag Talk" and Feminization

Hegemonic masculinity is not easily attainable—indeed, most males will never accomplish it. But it serves as a ready-made tool that can be used by anyone to police a male's masculinity. Questioning a male's manhood serves a similar purpose to Pascoe's "fag talk": it is a disciplinary mechanism to regulate boys' doing gender. Of course, characters on these G-rated children's shows did not actually call each other "fags." Instead, they feminized each other, which paralleled "fag talk." One way that characters on the series indicted someone's masculinity was to tell him to "man up." For example, on *Hannah*, Robby Ray nagged Jackson for sleeping until 2 pm: "It's time for you to cowboy up and act like a man." On *Wizards*, Justin announced that he was going to perform the "Thin Man" spell (S2, E3). Alex laughed: "Great! It's a spell that will make Justin thin *and* a man." Everyone laughed, including their father. On *iCarly*, Sam called Freddy, Spencer and Carly "a bunch of prancies" when they criticized her. On *Suite Life*, Marcus complained that Woody got him a cranberry hat instead of a magenta hat, to wear while judging the beauty pageant. Woody said, "You are such a diva! Other divas look at you and say, 'Wow, what a diva!'" Feminizing boys was a central part of these shows' humor, and it functioned like "fag talk."

On one episode of *Suite Life*, Woody arm-wrestled a female classmate (S2, E21). She slammed his arm down so hard that he fell out of his desk. He laid on the floor in a daze. Victorious, she raised her fists and yelled, "In your face! Eighty-three pounds of pure power!" Cody said, "Dude, you just got beat by a girl who can fit in a keyhole." Their teacher asked Woody what he was doing on the floor. Zack said, "Looking for his pride." Woody called out, "Can't find it! Oo, but I found a piece of gum!" He peeled the gum from beneath his desk and popped into his mouth, grinning goofily at the onlookers. Woody's repeated failings at masculinity provided dependable comic fodder for this series.

In another example, on *Suite Life*, Cody recreated a country fair to cheer up Bailey, who was homesick (S1, E19). Bailey's ex-boyfriend, Moose (played by Hutch Dano), came to visit during the fair. Moose—a hegemonic character, as implied by his name—beat Cody at every single game, including arm-wrestling, bobbing for corncobs, and "even something cerebral, like chess." Cody confided in Zack that he was worried Moose would win Bailey too. Zack sneered, "If the next competition is whining like a girl, you're gonna win by a mile!" Cody said, "Ok slightly harsh, but I guess I needed to hear that. I'm going to show Bailey that I'm ten times the man that Moose is. Right after I floss." He flossed his teeth and said, "Ow. Floss burn!" The audience laughed.

Gender Crossing: Boys in Drag

On the shows, a common comedic ploy involved dressing male characters in women's clothing. Sometimes boys would just appear in women's clothes momentarily. For example, on *Suite Life*, Cody tripped and fell into a rack of clothes in a boutique (S2, E5).When he stood back up, he wore a pink feather boa. He immediately took it off, but not before the audience laughed. On another episode, Woody opened a package from his mom to find a muumuu, which she accidentally sent to him instead of his sister (S1, E19). Zack saw him holding it up and quipped, "Nice dress Woody. Really brings out your eyes." Neither incident was central to the story line. They were just gratuitous episodes of unintentional gender crossing.

On these television shows, drag did call attention to the gender binary, but *not* so as to undermine the naturalness of gender. Drag was not counter-hegemonic, but a comedic tool for ultimately re-inscribing the binary. Drag made a spectacle out of crossers not to celebrate them, but to punish them.

Homoeroticism

On *Suite Life*, Cody and Moose's country-fair competition was tinged with homoeroticism (S1, E19). As already mentioned, one of the contests was bobbing for corn cobs. The boys went under water and came out with cobs—sometimes two at a time—sticking lengthwise from their mouths. The sight of the phalluses protruding from their mouths was borderline pornographic, underscored by their bawdy dialogue: Zack told Cody, "You really want to impress Bailey. Get in there and bob for a cob." Cody nodded and said to Moose: "You better kiss your kernels goodbye, pal, because you're going down." Moose said, "We both are going down. That's how you pick up the corn." Here, Cody likened Moose's testicles to corn kernels, underscoring the impression that the cobs were meant to represent phalluses. And the boys' use of the phrase "going down"—which often refers to oral sex—further punctuated the homoerotic undertones of the interchange. Later, Cody lost to Moose in chess and said, "Well, kiss my bishop!" Again, because of the phallic shape of the bishop and the larger context of their competition, this comment renewed the homoerotic tension between Moose—the strong, hegemonic boy—and Cody—the non-hegemonic, feminized boy.

In a bizarre incident on *iCarly*, Spencer hired a surly old cowboy, Bucky, to teach him to ride a mechanical bull (S3, E5). Bucky insisted that the only way Spencer would learn to ride the bull was to learn to *act* like the bull:

Bucky: "Get down on your hands and knees."
Spencer: "I'm sorry?"
Bucky: "GET DOWN!"
Spencer got on all fours.
Bucky: "Now when I climb on you, I want you to try to throw me off."
Spencer, rising up: "I don't think this is a good idea."
Bucky forced him back down: "Do you want to learn to ride that tin can or don't ya?"

Spencer: "I'm not sure any more!"
Spencer tried to throw Bucky off.
Bucky: "Come on boy! You can do better than that!"
Spencer: "I don't know! This is so new to me!"

This scene felt more like a sexual assault than homoerotic, as Bucky forced Spencer into unwanted, unequal physical intimacy. It embodied the masculine hierarchy, with a hegemonic male mounted upon a non-hegemonic male. Spencer was clearly bothered by the experience. When he ran into Carly at the smoothie shop, she said, "What are you doing here? I thought you had a bull riding lesson." Spencer said, "I did. And my teacher put his *butt* on me. I never want to think about him or that stupid bull ever again. That thing's an instrument of torture." He felt victimized and gave away his mechanical bull.

By allowing male characters to interact in intimate ways, these shows flirted with homoeroticism, which is definitely counter-hegemonic in a homophobic culture. These shows had the opportunity to introduce viewers to alternative ways for boys to interact, beyond competition and violence. Yet, for the most part, homoerotic moments were not presented as serious possibilities. They were humorous, disruptive, and in Spencer's case, harmful. Thus, homoeroticism was a tool for underscoring homophobia and competition among males.

Mask-ulinity Play

As mentioned above, the literature on non-hegemonic boys shows that, rather than undermining the hegemonic gendered order, non-hegemonic boys actually reinforce hegemony by valorizing hegemonic masculinity themselves (Pascoe, 2003; Renold, 2004). Non-hegemonic characters on these shows did the same thing: they temporarily crossed into hegemonic territory, and then crossed back (see also Thorne, 1993). Occasionally, these otherwise non-hegemonic males donned a "mask" of masculinity (Pollack, 1998), and asserted themselves over others in hegemonic, domineering ways.

On one episode of *iCarly*, Gibby transformed from passive heterosexual failure to hyperheterosexual brute. The friends were surprised to hear that Gibby had a girlfriend, but they were shocked when they met her: Tasha (Emily Ratajkowski) was a tall, beautiful brunette. Freddy stared at her, mouth agape, and said, "Why can't *I* have one of those?" Gibby, usually demonstrative and goofy, began speaking in monotonal monosyllables, grunting orders at Tasha. In a series of misunderstandings, Gibby thought he saw Freddy kiss Tasha. He flew into a jealous rage, broke up with Tasha and promised retribution. Gibby kicked a beanbag chair across the room and told him Freddy would "beat him down." Gibby told Freddy to "bring a mop for your blood!" Sam intervened before Gibby and Freddy actually fought, clearing up the misunderstanding. Gibby apologized but remained aloof: he shook hands with Freddy, and said, "Bros?" Freddy agreed, "Bros." Tasha whined, "What about me?" Gibby nodded and said, "You're back in." She squealed, "Oh thank you!" In this episode, Gibby acted like a completely different boy than in any other episode. He intimidated and impressed his peers. Hegemonic masculinity was an effective, temporary tool for him to manage a particular situation.

Carly and Nevel agreed to meet in an alley behind her apartment building. Nevel brought big, thuggish men to stand at each entrance to the alley, preventing Carly from escaping. He said, "You look wonderful in low light." He prepared to kiss her: "First, this": applying lip balm with his pinky. Carly outsmarted him and avoided the kiss. Infuriated, Nevel waved his fist and yelled, "I declare that you'll rue this day! You'll rue it!" Nevel was unable to conquer Carly, and his enactment of hegemonic masculinity failed as well.

Discussion and Conclusion

These television shows offered a variety of masculinities for audiences of children and adults. Hegemonic boy characters did exist—and girl characters found them irresistible. But most (88%) male characters tended toward a non-hegemonic, even feminized masculinity: they were sensitive, non-athletic, and unsuccessful with girls. Casual viewers might conclude that these shows have rewritten male characters in a way that undermines the traditional gender order, allowing for a broader, more feminist conceptualization of masculinity. Given the popularity of these shows, these counter-hegemonic masculinities could help alter gendered expectations among a group of young people, who might become more tolerant of non-conformists (Butler, 1999).

Although the potential for reconceptualizing gender existed—through the use of non-hegemonic protagonists, drag, and homoeroticism—these incidents were largely comedic, rather than serious challenges to the gender order. Systematic analysis of the portrayal of masculinity on these programs reveals a *leger de main*: non-hegemonic boys were not heroic, but clowns, serving as foils for hegemonic masculinity. Comedy centered on the ways that these boys failed at masculinity. Humor was used throughout the programs, disguising hegemonic messages as benign. Walsh et al. (2008, p. 132) write, "As the male protagonists remain likable characters, sexism is reduced to only a momentary digression, easily laughed off, as opposed to part of a systemic repressive ideology."

Pascoe (2003) and Renold (2004) argue that non-hegemonic boys participate in the hierarchy by approximating hegemonic masculinity, by donning the mask of hegemonic masculinity (Pollack 1998). In these shows, boys' masculinity-play suggests that hegemonic masculinity is a resource for all boys, a "patriarchal dividend" (Connell, 1995) regardless of where they fall in the hierarchy. They can use hegemonic masculinity to correct power imbalances—particularly over girls, as seen in these examples—and secure their relative status, even if they are lower status males. Hegemonic boy characters used non-hegemonic males to underscore their own dominance (Connell & Messerschmidt, 2005). Even though most characters were not hegemonic, hegemonic masculinity was a resource to be deployed by anyone at any time, to regulate a boy's gender enactment.

Rather than truly celebrating non-hegemonic masculinity, hegemonic masculinity remained the standard. There were consequences for challenging the gendered binary. Characters who flirted with non-hegemonic masculinities were policed—sometimes literally—for their transgressions. In post-feminist fashion (McRobbie, 2004; Ringrose, 2007; Walsh et al., 2004), the masculine hierarchy was highlighted, reinscribing a hierarchy in which hegemonic boys ruled over girls and boys of lesser status. Because hegemonic masculinity is an especially damaging incarnation of gender, these findings are troubling.

The effects of this gender frame (Ridgeway, 2011) are widespread due to the massive audience who consume these messages daily. The television programs are part of the regional construction of masculinity that reflects the larger American culture. If Connell and Messerschmidt (2005) are correct in their supposition that people's local, face-to-face interactions are shaped by culture, then everyday children will police each other in ways that they see on television (see also Corsaro, 1997). My own research reveals that children invoke these images and use them to police each other (Myers & Raymond, 2010). By valorizing hegemonic masculinity, children's' television programming missed an opportunity to transform and expand—in a positive light—cultural representations of boyhood and masculinity. Rather than contributing a feminist portrayal of gender, these shows could be characterized as "postfeminist" (McRobbie, 2004). These negative cultural meanings propagated by television have real-life consequences for everyday young people, limiting their imaginations (Butler, 2004) to "patriarchal constellations" (Walsh et al., 2008, p. 125).

References

Baker-Sperry, L. (2007). The production of meaning through peer interaction. *Sex Roles, 56,* 717–727.

Baraldi, C. (2008). Promoting self-expression in classroom interactions. *Childhood, 15,* 238–257.

Bereska, T. (2003). The changing boys' world in the 20th century. *The Journal of Men's Studies, 11,* 157–174.

Bragg, S., & Buckingham, D. (2004). Embarrassment, education, and erotics. *European Journal of Cultural Studies, 7,* 441–459.

Butler, J. (1999). *Gender trouble.* New York: Routledge.

Butler, J. (2004). *Undoing gender.* New York: Routledge.

Connell, R. W. (1987). *Gender and power.* Stanford University Press.

Connell, R. W. (1995). *Masculinities.* Cambridge: Polity Press.

Connell, R. W., & Messerschmidt, J. W. (2005). Hegemonic masculinity. *Gender & Society, 19,* 829–859.

Corsaro, W. (1997). *The sociology of childhood.* Berkeley: Pine Forge Press.

DeMol, J., & Buysse, A. (2008). Understanding children's influence in parent–child relationships. *Journal of Social and Personal Relationships, 25,* 359–379.

Epstein, D. (1997). Boyz' own stories. *Gender and Education, 9,* 105–115.

Fausto-Sterling, A. (2000). *Sexing the body.* New York: Basic Books.

Ferris, K. (2001). Through a glass darkly. *Symbolic Interaction, 24,* 25–47.

Fingerson, L. (1999). Active viewing. *Journal of Contemporary Ethnography, 28,* 389–418.

Goffman, E. (1974). *Frame analysis.* New York: Northeastern University Press.

Haywood, C. (1996). Out of the curriculum. *Curriculum Studies, 4,* 229–251.

Keddie, A. (2003). Little boys: Tomorrow's macho lads. *Discourse: Studies in the Cultural Politics of Education, 24,* 289–306.

Kelley, P., Buckingham, D., & Davies, H. (1999). Talking dirty: Sexual knowledge and television. *Childhood, 6,* 221–242.

Kimmel, M. (2006). A war against boys? *Dissent, 53,* 65–70.

Korobov, N. (2005). Ironizing masculinity. *The Journal of Men's Studies, 13,* 225–246.

Kurasaki, K. (2000). Intercoder reliability for validating conclusions drawn from open-ended interview data. *Field Methods, 12,* 179–194.

Kuypers, J. (2009). *Rhetorical criticism: Perspectives in action.* New York: Lexington Press.

Lofland, J., Snow, D., Anderson, L., & Lofland, L. (2005). *Analyzing social settings.* New York: Wadsworth.

Lotz, A., & Ross, S. (2004). Bridging media-specific approaches: The value of feminist television criticism's synthetic approach. *Feminist Media Studies, 4,* 185–202.

Ludvigsen, A., & Scott, S. (2009). Real kids don't eat quiche. *Food, Culture & Society, 12,* 417–436.

Martin, K., & Kazyak, E. (2009). Hetero-romantic love and heterosexiness in children's G-rated films. *Gender & Society, 23,* 315–336.

McAllister, M., & Giglio, M. (2005). The commodity flow of U.S. children's television. *Critical Studies in Media Communication, 22,* 26–44.

McRobbie, A. (2004). Notes on postfeminism and popular culture. In A. Harris (Ed.), *All about the girl* (pp. 3–14). New York: Routledge.

Messner, M. (1990). Boyhood, organized sports, and the construction of masculinities. *Journal of Contemporary Ethnography, 18,* 416–444.

Myers, K., & Raymond, L. (2010). Elementary school girls and heteronormativity: The girl project. *Gender & Society, 24,* 167–188.

Neitzel, C., & Chafel, J. (2010). "And no flowers grow there and stuff": Young children's social representations of poverty. *Sociological Studies of Children and Youth, 13,* 33–59.

Oransky, M., & Marecek, J. (2009). I'm not going to be a girl. *Journal of Adolescent Research, 24,* 218–241.

Pascoe, C. J. (2003). Multiple masculinities? *American Behavioral Scientist, 46,* 1423–1438.

Pascoe, C. J. (2005). Dude, you're a fag. *Sexualities, 8,* 329–346.

Pollack, W. S. (1998). *Real boys.* New York: Henry Holt.

Powell, K., & Abels, L. (2002). Sex role stereotypes in TV programs aimed at the preschool audience. *Women and Language, 25,* 14–22.

Ramlow, T. (2003). Bad boy. *GLQ, 9,* 107–132.

Renold, E. (2004). "Other" boys: Negotiating non-hegemonic masculinities in the primary school. *Gender and Education, 16,* 247–266.

Renold, E. (2007). Primary school "studs": (De)constructing young boys' heterosexual masculinities. *Men and Masculinities, 9,* 275–297.

Ridgeway, C. (2011). *Framed by gender.* New York: Oxford.

Ringrose, J. (2007). Successful girls? *Gender and Education, 19,* 471–489.

Risman, B., & Seale, E. (2010). Be twixt and between. In B. Risman (Ed.), *Families as they really are* (pp. 340–361). New York: Norton.

Thorne, B. (1993). *Gender play.* Rutgers University Press.

Van Ausdale, D., & Feagin, J. (2002). *The first r.* New York: Rowman & Littlefield.

Walsh, K., Fursich E., & Jefferson, B. (2008). Beauty and the patriarchal beast. *Journal of Popular Film and Television, 36,* 123–132.

Warren, C., & Karner, T. (2009). *Discovering qualitative methods.* New York: Oxford University Press.

West, C., & Zimmerman, D. (1987). Doing gender. *Gender & Society, 1,* 125–151.

CHAPTER 8

"We Wear No Pants"

Selling the Crisis of Masculinity in the 2010 Super Bowl Commercials

Kyle Green and Madison Van Oort

"Hello friends, we have an injury report on Jason Glaspie," sportscaster Jim Nantz informs us in a soft, deep voice as he casually approaches the camera. Behind him, we see Jason in the apparent torture chamber of the masculine psyche: the mall. His shoulders slump from carrying dozens of shopping bags, while a bright red bra drapes his shoulder. "As you can see, his girlfriend has removed his spine, rendering him incapable of watching the game." Just as Jason catches a glimpse of the big football game on TV, his girlfriend snatches him away, dragging him to the perfume counter. Jim Nantz guides our judgment, voicing disgust at Jason's actions. "That's hard to watch." In the end, Nantz implores: "Change out of that skirt Jason."

—Flo TV (2010)

Jason Glaspie, in his proverbial skirt, exemplifies the mass marketing of the crisis of masculinity in the commercials shown during the 2010 Super Bowl—the most watched event in television history (Nielson Company 2010). Viewers were bombarded with images of feminized, aging, and ultimately powerless male bodies, images that both implicitly and explicitly signaled a much broader crisis wherein the constitutive ingredients of hegemonic masculinity have supposedly been lost, stolen, or otherwise altered. "Take off that skirt!" "Put on the pants!" "Man's last stand!" These were the rallying cries of Super Bowl 2010. While the discursive terrain of the so-called crisis of masculinity has emerged in other cultural and political arenas, in 2010 the crisis overtly pervaded a substantial portion of the Super Bowl programming.

Our goal for this article is to examine the narrative of the crisis of masculinity in the 2010 Super Bowl commercials. We begin with a review of literature on advertising, gender, and the body. Next, we discuss a few commercials from 2009, highlighting the distinct ways in which elements of the crisis narrative begin to emerge through humorous injuries and nostalgia for childhood joys. We then engage in detailed analysis of three key commercials from 2010, in attempts to illuminate their strikingly overt attempt at mass marketing a crisis of masculinity.

The Discursive Structure of Advertising

In studying commercials we seek to explore the meaning attached to the products being sold and how advertising not only caters to but produces a particular group of consumers. Advertising has served as a key site for the dissemination of dominant discourses on masculinity.[1] As Michel Foucault

SOURCE: Green, K., and Van Oort, M. (2013). "We Wear No Pants": Selling the Crisis of Masculinity in the 2010 Super Bowl Commercials. *Signs*, 38, 695–719. Reproduced with permission from *Signs*.

explains, discourse can be understood as "practices that systematically form the objects of which they speak" (1972, 49).We focus on how discourse guides the meanings of certain images—like the portrayal of the lovable (male) loser. This approach does not treat advertising agencies as the sole creators of discourses on gender. Rather, they play a key role in filtering and disseminating discourse, and in doing so, they aid in stabilizing and building upon existing public sentiment.

In popular culture, sport has long been viewed as a bastion of masculinity and a site for the transmission and reproduction of what it means to be a man (Messner 1992; Burstyn 1999; Connell 2000), which makes sporting events singularly attractive to advertisers seeking the elusive young male demographic. For instance, the symbiotic relationship between beer, sports, and hegemonic masculinity has reached such heights that Lawrence A. Wenner and Steven Jackson (2009) described it as "a holy trinity" (25). Football, and the Super Bowl especially, serves as a particularly popular site for advertisements targeting men. We therefore treat the emergence of a discourse within Super Bowl advertisements as a seal of approval—a moment where the discourse ascends to the realm of other dominant discourses about what it means to be a man.

Crafting the Crisis of Masculinity as a Consumable Trope

Advertising, as a function of discourse, shapes what is knowable about social life and gender relations (Jhally 1987, 135). A large body of scholarship critiques the way advertisements depict women as passive subjects, needy girlfriends, or sexual objects to be consumed or won over by active men.[2] Women are active only to the extent that they must constantly monitor their bodies and work to make them more attractive. Even when women appear to defy gender roles, through drinking, smoking, or wearing masculine clothing, they are shown as merely imitating rather than challenging dominant masculinity (Barthel 1989). Thus, advertising largely reinforces sexist depictions of women.

Since the 1980s, however, advertisers have paid increasing attention to men as consumers of identity-related products (Patterson and Elliott 2002; Schroeder and Zwick 2004). In particular, there has been an exponential growth in advertising that seeks to build upon insecurities by encouraging men to view their own bodies as inadequate and in need of consumer-based improvements (Atkinson 2008). Advertisers have shaped masculinities to embrace styles and pleasures that were previously viewed as socially undesirable (Nixon 1996); beyond the "holy trinity," products like body wash, weight loss supplements, deodorant, and clothing are now being mass-marketed to male consumers. Whether this is an inversion of the male gaze (Patterson and Elliott 2002) or an expansion of it (Schroeder and Zwick 2004), it is clear that John Berger's famous observation that "men act and women appear. Men look at women. Women watch themselves being looked at" (1972, 45) no longer rings as true.

Susan Bordo's tour de force examination of the male body, *The Male Body: A New Look at Men in Public and in Private* (1999), chronicles the increasing visibility of and societal pressures on men. To be a man is to be hard in body and emotion, never showing pain, emotion, suffering, or physical weakness. The increased presence of nearly naked male models in advertising and the proliferation of men's "health" magazines ensure that eating disorders affect more than just women (Bordo 1999, 218). However, unlike the all-but-naked women that have become ubiquitous in television and print, the pressure is not for men to invoke sex through vulnerability. Rather, with men, dignity and strength remain: "the bodies are a kind of natural armor" (Bordo 1999, 30). The men of advertising are not objects ready to be simply enjoyed; their muscular exoskeleton and aggressive posture ensure that the audience does not forget that even in their current state of undress, the potential to dominate remains.

The current rendition of the crisis shares elements with the men's movements that arose during the 1980s—another time of insecurity that was more directly linked to the success of the feminist movement (Patterson and Elliott 2002, 235). Although not a uniform collective, with various subfactions like men's rights, mythopoetic, and profeminist men's movements, the cohesive element was a stated desire to repair the damage that had been done to men and their masculinity within the United States. The participants, often affluent, white males, attempted to restore the power, control, and independence once afforded to them by mainstream society by returning to a "lost era when men were men" (Kimmell and Kaufman 1995, 18). And again advertisers were quick to capitalize, presenting images in leisure magazines of hypermasculine men with bulging muscles (Connell 1987; Rutherford 1988).

In this study, we therefore seek to add to existing literature on gender and advertising by conducting a close, critical reading of the 2010 Super Bowl commercials. What does the marketing of masculinity look like in this contemporary moment? Which discursive tropes remain unchanged, and which new elements are being brought to the fore? What might these media strategies mean for gender relations in the United States? We illustrate the drama and the sensationalism advertisers use in these commercials to narrate a renewed crisis of masculinity, with a fierce emphasis on the importance of the physical body.

Methods

For this project, we watched every Super Bowl commercial presented from 2008 to 2010. We paid particular attention to the company, type of product, characters portrayed (in terms of race, class, and gender), dominant messages and themes, and discursive strategies employed (i.e., violence or humor) in the commercials. In analyzing our commercials we draw inspiration from semiotic analysis, and in particular from Judith Williamson's now classic semiotic study *Decoding Advertisements* (1978). Semiotics approaches focus on understanding signs, which are, in most simple terms, objects or images imbued with social meaning. Semiotic analysis allows us to pay attention to the ways in which layers of meaning become mapped and remapped onto the mundane, and as such, we see ourselves as archeologists of meaning, peeling back the layers of signs. These archeological formations are always changing, albeit slowly, while other images and meanings stick together for longer periods of time.

It follows that our sampling is theoretical and purposive rather than representative in nature, since we seek to analyze a significant discursive theme and its semiotic workings. We analyze three paradigmatic commercials from 2010 chosen because they all strongly suggest a broad crisis of masculinity of some kind. Traces of similar themes may be found in Super Bowl commercials from other years, but our viewing of commercials from a wide range of years, combined with other existing research on Super Bowl advertisements, suggests that the prominence of the crisis of masculinity trope in 2010 is indeed highly notable.

2010: The Year of Men

The Super Bowl, of course, has always been about men. The commercials, long filled with objects of desire (like beer and attractive women), have made little room for anything else. In 2010, though, men do not relish in their masculinity but instead scramble to salvage it. Numerous blogs and media outlets also caught on to the strong gender messages: feminist gossip blog *Jezebel* said the commercials sung the "woes of bros" (Smith 2010), *Slate* thought the misogyny was "rawer and angrier than usual" (Stevenson 2010), and the *Washington Post* pondered the "perpetual fear of emasculation" (Shales 2010).

The nuances of the crisis crystallize when situated within a broader sociopolitical context. Dominant masculinity in the United States is intertwined with nationalism and patriotism (Connell 2000), and in turn the 2010 Super Bowl commercials cannot be analyzed without taking into consideration the lingering economic recession. Beginning in 2008, the most recent economic crisis in the United

States has shaken individual lives, knocking millions out of their jobs and onto the streets. Numerous studies emerged in 2009 and 2010 claiming that the downturn more strongly hit men, with more women in the service sector holding onto their jobs, going so far as to dub the recession the "mancession" (Thompson 2009). Psychological studies pointed to increasing depression among men, stemming from their anxiety about maintaining their breadwinning role (Daily Mail Reporter 2009; Dunlop and Mletzko 2011). However, we now know that a veritable he-covery is taking over the supposed mancession, with women more slowly regaining employment (Kochar 2011). The mancession concept likewise obscures the extent to which men of color have long faced higher unemployment levels than whites (Lui et al. 2006; Cawthorne 2009), allowing us to reiterate the extent to which the crisis of masculinity as we see it in these Super Bowl commercials is a crisis of almost exclusively white middle-class masculinity.

In such a moment of perceived crisis, popular media could either place a newfound value on minority masculinities (see Halberstam's 2005 analysis of British masculinity, the unstable economic climate, and *The Full Monty*) or it could continue to use humor as a tool for attempting to uphold a masculinity now in peril. Part of the reason the 2010 Super Bowl commercials followed the latter path may also have something to do with an unmistakable right-wing backlash, most notably through the rise of the Tea Party movement. Not surprisingly, in addition to the commercials we analyze below, the 2010 Super Bowl included a pro-life advertisement from conservative football player Tim Tebow, while denying commercial airtime to a gay online dating service (CBS News 2010; Plocher 2010).

Perhaps unsurprisingly, nostalgia served an important role in comforting the aging male population through humor while reminding them of better times. For instance, a cell phone company remade the "Super Bowl Shuffle" rap, which was originally performed in 1985 by that year's Super Bowl champions, the Chicago Bears. Only this time, instead of rapping about being smooth or protecting their neighborhoods, the aging men, once revered for their strength, power, and unmatched ferocity, joke about their failing bodies. One player raps: "I still could play, if my groin didn't feel like paper maché. But it does. Ain't gettin any better." Even as older viewers laugh, their physical failure is brought to their attention. The younger generation is provided a warning of their bodies' impending failure, setting the stage for calls for more active and immediate action to reinforce their dominance.

The following three 2010 Super Bowl commercials serve as exemplars of the crisis, highlighting the theme of the diminishing power of men and men's bodies in contemporary society.* The significant differences in the commercials lie in how this crisis is explained. The first commercial, Dockers' "Wear No Pants," makes implied assumptions about class and body power. Next, Career Builders' "Casual Fridays" more explicitly lays blame on contemporary economic structures and cultures of flexibility and informality. Finally, Dodge Charger's "Man's Last Stand" overtly points to a combination of economic, cultural, and familial relations in disempowering middle-class men. It is in this last instance that the men most aggressively blame women for their unbearable pains.

Dockers' "I Wear No Pants" (2010)

A stout, pantless, middle-aged white man marches across the savanna. "I wear no pants!" he sings. Another pudgy man proudly sings along from another spot in the grass." I wear, I wear, I wear no pants!" (Dockers 2010). Finally, the group coalesces. The pack of fifteen pantless men march and shout, alone in the prairie. They are oblivious to their location, or the fact that birds ominously soar above their heads, cawing in warning. "Calling all men," an authoritarian narrator interrupts as the shot sweeps to a faceless, statuesque man standing in front of a brick wall. "It's time to wear the pants."

A closer reading of this commercial reveals the importance of men's bodies and their relationship to success. The failed men have soft, unkempt bodies. And while nature has long been seen as something for male domination, here the men roam aimlessly, as if they are animals themselves.

---

*EDITORS' NOTE: As a reference, we encourage you to view these commercials on YouTube.

The discursive implication is clear: the pantless men symbolize the professional class of men suffering from a shared delusion. They celebrate without shame, enjoying the open air in untucked dress shirts and underwear, an image usually used in movies to depict women following sex. These bodies signify failure on various levels: their middle-class status offers them no protection from the more primitive dangers of the natural world; their lack of pants implies their inability to head their families; and finally, the homosocial men quite literally dance on the border of homosexuality.

Most broadly, the failed bodies act as a sign of middle-class failure, leaving the men unable to dominate their surroundings or maintain their ideal muscular physique. The juxtaposition of the failing group of middle-class men with the clearly working-class single figure at the end—who is muscular, wearing a T-shirt and jeans, and safely bounded by the man-made brick wall—might initially be read as a desire to return to working-class status. However, we argue that the working-class man is less a sign of the working class itself than a sign of a particular masculine lifestyle. Men can still make money *and* wear Dockers, for as Williamson writes: "Products are thus set up as being able to *buy* things *you* cannot buy. This puts them in a position of replacing you. They do things you can't do, for you" (1978, 38). Thus middle-class men can still retain their capitalist gains without sacrificing the patriarchal power of wearing the pants. So while this commercial implies a waning of power for middle-class men, it calls on men to renew their power precisely through the capitalist system that failed them.

Career Builder's "Casual Fridays" (2010)

Career Builder, an Internet-based job search company, provides another humorous presentation of the erosion of traditional values in "Casual Fridays" (2010). The commercial opens with Terry, a rather ordinary-looking white man in a blue polo shirt, drinking a cup of coffee. His shoulders slump, his goatee shows signs of grey, and his body is beginning to sag. In the background we see a typical office, except the employees are wearing only their underwear. As the main character begins to explain his plight, his tone conveying defeat, "when I first started here . . . ," an old man in his underwear pushes a mail cart up to his desk and stops to sort the mail. The main character shields his eyes and explains, "I was like, casual Friday, awesome." From this opening scene we learn that the man is embarrassed by those who have embraced comfort and no longer make an effort to hide their failing, out-of-shape bodies. The commercial successfully invokes a sense of body horror so often seen in advertisements geared toward women, in which average bodies are repulsive and shameful.

In another scene, our narrator is greeted by a scrawny man who suavely rests his elbow on the water cooler. Terry bends down to grab his water but avoids grabbing the white cup, which is placed suspiciously close to the other man's white briefs, succeeding in what Williamson identifies as "connecting an object to a person" (1978, 22). The color of the cup and underwear perfectly match, and our narrator decides the risk is too great, for he might mistake the man's crotch for the cup and fall into a possibly queer space. Here, for the first time, we see the coworkers poking fun at the main character for being a prude and not letting his rigid heterosexual guard down. Our viewer response is guided by the reaction of the main character, who, instead of being swept along in the fun, is embarrassed and revolted.

The scene shifts to the conference room, where the boss announces, "we've decided to make casual Fridays . . . all week." Everyone in the office, save Terry, cheers and jumps. Two men sandwich Terry's head between their crotches while they stand to high-five, and our narrator again shows physical repulsion at his close proximity to another man's penis. A queer reading of this commercial might point out the joy of the men slamming crotches together, but the underlining point remains Terry's disgust at such behavior. Career Builder cashes in on a conservative backlash, as Terry longs for a return to normative, conservative, and hetero spaces.

"Of course, if it's mandatory, it can't be casual," notes the narrator, now standing alone with his coffee cup. The water cooler coworker begins to walk by, stops, and leans in: "Nice pants, Terry." Terry looks down at his pants and up again at the audience in despair. The tension has reached its climax, as the coworker points out that Terry no longer belongs. "Wearing the pants"—and, in particular, nice pants—comes to stand for everything Terry holds onto: manners, formality, tradition, and control (over his body, his space, and his sexuality). A voice-over states: "Expose yourself to something better. Career Builder. Start building."

As in "I Wear No Pants," the scantily clad men here are semiotically associated with a new masculinity and vulnerability. The underlying message is about a return to "real" masculinity, as Terry, alone in his pants, symbolizes classic hegemonic masculinity, old-time homophobia, and heterosexuality. In one telling scene, the main character is confronted with a fat woman in pearls who rushes past him, flesh and necklace bouncing, into the meeting room. He rolls his eyes as he makes a "go ahead" motion with his hand. He appears as disappointed in this woman's body as in the failing male bodies entering his space. The stripped figure thus generally signifies the failure of the strong, male physique, of his presumed heterosexuality (as in the water cooler scene) and of his ability or desire to act on his heterosexual urges (as with the woman in pearls). At the same time, though, Career Builder also equates the semiotic meaning of the near-nude men with what is wrong with corporate America. Instead of job insecurity, increasing hours, and declining wages, corporate disappointment is now linked with the changing social order. Universal Studios' "Universal Heroes" (2009) hinted at corporate dissatisfaction but told men simply to take a break, go to an amusement park, arm-wrestle with Popeye. In 2010 a more serious call is made: put the pants back on, or at least find—or "start building"—a place where wearing the pants is respected.

Dodge Charger's "Man's Last Stand" (2010)

Dodge offered the most explicit example of men's call to action in 2010. Here, instead of suffering from the delusions of Dockers' feminized field frolickers, the men individually reclaim what they think is rightfully theirs. The commercial presents head shots of diverse men, all disheveled, standing in traditionally feminine locations: the bedroom, the kitchen, the living room. Each man remains motionless while a narrator laments the daily struggles that men endure in modern life. The narrator, Michael C. Hall, also plays the doctor and serial killer in the TV series *Dexter*. As in Williamson's famous analysis of Catherine Deneuve and Chanel No. 5 (1978), the ad displays an assumption that the product and the celebrity are the same, when in fact the product gains its meaning precisely through the celebrity. In "Man's Last Stand," the Dodge Charger becomes synonymous with aggression through Michael C. Hall (as Dexter)'s voice. While the men in the commercial steer clear of murder, the semiotic association communicated in Hall's narration is obvious, highlighting the dangerously misogynistic tones of the advertisement.

The commercial begins with a shot of an attractive white man lying in bed, eyes open. The man looks straight into the camera and remains motionless as the narrator says, monotonously: "I will walk the dog at 6:30 a.m. I will eat some fruit as part of my breakfast. I will shave. I will clean the sink after I shave." Here, even the most basic domestic responsibilities, cleaning up after oneself, are presented as unreasonable burdens and affronts to masculinity. In general, fruit implies a pressure to be concerned with one's health and appearance, but here fruit further signifies both the feminine—delicate and unreasonable—and the threat to heteronormativity, as fruit is a classic sign for homosexuality.

The body here again signifies middle-class masculinity, but in a slightly different way than in the Dockers or Career Builder commercials. In those instances, the flabby, fleshy bodies are torn down in favor of a hard masculinity. This Dodge Charger commercial warns that, perhaps in response to the rising metrosexual image of recent years, too much concern with the body likewise throws men too far into femininity and queerness. These messages about appearance, when taken in tandem with the Dockers and Career Builder ads, illustrate somewhat contradictory tensions surrounding the male body. The body, as signifier for patriarchal, heteronormative power, must exude hardness, but not hyperawareness of itself (see also Bordo 1999).

The commercial continues, showing two other equally phlegmatic men while the narrator recites the daily drudgeries of conforming to the demands of work and women: "I will be at work at 8 a.m. . . . I will be civil to your mother." The final scene shows a fit man in a suit standing in front of a fireplace. "I will carry your *lip balm,*" the narrator enunciates with indignation. By now, all the audience can see are his furrowed brow and piercing eyes, a symbol Erving Goffman (1979) links to male aggression and power. "And because I do this . . ."

An engine revs, and the view of the camera switches from being on the men to being from their fantasy viewpoint, inside the car. "I will drive the car I want to drive." As in the Dockers commercial, the ideal man is never fully revealed; his humanity, his emotions, can never be fully accessible. The car speeds away into the distance. "Charger. MAN'S LAST STAND."

In this commercial, the sports car is a sign of status and escape, a phallic remedy to castration anxiety; men charge their way out of domestic life, running over everything in their path. The relationship between men and car advertising has been well documented (Barthel 1989), but in "Man's Last Stand" Dodge offers a narrative that differs in its level of bitterness and its astonishingly explicit call for escape (rather than getting the girl). The subtitle of the commercial on the Dodge Charger's website is clear: "You've sacrificed a lot, but surely there is a limit to your chivalry. Drive the car you want to drive." While the message presents a call to arms, the conclusion of this commercial is ultimately a sad one; the only solution to men's rage is individual consumption. The men are not shown coming together in resistance, and significantly, the war cry is not *men's* last stand, but *man's* last stand.

The relationship between the narrative message and the images is key to understanding the semiotic sleight of hand that attacks women. The linking between the narrative audio and the images should make a clear symbolic connection between the modern men and domesticity—"I will clean the sink after I shave"—but the anger in the narrator's voice undermines that semiotic connection; men aren't *really* meant to perform these frivolities. When the commercial turns in its conclusion to frantic anger as the engine revs, Dodge breaks the connection between men and femininity, relinking the men with traditional manhood and Dodge Charger. What's more, this semiotic move also points to modern women, who want men to perform a bigger share of housework, as the source of men's anger: "Surely, there is a limit to your chivalry."

While "Man's Last Stand" stands out in its inclusion of women as a source of suffering, it is not the only commercial to emphasize this variable. For instance, Flo TV's "Spineless" commercial, presented at the beginning of this article, serves as a suitable, although less intense, companion. Like the bodies of the men in the Dodge commercial, Jason's body is stationary, lacking any focus of attention. His lone moment of interest, when he sees a football game being shown on a television mounted on the wall, is only temporary as his girlfriend drags him over to an escalator. In this case, instead of escaping to a fast car, the solution is a mobile, handheld television, so that no matter what personal affront the faces, he retains his individual escape to a world of proper masculinity—live sports. Also, similar to the Dockers commercial, a change of clothing is imbued with meaning as Jason is urged to "change out of that skirt."

Consumerism, Anxiety, and the Body

In this article we argue that an explicit discourse of a crisis of masculinity emerges within the 2010 Super Bowl commercials. By providing in-depth analysis of the commercials, we are able to explicate a number of central themes involved in this crisis, including discontent over the loss of traditional patriarchal status and heteronormative family values, diminishing confidence in failing bodies, and uncertainty over the economy.

Beyond the collective body, the crisis also operates at the micro level of the physical body. The protruding midsections and flabby buttocks become signs for insecurity at multiple scales—the nation, the job, the family, and sexuality. The cult of hardness remains the underlying goal; however, it is now emphasized through a critical gaze toward failing bodies in "We Wear No Pants" and "Casual Friday" in addition to the metrosexuals implied in "Man's Last Stand." The wandering Dockers men, so fully human in their flawed bodies and flamboyant emotions, are called to imitate the anonymous final figure in all his physical glory, albeit through clothing purchases rather than through actual body-modifying lifestyle changes. Career Builder's "Casual Friday" tells aging, soft bodies to be ashamed of themselves, to hide their flaws and again any signs of happiness or excitement. These particular manifestations of the crisis are attributed to a separation from the body itself, a result of middle-class men being "increasingly defined as bearers of skill" and "separated by an old class division from physical force" (Connell 2005, 55). The separation from manual labor, combined with decreasing leisure time and increasingly unhealthy diets (Critser 2004), writes itself onto bodies that fall short of the traditional image of the powerful, dominant male (Bordo 1999).

Dodge Charger fosters anxiety by inverting the typical mode of men acting and women appearing (Berger 1972), instead narrating a tale in which frozen men succumb to the duties of modern domesticity, where the only acceptable emotional response is rage. But in contrast to the middle-class men of Dockers and Career Builder who have lost touch with their bodies, Dodge says that *women* have forced men to become all too aware of their physiques, and men now must maintain strength but not slip too far into metrosexuality. Nevertheless, throughout this group of commercials, the male body acts as the semiotic bedrock on which these messages about the crisis of masculinity rest.

While the 2010 Super Bowl commercials rehash many of the ideas about masculinity found in the men's movements, consumption is now woven into the discourse, offering itself as a solution and replacing the emphasis on spiritual growth. In this shift, many of the binaries established during early forms of the discourse are altered. Nature no longer has restorative powers; instead, as seen in the Dockers commercial, it represents confusion and lack of purpose, where the men wander in the fields like cows. Instead of following Robert Bly's (1990) prescription of guys' clubs, drum circles, and sweat lodges as productive outlets and a chance for spiritual growth (Magnuson 2008), the 2010 solution is individualized, as seen in the lone rotating figure in the Dockers commercial, the rage-filled Dodge Charger driver, or even the prescription for Jason to watch football on a viewing device made for one.

The 2010 Super Bowl discourse is a simpler, angrier one, crafted to galvanize men to buy. Dockers uses everyday white-collar men to signify collective idiocy and failing masculinity. Career Builder amplifies men's anxieties and semiotically links them with the failing economy, in which solving the crisis of masculinity will also renew faith in the corporate world. Dodge Charger, in the brashest communication of these worries, ultimately pins the crisis of masculinity on women and changing gender roles. Viewed together, these three commercials from 2010, along with advertisements showing women dragging their hubbies away from the big game or once powerful football players rapping about their aging bodies, create a strong intertextual message with men's bodies acting as the semiotic foundation on which this crisis is mounted. The 2010 Super Bowl tells men not to laugh with their buddies, but more importantly, to take charge of their bodies, change out of that skirt, and put on the pants.

Notes

1. "Discourse" is a term that is often used but less frequently understood. This is in part due to the varied usage of the term by different methodological and theoretical approaches. We understand discourse analysis as a study of power that explicates how knowledge and ways of seeing the world are organized. See Mills (1997) for an excellent introduction to the term and its varied use.

2. See Goffman (1979), Barthel (1989), Stern (1993), Bordo (1999), and Shields (2002).

References

Atkinson, Michael. 2008. "Exploring Male Femininity in the 'Crisis': Men and Cosmetic Surgery." *Body and Society* 14(1):67–87.

Barthel, Diane. 1989. *Putting on Appearances: Gender and Advertising.* Philadelphia: Temple University Press.

Berger, John. 1972. *Ways of Seeing: Based on the BBC Television Series.* London: British Broadcasting Corporation.

Bly, Robert. 1990. *Iron John: A Book about Men.* Reading, MA: Addison-Wesley.

Bordo, Susan. 1999. *The Male Body: A New Look at Men in Public and in Private.* New York: Farrar, Straus & Giroux.

Breazeale, Kenon. 1994. "In Spite of Women: *Esquire* Magazine and the Construction of the Male Consumer." *Signs: Journal of Women in Culture and Society* 20(1):1–22.

Burstyn, Varda. 1999. *The Rites of Men: Men, Manhood, Politics, and the Culture of Sport.* Toronto: University of Toronto Press.

Career Builder. 2010. "Casual Friday." YouTube video, 0:30, posted February 7 by "2010 SuperBowlIXLIV." http://www.youtube.com/watch?v5XjlAPEHm4Xs.

Cawthorne, Alexandra. 2009. "Weathering the Storm: Black Men in the Recession." Report, Center for American Progress, Washington, DC. http://www.americanprogress.org/issues/2009/04/pdf/black_men_recession.pdf.

CBS News. 2010. "Gay Dating Ad Sacked before Super Bowl." February 1. http://www.cbsnews.com/stories/2010/01/29/national/main6154905.shtml.

Connell, R. W. 1987. *Gender and Power: Society, the Person and Sexual Politics.* Cambridge: Polity.

———. 2000. *The Men and the Boys.* Berkeley: University of California Press.

———. 2005. *Masculinities.* Berkeley: University of California Press.

Critser, Greg. 2004. *Fat Land: How Americans Became the Fattest People in the World.* Boston: Houghton Mifflin.

Daily Mail Reporter. 2009. "Recession Depression: Men Are Twice as Likely to Suffer Stress in Silence." *Daily Mail Online,* May 11. http://www.dailymail.co.uk/health/article-1180366/Men-struggle-recession-depression-twice-likely-suffer-stress-silence.html.

Denny, Kathleen E. 2011. "Gender in Context, Content, and Approach: Comparing Gender Messages in Girl Scout and Boy Scout Handbooks." *Gender and Society* 25(1):27–47.

Dockers. 2010. "I Wear No Pants." YouTube video, 0:30, posted February 7 by "2010 SuperBowlIXLIV." http://www.youtube.com/watch? v=nys0i_FRjTI.

Dodge Charger. 2010. "Man's Last Stand." http://www.youtube.com/watch? V=hPmYxLUoZVc.

Duncan, Margaret C., and Alan Aycock. 2009. "'I Laughed until I Hurt': Negative Humor in Super Bowl Ads." In *Sport, Beer, and Gender: Promotional Culture and Contemporary Social Life,* ed. Lawrence A. Wenner and Steven J. Jackson, 243–59. New York: Peter Lang.

Dunlop, Boadie W., and Tanja Mletzko. 2011. "Will Current Socioeconomic Trends Produce a Depressing Future for Men?" *British Journal of Psychiatry* 198(3):167–68.

Flo TV. 2010. "Spineless." http://www.youtube.com/watch? v=5Mr31JemdOs.

Foucault, Michel. 1972. *The Archaeology of Knowledge.* Trans. A. M. Sheridan Smith. New York: Pantheon.

Gill, Rosalind, Karen Henwood, and Carl McLean. 2005. "Body Projects and the Regulation of Normative Masculinity." *Body and Society* 11(2):37–62.

Goffman, Erving. 1979. *Gender Advertisements.* New York: Harper & Row.

Halberstam, Judith. 1998. *Female Masculinity.* Durham, NC: Duke.

Halberstam. 2005. *In a Queer Time and Place: Transgender Bodies, Subcultural Lives.* New York: New York University Press.

Jhally, Sut. 1987. *The Codes of Advertising: Fetishism and the Political Economy of Meaning in the Consumer Society.* New York: Routledge.

Kimmel, Michael S. 1996. *Manhood in America: A Cultural History.* New York: Free Press.

Kimmel, Michael S., and Michael Kaufman. 1995. "Weekend Warriors: The New Men's Movement." In *The Politics of Manhood: Profeminist Men Respond to the Mythopoetic Men's Movement (and the Mythopoetic Leaders Answer),* ed. Michael S. Kimmel, 15–43. Philadelphia: Temple University Press.

Kochar, Rakesh. 2011. "Two Years of Economic Recovery: Women Lose Jobs, Men Find Them." Report, Pew Research Center, Washington, DC. http:// pewsocialtrends.org/2011/07/06/two-years-of-economic-recovery-women-lose-jobs-men-find-them/.

Lui, Meizhu, Bárbara Robles, Betsy Leondar-Wright, Rose Brewer, and Rebecca Adamson, with United for a Fair Economy. 2006. *The Color of Wealth: The Story Behind the U.S. Racial Wealth Divide.* New York: New Press.

Magnuson, Eric. 2008. "Rejecting the American Dream: Men Creating Alternative Life Goals." *Journal of Contemporary Ethnography* 37(3):255–90.

Messner, Michael. A. 1992. *Power at Play: Sports and the Problem of Masculinity.* Boston: Beacon.

Messner, Michael A., and Jeffrey Montez de Oca. 2005. "The Male Consumer as Loser: Beer and Liquor Ads in Mega Sports Media Events." *Signs* 30(3): 1879–1909.

Mills, Sara. 1997. *Discourse.* New York: Routledge.

Nielson Company. 2010. "SuperBowlXLIV Most Watched Super Bowl of All Time." Blog post, February 8. http://blog.nielsen.com/nielsenwire/media_entertainment/super-bowl-xliv-most-watched-super-bowl-of-all-time/.

Nixon, Sean. 1996. *Hard Looks: Masculinities, Spectatorship, and Contemporary Consumption.* New York: St. Martin's.

Patterson, Maurice, and Richard Elliott. 2002. "Negotiating Masculinities: Advertising and the Inversion of the Male Gaze." *Consumption, Markets, and Culture* 5(3):231–46.

Pepsi Max. 2009. "I'm Good." YouTube video, 0:33, posted February 1 by "reggiep08v2." http://www.youtube.com/watch? v=qUZaSf7T7ig&playnext =1&list=PLBD661EDEC86735DC.

Plocher, Carolyn. 2010. "USA Today Still Stomping on Tebow Ad." *NewsBusters.org,* February 16.

Putney, Clifford. 2001. *Muscular Christianity: Manhood and Sports in Protestant America, 1880–1920.* Cambridge, MA: Harvard University Press.

Rose, Gillian. 2001. *Visual Methodologies: An Introduction to the Interpretation of Visual Materials.* London: Sage.

Rutherford, Jonathan. 1988. "Who's That Man?" *In Male Order: Unwrapping Masculinity,* ed. Rowena Chapman and Jonathan Rutherford, 21–67. London: Lawrence & Wishart.

Schroeder, Jonathan E., and Janet L. Borgerson. 1998. "Marketing Images of Gender: A Visual Analysis." *Consumption, Markets, and Culture* 2(2):161–201.

Schroeder, Jonathan E., and Detlev Zwick. 2004. "Mirrors of Masculinity: Representation and Identity in Advertising Images." *Consumption, Markets and Culture* 7(1):21–52.

Shales, Tom. 2010. "Once Again, Letterman's 'Late Show' Promo Is Spot On." *Washington Post,* February 8. http://www.washingtonpost.com/wp-dyn/content/article/2010/02/07/AR2010020703677.html?wprss=rss_print/style.

Shields, Vickie Rutledge. 2002. *Measuring Up: How Advertising Affects Self-Image.* With Dawn Heinecken. Philadelphia: University of Pennsylvania Press.

Smith, Hortense. 2010. "The Woes of Bros: Super Bowl Ads Star Pathetic Men—and the Women Who Ruined Them." *Jezebel,* February 7. http://jezebel.com/5466296/woes-of-bros-super-bowl-ads-star-pathetic-men—and-the-women-who-ruined-them/gallery/?skyline=true&s=i.

Stern, Barbara B. 1993. "Feminist Literary Criticism and the Deconstruction of Ads: A Postmodern View of Advertising and Consumer Responses." *Journal of Consumer Research* 19(4):556–66.

Stevenson, Seth. 2010. "The Best and Worst Super Bowl Ads." *Slate,* February 8. http://www.slate.com/id/2243904/.

Thomas, Calvin. 2002. "Reenfleshing the Bright Boys; or, How Male Bodies Matter to Feminist Theory." In *Masculinity Studies and Feminist Theory: New Directions,* ed. Judith Kegan Gardiner, 60–89. New York: Columbia University Press.

Thompson, Derek. 2009. "It's Not Just a Recession: It's a Mancession!" *Atlantic,* July 9. http://www.theatlantic.com/business/archive/2009/07/its-not-just -a-recession-its-a-mancession/20991/.

Tsai, Wan-Hsui Sunny. 2010. "Assimilating the Queers: Representations of Lesbians, Gay Men, Bisexual, and Transgender People in Mainstream Advertising." *Advertising and Society Review* 11(1). http://muse.jhu.edu/journals /advertising_and_society_ review/v011/11.1.tsai.html.

Universal Studios. 2009. "Universal Heroes." YouTube video, 0:41, posted February 3 by "Super Bowl BestAds." http://www.youtube.com/watch? v=X2dIt _ykaK4.

Wenner, Lawrence A., and Steven Jackson. 2009. "Sport, Beer, and Gender in Promotional Culture: On the Dynamics of a Holy Trinity." In *Sport, Beer, and Gender in Promotional Culture and Contemporary Social Life,* 1–34. New York: Peter Lang.

Williams, Raymond. (1980) 2005. "Advertising: The Magic System." In *Culture and Materialism: Selected Essays,* 170–95. New York: Verso.

Williamson, Judith. 1978. *Decoding Advertisements: Ideology and Meaning in Advertising.* London: Boyars.

CHAPTER 9

Bitch, Slut, Skank, Cunt

Patterned Resistance to Women's Visibility in Digital Publics

Sarah Sobieraj

Introduction

The threat of unwanted sexual attention and violence has long constrained women's use of public space. Whether via the fear of sexual assault that hovers over women in nature (Clark, 2015; Roper, 2016; Wesely & Gaarder, 2004), the sense of vulnerability and embarrassment that accompany street harassment (Fairchild & Rudman, 2008; Gardner, 1995; Miller, 2008; Nielsen, 2009), or the labyrinthine challenges presented by sexual harassment in the workplace (see McLaughlin, Uggen, & Blackstone, 2012; Sojo, Wood, & Genat, 2016; Welsh, 1999; Williams, Giuffre, & Dellinger, 1999), women's use of public space is shaped by the looming possibility of gender-based incidents that threaten to undermine their freedom, comfort, and safety.

New internet and communications technologies (ICTs) have facilitated the construction of new public spaces—digital publics—with the potential for great inclusivity. Ideally these tools allow users to establish discursive arenas where women, and men from marginalized groups, whose freedom in public spaces has always been precarious, can enter, explore, and share freely. To some extent, this is true. Such spaces have proven to be valuable sources of solidarity for those from disadvantaged groups (e.g., Bonilla & Rosa, 2015; Keller, 2012; Rapp, Button, Fleury-Steiner, & Fleury-Steiner, 2010). As digital publics mature, however, it becomes increasingly clear that these are new cites of contention over power and meaning, where inequalities can be eroded, but also reinforced.

In terms of gender inequality, digital publics are rife with male resistance to women's involvement in public life. There is a steady drumbeat of sexism directed at many women who participate in public discourse. Female journalists, academics, political figures, activists, and bloggers, for example, often find themselves targeted for abuse. Myriad other women using social networking services, playing games, and participating in digital communities also find themselves on the receiving end of vitriolic, gender-based backlash. The abuse can be particularly burdensome for women of color who receive racialized gender-based attacks and race-based attacks in addition to the kinds of harassment white women experience (Gray, 2012, 2014). Lesbian and trans women of all races are also frequent targets (Citron, 2009; Finn, 2004). Research suggests digital misogyny is particularly common among young women, over a quarter of whom report having been sexually harassed online (PEW, 2014).[1] Indeed, identity-based attacks have become so common that they have been normalized as inevitable, something that 'goes with the territory' if you are a woman participating in digital publics.

SOURCE: Sobieraj, S. (2017). Bitch, Slut, Skank, Cunt: Patterned Resistance to Women's Visibility in Digital Publics. *Information, Communication & Society*, 1–15. doi: 10.1080/1369118X. Reproduced with permission from Taylor and Francis.

Nearly 30 years ago geographer Gill Valentine studied the way women felt about and used physical public spaces, noting that women were constrained by mental maps of public space they constructed based on their fear of male violence. This sense of danger impedes women's independence and freedom, shaping where they go, at what times, and with whom. Gill concludes, '. . . this cycle of fear becomes one subsystem by which male dominance, patriarchy, is maintained and perpetuated' (1989, p. 389). Similarly, gender-based attacks against women online must be understood as patterned resistance to women's public voice. Just as inhibited use of physical public spaces is a spatial expression of gender-based oppression, inhibited use of chat rooms, social media platforms, blogs, vlogs, and online gaming must be understood as a digital expression of these power dynamics.

Reflecting on two years of in-depth interviews with women who have been on the receiving end of gender-based digital abuse ($n = 38$), conversations with industry professionals working in content moderation and digital safety, the extant literature, and news stories about digital attacks against women, I offer a typology of digital sexism showing that aggressors draw upon three overlapping strategies—intimidating, shaming, and discrediting—to limit women's impact in digital publics.

In this paper, I explore attempts to constrain and inhibit women's digital presence, showing that gender is enmeshed not only in the propensity of a person to *be* an attacker or to *be* a target, but that it is also at the very center of the attacks themselves. Femininity and femaleness are the weapons of choice used to undermine women's participation and contributions, and—as in physical publics—the body is the locus of abuse. I argue that men call attention to women's physicality as a way to pull gender—and the male advantage that comes with it—to the fore in digital exchanges.

To the extent that digital sexism succeeds in pressing women out of digital spaces, or constrains the topics they address publicly or the ways they address them, it requires that we consider the democratic costs of the harassment, in addition to the personal ones.

Digital Publics and Inequities

The participatory media environment facilitated by new ICTs has been offered new avenues for people from marginalized groups. Social networking services and user-generated content platforms have helped flatten—though not eliminated—barriers to access; it is easier and far less costly to start a blog than to launch a newspaper. This accessibility has opened the doors to a greater diversity of voices.[2] Participatory online spaces such as comment sections, blogs, Facebook, Twitter, and YouTube now serve as digital public spheres. The term 'public sphere' refers to the practice of open discussion about matters of common concern as well as to the public spaces that serve as settings for such dialogue, such as parks, community centers, and plazas (Habermas, [1962] 1989). While such discourse can transpire face to face, as when we discuss neighborhood issues in community centers, the mass media serve as core venues for public discussion in contemporary political culture.

Mediated public conversations transpired in legacy media as well, on op-ed pages and through radio call-in programs, for example, but ICTs have supported the proliferation of new spaces for public discussion about matters of common concern. Not only do they provide spaces to talk, they help facilitate what Shirky (2008) refers to as the self-synchronization of latent groups. In other words, they help people with interests or attributes in common find one another. With these tools, geographically dispersed strangers can find one another to explore and discuss any number of shared interests, concerns, or identities.

Digital publics are of great import in the context of conventional public spheres, which have always been exclusionary. There has never been equal access to mainstream publics, nor have all voices or styles of communication been valued equally when included in the conversation.[3] The micro-publics that we find online are new incarnations of the subaltern counter publics valued by Fraser (1990) and others, who see them as spaces for articulating marginalized interests and viewpoints, building social cohesion, and establishing alternative interpretations of unfolding events and existing social arrangements. What's more, niche publics can serve as staging grounds for the development of strategies to inject these marginalized interests and views into mainstream public discourse.[4] In other words, to the extent that digital spaces—chat rooms, twitter networks, Tumblr communities, and the like—serve as micro-publics, they can provide safe havens and support for those from marginalized groups or with minority viewpoints, and facilitate collaboration among participants as they work to expand mainstream discursive space to create room for their issues and voices.[5] These niche publics, therefore, serve as sanctuaries, but also as incubators for engagement with outsiders.

So-called 'hashtag activism' is one such form of outreach. For example, we have seen struggles over racial inequality in the use of the #blacklivesmatter hashtag as well as in the pushback from those responding with #alllivesmatter. But hashtag activism is only one part of the story. Sometimes digital micro-publics launch coordinated efforts to reach elected officials, start boycotts, or find co-complainants for class action lawsuits. And at times these geographically dispersed groups coalesce into collective action in the traditional social movement sense, spawning marches and rallies, as seen in the wake of Donald Trump's inauguration.

Perhaps nowhere is the utility of new ICTs for those from disadvantaged groups more apparent than in efforts for cultural visibility. In contrast to efforts that seek legislative or judicial change, campaigns with visibility as their primary end-goal are tailor-made for this media environment. Social networking services and user-generated content platforms facilitate self-publishing, if not instant distribution (which requires access to a substantial marketing budget, or a combination of skill, persistence, unusually extensive social networks, and serendipity). Having a platform is a start. What's more, digital interventions occasionally capture the attention of conventional media, extending their reach when stories about their actions appear in print, on TV, or the radio. Consider the visibility secured for the racial imbalance in Hollywood launched by the hashtag #oscarssowhite in 2016 (and to a lesser extent in 2015), which was featured in myriad news outlets. These digital publics, then, can ultimately serve not only as an alternative to relying on mainstream news coverage, but as a potential path to obtain it.

Whether or not efforts to shape mainstream discursive spaces and publics succeed, the attempts to do so and the resistance that emerges in their wake, remind us that the elaborate and overlapping digital spaces introduced by new ICTs are best understood not as refreshingly democratic playing fields, but as consequential and contested cultural terrain where struggles to reproduce as well as erode existing social hierarchies are waged. In this sense, they have much in common with conventional media, such as film and television.

The spheres of publicity made available via digital life radically improve access to information for those at the margins and create new platforms from which to speak, but the entrenched inequalities (e.g., those of race, class, gender, sexual orientation, ability, and national origin) that we find offline reappear in and across digital arenas. Barriers to entry are lowered by new ICTs, but access remains unequal. And the digital production gap has been particularly resilient (Schradie, 2011). Even when digital publics include a diversity of participants, inequities shape participants' comfort, involvement, and social power (Herring, 1996, 1999; Milner, 2013).

Despite some early imaginings that digital technologies would liberate women by allowing them to transcend gender and disrupt patriarchal arrangements (Braidotti, 1996; Haraway, 1987; Plant, 1997), technologies are neither universally liberating nor oppressive (Daniels, 2009b). Instead, technologies—digital and otherwise—are social constructions that are malleable, open to interpretation, and context dependent. Further, technology and gender are not separate entities, but are rather coproduced. Technology is 'a source and consequence of gender relations' (Wajcman, 2004, 2010, p. 148). Gender inequalities, then, are reflected in digital technologies, and those technologies are platforms where gender inequities are recreated and reformed, as well as resisted.

These gender inequalities take a variety of digital forms. Some digital communities are androcentric, informally excluding women by creating an unwelcoming climate (Herring, 1996; Kendall, 2002;

Martin, Vaccaro, Heckert, & Heasley, 2015; Reagle, 2012; Turkle, 1984). While much of this androcentrism is overt, it can also can be subtle—accomplished through the over valuing of men's input and expertise and devaluing those of women (Korn, 2016). In some instances, familiar forms of violence against women found in physical spaces, such as stalking, sexual harassment in the workplace, and sexual assault, are facilitated by ICTs. This digital component often heightens the suffering experienced by victims. Think, for example, about the ways digital documentation of rape and sexual assault re-traumatize survivors through public shaming and humiliation facilitated by sharing technologies (Henry & Powell, 2015).[6] Women also bear the brunt of digital hate—freely flung insults, threats, and abuse (Citron, 2014; Herring, 2002; Herring, Job-Sluder, Scheckler, & Barab, 2002; Phillips, 2015), many of which are shamelessly misogynistic, racist, and heterosexist (Filipovic, 2007; Finn, 2004; Gray, 2014; Jane, 2014b; Sills et al., 2016).

Data-Based Reflection

How women navigate and respond to sexism in digital publics is the focus of a larger project that I have underway. The observations made in this paper draw on the in-depth qualitative interviews I have conducted for that research (*n* = 38), with women who have been on the receiving end of gender-based attacks online, as well as extended informal conversations I have had with professionals working in content moderation and internet safety, the extant literature, and an examination of cases of digital sexism in the news and popular media. More data are necessary to capture internal variation across axes of race and sexual orientation, but several clear patterns in the abuse itself have already become visible through participants' accounts, media coverage, the literature, and the stories of professionals in the industry, are noteworthy. The consistency is so striking that philosophers Emma Tom and Nicole Vincent created a slot machine–style 'Random Rape Threat Generator' that builds rape threats out of randomly selected snippets of 'real-life cyberhate received by real-life women' to illustrate the ways such attacks, which feel personal, are largely *im*personal and, as they hope to illustrate, literally interchangeable. What I offer here, then, is not systematic data analysis, but some lenses to help us think through the patterns that emerge over and over again in digital abuse directed at women.

Gender-Based Attacks Against Women Online

Entering and using digital publics to share work, ideas, opinions, and experiences often comes at great cost for women. Aggressors repeatedly draw upon three overlapping strategies intimidating, shaming, and discrediting—to silence women or to limit their impact in digital publics. With intimidation, attackers often draw upon women's fear of rape and physical violence. Public shaming attempts regularly exploit double standards about women's sexual behavior and physical appearance to taint targets. And efforts to discredit often employ sexist stereotypes to devalue the ideas and contributions of the woman under fire. Although these three tactics are deeply entwined and not mutually exclusive, I address them separately for analytic purposes.

Attackers often try to *intimidate*. Intimidation appears in threats of physical violence, such as death and rape threats, as well as in intimations that the attacker knows where the person lives or works, and vague but frightening missives indicating that the target should shut up or their families could be affected. Sometimes Denial of Service (Dos) and Distributed Denial of Service (Ddos) attacks are also used to make the target feel vulnerable and to effectively, if temporarily, restrict their access to the web (or a particular website), show network performance, or bombard their email account with spam. 'Swatting' is another, albeit far less common, intimidation tactic, in which attackers make false emergency calls to the police indicating that an imminent threat exists at the target's location (e.g., a hostage situation, a bomb threat, or an active shooter). The goal is to terrify the target when a swat team descends upon them. Although swatting is often referred to as a prank, the label belies the gravity of the experience. As described in a *New York Times* piece from 2015,

> K. says she opened the door of her Florida apartment one evening to find a dozen SWAT officers lined up on the stairs with riot shields and black guns pointed at her. She froze and thought of the metal belt buckle she happened to be clutching in her left hand. *They're going to think I have a weapon in my hand. They're going to shoot me.* (Fagone, 2015)

'Doxing' (short for dropping documents) is another intimidation tactic used in which attackers compile personal information about a target and publish it without their consent, with the intent of opening the door for other harassers. One woman I interviewed who had been the subject of an intense wave of digital hostility discovered that her home address, the floor plans to her house, and photos of her car and pets had all been published online. Such efforts escalate the fear of physical violence, by implying (and making more feasible) that threats made online might translate into rape or other physical violence. Sometimes doxing involves revealing the identity of someone who had been using a pseudonym for privacy. Here we see how closely linked and overlapping these three tactics can be. Threatening to dox is perhaps best understood as intimidation, but actually doing so can intimidate through heightening the fear of violence or—especially in the case of exposing some-one's identity—can be a form of shaming or discrediting.

Attacks against women online often involve attempts to publicly *shame* them. Missives drawing upon public shame strive to contaminate the public perception of the target. This can take a variety of forms. Harassers sometimes seek to do this by disclosing private information intended to humiliate their mark. Unauthorized pornography: the public posting of nude or otherwise compromising pic-tures originally taken with an understanding that they would remain private (often obtained through hacking or via former intimate partners), or revealing photos or videos taken without consent (e.g., captured by hidden cameras or while the target was incapacitated) and then posted are image-based examples of shame techniques. When combined with doxing, unauthorized pornography can not only humiliate the target, but open the floodgates for an onslaught of digital harassment. Public shame attempts may also involve circulating false information that attackers hope others will find reprehensible (e.g., making allegations about their sexual history) and/or efforts to recast actions that were originally public in a markedly negative light. At its heart, all three variants involve attempts to take control of how the target wishes to be seen in an effort to humiliate or, as is often the goal, dis-credit her.

Efforts to *discredit* women are extremely common online. These dispatches regularly draw on gender-based stereotypes that suggest the target cannot possibly have anything worthwhile to contribute or that she is not a credible source. Often she is described as incapable of an unbiased opinion or perspec-tive because she is a bitch, a ditz, emotional, needs to get laid, a dumb blonde, a whore, or suffering from PMS, to offer a few examples. In many cases, attackers suggest that personal accounts, political views or concerns about social arrangements cannot be taken seriously because she has an ulterior motive (e.g., she is a gold-digger, a feminazi, or a 'social justice warrior'). Taken together, these three strategies strive to devalue the knowledge, opinions, and experiences of women in digital publics.

This is what resistance to women's voice and visibility looks like.

Importantly, gender shapes the propensity of a person to be an attacker or be a target, but gender is also at the center of the attacks themselves. Whether they are working to intimidate, shame, or discredit their target, when people (mostly men) lash out at women, they use their femaleness against them. In other words, gender is implicated in the tools that are used to attack, not only in the actors who use them. Women with visibility are often deluged by vitriolic tweets, emails, and comments that draw on sexist name-calling, negative stereotypes of women, double standards, and sexual objectification. Cuen and Evers (2016) analysis of 80,000 tweets directed at Megyn Kelly's twitter handle over the 24-hour period after Donald Trump announced that he would not participate in a televised debate she was moderating serves as a useful illustration. In that brief window of time, tweets directed at Kelly included the words bitch ($n = 423$), bimbo ($n = 404$), blonde (128), whore ($n = 88$), cheap ($n = 66$), ugly ($n = 59$), skank ($n = 39$), cunt ($n = 34$), slut ($n = 27$), and hooker ($n = 13$).

The language is explicitly gender-based, dominated by the use of misogynistic epithets, evaluations of her sexual value, and sexist stereotypes (e.g., the dumb blonde). Substantive commentary is noticeably absent. Language of potentially relevant journalistic critiques—assertions that she is 'biased', 'unfair', or 'hostile', for example—is less common than language suggesting that she is a woman and thus without value or that she is the kind of woman who has no value. Kelly's alleged sexual behavior and physical appearance, which have nothing to do with her skills as a journalist or moderator, become the central grounds for condemnation. This is indicative of a broader pattern in which a woman's physical appearance and sexual propriety are treated as universally relevant. It is particularly noteworthy that no evidence is offered to support these claims; the allegation alone is treated as reason Kelly should be viewed with contempt.

Reading the unsettling examples of gender-based attacks against women detailed by scholars such as Jane (2014a), Citron (2014), Garde-Hansen and Gorton (2013), and in listening to the stories shared by the participants in my ongoing research, I am stuck by their vulgarity, cruelty, and violence. But I am also struck by the way they so pointedly use women's bodies as leverage to intimidate, shame, and discredit. A preponderance of the instances incorporate one or more of the following: rape threats, graphic descriptions of sexual torture, commentary about the person's presumed sexual behavior (e.g., whore, slut, prude), commentary about the person's physical appearance (often amounting to whether the women in question is even 'worth raping'), racialized commentary about their bodies or sexual behavior, seething statements about sexual orientation, preferences, or fetishes, use of the c-word, descriptions of nonsexual violence or torture, use of pornographic imagery, use of doctored images of the target (often sexualized and humiliating), the circulation of revenge pornography, etc.

By way of extreme example, consider the experience of feminist media critic, Anita Sarkeesian, who found herself at the center of the #GamerGate harassment in 2014, which reached such a fever pitch that safety concerns temporarily forced her to leave her home. Sarkeesian received death and rape threats for well over two years in response to a series of short videos she created that discuss sexism in video games. Her body was at the center of the abuse. One attacker created a video game where players could give Sarkeesian digital punches in the face and watch as her image became bloody, swollen, and bruised. Some attackers edited pornographic images of women in humiliating situations to bear her likeness. And among a random week of abusive twitter @mentions that Sarkeesian published on her website in 2015 are tweets such as:

> @femfreq You are a despicable whore
> @femfreq uh boohoo stop crying you selfish faking bitch and get over it who would rape you your fucking ugly you Arab bitch
> @femfreq I hope you get raped by 4 men with 9 inch cocks
> @femfreq you're a stupid fat cunt die pls?
> @femfreq BITCH WERE NOT TALKING ABOUT THAT SO I HOPE YOU GET RAPED U FUCKING WHORE.
> @femfreq im gonna bust dem sugar walls leave an aids load in der

These tweets give a sense of the vulgar and ad hominem nature of the attacks—these are hardly rebuttals of her ideas—as well as the gendered and body-centric nature of the abuse. It is remarkable that misogynist epithets such as cunt and bitch, intimations of sexual violence, commentary on her physical appearance, and the suggestion that she is not 'rapeable' can even fit into so few keystrokes.

We also see an example of racialized misogyny; Sarkeesian is not simply called a bitch, she is an Arab bitch. At times this body centrism includes references to a woman being 'fuckable' and descriptions of what the attacker would like to do to her, but more often the focus is on the target as a tainted woman. Such failed women are rendered contemptible by virtue of their physical appearance, alleged history of sexual behavior, race, ethnicity, religion, or sexual identity. Or she is marked for a comeuppance, usually to be delivered through gendered humiliation or some sort of sexual or physical violence.

Understanding the Centrality of Women's Bodies

There is a long history of women's objectification and sexualization, but I would argue that bodily references are especially common in digital spaces because they help reinforce the salience of gender in the digital arena.[7]

Research suggests that computer mediated communication reduces status inequality because we have a smaller number of social cues available (particularly in text-based exchanges), signals that might convey information about an interlocutor's race, age, gender, class, level of education, sexual orientation, ethnicity, and the like. This is referred to as the 'equalization hypothesis'. Proponents find that this leveling makes electronic communications somewhat more equitable than face-to-face communications (visible in who influences who, who dominates conversation, etc.). Although there is disagreement about the specific contexts in which status becomes less germane, we often feel and communicate as though we are on more level footing when we enter digital arenas (Boucher, Hancock, & Dunham, 2008; Dubrovsky, Kiesler & Sethna, 1991; George, Easton, Nunamaker Jr, & Northcraft, 1990). Such status leveling may not sit well with members of groups accustomed to having the upper hand.

Gender permeates digital life, but digital arenas preclude some of the physical strategies men use to control interactions and display dominance in the physical world. Differences in stature that often advantage men are not relevant in digital exchanges, nor can men rely upon body postures that command physical space, nonverbal gestures that signal dominance (e.g., invasive touch), or communicative habits such as interruption or amplification to maximize their influence and command attention. More overt tactics for exerting influence, such as physical intimations that suggest the threat of violence and the exploitation of power differentials emerging from employment or position, are also often out of the equation in the comments sections, chat rooms, on twitter, or the world of online games. As a result, the unspoken and often unrecognized communicative advantages of white masculinity in social interaction are subtly destabilized in digital publics. This is likely to feel particularly disorienting in digital publics with a history of being predominantly male and/or those that focus on topics that are usually the province of men.[8]

I would argue that these sexist missives take the form of body-based commentary because talking about women's bodies—about their sexuality, appearance, and physical vulnerability—is a shortcut that works to force gender into the conversation. They can be understood as flailing attempts to reassert the centrality of gender difference—and the gender inequality that comes with it—in spaces where its grip, though powerful, may feel feebler. Such gender billboards are important in digital arenas. Tim Jordan writes, 'Online markers of identity—because they are inherently unstable, unlike the body or timbre of a voice—have to be stabilized by being heard consistently . . .' (Shepherd, Harvey, Jordan, Srauy, & Miltner, 2015, p. 3). As Lois McNay reminds us, gender is accomplished through lived social relations that are negotiated and renegotiated (2004). That the locus of attack is the body, then, is instrumental rather than coincidental. Words such as cunt, dyke, and whore are shorthand for: 'This is a woman.' 'You are a woman.' 'She is a woman'.

The Costs of Gender-Based Attacks Against Women Online

Public harassment of women, and of men from marginalized groups, has long been a geographic expression of social inequality and an effective means for dominant groups to maintain control of public space. Street and sexual harassment are nearly universal experiences for women, and are particularly prevalent in the lives of black and Latina women and poor women of all races and ethnicities (Gardner, 1995; Miller, 2008; Nielsen, 2009). And while women certainly continue to use public space, research shows that they constrain their behaviors in response to prior experiences with harassment and the fear of sexual intimidation and violence (Fairchild & Rudman, 2008; Gardner, 1995; Hollander, 2001; Meyer & Grollman, 2014, Riger & Gordon, 1981; Wesely & Gaarder, 2004). Indeed, Gardner (1995) finds that harassment inhibits women's use of public space, *even when no harassment transpires*, as fear that it might occur diminishes their comfort and freedom, acting as a form of oppression even in absentia.

Women strategize their way around uncomfortable and frightening public spaces when they can, to avoid the threat of male violence and sexual intimidation. They make the mental maps described by Valentine (1989). Where is it safe to go? When is it safe to be there? How should I behave to minimize the likelihood of harassment? How will I react if something happens? Women of privilege have more options. They may opt to drive, be able to avoid communities they see as dangerous, take a taxi, or even hire a bodyguard. For women, the threat of abuse is part of the physical landscape, and circulating notions about gender suggest that it is women's responsibility to navigate around it. Was she alone? What was she doing in that part of town? What was she wearing?

The threat of abuse is increasingly becoming part of the digital landscape women navigate. Digital sexism is so common that when I talk informally with women about whether they have received gendered backlash, it is common for them to tell me no, or indicate that they've 'been really lucky' only to thereafter offer that 'of course' they have been called a bitch or a slut and been sent dick pics. This minimization and normalization of abuse suggests that while gender-based attacks are perceived as tedious and gross, they are seen as par for the course. This is also often the way digital misogyny is viewed by law enforcement (Citron, 2014). This persistent 'if you can't stand the heat, get out of the kitchen' mentality is not helpful in a world where social, educational, and professional life often require involvement in digital publics, nor is it effective, as one need not even be present to experience gender-based attacks online (Citron, 2014).

In looking at digital abuse leveled at feminists, particularly her own harassment on the law school rumor mill AutoAdmit and the harassment received by feminist bloggers working for the John Edwards presidential campaign, Filipovic argues that Internet misogyny parallels gendered harassment in physical spaces, suggesting that the heart of men's aggression toward women is a "generalized offense at women's public presence in 'men's' spaces—in politics, at law schools, online" (2007, p. 298). Indeed, the contours of digital harassment as I see them bear out her assertion. For example, digital hostility is particularly virulent for female journalists, bloggers, and vloggers who work on technology, science, and sports.[9] And extraordinary venom is saved for feminists and women who are otherwise noncompliant with gendered expectations, such as those who are overweight and body positive, women in positions of power, etc. Given these two hotbeds of resistance—against women entering male-dominated spaces on the one hand, and against women who are feminist or otherwise challenge gender norms on the other—it is of little surprise that successfully bringing attention to feminist issues in a male-dominated space, as Anita Sarkeesian was able to do in gaming, would be a phyrric victory. This parallels the experiences of women in the workplace, who face pronounced sexual harassment when they are in positions of authority and/or in male-dominated employment contexts such as the military, law enforcement, and construction (Konik & Cortina, 2008; McLaughlin et al., 2012; see also Welsh, 1999, for a full review).

Clearly, many women are using and relishing digital platforms, but it is not difficult to imagine why women might begin making mental maps of the digital landscape and navigating around high risk arenas. Digital sexism has cost victims their jobs, forced them to move, jeopardized their mental health, placed them at risk of physical violence, and caused irreparable social damage (Barak, 2005; Bates, 2017; Citron, 2014). Even when women do not worry about such dramatic risks, some decide that the constant irritation and inconvenience (e.g., sifting through the barrage of sexist hostility to find the more meaningful responses, being upset by feedback, needing to block people on social media services, etc.) is simply too tedious to tolerate.

When effective, intimidating, shaming, and discrediting can silence women, undermine their contributions to digital discourse, press them of out of valued digital publics, and create a climate of self-censorship that mirrors the calculations women make in physical public spaces about what is safe and what is risky. What are the conditions under which it is safe(r) to share your ideas, opinions, preferences, expertise, and experiences online? What topics are likely to rile the trolls? How does the specter of digital misogyny hover over the keyboard? To what extent does the looming threat of digital misogyny serve as a cautionary tale, creating a chilling effect even for women who have not personally been on the receiving end of this kind of abuse?

It is vital to consider the impact identity-based attacks in general and gender-based attacks in particular have on those who confront them, but we must also be cognizant of the concomitant societal-level costs. If the inclusion proffered by new ICTs places those who use them in harm's way, we lose the democratizing potential these tools can provide. Tools that support voice and visibility are not useful if voice and visibility are dangerous. Abuse that distorts political discourse such that the most visible representatives of key constituencies withdraw from fatigue, free speech is raced, classed, and gendered, the range of issues open for public discussion shrinks for fear of retaliation, and 'high risk' perspectives go unspoken thwarts not only those who opt to avoid risk, but democratic discourse writ large.

Future research is needed to evaluate the ways women and men from historically underrepresented groups navigate these hostile waters, how the threat of digital abuse transforms digital discourse, the consequences of normalizing extreme incivility as a mode of political exchange, and how best to support safe, inclusive publics.

Notes

1. The full PEW study explains that women ages 18–24 are more likely than others to experience some of the more severe forms of harassment. They are particularly likely to report being stalked online (26% said so) and sexually harassed (25%). In addition, they are also the targets of other forms of severe harassment like physical threats (23%) and sustained harassment (18%) at rates similar to their male peers (26% of whom have been physically threatened and 16% of whom have been the victim of sustained harassment). In essence, young women are uniquely likely to experience stalking and sexual harassment, while also not escaping the high rates of other types of harassment common to young people in general. (2014, p. 3)

2. Of course, the irony is that the same attributes—low cost, the chance to be anonymous if one chooses, and the limited oversight and regulation in many of these arenas—that render these platforms accessible to those from marginalized groups, also open the floodgates for those who may abuse them.

3. On these inequities see Benhabib (1996), Fraser (1990), Mansbridge (1990), and Young (2002).

4. Aronwitz (1995), Burrows (2010), Eckert and Chadha (2013), Graham and Smith (2016), Gregory (1994), Jacobs (2000), Simone (2006), and Squires (2000) all provide illustrations.

5. Of course, these marginalized views are not always pro-social. Jessie Daniels' work on white supremacist groups online serves as one powerful example (Daniels, 2009a).

6. The suicides of young teens Rehtaeh Parsons and Audrie Potts, both of whom took their lives after being humiliated by digital images of their sexual assaults, stand out as examples from the headlines.

7. Digital life is, of course, rife with gender. Niles Van Doorn uses three case studies to show the way 'online articulations of gender, sexuality, and embodiment are intricately woven with people's physical embeddings in everyday life, as well as in the new media technologies they employ . . .' (2011, p. 532). The gendered body is often visible in digital publics through photos and videos, but gender remains a focal point even when it is not visually referenced. Research suggests that rather than using online spaces as a way to 'change' or conceal our gender or racial identities, we use them to reach out to others, seek affirmation, and build relationships (Daniels, 2009b). What's more, many of the most popular platforms build gender relevance into their architecture, requiring registrants to identify by gender. For example, Facebook requires that you choose a gender category (either male or female) when you register. Since 2013, members have been able to then change their gender to a custom option, and choose a preferred pronoun. This more inclusive turn has broadened the range of options, yet not reduced the salience of gender categorization (see Bivens, 2017 for a discussion of misgendering in Facebook).

8. Interestingly, this disease may not be necessary. Jenny Korn's work on PLATO in the 1970s shows the way even 'genderless' online spaces are rife with gender inequality.

9. See Wallace's (2014) op-ed for the *New York Times*: 'Life as a Female Journalist: Hot or Not?'.

References

Aronowitz, S. (1995). Against the liberal state: ACT-UP and the emergence of postmodern politics. In L. Nicholson & S. Seidman (Eds.), *Social postmodernism: Beyond identity politics* (pp. 357–383). Cambridge: Cambridge University Press.

Barak, A. (2005). Sexual harassment on the Internet. *Social Science Computer Review*, 23(1), 77–92.

Bates, S. (2017). Revenge porn and mental health: A qualitative analysis of the mental health effects of revenge porn on female survivors. *Feminist Criminology*, 12(1), 22–42.

Benhabib, S. (Ed.). (1996). *Democracy and difference: Contesting the boundaries of the political.* Princeton University Press.

Bivens, R. (2017). The gender binary will not be deprogrammed: Ten years of coding gender on Facebook. *New Media & Society*, 19(6), 880–898.

Bonilla, Y., & Rosa, J. (2015). # Ferguson: Digital protest, hashtag ethnography, and the racial politics of social media in the United States. *American Ethnologist*, 42(1), 4–17.

Boucher, E. M., Hancock, J. T., & Dunham, P. J. (2008). Interpersonal sensitivity in computer-mediated and face-to-face conversations. *Media Psychology*, 11(2), 235–258.

Braidotti, R. (1996). Cyberfeminism with a difference. In M. Peters, M. Olssen, & C. Lankshear (Eds.), *Futures of critical theory: Dreams of difference* (pp. 239–259).

Burrows, E. (2010). Tools of resistance: The roles of two indigenous newspapers in building an indigenous public sphere. Australian *Journalism Review*, 32(2), 33.

Citron, D. K. (2009). Law's expressive value in combating cyber gender harassment. *Michigan Law Review*, 373–415.

Citron, D. K. (2014). *Hate crimes in cyberspace.* Cambridge, MA: Harvard University Press.

Clark, S. (2015). Running into trouble: Constructions of danger and risk in girls' access to outdoor space and physical activity. *Sport, Education and Society*, 20(8), 1012–1028.

Cuen, L., & Evers, J. (2016). Donald Trump fans attack Megyn Kelly with sexist slurs. *Vocativ*. Retrieved from http://www.vocativ.com/276256/donald-trump-megyn-kelly/

Daniels, J. (2009b). Rethinking cyberfeminism(s): Race, gender, and embodiment. *WSQ: Women's Studies Quarterly*, 37(1), 101–124.

Daniels, J. (2009). *Cyber racism: White supremacy online and the new attack on civil rights.* Lanham, MD: Rowman & Littlefield Publishers.

Dubrovsky, V. J., Kiesler, S., & Sethna, B. N. (1991). The equalization phenomenon: Status effects in computer-mediated and face-to-face decision-making groups. *Human-Computer Interaction*, 6(2), 119–146.

Eckert, S., & Chadha, K. (2013). Muslim bloggers in Germany: An emerging counter public. *Media, Culture & Society*, 35(8), 926–942.

Fagone, J. (2015, November). The serial swatter. New *York Times Magazine*, p. MM32.

Fairchild, K., & Rudman, L. A. (2008). Everyday stranger harassment and women's objectification. *Social Justice Research*, 21(3), 338–357.

Filipovic, J. (2007). Blogging while female: How internet misogyny parallels real-world harassment. *Yale JL & Feminism*, 19, 295.

Finn, J. (2004). A survey of online harassment at a university campus. *Journal of Interpersonal Violence*, 19(4), 468–483.

Fraser, N. (1990). Rethinking the public sphere: A contribution to the critique of actually existing democracy. *Social Text*, 25/26, 56–80.

Garde-Hansen, J., & Gorton, K. (2013). *Emotion online: Theorizing affect on the internet*. Houndmills, Basingstoke, Hampshire: Palgrave MacMillan.

Gardner, C. B. (1995). *Passing by: Gender and public harassment*. Berkeley, CA: University of California Press.

George, J. F., Easton, G. K., Nunamaker, J. F., Jr., & Northcraft, G. B. (1990). A study of collaborative group work with and without computer-based support. *Information Systems Research*, 1(4), 394–415.

Graham, R., & Smith, S. (2016). The content of our# characters black Twitter as counterpublic. *Sociology of Race and Ethnicity*, doi:2332649216639067

Gray, K. L. (2012). Intersecting oppressions and online communities: Examining the experiences of women of color in Xbox live. *Information, Communication & Society*, 15(3), 411–428.

Gray, K. L. (2014). *Race, gender, and deviance in Xbox live: Theoretical perspectives from the virtual margins*. New York, NY: Routledge.

Gregory, S. (1994). Race, identity and political activism: The shifting contours of the African American public sphere. *Public Culture*, 7(1), 147–164.

Habermas, J. ([1962] 1989). *The structural transformation of the public sphere: An inquiry into a category of Bourgeois Society*. Cambridge, MA: The MIT Press.

Haraway, D. (1987). A manifesto for cyborgs: Science, technology, and socialist feminism in the 1980s. *Australian Feminist Studies*, 2(4), 1–42.

Henry, N., & Powell, A. (2015). Embodied harms: Gender, shame, and technology-facilitated sexual violence. *Violence Against Women*, 21(6), 758–779.

Herring, S. C. (Ed.). (1996). *Computer-mediated communication: Linguistic, social, and cross-cultural perspectives* (Vol. 39). Amsterdam: John Benjamins Publishing.

Herring, S. C. (1999). The rhetorical dynamics of gender harassment on-line. *The Information Society*, 15(3), 151–167.

Herring, S. C. (2002). Computer-mediated communication on the Internet. *Annual Review of Information Science and Technology*, 36(1), 109–168.

Herring, S., Job-Sluder, K., Scheckler, R., & Barab, S. (2002). Searching for safety online: Managing 'trolling' in a feminist forum. *The Information Society*, 18(5), 371–384.

Hollander, J. A. (2001). Vulnerability and dangerousness: The construction of gender through conversation about violence. *Gender & Society*, 15(1), 83–109.

Jacobs, R. N. (2000). *Race, media, and the crisis of civil society: From Watts to Rodney King*. Cambridge, England: Cambridge University Press.

Jane, E. A. (2014a). 'Back to the kitchen, cunt': Speaking the unspeakable about online misogyny. *Continuum*, 28(4), 558–570.

Jane, E. A. (2014b). 'You're a ugly, whorish, slut' understanding E-bile. *Feminist Media Studies*, 14(4), 531–546.

Keller, J. M. (2012). Virtual feminisms: Girls' blogging communities, feminist activism, and participatory politics. *Information, Communication & Society*, 15(3), 429–447.

Kendall, L. (2002). *Hanging out in the virtual pub: Masculinities and relationships online*. Berkeley, CA: University of California Press.

Konik, J., & Cortina, L. M. (2008). Policing gender at work: Intersections of harassment based on sex and sexuality. *Social Justice Research*, 21(3), 313–337.

Korn, J. U. (2016). 'Genderless' online discourse in the 1970s: Muted group theory in early social computing. In R. Hammerman & A. L. Russell (Eds.), *Ada's legacy: Cultures of computing from the Victorian to the digital age* (pp. 213–230). New York, NY: Morgan & Claypool Publishers.

Mansbridge, J. J. (Ed.). (1990). *Beyond self-interest*. Chicago, IL: University of Chicago Press.

Martin, J. S., Vaccaro, C. A., Heckert, D. A., & Heasley, R. (2015). Epic Glory and manhood acts in fantasy role-playing Dagorhir as a case study. *The Journal of Men's Studies*, 23(3), 293–314.

McLaughlin, H., Uggen, C., & Blackstone, A. (2012). Sexual harassment, workplace authority, and the paradox of power. *American Sociological Review,* 77(4), 625–647.

McNay, L. (2004). Agency and experience: Gender as a lived relation. *The Sociological Review,* 52(2), 173–190.

Meyer, D., & Grollman, E. A. (2014). Sexual orientation and fear at night: Gender differences among sexual minorities and heterosexuals. *Journal of Homosexuality,* 61(4), 453–470.

Miller, J. (2008). *Getting played: African American girls, urban inequality, and gendered violence.* New York, NY: NYU Press.

Milner, R. M. (2013). Hacking the social: Internet memes, identity antagonism, and the logic of lulz. *Fibreculture Journal,* 22, 61–91.

Nielsen, L. B. (2009). *License to harass: Law, hierarchy, and offensive public speech.* Princeton, NJ: Princeton University Press.

Online Harassment. Pew Research Center. (2014). Retrieved April 3, 2016, from http://www.pewinternet.org/2014/10/22/online-harassment/

Phillips, W. (2015). *This is why we can't have nice things: Mapping the relationship between online trolling and mainstream culture.* Cambridge, MA: MIT Press.

Plant, S. (1997). *Zeros and ones: Digital women and the new technoculture.* New York, NY: HarperCollins.

Rapp, L., Button, D. M., Fleury-Steiner, B., & Fleury-Steiner, R. (2010). The internet as a tool for black feminist activism: Lessons from an online antirape protest. *Feminist Criminology,* 5(3), 244–262.

Reagle, J. (2012). Free as in sexist? Free culture and the gender gap. *First Monday,* 18(1), doi:10.5210/fm.v18i1.4291

Riger, S., & Gordon, M. T. (1981). The fear of rape: A study in social control. *Journal of Social Issues,* 37(4), 71–92.

Roper, E. A. (2016). Concerns for personal safety among female recreational runners. *Women in Sport and Physical Activity Journal,* 24(2), 91–98.

Schradie, J. (2011). The digital production gap: The digital divide and Web 2.0 collide. *Poetics,* 39(2), 145–168.

Shepherd, T., Harvey, A., Jordan, T., Srauy, S., & Miltner, K. (2015). Histories of hating. *Social Media + Society,* 1(2), 1–10.

Shirky, C. (2008). *Here comes everybody: The power of organizing without organizations.* New York, NY: Penguin Press.

Sills, S., Pickens, C., Beach, K., Jones, L., Calder-Dawe, O., Benton-Greig, P., & Gavey, N. (2016). Rape culture and social media: Young critics and a feminist counterpublic. *Feminist Media Studies,* 12, 1–17.

Simone, M. (2006). CODEPINK alert: Mediated citizenship in the public sphere. *Social Semiotics,* 16(2), 345–364.

Sojo, V. E., Wood, R. E., & Genat, A. E. (2016). Harmful workplace experiences and women's occupational well-being: A meta-analysis. *Psychology of Women Quarterly,* 40(1), 10–40.

Squires, C. R. (2000). Black talk radio defining community needs and identity. *The Harvard International Journal of Press/Politics,* 5(2), 73–95.

Turkle, S. (1984). *The second self: Computers and the human spirit.* Cambridge, MA: MIT Press.

Valentine, G. (1989). The geography of women's fear. *Area,* 4, 385–390.

Van Doorn, N. (2011). Digital spaces, material traces: How matter comes to matter in online performances of gender, sexuality and embodiment. *Media, Culture & Society,* 33(4), 531–547.

Wajcman, J. (2004). *Technofeminism.* Cambridge, UK: Polity Press.

Wajcman, J. (2010). Feminist theories of technology. *Cambridge Journal of Economics,* 34, 143–152.

Wallace, A. (2014, January 19). Life as a female journalist: Hot or not? *New York Times,* p. A17.

Welsh, S. (1999). Gender and sexual harassment. *Annual Review of Sociology,* 25(1), 169–190.

Wesely, J. K., & Gaarder, E. (2004). The gendered 'nature' of the urban outdoors: Women negotiating fear of violence. *Gender & Society,* 18(5), 645–663.

Williams, C. L., Giuffre, P. A., & Dellinger, K. (1999). Sexuality in the workplace: Organizational control, sexual harassment, and the pursuit of pleasure. *Annual Review of Sociology,* 25(1), 73–93.

Young, I. M. (2002). *Inclusion and democracy.* Oxford, UK: Oxford University Press.

CHAPTER 10

#TheFappening

Virtual Manhood Acts in (Homo)Social Media

Mairead Eastin Moloney and Tony P. Love

On August 31, 2014, a flood of nude photos emerged from the dimly lit corners of the Internet. These photos had two things in common: (1) they were stolen from private, password-protected accounts and personal devices and (2) with rare exception, they were images of white, heterosexual female celebrities. Over 100 individuals, including actors, models, and athletes—many with A-list name recognition—were targeted (Buchanan 2014). Within hours, the photo leak was dubbed "The Fappening," a combination of "fapping" (slang term for male masturbation) and "The Happening."

Although originally posted on the online message board 4chan, the photos quickly spread to countless other websites. On Twitter, an online social networking service that allows participants to read and post 140-character "tweets," reaction was swift and mostly enthusiastic. One user wrote, "This is the greatest day of the Internet." Others declared The Fappening an historical event: "August 31st 2014, or as it will be known in the history books, The Fappening." Many made their specific interest in the photos unambiguous (e.g., "Eat, sleep, fap, repeat #thefappening"). With rapidity only possible in the Internet Age, Twitter became clogged with Fappening-related jokes, commentary, and memes. The common denominator among Fappening fans? Their use of manhood acts to signal a masculine persona (MP).

While some see The Fappening as an iCloud security breach with a juvenile name, we argue that it is a timely case study in modern manhood acts. This article contributes to our understanding of the homosocial reproduction of manhood and its linkages to the oppression of women. While important research has examined ways men signal a masculine self through face-to-face interactions (Connell and Messerschmidt 2005; Eastman 2011; Ezzell 2012; Kehily and Nayak 1997), our work analyzes interactions that occur online and are typically faceless. As we demonstrate, individuals modify in-person manhood acts to convey MPs via *virtual manhood acts*. We assert that these symbolic selves are intimately linked to patriarchal hierarchies of power (Connell 2005; Johnson 2014).

Using an interactionist perspective (Berger and Luckmann 1966; Blumer 1969), we analyze publicly available data from Twitter to track real-time reactions from individuals participating in or commenting on The Fappening. Broadly speaking, these data provide insights into an array of gendered norms. However, the interactionist framework enables us to hone in on how manhood acts—like all facets of gender—are performative cues intended to convey a particular definition of self. Unlike all gender performance, however, manhood acts oppress women and thus "do" dominance (Schrock and Schwalbe 2009; Schwalbe 2014). In addition to expanding the literature on men and masculinity(ies), our data contribute to emergent understandings of manhood acts performed in virtual social spaces. We ask: "Related to The Fappening, what manhood acts are employed in virtual social space?"

SOURCE: Moloney, M. E., and Love, T. P. (2017). #TheFappening: Virtual Manhood Acts in (Homo)Social Media. *Men and Masculinities*. doi:10.1177/1097184X17696170. Reproduced with permission.

Masculinity and Manhood Acts

Gendered selves are "imagined qualit[ies] of character imputed to individuals based on their expressive behavior" (Schwalbe 2014, 49). "Doing gender" is a dramaturgical achievement (Goffman 1977; West and Zimmerman 1987) that often depends on physical characteristics (diffuse characteristics) or props that are readily observable, but behavioral characteristics are also important cues (Schrock and Schwalbe 2009). Typically, one does not attempt to prove possession of a male or female body through the display of anatomical features. Rather, one "acts like a man" or "acts like a woman" via preset social scripts (Kivel 1984). Because we live in patriarchy, the configuration of practice understood as "masculinity" offers the preferred and more powerful gendered script (Johnson 2014).

Masculinity does not exist in a singular form and has multiple definitions (Bridges and Pascoe 2014; Connell and Messerschmidt 2005; Messner 1990; Schrock and Schwalbe 2009; West and Zimmerman 1987). Previous definitions, wherein masculinity is any action performed by a male body, are too broad to be meaningful (Ezzell 2016). Schrock and Schwalbe (2009) have called for scholars to shift their analytic focus from masculinity to manhood acts. Manhood acts are cultural practices or individual actions—performed by men—that signify a masculine self, distinguish males from females, signal control, and *advantage men at the expense of women* (Schrock and Schwalbe 2009, 278). Manhood acts align with the interactionist understanding of gender as action, not an inherent characteristic of individuals (Ezzell 2016; West and Zimmerman 1987). These acts may be carried out individually but, since it is men who control the status of other men, they are typically homosocial and collaborative in nature (Flood 2008).

Utilizing this configuration of practices ensures the superiority of men within the gender order and allows men to strive for manhood status, a subjective yet desirable social value (Schwalbe 2014, 31). Analyzing manhood acts addresses the "Why should we care?" question of gendered practice generally and masculine practice in particular. Manhood acts deserve greater scrutiny not just for the way they imbue *difference* but for the way they create *inequality* (Ezzell 2016; Johnson 2014; Schrock and Schwalbe 2009).

Men may signal a masculine self via a variety of strategies including aggression, emotional control, and reification of sexist and heterosexist ideals (Kivel 1984; Pascoe 2007). These actions take on additional significance for men who do not meet hegemonic ideals (e.g., minority, gay, poor). Marginalized men leverage these actions as "compensatory" manhood acts (see Eastman 2011; Ezzell 2012; Sumerau 2012).

A commonality of previously studied manhood acts is their *embodied nature.* For instance, young boys learn that both the physical act of fighting and suppression of emotional reaction to injury are demonstrations of masculine selves (Morris 2012). In Southern male "rebel" culture, manhood acts are embodied by an explosive mixture of drunkenness and violent aggression (Eastman 2011). Men who are impeded from physical violence may signal their willingness to fight via verbal aggression and confrontation (Ezzell 2012). Connell (2005) speaks of the body as a site around which various masculine tensions are managed. In this view, the body is not only an object of, but also an agent in, the creation of the social structures responsible for the definitions, categorizations, and expectations that we place on them. He calls this recursive pattern "body-reflexive practices."

Body-reflexive practices are the avenues through which the body becomes a participant in social interaction as it generates and shapes "courses of social conduct" (Connell 2005, 60). For example, the classic insult, "You throw like a girl," includes not only symbolic gender stereotypes but also a concrete observation of a real body and an evaluation of how the body should move in association with these stereotypes. Gender is vulnerable when bodily performance cannot be sustained. In online social spaces, the body is absent and the recursive loop is broken. Thus, it is necessary to construct a virtual reflexive site and attempt to make the body "visible" online (Boero and Pascoe 2012). Although we might expect references to the body to be at once more prevalent and explicit in online masculine performances, data on manhood acts in virtual space are relatively rare (for exceptions, see Garcia-Favaro and Gill 2016; Jane 2014; Massanari 2015).

To address this literature gap, we ask: "Related to The Fappening, what manhood acts are employed in virtual social space?" We identify four virtual manhood acts commonly employed to signify elevated membership in the heterosexist hierarchy. These acts include (1) creation of homosocial, heterosexist space; (2) sexualization of women; (3) signaling possession of a heterosexual, male body; and (4) humor as a tool of oppression. From a strictly interactionist perspective, all actors engaging in manhood acts are "men" and all masculine selves are essentially virtual (Schrock and Schwalbe 2009). However, online actors may find it easier to convincingly "be a man" and claim the benefits of this status within the liminal space of virtual interactions. Thus, we introduce the term masculine persona (MP) to underscore the performative nature of this gender-identity claim in the specific context of online social spaces.

We also emphasize that manhood acts performed by MPs are intimately linked with the reproduction of gender inequality. For instance, the creation of homosocial, heterosexist space—wherein men perform manhood acts for the gaze of other men—serves to reproduce "structures of inequality *within* as well as *across* the socially constructed gender divide between men and women" (Grazian 2007, 224). Sexualization strips women of any worth beyond sexual desirability and is thus also used as a means for men to (re-) assert their dominance, heterosexual power, and/or sexual competence (Flood 2008; Grazian 2007). Male bodies generally, and heterosexual male bodies in particular, are socially structured as normative and dominant (Johnson 2014; Pascoe 2007). Laying claim to such a body—even if it cannot be visually confirmed—signals power and control. Finally, while humor has many functions in interpersonal interactions, it may be used in gendered interactions to subordinate others or reify existing social stratification (Martineau 1972).

Gender, Virtual Spaces, and Power

Living in patriarchy means that women in "real life" are routinely dismissed, silenced, harassed, threatened, beaten, raped, and murdered (Johnson 2014). Virtual social spaces, in theory, encourage more egalitarian and less gendered interactions (Bartlett et al. 2014). But a growing body of research finds that gendered power differentials are not merely replicated online, they are magnified (Henry and Powell 2015; Filipovic 2007; Shaw 2014). Anonymity and the real or perceived lack of consequences—"the online disinhibition effect"—(Suler in Thompson 2016) appears to fuel virtual gendered violence (Massanari 2015; Penny 2013). Misogyny and violence range from subtle (sexting) to overt (online threats of rape or murder directed at women perceived as "feminist") (Garcia-Favaro and Gill 2016; Jane 2014).

On Twitter, misogyny is alive and well, even if limited to 140 characters or less (Cole 2015). One study found that between December 2013 and February 2014, about 2.7 million English-language tweets used the word "rape"; over six million tweets used the words "slut" or "whore" (Bartlett et al. 2014). More than half the time, these tweets were misogynistic, abusive, or related to pornography (Bartlett et al. 2014). In an effort to push back against this misogyny, gender-relevant hash-tags have emerged and are often used to expose gendered violence or create a space for solidarity (Berridge and Portwood-Stacer 2015; Eagle 2015; Rentschler 2015). Still, "gendertrolling"—the use of specific, and often explicit, gender-based insults and threats—is prevalent (Mantilla 2013).

While it is tempting to target technology as a source of misogyny, we assert that technology is merely an enabling tool. To understand online misogyny is to shed light on deeply embedded gendered norms and societal power dynamics. To that end, we begin the process of analyzing virtual manhood acts that systematically disempower women and reify the hegemony of men (Hearn 2004).

This article answers Schrock and Schwalbe's (2009, 289–90) call to document and examine "how males use the interaction order collaboratively to construct manhood acts, how they police and support each other's acts, and how they create and share the material and symbolic resources that enable various kinds of manhood acts." In the following pages, we demonstrate that a variety of virtual manhood acts are employed to maintain the heterosexist hierarchy. Although Twitter may be anonymous in nature, the tweets we highlight use unambiguous textual and visual strategies to signal manhood status.

Data and Methods

Twitter.com is a social media website geared toward communication. Through the website and its various other forms (i.e., mobile apps), Twitter users can create, share, and engage in discussion 140 characters at a time using text, pictures, and web links. An estimated 23 percent of all online adults and 20 percent of the entire United States adult population used Twitter in September 2014, the time frame of our analyses. Of the Internet users in the United States, approximately 25 percent of men and 21 percent of women interact with Twitter. Of Internet users who use Twitter about 20 percent are white non-Hispanic, 28 percent are black non-Hispanic, and 28 percent are Hispanic. The majority of Twitter users are 18–49 years of age and live in urban or suburban areas. Of Twitter users, 38 percent report using Twitter daily, 21 percent weekly, and 44 percent less often than weekly. In comparison, 71 percent of Facebook users reported engaging with Facebook daily (Duggan 2015).

As an online social space, Twitter possesses its own culture, including its own language conventions (Zhang et al. 2011). Examples include "tweet" (a block of text no longer than 140 characters), "RT" (indicating that a user has repeated or "retweeted" a previous tweet), and "#" ("hashtag", used to organize tweets according to topics (e.g., #fappening)). Additionally, symbols called "emoticons" or "emojis" are frequently used to convey feelings or emotions.

Using Twitter provides a unique opportunity to engage in textual ways of knowing that is highly dependent on the constantly shifting stream of twenty-four-hour media and access to shared digital knowledge. Sociologically, it provides a useful, if currently underutilized, tool in capturing public opinion on current events, as it occurs in "real time." Using Twitter for research also avoids a host of problems that plague traditional social science research, including recruitment, social acceptability bias, and recall bias (Miller and Duffy 2014). Tweets are digitally archived by the United States Library of Congress and widely considered to be a publicly available data source (Zimmer and Proferes 2014). Additionally, passive information gathering, or data mining, involves no interaction or intervention with individuals. Our university Institutional Review Board waived the approval requirement.

We identified The Fappening as an event that could provide a rich data set of gendered performance in virtual space. Using search terms for "fappening" or "#thefappening", we collected tweet data from Topsy.com, a web service that archives all tweets since 2006. We analyzed data over a thirty-day period from 12 a.m. August 31, 2014, to 12 a.m. October 1, 2014, using automated web scraping techniques. Web scraping (web harvesting or web data extraction) is the process of implementing software to examine a webpage and catalog data. We employed Web Scraper, an extension for Google's Chrome browser. The scraper software deciphers cues from the user to pinpoint locations in the source code from which to extract text and catalog the selection in a database file.

We attempted to collect 100 tweets per hour for our target period; in some instances, 100 unique tweets were not present. In this case, all tweets during that hour were included in our study population. In other instances, the 100 tweets represent a sample of all existing tweets. Although there was potential to collect 2,400 tweets per day, we averaged approximately 1,700 tweets each day, with a maximum of 2,400 and a minimum of 592.

. . . [W]e chose to analyze a subsample of fifteen days within the month. We analyzed 50 percent of the tweets from the day of the leak, August 31, and September 1, 2, 3, 4, 6, 7, 8, 11, 14, 21, 22, 23, 26, and 30 (*N* = 9,750). The first author reviewed preliminary data from August 31 and September 7 to construct a first-pass code list. Both authors then fully coded a subsample of days (August 31, September 7, and September 14) for the purposes of code reconciliation as well as to generate and reconcile emergent codes. A total of ninety-two codes were created, and the authors used this full code list to code the days selected for this analysis.

To aid in coding, memo writing, and analysis, we used NVivo 10 (2012) software. NVivo allowed us to create and utilize a mixture of researcher-designated codes (e.g., codes linked to the sexualization definition) as well as code "in vivo" wherein codes are created directly from the text. We shared coding and produced reports that illuminated complex thematic connections.

In addition to coding tweet text, we followed many of the links embedded in tweets and coded those containing Fappening-related content. Some links appeared to be piggybacking off the popularity of #thefappening and used the hashtag as clickbait to sell products or pornography. The content of these links was not directly Fappening related and in an effort to focus our analytic efforts, we did not follow these links.

Analyses were informed by grounded theory, and we used a multistage coding process (Strauss and Corbin 1998) that is both deductive and inductive. This method allowed us to focus our analytic gaze on gender performance while still remaining open to tangential and emergent themes (Charmaz 2014). Of the ninety-two codes that emerged, most related to the performance of manhood. In the following pages, we explicate the four most commonly utilized manhood acts and use specific tweet examples to connect individual sentiments to the large-scale creation of a hetero-sexist, homosocial virtual space. Our qualitative findings are not intended to be generalizable to the population at large, but these data do not need to be statistically generalizable for us to draw inferences about gendered inequality and its reproduction in online social spaces (Charmaz 2014).

Virtual Manhood Acts

We analyze how individuals signaled a MP as they commented on or participated in The Fappening, thus signifying masculine selves without benefit of the most obvious marker of manhood—a physical body. Rather than provide numerous example quotes, we present excerpts that exemplify common strategies intended to lay claim to manhood status. Interactions within this online social space were structured to welcome "real men" and leave women or gay men feeling rejected or uncomfortable. MPs also signaled their masculine selves through tweets connoting a heterosexual male body; explicitly carnal imagery and words were frequently utilized. To emphasize their sexual potency and distance themselves from the feminine, MPs sexualized the Fappening victims and other women. Finally, humor was used to trivialize the degradation and exploitation of women. Viewed separately, each act signals a claim to manhood status and the accompanying power and privileges. Taken together, these virtual acts affirmed privileges of manhood while oppressing and debasing women.

Creating a Homosocial, Heterosexist Space

MPs signified that The Fappening was a celebratory event controlled by and created for heterosexual men. A successful homosocial space conforms to gendered performance expectations. Participants must avoid any hint of femininity (i.e., weakness) by adhering to the scripts of misogyny and homophobia (Kimmel 2008; Schrock and Schwalbe 2009). By keeping girls and gays out, "real" men can successfully police manhood acts and ensure that dominant ideals about male superiority and female inferiority are preserved. In other words, the creation of a "boys only" space is just as much about keeping women (down and) *out* as it is keeping men *in* (and in line).

In Fappening-related tweets, MPs used hashtags #fappening and #thefappening to signal group identity. Text and images accompanying the hashtag displayed a world-view that was male- and hetero-centric. Much like men and boys in face-to-face interactions (see Kimmel 2008; Pascoe 2007), MPs used gendered language, signaled in-group status, and reacted negatively to the smattering of nonfemale nudes. Early tweeters shouted from the virtual rooftops, urging all men to check out The Fappening. Male identifiers, including "lads," "bruh," and "guy(s)," were commonly employed. Using noninclusive language helped underscore that The Fappening was created for, and intended to benefit, only heterosexual men. Gendered language served as the virtual equivalent of a "Boys Only!" sign on a teenager's door.

One participant wrote: "If you're a guy, Google the Fappening RIGHT NOW. You're welcome." Proclaimed another: "Fellow guys!!! Check it out! The fappening is happening! Enjoy and thank me later! reddit.com/r/TheFappening . . ." Said a third: "Lads in case you didn't know. Remember this day. THEFAPPENING 2014."

The Fappening, moreover, was associated with real manhood ("August 31st 2014 a day no red blooded male will ever forget thank god for the Internet #TheFappening!") and posited as a "victory" for men ("The day men won the Internet. Never forget 8/31/2014. #TheFappening"). MPs not only reified hegemonic ideals of real men but reminded participants that in patriarchy men are the representative of all people (Johnson 2014). For example, "The fappening . . . still gives me hope in mankind." Since men are central to patriarchy's narrative, it follows that "the world" would be "uplifted" by stolen female nudes: "With all the bad news (wars, terrorists), we have to admit that #thefappening has uplifted the morale of the world #jenniferlawerence."

Many tweets signaled participation in the viewing and/or collection of hacked photos. We coded these quotes "participation ribbon" to underscore that these proclamations were a form of identity work rooted in virtual interaction. By asserting heterosexual desire for nude female images, these MPs established "a sort of baseline masculinity" (Pascoe 2007, 87). Participation ranged from gawping decrees ("I SAW EVERYTHING #TheFappening") to indicating shared experience ("So how many people here still haven't slept. #TheFappening"). Others demonstrated "Fear of Missing Out or FOMO": "Yup, bringing my laptop while reviewing. Can't miss #TheFappening."

In order to underscore the homosocial nature of The Fappening, some MPs name-checked specific friends. Said one: "So @[redacted] sent me a glorious compilation of nudes from #TheFappening phenomenon. Good job! Hahaha. Aaaand goodnight!" Others offered to share their links: "A good friend has just sent me the Fappening. Posting the link in the chat in my hitbox.tv/[redacted]." Another wrote simply, "Lemme know if you wanna see those leaked nudes. #thefappening."

An unsettling theme that emerged was curating behavior, or "women as collectible objects." Objectification is key to dominant-subordinate relationships inherent in patriarchy, as it strips women of personhood and creates critical cognitive and emotional distance (Johnson 2014). One MP wrote, "#TheFappening is the new Pokemon game #Gottacatchemall." Another wondered: "Anyone else having trouble keeping track of the updates to #TheFappening? I want to have a complete set, like Flintstones jelly jars." Some MPs bragged about their "collections." For instance, "@[Name Redacted] I have them all now mate #TheFappening."

MPs also engaged in gendered identity work by loudly rejecting the (very rare) inclusion of male bodies. Justin Verlander, an athlete, was featured in a handful of the hacked nudes though his girlfriend, model Kate Upton, was the clear target. Said one MP: "All I've learned from #TheFappening is that Justin Verlander's dick sucks." Another complained: "I'm having nightmares about Kate Upton's Fappening pictures." Others took the opportunity to make fun of Mr. Verlander. For example, "Saw Verlander on TV. Laughed for 90 seconds. #TheFappening" and "Justin Verlander has just passed Donald Sutherland as the Most Awkward Naked Man on Film Ever."

MPs also used the "fag discourse" (see Pascoe 2007) to affirm their heterosexuality. Responding to a tweet suggesting that the hacker should share his nudes, one MP huffed, "Hahaha Jennifer Lawrence on why no dude selfies. Come on the Hacker was a dude. Would be rather gay for him to post male #TheFappening."[1] *Non*participation in the Fappening was seen as clear evidence of homosexuality. For instance, "You know you're gay when you stayed limp during the Fappening."

In sum, MPs created a homosocial, heterosexist space by broadcasting the events of The Fappening to the public at large as well as targeted others. The homosocial nature of the event is underscored by the willingness of veteran photo collectors to lend a helping hand to others seeking to secure the pictures. Other MPs received these messages and reproduced them. Although we acknowledge that Fappening-related tweets were not exclusive to MPs, they set the tone and enacted strict boundary maintenance of gendered norms. Images of female bodies were curated and objectified while images of male bodies were eschewed, as exemplified by the strong negative sanctions against a single nude male body (Justin Verlander) and utilization of the "fag" discourse. These broadcasting, organizing, and excluding behaviors simultaneously increased awareness of the existence of the nude photo leak and set the expectations for the tenor of the conversation. MPs posited this predatory event as a celebration and victory created by, and intended for, heterosexual men only. Regardless of motive (e.g., fear of being left out, excited by the opportunity to participate, etc.), these collective actions and interactions served to create a collaborative, homosocial event that reified and normalized a cyber-sex crime.

Signifying Possession of a Heterosexual Male Body

As noted, a unique feature of this study is the anonymous and disembodied nature of the participants. While it could be argued that these features are a limitation of our data set, we assert that the *claiming* of a masculine self, done thousands of time post-Fappening, is more interesting and important than whether or not the participant's sex matches their gender performance. While it's true that virtual spaces pose obvious challenges to "proving" one's manhood, MPs found unambiguous ways to signify a masculine self and suggest possession of a heterosexual male body. We assert that the emphasis on the body is no accident and in fact aligns with recent observations that the modern male body is portrayed as significantly larger and more aggressive compared to previous generations (Earp and Katz 1999). Some propose that increased emphasis on male physique is a reaction to the "crisis of masculinity" wherein men are increasingly challenged by women for roles in educational, social, and occupational spaces (Earp and Katz 1999; Vaccaro 2011).

Lacking the ability to give off the impression of a male body via diffuse status characteristics or physical performances, MPs made explicit references to male anatomy and/or signaled participation in activities that require a male body. The most common ways of signaling possession of a heterosexual male body were masturbatory comments, jokes, and images. Some tweets were the virtual version of a sly wink ("Big night for Kleenez [sic] and Jergens last night/this morning."). But many MPs used unambiguous slang terms (e.g., "cumming," or "jizzing" and "fapping"[2]) to describe their highly sexualized response to The Fappening. One MP stated, "I had a very busy weekend of fappin to J. Lawrence and Kate Uptons nudes." The following comments were frequently retweeted: "#The-Fappening all these photo leaks have caused me to leak something as well . . . my jism!" and, "Wat's fappening? A lot of ppl right now—omg I feel so bad for Jennifer Lawrence!! fap-fap-fap." These latter tweets signal more than mere sexual desire, they naturalize the assumption that men are incapable of exercising sexual self-control—an assumption central to rape culture. Many tweets reified this assumption. For instance: "A healthy reminder to those closely monitoring #TheFappening: please stay hydrated, pervs," "Day 2 of #TheFappening prepare your lotion and clear your schedules we don't know I [sic] who is next," "RIP the hands of my fellow men," and "We have now reached a new time era where no male hand is safe."

These public proclamations of masturbation are examples of "compulsive heterosexuality" wherein men engage in public displays of heterosexuality, demonstrate their ability to "work their will upon the world around them," and align their personas with dominant practices typically coded as masculine (Pascoe 2007, 86). As Pascoe explains, actions stemming from compulsive heterosexuality both "are and are not" about sex (2007, 85); at their core, these acts are about power. In addition to textual displays of dominance, MPs frequently posted and retweeted masturbatory images or "memes." Perhaps the most retweeted image during our period of analysis is a cartoon image of Glenn Quagmire, a character from the adult cartoon "Family Guy."

In this still, Glenn stands on his front stoop, unshaven and wearing pajamas, his left arm huge and muscular, and his right arm thin and limp. The implication is that Glenn has been copiously masturbating with the noticeably larger arm. Commentary accompanying this image was typically along the lines of "Me, after the Fappening." Or, "Guys, after the Fappening." Another commonly retweeted link takes the viewer to an animated meme. In this looping image, a shovel is seen scooping up a mass of sticky white substance from a bathroom floor. It is simply captioned, "The Fappening Aftermath." Although intended to be a source of humor (more on that later), what these images actually portray is a world that is ruled by sexually voracious men who feel entitled to use the criminally acquired images of women for their sexual self-pleasure.

Although masculine practices are not confined to actors with male bodies, a penis may be viewed as a "semiotic asset" (Schwalbe 2014, 55). Further, "[b]odies are the vehicles though which we express gendered selves; they are also the matter through which social norms are made concrete" (Pascoe 2007, 12). Notably, Fappening participants blurred the lines between "front stage" and "backstage" behaviors (Goffman 1959) and demonstrated evolving conceptions of what it means to "own" a male body. Nineteenth- and early twentieth-century conceptualizations of masturbation as "self-abuse" linked the act to disease, insanity, and the degradation of the era's "true" masculine ethos (Hall 1992). As Hall writes, "'real men' had sexual urges . . . a true man was able to control these" (1992, 375). The pendulum has swung; signaling a *lack* of self-control and *use of/control over* women's bodies is central to conveying a heterosexual, male body in 21st century cyberspace.

Sexualization of Women

Related to, but distinct from, the manhood act of signaling a heterosexual male body is the process of sexualization. Sexualization is a multifaceted process occurring when an individual's value and worth come solely from his or her sexual appeal; one is objectified or regarded as an item for another's sexual use; an individual is held to a narrow standard that equates attractiveness with sexiness; or sexuality is inappropriately imposed upon an individual (APA Task Force 2010). By reducing women to sexual objects, MPs implied sexual potency, differentiated themselves from the feminine, and signaled domination over women. Sexualization was evident in tweets that signaled narrow standards for appearance, objectification, sexual appeal as victim's sole worth, imposition of sexuality, and entitlement to women's bodies.

The underlying message of sexualization is: "You're not good enough" (Moloney and Pelehach 2014). Women are informed, early, often, and in myriad ways, that their appearance should mirror a particular, difficult-to-achieve set of cultural expectations. These unrealistic expectations are based on dominant racist, classist, and ageist views (APA Task Force 2010). Despite the fact that many of The Fappening victims serve as the literal embodiment of our cultural standards of beauty (youthful, light-skinned, thin-yet-curvy, blonde, etc.), MPs on Twitter routinely critiqued their appearance. For instance, commenting on Oscar winner and frequent magazine cover girl Jennifer Lawrence, one MP scoffed: "There are literally dozens of porn stars who are hotter than Jennifer Lawrence. #TheFappening is overrated." Another MP wrote, referring to one of the world's top models, "Kate Upton has a weird ass body #lol #TheFappening." Tweeters were also quick to hone in on specific physical features that didn't meet their standards. Wrote one: "Who's this bitch with the saggy boobs who keeps popping up? Put them away!" Said another, "Kim Kardashian got those DINNER PLATES for nipples." The manifest function of these tweets is to critique the appearance of these women, but the latent function harkens to the central purpose of manhood acts—enacting control and domination over women and women's bodies (Johnson 2014).

In addition to imposing incredibly narrow aesthetic standards, sexualization strips women of their intellect, autonomy, and achievements. What's left is a "thing" meant for others' sexual use (APA Task Force 2010). This reductionist process was evident in many MP comments; high-achieving women were portrayed as objects to be consumed without consent. For instance, "I'd beat it so hard to a @DanicaPatrick sex tape. Why couldn't she have been leaked on #TheFappening?" Other commenters reduced women even further, to just body parts, including "boobs," "booties," and "titties" (e.g., "So many boobs 👀"). One enthusiastic pornography site hash-tagged a string of objectifications in an attempt to lure clicks, "#Nude #Naked #Girls #Pictures #Pussy #Ass #Boobs #datass #Leaked #Celebrity #TheFappening."

MPs also imposed their sexual desires on the Fappening victims; some depicted imagery wherein they had full access to these women's bodies and imagined themselves in intimate acts. For instance, "Everytime I see that Jennifer Lawrence all I can picture is a dirty sket covered in Jizz 😂." MPs also underscored that the sole worth of these women came from their sexual appeal. One MP said: "If anything i hope #TheFappening shows pop stars and actresses how much more money and fame they could be getting by simply doing porn." Another suggested: "Just own it, and be graceful. Ask us how we liked [the pictures], and then release more on your own." Incredibly, one MP wrote: "Maybe if these bitches would have shown their tits two weeks ago Robin Williams wouldn't have killed himself." These tweets exemplify masculine social norms where men are "encouraged to bond around a common view of women as objects to be competed for, possessed and used" (Johnson 2014, 56).

In addition to implying that women are only good for sexual titillation and service, MPs demonstrated a sense of entitlement to these illegally gained images. MPs voiced threats ("the fappening better still be happening."), demands ("Show us the photos we want to see"; "LET THE FAPPENING COMMENCE"; "LET THE FAPPENING RESUME!!!!!!"), and an appetite for even more graphic material ("U have to go to the next level, the street wants sextapes"; "It's horrible to say but . . . I hope there's more . . . and videos too"; "Keeping my fingers crossed for more #Selena-Gomez and #ArianaGrande #TheFappening oh and #kateupton vids too"). The connection between these stolen, private images and MPs appetite for pornography was made explicit by one Tweeter: "yeah, the fappening is great and all but the more I look at these pics of the women I've fantasized about the more I wanna watch real porn." While this is not the place to engage in a thorough discussion of pornography, it is noteworthy that most, if not all, of these commenters were mere clicks away from real porn. So, what was it about The Fappening victims that served to "break the Internet"?

We argue that these tweets reveal less about sexual desire and more about the ability to exercise dominance over women's bodies (Pascoe 2007, 85-86). In this case, MPs found it exciting or rewarding to figuratively dominate bodies of women who had achieved power in an otherwise male-dominated society. These accomplished women—actors, athletes, and musicians—were reduced to objects, good only for sexual consumption. Further, MPs signaled domination by asserting that women's worth lay solely in their sexual appeal while simultaneously imposing impossible aesthetic standards. Finally, they demonstrated a deeply embedded sense of entitlement to the use of these stolen images for their sexual pleasure. As one participant rejoiced, "Not even apple's new IOS8 can save these celebrities from The Fappening. 🙌"

Humor as a Tool of Oppression

A common theme throughout these data, and in other studies of masculine performance, is the presence of humor. Humor permeates male subjects' recollections of sexual encounters in Connell's (2005) foundational work. It is interwoven into the ethnographic accounts and interviews in Pascoe's

(2007) study of sexuality in high school and Kimmel's (2008) study of men negotiating young adulthood. Humor is a staple of masculine performance.

Humor typically acts in two ways to aid oppression: (1) as a smokescreen for oppressive discourse and (2) as a neutralization technique for discordant self-evaluations. As to the former, humor can be a "very effective way of 'doing power' less explicitly" (Holmes 2000, 165). In the case of gendered interactions, humorous speech is often a vehicle for misogynistic messages establishing males as privileged and powerful in the heterosexual hierarchy (Kehily and Nayak 1997). Masculine comic displays are sometimes used to "blur the boundaries between humor and harassment" (Kehily and Nayak 1997, 81). Furthermore, humorous insults can be employed not only to affect the individual target of the discourse but serve the larger purpose of boundary maintenance and social control.

Fappening-related humor had two primary aims: to claim a masculine self and to trivialize the exploitation and oppression of women. In terms of claiming masculine status, humor was often used when signifying a male, heterosexual body. For instance, "The fappening is a real hard time for us all" reifies the universality of the male body and makes an erection-related double entendre. The tweet "that's one small step for a man, a giant leap for all of us wankers!:-)," accomplishes multiple tasks. It establishes the tweeter as having a male body, one specifically used to masturbate to the images of women. It also suggests the tweeter is a member of the "in" group. Other tweets also underscore what a "gift" The Fappening was to the in-group (e.g., "The Fappening. Proof that god exists and he loves us"). Masculine performance was linked to the trope of the sexually insatiable man. Even the president of the United States was jokingly presumed, via his male status, to be participating in The Fappening: "@BarackObama u making a statement about #TheFappening nude celeb photo leak or are you still jackin?"

Humor is not used only as a cover for direct assaults. Humor aids oppression when it serves as a neutralization tool that partially absolves an oppressor from conflicted feelings or sympathy for the oppression target. This is similar to the way that Goffman views humor and its relation to role distance (Coser 1966). Examples of this distancing are rife throughout these data. Most commenters expressed that they found the whole event "hilarious" (e.g., "Lol this whole fappening thing is mad fuckin funny"). Others managed to downplay the ways in which The Fappening was a violation. For instance, "The funniest comment I read on Jennifer Lawrence's leaked nudes is, 'I bet her breasts taste like love & understanding.'" While this tweet is actually describing an incredibly invasive and sexually aggressive act, the MP pitches it as "funny."

Other examples of humor use frequently invoked ambivalence. For instance, "On one hand, it's a huge violation of privacy. On the other . . . well, the other hand is busy." And, "I feel bad for these women! (I keep looking) What kinda guy does this? (I keep looking) I feel creepy. #iKeepLooking #TheFappening." Waffling between aggression and remorse allowed these MPs to ignore their heterosexist actions and create distance between themselves and the hacking victims. Sarcasm was also used to demonstrate lack of empathy (e.g., "Check out all these celebrities, thinking they're people. #TheFappening").

In sum, many MPs used humor to claim masculine status, in turn oppressing women and reifying existing gendered inequalities. Humor in this context serves not just to reify power differentials between men and women but to *trivialize* the negative, aggressive, and degrading harms done *by* men *to* women. Although comic displays were primarily intended to gain group acceptance, they had a secondary purpose: to enable users to inhabit a liminal space between innocence and aggression. Within this liminal space, MPs were excused from having to take responsibility for their oppressive actions. They could claim every bully's favorite retort: "It was just a joke. Grow thicker skin." Thus, humor may be used as a technique to shift the responsibility back on women to be "good" objects, to submit to the male gaze, and to keep any negative responses to themselves.

Discussion

Through the qualitative coding of Fappening-related tweets, we studied the creation and maintenance of a homosocial heterosexist virtual space. Within this space, MPs engaged in virtual manhood acts that signified their masculine selves, reified current gender hierarchies, and oppressed out-group members. In addition to the creation of a homosocial, heterosexist space, specific virtual manhood acts included the sexualization of women, signaling possession of a heterosexual, male body and using humor as a tool of oppression.

As previously stated, all manhood acts are, in essence, virtual (Schrock and Schwalbe 2009). Manhood acts are meant to create and support an abstract definition of self (or "front" to use Goffman's term) around which others organize their reactions and reflect appraisals congruent with an MP (Pascoe 2007). This characteristic of manhood acts (and other social acts) lends support to the viewpoint that distinctions between real world and virtual scenarios are blurred, overlapping, and possibly unhelpful. After all, even if these aggressively masculine tweets come from people who would never act this way face-to-face, the enforcement of gender inequality remains impactful. In short, manhood acts performed online *or* face-to-face reproduce gender inequality.

Like all research, our study has noteworthy limitations. Our search terms (fappening and #thefappening) were the most appropriate choices to ensure that tweet text procured was directly relevant to The Fappening. Related search terms like "Jennifer Lawrence" and "hacking" also returned thousands of tweets, but we quickly realized that much of the text was unrelated to The Fappening. Still, limiting our terms narrowed the breadth of tweets available for analysis and likely skewed our results toward tweeters who were somewhat in favor of The Fappening. Conversely, this limitation may also be viewed as a strength, given that the term and hashtag were used to aid in carving out a homosocial, heterosexist space in which we could more readily observe these virtual manhood acts.

Despite its limitations, our research serves as a timely case study in the execution of modern manhood. Building on the interactionist perspective, we demonstrate how gender is both a performance and a master status that belies the presence of a visual sex category (West and Zimmerman 1987; Ridgeway 2011). We introduce the concept of virtual manhood acts and identify four specific manhood acts used to claim membership in the heterosexist hierarchy and reproduce gendered inequality. These data demonstrate the ways in which homosocial space, collective action, and gender identity intersect to reify power hierarchies. It also builds on sexualization literatures by specifically connecting masculine norms to the sexualization process. Further, it highlights major shifts in the conceptualization and utility of the male body. In addition, it builds on previous work that demonstrates the use of humor in constructing and reinforcing heterosexist hierarchies. In our study, humor served not only as a masculine signal but as a tool to actively trivialize the oppression and exploitation of women. We also expand beyond the ethnographic studies that have thus far typified research on manhood acts. While ethnography is an important method that provides rich, nuanced insights, Twitter is a novel social space and largely untapped data source that may be used to capture reaction to social phenomenon occurring in real time.

Virtual manhood acts are noteworthy in their ability to overcome the absence of physical male characteristics while projecting a MP. These virtual acts appear to be taken at face value by observers, despite a tacit understanding that the presence of visual cues may be contradictory to one's claim of status. However, the lack of information from physical characteristics, in this case study at least, leads to personas overtly making mention of ownership of male anatomy. Perhaps this is because suggesting possession of a heterosexual male penis, and thus the ability to "fap," enables the MP to quickly assert a masculine self in a way that does not easily lend itself to challenge.

Like in-person manhood acts, virtual manhood acts may be either performative (remind/assure/convince your audience you are a man) or compensatory (compensate for lower social status by laying claim to masculine power). The anonymity and disembodied nature of social media creates environments wherein individuals may lay claim to any identity imaginable. But choice of gendered expression—particularly a masculine self—does not appear to be randomly ordered. Manhood acts are linked not just with defining differences between men and women but with establishing an innate and "natural" order wherein men are dominant and women are oppressed (Schrock and Schwalbe 2009). Although there is nothing natural or pre-ordered about the virtual spaces created on social media, the fact that so many Fappening commentators chose to claim heterosexual manhood status is a clear reflection on deeply embedded societal gender dynamics. By documenting specific manhood acts carried out by MPs in virtual social space, we also strive to bridge the false cleavage between masculinity as a theoretical construct and the problematic—and very real—practices of men (Hearn 2004; McCarry 2007).

Virtual identities may be relatively nascent, but they appear to be here to stay. In a place where there is little or no imagery or where the (given off) image of the body can be controlled and manipulated to show any and all variations, it is possible to credibly perform (or "pass") as any gender. As human interaction continues to migrate to virtual social spaces, the reproduction—or disruption—of inequality in these spaces must become a central research focus for social scientists. Future work should consider examination of other online spaces, and the gendered identities and hierarchies present. These gendered identities should be considered in context with intersectional factors of race, class, and age. While the technologically facilitated mediums of social media are new, the sexist ideologies and social hierarchies reinforced by virtual manhood acts are ancient and deeply entrenched in society.

Notes

1. Although an assumption at the time, the individuals thus far charged and/or under investigation for The Fappening are men. http://heavy.com/news/2016/03/ryan-collins-celeb gate-fappening-hacker-lancaster-pennsylvania-celebrity-phones-photos-phishing-photos-family-documents/

2. "Jizzing" and "Fapping" are male-only terms for orgasm and masturbation, respectively. To our knowledge, there is no widely accepted female-specific term for masturbation. Thus, a male-body focus is central to the name of this online event.

References

American Psychological Association, Task Force on the Sexualization of Girls. 2010. *Report of the APA Task Force on the Sexualization of Girls.* Washington, DC: American Psychological Association. Accessed November 4, 2010. http://www.apa.org/pi/women/pro grams/girls/report-full.pdf.

Bartlett, Jamie, Richard Norrie, Sofia Patel, Rebecca Rumpel, and Simon Wibberly. 2014. *Misogyny on Twitter.* London, UK: Demos. Accessed November 9, 2015. http://www.demos.co.uk/files/MISOGYNY_ON_TWITTER .pdf?1399567516.

Berger, Peter L., and Thomas Luckmann. 1966. *The Social Construction of Reality: A Treatise in the Sociology of Knowledge.* Garden City, NY: Doubleday.

Berridge, Susan, and Laura Portwood-Stacer. 2015. "Feminism, Hashtags and Violence against Women and Girls." *Feminist Media Studies* 15:341.

Blumer, Herbert. 1969. *Symbolic Interactionism.* Englewood Cliffs, NJ: Prentice Hall.

Boero, Natalie, and C. J. Pascoe. 2012. "Pro-anorexia Communities and Online Interaction: Bringing the Pro-ana Body Online." *Body and Society* 18:27–57.

Bridges, Tristan, and C. J. Pascoe. 2014. "Hybrid Masculinities: New Directions in the Sociology of Men and Masculinities." *Sociology Compass* 8:246–58.

Buchanan, Rose Troup. 2014. "Jennifer Lawrence Nude Pictures Leak Sparks Fear of More Celebrity Hackings: 'A Flagrant Violation of Privacy.'" *The Independent.* Accessed September 1, 2014. http://www.independent.co.uk/news/people/jennifer-lawrence-naked-photos-spark-fear-of-mass-celebrity-hacking-9702902.html.

Charmaz, Kathy. 2014. *Constructing Grounded Theory,* 2nd ed. Los Angeles, CA: Sage.

Cole, Kirsti K. 2015. "'It's Like She's Eager to Be Verbally Abused': Twitter, Trolls, and (En)Gendering Disciplinary Rhetoric." *Feminist Media Studies* 15:356–58.

Connell, Raewyn W. 2005. *Masculinities,* 2nd ed. Berkeley: University of California Press.

Connell, Raewyn W., and Jason W. Messerschmidt. 2005. "Hegemonic Masculinity: Rethinking the Concept." *Gender and Society* 19:829–59.

Coser, Ruth Laub. 1966. "Role Distance, Sociological Ambivalence, and Transitional Status Systems." *American Journal of Sociology* 72:173–87.

Duggan, Maeve. 2015. "Mobile Messaging and Social Media 2015." *Pew Internet & American Life Project.* Accessed October 14, 2015. http://www.pewinternet.org/2015/ 08/19/mobile-messaging-and-social-media-2015/.

Eagle, Ryan B. 2015. "Loitering, Lingering, Hashtagging: Women Reclaiming Public Space Via #Boardthebus, #Stopstreetharassment, and the #Everydaysexism Project." *Feminist Media Studies* 15:350–53.

Earp, Jeremy, and Jackson Katz. 1999. *Tough Guise: Violence, Media and the Crisis in Masculinity.* DVD. Northampton, MA: Media Education Foundation.

Eastman, Jason T. 2011. "Rebel Manhood: The Hegemonic Masculinity of the Southern Rock Music Revival." *Journal of Contemporary Ethnography* 41:189–219.

Ezzell, Matthew B. 2012. "'I'm in Control': Compensatory Manhood in a Therapeutic Community." *Gender and Society* 26:190–215.

Ezzell, Matthew B. 2016. "Healthy for Whom?—Males, Men, and Masculinity: A Reflection on the Doing (and Study) of Dominance." In *Exploring Masculinities: Identity, Inequality, Continuity, and Change,* edited by C. J. Pascoe and T. Bridges, 188–97. New York: Oxford University Press.

Filipovic, Jill. 2007. "Blogging While Female: How Internet Misogyny Parallels Real-world Harassment." *Yale Journal of Law and Feminism* 19:295–303.

Flood, Michael. 2008. "Men, Sex, and Homosociality: How Bonds between Men Shape Their Sexual Relations with Women." *Men and Masculinity* 10:339–59.

Garcia-Favaro, Laura, and Rosalind Gill. 2016. "'Emasculation Nation Has Arrived': Sexism Rearticulated in Online Responses to Lose the Lads' Mags Campaign." *Feminist Media Studies* 16:379–97.

Goffman, Erving. 1959. *The Presentation of Self in Everyday life.* New York, NY: Anchor Books.

Goffman, Erving. 1977. "The Arrangement between the Sexes." *Theory and Society* 4:301–31.

Grazian, David. 2007. "The Girl Hunt: Urban Nightlife and the Performance of Masculinity as Collective Activity." *Symbolic Interaction* 30:221–43.

Hall, Lesley A. 1992. "Forbidden by God, Despised by Men: Masturbation, Medical Warnings, Moral Panic and Manhood in Great Britain, 1850–1950." *Journal of History and Sexuality* 2:365–87.

Hearn, Jeff. 2004. "From Hegemonic Masculinity to the Hegemony of Men." *Feminist Theory* 5:49–72.

Henry, Nicola, and Anastasia Powell. 2015. "Embodied Harms: Gender, Shame, and Technology-facilitated Sexual Violence." *Violence Against Women* 21:758–79.

Hentemann, Mark, and James Purdum. 2009. "Family Goy." In Seth MacFarlane's *Family Guy* Season 8, Episode 2. Los Angeles, CA: Fox Broadcasting Company.

Holmes, Janet. 2000. "Politeness, Power, and Provocation: How Humour Functions in the Workplace." *Discourse Studies* 2:159–85.

Jane, Emma Alice. 2014. "'Back to the Kitchen, Cunt': Speaking the Unspeakable about Online Misogyny." *Continuum: Journal of Media & Cultural Studies* 28:558–70.

Johnson, Allan G. 2014. *The Gender Knot.* Philadelphia, PA: Temple University Press.

Kehily, Mary Jane, and Anoop Nayak. 1997. "'Lads and Laughter': Humour and the Production of Heterosexual Hierarchies." *Gender and Education* 9:69–87.

Kimmel, Michael. 2008. *Guyland: The Perilous World Where Boys Become Men.* New York, NY: Harper.

Kivel, Paul. 1984. "Act Like a Man Box." Accessed April 3, 2012. http://paulkivel.com/component/jdownloads/finish/2/58/0.

Mantilla, Karla. 2013. "Gendertrolling: Misogyny Adapts to New Media." *Feminist Studies* 39:563–70.

Martineau, William. 1972. "A Model of the Social Functions of Humor." In *The Psychology of Humor,* edited by J. Goldstein and P. E. McGhee, 101–25. London, UK: Academic Press.

Massanari, Adrienne. 2015. "#Gamergate and The Fappening: How Reddit's Algorithm, Governance, and Culture Support Toxic Technocultures." *New Media and Society* October 9:1–18.

McCarry, Melanie. 2007. "Masculinity Studies and Male Violence: Critique or Collusion?" *Women's Studies International Forum* 30:404–15.

Messner, Michael. 1990. "Boyhood, Organized Sports, and the Construction of Masculinities." *Journal of Contemporary Ethnography* 18:416–14.

Miller, Carl, and Bobby Duffy. 2014. "The Birth of Real-time Research." *Demos Quarterly.* Accessed April 24, 2014. http://quarterly.demos.co.uk/article/issue-2/the-birth-of-real-time-research/.

Moloney, Mairead E., and Lisa J. Pelehach. 2014. "'You're Not Good Enough': Teaching Undergraduate Students about the Sexualization of Girls and Women." *Teaching Sociology* 42:119–29.

Morris, Edward W. 2012. *Learning the Hard Way: Masculinity, Place, and the Gender Gap in Education.* New Brunswick, NJ: Rutgers University Press.

NVivo Qualitative Data Analysis Software. 2012. QSR International Pty Ltd, Version 10.

Pascoe, C. J. 2007. *Dude, You're a Fag.* Los Angeles: University of California Press.

Penny, Laurie. 2013. *Cybersexism: Sex, Gender and Power on the Internet.* London, UK: A & C Black.

Rentschler, Carrie. 2015. "#Safetytipsforladies: Feminist Twitter Takedowns of Victim Blaming." *Feminist Media Studies* 15:353–56.

Ridgeway, Cecilia L. 2011. *Framed by Gender: How Gender Inequality Persists in the Modern World.* New York, NY: Oxford University Press.

Schrock, Douglas, and Michael Schwalbe. 2009. "Men, Masculinity, and Manhood Acts." *Annual Review of Sociology* 35:277–95.

Schwalbe, Michael. 2014. *Manhood Acts: Gender and the Practices of Domination.* Boulder, CO: Paradigm.

Shaw, Adrienne. 2014. "The Internet Is Full of Jerks, because the World Is Full of Jerks: What Feminist Theory Teaches Us about the Internet." *Communication and Critical/Cultural Studies* 11:273–77.

Strauss, Anselm, and Juliet M. Corbin. 1998. *Basics of Qualitative Research: Techniques and Procedures for Developing Grounded Theory.* Thousand Oaks, CA: Sage.

Sumerau, J. Edward. 2012. "'That's What a Man Is Supposed to Do': Compensatory Manhood Acts in an LGBT Christian Church." *Gender and Society* 26:461–87.

Thompson, Laura. 2016. "#Dick-pics Are No Joke: Cyberflashing, Misogyny and Online Dating." Accessed July 15, 2016. https://theconversation.com/dickpics-are-no-joke- cyber-flashing-misogyny-and-online-dating-53843.

Vaccaro, Christian Alexander. 2011. "Male Bodies in Manhood Acts: The Role of Body-talk and Embodied Practice in Signifying Culturally Dominant Notions of Manhood." *Sociology Compass* 5:65–76.

West, Candace, and Don H. Zimmerman. 1987. "Doing Gender." *Gender and Society* 1:125–51.

Zhang, Lei, Ghosh Riddhiman, Dekhil Mohamed, Hsu Meichun, and Bing Liu. 2011. "Combining Lexicon-based and Learning-based Methods for Twitter Sentiment Analysis." Hewlett-Packard Technical Report. Accessed October 14, 2015. http://www.hpl.hp.com/techreports/2011/HPL-2011-89.pdf.

Zimmer, Michael, and Nicholas John Proferes. 2014. "A Topology of Twitter Research: Disciplines, Methods, and Ethics." *Aslib Journal of Information Management* 66:250–61.

PART III

Politics and Nationhood

In his book *Hegemonic Masculinities and Camouflaged Politics,* James W. Messerschmidt describes how U.S. president George W. Bush engaged in a project to reconstruct hegemonic masculinity following the 9/11 terrorist attacks. During a profound political and ideological crisis, the former president, Messerschmidt argues, articulated a heroic masculinity needed to defeat a "global war on terror." This reconstructed hegemonic masculinity positioned foreign (non-Western) enemies as uncivilized threats in need of vanquishing and infantile populations in need of rescue. Bush averred that the United States possessed a superior morality and a heroic masculinity, and was ready once again to take up the mantle of "masculine protector" (Young 2003) and defender of the free world. As Messerschmidt and others have demonstrated, hegemonic masculinity in the United States links gender, race, and nation.

The five readings in this section explore the deeply masculine realms of domestic and international politics. Readings no. 11, no. 12, and no. 13 focus on the gendered (and racialized) lives and times of three major U.S. politicians: two presidents and one celebrity-turned-governor. As Raewyn Connell wrote in reading no. 1, hegemony is more likely to be secured when there is a "correspondence between cultural ideal and institutional power." Therefore, presidents especially have served as exemplars of hegemonic masculinity. The historian Gail Bederman, the author of the first reading in this section, offers a rich analysis of perhaps the most famously masculine of all U.S. presidents: Theodore Roosevelt. Bederman chronicles Roosevelt's transformation from a sickly, effeminate boy to an avid big-game hunter and hero of white American masculinity, or what Bederman calls "the virile cowboy on the Western frontier." Not unlike what George W. Bush would later do during the "war on terror," Roosevelt linked race and gender to assert that a white masculinity deserved to lead the nation against nonwhite enemies and other threats viewed as degenerate, savage, and uncivilized.

The next reading (no. 12) by Frank Rudy Cooper turns to a quite different commander-in-chief: Barack Obama, the first African-American president of the United States. During his rise to the nation's top office, Obama was forced to take part in a delicate balancing act. Cooper calls this, somewhat provocatively, a "unisex" identity. On the one hand, a destructive historical narrative of the "angry Black man" meant that Obama could be derided and feared for his toughness, but he also had to learn to appear not too weak. On the other hand, as Obama learned to cultivate a calm demeanor, appearing too "feminine" carried risks. By showing how race and gender interpenetrate, Cooper's analysis complicates our understanding of the masculine privilege typically afforded to presidents and other leading figures.

Reading no. 13, "The Masculinity of the Governator" by Michael A. Messner, takes us to another unique political figure. Arnold Schwarzenegger came to the United States as an Austrian immigrant, starred in movies such as *The Terminator* series and *Kindergarten Cop,* and then became governor of the country's most populous state. Messner argues that Schwarzenegger's political popularity was partly the result of a hybrid masculinity (see reading no. 5) that Messner calls a "Kindergarten Commando." Messner makes a similar observation as Messerschmidt from earlier in this Introduction. In the wake of 9/11, Schwarzenegger capitalized on widespread fear by drawing on his "Terminator" symbolism to "outmuscle" his opponents. However, Schwarzenegger learned to soften his image with momentary displays of compassion.

The last two readings in this section shift attention to how ordinary men link race, gender, and nation in taking up arms. Michael Kimmel and Abby L. Ferber's "White Men Are This Nation" (reading no. 14) assess the rise of the right-wing militia in rural stretches of the U.S. These predominantly white and Christian anti-government paramilitary groups, Kimmel and Ferber argue, stand ready to defend their vision of an "American Eden." Membership in militia groups enable these men to regenerate masculinity in the face of a threateningly feminized and multicultural society. Finally, reading no. 15, "Mourning Mayberry" by Jennifer Carlson, is a case study of male gun carriers in Michigan. In the first decade of the 21st century, Michigan passed a law that has expanded the number of residents who carry concealed guns, just as the state was undergoing severe socioeconomic decline. What consequences have these developments had for men? Carlson argues that men take up arms to assert their masculinity when socioeconomic insecurity threatens traditional male breadwinner roles. Like Messner, Carlson draws on Iris Marion Young's (2003) notion of "masculinist protection" and argues that these men view guns as a way of protecting both their loved ones and a nostalgic vision of small-town America.

Questions to Ponder

1. The term *hegemonic masculinity* does not appear in Bederman's chapter. Yet how did Theodore Roosevelt both embody and construct hegemonic masculinity? What consequences do you think this had for ordinary citizens?

2. Several of these chapters analyze how men (including President Theodore Roosevelt, Governor Arnold Schwarzenegger, members of a right-wing rural militia, and gun carriers in Michigan) responded to crisis and social upheaval by reconstructing masculinity. What is similar and different about these various responses?

3. The readings by Cooper and Messner argue that President Obama and Governor Schwarzenegger, respectively, "softened" their image. However, this softening impacted Obama and Schwarzenegger quite differently. How so? What explains these differences?

4. Both Messner and Carlson explicitly, and Kimmel and Ferber implicitly, identify the harm posed by an ethos of "masculinist protection." Can you think of other examples of how politicians and others draw on this ethos? Finally, Messner argues for a politics of caring and compassion. What are some additional gendered obstacles to these goals, and what will it take to accomplish greater compassion in politics?

5. The president, of course, is the commander-in-chief of the armed forces, and so the military emerges as a main protagonist across these readings. How do military ideals, philosophies, and interests shape masculinity and gender in other social domains such as sports and schools?

Key Concepts

Civilization and nation	Masculinist protection	Unisex identity
Kindergarten commando	Right-wing militias	

References

Messerschmidt, James W. 2010. *Hegemonic Masculinities and Camouflaged Politics: Unmasking the Bush Dynasty and Its War Against Iraq.* London: Routledge.

Young, Iris Marion. 2003. "The Logic of Masculinist Protection: Reflections on the Current Security State." *Signs: Journal of Women in Culture and Society* 291:1–25.

CHAPTER 11

Theodore Roosevelt

Manhood, Nation, and "Civilization"

Gail Bederman

In 1882, a newly elected young state assemblyman arrived in Albany. Theodore Roosevelt, assuming his first elective office, was brimming with self-importance and ambition. He was only twenty-three—the youngest man in the legislature—and he looked forward to a promising career of wielding real political power. Yet Roosevelt was chagrined to discover that despite his intelligence, competence, and real legislative successes, no one took him seriously. The more strenuously he labored to play "a man's part" in politics, the more his opponents derided his manhood.[1]

Daily newspapers lampooned Roosevelt as the quintessence of effeminacy. They nicknamed him "weakling," "Jane-Dandy," "Punkin-Lily," and "the exquisite Mr. Roosevelt." They ridiculed his high voice, tight pants, and fancy clothing. Several began referring to him by the name of the well-known homosexual Oscar Wilde, and one actually alleged (in a less-than-veiled phallic allusion) that Roosevelt was "given to sucking the knob of an ivory cane."[2]

Above all other things, Roosevelt desired power. An intuitive master of public relations, he knew that his effeminate image could destroy any chances for his political future. Nearly forty years before women got the vote, electoral politics was part of a male-only subculture, fraught with symbols of manhood.[3] Besides, Roosevelt, who considered himself a man's man, detested having his virility impugned. Although normally restrained, when he discovered a Tammany legislator plotting to toss him in a blanket, TR marched up to him and swore, "By God! if you try anything like that, I'll kick you, I'll bite you, I'll kick you in the balls, I'll do anything to you—you'd better leave me alone!"[4] Clearly, the effeminate "dude" image would have to go.

And go it did. Roosevelt soon came to embody powerful American manhood. Within five years, he was running for mayor of New York as the "Cowboy of the Dakotas." Instead of ridiculing him as "Oscar Wilde," newspapers were praising his virile zest for fighting and his "blizzard-seasoned constitution."[5] In 1898, after a brief but highly publicized stint as leader of a regiment of volunteers in the Spanish American War, he became known as Colonel Roosevelt, the manly advocate of a virile imperialism. Never again would Roosevelt's name be linked to effeminacy. Even today, historians invoke Roosevelt as the quintessential symbol of turn-of-the-century masculinity.[6]

Roosevelt's great success in masculinizing his image was due, in large part, to his masterful use of the discourse of civilization. As a mature politician, he would build his claim to political power on his claim to manhood. Skillfully, Roosevelt constructed a virile political persona for himself as a strong but civilized white man.

SOURCE: Bederman, G. (1996). Theodore Roosevelt: Manhood, Nation, and "Civilization." In *Manliness & Civilization*. Chicago, IL: University of Chicago Press. Reproduced with permission from the University of Chicago Press.

Yet Roosevelt's use of the discourse of civilization went beyond mere public relations: Roosevelt drew on "civilization" to help formulate his larger politics as an advocate of both nationalism and imperialism. As he saw it, the United States was engaged in a millennial drama of manly racial advancement, in which American men enacted their superior manhood by asserting imperialistic control over races of inferior manhood. To prove their virility, as a race and a nation, American men needed to take up the "strenuous life" and strive to advance civilization—through imperialistic warfare and racial violence if necessary.

Thus, TR framed his political mission in terms of race and manhood, nationalism and civilization. Like G. Stanley Hall and Charlotte Perkins Gilman, Roosevelt longed to lead evolution's chosen race toward a perfect millennial future. Yet Roosevelt harbored larger ambitions than either Hall or Gilman. Hall merely wanted to develop a pedagogy that would produce the "super-man." Gilman only wanted to revolutionize society by civilizing women. Roosevelt, on the other hand, yearned to be the virile leader of a manly race and to inspire his race to wage an international battle for racial supremacy. He hoped that, through this imperialistic evolutionary struggle, he could advance his race toward the most perfect possible civilization. This, for Roosevelt, was the ultimate power of manhood.[7]

Civilized Manliness and Violent Masculinity: Claiming the Power of a Man

From early boyhood, Roosevelt longed for the authority of a powerful man. Like the young G. Stanley Hall, young Roosevelt learned early that achieving real manhood required serious attention and strenuous effort. The boy Teedie (as Theodore was called as a child) learned that male power was composed of equal parts kindhearted manly chivalry and aggressive masculine violence.[8]

On the one hand, Roosevelt grew up committed to Victorian codes of bourgeois manliness. He identified this Victorian moral manliness with his adored father, "the best man I ever knew. He combined strength and courage with gentleness, tenderness and great unselfishness. . . . He made us understand that the same standard of clean living was demanded for the boys as for the girls; that what was wrong in a woman could not be right in a man."[9] His father's unselfish, self-restrained manliness expressed itself, in part, through an upper-class sense of noblesse oblige: the senior Roosevelt devoted himself extensively to philanthropic activity, especially on behalf of New York's poor street urchins.[10] Yet Roosevelt's father also taught his son that this unselfish, charitable manliness implied a certain authority over the lower orders. On a trip to Italy, for example, he showed eleven-year-old Teedie a game of tossing broken pieces of cake into the open mouths of a crowd of hungry beggars.

At the same time young Teedie was learning the virtues of unselfish, moral Victorian manliness, he was also attracted to a more violent masculinity. Like other exponents of "natural man," Teedie associated this sort of masculinity with "nature." One morning in 1865, when Teedie was about seven, he suddenly came upon the body of a dead seal, laid out on a slab in a Broadway market. The little boy was enthralled, and later described discovering the seal as an epiphany—the adventure which started him on his career as a naturalist. To the delicate, sickly boy, the dead animal seemed a tangible link to the aggressive, masculine world of boys' adventure novels. "That seal filled me with every possible feeling of romance and adventure," he recalled. "I had already begun to read some of Mayne Reid's books and other boys' books of adventure, and I felt that this seal brought all these adventures in realistic fashion before me."[11]

Why should a young boy see a dead animal as a representation of "romance and adventure"? To understand why Teedie associated dead animals, "nature," and manhood, we can look at Mayne Reid's *The Boy Hunters; or Adventures in Search of a White Buffalo*, one of Teedie's favorite books.[12] Reid's three young heroes are "hunter-naturalists" who travel alone from Louisiana to Texas to kill and skin an albino buffalo. On the way, they have many thrilling adventures: they are attacked by cougars, shoot antelope and cimmaron, kill an attacking grizzly bear, and finally face down hostile Indians. *The Boy Hunters*, then, is a traditional Western adventure, in which white men (or boys) prove their manhood by fighting and vanquishing Indians and wild beasts.

To show how the boy hunters become men, Reid draws on two larger subthemes. First, *The Boy Hunters* draws unmistakably on a wider tradition of Western stories in which, as Richard Slotkin has shown, white heroes achieve manhood by becoming "like" Indian warriors, while nonetheless remaining unmistakably white. Indeed, the very quest for a white buffalo mentioned in Reid's title typifies this tradition: the boys hunt a buffalo, the stereotypical quarry of Indians, yet they hunt a buffalo which is rare and superior because it is white. Similarly, at the novel's climax, the boy hunters are on the verge of being tortured and executed by Indians when, suddenly, the boys are revealed to possess the long-lost pipe of Tecumseh's brother, who was a friend of their father's. Recognizing this as a basis for kinship with the boys, the Indians are filled with "astonishment as well as admiration for [their] courage."[13] The boys' simultaneous kinship and superiority to the Indians implicitly tie them to the American national myth of the frontier, in which manly Indian fighters like Daniel Boone and Davy Crockett forge an American nation.[14]

Yet if Indian frontier mythology was one subtheme of *The Boy Hunters*—and one element of the romance Teedie saw in the dead seal—the masculine "naturalness" of violence was an even stronger subtheme. Reid laces his adventures with natural history lessons stressing how predatory "nature" was. He dramatizes this predation in "The Chain of Destruction," a chapter in which the boy hunters observe a virtual feeding frenzy: A hummingbird hunting for insects is killed by a tarantula, which is in turn killed by a chameleon, and so on. When the hero Basil shoots and kills the last creature, a thieving eagle, Reid italicizes the moral: "This was the last link in the *chain of destruction!*"[15] In nature, the large animals hunt the smaller—and man is the fiercest, most powerful animal of all.

"Eat or be eaten" was the lesson Mayne Reid drew from nature, but it is not the only lesson one might draw from stories about animal life. "Nature" is a cultural construct, not a transparent fact to be reported. Reid's lesson about nature's violence enthralled the sheltered, sickly young Roosevelt, however. When he saw the body of the dead seal in the marketplace, he felt he had suddenly come face-to-face with a distant, romantic world of powerful and violent masculinity. He was fascinated. "As long as that seal remained there, I haunted the neighborhood of the market day after day." Emulating Lucien, the Boy Hunter who carried a notebook to annotate his observations, he returned to the market with a ruler and notebook, took a series of "utterly useless" measurements, and "at once began to write a natural history of my own, on the strength of that seal." By playing at being a naturalist, young Teedie brought himself into imaginary contact with the aggressive, masculine nature he identified with the fictional Western frontier, where boys demonstrated their heroic masculinity by killing fierce animals and battling wild Indians.

Stories like Mayne Reid's "Chain of Destruction," depicting nature as red in tooth and claw, predisposed young Teedie to embrace Darwinism. By age ten the budding boy-naturalist had discovered Darwin's *Origin of Species*, and he soon became familiar with evolutionary theory.[16] *The Boy Hunters*, written seven years before Darwin published *Origin of Species*, was not in itself Darwinistic. While Reid's "chain of destruction" affirmed man as the apex of creation, it ascribed no cosmic meaning to man's superiority. But Darwinism provided a millennial purpose for Reid's chain of destruction—it was the engine which drove evolution. Like G. Stanley Hall and Charlotte Perkins Gilman, Roosevelt believed that bitter evolutionary conflict allowed the fittest species and races to survive, ultimately moving evolution forward toward its ultimate, civilized perfection.[17]

The sickly seven-year-old boy measuring the seal in the Broadway market is the earliest glimpse we have of the strenuous adult man who would slaughter African lions and elephants in the name of science and construct himself as a virile cowboy on the Western frontier.

Eighteen years after encountering the seal, now a budding young politician, Roosevelt was accused of effeminacy, and once again he constructed a powerful male identity for himself in the terms of the

Western adventure story. What better way to counter his Oscar Wilde image than to replace it with the image of the masculine Western hero? Although this was clearly a smart political move on TR's part, it was no cynical pose. Roosevelt had been enthralled by the masculine aggressiveness of Western fiction ever since he was a small boy reading *The Boy Hunters*. On his first trip to the Badlands in 1883, he was giddy with delight and behaved as much like a Mayne Reid hero as possible. He flung himself into battle with nature and hunted the largest and fiercest game he could find. Now, shooting buffalo and bullying obstreperous cowboys, he could style himself the real thing.[18]

Although most of his biographers date his transformation into a "Western man" from his retreat to South Dakota following the tragic death of his wife in 1884, Roosevelt had already bought his ranch and begun to transform himself into a Western rancher while Alice Lee was very much alive. On his very first trip to the Badlands in 1883, Roosevelt—although chronically short of cash—committed himself to spending forty thousand dollars to buy a South Dakota cattle ranch. Financially this was a foolhardy and risky investment, as Edmund Morris has pointed out; yet politically it was a brilliant step to transform his image from effeminate dude to masculine cowboy.[19]

Alice's death completely devastated TR, but it also freed him to construct himself as a cowboy far more completely than he had previously planned.[20] Even in his grief, and during his temporary withdrawal from politics, Roosevelt made certain the folks back East knew he was now a masculine cowboy. On his way to take up "permanent" residence on his Dakota ranch in 1884, he gave a "final" interview to the *New York Tribune*.

> It would electrify some of my friends who have accused me of representing the kid-glove element in politics if they could see me galloping over the plains, day in and day out, clad in a buckskin shirt and leather chaparajos, with a big sombrero on my head. For good healthy exercise I would strongly recommend some of our gilded youth go West and try a short course of riding bucking ponies, and assist at the branding of a lot of Texas steers.

Let no one think that TR remained a gilded youth or effeminate dude. He was now a denizen of (as he would later put it) "Cowboy Land."[21]

Six months later, Roosevelt was back in New York writing *Hunting Trips of a Ranchman,* the first of three books detailing his thrilling adventures as a Western hero.[22] TR intended *Hunting Trips* to establish his new identity as a heroic ranchman. He even included his new "ranchman" identity in the title. But lest the reader miss the point, TR included a full-length engraved portrait of himself as ranchman opposite the title page.[23] Sans eyeglasses (which would mark his body as imperfectly evolved), TR stands in a woodland setting, wearing a fringed buckskin suit. His face is grave, restrained, resolute—manly—and he grips a long rifle. Yet, although he bears the weapons and manly demeanor of civilized man, he wears the clothing of savages.[24] Like the Boy Hunters tracking the albino buffalo, he is at once like the Indians and superior to them.

TR's second Western book, *Ranch Life and the Hunting Trail,* published three years later, continued to portray him as a heroic and manly Western rancher, this time drawing more explicitly on the discourse of civilization. TR depicted ranchers like himself as pivotal characters in the evolutionary struggle between civilization and savagery—the struggle to establish the American nation. On the one hand, they embodied all the virtues of upright civilized manliness. A rancher "must not only be shrewd, thrifty, patient, and enterprising, but he must also possess qualities of personal bravery, hardihood, and self-reliance to a degree not demanded in the least by any mercantile occupation in a community long settled."[25] Yet the rancher's location on the frontier between civilization and savagery also allowed him to share the savage's primitive masculinity: By telling a few stories about his run-ins with Indians, in which only his own manly coolness and facility with a rifle saved his scalp, Roosevelt further cemented his new identity as a modern Western hero.[26]

TR's efforts to transform his Jane-Dandy political image succeeded brilliantly. In 1886, when he ran for mayor of New York as the "Cowboy of the Dakotas," even the Democratic *New York Sun* lauded

FIGURE 11.1

Source: Stringer/Contributor/Getty Images.

his zest for fighting and his "blizzard-seasoned constitution" instead of ridiculing him as "Oscar Wilde."[27] Throughout his political life TR would actively cultivate this political persona of masculine denizen of "Cowboy Land."[28]

Yet Roosevelt's ranchman identity was not a merely a case of cynical political packaging. It stemmed from Roosevelt's understanding of the higher significance of his political leadership. Despite his single-minded quest for political power, TR never believed he craved power for its own sake. As he saw it, his political ambitions ultimately served the purposes—not of his own selfish personal advancement—but of the millennial mission to advance his race and nation toward a more perfect civilization.

The Winning of the West: Race War Forges the Identity of the Manly American Race

At the same time that Roosevelt was engaged in constructing himself as a manly Western hero, he was also writing a history which explained the larger significance of his new frontiersman identity to the advancement of civilization. In *The Winning of the West*, Roosevelt depicts the American West as a crucible in which the white American race was forged through masculine racial conflict. By applying Darwinistic principles to the Western tradition, Roosevelt constructed the frontier as a site of origins of the American race, whose manhood and national worth were proven by their ability to stamp out competing, savage races.[29]

Even in these scholarly historical tomes, Roosevelt invoked his own persona as a manly frontiersman to signify that he, himself, shared his race's virility, as well as its manly racial destiny.[30] At the very outset of *The Winning of the West*, TR makes his personal connection with the frontier explicit: "For a number of years I spent most of my time on the frontier, and lived and worked like any other frontiersman. . . . We guarded our herds of branded cattle and shaggy horses, hunted bear, bison, elk, and deer, established civil government, and put down evil-doers, white and red . . . exactly as did the pioneers."[31] This stretches the truth: Roosevelt never spent "most of his time" on the frontier.

Like Mayne Reid's *Boy Hunters* and other Western adventures, Roosevelt's *Winning of the West* told a story of virile violence and interracial conflict. Yet while the hero of the traditional Western adventure was a *man* whose race was implicitly white, the hero of Roosevelt's story was a *race* whose gender was implicitly male. The hero of *The Winning of the West* was the manly American race, which was born in violence on the Western frontier.

The *Winning of the West* then narrates, in much greater detail, a similar origin tale for the American race as it began in the forests of Kentucky, overran the American continent, and began to establish itself as the great United States. The settlement of the American West, according to Roosevelt, echoed the establishment of ancient England in that a race of primarily Germanic descent reconstituted itself in an extended act of racial conquest. As Roosevelt saw it, this act of manly conquest established the American race as a race apart—a race different from its English parent.[32]

TR made much of this point: The American race was not the same as the English race, since it had been reconstituted of new racial stock in the act of winning a new and virgin continent. Americans were literally of a different blood than the British. However, since most of the new, immigrant additions to English stock in America had come from the same superior Germanic and Celtic races that had long ago formed the British race (Germans, Scandinavians, Irish, and Dutch), the new American race retained all the superior racial traits of the older British race. In other words, the American race was a brand new race, but it shared both ancestry and "blood" with the English race.

Yet although the manly American race was forged of various immigrant races, all of those contributing races were European. Black Americans played no part in TR's frontier history, nor did he consider them part of the American race. As he saw it, African Americans were racial inferiors whose presence in America could only damage the real (that is, white) American race. TR lambasted slave importers as "the worst foes, not only of humanity and civilization, but especially of the white race in America." Slave importation was not only "ethically aberrant," it was a biological crime because it encouraged non-eugenic interbreeding. In short, in constructing his racial hero, TR envisioned an American race that was exclusively white.[33]

The logic behind TR's story of heroic racial formation revolves around "civilization's" three basic aspects: race, gender, and millennialism. The millennial evolutionary imperatives behind nature's quest to develop the most perfect men and women demanded that white Americans and Indians, thrown together on one continent, compete to establish which race had the strongest, most powerful men. Warfare between the white man and the Indian was thus, as TR repeatedly put it, "inevitable."[34] Only virile, masculine combat could establish whose men were superior and deserved to control the land and its resources. But the outcome was never in doubt. The new American race, able to advance civilization to ever greater heights, was "predestined" to prevail against the barbarous Indians.[35] Thus, in the violence of race war, the manly American race was born.

Manhood was the key to the American frontiersmen's victory in this race war, just as it had been the key to Roosevelt's own frontiersman identity. "The west would never have been settled save for the fierce courage and the eager desire to brave danger so characteristic of the stalwart backwoodsmen." Like the heroes of Western novels, these virile frontiersmen were bold, resourceful and self-reliant.[36] Moreover, the men and women of the American race clung tenaciously to "natural" sex roles: "The man was the armed protector and provider, the woman was the housewife and child-bearer."[37] As TR described the virile backwoodsmen, in another context, they were "every inch men," whose manhood was essential to their racial character.

TR repeatedly contrasts the virile manliness of the Americans to the brutal unmanliness of the Indians.[38] Manhood was the essential characteristic of the American race, whereas Roosevelt's Indians "seemed to the white settlers devils and not men." These devilish nonmen "mercilessly destroyed all weaker communities, red or white" and "had no idea of showing justice or generosity towards their fellows who lacked their strength."[39] Manliness meant helping the weak; Indians attacked the weak. Therefore, Indians—like the Negro rapists in contemporary reports of lynching—were the opposite of manly. Indeed, Roosevelt repeatedly described Indians as brutal despoilers of women and children, invoking (like so many of his contemporaries) the ubiquitous cultural figure of the savage primitive rapist.

Roosevelt described this savage unmanliness in pornographic detail, lumping together every Indian atrocity he had ever heard of—events occurring years apart, in different parts of the country— so that it appeared that Indians were typically rapists and baby killers.[40] Drawing on the discourse of civilization, TR constructed his Indians in the same terms which were currently depicting African Americans as unmanly, congenital rapists.

Yet civilized manliness was not the only thing that made the American race superior to the barbarous Indians. The American frontiersmen also proved their racial superiority by the potency of their violent masculinity—their ability to outsavage the savages. Although the primitive Indians were powerfully violent foes, Roosevelt depicted the white frontiersmen's violence as even more powerful: "Their red foes were strong and terrible, cunning in council, dreadful in battle, merciless beyond belief in victory. The men of the border did not overcome and dispossess cowards and weaklings; they marched forth to spoil the stout-hearted and to take for a prey the possessions of the men of might."[41] Again, the virile white man is both like the Indians and superior to them.

One might think that by regressing to brutal savagery, American men might be devolving toward a lower evolutionary stage, instead of advancing to a higher civilization. And Roosevelt conceded that, in the short run, this brutal race war was more likely to retrograde than to advance manliness and civilization. "A sad and evil feature of such warfare is that the whites, the representatives of civilization, speedily sink almost to the level of their barbarous foes, in point of hideous brutality."[42] Yet, as Roosevelt saw it, this regression to savagery was only temporary and proved the Americans' racial superiority. Since the Indian men fought at the brutal level of savagery, it was they who forced the white men into equal brutality in order to prevail in the struggle for survival. The superior race needed to match their red foes' masculine savagery in order to win the war and safeguard the future of civilization.[43] Having met the savages on their own primitive ground and having proven themselves the fitter race and the better men, the American men could claim their continent and reclaim their place as the most advanced of civilized races.

The Meaning of the Strenuous Life

Roosevelt never had the time to write the two final volumes of *The Winning of the West*. Instead, he took up the mantle of his heroic Indian fighters himself, urging American men to embrace a virile imperialism for the good of the race and the future of all civilization. Beginning in 1894, unhappy with President Cleveland's reluctance to annex Hawaii, Roosevelt began to exhort the American race to embrace a manly, strenuous imperialism, in the cause of higher civilization.[44] In Roosevelt's imperialistic pronouncements, as in *The Winning of the West*, issues of racial dominance were inextricably conflated with issues of manhood. Indeed, when Roosevelt originally coined the term "the strenuous life," in an 1899 speech, he was explicitly discussing only foreign relations: calling on the United States to build up its army and to take imperialistic control of Cuba, Puerto Rico, and the Philippines. Ostensibly, the speech never mentions gender at all. Yet the phrase "the strenuous life" soon began to connote a virile, hard-driving manhood which might or might not involve foreign relations at all.

For Roosevelt, the purpose of American expansionism and national greatness was always the millennial purpose behind human evolution—human racial advancement toward a higher civilization. And the race that could best achieve this perfected civilization was, by definition, the one with the most superior manhood.

The Dangers of Unmanly Overcivilized Racial Decadence

It was not coincidental that Roosevelt's advocacy of manly imperialism in the 1890s was contemporaneous with a widespread cultural concern about effeminacy, overcivilization, and racial decadence. Roosevelt shared many of his contemporaries' fears about the future of American manly power; and this gave his imperialistic writings an air of especial urgency.[45]

Although Roosevelt never despaired about the future of American civilization, he believed racial decay was distinctly possible. He warned the nation that overcivilized effeminacy could threaten the race's fitness to engage in the sort of race wars he had described in *The Winning of the West*. He fretted over "a certain softness of fibre in civilized nations, which, if it were to prove progressive, might mean the development of a cultured and refined people quite unable to hold its own in those conflicts through which alone any great race can ultimately march to victory."[46]

As he had shown in *The Winning of the West*, TR believed that manly racial competition determined which race was superior and deserved to control the earth's resources. A race which grew decadent, then, was a race which had lost the masculine strength necessary to prevail in this Darwinistic racial struggle. Civilized advancement required much more than mere masculine strength, of course; it also required advanced manliness. Intelligence, altruism, and morality were essential traits, possessed by all civilized races and men. Yet, as important as these refined traits were, they were not enough, by themselves, to safeguard civilization's advance and prevent racial decadence. Without the "virile fighting virtues" which allowed a race to continue to expand into new territories, its more civilized racial traits would be useless. If American men lost their primal fighting virtues, a more manful race would strip them of their authority, land, and resources. This effeminate loss of racial primacy and virility was what Roosevelt meant by overcivilized racial decadence.

In order to help American men ward off this kind of racial decadence, Roosevelt wrote a series of articles exhorting American men to eschew over-civilized effeminacy. In 1893, for example, he suggested in *Harper's Weekly* that athletics might be one way to combat excess civilization and avoid losing Americans' frontier-bred manliness:

In a perfectly peaceful and commercial civilization such as ours there is always a danger of laying too little stress upon the more virile virtues—upon the virtues which go to make up a race of statesmen and soldiers, of pioneers and explorers. . . . These are the very qualities which are fostered by vigorous, manly out-of-door sports, such as mountaineering, big-game hunting, riding, shooting, rowing, football and kindred games.[47]

Elsewhere he urged men to take up politics in order to cultivate "the rougher, manlier virtues. . . ."[48] Decadence could only be kept at bay if American men strove to retain the virile fighting qualities necessary for a race of soldiers and pioneers.

This concept of overcivilized decadence let Roosevelt construct American imperialism as a conservative way to retain the race's frontier-forged manhood, instead of what it really was—a belligerent grab for a radically new type of nationalistic power. As Roosevelt described it, asserting the white man's racial power abroad was necessary to avoid losing the masculine strength Americans had already established through race war on the frontier.

By depicting imperialism as a prophylactic means of avoiding effeminacy and racial decadence, Roosevelt constructed it as part of the status quo and hid the fact that this sort of militaristic overseas involvement was actually a new departure in American foreign policy. American men must struggle to retain their racially innate masculine strength, which had originally been forged in battle with the savage Indians on the frontier; otherwise the race would backslide into overcivilized decadence. With no Indians left to fight at home, then, American men must press on and confront new races, abroad.

Imperialism: The Masterful Duty of the Manly Race

From 1894 until he became president in 1901, Roosevelt wrote and lectured widely on the importance of taking up what Rudyard Kipling, in 1899, would dub "the White Man's burden." Kipling coined this term in a poem written to exhort American men to conquer and rale the Philippines. In "The White Man's Burden," Kipling used the term in all these senses to urge white males to take up the racial burden of civilization's advancement. "Take up the White Man's burden," he wrote, capitalizing the essential term, and speaking to the manly civilized on behalf of civilization. "Send forth the best ye breed"—quality breeding was essential, because evolutionary development (breeding) was what gave "the White Man" the right and duty to conquer uncivilized races.

> *Go bind your sons to exile*
> *To serve your captives need;*
> *To wait in heavy harness,*
> *on fluttered folk and wild—*
> *Your new-caught, sullen peoples,*
> *Half-devil and half-child.*[49]

Like Teedie throwing cake in the mouths of hungry beggars, manly men had the duty of taking unselfish care of those weaker than themselves—to "wait in heavy harness" and "serve their captives' need." And by calling the Filipinos "half-devil and half-child," Kipling underlined the essential fact that whatever these races were, they were not *men*.

Roosevelt called Kipling's poem "poor poetry but good sense from the expansionist standpoint."[50] Although Roosevelt did not use the term "the white man's burden" in his writings on imperialism, he drew on the same sorts of race and gender linkages which Kipling deployed in his poem. TR's speeches of this period frequently conflate manhood and racial power, and draw extended analogies between the individual American man and the virile American race.

For example, "National Duties," one of TR's most famous speeches, represents both American men and the American race as civilized entities with strong virile characters—in popular parlance, both were "the white man." Roosevelt begins by outlining this racial manhood, which he calls "the essential manliness of the American character."[51] Part of this manliness centered around individual and racial duties to the home. On the one hand, individual men must work to provide for the domestic needs of themselves and their families. On the other hand, the men of the race must work to provide for their collective racial home, their nation.[52]

Yet laboring only for his own hearth and nation was not enough to satisfy a real man. Virile manhood also required the manly American nation to take up imperialistic labors outside its borders, just as manhood demanded individual men to labor outside the home: "Exactly as each man, while doing first his duty to his wife and the children within his home, must yet, if he hopes to amount to much, strive mightily in the world outside his home, so our nation, while first of all seeing to its own domestic well-being, must not shrink from playing its part among the great nations without."[53] It would be as unmanly for the American race to refuse its imperialist destiny as it would be for a cowardly man to spend all his time loafing at home with his wife.

After setting up imperialism as a manly duty for both man and race, Roosevelt outlines the imperialist's appropriate masculine behavior—or, should we say, his appropriate masculine appendage? Roosevelt immediately brings up the "big stick." It may be a cheap shot to stress the phallic implications of TR's imagery, yet Roosevelt himself explained the meaning of the "big stick" in terms of manhood and the proper way to assert the power of a man: "A good many of you are probably acquainted with the old proverb: 'Speak softly and carry a big stick—you will go far.' If a man continually blusters, if he lacks civility, a big stick will not save him from trouble; and neither will speaking softly avail, if back of the softness there does not lie strength, power."[54]

This imperialistic manliness underlay the virile power of both man and race; yet it was not self-seeking. It was intended only for the advancement of civilization. Therefore, Roosevelt insisted, Americans never directed their virile expansionism against any civilized race. "No nation capable of self-government and of developing by its own efforts a sane and orderly civilization, no matter how small it may be, has anything to fear from us."[55] Only barbarous nations incapable of developing "a sane and orderly civilization"—for example, the Hawaiians and the Filipinos—required the correction of the manly American race.

Unfortunately, Roosevelt conceded, this unselfish civilizing duty might well become bloody and violent. Civilized men had a manly duty to "destroy and uplift" lesser, primitive men, for their own good and the good of civilization: "It is our duty toward the people living in barbarism to see that they are freed from their chains, and we can free them only by destroying barbarism itself. The missionary, the merchant, and the soldier may each have to play a part in this destruction and in the consequent uplifting of the people."[56] Yet this unselfish racial uplift would be worth the bloodshed, even for the destroyed barbarians themselves. Both Indians on the Great Plains and the Tagalogs in the Philippines—at least, those who still survived—would be far happier after the white man had conquered them, according to Roosevelt.[57]

Roosevelt closed his speech by reiterating his analogy between the manful race and the race's men. By conquering and civilizing primitive races, the American nation was simply girding up its racial loins to be "men" of the world, just as they had long been "men" at home in the United States: "We gird up our loins as a nation, with the stern purpose to play our part manfully in winning the ultimate triumph; and therefore . . . with unfaltering steps [we] tread the rough road of endeavor, smiting down the wrong and battling for the right, as Greatheart smote and battled in Bunyan's immortal story."[58] In its imperialist glory, the virile American race would embody a warlike manliness, smiting down and battling its unmanly foes in the primitive Philippines.

The Rough Rider: The War Hero Models the Power of a Manly Race

Roosevelt was not content merely to make speeches about the need for violent, imperialistic manhood. He always needed to embody his philosophy. The sickly boy had remade himself into an adventure-book hunter-naturalist; the dude politician had remade himself into a heroic Western rancher. The 1898 outbreak of the Spanish-American war—for which he had agitated long and hard—let Roosevelt remake himself into Colonel Roosevelt, the fearless Rough Rider.

Reinventing himself as a charismatic war hero allowed Roosevelt to model the manful imperialism about which he had been writing for four years. TR became a walking advertisement for the imperialistic manhood he desired for the American race. In late April 1898, against all advice, Roosevelt resigned as assistant secretary of the navy and enlisted to fight in the just-declared war on Spain. Aged thirty-nine, with an important subcabinet post, a sick wife, and six young children, no one but Roosevelt himself imagined he ought to see active service. Roosevelt's decision to enlist was avidly followed by newspapers all over the country. Several editorialized against his enlistment, saying he would do more good for the war effort as assistant secretary of the navy. Roosevelt enlisted nonetheless and lost no opportunity to publicize his reasons to friendly newspapers. As he explained to the *New York Sun,* it would be unmanly—hypocritical—to allow other men to take his place on the front lines after he had agitated so strenuously for war. "I want to go because I wouldn't feel that I had been entirely true to my beliefs and convictions, and to the ideal I had set for myself if I didn't go."[59]

Roosevelt, commissioned at the rank of lieutenant colonel, raised a volunteer cavalry regiment which he described as "peculiarly American."[60] It was designed to reflect Americans' masculine racial power as well as their civilized manly advancement. TR accepted only a fraction of the host of men who tried to enlist in his well-publicized regiment. Most of those he accepted were Westerners— rough cowboys and frontiersmen, the heirs and descendants of the masculine Indian fighters who had been forged into the American race on the Western frontier. But, to emphasize the American race's civilized superiority to the Spanish enemy, TR also enlisted several dozen young Ivy League college graduates, many of them athletes. These Harvard and Yale men, presumably the beneficiaries of the race's most advanced moral and intellectual evolution, represented the ever-advancing heights of civilization to which the manly American race could aspire. The regiment's combination of primitive Western masculinity and advanced civilized manliness dramatized the superior manhood of the American race.

The press, fascinated by the undertaking, christened the regiment "Roosevelt's Rough Riders."[61] Roosevelt's heroic frontiersman identity thus came full circle, as he no doubt intended. As Richard Slotkin has pointed out, the term "Rough Riders" had long been used in adventure novels to describe Western horsemen. Thus, by nicknaming his regiment the "Rough Riders," the nation showed it understood the historical connections Roosevelt always drew between Indian wars in the American West and virile imperialism in Cuba and the Philippines.[62]

But lest anyone miss the connections he was trying to draw between continued manhood and racial expansion, Roosevelt made certain the press, and thus the public, remained fully informed about the Rough Riders' doings. He encouraged several journalists to attach themselves to the regiment throughout its sojourn in Cuba and even rounded up an interested motion-picture crew.[63] The public avidly followed the newspaper reports of the Rough Riders' masculine cowboy heroics, manly collegiate athleticism, and overall wartime heroics.

Roosevelt, himself, was the core of the Rough Riders' popularity—he embodied the whole manly, imperialistic enterprise. Like his Western recruits, Roosevelt was both a masculine cowboy-hero and (by reputation and association, although not in reality) an Indian fighter. But TR was also a civilized Harvard man, manfully sacrificing his life of ease and privilege to take up the white man's burden and do his duty by the downtrodden brown Cubans. According to Edmund Morris, when Roosevelt returned from the war he was "the most famous man in America."[64]

After his mustering out, TR the politician continued to play the role of virile Rough Rider for all he was worth. In November, he was elected governor of New York, campaigning as a war hero and employing ex–Rough Riders to warm up the election crowds. By January 1899, his thrilling memoir, *The Rough Riders,* was appearing serially in *Scribner's Magazine.* And in 1900 his virile popularity convinced Republican party leaders that Roosevelt could counter Bryan's populism better than any other vice-presidential candidate. Roosevelt had constructed himself and the Rough Riders as the epitome of civilized, imperialistic manhood, a model for the American race to follow.

"Civilization" in the White House: Race Policy and Race Suicide

In 1901, Theodore Roosevelt finally grasped the ultimate manhood which he had sought for so long: to be the preeminent manly leader of the virile American race. As president, TR believed his duty was to usher the manly American nation ever closer to the racial preeminence and perfect civilization he had long predicted for it. Not surprisingly, then, considerations of manhood, race, and "civilization" shaped many of Roosevelt's presidential policies.

Internationally, as Frank Ninkovich has so eloquently shown, Roosevelt relied on the ideology of civilization to frame his foreign policy. Ninkovich refutes those historians who see TR as engaging in realpolitik or upholding balances of power between the European nations, and argues that TR's concern was always to uphold the interests of "civilization."

As Roosevelt described it in his *Autobiography*, this diplomacy of "civilization" was essentially a diplomacy of manliness. "In foreign affairs, the principle from which we never deviated was to have the Nation behave toward other nations precisely as a strong, honorable, and upright man behaves in dealing with his fellow-men."[65] Like the manly man, the manly nation kept its promises, fearlessly faced down strong, civilized nations, and was patient with weak, barbarous ones.[66] For example, Roosevelt wrote that the Monroe Doctrine was intended to apply, not to "civilized commonwealths" like Canada, Argentina, Brazil, or Chile (all with large white populations), but only to uncivilized "tropical states" which (like unmanly men) were too "impotent" to do their own duty or defend their own independence.[67]

President Roosevelt's belief in manly civilization shaped his domestic policies, too, especially regarding interracial relations. His actions toward both Japanese immigrants and African Americans were shaped by his long-standing assumption that when men of different and incompatible races lived together, they would battle until one race reigned supreme, just as they had on the American frontier.[68] Yet although TR believed that African American and Japanese men both presented a racial challenge to white American men, his policies toward the two races differed because, as he saw it, the two races had attained different degrees of civilization.

Roosevelt believed that "Negroes" were the most primitive of races—"a perfectly stupid race."[69] As he had written in *The Winning of the West*, he always believed that their very presence in the United States was a tragic but irreversible historical error.[70] Black Americans were somewhat less backward than "Negroes" anywhere else in the world because they had extensive contact with civilization in the United States. Yet even so, Roosevelt warned, it might take "many thousand years" before "the descendant of the Negro" in the United States evolved to become even "as intellectual as the [ancient] Athenian."[71]

The disparity in racial capacity between black and white threatened the nation with race war, since the "fundamental . . . fact of the conflict between race and race" at such different evolutionary points inevitably led men into racial violence.[72] TR deplored such racial violence as uncivilized and made headlines in 1903 and 1906 by denouncing lynching. Yet, although he deplored lynching, Roosevelt assumed racial violence was all but inevitable when men of such dissimilar races lived together.[73]

Thus Roosevelt saw the "Negro Problem" as a question of male power. The men of the masterful white American race had an irresistible evolutionary imperative to assert control over any race of inferior men in their midst. The Negro race was, unfortunately, permanently resident in the United States. Racial violence was thus a natural and inevitable part of manhood in a racially diverse society. Yet this posed another problem, because violence was itself barbarous and incompatible with a highly advanced civilization.

The only way to solve this dilemma, Roosevelt believed, was to focus explicitly on manhood. Because race difference was extreme and inescapable, the only solution was to pretend races did not exist, and invoke a democratic individualism which would allow each man (however racially unequal) to compete as a man.

Racial strife was unavoidable; racial inequality a terrible and immutable fact. The only solution was to trust to manhood and natural selection, allowing each man to compete fairly, as a man facing other men, regardless of race. If any African American man proved himself as manly as white American men in fair competition, he should be given an equal chance.

In other words, where African Americans were concerned, Roosevelt substituted an individual contest between men—the democratic merit system—for a collective contest between men—race war. To carry out this substitution, Roosevelt made ostentatious efforts to appoint blacks to federal positions, though he always complained qualified black candidates were inordinately difficult to find. But although Roosevelt championed the right of individual, superior black men to compete with white men, he was confident that the Negro race, as a whole, was so far inferior to the white American race that no real evolutionary challenge would ensue.[74]

He was less confident about the Japanese. He believed them "a great civilized power of a formidable type; and with motives and ways of thought which are not quite those of the powers of our race."[75] Because Japanese men were civilized, they were serious contenders for evolutionary supremacy and could pose a threat to white Americans' manly dominance. After all, they too had proven their masculinity through imperialistic race war, defeating the Russians in 1904, as the American frontiersmen had defeated the Indians. Yet, however advanced, Japanese civilization was nonetheless both inferior to and incompatible with white American civilization.

Thus, it would be extremely dangerous to allow Japanese men to immigrate freely into the United States. On the one hand, the less civilized Japanese men were less manly and so willing to work for lower wages than American men. On the other hand, the Japanese were somewhat civilized and so were desirable and competent workers. Here was a particularly dangerous situation: If Japanese workingmen were allowed to settle in the United States, they could emasculate American men as breadwinners. Allowing Japanese men to immigrate and compete with white American men would thus be, as TR put it, "race suicide."[76]

In order to avoid this masculine racial competition, with its threat of race suicide, Roosevelt stood firm on proscribing all permanent Japanese immigrants, although temporary Japanese visitors—for example, students and tourists—would be acceptable.[77] The men of such totally different and unassimilable civilizations, living side by side, must inevitably compete in the daily struggle for economic survival and eventually battle for control of the American land and resources. "To permit the Japanese to come in large numbers into this country would be to cause a race problem and invite and insure a race contest."[78]

TR's views on manhood and civilization thus shaped his presidential policies toward both African Americans and Japanese immigration, but in contrasting ways. Because TR believed African Americans already resident in the United States in large numbers, were generally primitive and inferior, he was willing to make a virtue of necessity by allowing black men to compete with white American men on an equal basis. He believed that if natural selection took its course, African American men would be weeded out as unfit, and the manly white American race would remain supreme. Japanese men, however, were civilized, and thus formidable manly competitors. To allow natural selection to work— to allow Japanese men to compete, as men, with white American men—would be dangerous to the white American race's supremacy "Civilized" Japanese men, thus, should be excluded, while "primitive" African American men should be allowed to compete.[79]

Allowing Japanese immigration was not the only way the white American race could commit race suicide, however. Roosevelt was even more worried about a similarly suicidal racial tendency: native-born white Americans' falling birth rate. In his warnings about racial decadence, Roosevelt had always insisted that women's reluctance to breed was as dangerous to the race as men's reluctance to fight. Either way, a race would lose power and allow inferior races to surpass it in the Darwinistic quest for global supremacy.

Although historians today usually think of race suicide purely in terms of the birthrate controversy, the issue was tied to a host of broader fears about effeminacy, overcivilization, and racial decadence. The term "race suicide" was first coined in 1901 by sociologist Edward A. Ross. In his address "The Causes of Race Superiority," Ross raised all the fears of decadent manhood that had been so often evoked throughout the 1890s.[80] He delineated the racial characteristics which had made white

Americans superior to all other races—self-reliance, foresight, the ability to control their passions—in short, manliness. Yet, Ross argued, when faced with competition from less manly, racially inferior immigrants, these manly traits would prove the superior race's undoing. As it competed with these immigrants, the "very foresight and will power that mark the higher race dig a pit beneath its feet."[81] The superior race's manly self-denial gave it the drive to provide a rising standard of living for its children. But when manly white men competed for a livelihood with their racial inferiors, the inferior men, able to survive on less, would drive down wages; and the superior race's standard of living would decline. Unwilling to sire children they could not provide for, the superior American men would have fewer and fewer children. Thus manfully controlling their emotions, American men would "quietly and unmurmuringly eliminate" themselves.[82]

Race suicide thus expressed the ultimate racial nightmare—impotent, decadent manhood. In Ross' vision, the same manly traits which allowed a superior race to develop the most advanced civilization would leave it unable to compete with more primitive, less manly races. Civilized races' *manliness* thus threatened to destroy their *virility*.

Roosevelt shared Ross' concern about the dangers of a falling birthrate.[83] TR had first voiced concern about the birthrate in 1894, about the same time he began to worry about national decadence and to agitate for a more vigorous imperialism. "Unquestionably, no community that is actually diminishing in numbers is in a healthy condition; and as the world is now, with huge waste places still to fill up, and with much of the competition between the races reducing itself to the warfare of the cradle, no race has any chance to win a great place unless it consists of good breeders as well as of good fighters," he warned.[84] In the midst of chronicling the manly American race's heroic conquest of savage Indians, the author of *The Winning of the West* fretted that "the warfare of the cradle" could undo the warfare of the frontier.

Roosevelt's personal dismay about the falling birthrate remained relatively private until 1903 when, as president, he allowed a letter expressing his fears about race suicide to be published. In October 1902 Roosevelt had written author Bessie Van Vorst, praising her *The Woman Who Toils*, an exposé of the hardships faced by women factory workers, then running serially in *Everybody's Magazine*. Van Vorst scarcely mentioned the birthrate, but she did suggest that factory girls liked the independence of wage work and thus were in no hurry to marry. This elicited a Rooseveltian tirade against race suicide. Possibly hoping to bolster sales, Van Vorst obtained TR's permission to reprint his letter as a preface to her book. Thus the nation became acquainted with Roosevelt's views, and the phrase "race suicide" came before the general public for the first time.[85]

Denouncing the selfish wish to live for individual pleasure, TR called instead for "the strong racial qualities without which there can be no strong races"—courage, high-mindedness, unselfishness. The absence of these sorts of virtues showed a reprehensible inability to consider the good of the race and was a symptom of "decadence and corruption in the nation." A man or woman who, considering only his or her own individual convenience, deliberately avoided having children was "in effect a criminal against the race, and should be an object of contemptuous abhorrence by all healthy people." Men must be "ready and able to fight at need, and anxious to be fathers of families," just as women must "recognize that the greatest thing for any woman is to be a good wife and mother." Refusing to bear children was the same sort of racial crime as refusing to fight for racial advancement; for no matter how refined its civilization, a race which refused to fight or breed was doomed to racial extinction.[86] The masterful American race could regain its manly primacy through willful procreative effort.

Elite magazines' discussions mostly revolved around how to keep civilization manly and powerful. Many commentators accepted Roosevelt's argument and wrung their hands over civilization's future. Some complained that less civilized races outbred the native-born whites.[87] Others claimed a decadent love of luxury was sapping white Americans' will to sacrifice for their children. Some fretted that the white American race, like an overbred hybrid, had simply become sterile.[88] The anti-imperialist *Nation* agreed that a negative birthrate heralded national decadence, but it turned race suicide into an argument against TR's imperialism, suggesting that "a people who cannot bring to maturity an average of more than nineteen children to twenty parents ought not to think of having colonies and of civilizing inferior races."[89] Although feminists objected that TR's pronouncements limited women to earning their "right to a footing on earth by bearing children and in no other way," and questioned "the note of savagery that rings in [TR's] voice when he discusses war and 'race suicide,'" they had little impact on the national debate.[90]

Outside the genteel press, however, the race suicide debates developed unexpectedly into a new and respectable way to celebrate masculine sexuality. In April 1903, only two months after his letter was published, Roosevelt embarked on a Western speaking tour and was delighted to discover that the public now saw him as a patron saint of large families: "I found to my utter astonishment that my letter to those Van Vorst women about their excellent book had gone everywhere, and the population of each place invariably took the greatest pride in showing off the children."[91] Always the resourceful publicist, TR grabbed the chance to encourage the American race to breed. Throughout TR's presidency, Americans deluged the White House with letters and photographs of their large families, receiving in reply presidential letters of congratulations.[92]

In these exchanges Roosevelt and his audience affirmed the potency of their civilization by affirming the sexual power of American manhood. By repeatedly invoking multitudes of rosy, white, native-born children, these cries of "No race suicide here!" joyfully reassured men that white American manhood was not growing decadent or overcivilized—just look what American paternity could produce! As these humorous protestations multiplied, they took on a ritual quality. At one typical interchange in 1905, Roosevelt was preparing to address the Society of Friendly Sons of St. Patrick at Delmonico's in New York when he was handed a telegram. During the course of the banquet one of the diners, Peter McDonnell, had become a grandfather, and his son Robert had cabled him the good news. TR jocularly announced that "as a sop to certain of my well-known prejudices," he had been shown the telegram, and he then read it aloud to the assembled Friendly Sons. "Patrick just arrived. Tired after parade. Sends his regards to the President. . . . No race suicide in this family." According to the *New York Times*, "Pandemonium resulted. Men yelled and laughed and waved flags and behaved like boys on a lark."[93] As TR beamed down on the ecstatic gathering, the message was clear. Overcivilized effeminacy be damned—*they* were men.

Conclusion

Theodore Roosevelt is often invoked as turn-of-the-century America's prime example of a new and strenuous manhood. This chapter has attempted to show that one cannot understand Theodore Roosevelt's evocation of powerful manhood without understanding that, for Roosevelt, race and gender were inextricably intertwined with each other, and with imperialistic nationalism. In an era when traditional ideologies of manhood were being actively renegotiated, Roosevelt reinvigorated male authority by tying it to white racial supremacy and to a militaristic, racially based nationalism.

Theodore Roosevelt was not a representative American man. He was privileged and powerful, and some of his views were surely idiosyncratic. Yet, as we have seen, his impulse to remake male power by linking it to racial dominance using the discourse of civilization was not unusual. In diverse ways throughout the United States, men who felt the loss of older ideas of male authority—who feared that Victorian manliness was no longer enough to explain the source and workings of male power—turned to ideas of white supremacy. *Men's* power was growing murky. But *the white man's* power, the power of civilization, was crystal clear. And as race became interwoven with manhood through discourses of civilization, Americans' assumptions about manhood moved ever closer, to what twentieth-century men would recognize as "masculinity."

Notes

1. Edmund Morris, *The Rise of Theodore Roosevelt* (New York: Ballantine, 1979), 159–202, 227–70.

2. Mark Sullivan, *Our Times: The United States 1900–1925* (New York: Charles Scribner's Sons, 1927), 2:226–9; Morris, *Rise*, 162; David McCullough, *Mornings on Horseback* (New York: Simon and Schuster, 1981), 256.

3. Paula Baker, "The Domestication of Politics: Women and American Political Society, 1780–1920," *American Historical Review* 89 (June 1984): 620–47, esp. 628–30; *Paula Baker, The Moral Framework of Public Life: Gender, Politics, and the State in Rural New York, 1870–1930* (New York: Oxford University Press, 1991), 24–55.

4. Morris, *Rise*, 166.

5. Ibid., 349–53.

6. See, e.g., Peter G. Filene, *Him/Her/Self: Sex Roles in Modern America* (Baltimore: Johns Hopkins University Press, 1986), 69–93, 71, 73; Joe L. Dubbert, *A Man's Place: Masculinity in Transition* (Englewood Cliffs, N.J.: Prentice-Hall, 1979) 131–3; and Harvey Green, *Fit for America: Health, Fitness, Sport and American Society* (Baltimore: Johns Hopkins University Press, 1986), 235–8.

7. For a fine discussion of many of the same themes from a slightly different angle, see Donna Haraway, "Teddy Bear Patriarchy: Taxidermy in the Garden of Eden, New York City, 1908–36," in *Primate Visions: Gender, Race, and Nature in the World of Modern Science* (New York: Routledge, 1989), 26–58.

8. Anthony Rotundo, *American Manhood: Transformations in Masculinity from the Revolution to the Modern Era* (New York: Basic, 1993), 31–55.

9. Theodore Roosevelt, *An Autobiography* (1913; New York, De Capo Press, 1985), 7.

10. Ibid., 10; McCullough, *Mornings*, 28–9.

11. Roosevelt, *Autobiography*, 14; McCullough, *Mornings*, 115; and Morris, *Rise*, 46.

12. Captain Mayne Reid, *The Boy Hunters; or Adventures in Search of a White Buffalo* (Boston: Ticknor and Fields, 1852); Paul Russell Cutright, *Theodore Roosevelt: The Making of a Conservationist* (Urbana: University of Illinois Press, 1985), 5.

13. Reid, *Boy Hunters*, 363.

14. Richard Slotkin, *Regeneration through Violence: The Mythology of the American Frontier, 1600–1860* (Middletown, Conn: Wesleyan University Press, 1973); and Richard Slotkin, *The Fatal Environment: The Myth of the Frontier in the Age of Industrialization, 1800–1890* (New York: Atheneum, 1985).

15. Reid, *Boy Hunters*, 90–114, 120, emphasis in the original; see also McCullough, *Mornings*, 116.

16. McCullough, *Mornings*, 116.

17. Darwin himself, of course, was far less eager to embrace violence as the engine of evolutionary progress than some of his "Darwinistic" followers.

18. On Roosevelt's first trip west, see Morris, *Rise*, 202–25.

19. Morris, *Rise*, 222–3.

20. On Alice Lee's death, see Morris, *Rise*, 221–5, 284–5.

21. Interview, *New York Tribune* (28 July 1884), quoted in Morris, *Rise*, 281. For "Cowboy Land," see Theodore Roosevelt, "In Cowboy-Land," *Century* 46 (June 1893): 276–84; and Roosevelt, *Autobiography*, 94–131.

22. Morris, *Rise*, 297.

23. Theodore Roosevelt, *Hunting Trips of a Ranchman* (New York: G. P. Putnam's Sons, 1885), frontispiece.

24. See Theodore Roosevelt, *The Winning of the West*, 4 vols. (New York: G. P Putnam's Sons, 1889–96), 1:114–5.

25. Roosevelt, *Ranch Life and the Hunting Trail* (New York: Winchester Press, 1969), 7.

26. Ibid., 102–4.

27. Morris, *Rise*, 349–53.

28. See, for example, "The President Talks on the Philippines," *New York Times*, 8 April 1903, 3; "Mr. Roosevelt Sees a Cowboy Festival," *New York Times*, 26 April 1903, 1; and "President Calls for a Larger Navy," *New York Times*, 23 May 1903, 2.

29. Michel Foucault, "Nietzsche, Genealogy, History," in *Language, Counter-Memory, Practice: Selected Essays and Interviews*, ed. Donald F Bouchard (Ithaca, N.Y. Cornell University Press, 1977), 139–64, esp. 139–45.

30. Roosevelt, *Winning*, l: xiv. For other discussions of *The Winning of the West*, which properly define it as a story of racial origins, see Thomas G. Dyer, *Theodore Roosevelt and the Idea of Race* (Baton Rouge: Louisiana State University Press, 1980), 54–67; Morris, *Rise*, 462–5; and especially Richard Slotkin, *Gunfighter Nation: The Myth of the Frontier in Twentieth Century America* (New York: Atheneum, 1992), 42–51, and Richard Slotkin, "Nostalgia and Progress: Theodore Roosevelt's Myth of the Frontier," *American Quarterly* 33 (Winter 1981): 608–37.

31. Roosevelt, *Winning*, l: xiv.

32. Ibid., 1:1–27.

33. Ibid., 3:28–9; 1:8.

34. Ibid., 1:87; 3:40, 326.

35. Ibid., 3:1.

36. Ibid., 1:124.

37. Ibid., 1:113.

38. Ibid., 1:106.

39. Ibid., 1:69.

40. Slotkin, "Nostalgia and Progress," 623–34.

41. Roosevelt, *Winning*, 1:110

42. Ibid., 3:36.

43. Ibid., 2:230–1.

44. Morris, *Rise*, 471.

45. Theodore Roosevelt, "The Monroe Doctrine" (1896), in *American Ideals and Other Essays, Social and Political* (New York: G. P Putnam's Sons, 1897), 2:58–9.

46. Theodore Roosevelt, "The Law of Civilization and Decay," *Forum* 22 (January 1897): 579.

47. Theodore Roosevelt, "Value of an Athletic Training," *Harper's Weekly* 37 (23 December 1893): 1236.

48. Theodore Roosevelt, "The Manly Virtues and Practical Politics," *Forum* 17 (July 1894): 555.

49. Rudyard Kipling, "The White Man's Burden," in *The Five Nations: The Works of Rudyard Kipling*, 30 vols. (New York: Scribner's, 1903), 21:78.

50. Quoted in Willard Gatewood, *Black Americans and the White Man's Burden* (Urbana: University of Illinois Press, 1975), 183. See also 183–6 for a fine discussion of African Americans' scathing parodies and reactions to Kipling's poem.

51. Theodore Roosevelt, "National Duties," in *The Strenuous Life: Essays and Addresses* (1901; St. Clair Shores, Mich.: Scholarly Press, 1970), 280.

52. Ibid., 282.

53. Ibid., 287.

54. Ibid., 288.

55. Ibid., 291.

56. Ibid., 293–4.

57. Ibid., 292–6.

58. Ibid., 296–7.

59. Roosevelt to Paul Dana [editor of the *New York Sun*], April 18, 1898, in *Letters*, 2:817.

60. Quoted in Morris, *Rise*, 673.

61. Morris, *Rise*, 614. For the full story of the Rough Riders, see Morris, *Rise*, 615–61.

62. Slotkin, *Gunfighter Nation*, 79–87; see also 101–6.

63. Morris, *Rise*, 629.

64. Ibid., 665.

65. Roosevelt, *Autobiography*, 398–9.

66. Ibid., 516–7.

67. Ibid., 520–1.

68. John R. Jenswold, "Leaving the Door Ajar: Politics and Prejudices in the Making of the 1907 Immigration Law," *Mid-America* 67 (January 1985): 3–22; and Dyer, *Roosevelt and the Idea of Race*, 129–34.

69. Theodore Roosevelt, "National Life and Character" (1894) in *American Ideals and Other Essays, Social and Political* (New York: G. P Putnam's Sons, 1897), 1:109. For a comprehensive discussion of Roosevelt's ideas about African Americans, see Dyer, *Roosevelt and the Idea of Race*, 89–122; and George Sinkler, *The Racial Attitudes of American Presidents* (Garden City, N.Y.: Doubleday, 1971), 341–73.

70. Roosevelt to Albion Winegar Tourgée, 8 November 1901, in *Letters* 3:190; Roosevelt, *Winning*, 3:28–9.

71. Theodore Roosevelt, "The Negro in America," (4 June, 1910) in *The Works of Theodore Roosevelt*, Memorial Ed., 24 vols. (New York: Charles Scribner's Sons, 1925), 14:194; Roosevelt, "National Life and Character," 110–1.

72. Roosevelt to Ray Stannard Baker, 3 June 1908, in *Letters*, 6:1047–8.

73. Roosevelt to Charles Henry Pearson, 11 May 1894, in *Letters*, 1:376–7.

74. Roosevelt to Charles Henry Pearson, 11 May 1894, in *Letters*, 1:376–7.

75. Roosevelt to Cecil Arthur Spring Rice, 16 June 1905, in *Letters*, 4:1233–4.

76. Roosevelt to James Wilson, 3 February 1903, in *Letters*, 3:416.

77. Roosevelt to William Kent, 4 February 1909, in *Letters*, 6:1503. See also Theodore Roosevelt, "The Japanese Question," in *Works*, National Ed., 16:289; originally published in the *Outlook*, 8 May 1909.

78. Roosevelt to Philander Chase Knox, 8 February 1909, in *Letters*, 6:1511. See also Roosevelt, *Autobiography*, 392–3, 396.

79. Sinkler, *Racial Attitudes*, 317–8.

80. Edward A. Ross, "The Causes of Race Superiority," *Annals of the American Academy of Political and Social Science* 18 (July 1901): 67–89.

81. Ibid., 86.

82. Ibid., 88.

83. Dyer, *Roosevelt and the Idea of Race,* 143–67. See also Sinkler, *Racial Attitudes,* 337–40.

84. Roosevelt, "National Life and Character," 2:117.

85. Bessie and Marie Van Vorst, *The Woman Who Toils: Being the Experience of Two Ladies as Factory Girls* (New York: Doubleday, Page, 1903), 1–2; for the uncut letter, see Roosevelt to Bessie Van Vorst, 18 October 1902, in *Letters,* 3:355–6. This was the beginning of Roosevelt's public attack on race suicide, not his March 1905 speech to the National Congress of Mothers, as Linda Gordon has suggested in *Woman's Body,* 136–7, 142.

86. Roosevelt to Bessie Van Vorst, 18 October 1902, in *Letters,* 3:355.

87. See, e.g., A. C. R., "Race Preservation," *New York Times,* 7 June 1903, 14. Actually, while the birthrate of African Americans was somewhat higher than that of white Americans, it was falling far more rapidly. See *Men's Ideas/Women's Realities,* ed. Newman, 120.

88. "Race Suicide," *Independent* 55 (May 21, 1903): 1220–1; "Topics of the Times: Presenting a Few of the Facts," *New York Times,* 1 May 1905, 8.

89. "The Question of the Birthrate," *Nation* 76 (11 June 1903): 469.

90. Reason vs. Instinct [pseud.], "No Fear of 'Race Suicide,'" *New York Times,* 4 March 1903, 8. See also Lydia Kingsmill Commander, "Has the Small Family Become an American Ideal?" *Independent* 56 (14 April 1904): 837–40.

91. Roosevelt to John Hay, 9 August 1903, in *Letters,* 3:549.

92. "Mr. Roosevelt's Views on Race Suicide," *Ladies' Home Journal* 23 (February 1906): 21; Roosevelt to Mr. and Mrs. R. T. Bower, 14 February 1903, in *Letters,* 3:425; "Roosevelt Thanks a Father," *New York Times,* 21 July 1904, 5.

93. Theodore Roosevelt, "Americans of Irish Origin," *Works,* National Ed., 16:39–40; "Roosevelt Praises the Hardy Irish," *New York Times,* 18 March 1905, 1.

CHAPTER 12

Our First Unisex President?

Black Masculinity and Obama's Feminine Side

Frank Rudy Cooper

Introduction

During the 2008 Democratic Presidential primaries and general election there was a whole discourse in the media about Senator Barack Obama's (D-IL) femininity. When he faced Senator Hillary Clinton (D-NY) in the primaries, the head of a women's non-profit said, "He's the girl in the race."[1] The magazine *Marketing* said, "In swept Barack Obama with what could be described as a classically feminine campaign. . . . The values he represented contrasted with Clinton in being more collaborative, more human, more feelings-led and people-focused."[2] The idea was that while Clinton was tough and hawkish, Obama was empathetic and inclusive.[3] Carol Marin expressed that point of view in an editorial in the *Chicago Sun Times*:

> If Bill Clinton was once considered America's first black president, Obama may one day be viewed as our first woman president. While [Hillary] Clinton, the warrior, battles on, talks about toughness, and out loud considers nuking Iran, it is Obama who is full of feminine virtues.
>
> Consensus. Conciliation. Peace, not war.[4]

For those reasons, a number of people (half-jokingly) refer to Obama as our first female president.[5]

A caveat: In order to evaluate Obama's status as our first female President, we must ask, what does it mean to say that a Presidential candidate acted "feminine" or "masculine" during the campaign? Even someone who believes in a version of cultural feminism has to acknowledge that "masculine" qualities are hardly limited to men and "feminine" qualities are not limited to women.[6] Cultural feminism is the theory that women tend to have certain cultural traits that are most prevalent among women, such as focusing on nurturing relationships rather than applying hierarchical principles in a zero-sum game.[7] Still, "masculine" and "feminine" qualities are nothing more than shared understandings about what it means to act like a man or woman.[8] They are not reflective of stable essences of man or woman as such.[9] Their definitions are subject to change over time and in different cultural contexts.[10] Nonetheless, the discourse in the popular media

SOURCE: Cooper, F. R. (2008). Our First Unisex President? Black Masculinity and Obama's Feminine Side. *Denver University Law Review, 86,* 633–661. Reproduced with permission from the *Denver University Law Review.*

used these concepts to describe the presidential candidates. Accordingly, I[11] will analyze what it meant that Obama displayed qualities the media calls feminine during his campaign for the Presidency.

In order to analyze the significance of Obama's feminine side, I will turn to theories of identity. Identity performance theory says that people make choices about how to present themselves that position their identities against the backdrop of social expectations.[12] Critical race theory explores the ways that race is simultaneously non-existent and materially consequential.[13] Masculinities studies says that assumptions about the meaning of manhood influence behaviors, ideologies, and institutions.[14] Together, these theories will help us analyze how Obama's Presidential campaign influenced popular understandings of femininity and of black male identity.

I argue that Obama was more feminine than most mainstream candidates because he is a black male.[15] I base this argument on my theory of the "bipolarity" of media representations of black men.[16] We are typically described as either the completely threatening Bad Black Man or the fully assimilationist Good Black Man. The Bad Black Man is a criminal you might see on the local news or a race-conscious black leader you might see in other shows.[17] The Good Black Man is a token member of the corporate world or a conservative post-race spokesman.[18] A prime stereotype of the Bad Black Man that Obama must avoid is the stereotype of the angry black man.[19] One way to counter this stereotype is to be unusually calm. Obama has that quality, as well as a penchant for negotiation over imposition. Together, those qualities seem to be the source of claims that he would be our first female president.[20]

Obama's calmness has roots in the general need of black men to be non-threatening in order to achieve mainstream success. As a youth, Obama learned to be calm in order to assimilate.[21] During the Presidential campaign, Obama's calmness in the face of attacks was strategic in order to prevent whites from associating him with the angry black man stereotype.[22] Obama's feminine qualities are thus revealed to have been necessitated in part by his desire to avoid a stereotype of the Bad Black Man.[23]

Obama's feminization strategy was potentially dangerous, however, since femininity is still a slur in our male-dominated culture. Obama had to engage in a balancing act. He could not be too masculine because that would trigger the Bad Black Man image but he could not be too feminine because that would have looked unpresidential.

Obama seems to have resolved that conflict by being masculine enough to pass the Commander-in-Chief test yet feminine enough to make people comfortable with his blackness.[24] He tried to place himself more toward the middle of the general gender continuum, rather than the masculine end that most Presidential candidates frequent, as a means of showing that he was on the good side of the specific black masculinity continuum. The appropriate term for Obama's feminine-but-not-too-much-so style seems to be "unisex."[25] A unisex style is one that is "designed to be suitable for" either gender.[26] A unisex style can swing both ways, creating the overall impression of being in the middle of the gender continuum. Obama's style was unisex in that he moved from more masculine to more feminine depending on the context.

While there is some implication that a unisex style is one that lacks the characteristics of either sex, I am emphasizing the fact that a unisex style is one that a member of either gender can adopt.[27] Often the term applies to clothing that can be worn by either men or women. The example that comes to mind is the blue jean, which can be masculinized or feminized to suit the wearer's needs on the particular occasion.[28] A unisex style fits between the two genders, but not in the sense of being asexual. Obama was more feminine than most Presidential candidates, but hardly non-gendered, like "Pat" from the famous *Saturday Night Live* skit.[29] Obama's style ranged from his tough guy acceptance speech at the Democratic convention[30] to his playing of feminist folk songs at his rallies.[31] Accordingly, I argue that Obama was not our first female Presidential candidate, but our first unisex Presidential candidate.

I. Theories of Identities

My methodology in this essay is rather simple. I have reviewed the news stories on LEXIS/NEXIS that discuss Obama and femininity.[32] I have analyzed those stories using the lenses of critical race theory and masculinities studies.

A. Some Tenets of Critical Race Theory

With those shared understandings of identities in mind, I now turn to the task of summarizing critical race theory. Critical race theory is an interdisciplinary field that draws heavily upon ethnic studies, history, and sociology, among other fields. The editors of the legal academy's most important anthology of critical race theory texts define this school of thought as "challeng[ing] the ways in which race and racial power are constructed and represented in American legal culture and, more generally, in American society as a whole."[33] In this section of the essay, I will review some tenets of critical race theory.[34]

The first tenet of critical race theory is that it is founded on the need to unpack the ways in which race and other identities are both socially constructed and materially consequential.[35] Proponents of social construction accept Michael Omi and Howard Winant's theory that race is "formed." That is, bases for racial stratification are ideologically constructed, or formed, and then used to justify particular social orders.[36] Race and masculinity, and thus black maleness, do not actually exist. At best, they are biological configurations that in no way dictate personalities. Society "forms" the meanings of identity positions, such as heterosexual black maleness, and people then adopt the practices associated with those positions.[37] However, the status of being black and male is materially consequential in that it triggers a whole host of stereotypes, such as the angry black man stereotype that I discuss further in Part II. Those stereotypes are materially consequential in that they influence the distribution of social goods.[38]

A second tenet of critical race theory is that the racial status quo is often perpetuated by bias that is implicit rather than explicit. Accordingly, Jerry Kang and Mahzarin Banaji apply implicit bias theory to argue that, rather than traditional affirmative action, what we need are "debiasing agents."[39] These are people whose identities contradict biases about who would, and would not, hold certain positions.[40] As a black President, Obama could serve as a debiasing agent for the whole country by changing expectations about what types of people can hold that position. In my conclusion, I will both note Obama's debiasing effect and discuss the ways that Obama does and does not change expectations for performances of race and gender in general.

As this focus on how identity characteristics matter suggests, a third tenet of critical race theory is the critique of colorblindness. As presently used, colorblindness is a perversion of the first Justice Harlan's statement that "our constitution is colorblind"[41] and Martin Luther King, Jr.'s statement that blacks should be judged by the "content of their character."[42] Those statements have been translated into the proposition that merely acknowledging someone's race is invidious racism.[43] Accordingly, schools cannot consider how a student's racial identity has negatively affected or enriched her experiences.[44] Elsewhere, I have noted that accepting colorblindness seems to be an implicit requirement for black men to be able to advance in corporations.[45] In Part II of this essay I will argue that during the campaign Obama was subject to assimilationist pressure to pretend that race does not matter. For now, it suffices to say that critical race theory refuses to view black men as if our race were inconsequential to the expectations that people have of us.

Taken together, the principles of identity theories in general and these three tenets of critical race theory in particular describe a perspective that can be brought to bear on the question of how black men are understood in popular culture. In my article, *Against Bipolar Black Masculinity: Intersectionality, Assimilation, Identity Performance, and Hierarchy*, I critically reviewed scholarship on media representations of black men and found that they

> depict us as either the completely threatening Bad Black Man or the fully assimilationist Good Black Man. The Bad Black Man is animalistic, sexually depraved, and crime-prone. The Good Black Man distances himself from black people and emulates white views. The images are bipolar in that they swing from one extreme to another with little room for nuanced depictions. Threatened with the Bad Black Man image, black men are provided with an "assimilationist incentive" to pursue the Good Black Man image.[46]

It may be helpful to emphasize some points about the bipolarity of black masculinity. First, similar phenomena play out with respect to other denigrated groups. For instance, Mahmood Mamdani discusses a good muslim, bad muslim dichotomy in post-9/11 representations of Islam.[47] Second, I identify race consciousness as a trait of the Bad Black Man because the bipolarity of black masculinity has the purpose of forcing assimilation to the mainstream norm. The assimilationist model makes no room for race consciousness, let alone racial loyalty. Since the default position on black men is that we are bad, we must defeat that presumption to gain mainstream acceptance.[48] While the criminal is the paradigmatic Bad Black Man, the race-conscious black man also fails to defeat that presumption.

Because the default position on black men is that we fit the Bad Black Man stereotype, we are incentivized to demonstrate our assimilation.[49] A primary means for the Good Black Man to distinguish himself from the Bad Black Man is to respond to the assimilationist incentive by engaging in race-distancing acts.[50] Race-distancing acts, such as adopting the colorblind stance that one does not even notice the color of the people one interacts with, are ways of performing one's identity that respond to the assimilationist incentive. Such race-distancing in order to assimilate is problematic, though, since it suggests that only blacks who act white deserve mainstream success.[51] As a mainstream candidate, Obama would seem to have been especially subject to the assimilationist incentive. I will apply this theory of bipolar black masculinity to Obama in Part II of this essay by arguing that his feminine style was a choice about how to perform his identity that had strategic benefits.

B. Some Tenets of Masculinities Studies

We can best define masculinities studies as the interdisciplinary field that describes the ways assumptions about the meanings of manhood are used to justify particular ideas, behaviors, and institutions.[52] Masculinities studies is interdisciplinary in that it draws heavily upon feminist theory, sociology, and queer theory, among other fields. I will describe the contours of this field by reviewing some of masculinities studies' basic tenets.[53]

The first tenet of masculinities studies is that the principal message that masculinity norms send is that masculinity is to be privileged over femininity. For example, Deborah Brake has described the privileging of men in athletics.[54] Ann C. McGinley has discussed the privileging of masculinity in the very structure of work.[55] Valerie Vojdik has discussed male privileging in the rituals of all-male educational institutions.[56] Throughout Western civilization men have generally been the leaders and have generally relegated women to the private sphere.[57] Here, that privileging is seen in the fact that Obama was often denigrated for having feminine traits, as I will describe in Part II of this essay.[58]

A second tenet of masculinities studies is that men have a constant need to prove to other men that they possess the normative masculinity, which leads to an ongoing masculine anxiety.[59] That is so because the rules of the hegemonic, or dominant, form of masculinity[60] are unrealizable.[61] Manhood is a relentless test of how close you are to the ideal.[62] Men must constantly re-prove that they possess the hegemonic form of masculinity.[63] We are thus placed in a state of constant anxiety over our masculinity.[64]

A third tenet of masculinities studies is that norms of masculinity constrain men's performances of their identities. The first constraint on men's identity performances is the need to denigrate contrast figures. As Mutua says, "the central feature of masculinity is the domination and oppression of others; namely women, children, and other subordinated men."[65] Since the idealized figure of the powerful white male is the model for hegemonic masculinity, demonstrating that you fit the hegemonic pattern of U.S. masculinity involves a repudiation of that model's contrast figures, most notably, women, gays, and racial minorities.[66]

A second constraint on men's identity performance stems from the first: a competitiveness reflected in a need to dominate other men. Behaviors that seek to express dominance over other men, such as aggression, are part of the project of establishing that one possesses the hegemonic form of U.S. masculinity.[67] Given that hegemonic masculinity is associated with economic success, it might seem strange that a low-brow quality like aggression is so prized. As Jewel Woods notes, however,

> Despite the economic trend away from blue-collar jobs, many of the most powerful expressions of masculinity within contemporary American society continue to be associated with blue-collar imagery. . . .
>
> . . . At the very same time society is becoming less reliant on male brawn, the dominant cultural images of masculinity are largely derived from the "traditional" ideas of maleness.[68]

So, there is a nostalgia for blue-collar aggression. The expectation that a man will display an aggressive demeanor is so pervasive that it stands as a second constraint on men's performances of their identities. This fact was reflected in the many criticisms of Obama for not striking back more aggressively when attacked by Hillary Clinton or McCain, which I will analyze in Part II of this essay.[69]

II. Analyzing Obama's Femininity

As sociologist Michael Kimmel has noted, "From the founding of the country, presidents of the United States have seen the political arena as a masculine testing ground."[70] It is thus appropriate that the *Orlando Sentinel* presented the 2008 Presidential general election as a referendum on whether we wanted masculine leadership or feminine leadership. It said, "Now that the actual [P]residential campaign is under way, we have the traditionally 'masculine' style, embodied by John McCain, emphasizing experience, toughness, feistiness, stubbornness, grit, exclusivity, etc., and the newly emergent 'feminine' managerial style practiced by Obama and emphasizing communication, consensus, collegiality and inclusivity."[71] Prior to that editorial, the *New York Post* ran an editorial suggesting that Obama would be "our first woman president."[72] There are more examples of the gendered framing of this race in the media, which I will address later.[73]

Obama was called feminine because of his restraint, calm demeanor, collaborative style, willingness to speak with enemies, and finely honed language.[74] Those characterizations of Obama as feminine, while melodramatic, did seem to capture real differences between Obama and his opponents. The media has recognized that Obama has "an unusual blend of traditionally masculine and feminine skills at work in him."[75] Further, there is reason to believe Obama's feminization was conscious:[76] Obama's feminine style was unlikely to be accidental given the meticulous planning that goes into every move of a Presidential candidate.[77] The media's gendered framing of Obama thus had some basis in Obama's actions.

The identity theories that I outlined in Part I will prove helpful in analyzing Obama's feminine style. First, this election gave us a chance to observe the processes of the social construction of the meanings of black masculinity and of femininity in action. Since the Presidency is a bully pulpit that influences how people think about themselves and others, I expect that Obama's election will influence people's expectations for performances of race and gender. Second, we see both the multiplicity and the hierarchy of masculinities in the different constraints (and privileges) placed on Obama because he is a black male. McCain could be angry, but Obama could not.[78] Ironically, Obama's status as a minority male may have given him more leeway to feminize himself than McCain because of the assumption that black men are already overly masculine.[79] With those general identity theory insights in mind, I now turn to specific critical race theory and masculinities studies analyses of Obama's femininity.

A. Critical Race Theory and Obama as a Good Black Man

Does the bipolar black masculinity thesis that I described in Part I of this essay apply to the 2008 election? Seemingly, yes. The media has sometimes acknowledged Obama's bipolarity problem. In an article in the *Washington Post*, journalist Courtland Milloy says, "You can walk a fine line between being too black for whites and not black enough for blacks."[80] That is the basic problem Obama faced, even though he largely had blacks locked into voting for him given that Republican John McCain was not seen as a viable alternative. I suspect that many whites would have been less interested in Obama if he were seen as an inauthentic black man or downright collaborator with white supremacy. Obama thus had to navigate between poles of blackness and whiteness.

As the Good Black Man image would dictate, Obama consistently downplayed his race and avoided racial issues.[81] For instance, David Axelrod, a significant Obama campaign official, was quoted as saying, "[W]e're focusing not on his race but the qualities of leadership that he would bring to this country."[82] Such statements are problematic because, in the context of Obama's refusal to mention race even as he made racial history, they suggest that he was engaging in the type of race distancing acts that the Good Black Man model calls for.[83] That conclusion is supported by the fact that Obama seemingly tied himself to color blindness,[84] another characteristic of the Good Black Man.[85] Obama often said things like, "There's not a black America and white America and Latino America and Asian America—there's the United States of America."[86]

My analysis of Obama as a potential Good Black Man also seems to be supported by the general tone of Obama's campaign. As others have noted, Obama cultivated a "post-racial" image.[87] While Obama did explicitly mention race during the controversy over his former pastor, Jeremiah Wright, he only did so when race was unavoidable and precisely in order to take race off the table. In a post-election *New Yorker* article, journalist David Remnick said "[t]he speech in Philadelphia did more than change the subject."[88] But changing the subject was the speech's primary goal.

The bigger problem for Obama, though, was his need to reject linkage with the Bad Black Man. This explains why he denigrated black fathers and repudiated Wright. First, in his Father's Day speech to a black audience, Obama scolded fathers, but especially black fathers, for being "missing in action."[89] It is hard not to believe that such statements were meant to distance Obama from the Bad Black Man image. As civil rights leader Julian Bond told Remnick, "Jesse [Jackson, Sr.] had the feeling that Obama played to white Americans by criticizing black Americans, for not doing enough to help ourselves. . . ."[90] When Jackson had to apologize for the crude form of such a criticism, it gave Obama the opportunity to distance himself from a famously race-affirming black man.[91]

Having seen the applicability of the bipolar black masculinity thesis, we can now see that Obama's post-racial Good Black Man approach is related to his feminine style. The best example of this is the fact that, as a black man, Obama had to soften his approach or be deemed an angry black man. During the campaign, Milloy said that Obama was being called on to prove he was man enough for the

Presidency, but "without coming off as an angry black man."[92] That stereotype may be related to the image of black men as overly masculine since anger is an extreme form of the aggressiveness expected of men.[93] People fear that black men will easily lose their tempers and become out of control.[94] *Time Magazine* made this point a month before the general election.[95]

I speculate that Obama's preternaturally calm demeanor originated in his need to counter the stereotype of the angry black man. Anecdotes from Obama's autobiography, *Dreams From My Father: A Story of Race and Inheritance*, support that view. Remnick concludes that as an undergraduate, "What Obama did learn in those days was the strategic benefit of a calm and inviting temperament."[96] Obama learned that people like a calm black man; "such a pleasant surprise to find a well-mannered young black man who didn't seem angry all the time."[97] Remnick's statements are consistent with what we know about how young black men are raised. We are often warned to be non-threatening in order to avoid police brutality, which is disproportionately visited upon young black males.[98] Obama was certainly aware that black men are often viewed as threatening since he mentioned his grandmother's fear of black men during his campaign speech on race.[99]

My argument is not that Obama was in fact an angry black man who hid his anger during the campaign. Rather, I argue that Obama became a calm black man much earlier in life because he learned that angry black men are not acceptable in elite mainstream environments. Further, the reason angry black masculinity is unacceptable is because it is associated with a race-affirming position. For example, even when Obama wanted to infuse race into the conversation, he found that whites would not allow him to do so. As Remnick reports, the campaign noted a decline in Obama's poll numbers after he repeatedly stated that he did not look like the other Presidents on U.S. currency during his European tour.[100] Obama immediately ceased and desisted from race talk.[101] Consequently, Obama's refusal to get angry even in the face of attacks, which contradicts hegemonic masculinity's call for aggressiveness and is a primary basis for his being called feminine, should be deemed to be the result of special constraints on the performance of black male identity. The principal reason Obama was more feminine than other Presidential candidates was to avoid a pervasive stereotype associated with the Bad Black Man. As I will demonstrate, however, that feminization strategy came with risks.

B. Masculinities Studies and the Dangers of Obama's Feminization

Obama's conundrum was that he had to feminize himself in order not to be seen as an angry black man, but femininity is still a slur. People do not fully believe that women can lead or that feminine styles can show strength.[102] Despite his masculine traits, such as being an avid sports fan[103] and his seemingly traditional relationship with his wife Michelle,[104] Obama had a feminine style in the ways I have discussed. History professor Estelle Freedman fleshed out Obama's gender problem. She said, "Some of the criticism of Obama as being too aloof, or not going after red meat enough, or not being aggressive enough, are really questioning his masculinity in some ways."[105] So, Obama's restrained style could have proven unacceptable to too many people because it was a break with the masculine style traditionally associated with the Presidency.

The masculinities studies tenets I noted earlier elucidate the aspects of Obama's feminine style that proved problematic. First, the privileging of masculinity is clearly seen in the denigration of Obama for his feminine style. For example, MSNBC talk show host Joe Scarborough called Obama "prissy" and insinuated that Obama is not "a real man" because he is not good at bowling.[106] That denigration of Obama's perceived feminine qualities was consistent with hegemonic masculinity's privileging of masculinity. The persistence of associations between the Presidency and masculinity suggests that we still have a long way to go on gender.

Second, we see masculine anxiety in the hand-wringing about the possibility that an Obama presidency might be a feminized presidency. Recall that a need to prove that one is sufficiently masculine is built into the structure of masculinity.[107] Recall further that many people implicitly expect to be able to bask in the nation's reflected masculinity.[108] By virtue of his feminine style, Obama risked failing to satisfy people's needs to soothe their anxiety over our nation's masculinity. His calmness and openness to negotiating rather than imposing his will made some people worry he was not tough enough to be President.[109] That anxiousness was gendered.

Third, the criticism of Obama's lack of manliness reflects hegemonic masculinity's constraint of requiring the denigration of contrast figures. In contravention of the dictates of hegemonic masculinity, whereby masculinity is achieved by not "acting like a woman,"[110] Obama did not attempt to distance himself from his feminine tendencies.[111] Given the need to denigrate contrast figures that inheres in hegemonic masculinity, Obama put his masculinity in question when he acted inclusive rather than exclusive. As I suggested when discussing the constraints on the performance of masculinity, hegemonic masculinity calls on men to reject femininity.[112] Obama's failure to do so may explain why he was often criticized as unmanly.

Fourth, a further constraint on Obama's performance of his identity is that, given the premium that hegemonic masculinity places on aggressiveness, Obama's empathetic style is antimasculine.[113] This was reflected in the calls for Obama to be tougher in responding to attacks. The title of one editorial captures the spirit of this criticism: *Where's His Right Hook? Barack Obama Seems Refreshingly Decent. Can He Survive Hardball Politics?*[114] That attitude about Obama's candidacy was reflective of the expectation that men will maintain an aggressive demeanor, especially in the face of attacks.[115] Calls for Obama to be more aggressive were also reflective of Democrats' desires to "fight the last war" by not having their candidate "get swift-boated."[116] But the intensity of the calls for aggressiveness, in conjunction with general calls for Obama to be more manly, suggests that gender, and not just political effectiveness, was at issue.

Finally, we might note that despite the dangers that Obama's feminization presented for him, his ability to feminize was bolstered by certain stereotypes. As a man, Obama had more room to feminize without seeming too feminine than female politicians. Moreover, the stereotypes of black men as overly masculine meant people still took Obama to be sufficiently masculine. In contrast, Hillary Clinton clearly felt the need to out-macho Obama during their Democratic primary contests.[117] As professor Georgia Duerst-Lahti says, "The first woman has to out masculine the man, kind of like Margaret Thatcher did. . . . Men have a lot more latitude."[118] As a man, and a black man in particular, Obama had more room to negotiate a partly feminized masculinity.[119]

C. Obama Had to Be Unisex

So, why do I suggest that Obama is our first "unisex" President? Because Obama could not be too masculine, even as he had to prove he was not too feminine. Perhaps, then, Obama's masculinity problem is really a refracted version of his bipolar black masculinity problem. Just as Obama had to navigate between the shoals of blackness and whiteness, he had to position himself as feminine, but not too much so. He had to be unisex.

Use of the term unisex is especially appropriate in this context because it captures the performative nature of race and gender. If Obama was unisex in the sense that blue jeans are unisex, the strategic nature of his choices of when to act more feminine or more masculine comes into high relief. He sometimes chose to be more feminine than other Presidential candidates in order to be racially palatable. He sometimes chose to be more masculine in order to project the ability to be Commander-in-Chief. The overall effect was to place him in the middle of the gender continuum that we might expect from a Presidential candidate rather than on the more masculine end.

III. Conclusion: The Possibilities of a Unisex Presidency

I did not imagine I would live to see a black President (and I am not especially old). Nor did I expect to see anything but a macho man (or woman) win the Presidency in our recent climate. Given the symbolic power of the Presidency, one would expect Obama's election to influence how people think about race and gender. In this concluding section of the essay, I speculate about the impact of Obama's unisex style.

Freedman suggests a racial problem with Obama's feminization: "Obama has been successful because he embodies an earlier model of black male politicians for whom respectability and reason were tickets into full citizenship.[120] The politics of respectability that Freedman refers to is dangerous for the same reason that playing the Good Black Man game is dangerous. Striving to prove one's exceptional respectability accepts that only special blacks merit inclusion while the dregs of the race are to be left behind.[121] Freedman was right that the media was questioning Obama's masculinity.[122] If the only answer was for Obama to play the politics of respectability, his feminization served as a similar type of race-distancing act as bipolar black masculinity has always required.

Nonetheless, there is some reason for optimism. The potential for Obama to change what is an intelligible performance of black masculinity has been recognized by black men:

> For African-American men, Obama has accomplished something even more extraordinary. He has arguably single-handedly transformed the black public sphere. In their eyes, it is no longer "easy" to view black men solely through the lens of deficiencies, bad behavior, their bodies or even their relationship to black women.[123]

In the simplest sense, then, black male identity has already been reconstructed by Obama's success since it is now possible to imagine a black man as a president. In addition to that opening up of images of black men, there may also be a shutting down of images. After Obama, many people's dominant image of black men will be of calmness rather than anger. Obama thus has a debiasing effect on racial stereotypes. Further, Obama will create new images of black masculinity that will help to construct the future expectations of black men. For black men, therefore, Obama stands as a redemptive figure for our attributed identities. This is the racial payoff of Obama's success.[124]

The gender payoff of Obama's success is that it could remove some of the stigma from femininity. Taken together, the tenets of masculinity describe a privileged but anxious status that may constrain men nearly as much as it empowers them. This is why men, who are clearly privileged as a group, sometimes feel disempowered as individuals.[125] This creates a tension in masculinity whereby masculinity is both something people expect you to demonstrate and something some people might want to escape. This may be the genius of Obama's feminization: it allows us to have it both ways on masculinity. While Obama is hardly effeminate, he seems unusually non-anxious about his masculinity. As *MS. Magazine* recently put it on their cover, perhaps Obama is "what a feminist looks like."[126] He certainly seems to be a man who is comfortable with the fact that he has a feminine side. There is certainly reason to believe that Obama may be a harbinger of a move toward "progressive black masculinities" that are not based on the denigration of femininity.[127] As a result, the potential is there for Obama's example to allow all men greater movement along the gender continuum.

However, while Obama is not exactly "metrosexual," that genderbending status suggests a cautionary note. Metrosexuals have been accused of taking advantage of their privileged heterosexual status in order to dabble in gay style when it is convenient.[128] To the extent that Obama's feminization was only enabled by his male (and even black male) privilege, his being unisex does not necessarily portend the loosening of identity constraints.

Ultimately, though, I expect Obama's unisex performance on the world's biggest stage to free up all sorts of people to perform their identities against the grain. Butler might say that Obama has cited norms of black masculinity and Presidential masculinity with a difference and thereby created new performative possibilities. In a small way, but at a fundamental level, Obama's refusal to accept that a

Presidential demeanor requires a hyper-masculine style challenges the assumptions of the hegemonic form of masculinity. If the President can be both black and unisex, maybe we are all more free to perform our identities as we see fit than we had imagined.[129]

Notes

1. See Amy Sullivan, Gender Bender, *Time*, June 16, 2008, at 36 (analyzing why Hillary Clinton did not win Democratic Presidential primary) (quoting Marie Wilson).

2. Philippa Roberts & Jane Cunningham, Feminization of Brands, *Marketing*, Sept. 3, 2008, at 26.

3. See Martin Linsky, Op-Ed., The First Woman President? Obama's Campaign Bends Gender Conventions, *Newsweek*, Feb. 26, 2008, available at http://www.newsweek.com/id/115397/page/l (arguing that Obama advocates conversation and collaboration while Hillary Clinton supports realism).

4. Carol Marin, Editorial, Thanks to Hillitary for Being a Winner at Heart, *Chi. Sun Times* May 11, 2008, at A17.

5. See, e.g., Lucy Berrington & Jeff Onore, Op-Ed., Bam: Our 1st Woman Prez?, *N.Y. Post*, Jan 7, 2008, available at http://tinyurl.com/cd4d8s (noting Obama's feminine style); Linsky, supra note 3 (same); Marin, supra note 4, at A17 (same); Roberts 7 Cunningham, supra note 2, at 26 (same).

6. See Nancy Ehrenreich, Disguising Empire: Racialized Masculinity and the "Civilizing" of Iraq, 52 *Clev. St. L. Rev.* 131, 132 (2005) (noting both sexes can bask in reflected masculinity).

7. See Martha Chamallas, *Introduction To Feminist Legal Theory* 53–60 (2d ed., Aspen 2003) (describing the rise of difference feminism).

8. See Michael S. Kimmel, Masculinity as Homophobia, in *The Gender of Desire: Essays on Male Sexuality* 25, 26 (2005) [hereinafter Kimmel, *Masculinity as Homophobia*] (declaring that "manhood is socially constructed and historically shifting").

9. Athena D. Mutua, Theorizing Progressive Black Masculinities, in *Progressive Black Masculinities* 3, 12 (Athena D. Mutua ed., 2006). See also discussion infra notes 40–50 (explicating Judith Butler's theory of gender).

10. See generally Devon W. Carbado & Mitu Gulati, Working Identity, 85 *Cornell L. Rev.* 1259 (2000) [hereinafter Carbado & Gulati, Working Identity] (developing a theory of identity performance).

11. I sometimes use the first person in this essay because that is consistent with poststructuralist feminist methodology. See Michael Awkward, A Black Man's Place in Black Feminist Criticism, in *Black Men on Race, Gender, and Sexuality: A Critical Reader* 362, 362 (Devon W. Carbado ed., 1999) (arguing for autobiographical stance in male feminism).

12. See Frank Rudy Cooper, Cultural Context Matters: Terry's "Seesaw Effect," 56 *Okla. L. Rev.* 833, 843 (2003) [hereinafter Cooper, Cultural Context Matters] (arguing identity negotiation is influenced by social expectations). For some recent thoughts on identity performance, see Russell K. Robinson, Uncovering Covering, 101 *Nw. U. L. Rev.* 1809 (2007), critically reviewing identity performance theory, and Holning Lau, Tailoring Equal Protection to Address Today's Democratic Deficit (manuscript on file with author), applying identity performance theory to equal protection doctrine.

13. See Frank Rudy Cooper, The "Seesaw Effect" from Racial Profiling to Depolicing: Toward Critical Cultural Theory, in *The New Civil Rights Research: A Constitutive Approach* 139, 148 (Benjamin Fleury-Steiner & Laura Beth Nielsen eds., 2006) [hereinafter Cooper, The "Seesaw Effect"] (defining critical race theory).

14. See generally Frank Rudy Cooper, 'Who's the Man?': Masculinities and Police Stops (Soc. Sci. Research Network, Research Paper No. 08–23, 2008), available at http://ssrn.com/abstract=1257183 [hereinafter Cooper, 'Who's the Man?'] (defining and applying masculinities studies).

15. Obama is half-black. Historically, however, one drop of black blood has made you black in the United States. Further, Obama's skin tone made it hard for him to emphasize his whiteness. And Obama seems

to have usually chosen to accept descriptions of himself as black. It is possible that his whiteness nonetheless made him more palatable to some voters. Still he seems to have generally been perceived as black, not black and white.

16. See generally Frank Rudy Cooper, Against Bipolar Black Masculinity: Intersectionality, Assimilation, Identity Performance, and Hierarchy, 39 *U.C. Davis L. Rev.* 853 (2006) [hereinafter Cooper, Against Bipolar Black Masculinity] (arguing media depicts black men in either/or fashion).

17. See id. at 875–79 (defining Bad Black Man). Jerry Kang argues that the local news is full of stories about violent crimes prominently featuring African Americans as the perpetrators. Jerry Kang, Trojan Horses of Race, 118 *Harv. L. Rev.* 1489, 1490 (2005) (summarizing research on implicit bias and arguing racism in news is insidious and pervasive). Individuals rely on and trust their local news, and thereby internalize these images, which exacerbate their implicit biases about black men. *Id.*

18. See Cooper, Against Bipolar Black Masculinity, supra note 16, at 879–86 (defining Good Black Man). An example of a conservative post-race spokesman is Shelby Steele. See generally Shelby Steele, *A Bound Man: Why We Are Excited About Obama And Why He Can't Win* (2008) (arguing Obama should take stances that go against the views of the overwhelming majority of blacks).

19. See Courtland Milloy, Maybe It's Time We Redefined Manliness, *Wash. Post*, Sept. 10, 2008, at B1 (analyzing masculinity in the Presidential contest).

20. See, e.g., Linsky, supra note 3 (contrasting Obama's non-confrontational approach with Hillary Clinton's more masculine approach).

21. See David Remnick, The Joshua Generation, *New Yorker*, Nov. 17, 2008, at 68, 71–72 (suggesting that Obama adopted his calm demeanor in order to counter stereotypes of black men); see also discussion infra notes 140–43 and accompanying text (locating roots of Obama's calmness in his youth).

22. See discussion infra notes 117–45 and accompanying text (applying bipolar black masculinity thesis to Obama).

23. I cannot definitively prove that Obama thought about being feminine as a means of avoiding the angry black man stereotype. There is some evidence of such thinking. See Joe Klein, Anger vs. Steadiness in the Crisis, *Time*, Oct. 2, 2008, available at http://content.time.com/time/magazine/article/0,9171,1846723,00.html (mentioning angry black man stereotype in discussing how Obama thinks about the campaign). However, little that a Presidential candidate does is unplanned. It is possible that Obama's camp was only subconsciously aware of the need to avoid the angry black man stereotype. Regardless, speculating about the identity constraints Obama faced reveals interesting things about race and gender.

24. In this sense, Obama was engaged in what Carbado and Gulati call a "comforting strategy." See Carbado & Gulati, Working Identity, supra note 10, at 1301–04 (describing potential strategies for subordinated group members who wish to be accepted in mainstream environments).

25. One could suggest that Obama's style was "metrosexual," but I do not believe that label fits. The term is "generally applied to heterosexual men with a strong concern for their appearance, and/or whose lifestyles display attributes stereotypically attributed to gay men." Wikipedia, http://en.wikipedia.org/wiki/Metrosexual (last visited Nov. 21, 2008). While feminine styles are often associated with homosexuality, having a more feminine political approach is not the same as being metrosexual. See Kimmel, Masculinity as Homophobia, supra note 8, at 38 (discussing homophobia, as fear of being unmasked as unmanly, as a source of denigration of femininity). At heart, metrosexuality creates the appearance that the individual could possibly be gay or bisexual. See Wikipedia, supra ("Rising popularity of the term followed the increasing integration of gay men into mainstream society and a correspondingly decreased taboo towards deviation from existing notions of masculinity."); see also Bernard E. Harcourt, Foreword: "You Are Entering a Gay and Lesbian Free Zone": On the Radical Dissents of Justice Scalia and Other (Post) Queers. [Raising Questions about Lawrence, Sex Wars, and the Criminal Law], 94 *J. Crim. L. & Criminology* 503, 516 (2004) (defining "metrosexuals" to refer to "generally heterosexual practicing males—sometimes hyper-heterosexual—who share aesthetic sensibilities with the more traditional stereotype of the gay male"). Obama's style makes no such suggestion.

26. See *Shorter Oxford English Dictionary* 3447 (5th ed. 2002) (defining "unisex").

27. See id. (defining "unisex").

28. "Unisex" means different things for people with different identities. Hillary Clinton's version of going unisex was to wear pant suits with conservative blouses. See Robin Givhan, The Frontrunners: Fashion Sense, *Wash. Post*, Dec. 18, 2007, http://www.washingtonpost.com/wpdyn/content/discussion/2007/12/16/DI2007121601778.html (mentioning Hillary Clinton's pant suits and the controversy over her revealing cleavage during one press conference). Being unisex, in the asexual sense of the term, is demanded of a white woman candidate in a way that is not expected of a black man.

29. See Wikipedia.org, Pat (Saturday Night Live), http://en.wikipedia.org/wiki/Pat_ (last visited Mar. 31, 2009) (describing the character).

30. See Carla Marinucci, Obama Promises to Restore promise of the U.S., *S.F. Chron.*, Aug. 29, 2008, at A1 (describing Obama's speech as "tough" on McCain).

31. Michael Scherer, Hillary is from Mars, Obama is from Venus, *Salon.com*, July 12, 2007, http://www.salon.com/news/feature/2007/07/12/obama_hillary/print.html (noting Obama rallies sometimes play Indigo Girls music).

32. I used the following two searches under the terms and connectors method: "obama /s masculine or feminine" and "obama /s 'first female president,'" then supplemented those searches with a variety of searches for specific propositions.

33. Kimberle Crenshaw et al., *Introduction to Critical Race Theory: The Key Writings That Formed The Movement* xiii, xiii (Kimberle Crenshaw et al. eds., 1995). For a more recent compilation of articles, legal cases, and other materials, see Juan Perea et al., *Race and Races: Cases and Materials for a Diverse America* (2d ed. 2007) (collecting materials for a law course on identities).

34. These are not nearly all of the tenets of critical race theory, but they are the ones that are relevant to this essay. Some additional projects of critical race theory include the critique of the black-white binary paradigm of race, the critique of the intentional model of discrimination, and exploration of the place of autobiography in critique.

35. Cooper, The "Seesaw Effect," supra note 13, at 148.

36. See generally Michael Omi & Howard Winant, *Racial Formation in the United States: From the 1960s to the 1990s* (1994) (defining and applying concept of racial formation).

37. See Anna Marie Smith, Laclau & Mouffe: *The Radical Democratic Imaginary* 61 (1998) (arguing identity is a discursive construct).

38. See, e.g., Carbado & Gulati, Working Identity, supra note 10, at 1267–70 (linking stereotyping to workplace discrimination based on identity performance).

39. See Jerry Kang & Mahzarin R. Banaji, Fair Measures: A Behavioral Realist Revision of "Affirmative Action," 94 *Cal. L. Rev.* 1063,1066 (2006) (introducing term).

40. See id. at 1109–11 (defining debiasing agent's role).

41. *Plessy v. Ferguson,* 163 U.S. 537, 559 (1896) (Harlan, J., dissenting).

42. See Crenshaw et al., supra note 63, at xv (decrying misappropriation of Martin Luther King, Jr.'s language).

43. See id. at xiv (critiquing mainstream perspective on civil rights).

44. See Darnell M. Hunt, UCLA's Process Rights a Wrong, *L.A. Times*, Sept. 7, 2008, at A34 (reporting Ward Connerly's complaint that colleges are considering race as revealed in essay statements, allegedly in contravention of Prop. 209's prohibition on affirmative action).

45. Cooper, Against Bipolar Black Masculinity, supra note 16, at 884.

46. Id. at 857–58; see also D. Aaron Lacy, The Most Endangered Title VII Plaintiff?: Exponential Discrimination Against Black Males, 86 *Neb. L. Rev.* 552, 566 (2008) (contending black men are subject to Good Black Man and Bad Black Man depictions); cf. Devon W. Carbado, (E)Racing the Fourth Amendment, 100 *Mich. L.*

Rev. 946, 1034–43 (2002) (describing ways that the ACLU makes the argument against racial profiling depend on whether black men are "good").

47. See generally Mahmood Mamdani, *Good Muslim, Bad Muslim: America, the Cold War, and the Roots of Terror* (2004) (discussing dichotmony popularly made between Westernized and medieval Muslims and connecting radical Islam to Western cold war manipulation in the middle east).

48. Cf. Carbado, supra note 76, at 968–69 (noting Court's "perpetrator perspective" causes it to presume all police are "racially good" unless proved "racially bad").

49. See Cooper, Against Bipolar Black Masculinity, supra note 16, at 887 (identifying default position on black men).

50. See id. (describing incentive to engage in race-distancing acts).

51. See id. at 893–95 (declaring the assimilationist incentive to provide a false inclusiveness).

52. See generally Cooper, 'Who's the Man?', supra note 14 (defining masculinities studies, applying it to police stops, proposing reforming police training).

53. There are other tenets, but these are the ones most useful to my current project.

54. See, e.g., Deborah Brake, The Struggle for Sex Equality in Sports and the Theory Behind Title IX, 34 U. *Mich. J.L. Reform* 13, 92–93 (2001) (explaining masculinity and male dominance in male athletics).

55. See Ann C. McGinley, Masculinities at Work, 83 *Or. L. Rev.* 359 (2004) (applying masculinities studies to workplace norms).

56. See Vojdik, supra note 51, at 71, 75 (criticizing male dominance in the male military academies).

57. See Lorna Fox, Re-Possessing "Home": A Re-Analysis of Gender, Homeownership, and Debtor Default for Feminist Legal Theory, 14 *Wm. & Mary J. Of Women & L.* 423, 437 (2008) (arguing that the association of women and home confined women to the private sphere and inhibited female development outside the home); see also Judith Koons, "Just" Married?: Same-Sex Marriage and a History of Family Plurality, 12 *Mich. J. Gender & L.* 1, 11–12 (2005) (arguing that the family construct is fundamental to women's confinement to private sphere); see also Gila Stopler, Gender Construction and the Limits of Liberal Equality, 15 *Tex. J. Women & L.* 43, 46 (2005) (distinguishing the feminine private sphere of the family and the masculine public sphere of the market and politics).

58. A related tenet of masculinities studies is that what makes this privileging of masculinity over femininity all the more insidious is the fact that it has been invisible. When I say masculinities have been invisible, I mean this in the way Barbara Flagg talks about "white transparency." Flagg's point is that whites sometimes operate from perspectives that are widely shared by whites but not widely shared by nonwhites without acknowledging that they are utilizing a particular perspective. See generally Barbara J. Flagg, "Was Blind, But Now I See": White Race Consciousness and the Requirement of Discriminatory Intent, in *A Reader On Race, Civil Rights, And American Law: A Multiracial Approach* 33 (Timothy Davis et al. eds., 2001). Similarly, men may often operate from a male perspective while thinking they are operating from a neutral perspective. See Cooper, "Who's the Man?", supra note 14 (making this argument).

59. See Kimmel, Masculinity as Homophobia, supra note 8, at 33 (defining masculinity as "homosocial" in this sense).

60. Kimmel's rules of hegemonic masculinity are (1) never act feminine, (2) accrue power, success, wealth, and status, (3) always hold your emotions in check, and (4) always exude an aura of daring and aggression. Id. at 30–31.

61. Id. at 31.

62. Id.

63. See id. at 36 ("The possibilities of being unmasked are everywhere.").

64. See id. at 37 (defining homophobia as omnipresent fear of being unmasked as less than masculine).

65. Mutua, supra note 9, at 5.

66. Id. at 24–25.

67. See Patricia Hill Collins, A Telling Difference: Dominance, Strength, and Black Masculinities, in *Progressive Black Masculinities*, supra note 9, at 73, 86 ("Physical dominance, aggressiveness, and the use of violence to maintain male power constitute a central feature in the definitions of hegemonic white masculinity. . . .").

68. Jewel Woods, Editorial, Why Guys Have a Man-Crush on Obama; Sure Women Swoon, But Modern Men Seem Weak-Kneed, Too, *Chicago Sun-Times*, July 24, 2008, at 25.

69. See, e.g., Maureen Dowd, Editorial, Where's His Right Hook? Barack Obama Seems Refreshingly Decent. Can He Survive Hardball Politics?, *Pittsburgh Post-Gazette*, Mar. 5, 2007, at B7 [hereinafter Dowd, Where's His Right Hook?]; Milloy, supra note 19, at B1 (noting criticism of Obama for not being aggressive enough); Amy Alkon, *Advice Goddess Blog*, The Self-Help President, (Aug. 26, 2008) http://www.advice-goddess.com/archives/2008/08/26/the_selfhelp_pr.html (criticizing Obama for seeming less masculine than his wife). The expectation of aggression can be thought of as stemming from our "culture of honor." See generally Dov Cohen & Joe Vandello, Social Norms, Social Meaning, and the Economic Analysis of Law, 27 *J. Legal Stud.* 567 (1998) (defining cultures of honor); Cooper, "Who's the Man?", supra note 14 (discussing cultures of honor).

70. Michael Kimmel, Integrating Men into the Curriculum, 4 *Duke J. Gender L. & Pol'y* 181, 183(1997).

71. The Macho Factor, *Orlando Sentinel*, Sept. 1, 2008, at A18.

72. Berrington & Onore, supra note 5.

73. See, e.g., Ellen Goodman, Editorial, Trading Places; Obama is the Woman, *Pittsburgh Post-Gazette*, Feb. 22, 2008, at B7 [hereinafter Goodman, Trading Places] (saying Obama was the "Oprah candidate"); Milloy, supra note 19, at B1 (portraying Obama as aloof and non-aggressive while describing Sarah Palin as a "masculine . . . moose hunter," "hockey mo[m]," and "pit bull").

74. See Goodman, Trading Places, supra note 93, at B7.

75. Christi Parsons, Women Lean Toward Obama; But McCain to Fight for Clinton Backers, *Chi. Trib.*, June 18, 2008, at C1.

76. See Linda Valdez, Editorial, We Need a President with Both Masculine, Feminine Values, *Ariz. Republic*, May 8, 2008, at 4 ("Barack Obama understands that real strength comes from a blending of die masculine and feminine.").

77. Obama may have found it strategic to demonstrate a feminine side to the disproportionately female Democratic electorate.

78. See, e.g., Steve Chapman, John McCain, Reveling in Anger, *Cm. TRIB.*, Oct. 14, 2008, at C33 (describing McCain as an anger-based candidate).

79. See Kimmel, Masculinity as Homophobia, supra note 8, at 38 (describing construction of black men as hypermasculine). Ann C. McGinley reminds me that McCain faced his own identity constraints, as his age threatened to demasculinize him. McGinley, supra note 85, at 376. That fact helps explain McCain's emphasis on his military experience and his "maverick" tendencies.

80. Milloy, supra note 19, at B1.

81. Cooper, Against Bipolar Black Masculinity, supra note 16, at 887 (stating the Good Black Man must downplay his blackness and avoid racial issues in general).

82. Christi Parsons & John McCormick, Obama, Huckabee Strike First with Iowa Victories; Edwards Ekes by Clinton for 2nd Amid Huge Turnout, *Chi. TRIB.*, Jan. 4, 2008, at Nl (quoting David Axelrod); see also Susan Page & William Risser, Beyond Black and White; Obama's Rise Spotlights Gains in Race Relations and How Ethnicity Remains a Dividing Line on Some Issues, *USA Today*, Sept. 23, 2008, at 1A (noting that Obama usually does not emphasize his race); Joseph Williams, Changing of the Guard; New Generation Replaces Past Civil Rights Leaders, *Boston Globe*, Aug. 28, 2008, at Al ("'Obama's success running a race-neutral campaign has set the standard for ambitious African-American politicians.") (quoting Michael Cobb).

83. See EUR Political Analysis: Obama Hit for not Mentioning Dr. King's Name During Acceptance Speech, *Electronic Urb. Rep.*, Sept. 2, 2008, http://www.eurweb.com/story/eur46705.cfm (criticizing Obama's refusal to mention Martin Luther King's name during acceptance speech).

84. See Frank & McPhail, supra note 118, at 583–84 (criticizing Obama's speech to the 2004 DNC for inviting "the erasure of race"). In a future article, I will explore whether Obama has adopted a colorblind position on affirmative action.

85. See Cooper, Against Bipolar Black Masculinity, supra note 16, at 884.

86. John Aloysius Farrell, Obama Revives MLK's Dream, *Denv. Post*, Aug. 1, 2004, at A25 (quoting Barack Obama); see also Peter Wehner, Why Republicans Like Obama, *Wash. Post*, Feb. 3, 2008, at B7 ("I did not travel around this state over the last year and see a white South Carolina or a black South Carolina . . . I saw South Carolina.") (quoting Barack Obama).

87. See Matt Bai, Post-Race, *N.Y. Times*, Aug. 10, 2008, at MM8, *available at* http://www.nytimes.com/2008/08/10/magazine/10politics-t.html (describing potentially post-racial generation of black politicians).

88. Remnick supra note 21, at 79.

89. Michael McAuliff, Bam Slams AWOL Fathers, *Daily News* (N.Y.), June 16, 2008, at 8 ("Father's Day turned out to be family values day for Barack Obama, who went home to a Chicago church to scold 'MIA' dads, especially in the black community."); see also Julie Bosman, Obama Calls for More Responsibility from Black Fathers, *N.Y. Times*, June 16, 2008, at A15 ("Addressing a packed congregation at one of the city's largest black churches, Senator Barack Obama on Sunday invoked his own absent father to deliver a sharp message to black men. . . ."); Juliet Eilperin, Obama Discusses Duties of Fatherhood, *Wash. Post*, June 16, 2008, at A7 ("Calling himself 'an imperfect father,' Sen. Barack Obama (D-Ill.) spoke of the need for more African American men to live up to their responsibilities in a Father's Day sermon yesterday."); Abdon M. Pallasch, Obama Urges Fathers to Step Up, *Chi. Sun-Times*, June 16, 2008, at 2 ("White House hopeful Barack Obama gave a tough-love but optimistic Father's Day sermon at the Apostolic Church of God on Sunday, exhorting other fathers, especially African Americans, to meet their responsibilities.").

90. Remnick, supra note 21, at 79 (quoting Julian Bond); see also Gregory Scott Parks & Jeffrey J. Rachlinski, A Better Metric: The Role of Unconscious Race and Gender Bias in the 2008 Presidential Race, *Cornell Legal Studies Research Paper No. 08–007*, at 23–24 (2008), available at http://ssrn.com/abstract=l 102704 (warning that blacks would deem Obama insufficiently black if he were perceived to be chastising blacks in order to curry favor with whites).

91. See Remnick, supra note 21, at 79 (describing Jackson's criticism of Obama).

92. See Milloy, supra note 19, at Bl (considering Obama).

93. See Kimmel, Masculinity as Homophobia, supra note 8, at 38 (describing images of black men as hyper-masculine); see also discussion supra notes 104-06 and accompanying text (identifying expectation of aggressiveness as a constraint on men's identity performances).

94. See U.S. Glass Ceiling Comm'n, Good For Business: Making Full Use of the Nation's Human Capital 71 (1995) (documenting stereotypes of black males as "aggressive," "undisciplined," "violent," "confrontational," "emotional," "hostile," and so on). On stereotyping of Black males, see generally Floyd D. Weatherspoon, *African-American Males and the Law: Cases and Materials* (1998).

95. See Klein, supra note 23 ("Part of Obama's steadiness is born of necessity: An angry, or flashy, black man isn't going to be elected President.").

96. Remnick, supra note 21, at 71.

97. Id. (quoting Barack Obama, *Dreams From My Father: A Story of Race and Inheritance* (1996)).

98. See Carbado, supra note 76, at 954-53 (relating Kenneth Meeks' warnings to black men who are stopped for "driving while black").

99. See Michael McAuliff & Michael Saul, Bam Jam Over "Typical White" Folk Talk in Philly, *Daily News* (N.Y.), Mar. 21, 2008, at 9 (noting use of grandmother anecdote in speech).

100. See Remnick, supra note 21, at 78.

101. Id.

102. See Laura Padilla, A Gendered Update on Women Law Deans: Who, Where, and Why Not?, 15 *Am. U. J. Gender Soc. Pol'y & L.* 443, 485 (2007) (arguing that negative attitudes and stereotypes about women leaders prevail despite the women's rights movement); Mary Radford, Sex Stereotyping and the Promotion of Women to Positions of Power, 41 *Hastings L.J.* 471, 490–91 (1990) (noting Western perception that males are dominant, self-confident leaders and women are docile, gentle followers); Deborah Rhode, The Difference "Difference" Makes, 55 *Me. L. Rev.* 15, 17 (2003) (arguing that gender stereotypes create obstacles to female advancement).

103. See Jonathan Martin, First Fan Obama takes aim at the BCS, *Politico.com*, Jan. 11, 2009, http://www .politico.com/news/stories/0109/17313.html ("Obama is seemingly as sports crazed as the city from which he hails. . .").

104. See Christi Parsons, Is Michelle Obama really in the kitchen?, *L.A. TIMES*, Feb. 23, 2009, at A9, available at http://www.latimes.com/news/nationworld/nation/la-na-michelle-obama232009feb23,0,2585916. story ("Is her goal to become a symbol of the traditional wife and mother?"). Of course, this is also about Obama's heteronormativity, which is an important subject that I do not address in this essay.

105. See Milloy, supra note 19, at B1 (quoting Estelle Freedman, Professor of history, Stanford University).

106. *Morning Joe* (MSNBC television broadcast Mar. 31, 2008), available at http://mediamatters.org/ items/2O0803310oO7.

107. See discussion supra notes 89–97 and accompanying text (discussing masculine anxiety).

108. See Ehrenreich, supra note 6, at 132 (detailing reflected masculinity thesis).

109. See Linda Killian, Obama's Tough Talk Falls Short, *Politico.Com*, Aug. 2, 2007, http://www.politico.com/ news/stories/0807/5222.html (criticizing Obama for lacking toughness).

110. See Angela Harris, Gender, Violence, Race, and Criminal Justice, 52 *Stan. L. Rev.* 777, 785 (2000) (discussing how men prove their masculinity).

111. Obama did denigrate his female opponent, Hillary Clinton—"You're likable enough"—but that is not the same thing as denigrating femininity. See Steve Huntley, Despite Divisions, Dems on Top, *Chi. Sun-Times*, Feb. 10, 2008, at A27 (noting Obama's comment during a debate). Given pervasive fears amongst whites that Obama would be race-loyal, he may have been in a position where it was better to be criticized for being feminine because he was inclusive rather than being seen as exclusive in the sense of race-loyalty.

112. See, e.g., I. Bennett Capers, Sex(ual) Orientation and Title VII, 91 *Colum. L. Rev.* 1158, 1171–72 (1991) (noting that women may face employment barriers if perceived as cooperative, sensitive, and submissive); Jane Maslow Cohen, Equality for Girls and Other Women: The Built Architecture for the Purposive Life, 9 *J. Contemp. Legal Issues* 103, 106 (1998) (explaining critiques of andocentrism for valorizing the male condition and denigrating the female condition); Barbara Stark, Guys and Dolls: Remedial Nurturing Skills in Post-Divorce Practice, Feminist Theory, and Family Law Doctrine, 26 *Hofstra L. Rev.* 293, 336 (1997) (recognizing law's failure to value traditionally feminine attributes such as intimacy and empathy).

113. See Mary Becker, Patriarchy and Inequality: Towards a Substantive Feminism, 1999 *UCHI. Legal. F.* 21, 27 (1999) (observing that patriarchal cultures idealize women as "dependent, vulnerable, pliant, weak, supportive, nurturing, intuitive, emotional, and empathic"); Amy Cohen, Gender: An (Un)Useful Category of Prescriptive Negotiation Analysis?, 13 *Tex. J. Women & L.*169, 173, 175 (2003) (arguing that feminine characteristics such as inclusivity and empathy are "denigrated in negotiation theory and practice"); Emma Lindsay, Lysistrata, Women & War: International Law's Treatment of Women in Conflict and Post-Conflict Situations, 12 *Tex. Wesleyan L. REV.* 345, 351 (2005) (associating female characteristics such as submissiveness, passivity, and inclusivity with weakness).

114. Dowd, Where's His Right Hook?, supra note 106, at B7; see also Alkon, supra note 89 (criticizing Obama for seeming less masculine than his wife); Milloy, supra note 19, at Bl (noting criticism of Obama for not being aggressive enough).

115. See discussion supra notes 104–06 and accompanying text (arguing an expectation of aggressiveness constrains men's identity performances).

116. See, e.g., E.J. Dionne, Editorial, Finally, Jinxed Month of August is Almost Over, *Charleston Gazette* (W. Va.), Aug. 23, 2008, at 4A (raising the issue of Obama's ability to head

117. See Richard Ruelas, Must Hillary Walk "Man Enough" Line?, *Ariz. Republic*, March 4 2008, at 1 (noting Hillary's dilemma of how masculine to be). Palin, while feminine in many ways, was also masculine in many ways. See Milloy, supra note 19, at B1 (calling Sarah Palin a masculine moose hunter, hockey mom, and pitbull"). Whether Palin was also trying to be unisex in the sense of being male-enough to be Presidential and female-enough to make people comfortable is an interesting question for another day.

118. Michael Scherer, Hillary is from Mars, Obama is from Venus, *Salon.com*, July 12, 2007, http://www.salon .com/news/feature/2007/07/12/obama_hillary/print.html.

119. For examples of how Hillary Clinton and other prominent women had their identity performances constrained during the 2008 campaign, see Ann C. McGinley's excellent essay in this symposium. Ann C. McGinley, Hillary Clinton, Sarah Palin, and Michelle Obama: Performing Gender, Race, and Class on the Campaign Trail, 86 *Denv. U. L. Rev.* 709 (2009).

120. Milloy, *supra* note 19, at Bl (quoting Estelle Freedman, Professor of history, Stanford University).

121. See Cooper, Against Bipolar Black Masculinity, supra note 16, at 892 (arguing triumphalism about assimilated black successes assumes the "dregs" of the black community deserve their fate).

122. See discussion supra note 149 and accompanying text (quoting Estelle Freedman, Professor of history, Stanford University).

123. Woods, supra note 105, at 25.

124. A remaining concern, however, is that Obama may be framed as a special case that proves nothing about the abilities and characters of black men in general.

125. See Kimmel, Masculinity as Homophobia, supra note 8, at 40 (noting that chauffeurs can feel disempowered even as others are pedestrians).

126. See http://msmagazine.com/ (last visited January 28, 2009) (showing cover of latest issue with Obama wearing a "This is what a feminist looks like" t-shirt).

127. Mutua, supra note 9, at 7.

128. See José Gabilondo, Irrational Exuberance About Babies: The Taste for Heterosexuality and Its Conspicuous Reproduction, 28 *B.C. Third World L.J.* 1, 64 (2008) (suggesting that heterosexuals stand to gain from copying homosexuals).

129. Again, I do not mean that we are free in a transcendental sense. I mean only that, after the election of a black and unisex President, it is easier to imagine that we can break down other assumptions.

CHAPTER 13

The Masculinity of the Governator

Muscle and Compassion in American Politics

Michael A. Messner

Arnold Schwarzenegger's celebrity status allowed him to project a symbolic masculine persona that was effective in gaining political power as California governor. The well-known violent tough-guy persona that Schwarzenegger developed in the mid-1980s contributed to a post–Vietnam era cultural remasculinization of the American man. But this narrow hyper-masculinity was often caricatured in popular culture and delegitimized. In the 1990s and 2000s, Schwarzenegger forged a credible masculine imagery by introducing characters who were humorously self-mocking and focused on care and protection of children. Schwarzenegger's resultant hybrid masculinity, the "Kindergarten Commando," represents an ascendant hegemonic masculinity always foregrounding muscle, toughness, and the threat of violence and following with situationally appropriate symbolic displays of compassion. The equation of toughness plus compassion composing the Kindergarten Commando is asymmetrical, with toughness eclipsing compassion; this has implications for the kinds of policies that U.S. elected leaders advocate. Republicans utilize this masculine imagery in national politics to gain voters' trust in times of fear and insecurity and continue to employ a strategy that projects a devalued feminized stigma onto more liberal candidates.

The big news story on November 7, 2006, was that voters had returned control of the U.S. Congress to the Democrats. This represented a dramatic turning of the electoral tide against the policies of Republican President George W. Bush—especially against his stubborn mantra to "stay the course" in the war on Iraq. But apparently swimming against this tide was another story. On that same day, Republican Arnold Schwarzenegger was reelected as California governor by a landslide, winning 56 percent of the vote over Democratic challenger Phil Angelides's mere 39 percent. During a year of resurgent Democratic strength nationally, in a solidly Democratic state, and only a year after his popularity had plummeted with voters, how do we explain Schwarzenegger's resounding victory? In this article, I will explore this question by examining Schwarzenegger's public masculine image.

A key aspect of Schwarzenegger's public image, of course, is his celebrity status, grounded first in his career as a world champion bodybuilder and even more so in his fame as one of the most successful action film stars of his generation (Boyle 2006). My aim here is not to analyze Arnold Schwarzenegger's biography. Nor do I intend to offer a critical analysis of his films—I confess, I have watched some of them and not others (and I enjoy the ones that I have seen). Instead, my aim is both practical and theoretical: I will outline the beginnings of a cultural analysis of how and why Schwarzenegger rose to political power, what his appeal was and is, and how some current debates in gender theory might be useful in informing these questions. I will consider what Schwarzenegger's deployment of a shifting configuration of masculine imagery tells us about the limits and possibilities in current U.S.

SOURCE: Messner, M. A. (2007). The Masculinity of the Governator: Muscle and Compassion in American Politics. *Gender & Society, 21*(4), 461–480. Reproduced with permission.

electoral politics. And I will deploy the concept of "hegemonic masculinity" to suggest how Schwarzenegger's case illustrates connections between the cultural politics of gender with those of race, class, and nation. In particular, I hope to show how, when symbolically deployed by an exemplar like Arnold Schwarzenegger, hegemonic masculinity is never an entirely stable, secure, finished product; rather, it is always shifting with changes in the social context. Hegemonic masculinity is hegemonic to the extent that it succeeds, at least temporarily, in serving as a symbolic nexus around which a significant level of public consent coalesces. But as with all moments of hegemony, this consent is situational, always potentially unstable, existing in a dynamic tension with opposition.

Masculinities and Politics

Since the late 1980s, sociologists have tended to agree that we need to think of masculinity not as a singular "male sex role" but as multiple, contextual and historically shifting configurations. At any given moment, a dominant—or hegemonic—form of masculinity exists in relation to other subordinated or marginalized forms of masculinity and in relation to various forms of femininity (Connell 1987). Very few men fully conform to hegemonic masculinity. In fact, it is nearly impossible for an individual man consistently to achieve and display the dominant conception of masculinity, and this is an important part of the psychological instability at the center of individual men's sense of their own masculinity. Instead, a few men (real or imagined) are positioned as symbolic exemplars for a hegemonic masculinity that legitimizes the global subordination of women and ensures men's access to privilege. What makes this masculinity hegemonic is not simply powerful men's displays of power but also, crucially, less powerful men's (and many women's) consent and complicity with the institutions, social practices, and symbols that ensure some men's privileges (Messner 2004). To adapt a term that is now popular in market-driven bureaucracies, hegemonic masculinity requires a "buy-in" by subordinated and marginalized men, and by many women, if it is to succeed as a strategy of domination.

Thus, the concept of hegemonic masculinity is most usefully deployed when we think of it not as something that an individual "has"—like big muscles, a large bank account, or an expensive car. But then, what is it? Where does it reside? Can we define it, or is it something about which we simply say, "I know it when I see it"? To ask these kinds of questions, we need to develop ways of thinking about gender that are global, both in the geographic and in the conceptual senses of the word. Here, I want to explore the ways that we can think about hegemonic masculinity as a symbolically displayed "exemplar" of manhood around which power coalesces—and, it is important to note, not just men's power over women but also power in terms of race, class, and nation (Connell and Messerschmidt 2005). I will suggest that it is in the symbolic realm where an apparently coherent, seemingly stable hegemonic masculinity can be forged (Gomez-Barris and Gray 2006). We can track this symbolic masculinity as it reverberates into institutions—in the case of Arnold Schwarzenegger, into the realm of electoral politics—and we can see how hegemonic masculinity works in relation to what Collins (1990) calls a "matrix of domination," structured by race, class, gender, and sexuality.

Terminating the Feminized American Man

Arnold Schwarzenegger began his public career as a world champion bodybuilder. Many people mark his starring role in the award winning 1977 documentary on bodybuilders, *Pumping Iron*, as his film debut. However, Schwarzenegger actually appeared in a few other television and B film roles before that, including a typecast role in the 1970 film *Hercules in New York*. Schwarzenegger's celebrity star rose rapidly in the early 1980s, with a series of films that featured his muscular body as the ultimate fighting machine: *Conan: The Barbarian* (1982), *Conan: The Destroyer* (1984), *Red Sonja* (1985), *Commando* (1985), and *Predator* (1987). Among these popular 1980s films, it is *The Terminator* (1984) that most firmly established Schwarzenegger as a major film star and as king of a particular genre.

Conan, Commando, and the Terminator appear in the 1980s, at the same time that Rambo and other hard, man-as-weapon, man-as-machine images filled the nation's screens. Susan Jeffords (1989) calls this cultural moment a "remasculinization of America," when the idea of real men as decisive, strong, and courageous arose from the confusion and humiliation of the U.S. loss in the Vietnam war, and against the challenges of feminism and gay liberation. Jeffords's analyses of popular Vietnam films are especially insightful. The major common theme in these films is the Vietnam veteran as victimized by his own government, the war, the Vietnamese, American protestors, and the women's movement—all of which are portrayed as feminizing forces that have shamed and humiliated American men. Two factors were central to the symbolic remasculinization that followed: First, these film heroes of the 1980s were rugged individuals who stoically and rigidly stood up against bureaucrats who were undermining American power and pride with their indecisiveness and softness. Second, the muscular male body, often with massive weapons added as appendages, was the major symbolic expression of remasculinization. These men wasted very few words; instead, they spoke through explosive and decisively violent bodily actions. Jeffords argues that the male body-as-weapon serves as the ultimate spectacle and locus of masculine regeneration in post–Vietnam era films of the 1980s. There is a common moment in many of these films: The male hero is seemingly destroyed in an explosion of flames, and as his enemies laugh, he miraculously rises (in slow motion) from under water, firing his weapon and destroying the enemy. Drawing from Klaus Theweleit's (1987) analysis of the "soldier-men" of Nazi Germany, Jeffords argues that this moment symbolizes a "purification through fire and rebirth through immersion in water" (Jeffords 1989, 130). During this historical moment of cultural remasculinization, Schwarzenegger was the right body at the right time. Muscular Arnold, as image, reaffirmed the idea of categorical sex difference in an era where such difference had been challenged on multiple levels. In this historical moment, the Terminator's most famous sentence, "I'll be back," may have invoked an image of a remasculinized American man, "back" from the cultural feminization of the 1960s and 1970s, as well as a resurgence of American power in the world.

It is possible to look at this remasculinized male subject in 1980s films as a symbolic configuration of hegemonic masculinity that restabilizes the centrality of men's bodies and thus men's (at least white U.S. men's) power and privilege. Indeed, Messerschmidt's (1993, 82) statement that "hegemonic masculinity . . . emphasizes practices toward authority, control, independence, competitive individualism, aggressiveness, and the capacity for violence," seems to describe precisely the masculinity displayed by Schwarzenegger and Stallone in these 1980s films. But we need to be cautious about coming up with such a fixed definition of hegemonic masculinity. Although it clearly provided symbolic support for the resurgent conservatism of the Reagan era, this simplistic reversion to an atavistic symbology of violent, stoic, and muscular masculinity probably fueled tensions in gender relations as much as it stabilized them. As Connell and Messerschmidt (2005, 853) note, "gender relations are always arenas of tension. A given pattern of hegemonic masculinity is hegemonic to the extent that it provides a solution to these tensions, tending to stabilize patriarchal power or reconstitute it in new conditions. A pattern of practice (i.e., a version of masculinity) that provided such a solution in past conditions but not in new conditions is open to challenge—in fact is certain to be challenged."

There is plenty of evidence that by the end of the 1980s, the remasculinized muscular hero who wreaks havoc with his guns (biceps and bazookas) while keeping verbal expression down to a few grunts or occasional three-word sentences delivered in monotone was not playing well in Peoria. The 1988 final installment of *Rambo* (*Rambo III*) was listed by the 1990 *Guinness Book of World Records* as the most violent movie, with 221 acts of violence and more than 108 deaths. Despite (or because of?) this carnage, the film did not do well: Its gross in the United States was $10 million less than the film's overall budget, and Stallone's tired one-liners (Zaysen: "Who are you?" Rambo: "Your worst nightmare") reportedly left audiences laughing derisively. Other icons of heroic masculine invulnerability tumbled from their pedestals: One of the actors who played the Marlboro man in cigarette ads died from lung cancer. By the late 1980s and early 1990s, the idea of men as invulnerable, nonemotional, working and fighting machines was frequently caricatured in popular culture and made fun of in everyday life. Health advocates grabbed onto this caricature with "culture jamming" counteradvertisements aimed at improving men's health. For instance, a counterad distributed by the California Department of Health Services referenced years of "Marlboro Country" ads by depicting two rugged cowboys riding side by side on their horses, with a caption that read, "Bob, I've got emphysema." These sorts of ads invert the intended meanings of the Marlboro Man, illustrating how narrow cultural conceptions of masculinity are unhealthy—even deadly—for the men who try to live up to them. This new cultural sensibility is a direct legacy of the feminist critique of hypermasculinity. By the 1990s, these kinds of counterads could rely on readers to make the ironic connections, drawing on their own familiarity with the straight tobacco ads that were referenced, in addition to their familiarity with the increasingly prevalent cultural caricatures of hypermasculinity as dangerous, self-destructive, and (often) ridiculously laughable.

The Birth of the Kindergarten Commando

Many professional-class white men in the 1980s and 1990s began to symbolically distance themselves from this discredited view of traditional masculinity and forged new, more sensitive forms of masculinity. But this is not to say that successful and powerful men have fully swung toward an embrace of femininity and vulnerability. Some men's brief flirtations with soft, "new man" styles in the 1970s—the actor Alan Alda comes to mind—were thoroughly discredited and marginalized. Instead, we have seen the emergence of a symbology of masculinity that is hybrid: Toughness, decisiveness, and hardness are still central to hegemonic masculinity, but it is now normally linked with situationally appropriate moments of compassion and, sometimes, vulnerability. The 1980s and 1990s saw the increasingly common image of powerful men crying—not sobbing, but shedding a tear or two—in public: President Ronald Reagan in speaking of soldiers' sacrifices after the 1983 U.S. invasion of Grenada, General Norman Schwarzkopf at a press conference noting U.S. troops killed during the 1990–1991 Gulf War, basketball player Michael Jordan in the immediate aftermath of winning his first NBA championship in 1991. These emotional displays may have been fully genuine, but I emphasize that they were not delivered in the aftermath of a loss, in a moment of vulnerability, failure, or humiliation. Try to imagine for a moment superstar NBA player Dirk Nowitzki, after the Dallas Mavericks' 2006 loss in the NBA Finals, dropping to his knees at center court, overcome with grief, weeping openly with his face buried in his hands. That is not likely to happen. Tears are appropriate as public masculinity displays in the immediate aftermath of winning an NBA championship, or of having just successfully overrun a small Third World country with virtually no military. Powerful men have found it most safe to display public grief or compassion not in relation to their own failures or to the pain of other men—this might be perceived as weakness—and not in terms of women's struggles for respect and equality—this might be perceived as being "pussywhipped" (a recently revived epithet in pop culture). Rather, the public compassion of this emergent masculinity is most often displayed as protective care—often for children—which brings us back to the Governator.[1]

Schwarzenegger's original *Terminator* character was an unambiguously violent male-body-as-weapon, severed from any capacity for human compassion. But in the late 1980s, this image began to be rounded out by—not replaced with—a more compassionate persona. We can actually watch this transformation occur in *Terminator II: Judgment Day* (1991). In this film, Schwarzenegger, although still a killing machine, becomes the good guy, even showing occasional glimpses of human compassion. And significantly, it is his connection with a young boy that begins to humanize him. Taken together, Schwarzenegger's films of the 1990s display a masculinity that oscillates between his more recognizable hard guy image and an image of self-mocking vulnerability, compassion, and care, especially care for kids (e.g., *Kindergarten Cop,* 1990; *Jingle All the Way,* 1996). I call this emergent hybrid masculinity "The Kindergarten Commando." Indeed, in Schwarzenegger's first major foray into California politics in 2002, he plugged his ballot initiative for after-school activities for kids by saying that he had been "an action hero for kids in the movies; now I want to be an action hero for kids in real life." In the 1994 comedy *Junior,* Schwarzenegger appropriates an ultimate bodily sign of femaleness: pregnancy and childbirth. But Schwarzenegger's gender hybridity could never be mistaken as an embrace of a 1970s styled androgyny. Instead, in the Kindergarten Commando masculinity of Arnold Schwarzenegger, we see the appropriation and situational display of particular aspects of femininity, strategically relocated within a powerfully masculine male body.

In his initial 2003 run for California governor, Schwarzenegger positioned himself as a centrist unifier, and his film-based masculine imagery supported the forging of this political image. Hardness and violence, plus compassion and care, is a potent equation for hegemonic masculinity in public symbology today. And what tethers these two seemingly opposed principles is protection—protection of children and women from bad guys, from evil robots from the past, or from faceless, violently irrational terrorists from outside our borders.

The post–9/11 world has provided an increasingly fertile ground for the ascent of the Kindergarten Commando as compassionate masculine protector. Iris Marion Young (2003) has argued that the emergent U.S. security state is founded on a renewed "logic of masculine protection." And as Stephen Ducat (2004) has argued in his book *The Wimp Factor,* right-wing movements have seized this moment to activate a fear among men of "the mommy state"—a bureaucratic state that embodies weakness, softness, and feminist values. The desire for a revived "daddy state" is activated through a culture of fear: Only the man who really cares about us, and is also tough enough to stand up to evil, can be fully trusted to lead us in these dangerous times. The ascendance of this form of hegemonic masculinity is a response to feminist and other critiques of the limits of a 1950s John Wayne–style masculinity, and it thrives symbiotically with pervasive fears of threats by outsiders.

This is not a symmetrical symbiosis, though: In a male political leader today, compassion and care seem always to be subordinated to toughness, strength, and a single-minded resolve that is too often called "decisiveness" but that might otherwise accurately be characterized as stubborn narrow-mindedness. This asymmetry is reflected in Schwarzenegger's recent films, in which the violent, tough-guy hero has never been eclipsed by the vulnerable kid-loving guy: in *End of Days* (1999), Schwarzenegger saves the world from no less a force of evil than Satan himself. The emergent Kindergarten Commando masculinity is forged within a post-9/11 context in Schwarzenegger's 2002 film *Collateral Damage.* Here, firefighter Gordon Brewer is plunged into the complex and dangerous world of international terrorism after he loses his wife and child in a terrorist bombing. Frustrated with the official investigation and haunted by the thought that the man responsible for murdering his family might never be brought to justice, Brewer takes matters into his own hands and tracks his quarry ultimately to Colombia. When *Terminator III: Rise of the Machines* hit the theatres in 2003, Schwarzenegger was running for governor of California. In *T3,* it was clear that the hero, though still an admirably efficient killing machine, had mobilized his human compassion to fight for humanity against the evil machines.

Hegemonic Masculinity in a Matrix of Domination

My argument thus far is that the currently ascendant hegemonic masculinity constructed through a combination of the film images of Arnold Schwarzenegger is neither the stoic, masculine, postwar hero image of John Wayne nor the 1980s remasculinized man-as-machine image of Rambo or the

Terminator. These one-dimensional masculine images, by the 1990s, were laughable. Instead, the ascendant hegemonic masculinity combines the kick-ass muscular heroic male body with situationally expressive moments of empathy, grounded in care for kids and a capacity to make us all feel safe. Feminism, antiwar movements, health advocates, and even modern business human relations management have delegitimized pure hypermasculinity. But many people still view effeminacy as illegitimate in men, especially those who are leaders. So, neither hard nor soft is fully legitimate, unless the two are mixed, albeit with a much larger dose of the former than of the latter. And commercial interests have fruitfully taken up this hybrid masculine image: Heterosexual men, as we saw in the TV show *Queer Eye for the Straight Guy*, are seen as more attractive to women when softened—provided they still have power, muscles, and the money to purchase the correct draperies, fine cuisine, clothing, cosmetics, and other body-management products. Arnold, of course, has all of this. His masculinity displays were effective in securing power. But toward what ends? What do we see in the play of hard and soft, in strength and compassion in terms of what he does as governor? Three events are very revealing, and I will discuss them very briefly: first, the governor's playfully aggressive use of references to his film and bodybuilder careers in his ongoing budget battles with the Democrats; second, his class politics—particularly in his dealings with business and labor interests in California; and third, the "woman problem" that emerged during his first election.

Girlie Men and Political Intertextuality

During his earliest days in office, Schwarzenegger famously mobilized the "girlie men" epithet and turned it on his Democratic opponents in the California legislature. In doing so, he deployed references to his own *Terminator* films (urging voters to "terminate" his democratic opponents), and the "girlie men" comments referenced the *Saturday Night Live* skit that had originally spoofed him. This illustrates the often-noted fact that cultural symbols do not float free: They emerge from and in turn enter into social relations. Schwarzenegger strategically deployed the imagery of the Kindergarten Commando to get himself elected. But in the real life of governing, when push came to shove, he fell back on the Terminator, not the lovable *Kindergarten Cop* protector of children, as a strategy for deploying power.

Schwarzenegger's girlie man taunt is not the first time that a politician has drawn from popular commercial culture to invoke an image aimed to undermine his opponents. Recall, for instance, then vice president Walter Mondale's 1984 attempt to attack his Republican presidential race opponent's lack of substantive ideas by humorously deploying a "where's the beef?" chant that referenced the then-popular Wendy's hamburger commercial. However, by comparison, Schwarzenegger's girlie man insult is a rather unprecedented multilevel image: It is a veritable Möbius strip of meanings, with life imitating ironic schlock, imitating life, imitating more schlock.

Audiences get a sense of pleasure and power—a sense of authorship—from being insiders as they participate in decoding familiar intertextual messages such as "where's the beef?" "girlie man," or "I'll be back!" And if we think of the electorate as an audience (and certainly political parties use all the advertising expertise that they can muster), an election can be seen as a sort of poll of the audience's preferences. The electorate is buying a particular candidate who has been sold to them. Schwarzenegger's reference to girlie men and to *The Terminator* appealed to his supporters, but it also set off a firestorm of criticism from feminists, gay/lesbian organizations, and Democratic legislators. The governor's plea to voters to "terminate" his Democratic foes in November not only disrupted his thus-far carefully crafted image of the bipartisan get-it-done compromiser but also indicated the reemergence of a gloves-off muscular masculinity behind which the kind and compassionate Kindergarten Cop receded into the background. And this spelled some trouble for the Governor.

The symbolic symmetry of the new man—the Kindergarten Commando—was broken, leaving Schwarzenegger once again vulnerable both to sarcastic media caricature and to open questioning about the misogyny and homophobia that might lie behind the warm smile. However, the fact that Schwarzenegger's power was anchored so much in the symbolic realm facilitated his ability to deploy his power in a form that allowed for humorous, ironic interpretation; the implied self-mocking in his girlie man comments gets him off the hook, perhaps, from otherwise coming across as a bully: Democrats who decry the sexism or homophobia embedded in the girly man comment appear perhaps to have no sense of humor. In the vernacular of the shock radio so popular with many young white males today, people who object to Schwarzenegger's comments as sexist or homophobic are "feminazis"; they just don't get the joke (Benwell 2004; Messner and Montez de Oca 2005).

Hegemonic Masculinity and Class Politics

Meanwhile, though, it is clear that the joke was on some of the most vulnerable people of California. My second example concerns Schwarzenegger's class politics. In August 2004, he vetoed a minimum wage increase. Simultaneously, he supported Walmart's economic colonization of the California retail industry. Walmart's importation of notoriously low-waged jobs has been resisted by organized retail unions and by several California cities and towns, yet it was clear which side Schwarzenegger took in this struggle. This illustrates how hegemonic masculinity enters class relations: If there was compassion here, it was compassion for big business; if there was muscle to be deployed, it was against the collective interests of working people, defined by the governor's business logic as special interests.

Governor Schwarzenegger also attacked public employees' unions in his effort to control state spending. A National Public Radio story on March 15, 2005 noted that members of the California Nurses Association were showing up and protesting in every public venue in which he appeared. As he was giving a speech to supporters, one could hear the voices of the nurses chanting something in the background. Schwarzenegger commented to a cheering crowd, "Pay no attention to them. They are the *Special Interests.* They don't like me in Sacramento, because I am always kicking their butts!" Indeed, earlier that year, Schwarzenegger had vetoed the rule that mandated a lower nurse/doctor ratio and also took $350,000 in campaign contributions from pharmaceutical companies while opposing a prescription drugs law that would have helped consumers.

His proposed 2005 budget included cuts in welfare, cuts in dental aid for the poor, cuts in the state's contribution to caregivers for the disabled and the elderly, and a scaling back of retirement plans for state workers. By 2005, children in the California public schools had good reason to suspect that the protective Kindergarten Commando had morphed into the Kindergarten Terminator. Despite a previous promise not to cut education spending, his proposed budget included $2.2 billion in education cuts while holding firm on his promise not to raise taxes.

The ideological basis of these class politics—and their links to the politics of race and immigration— was further demonstrated in Schwarzenegger's speech at the 2004 Republican National Convention. Here, he told his own rugged individualist immigrant story, with clear pull-yourself-up-by-your-bootstraps, Horatio Alger themes. While positioning himself on the surface as someone who cares about and understands immigrants, his story reiterated conservative themes that are grounded in the experience of white ethnics rather than in that of the vast majority of California's current immigrant population who deal daily with poverty, institutionalized racism, and escalating xenophobia. Schwarzenegger's narrative thus helps to reconstruct a white male subject and demonstrates how hegemonic masculinity is never just about gender: It is also about race and nation (Montez de Oca 2005).

Hegemonic Masculinity as Heterosexy

My third example concerns Schwarzenegger's woman problem. During the final weeks of the 2003 election, the *Los Angeles Times* broke a series of stories indicating that several women had complained of Schwarzenegger's having sexually harassed and humiliated them in various ways over the years.

The women's claims were quickly trivialized by being more benignly defined as "unwanted groping." Ironically, these accusations probably enhanced Schwarzenegger's status with many men and may have helped to secure the complicity of many women, as evidenced by the "Arnold, Grope Me!" signs seen at some of his rallies in the final days of his run for governor. Here, we can see that the hegemonic masculinity created by Schwarzenegger's symbolic fusing of opposites also involves the construction of a particular form of masculine heterosexuality. We should not underestimate the extent to which the imagery of hegemonic masculinity is electrified with an erotic charge—a charge that serves as a powerful linking process in constructing dominant forms of femininity—and through that, the consent of many women. In fact, it is likely that while the groping charges solidified an already-existing opposition to Schwarzenegger, they also pulled some voters more solidly into his camp.

A comparison with former president Bill Clinton is useful in this regard. Stephen Ducat (2004) discusses how during his first term as president, Clinton was vulnerable to questions about his masculinity due to his lack of military service, his support for women's and gay issues, and especially the perception that his wife Hillary "wore the pants" in his family. Clinton, according to Ducat, lacked symbolic ownership of the phallus, necessary for a man with power. Attempts by Clinton's handlers to symbolically masculinize Bill and to feminize Hillary did little to help either of their images.

However, in the aftermath of the scandals surrounding Bill Clinton's sexual relations with White House intern Monica Lewinsky, Clinton's poll numbers skyrocketed. A 1998 Gallup poll conducted after the scandal broke found that Americans saw him as the most admired man in the world. He had morphed, in Ducat's (2004) words, from "emasculated househusband to stud muffin," from "pussy" to "walking erection." Hillary Clinton's "stand by your man" posture apparently enhanced her popularity, too.

As governor, Schwarzenegger's virile sexual image has been stabilized in large part by his famous Democratic wife Maria Shriver's steadfastly supportive presence. The story of his past sexual indiscretions was quickly dropped by the media, apparently seen as (1) just another example of a woman (in this case almost a dozen separate women!) trying to bring down a powerful man with a sex scandal, or (2) an example of certain sexual conventions being acceptable in one context (Hollywood) and not in others, and/or (3) something that, while regrettable, is now all in the past, perhaps like Schwarzenegger's past statements of admiration for Adolph [sic] Hitler.

Hegemonic Masculinity and Women in Politics

To summarize, Arnold Schwarzenegger's sexy, hybrid mix of hardness and compassion is currently a configuration of symbols that forge a masculinity that is useful for securing power among men who already have it. But for a woman striving for power—at least in the context of the United States' current gender order—these opposites do not mesh as easily. Strength and compassion, when embodied in a woman leader, still appear to clash in ways that set her up for public crucifixion: U.S. Congresswoman Pat Schroeder's brief flirtation with a presidential run in 1988—derailed by a public tear—comes to mind. Although Schroeder's many successful years in Congress, and especially her position as head of the Congressional Armed Services Committee, might have made her seem a serious candidate for the presidency, one public tear made her seem perhaps too feminine to become president. By contrast, during her years as first lady, Hillary Clinton was pilloried for her supposed ballbusting of her husband and for having her own ambitions to gain political power—in short, for being too much like a man. Former British prime minister Margaret Thatcher is no exception; she proves the rule. Thatcher was notoriously conservative with respect to slashing the British welfare state, and she complemented then U.S. president Ronald Reagan with her militaristic saber rattling. An individual woman can occasionally out-masculine the men and be a strong leader. But as with Thatcher, she had better leave compassion and caring for the poor, for the sick, and for the aged literally at home. That is why I have been predicting for some time that our first woman president, or vice president, will be a Republican. To be seen as a credible candidate, a woman candidate might downplay the politics of compassion and care and instead present herself as an advocate for, and leader of, the daddy state.

The Dangers of a Compassionate Masculinity

Arnold Schwarzenegger is not the first male politician to attempt to craft a postfeminist hybrid symbology of hegemonic masculinity. George Bush Sr. battled his own reputation as a bureaucratic wimp with a masculinizing project of waging war against Saddam Hussein. He signaled his compassionate side with speeches encouraging others (instead of the government) to be "a thousand points of light" to help the poor and homeless. And the 2004 presidential election between Kerry and Bush seemed to devolve into another old *Saturday Night Live* satire: *Quien es mas macho?* This reveals something important about the ascendant hegemonic masculinity: It did not seem to matter to many voters that Bush had been a lousy student who partied his youth away and only escaped the shame of a drunk driving conviction, Vietnam War service evasion, and possible desertion from his National Guard service through his born-with-a-silver-spoon family connections. Nor did it seem to matter to many voters that John Kerry had served willingly in Vietnam and had been honored for bravery and war wounds. Kerry was still—with enough success to neutralize this apparent war hero advantage—stained by his association with elite liberalism.

This is nothing new. Adlai Stevenson's unsuccessful runs for the presidency in 1952 and 1956 offer a good case in point. The conservative attack on Stevenson can be seen as part of the postwar hysteria about reds and homosexuals. Kimmel (1996, 237) notes, "Not only was Stevenson labeled 'soft' on communism, but he was the classic 'egghead.' The candidate whom the *New York Daily News* called 'Adelaide' used 'tea cup words,' which he 'trilled' with his 'fruity' voice, and was supported by 'Harvard lace cuff liberals' and 'lace panty diplomats.'" A month before the 1952 Democratic Convention, FBI head J. Edgar Hoover ordered a "blind memorandum" be prepared on Stevenson. The "investigation" concluded that Stevenson was "one of the best known homosexuals" in Illinois (Theoharis 2002, 180). Although the FBI memorandum was not made public at the time, attacks on Stevenson's masculinity (linked with his liberalism and intellectualism) formed a core of the contrast that Republicans successfully drew between Stevenson and war hero General Dwight D. Eisenhower, who handily won the election—and reelection four years later. For the past half century, conservatives have used a version of this same gender strategy to wage a successful symbolic campaign that links liberalism with softness: Book learning and intellectual curiosity are viewed as a lack of inner strength and determination. Seeing the complications and gray areas in any public debate is viewed as a sign of waffling and a lack of an inner values–based compass. And compassion for the pain of others is seen as weakness.

To be sure, as President George W. Bush's slogan about "compassionate conservatism" showed, conservatives have incorporated the language of care into their project. As I have argued, a leadership masculinity without compassion is now symbolically untenable. But the new hybrid hegemonic masculinity always leads with the muscle. Muscle must first and foremost be evident; compassion is displayed at appropriate symbolic moments, suggesting a human side to the man. Liberalism suffers from the fact that it seems too often to lead with compassion, not with muscle. So when liberals try to look muscular, they are much more easily subjected to ridicule, like they are in some sort of gender drag, as evidenced by the infamous moment when 1988 Democratic presidential candidate Michael Dukakis tried to dress up like a commander-in-chief but ended up looking more like a schoolboy taking a joyride in a tank while wearing a too-large military costume.

George W. Bush's love of military dress-up did not draw the same kind of ridicule. Or at least it can be said that this kind of ridicule does not seem to stick in the way it does when aimed at a supposed liberal. And so, very sadly I think, in recent presidential campaigns, we saw both candidates trying their hardest to appear tough, strong, decisive, athletic, and militaristic, while suggesting—parenthetically, almost as an afterthought—that they care about all of us, that seniors should get prescription drugs, that no child should be left behind. The asymmetries in the ways that these two candidates were able to deploy this hybrid masculinity were apparent: When Kerry said that smart leadership would lead to a "more sensitive" waging of the war in Iraq, it was the only opening that any manly hunter would need: Vice President Dick Cheney needed no shotgun to jump right on this opportunity to blast the war hero with the feminized symbolism of weakness and liberalism.

Gender, Politics, and Justice

The accomplishment of a stable hegemonic masculinity by an individual man in daily interactions is nearly impossible. But what helps to anchor an otherwise unstable hegemonic masculinity is the play of masculine imagery in the symbolic realm. Today, for the moment, the gender imagery seen in the combined films of Arnold Schwarzenegger creates a hybrid masculinity I am calling the Kindergarten Commando. This image, when deployed in the realm of electoral politics, secures power and privilege in a moment of destabilized gender and race relations, economic insecurity, and concerns about immigration, all permeated with a culture of fear.

The widespread consent that accumulates around this form of masculinity is, I suggest, an example of hegemony at work. And—it is important to note—the power and privilege that this hegemonic masculinity secures is not necessarily or simply men's power over women. The erotically charged masculinity of the famously cigar-loving Governator was effective in securing power in terms of race and nation, and in class relations in California. What I am suggesting here is that the public symbolism of hegemonic masculinity is a means of consolidating power in a matrix of class, race, and international politics. For California in 2004, it was Arnold Schwarzenegger's combination of muscle, heterosexuality, and whiteness—particularly the way his story reiterated the white European melting pot story of individualism and upward mobility in a meritocratic America—that formed a successful symbolic package that enough voters liked. As governor, Schwarzenegger mobilized this package first and foremost to wage class war on California's public workers and poor. But as Connell and Messerschmidt (2005) point out, hegemonic masculinity is always contingent and contextual. As contexts change, challenges are possible, perhaps inevitable. And California during the past few years has certainly been a site of rapid shifts and conflicts.

Schwarzenegger's attack on the underprivileged left him open to criticism of his own privilege and the possible use of his office to further his own interests. Opposition to Schwarzenegger mounted in 2005, as organized California teachers, nurses, firefighters, and other public employees waged massive protests and media campaigns against the governor. His having flexed his Terminator muscles left him open to questioning about whether he really cared about the elderly. Health activists and advocates for the elderly railed at the large donations he had accepted from the insurance and pharmaceutical industries and his decisions that reflected those links. Perhaps, at least in California, a less conservative state than most, many of the governor's constituents wanted to see care and compassion reflected in actual policies rather than simply in some of his movies.

And so, after the ballot initiatives that he had sponsored were soundly defeated in the 2005 special election that he had called for, Schwarzenegger immediately shifted his strategy, leaving his combative Terminator persona behind and returning to the Kindergarten Commando. He began to promote some liberal issues, including signing landmark legislation to control global warming. He finally agreed to sign legislation to authorize a modest raise in California's minimum wage. But he also advocated cutting thousands of poor off of the welfare rolls and continued his ties with corporate elites in the pharmaceutical industry. Perhaps the new model for Schwarzenegger might be closer to the masculinity of Bill Clinton—combining a moderate liberalism on social issues like women's and gay rights with a fiscal conservatism that continues to enlarge the gap between rich and poor. The success of this new man leadership style is at once a visible sign of the ways that liberal feminist critiques of hypermasculinity have been incorporated and embodied into many professional-class men's interactional styles and displays. What results is a rounding of the hard edges off of hypermasculinity and a visible softening of powerful men's public styles and displays. But this should not be seen necessarily as a major victory for feminism. Rather, if I am correct that this more sensitive, new man style tends to facilitate and legitimize privileged men's wielding of power over others, this is probably better seen as an example of feminism's being co-opted into new forms of domination—in this case, class and race domination.

Schwarzenegger's return to Kindergarten Commando masculinity appears to have worked. His shift to more centrist stands—undoubtedly influenced by his more liberal wife, Maria Shriver—has calmed the anti-Arnold storms of 2005. And clearly, the muscle still matters: One of the largest advantages he had over his Democratic opponent in 2006 was that voters saw Schwarzenegger as a much stronger leader. A preelection poll conducted by the *Los Angeles Times* found that 60 percent of likely voters saw Schwarzenegger as a "strong leader" while only 20 percent viewed Phil Angelides as strong.

In short, I speculate that Governor Schwarzenegger's 2004–2005 rejection of the hybrid Kindergarten Commando masculine imagery that had gotten him elected contributed to a dramatic decline in his popularity and to his thrashing in the special election of 2005. When he dropped the oppositional tough-guy approach, and redeployed the Kindergarten Commando, his popularity again soared in 2006, contributing to his landslide reelection.

Conclusion

If we are to work toward economic justice for working people, immigrants, and the aged; equality for women and racial and sexual minorities; and the creation of a more just and peaceful world, we need to tackle head-on the ways that dominant forms of masculinity—while always contested and shifting—continue to serve as a nexus of power that secures the privileges of the few at the expense of the many. Governor Arnold Schwarzenegger's strategic shifting of his public persona from Kindergarten Commando to Terminator and then back to Kindergarten Commando illustrates how, in the realm of electoral politics, hegemonic masculinity is a malleable symbolic strategy for wielding power.

In electoral politics, men's militaristic muscular posturing in seeking office limits women's abilities to seek high office in much the same ways that narrow masculine displays of dress, demeanor, voice, and style narrow women's chances in corporate or professional occupations. Women's activism in public life challenges these limitations, but if meaningful change is to occur, men leaders must also stop conforming to a singular masculine style of dress, demeanor, or leadership style. When men create a wider range of alternative masculine styles of leadership, it opens space for women (and for other kinds of men). Ironically, Arnold Schwarzenegger is perfectly positioned in 2007 and beyond to model a different kind of masculinity and a different kind of leadership. The social and political context of California (and perhaps his more liberal wife) have already pushed him to the Left—even to the point where by early 2007, members of his own party had begun to complain that he, in effect, had become a Democrat. And Schwarzenegger's public image has softened, partly in response to several widely distributed photos of him on a beach, showing a flabby middle, sagging pectoral muscles, and arms far thinner than the guns he proudly displayed in his bodybuilding and film careers. Schwarzenegger is aging; he attended his own inauguration on crutches in the aftermath of a skiing injury. The mass media are reporting that he is depressed by the decline of his own body and is speculating that his health problems may be related to his earlier use of steroids. Although this creates a potential opportunity for Schwarzenegger, it would be foolhardy for anyone to look hopefully to him to create a counterhegemonic gender symbolism.

In fact, it is unlikely that new, expansive, and progressive imagery will emanate from top male politicians. It is more likely that some men who seek high office but have progressive (even feminist) values may try to be "stealth feminists"—while posturing in military garb (Dukakis in 1988), downplaying a deep commitment to reversing the human destruction of the environment (Gore in 2000), or overemphasizing long past military accomplishments (Kerry in 2004) instead of focusing on issues and values that they cherish. This does not work, partly because it is bad theatre. Even if this strategy succeeds in getting someone elected, it is unlikely that stealth feminism will work; men who get to the top using masculine muscle will rightly assume that once in office, their constituents expect them to flex those muscles (e.g., President Jimmy Carter's ill-fated use of military power in 1980 in his attempt to end the Iran hostage crisis).

Are there alternatives? Think of former president Jimmy Carter, and more recently former vice president Al Gore in their postelectoral politics lives. They have both done brave and important work, work grounded in compassion for peoples of the world, for peace, and for the environment. When I reflect on their failures in electoral politics, I cannot help but wonder if this is a case of the clothes not having fit the men. Clearly, instead of the man (or the woman) having to adopt a ridiculous drag to be taken seriously as a leader, or as a potential leader, we need to change the clothes of politics so that they better suit the kinds of leaders we need: smart, literate, visionary, compassionate leaders who shape and fight for policies that help everyday people, not just here in the United States but globally. Carter and Gore have found roles that suit them, postpolitics, and have done good work. But we cannot accept it as good enough that national leaders can live out their compassionate and progressive values only after leaving national office. There must be alternatives.

What we need is a renewed movement of ordinary women and men working side by side to push assertively for an ideal of the public that is founded first and foremost on compassion and caring. The seeds of such a movement currently exist—in feminist organizations, in the peace movement, in religious-based immigrant rights organizations, in union-based organizing for the rights of workers. A coalition of these progressive organizations can succeed in infusing local and national politics with the values of public compassion. This will not happen easily, or without opposition. We need to expect that such a movement will have to be tough and will have to fight—against entrenched privilege and against the politics of fear—to place compassion and care at the top of the public agenda. Out of such a movement, we can generate and support women and men who will lead with love and compassion and follow with the muscle.

Note

1. The term "Governator" became a widely used way to refer to Arnold Schwarzenegger in the popular media and among Californians in the aftermath of his election as California governor. The term symbolically links his job as governor with his best-known film role in *The Terminator* and speaks to the successful construction of a hybrid celebrity personality that I discuss in this article.

References

Benwell, Bethan. 2004. Ironic discourse: Evasive masculinity in men's lifestyle magazines. *Men and Masculinities* 7:3–21.

Boyle, Ellexis. 2006. Memorializing muscle in the auto/biography(ies) of Arnold Schwarzenegger. Paper presented at the annual meetings of the North American Society for the Sociology of Sport, Vancouver, BC, Canada, November 4.

Collins, Patricia Hill. 1990. *Black feminist thought: Knowledge, consciousness, and the politics of empowerment.* Boston: Unwin Hyman.

Connell, R. W. 1987. *Gender & power.* Stanford, CA: Stanford University Press.

Connell, R. W., and James W. Messerschmidt. 2005. Hegemonic masculinity: Rethinking the concept. *Gender & Society* 19:829–59.

Ducat, Stephen J. 2004. *The wimp factor: Gender gaps, holy wars, and the politics of anxious masculinity.* Boston: Beacon.

Gomez-Barris, Macarena, and Herman Gray. 2006. Michael Jackson, television and post-op disasters. *Television and New Media* 7:40–51.

Jeffords, Susan. 1989. *The remasculinization of America: Gender and the Vietnam War.* Bloomington: Indiana University Press.

Kimmel, Michael. 1996. *Manhood in America: A cultural history.* New York: Free Press.

Messerschmidt, James. 1993. *Masculinities and crime.* Lanham, MD: Rowman & Littlefield.

Messner, Michael A. 2004. On patriarchs and losers: Rethinking men's interests. *Berkeley Journal of Sociology* 48:76–88.

Messner, Michael A., and Jeffrey Montez de Oca. 2005. The male consumer as loser: Beer and liquor ads in mega sports media events. *Signs: Journal of Women in Culture and Society* 30:1879–1909.

Montez de Oca, Jeffrey. 2005. "As our muscles get softer, our missile race becomes harder": Cultural citizenship and the muscle gap. *Journal of Historical Sociology* 18:145–71.

Theoharis, Athan. 2002. *Chasing spies.* Chicago: Ivan R. Dee.

Theweleit, Klaus. 1987. *Male fantasies.* Vol. 1, *Women, floods, bodies, history.* Minneapolis: University of Minnesota Press.

Young, Iris Marion. 2003. The logic of masculinist protection: Reflections on the current security state. *Signs: Journal of Women in Culture and Society* 29:1–25.

CHAPTER 14

"White Men Are This Nation"

Right-Wing Militias and the Restoration of Rural American Masculinity

Michael Kimmel and Abby L. Ferber

In a 1987 illustration in *W.A.R.*, the magazine of the White Aryan Resistance, a working-class white man, in hard hat and flak jacket, stands proudly before a suspension bridge while a jet plane soars overhead. "White Men *Built* This Nation!!" reads the text. "White Men Are This Nation!!!" Most observers see the statement's racist intent immediately, but rarely do we see its deeply gendered meaning. Here is a moment when racial and gendered discourses fuse, when both race and gender are made visible. "This nation," we now understand, "is" neither white women nor non-white people of either gender.

The White Aryan Resistance that produced this illustration is situated on a continuum of the far right that runs from older organizations, such as the John Birch Society, the Ku Klux Klan, and the American Nazi Party, to Holocaust deniers, neo-Nazi or racist skinheads; white power groups like Posse Comitatus and White Aryan Resistance; and radical rural militias like the Wisconsin Militia and the Militia of Montana. This last set of organizations, the rural militias, appeared in the 1990s in the farm belt (and Rust Belt) and became especially visible after the standoffs in Ruby Ridge, Idaho, and the bombing of the federal building in Oklahoma City.

In this chapter we examine the ideology and organization of the rural militia movement, which reached its peak in the mid-1990s. First, we locate the emergence of this movement in the farm crisis of the 1980s. Second, we describe the movement's social composition. Finally, we explore its ideology. We argue that the militias, like many far-right groups, are both fiercely patriotic and simultaneously against capitalism and democratic government—or, more accurately, against corporate capitalism and federal government. To resolve that apparent contradiction, the militias, like other groups, employ a gendered discourse about masculinity both to explain the baffling set of structural forces arrayed against them and to provide a set of "others" against which they can project a unifying ideology.

The Rural Context

The economic restructuring of the global economy has had a dramatic effect on rural areas throughout the industrial world.[1] The Reagan Revolution in general meant corporate downsizing, declining real wages, changing technology, an increasing gap between the wealthy and everyone else,

SOURCE: Kimmel, M., and Ferber, A. L. (2006). "White Men Are This Nation": Right-Wing Militias and the Restoration of Rural American Masculinity. *Country Boys: Masculinity and Rural Life*. Pennsylvania State University Press. Reproduced with permission from John Wiley & Sons.

uncertainty in the stock market, new waves of Latino and Asian immigrants to the United States, and a steady decline in manufacturing jobs (typically replaced by lower-paying jobs in the service sector). Increased capital mobility and the elimination of tariff barriers have also weakened the bargaining power of labor and left the average American worker feeling vulnerable and betrayed.[2] Between 1980 and 1985 alone, 11 million American workers lost their jobs through plant closures and layoffs. Of those who found new jobs, more than half experienced downward mobility.[3] Rural Americans in particular have found their economic insecurity compounded by threats to traditional Western industries like logging, mining, ranching, and farming, where consolidation has also proceeded rapidly and markedly.[4] Squeezed between corporate capital (agribusiness) and federal government (regulations, environmentalism, and the like), many farmers feel themselves to be the "victim[s] of the global restructuring of the rural world."[5]

Since 1980, America has lost nearly 750,000 of its small and medium-size family farms. During the farm crisis of the 1980s, Linda Lobao and Katherine Meyer point out, "farmers faced the worst financial stress since the Great Depression."[6] For affected farmers, this economic disaster dashed the American Dream of upward mobility and replaced it with the stark reality of downward mobility. As Osha Davidson notes, "Many of the new rural poor had not only shared American cultural goals— they had achieved them for a time. They had been in the middle class, of the middle class. They had tasted the good life and then had fallen from it." Davidson also notes the irony—crucial to our analysis—that "the victims of this blight, the inhabitants of the new rural ghettos, have always been the most blindly patriotic of Americans, the keepers of the American dream."[7] This state of rural crisis continues today as "family farms, which use little hired labor and whose households are sustained through farming alone, are being edged out."[8] While many may speak of a "new farm crisis," it is more accurate to say that the crisis of the 1980s never truly ended.[9]

For many, the continuing farm crisis is also a gender crisis, a crisis of masculinity. Many white, rural American men feel under siege and vulnerable, unsure of their manhood. They are furious and are looking for someone to blame. Some direct their rage inward, even to the point of suicidal thoughts and actions; others direct it outward. "Many debt ridden farm families will become more suspicious of government, as their self-worth, their sense of belonging, their hope for the future deteriorates," predicted Oklahoma psychologist Glen Wallace in 1989. "The farms are gone," writes Joel Dyer, "yet the farmers remain. They've been transformed into a wildfire of rage, fuelled by the grief of their loss and blown by the winds of conspiracy and hate-filled rhetoric."[10] Rural men are not alone in facing wrenching economic transformations, however. Many urban men, too, have tasted the good life and fallen from it. "It is hardly surprising, then, that American men—lacking confidence in the government and the economy, troubled by the changing relations between the sexes, uncertain of their identity or their future—began to *dream*, to fantasize about the powers and features of another kind of man who could retake and reorder the world. And the hero of all these dreams was the paramilitary warrior."[11] The militia movement is one embodiment of this dream, one that is strikingly rural both in the population from which it draws and in the location of most of its activities.

The Militia Movement

The militia movement is not easy to define. There is no central organization or leadership; rather, the movement is composed of loosely connected paramilitary organizations that "perceive a global conspiracy in which key political and economic events are manipulated by a small group of elite insiders."[12] These numerous unrelated groups form private armies, mistrust the government, and have armed themselves to fight back. According to the Militia Watchdog, an internet organization that tracks the movement, the militias grew out of the Posse Comitatus and the Patriot movement, which were strong in the 1970s and 1980s. (The Southern Poverty Law Center, which tracks right-wing extremist groups, lists the militias as a subset of the Patriot movement.)

Like their predecessors, militia members believe that the U.S. government has become totalitarian and seeks to disarm its citizenry and create a "one-world government." Militia members believe that traditional political reform is useless and that they must resist U.S. laws and attack the government. They believe that armed confrontation is inevitable. While not unified in any traditional sense, the movement nonetheless is tied together through the internet, where groups and individuals share stories and advice. At survivalist expositions and gun shows, they sell literature, recruit new members, and purchase arms and survivalist gear.[13] Some groups sell their wares via mail-order catalogs, and many meet on the weekends to train in guerrilla warfare tactics. Militia organizations subscribe to the magazine *Soldier of Fortune,* frequent *Soldier of Fortune* conventions, and draw members from *Soldier of Fortune* enthusiasts. The Militia of Montana has had booths at *Soldier of Fortune* expositions, where it peddles T-shirts reading "Angry White Guy" and bumper stickers proclaiming, "I Love my Country, but I Hate my Government."[14]

The Militia of Montana (with the deliciously unironically gendered acronym MOM) provides us with a "prototype" of the American militia. Founded by former Aryan Nations member John Trochman, his brother, and his nephew in the aftermath of Ruby Ridge, MOM was the first significant militia organization and the largest national distributor of militia propaganda.[15] At MOM meetings and through mail-order distribution it sells its own manuals, as well as a variety of books and videos, including *A Call to Arms, Battle Preparations Now, The Pestilence* (AIDS), *America in Crisis, The Illuminati Today, Booby Traps,* and *Big Sister Is Watching You* (discussed below). Their numerous manuals encourage and train readers in kidnapping, murder, and explosives, urging acts of terrorism.[16]

Estimates about the size and appeal of such militias vary. Since the first modern-day militias began appearing in the early 1990s, their numbers have expanded to include between 50,000 and 100,000 members in at least forty states.[17] In 1996 the number of militias and similar Patriot groups hit an all-time high of 858, with militia units or organizers in every state.[18] That number declined to 435 in 1998, of which 171 were classified as militias, and in 2001 only 158 Patriot groups remained active, with 73 classified as militias. We attribute this decline to a variety of factors. According to Mark Potok of the Southern Poverty Law Center, "They have gone home, disillusioned and tired of waiting for the revolution that never seems to come. They have been scared off, frightened by the arrests of thousands of comrades for engaging in illegal 'common-law' court tactics, weapons violations and even terrorist plots. And they have, in great numbers, left the relatively nonracist Patriot world for the harder-line groups that now make up most of the radical right."[19]

Few sharp divisions separate the various subgroups of the radical right. People flow between groups and have overlapping memberships and allegiances.[20] At the peak of the militia movement, one observer wrote, "It is the convergence of various streams of fanatical right wing beliefs that seems to be sweeping the militia movement along. Overlapping right wing social movements with militant factions appear to be coalescing within the militias."[21] This demonstrates the important point that far-right groups are intricately interconnected and share a basic antigovernment, anti-Semitic, racist, and sexist/patriarchal ideology. Equally, the extent of involvement in the movement varies; some men simply correspond over the internet and read militia literature; others attend training sessions, stockpile food supplies and weapons, and resist paying taxes. In its most dangerous form, small, secret cells of two to ten people plan sabotage and terrorism. These cells have been linked to several terrorist acts, including the Oklahoma City bombing, the derailment of an Amtrak train in Arizona, and multiple bomb plots targeting "the Southern Poverty Law Center, offices of the Anti-Defamation League, federal buildings, abortion clinics and sites in the gay community."[22]

As these activities suggest, militias provide training in, among other things, weapons use, target practice, intelligence gathering, encryption and decryption, field radio operation, navigation, unarmed defense, the manufacture of explosives, and demolition.[23] Vietnam War veterans, Gulf War veterans, and active military and law enforcement officers provide much of the instruction.

Social Composition of the Militias

Who are militia members? While no one has undertaken a formal survey of the militias (for obvious reasons), we can nonetheless discern several demographic characteristics. First and most obviously, militia members are overwhelmingly white and male. These white men, moreover, are commonly rural men. Numerous researchers have documented the rural nature of the militia movement; its roots are strongest, for instance, in the intermountain Montana and Idaho panhandle.[24] Potok similarly notes that the militia movement is "almost entirely rurally based."[25] Historian Carol McNichol Stock situates the militia movement within the historical tradition of rural radicalism on both the left and the right, a tradition rooted in the values of producerism and vigilantism. Stock explores what she labels the "ideology of rural producer radicalism." "The desire to own small property, to produce crops and foodstuffs, to control local affairs, to be served but never coerced by a representative government, and to have traditional ways of life and labor respected," she writes, "is the stuff of one of the oldest dreams in the United States."[26]

Many militia members are also military veterans. Several leaders served in Vietnam and were shocked by the national disgust that greeted them as they returned home after the debacle.[27] Some veterans believed the government sold them out, caving in to effeminate, cowardly protesters; they no longer trust the government to fight for what is right. Louis Beam, for example, served eighteen months in Vietnam before returning to start his own paramilitary organization, which was broken up in the 1980s by lawsuits. He now advocates "leaderless resistance," the formation of underground terrorist cells.

Another militia member, Bo Gritz, a former Green Beret in Vietnam, returned to Southeast Asia several times on clandestine missions to search for prisoners of war and provided the real-life basis for the film *Rambo*. He used his military heroism to increase his credibility among potential recruits—one brochure describes him as "this country's most decorated Vietnam veteran," a man who "killed some 400 Communists in his illustrious military career."[28] In 1993 Gritz began a traveling SPIKE (Specially Prepared Individuals for Key Events) training program, a rigorous survival course in paramilitary techniques. Gritz and colleague Jack McLamb, a retired police officer, created their own community, "Almost Heaven," in Idaho. Gritz embodies the military element of the militias; he represents men who believe they are entitled to be hailed as heroes, like earlier generations of American veterans, not scorned as outcasts. He symbolizes "true" warrior-style masculinity, the reward for men who join the militia.

The militias are also Christian, and thus the movement is strongest in states with high concentrations of fundamentalist Christians. Many have embraced Christian Identity theology, which gained a foothold on the far right in the early 1980s. About half of the militia members in South Carolina, for example, are also followers of Christian Identity.[29] Christian Identity's focus on racism and anti-Semitism provides the theological underpinnings for the shift from a more "traditional agrarian protest" to the paramilitarism of the militias.

According to several researchers, actual militia members tend to range in age from the late thirties to fifties, while the active terrorists tend to be somewhat younger—in their twenties.[30] Many teenagers who commit hate crimes "graduate" to militias and other far-right organizations when they reach their twenties.[31] Like other groups of ethnic nationalists, the militias and their followers consist of two generations of dispossessed and displaced lower-middle-class men—small farmers, shopkeepers, craftsmen, and skilled workers. Some are men who have worked all their adult lives, hoping to pass their family farm to their sons and retire comfortably. Tom Metzger, head of the White Aryan Resistance, for instance, estimates that while 10 percent of his followers are skinheads, most are "businessmen and artisans."[32] These men believed that if they worked hard, their legacy would be assured, but they are able to leave their sons little but foreclosures, economic insecurity, and debt. As Timothy McVeigh, from Lockport, New York, wrote in a letter to the editor in his hometown paper a few years before he blew up the federal building in Oklahoma City, "the American dream of the middle class has all but disappeared, substituted with people struggling just to buy next week's groceries."[33] The sons of these farmers and shopkeepers expected to—and felt entitled to—inherit their fathers' legacy.[34] And when they realized the extent of their dispossession, some became murderously angry—at a system that not only emasculated their fathers but also threatened their own manhood.

Of course, the militias are not composed entirely of "sons." Lori Linzer, a militia researcher at the Anti-Defamation League, found that there are a few women involved in the movement. These women, however, are most likely to become involved with internet discussions and websites and less likely to be active in paramilitary training and other militia activities. Although some women are actively involved in the movement, their presence does not change the fact that most militias are "vastly, mainly, white Christian men."[35]

This demographic certainly coincides with the dominant gender ideology in rural areas. U.S. farming communities are characterized by a prevalent "domestic ideology" that depicts men as farmers and women as their helpmates.[36] This ideology erases the significant labor of women on farms from view and reinforces a sexual division of labor that defines different areas of work for men and women.[37]

While many members of the militia movement were not born or raised in rural areas many have moved to such areas because they seek companionship with like-minded fellows. Moreover, in relatively remote areas, far from large numbers of nonwhites and Jews, they can organize, train, and build protective fortresses. Many groups thus seek to establish a refuge in rural communities where they can practice military tactics, stockpile food and weapons, hone their survivalist skills, and become self-sufficient in preparation for Armageddon, the final race war, or whatever cataclysm they envision. For example, while preparing for Y2K, some groups set up "covenant communities," self-sufficient and heavily armed rural settlements of white people who feared that "when the computers crash, government checks to minorities in the inner cities will stop. Then starving Hispanics and blacks will flood into the rural parts of America, armed to the teeth and willing to stop at nothing in order to wrench food from the tables of white Christians."[38]

In addition, far-right extremist leaders see rural areas as strong potential recruitment bases. Accurately reading the signs of rural decline and downward mobility, these leaders "see an opportunity to increase their political base by recruiting economically troubled farmers into their ranks.[39] While Davidson explains that "the spread of far-right groups over the last decade has not been limited to rural areas alone," we can certainly see that "the social and economic unraveling of rural communities—especially in the Midwest—has provided far-right groups with new audiences for their messages of hate."[40] Many farmers facing foreclosure have responded to promises from the far right to help them save their land; extremist groups offer them various schemes and legal maneuvers to help prevent foreclosure, blaming the farmers' troubles on Jewish bankers and "one world government." In stark contrast to the governmental indifference many rural Americans encounter, a range of right-wing groups, most recently the militias, seem to provide support, community, and answers.

In this sense, the militias simply follow in the footsteps of the Ku Klux Klan, the Posse Comitatus, and other far-right groups that recruited members in rural America throughout the 1980s. In fact, rural America has an entrenched history of racism and an equally long tradition of collective local action and vigilante justice. There remains a widespread notion that "Jews, African-Americans, and other minority-group members 'do not entirely belong,'" which may, in part, "be responsible for rural people's easy acceptance of the far right's agenda of hate."[41] "The far right didn't create bigotry in the Midwest; it didn't need to," Davidson concludes. "It merely had to tap into the existing undercurrent of prejudice once this had been inflamed by widespread economic failure and social discontent."[42]

What characterizes these descendants of small-town rural America—both the fathers and the sons—is not only their ideological vision of producerism, threatened by economic transformation, or their sense of small-town democratic community, an inclusive community based on the exclusion of broad segments of the population (blacks, Jews, homosexuals, and so on), but their sense of entitlement to economic, social, political—and even military—power. To cast the straight, white, middle-class man as the hegemonic holder of power in America entirely misses the daily experience of these straight white men. They believe themselves *entitled* to power—by a combination of historical legacy, religious proclamation, biological destiny, and moral legitimacy; but they feel powerless. Power, in their view, has not only been surrendered by white men—their fathers—but stolen from them by a federal government controlled and staffed by legions of newly enfranchised minorities, women, and immigrants. Furthermore, they believe these minorities all serve the "omnipotent" Jews, who control international economic and political life. "Heaven help the God-fearing, law-abiding Caucasian middle class," said actor and NRA spokesman Charlton Heston to a Christian Coalition convention, especially the "Protestant or even worse evangelical Christian, Midwest or Southern or even worse rural, apparently straight or even worse admittedly [straight], gun-owning or even worse [National Rifle Association] card-carrying average working stiff, or even worst of all, male working stiff. Because not only don't you count, you're a downright obstacle to social progress."[43]

Downwardly mobile rural white men—those who lost the family farms and those who expected to inherit them—are squeezed between the omnivorous jaws of capital concentration and a federal bureaucracy that at best is indifferent to their plight and at worst gives them a solid push down the slippery slope.

Militia Ideology

Militia ideology reflects this squeeze yet cannot fully confront its causes. Rooted in heartland conservatism, the militias have no difficulty blaming the federal government for their ills, but they are less willing to blame capitalism. After all, in terms of capitalist economics, they are strong defenders of the self-made man,[44] and many have served in the armed forces defending the capitalist system that they believe ensures individual freedom. As a result, they must displace their potential criticism of capitalism onto another force that distorts and disfigures the pure capitalist impulse. Thus they combine racism, sexism, homophobia, and anti-Semitism into a rhetoric of emasculating "others" against whom the militias' fantasies of the restoration of American masculinity are played out.

The antigovernment position is central to the militia ideology. It is big government, not big capital, that is eroding Americans' constitutional rights. International economic arrangements, such as NAFTA (the North American Free Trade Agreement) and GATT (the General Agreement on Tariffs and Trade) are understood as politically disenfranchising white American workers. Recent governmental initiatives, such as the Brady Bill and the Crime Bill, which require a waiting period before handguns may be purchased and ban certain assault rifles, are seen as compromising the constitutional right to bear arms and are perceived as a threat to white men's ability to protect and defend their families. Gun control is seen as a further attempt by the government to emasculate white men. The 1993 FBI/ATF (Alcohol, Tobacco, and Firearms) shootout at the Branch Davidian compound in Waco, Texas, and the 1992 standoff and shootout with white separatist Randy Weaver at Ruby Ridge, Idaho (which resulted in the death of Weaver's wife and son), have further exacerbated distrust in the federal government.[45] Restrictions on the right to bear arms are perceived as just further steps in the government's attempt to disarm and eventually control all citizens, leading inevitably to a United Nations invasion and establishment of a totalitarian new world order.

Militia publications are replete with stories of government conspiracies, and many militia members believe that the U.S. government is working with international forces to control U.S. citizens. For example, some argue that black helicopters are spying on citizens, that monitoring devices are being implanted in newborns, that Hong Kong police forces are being trained in Montana to disarm U.S. citizens, and that markings on the back of road signs are secret codes to direct invading UN forces.[46] In response, militias have established "common-law courts"—self-appointed groups that usurp the authority of the law, stage their own trials, and issue their own legal documents.

In many respects, the militias' ideology reflects the ideologies of other fringe groups on the far right, from which they typically recruit and with which they overlap. While the militias may not be as overtly racist and anti-Semitic as some other white supremacist groups, many researched have docu-mented extensive links between the two.[47] For example, militia embrace white supremacist theories of the international Jewish conspiracy for world control. They likewise take their idiosyncratic reading of the Bible from Christian Identity groups, which hold that Jews are descendants of Satan (through Cain), that people of color are "pre-Adamic mud people," and that Aryans are the true people of God. Militia member Rodney Skurdal, for instance, uses Christian Identity theology to justify his refusal to pay taxes, arguing that if "we the white race are God's chosen people . . . and our Lord God stated that 'the earth is mine,' why are we paying taxes on 'His land'?"[48] And from all sides the militias take racism, homophobia, nativism, sexism, and anti-Semitism. Like antigovernment ideology, these discourses provide an explanation for militia members' feelings of thwarted entitlement and fix the blame squarely on "others" whom the state must now serve at the expense of white men.

Central to our analysis here is that the unifying theme of all these discourses, which have tradition-ally formed the rhetorical package Richard Hofstadter labeled "paranoid politics," is *gender*. Specifi-cally, it is by framing state policies as emasculating and problematizing the masculinity of "these various "others" that rural white militia members seek to restore their own masculinity. In this, mili-tias can claim a long historical lineage. Since the early nineteenth century American manhood has pivoted around status of breadwinner—the self-made man who supports his family by his own labor. The breadwinner is economically independent, long in his own castle, embedded in a political com-munity of like-minded and equally free men. When this self-made masculinity has been threatened, one response from American men has been to exclude others from staking their own claim to man-hood. Like the Sons of Liberty who threw off the British yoke of tyranny in 1776, these contemporary "patriots" see "R-2" (the second American Revolution) as restorative. Their goal is to reestablish tra-ditional masculinity on the exclusion of others.

That such ardent patriots as militia members are so passionately antigovernment might strike the observer as contradictory. After all, are these not the same men who served their country in Vietnam or the Gulf War? Are these not the same men who believe so passionately in the American Dream? Are they not the backbone of the Reagan Revolution? Indeed they are. As we have shown, militia members face the difficult theoretical task of maintaining their faith in America *and* in capitalism. Simultaneously they must aim to rationalize what seems at best an indifferent state, or at worst an actively interventionist one, coupled with contemporary versions of corporate capitalist logic that leave them, often literally, out in the cold.

It is through a decidedly gendered and sexualized rhetoric of masculinity that this contradiction between loving America and hating its government, loving capitalism and hating its corporate itera-tions, is resolved. First, like others on the far right, militia members believe the state has been captured by evil—even Satanic—forces; the original virtue of the American political regime has been deeply and irretrievably corrupted. In their view, environmental regulations, state policies dictated by urban and northern interests, and the Internal Revenue Service are the outcomes of a state now utterly controlled by feminists, environmentalists, blacks, and Jews.[49]

According to this logic, feminists have captured the welfare state, so that now, like all feminists and feminist institutions, it serves to emasculate white manhood. Several call for the repeal of the Thirteenth and Fourteenth Amendments, which eliminated slavery and provided equal protection for all.[50] One leader, John Trochman, argues that women must relinquish the right to vote and to own property.[51] Likewise, one book sold by the Militia of Montana, *Big Sister Is Watching You: Hillary Clinton and the White House Feminists Who Now Control America and Tell the President What to Do,* argues that during the Clinton era Hillary Clinton and her feminist co-conspirators were controlling the country and threatening Americans' rights and national sovereignty. The author, Texe Marrs, claims that "Big Sister" intends nothing short of a new world order, to be accomplished through a "10 Part Plan" that includes:

> the replacement of Christianity with feminist, new-age spirituality. . . . History will be rewritten,
> discarding our True heroes. . . . Homosexuality will be made noble, and the male-female

relationship undesirable. . . . Patriotism will be smashed, while multiculturalism shall be exalted, and the masses will come to despise white, male dominated society as a throwback to the failed age of militarism and conflict. The masses shall be taught to revile nationalism, patriotism, and family . . . abortion and infanticide . . . encouraged. . . . Women will dominate in all walks of life—in law, medicine, literature, religion, economics, entertainment, education, and especially in politics.[52]

In this vision, feminism, multiculturalism, homosexuality, and Christian-bashing are all tied together, part and parcel of the new world order. On the other hand, Christianity, traditional history, heterosexuality, male domination, white racial superiority and power, individualism, meritocracy, and the value of individual hard work all describe the true America that is at risk and must be protected. Because these facets are so closely intertwined, multicultural textbooks, women in government, and legalized abortion can all be taken as individual signs of the impending new world order.

This text suggests several themes of interest to us here. The notion that the state has been taken over means that it no longer acts in the interests of "true" American men. The state is an engine of gender inversion, masculinizing women through feminism and simultaneously feminizing men. Feminist women, it turns out, are more masculine than men are. Not only does this call the masculinity of white men into question, it uses gender as the rhetorical vehicle for criticizing "other" men.

The militia movement is also strongly anti-Semitic. According to militia logic, it is not capitalist corporations that have turned the government against them but the international cartel of Jewish bankers and financiers, media moguls, and intellectuals who have already taken over the United States and turned it into a ZOG (Zionist-Occupied Government). The Wisconsin Militia's pamphlet *American Farmer: 20th Century Slave* explains how banks have been foreclosing on farms because Jews, incapable of farming themselves, had to control the world's monetary system to control the global food supply.[53] "Is this what you work your fingers to the bone for—to pay usury to a private group of bankers who make up the Fed?" asks a militia publication, *Why a Bankrupt America?* Eustace Mullins, a popular speaker on the militia circuit and author of the anti-Semitic *Secrets of the Federal Reserve,* argues that militias are "the only organized threat to the Zionists' absolute control of the [United States]."[54]

Since Jews are incapable of acting like real men—strong, hardy, virtuous manual workers and farmers—a central axiom of the international Jewish conspiracy for world domination is their plan to "feminize White men and to masculinize White women."[55] *The Turner Diaries* similarly describes the "Jewish-liberal-democratic-equalitarian" perspective as "an essentially feminine, submissive worldview."[56] Embedded in this anti-Semitic libel is a critique of white American manhood as having already become soft, feminized, and weak—indeed, emasculated. According to *The Turner Diaries,* American men have lost the right to be free; slavery "is the just and proper state for a people who have grown soft."[57]

Militias and Manhood

For the men involved in the militia movement, the militias offer a way to restore and revive American manhood—a manhood in which individual white men control the fruits of their own labor and are not subject to the emasculation of Jewish-owned finance capital or a black- and feminist-controlled welfare state. This is the militarized manhood of the heroic John Rambo—a manhood that celebrates a God-sanctioned right to band together in armed militias if anyone (or any governmental agency) tries to take it away from them. If the state and capital emasculate them, and if the masculinity of "others" is problematic, then only "real White men" can rescue this American Eden from a feminized, multicultural, androgynous melting pot. The militias seek to reclaim their manhood gloriously, violently.

Notes

1. Bonanno, A., L. Busch, W. Friedland, L. Gouveia, and E. Mingione, eds. 1994. *From Columbus to Conagra: The Globalization of Agriculture and Food.* Lawrence: University Press of Kansas; Jobes, P. C. 1997. "Gender Competition and the Preservation of Community in the Allocation of Administrative Positions in Small Rural Towns in Montana: A Research Note." *Rural Sociology* 62:315–34, 331.

2. Gouveia, L., and M. O. Rousseau. 1995. "Talk Is Cheap: The Value of Language in the World Economy-Illustrations From the United States and Quebec." *Sociological Inquiry* 65:156–80.

3. Weis, L. 1993. "White Male Working Class Youth: An Exploration of Relative Privilege and Loss." In *Beyond Silenced Voices: Class, Race and Gender in United States Schools,* edited by L. Weis and M. Fine. Albany: SUNY Press.

4. Jobes (1997).

5. Dyer, J. 1997. *Harvest of Rage: Why Oklahoma City Is Only the Beginning.* Boulder: Westview; Ferber, A. L. 1998. *White Man Falling: Race, Gender and White Supremacy.* Lanham, MD: Rowman and Littlefield, 61.

6. Lobao, L. and K. Meyer. 1995. "Restructuring the Rural Farm Economy: Midwestern Women's and Men's Work Roles During the Farm Crisis Period." *Economic Development Quarterly 9* (1):60–73, 6.

7. Davidson, O. G. 1996. *Broken Heartland: The Rise of America's Rural Ghetto.* Iowa City: University of Iowa Press, 118–19.

8. Lobao and Meyer (1995, 61). See also Hanson, V. D. 1996. *Fields Without Dreams: Defending the Agrarian Idea.* New York: Free Press.

9. Bell, M. M. 1999. "The Social Construction of Farm Crises." Presented at the annual meetings of the Rural Sociological Society, August 5, Chicago.

10. Dyer (1997).

11. Gibson, J. W. 1994. *Warrior Dreams: Violence and Manhood in Post-Vietnam America.* New York: Hill and Wang, 11.

12. Junas, D. 1995. "The Rise of Citizen Militias: Angry White Guys With Guns." Pp. 226–35 in *Eyes Right: Challenging the Right Wing Backlash,* edited by C. Berlet. Boston: South End Press, 227.

13. Rand, K. 1996. *Gun Shows in America.* Washington, DC: Violence Policy Center.

14. Lamy, P. 1996. *Millennium Rage: White Supremacists and the Doomsday Prophecy.* New York: Plenum, 26.

15. The 1992 confrontation in rural Idaho between white separatist Randy Weaver and U.S. marshals and FBI agents resulted in the deaths of Weaver's wife and son. Department of Justice reports have since exposed government misconduct in the siege on Weaver's home.

16. Stern, K. S. 1996. *A Force Upon The Plain: The American Militia Movement and the Politics of Hate.* New York: Simon and Schuster, 78.

17. Potok, M. (Southern Poverty Law Center researcher). 1999. Telephone interview by A. L. Ferber, 21 July.

18. Southern Poverty Law Center (SPLC). 1999. *Intelligence Report.* Montgomery: SPLC.

19. Potok, M. (Southern Poverty Law Center researcher). 2002. Telephone interview by A. L. Ferber, 23 December.

20. Berlet, C., and M. Lyons. 1995. "Militia Nation." *The Progressive,* June, pp. 22–25.

21. Ibid., 24.

22. Southern Poverty Law Center (1999, 23).

23. Ibid., 20.

24. Corcoran, J. 1997. *Bitter Harvest: The Birth of Paramilitary Terrorism in the Heartland.* New York: Penguin; Dyer (1997); Stern (1996); Stock, C. M. 1996. *Rural Radicals: Righteous Rage in the American Grain.* Ithaca: Cornell University Press.

25. Potok (1999).

26. Stock (1996, 16).

27. Gibson (1994, 10).

28. Mozzochi, J., and L. E. Rhinegaard. 1991. *Rambo, Gnomes and the New World Order: The Emerging Politics of 'Populism.'* Portland, OR: Coalition for Human Dignity, 4.

29. Potok (1999).

30. Aho, J. A. 1990. *The Politics of Righteousness: Idaho Christian Patriotism.* Seattle: University of Washington Press; Linzer, L. (Anti-Defamation League researcher). 1999. Telephone interview by A. L. Ferber, 16 July.

31. O'Matz, M. 1996. "More Hate Crimes Blamed on Juveniles." *The Morning Call*, October 23.

32. Serrano, R. 1990. "Civil Suit Seeks to Bring Down Metzger Empire." *Los Angeles Times*, February 18.

33. Dyer (1997, 63).

34. Junas (1995).

35. Potok (1999).

36. Walter, G., and S. Wilson. 1996. "Silent Partners: Women in Farm Magazine Success Stories, 1934–1991." *Rural Sociology 61*:227–48; Jellison, K. 1993. *Entitled to Power: Farm Women and Technology, 1913–1963.* Chapel Hill: University of North Carolina Press.

37. Lobao and Meyer (1995); Walter and Wilson (1996).

38. Southern Poverty Law Center (1999, 13).

39. Young, T. J. 1990. "Violent Hate Groups in Rural America." *International Journal of Offender Therapy and Comparative Criminology 34*(1):15–21, 15.

40. Davidson (1996, 109).

41. Snipp, C. M. 1996. "Understanding Race and Ethnicity in Rural America." *Rural Sociology 61*:125–42, 127, 122.

42. Davidson (1996, 120).

43. Citizens Project. 1998–1999. *Freedom Watch.* Colorado Springs.

44. Kimmel, M. 1996. *Manhood in America: A Cultural History.* New York: Free Press.

45. Dees, M. 1996. *Gathering Storm: America's Militia Threat.* New York: Harper; Southern Poverty Law Center (SPLC). 1997. *False Patriots: The Threat of Antigovernment Extremists.* Montgomery: SPLC; Stern (1996).

46. Southern Poverty Law Center (1997).

47. Crawford, R., and D. Burghart. 1997. "Guns and Gavels: Common Law Courts, Militias and White Supremacy." Pp. 189–205 in The Second Revolution: States Rights, Sovereignty, and Power of the County, edited by E. Ward. Seattle: Peanut Butter Publishing, 190.

48. Stern (1996, 89).

49. Dyer (1997).

50. Stern (1996, 82).

51. Crawford and Burghart (1997); Stern (1996, 69).

52. Marrs, T. 1993. *Big Sister Is Watching You: Hillary Clinton and the White House Feminists Who Now Control America—And Tell the President What to Do.* Austin: Living Truth Publishers, 22–23.

53. Stern (1996, 120).

54. Mullins, E. n.d. *Vigilante Justice,* 28.

55. *Racial Loyalty.* 1991. 72, 3.

56. Pierce, W. 1978. *The Turner Diaries.* Hillsboro, VA: National Vanguard Books, 42.

57. Ibid., 33.

CHAPTER 15

Mourning Mayberry

Guns, Masculinity, and Socioeconomic Decline

Jennifer Carlson

"I don't carry a gun to kill people, I carry a gun to keep from being killed! Pure, plain and simple! Shit, if this was Mayberry, I'd be alright! But it's not."

—*Frankie*[1]

"Neither one of [my parents] related to guns or the use of force. . . . They were just peaceful middle-class folks . . . [but] I carry for my protection and the protection of my loved ones."

—*Nate*

Frankie and Nate have different social backgrounds: Frankie, an African American, is a retired welder from Detroit; Nate is a white lawyer who lives in the suburbs. Yet, they also have much in common: Both carry guns on a regular basis, and both explain their turn to guns using a narrative of American decline, alluding to a lost "Mayberry" America that implies well-paying jobs, safe communities, and cheap goods that support a breadwinner's masculinity. Frankie's and Nate's accounts are suggestive of studies that examine how American men positioned differently along the lines of race, class, marital, and criminal statuses have responded to the economic erosion of the breadwinner model (Chesley 2011; Randles 2013; Roy 2004; Townsend 2002). Yet their accounts also raise a question regarding masculine protectionism (Young 2003): Why do men as different as Frankie and Nate use guns to mourn the loss of this imagined Mayberry?

Since the 1970s, more than 40 states have dramatically loosened their restrictions, licensing citizens to carry concealed guns and expanding their legal ability to use them in self-defense. Alongside recently renewed calls for gun control in the wake of the Sandy Hook massacre and other shootings, at least eight million Americans are now licensed to carry guns according to the U.S. Government Accountability Office. As symbols of self-reliance, independence, and rugged individualism (Melzer 2009), guns carry powerful gendered meanings, and gun owners and carriers are overwhelmingly men who increasingly embrace gun ownership as self-protection (Pew 2013). In Michigan, men are four times more likely to have a permit to carry a gun than women, and as suggested by Nate and Frankie, white and African American residents are equally likely to have a permit (1 in 25 residents).

This article uses the case of gun carry to examine how American men negotiate their perceptions of decline and their position within that decline. Today, American men have a comparatively harder time finding and holding onto a job with sufficient wages to be a sole household breadwinner than men in the past. Attention to economic precarity, I argue, helps to clarify why not only white,

SOURCE: Carlson, J. (2015). Mourning Mayberry: Guns, Masculinity, and Socioeconomic Decline. *Gender & Society, 29*(3), 386–409. Reproduced with permission.

middle-class men but also poor and working-class white men and men of color turn to guns. Here, I use "precarity" to refer to a condition of *social* insecurity and instability, as opposed to "precariousness," which describes the ontological vulnerability of human life (Butler 2006). I argue that men use guns not simply to instrumentally address the threat of crime (crime levels are generally far below their peaks in the 1980s and 1990s); rather, the narrative of crime allows men to negotiate their own position within Michigan's socioeconomic decline by emphasizing their role as protector.

Focusing on 60 interviews with male gun carriers and participant observation conducted in Michigan, this is the first study to examine how socioeconomic decline shapes the appropriation of guns by men. As an extreme case of decline, Michigan provides a sobering view into the social fallout of declining wages, high unemployment rates, and an unraveling social safety net. American pro-gun sentiment is not new, nor is pro-gun sentiment exclusively mobilized through the processes of economic decline analyzed here: In the United States, guns carry a rich and enduring cultural and political history (Melzer 2009). Nevertheless, I argue that against a backdrop of decline, guns are mobilized as a "tool" with which to negotiate economic insecurities, allowing men to assert social relevance by embracing a duty to protect. For these men, this assertion takes on added urgency in contexts of economic decline: A downturn not only undercuts men's positions as family providers but it is also believed to increase crime, in turn threatening not only men but also their families, friends, and vulnerable "women and children."

Masculinity and Guns

From the myth of the cowboy (Melzer 2009) to the celebrated gangsta of contemporary hip hop culture (Collins 2004), violence is a means by which American men—symbolically and physically—attempt to establish their dominance (Katz 2003; Kimmel 2005). One linkage between masculinity and violence is captured in what Iris Marion Young calls "masculinist protection": "The 'good' man is one who keeps vigilant watch over the safety of his family and readily risks himself in the face of threats from the outside world in order to protect the subordinate members of his household. . . . [T]he role of this courageous, responsible, and virtuous man is that of a protector" (2003, 4). This emphasis on protection situates men in a privileged position in the gendered hierarchy by repackaging violence as a necessary, honorable social *duty* that men perform on behalf of women and children (Brown 1992, 24–25). This embrace of violence for the sake of protection allows men to distinguish themselves from hyperaggressive, violent men (who threaten them with chaotic, rather than controlled, violence) and from dependent women and children incapable of self-protection.

The intersection of violence and masculinity raises the important distinction between hegemonic masculinity and the hegemony of men (Hearn 2012): While men's power over women may be sustained through brute force and violence (i.e., the hegemony of men), protectionist masculinity (as a form of hegemonic masculinity) emphasizes men's violence in ideological terms, as a basis for consent rather than a vehicle of coercion. Hegemonic masculinity (Connell 2005) describes the idealized privileged form of masculinity in a given social context; an impossible and contextually dynamic ideal, no living, breathing man fully embodies hegemonic masculinity. Rather, the Gramscian term "hegemonic" signals both that masculinities exist within a *hierarchy* relative to other men and women and that hegemonic masculinity is a negotiated achievement, consolidated not simply through coercion but also through consent. Men's struggles to (re)define hegemonic masculinity are both an expression of gendered power relations and a way to constitute those relations by laying claim to one's position at the top of gender hierarchy. Hence, shifts in hegemonic masculinity represent the attempts of men (even precarious men) to negotiate, and express, the power relations they inhabit vis-à-vis other men and women, which are in turn structured along race, class, and other lines of difference.

As a form of hegemonic masculinity, masculine protectionism shapes contemporary American gun politics. Melzer (2009) shows that the National Rifle Association (NRA) promotes a mythologized frontier masculinity, which emphasizes men's heroic defense of the (white, heterosexual, conservative) social order. Various scholars have more broadly looked at the violent symbolism of the gun in American culture, which promises masculine empowerment through violence (Burbick 2006; Katz 2003; Kellner 2008), often in racialized terms pitting white heroism against Black criminality (Melzer 2009; O'Neill 2007; Stroud 2012). Such studies illuminate how guns are used to consolidate hegemonic masculinity by defining themselves in opposition to racialized criminal "others" and embracing guns as part of being a "good guy" (Stroud 2012).

Missing from these analyses of race, masculinity, and guns, however, is a sustained analysis of how these linkages are structured by class ideologies and inequalities. The specter of the Black urban criminal is also a *classed* image that presumes desperation and depravity conditioned by economic precarity (Wacquant 2009). Fears of urban criminals are a means of expressing broader insecurities about socioeconomic decline (Simon 2007). Moreover, previous studies overlook the historical and structural specificity of men's embrace of protection as a basis of masculinity. While Stroud (2012) shows that concealed carriers in Texas emphasize their roles as family protectors, for example, it is unclear in which social contexts protection becomes an important pillar of hegemonic masculinity. Does socioeconomic decline render alterative masculinities, beyond breadwinning, possible and attractive?

Mourning Mayberry

I use "Mayberry"—as Frankie did—to capture a nostalgic longing for a particular version of America. A fictional small North Carolina town on the long-gone *Andy Griffith Show*, Mayberry represents an idyllic space of single-family homes, community cohesion, and safety and security. This imaginary was rooted in a particular historical moment: the manufacturing-based economy that rose and fell in the United States in the early to mid-twentieth century and that was buttressed by men's ability to unionize, which excluded women from the workplace and guaranteed a "family wage" (Hartmann 1979; Townsend 2002). This imaginary celebrated the nuclear family, which reflected separate spheres ideology (by providing guidelines for men, as breadwinners, and women, as housewives, on their distinct but complementary roles within the household) and reproduced it (by socializing children into their respective gender roles). Built on this heteronormative foundation, Mayberry has been disproportionately available to white, middle-class Americans, who chased this version of America by fleeing en masse to the suburbs in the mid-twentieth century (Sugrue 2005). This in turn *protected* and *reproduced* racial and class inequalities, as the suburbanization of America led to mass divestment of urban areas with concentrated populations of poor, racial minorities (Sugrue 2005).

For many Americans today, Mayberry is either a "lost" America or an America that never existed (Coontz 1993; Heath 2012) because of the inaccessibility of the economic arrangement it depended on—the male breadwinner model. Under this model, men fulfill their masculine responsibilities primarily through *provision*, with men's familial contributions resting on productive activities outside of the home (Hartmann 1979).

Despite the ideological centrality of breadwinning to masculinity during the twentieth century, there has been a persistent gap between this ideology and the material reality for working-class families and families of color, where working women and female-headed households disrupted the breadwinning model of masculinity (Barrow 1986; Collins 2004; Steedman 1987). Moreover, over the past several decades, structural conditions have eroded the male breadwinner model across the board. Compared to 1960, when 95 percent of Americans of "prime working age" were employed, today this figure is just above 80 percent. In 1960, 70 percent of families were headed by a sole male breadwinner, as compared to 31 percent today (Wang, Parker, and Taylor 2013). These figures indicate two major changes: Men are facing eroding labor opportunities (Legerski and Cornwall 2010; Wilkie 1993), and women are increasingly entering the labor force as income earners due to both changing labor opportunities and cultural shifts in women's social status (Heath 2003).

The structural erosion of the male breadwinner model has led to a refashioning of hegemonic masculinity, or "repackaging the package deal" (Randles 2013; Townsend 2002). Examining how men negotiate their roles as men, husbands, and fathers, Wilkie (1993) found that the structural erosion of the single-provider family model has led men to increasingly embrace egalitarian attitudes, even as they still feel uniquely "responsible" for provision. Subsequent studies document how these negotiations unfold on the ground, refashioning the breadwinner model to emphasize engaged fatherhood and compassion. Roy (2004) finds that while stably employed fathers maintained an emphasis on provision, underemployed and unemployed fathers stressed paternal involvement (Chesley 2011; Gallagher and Smith 1999).

This literature has focused on repackaging masculinity toward care-work, but that is not the only way men negotiate their understanding of socioeconomic decline. In contrast, the "separate spheres" ideology that underpinned the breadwinning model may be redefined: As women become income earners and displace men as sole breadwinners, men may respond to their eroding labor opportunities and the changing social status of women by emphasizing protection. An emphasis on protection helps men claim a privileged relation vis-à-vis women and children (by protecting them) and vis-à-vis other men (by protecting against them) alongside, or even in place of, provision. In this way, masculine protectionism operates as a form of hegemonic masculinity, allowing some men to legitimate neo-patriarchal relationships. Indeed, even men's frequent encouragement that women arm themselves further deepened masculine protectionism, as they often treated women's guns as an extension of their prerogative to protect, describing guns as a stand-in for a missing male protector or claiming ownership over women's guns (Carlson 2014). In one revealing example, a gun carrier told me that after his license had expired, he made sure his wife carried a gun so that "if anything happens," "you have it with you, and then I can use it" (Carlson 2014, 71). Rather than rely on his wife for protection, he asserted masculine protectionism by claiming use of the very gun he encouraged her to carry.

In this way, guns provide another "tool" in the gendered "toolbox" for men to assert masculine status amid perceptions of socioeconomic decline—what I call "mourning Mayberry," which is inflected differently by the race and class positionalities of gun carriers. Working-class men of color and working-class white men tended to live in higher-crime neighborhoods, reported direct experiences of crime, and had precarious work situations. For them, carrying a gun was both instrumental *and* symbolic: Gun carriers attempted to address an immediate threat of crime, but they were also performing a kind of masculinity (West and Zimmerman 1987) that "includes protecting the family from threats, at times literally putting his body in the line of fire on the street," as Elijah Anderson describes fathers in "decent" families in West Philadelphia (Anderson 1999, 38).

Relatively privileged gun carriers—white gun carriers living in the suburbs—experienced economic decline more as anxiety than immediate threat. They tended to hear about crime mainly through newspaper headlines, local television broadcasts, and stories about crime and victimization. Economically, they were relatively secure with stable jobs, but they read their own trajectory through Michigan's broader economic decline and in relation to their parents' class positions. For many of these gun carriers, it was not their class position but their *economic imaginaries* that lead them to embrace guns and masculine protectionism, not unlike the Americans who have organized to symbolically defend white, middle-class social order in small-town America (Stein 2002) and along the U.S.–Mexico border (Shapira 2013) through homophobic and anti-immigrant politics. Here, guns are more symbolic than instrumental (insofar as a distinction can be drawn between the two).

Decline in Michigan: Race, Class, and Gender

As an extreme case (Burawoy 1998), Michigan's socioeconomic decline, combined with its recent passage of expanded concealed carry laws, provides a window into how pro-gun sentiment is mobilized to address social insecurity.[2] At one time, Michigan's prosperity and prominence in labor struggles helped create an idealized version of American citizenship: the male breadwinner. But with the unraveling of unions and the welfare state, American society has been increasingly characterized by neoliberal shifts toward privatization, deregulation, and automation. Michigan was the only state with a statewide decline in employment from 1990 to 2009. Manufacturing jobs declined from 2000 to 2009, with a loss of more than 435,000 jobs, according to the Bureau of Labor Statistics (Platzer and Harrison 2009). Union membership rates have decreased from 26 percent in 1989 to 16.6 percent in 2012, a steeper decline than the U.S. average (Bureau of Labor Statistics 2013). Meanwhile, Michigan's median household income has declined 19.2 percent from 2000 to 2012, the largest drop of any state (Wilson 2013).

Compared to whites elsewhere, Michigan's white workers were the second-hardest hit by the 2008 recession, trailing only Nevada in the number of quarters that white workers faced an unemployment rate greater than 9 percent (Gable and Hall 2013). But African Americans have borne the brunt of the recession in Michigan. From the 1950s to the present day, African Americans in the United States have had roughly twice the unemployment rate as whites (Desilver 2013), and data from 2007 to 2012 show that in Michigan this ratio has been closer to 2.5 (Gable and Hall 2013). The 2011 median household income in Detroit, a predominantly African American city, was just $25,193, while the poverty rate for families was 35.5 percent (compared to 11.7 percent in the United States; see Hajal 2012a). Once the manufacturing capital of the country, in July 2013 Detroit filed the largest bankruptcy case in U.S. history.[3]

Labor statistics illustrate Michigan's economic decline, but crime rates do not parallel the decline. As in the rest of the United States, violent crime rates in Michigan have generally been on a downward trajectory, from a peak of 803.9 violent crimes per 100,000 residents in 1986 to 454.5 in 2012,[4] and Michigan is not within the top 10 states with the most violent crime. However, crime is highly concentrated. Detroit and Flint frequently top lists of the United States' "most dangerous" cities (Hajal 2012b), and African American males in Michigan are *41 times* more likely to die from homicide than white males (Metzger 2013). As outliers, Detroit and Flint sustain popular imageries of Black criminals.

Against this backdrop, Michigan passed a watershed concealed carry law in 2001, which allows residents to carry a gun concealed on their person provided they have a clean criminal record, have taken a qualifying firearms course, and have paid an application fee. The number of concealed carriers has increased every year since. While this increase is partly explained by pent-up demand for such licenses, the steady increase over a decade later is in line with (or at least does not contradict) my argument that perceptions of socioeconomic decline enhance the appeal of guns. Based on data from the Michigan State Police in May 2013, there were 425,790 residents with concealed carry licenses; the vast majority of CPL-holders are white (75 percent) followed by African American (21 percent), the latter of whom comprise 14.3 percent of Michigan's population based on 2012 U.S. Census data. White gun carriers outnumber African American gun carriers by a ratio of 3.6 to 1, but when disaggregated by subpopulation, African Americans in Metro Detroit have higher per capita rates of concealed pistol licensing than their white counterparts.

Methods

This article is part of a broader study on the everyday politics of gun carry in Michigan. I conducted ethnographic research and in-depth interviews with gun carriers, engaging in five months of participant observation at activist events, shooting ranges, and concealed pistol licensing classes. My analysis here mainly relies on interviews with 60 men who carried firearms on a regular basis, including gun enthusiasts ($n = 40$) and firearms instructors ($n = 20$). The majority of interviewees were white (85 percent) ($n = 51$). The other 15 percent were Black ($n = 7$), Hispanic ($n = 1$), or multiracial ($n = 1$). Most were in their 40s, 50s, and 60s, and 23 percent were retired. The vast majority of interviewees were from southeastern Michigan, including Detroit, Flint, and Lansing. Interviewees were blue-collar workers in professions like welding or trucking (46 percent), white-collar professionals like lawyers, IT specialists, and administrative staff (37 percent), and security specialists, such as current or former police officers, self-defense instructors, or bouncers (12 percent). Based on their political identification and political views expressed during interviews, the vast majority were right-leaning conservatives and libertarians, in line with studies showing that right-leaning men exhibit the highest levels of pro-gun sentiment (Berlet and Lyons 2000; Jones 2013).

My sample is somewhat disproportionately composed of white-collar individuals who live in suburban areas; these data suggest that my interviewees are skewed toward the middle class, in line with survey data on legal gun owners (Gaeser and Glendon 1998). This skew is also likely shaped by the fact that the majority of interviewees were white. Though I did not survey interviewees on sexual identity, all interviewees presented as straight men when describing their families and relationships. My finding, that men use guns to emphasize their familial obligations as protectors, may be different for men who explicitly reject heteronormativity.

I met prospective interviewees through contacts with state-level, pro-gun organizations and firearms instructors. Although I used snowball sampling and, therefore, do not have a response rate, most prospective interviewees I approached agreed to be interviewed. My age, race, and gender (a white female in her 20s during fieldwork) allowed me to present myself as a nonthreatening, eager-to-learn novice. Many of the men I interviewed took a paternalistic stance toward me, explicitly encouraging me to purchase and carry a firearm for self-defense. My positionality probably encouraged gun carriers to emphasize that women should be armed (Carlson 2014) and to highlight their identities as fathers and husbands.

Narratives of Decline

When I met Joseph, a white gun carrier, I asked how he got involved in gun politics. He replied, "It probably became political for me right around '94, and I was just coming of age . . . when the Assault Weapons Ban passed." At first, I read Joseph's narrative of "coming of age" as an example of guns as a rite of passage noted by other scholars (Messner 2011). However, I soon realized that this narrative took on particular significance in Michigan: Perhaps decades ago, gun carriers like Joseph may have used this phrase to describe joining a union or beginning stable work in manufacturing. But today, Joseph supports conservative politicians not because they promise a return to Michigan's manufacturing heyday, but because they make a new promise (gun rights) that allows men to embrace a distinct brand of hegemonic masculinity (masculine protectionism) amid conditions of decline.

Gun carriers often used a narrative of crime to articulate their perceptions of socioeconomic decline. Frankie, a retired African American veteran who lives in Detroit, contrasted the city's former promise with its present-day reality: "I grew up in Detroit. It was a different era back then. It's not anything like it is today." He described the 1920s, when his parents migrated from the South: "Hell, you could make five dollars a day! $25 a week is almost like a thousand today!" As employees, each autoworker would receive a badge, which not only guaranteed their employment but also their attractiveness to women: "On the weekend, the guys would have their shirts and their suits, and they'd put their badge where their tie should be, and the women would just flock to them. Because they had a source of income, see what I mean?" Now, with jobs gone and crime rampant in Detroit, Frankie explains that the city is not "Mayberry": "I don't carry a gun to kill people, I carry a gun to keep from being killed! Pure plain and simple! Shit, if this was Mayberry, I'd be alright! But it's not." Referring to a breakdown in family, Frankie told me, "They had an old African proverb about how it takes a village to raise a child. Well, it does, and you got to look at what kind of village we're talking about. What if we're talking about a village with a deluge of shoot-outs, you know?"

Frankie's linking of families and social breakdown is embedded in a social ecology that concentrates marginalized African Americans in urban centers that reproduce cycles of poverty, crime, and violence (Anderson 1999; Tonry 1995). The strategies of survival he references (i.e., "a village to raise a child") are also characteristic of that milieu (Stack 1997). Gerald, an African American who lives in the suburbs but travels through Detroit regularly for work, likewise connects historical structural marginalization to crime rates:

> We have 30 percent unemployment, 75 percent high school drop-out rate in Detroit. And I think they're down to like a third of the schools: Two-thirds of the schools are closed down. So it's sad. . . . People that got all these different skills and education. And we just—fell off like that. But that's a whole 'nother conversation. If people would just educate themselves a little bit more, it [crime] wouldn't be so bad. But when people are poor, they can't eat—I don't know. You or I can't say we wouldn't do it [commit a crime]! Know what I mean?

Referencing Detroit's decline ("we just—fell off like that"), Gerald blames Detroiters who turn to crime by doubting their work ethic, but he also states that he *understands* why people join gangs or commit crimes: to eat. After all, "You or I can't say we wouldn't do it!"

White gun carriers also articulated a narrative of decline, but they did so from the perspective of a very different social ecology. Rather than urban decay, they emphasized a suburban decline represented by increased incivility and decreasing civic engagement (Putnam 2001). Fred, a white retired postal worker who lives in a rural area outside of Flint, explained the shift from idyllic American dream to its present-day condition:

> Right after WWII, the economy was going good, cars became cheap, and with the advent of the trailer, people were moving around. It was really kind of an Ozzie and Harriet[5] country, everybody was getting along, and cops were sitting in the doughnut shop because there wasn't anything else to do. Well, it's not that way anymore.

Fred laughed ironically as he contrasted past to present, and his explanation of the "doughnut-eating cop" stereotype[6] allowed him to create a nostalgic vision of crime control—with crime so low that police spent their shifts sitting in coffee shops.

More explicitly referencing a breakdown in civility, Christopher, a white gun carrier who lives in a Detroit suburb, blamed "the family unit that's no longer in existence":

> When I grew up—it was family dinners, it was a lot of family interaction, and there was always family involvement. Now, because of the economy, because of keeping up with the Joneses, you have two parents working one job, 12-, 14-plus-hour days, five to six days a week, and the kids are coming home and playing Xbox 360, then living on the Internet. . . . It's a complete breakdown in basic social skills and fundamentals. Nobody knows their neighbors. They go behind their locked doors and do their thing . . . it's a complete social breakdown.

Here, the problem is not joblessness but juggling multiple jobs to make ends meet. This is a different kind of social precarity than articulated by Frankie and Gerald, embedded in a "white spatial imaginary" (Lipsitz 2011) that emphasizes the struggles of an isolated, single-family household rather than Frankie's proverbial "village."

White gun carriers also talked about crimes committed due to workplace stress and job instability. Marlin, a white gun carrier, described a "typical" crime scenario as he sees it. Imagining a self-defense scenario, he alludes to a guy "who had a bad day at work":

> Say you're walking through whatever mall right now. A guy had a bad day at work, lost his job, grabbed his deer rifle, and he decided to have it at the mall manager and whoever was at the mall. And now you've got 300+ people [at risk].

The criminal imagined in this passage is implicitly white: he owns a deer rifle (whites are significantly more likely to own guns for sporting or hunting purposes), he lives near a mall (and therefore is likely to be suburban) and he has (or had) a job. Finally, Marlin's imagined criminal is activated by his economic situation—he "lost his job."

In contrast to Gerald and Frankie, who emphasize chronic unemployment as the entree to criminal activity, white gun carriers saw long-term low wages (even with a steady job) as connected to criminal behavior. Rusty, a white gun carrier who was laid off at General Motors and turned to moonlighting as a DJ, told me he understands the incentives of crime: "You know, a cop on the street makes forty grand a year, maybe, if you're lucky. So, a drug dealer wants to pay you more than they make in a year to look the other way. Yeah, take it, right? They'd be stupid not to." Thus, if gun carriers articulate common narratives of decline, they do so from very different racial vantage points, operating with different kinds of "racial logics" and "racial spatial imaginaries" (Lipsitz 2011): Gerald and Frankie from the standpoint of joblessness and unemployment, and Marlin and Rusty from the standpoint of job precarity and low wages.

My respondents identified multiple markers of decline: erosion in the economy and a breakdown in the nuclear family. This, gun carriers maintained, had resulted in a context ripe for rampant crime: Alongside racialized tropes to describe criminals (Carlson 2012; Stroud 2012), the "economy" was regularly used as a catch-all explanation for crime and the need to protect against it. The presumption that criminals are men (Carlson 2014) suggested that it was *men's* precarity that led them down the path of criminality. However, the gun carriers I interviewed were not immune to these conditions of economic decline: They saw themselves as intertwined in precarious employment situations that eroded their own claims to breadwinner status and placed them and their families at greater risk of criminal victimization. How did they articulate their own precarity?

Men's Direct Experiences of Decline

One of the first concealed carry classes I attended was led by Butch, a former U.S. Marine and staunch conservative who devoted his time to Second Amendment activism and gun instruction. Butch saw his gun as intertwined with a symbolic celebration of American rights and freedoms. Butch was not unusual in this regard: The other half-dozen military veteran men I interviewed as well as most of the non-veteran gun carriers tied their choice to carry a gun to the language of rights, citizenship, and American freedom promulgated by the National Rifle Association (Melzer 2009) and other pro-gun outlets. At the same time, Butch explained his embrace of guns as intimately connected to his current family situation. He introduced himself at that class as a "proud stay-at-home dad." Later, he told me he had divorced several times, and after a string of relationships, he is now with his wife—the breadwinner—while he runs a firearms business and raises their children. While his wife worked upstairs, he described her employment as "professional, upstanding job, well-paying," but was quick to point out that she lacked the "warrior mentality" that people (specifically men) need to succeed in the workplace. Butch's narratives revealed how men use guns to negotiate a second layer of social vulnerability: the erosion of a traditional basis of masculinity alongside expanding opportunities for women. Butch mobilized an enduring language of rights and citizenship to assert a sense of national pride and American identity, as well as to navigate his own masculine status within his family; dependent on the income of his wife, Butch emphasized his duty to protect. Here, Butch's navigation of care work reinforces gender inequalities in the home (England 2005; Hochschild and Machung 2003) by explicitly celebrating a "hardened" version of care work and implicitly devaluing more "feminine" forms of care work.

Butch was not the only gun carrier concerned about his own economic precarity. Brent and Austin, both white gun carriers, connected their experiences to the loss of well-paying, stable blue-collar jobs. They told of being laid off, reemployed, and forced to relocate. When I asked Austin, a divorced white gun carrier and father, to identify his hometown, he joked, "I've moved over 50 times, so I don't really know." He also changed jobs frequently; in the short period I knew him, Austin moved from truck driving to steel mill work. He explained that he first turned to guns for self-protection when he moved to Flint with his daughter. He told me that he used to carry a handgun on his person, even at home, and that "after dark in Flint in that area, I would not even go off my property." Tattooed with his daughter's name, Austin seemed to value his identity as a father. But he believed that his ability to provide was precarious: As he explained during the interview, he couldn't afford health insurance.

Brent also told a story of long-term instability: He went through three marriages and moved several times in search of work:

> I was laid off from General Motors, I worked at the plant in Ypsilanti, and . . . I finally was able to get a job in a plant up in Flint. So, I was riding with another guy who lived in Brooklyn, and he had to do a 100-mile trip to Flint every day for work. And uh, then I moved up into Flint. [Flint was] on the list of dangerous cities to live in at that time. There were dead people here, there, and everywhere. We were right in the middle of it. Got a 12-gauge. Had to pull it out a couple of times because people were running up and down the streets, yelling and screaming.

Austin's and Brent's stories were indicative of the lacking labor opportunities facing working-class men as the manufacturing bases of Michigan moved first south and then overseas, and these circumstances both revealed their own economic precarity as well as placed them in closer proximity to crime.

Whereas working-class men experienced job insecurity, middle-class men saw themselves as downwardly mobile from their parents and referenced a changing experience of what it means to be "middle class." Nate, a white gun carrier, intimated that his parents were sheltered from violence because they were just "peaceful, middle-class folks":

> I grew up in a lower-middle-class income, middle-class neighborhood. My dad worked in a shop, and he had an eighth-grade education. He worked in a factory that made machine parts, like airplane parts and automobile parts. My mom was a former judge's secretary. Her background was far different from my dad's. Neither one of them related to guns or the use of force—they were really protected from that kind of thing. Or at least felt that they were protected from that thing generally, because each of their backgrounds was a nonconfrontational background. Nobody got into fights or arguments or anything like that. They were just peaceful middle-class folks.

While Nate earns a middle-class income as a lawyer, he does not have the same middle-class life as his parents: The stark contrast he draws between his parents' "peaceful" lives and his own turn to guns for self-protection suggests that his sense of security—articulated through a class narrative—has eroded. While gun carriers often used phrases like "sheltered," "liberal," and "anti-gun" interchangeably to deride gun control advocates, only when discussing their anti-gun parents did they use these terms to highlight *classed* contrasts about their parents' "middle-class" or "upper-class" sentimentality: Anthony, a white gun carrier who was kicked out of his house at age 15 and worked three jobs while he graduated high school, told me that his parents were "very liberal," "anti-gun," and "upper-class, all prim and proper." Ted told me his parents, a social worker and middle school teacher, were "goody two-shoe" "middle-class" people with "sheltered" ideas about the need for guns. These contrasts allowed gun carriers to articulate their own downward mobility without undermining their masculinity: While they may not have the stable and secure middle-class life-styles available to their parents, they situate themselves as respectable men by embracing a duty to protect.

Masculine Protectionism

As shown above, the masculine status of gun carriers is "under attack" due to social decline from two mechanisms: Their ability to provide has eroded, and they face the problem of protecting their families. For much of my sample, these were symbolic, and not actualized, threats—especially for middle-class, white men who live in suburban areas and who experience economic decline mostly as perceived rather than actual economic decline. As in the fictionalized Mayberry, they rarely need to use their guns to ward off actual physical threats.

But what guns *did* protect against was a gendered threat: the threat of falling down the masculine hierarchy (represented by the threat of their own downward mobility), at the bottom of which lies the subjugated masculinities of lower-class, racialized, and hypermasculine criminals (which they construe as threats to themselves and their families). Through this implicit social distancing, guns provide a way for men to insist on their social relevance and usefulness. During my conversations and interviews, gun carriers told me they believed they had become *better people* because of their choice to carry guns.

As adults with families of their own, gun carriers consistently articulated their decision to carry as part of a fatherly duty (Stroud 2012). Jeremy, a white gun carrier, told me that having a gun made him feel he could fulfill his familial duties: "When I'm with my family, I could defend them. I'm not a karate expert, so I never had that feeling of safety until I had a firearm." Brad, a white truck driver, perhaps provided the clearest connection between arming himself and fulfilling his duties as a father:

> The child's born. Mortgage, marriage. I have a kid. I'm paying for all this stuff on a truck driver's wage; she's [his wife] a stay-at-home mom. And it wasn't where I expected her to be in the kitchen, you know. We both knew right off the bat that we were equal, but we had different purposes. I was good at making money, and my wife's good at tending to the kid, and I wanted to protect them all, so then a firearm comes along.

Brad presents himself in terms of his dual role as a *provider* (he is "paying for all this stuff on a truck driver's wage") and a *protector* ("I wanted to protect them all"), which together establish him as head of his household. Brad exemplifies how men's role as protector does not *replace* their role as provider but rather further *fortifies* their claims to the position of head of household. This mutually reinforcing relationship is further illustrated by the handful of gun carriers who have turned their commitment to protection into a profitable enterprise by opening firearms training academies. As gun sales and concealed permit applications increase, firearms buttress these men's capacities as both providers and protectors.

Arthur, a white gun carrier and truck driver, similarly explained heteronormative relations as rooted in men's ability to protect:

> All women deserve special treatment, especially mothers . . . Women should understand that they shouldn't fear men who are willing to protect them, men who are willing to stand up for them. And they should be willing to stand up for themselves and also carry guns, too.

Arthur is not just explicitly claiming his own role as protector but also implicitly assigning particular roles for women—in this case, as mothers. Embracing his obligation to protect asserts *simultaneously* gendered roles for men (as protectors) and women (as protected mothers and housewives) that harken back to the bygone era of masculine breadwinning.

While some gun carriers cautioned that "when you get the concealed pistol license, you are not automatically deputized to go out and save the world" (Craig, white gun carrier), many justified their decision to carry as benefiting society at large. Referring to one of his friends who carries and often goes on long walks with his wife, Paul, a white gun carrier and firefighter from Flint, told me that "it makes my wife safer. It makes you safer!" Ken, another white gun carrier, told me, "The more people who have licenses, the safer we all will be . . . I think it makes Michigan safer. I *know* it makes Michigan safer. Because criminals know what's going on." When I asked Billy, a white gun carrier, how often he carried and why, he responded that he carries every day, everywhere it is legal to do so: "I'm going to stay safe. Whoever is around me is going to be safe." In this way, gun carriers articulate their choice to be armed as a civic practice with positive social consequences, a view widely circulated in the pro-gun literature on the effects of guns on crime (Goss 2013).

The men I interviewed extolled a variety of virtues that come along with carrying guns, but celebration of these virtues does not occur in a vacuum. Shifts in the political economy of Michigan have galvanized concerns about crime (threatening men and their families) and undermined the breadwinner model (threatening men's positions *within* their families). Guns become a symbolic means of asserting masculine relevance amid this imaginary of decline.

Conclusions

This article examines how political economy shapes pro-gun sentiment. Against perceptions of decline, gun carriers use guns to assert themselves as good men, respectable husbands, and responsible fathers not necessarily because they can provide a middle-class lifestyle but because, they maintained, they can provide protection. Guns provide men with another "tool" in the gendered toolbox to assert their masculine identities within the context of the heteronormative family (Townsend 2002).

This article contributes to scholarship on masculinities, conservative politics, and gender inequality. It extends existing studies of the impact of American decline (and perceptions thereof) on how men "do" masculinities by adding to the literature on "repackaged" masculinities (Randles 2013). While much of the literature on the reconfiguration of American masculinities emphasizes shifting norms surrounding care work and provisions, this article shows that contemporary American masculinity is not necessarily "softened" in contexts of socioeconomic insecurity and shifting gender roles; it is also fortified in ways that recuperate men's privileged position as head of household—not just as *provider* but also as *protector*. In doing so, this article forges a new approach to the relationship between guns and gender inequality by highlighting how guns inform the nostalgia that many men feel for the breadwinner model, itself dependent on a heteronormative, separate spheres ideology (Heath 2012). Indeed, men's responses to socioeconomic decline can also be read as responses to shifts in women's participation in the family and in the labor market, shifts that are connected, but not reducible to, economic decline. Some men celebrated when women took on these stereotypic roles (e.g., Arthur), while others (e.g., Butch) seemed resentful that women's opportunities in the workforce exceeded their own. While research on low-income fatherhood suggests that poor and low-income men may embrace their ability to care for children in contexts of economic insecurity, men's strategies to navigate care work can also reinforce gender inequalities (England 2005; Hochschild and Machung 2003). The present study suggests that some men may participate in a "hardening" of care work by distancing themselves from, and implicitly devaluing, the traditional, "feminine" caregiving responsibilities of housework and direct child care and instead embracing the defense of themselves and their families as a central aspect of their identities as men, fathers, and husbands. Navigating the division of care work in this way, gun carriers can reinforce gender inequalities in the home.

Finally, this article provides new insight into the relationship between masculinity, on the one hand, and the rightward turn in American politics (Berlet and Lyons 2000) on the other. Specifically, this analysis sheds light on why states similar to Michigan—historically blue or purple states with strong manufacturing bases—are seeing increasing support among residents for gun legislation. Fifty years ago, being a pro-union democrat and sole breadwinner defined masculinity in these areas. Today, protecting one's family is viewed as an increasingly appealing way to achieve masculinity. While this may be compelled by declining economic opportunities facing men, the social implications may be far broader than economic decline. That is, guns may be involved in a broader reconfiguration of rights and citizenship—meaning that even though perceptions of decline play an important role in men's turn toward guns, the return of "good jobs" alone may not quell pro-gun sentiment.

Though limited in scope (this study examines one case—suburban and urban areas in Michigan—using in-depth interview and ethnographic data), this study also raises new avenues for future research. While this study is most directly generalizable to other Midwestern, rustbelt cities, future work may examine how socioeconomic decline impacts the use of guns in other regions of the United States, particularly the South, which has a strong culture of honor (Nisbett and Cohen 1996). To my knowledge, no study has examined the effect of broad-based socioeconomic decline (rather than socioeconomic status of individuals), and no research has studied the relationship between concealed carry rates and socioeconomic changes over time or across regions.[7] Future research should take advantage of the state-maintained databases of license holders to examine the relationships among socioeconomic decline, masculinity, and gun carry over time and across geographic region. Moreover, there is evidence that the decline of the farm industry (Gallaher 2003) and growing concern over methamphetamine-related crimes (Garriott 2011) parallel the dynamics I have unpacked here. Future research should examine how crime, protection, and masculine duty become co-articulated in rural contexts of decline.

In summary, I have used Young's (2003) term *masculine protectionism* to unpack the narratives of gun-carrying men. My analysis suggests that while guns figure throughout American history as masculine-marked objects, contemporary contexts of socioeconomic decline shape men's gender identities and, as a result, their turn to guns. When socioeconomic insecurity undermines men's role as provider (even if all men do not experience this directly), guns provide a means for men to prove their utility and relevance outside the breadwinner role. By pivoting hegemonic masculinity on men's capacity as protectors, gun-toting men are able to lay claim to a rendition of hegemonic masculinity that allows them to negotiate a sense of socioeconomic—and, therefore, gender—precarity.

Notes

1. Personal identifiers have been changed to protect participant confidentiality.

2. This is not to downplay the historic and present-day significance of race in co-constitutively shaping Michigan's decline: Starting with the Great Migration in the 1920s to the White Flight of the 1950s, 1960s, and 1970s, racial prejudice and institutionalized racism in Metro Detroit have shaped crime and insecurity in a myriad of ways, from people's perceptions of crime to the extent to which criminal justice institutions (such as police) are viewed as legitimate, just, and fair.

3. The figures cited here do not include unreported or undocumented sources of income.

4. See the FBI uniform Crime Report online database at http://ucrdatatool.gov/Search/Crime/Crime.cfm (accessed April 16, 2014).

5. *The Adventures of Ozzie and Harriet* was an American sitcom that aired in the 1950s and 1960s that chronicled the quotidian lives of the Nelson family in suburban Los Angeles and, like *The Andy Griffith Show*, it celebrated 1950s American values.

6. The stereotype of cops as "doughnut-eaters" most likely began because doughnut shops were convenient, late-night spots for cops to congregate on cold, graveyard shifts, not because police were driven to doughnuts out of boredom.

7. Most studies looking at the determinants and implications of legal gun availability in the United States focus on crime. The handful of studies that look beyond crime provide snapshot insights into racial attitudes, racial disparities, changes in racial demographics, political conservatism, and socioeconomic status (e.g., Costanza and Kilburn 2004; Thompson and Stidham 2010).

References

Anderson, Elijah. 1999. *Code of the street.* New York: Norton.

Barrow, Christie. 1986. Finding the support. *Social and Economic Studies* 35: 131–76.

Berlet, Chip, and Matthew Lyons. 2000. *Right-wing populism in America.* New York: Guilford.

Brown, Wendy. 1992. Finding the man against the state. *Feminist Studies* 18:7–34.

Burawoy, Michael. 1998. The extended case method. *Sociological Theory* 16: 4–33.

Burbick, Joan. 2006. *Gun show nation.* New York: Norton.

Bureau of Labor Statistics. 2013. Union membership in Michigan 2012. Bureau of Labor Statistics. http://www.bls.gov/ro5/unionmi.htm (accessed September 20, 2013).

Butler, Judith. 2006. *Precarious life.* New York: Verso.

Carlson, Jennifer. 2012. "'I Don't Dial 911!' American Gun Politics and the Problem of Policing." *British Journal of Criminology* 52(6): 1113–1132.

Carlson, Jennifer. 2014. The equalizer? Guns, vulnerability politics and the misrecognition of domestic violence. *Feminist Criminology* 9:59–83.

Chesley, Noelle. 2011. Stay-at-home fathers and breadwinning mothers. *Gender & Society* 25:642–64.

Collins, Patricia Hill. 2004. *Black sexual politics.* New York: Routledge.

Connell, Raewyn. 2005. *Masculinities.* Berkeley: University of California Press.

Coontz, Stephanie. 1993. *The way we never were.* New York: Basic Books.

Costanza, Stephen, and John Kilburn. 2004. Circling the welcome wagons. *Criminal Justice Review* 29:289–303.

Desilver, Drew. 2013. Black unemployment is consistently twice that of whites. Pew Research Center. http://www.pewresearch.org/fact-tank/2013/08/21/ through-good-times-and-bad-black-unemployment-is-consistently-double that-of-whites (accessed July 15, 2014).

England, Paula. 2005. Emerging theories of care work. *Annual Review of Sociology* 31:381–99.

Gable, Mary, and Douglas hall. 2013. Ongoing joblessness in Michigan. Washington DC: Economic Policy Institute. http://www.epi.org/publication/ongoing-joblessness-michigan-unemployment (accessed September 20, 2013).

Gaeser, Edward, and Spencer Glendon. 1998. Who owns guns? *American Economic Review* 88:458–62.

Gallagher, Sally, and Christian Smith. 1999. Symbolic traditionalism and pragmatic egalitarianism. *Gender & Society* 13:211–33.

Gallaher, Carolyn. 2003. On the fault line: Race, class, and the American Patriot Movement. New York: Rowman & Littlefield.

Garriott, William. 2011. *Policing methamphetamine.* New York: New York University Press.

Goss, Kristin. 2013. Why we need to talk about guns. *Newsweek Magazine.* http://www.thedailybeast.com/newsweek/2013/01/04/why-we-need-to-talk-about-guns.html (accessed September 20, 2013).

Hajal, Khalil Al. 2012a. Detroit has half the median income, three times the poverty rate of the nation, new Census numbers show. http://www.mlive.com/news/detroit/index.ssf/2012/09/detroit_has_half_the_ median_in.html (accessed April 16, 2014).

Hajal, Khalil Al. 2012b. Flint no. 1, Detroit second among nation's most violent cities. http://www.mlive.com/ news/flint/index.ssf/2012/06/flint_no_1_detroit_second_amon.html (accessed April 16, 2014).

Hartmann, Heidi. 1979. The unhappy marriage of Marxism and Feminism. *Capital & Class* 3:1–33.

Hearn, Jeff. 2012. A multi-faceted power analysis of men's violence to known women. *Sociological Review* 60:589–610.

Heath, Melanie. 2003. Soft-boiled masculinity. *Gender & Society* 17:423–44.

Heath, Melanie. 2012. *One marriage under God.* New York: New York University Press.

Hochschild, Arlie, and Anne Machung. 2003. *The second shift.* New York: Penguin.

Jones, Jeff. 2013. Men, married men, Southerners most likely to be gun owners. Gallup. http://www.gallup.com/ poll/160223/men-married-southerners-likely-gun-owners.aspx (accessed April 1, 2014).

Katz, Jackson. 2003. Advertising and the construction of violent white masculinity. In *Gender, race, and class in media: A text-reader,* edited by G. Dines and J. M. Humez. Thousand Oaks, CA: Sage.

Kellner, Douglas. 2008. *Guys & guns amok.* Boulder, CO: Paradigm.

Kimmel, Michael. 2005. *Men and masculinities.* Thousand Oaks, CA: Sage.

Legerski, Elizabeth, and Marie Cornwall. 2010. Working-class job loss, gender, and the negotiation of household labor. *Gender & Society* 24:447–74.

Lipsitz, George. 2011. *How racism takes place.* Philadelphia, PA: Temple University Press.

Melzer, Scott. 2009. *Gun crusaders.* New York: New York University Press.

Messner, Michael. 2011. *King of the wild suburb.* Austin, TX: Plain View.

Metzger, Kurt. 2013. Black males in Michigan die at an alarming rate. The Center for Michigan. http://bridgemi .com/2013/08/black-males-in-michigan-die-at-an-alarming-rate (accessed September 20, 2013).

Nisbett, Richard, and Dov Cohen. 1996. *Culture of honor: The Psychology of violence in the south.* New York: Westview.

O'Neill, Kevin. 2007. Armed citizens and the stories they tell. *Men and Masculinities* 9:457–75.

Pew. 2013. Why own a gun? Protection is now top reason: Overview. Pew Research Center. http://www.people-press.org/2013/03/12/why-own-a-gun-protection-is-now-top-reason (accessed September 20, 2013).

Platzer, Michaela D., and Glennon J. Harrison. 2009. The U.S. automotive industry: National and state trends in manufacturing employment. Washington. DC: Congressional Research Service. http://digitalcommons.ilr .cornell.edu/key_workplace/666 (accessed April 16, 2014).

Putnam, Robert. 2001. *Bowling alone.* New York: Simon & Schuster.

Randles, Jennifer. 2013. Repacking the "package deal." *Gender & Society* 27: 864–88.

Roy, Kevin. 2004. You can't eat love. *Fathering* 2:253–76.

Shapira, Harel. 2013. *Waiting for Jose.* Princeton, NJ: Princeton University Press.

Simon, Jonathan. 2007. *Governing through crime.* New York: Oxford University Press.

Stack, Carol. 1997. *All our kin.* New York: Basic Books.

Steedman, Carolyn. 1987. *Landscape for a good woman.* New Brunswick, NJ: Rutgers University Press.

Stein, Arlene. 2002. *Stranger next door.* New York: Beacon Press.

Stroud, Angela. 2012. Good guys with guns. *Gender & Society* 26:216–38.

Sugrue, Thomas. 2005. *The origins of urban crisis.* Princeton, NJ: Princeton University Press.

Swidler, Ann. 1986. Culture in action: Symbols and strategies. *American Sociological Review* 51:273–86.

Thompson, Joel, and Ronald Stidham. 2010. Packing heat in the Tar Heel State. *Criminal Justice Review* 35:52–66.

Tonry, Michael. 1995. *Malign neglect.* New York: Oxford University Press.

Townsend, Nicholas. 2002. *The package deal.* Philadelphia, PA: Temple University Press.

Wacquant, Loic. 2009. *Punishing the poor.* Durham, NC: Duke University Press.

Wang, Wendy, Kim Parker, and Paul Taylor. 2013. Breadwinner moms. Pew Research Center. http://www .pewsocialtrends.org/2013/05/29/breadwinner-moms (accessed September 20, 2013).

West, Candace, and Don Zimmerman. 1987. Doing gender. *Gender & Society* 1:125–51.

Wilkie, Jane Riblett. 1993. Changes in U.S. men's attitudes toward the family provider role, 1972–1989. *Gender & Society* 7:261–79.

Wilson, Reid. 2013. Household incomes stabilize, but still below 2000 levels. *The Washington Post*, September 19. http://www.washingtonpost.com/blogs/govbeat/wp/2013/09/19/household-incomes-stabilize-but-still-below-2000-levels (accessed April 16, 2014).

Young, Marion. 2003. The logic of masculinist protection. *Signs* 29:1–24.

PART IV

Masculine Strategies

Masculinity is achieved, not given. It is never fixed, never determined. People often think of men as stolid, implacable oaks that are impervious to threats. The projection of stability and control is foundational to manhood, but this foundation is much weaker than it first appears. In fact, men are constantly fearful of having their masculinity questioned. When masculine authority is challenged—whether by women, other men, institutional processes, or economic currents—men risk losing their status in the gender hierarchy, and they risk losing a significant share of the spoils of patriarchy. These pressures may sometimes prompt a reassessment and redefinition of masculinity. More often, however, men and boys respond to such challenges by doubling down on masculine dominance.

Strategies to assert and (re)claim masculinity include projections of risk-taking, toughness, defiance, and physical and emotional control over oneself, others, and the environment (see Schrock and Schwalbe, reading no. 3). As Sharon Bird discussed in reading no. 2, such strategies are often enacted with the help of other men and for the audience of other men to prove one belongs in the club and one should be privy to its membership benefits. In this pursuit, men and boys draw from the particular resources available to them—based on age, race, economic status, and so on—to project manly power. The readings in this section explore strategies through which different men and boys protect masculine status, particularly when this status may be compromised.

Reading no. 16, "The Sanctity of Sunday Football" by Douglas Hartmann, indicates how symbolic rituals and manly domains protect, reaffirm, and teach masculinity. Hartmann focuses on sports, a preeminent arena for broadcasting the "natural" power of male bodies. Sports serve as a homosocial space for men to bond, and the general popularity of male sports helps solidify men's cultural centrality. The remaining readings in this section focus on how boys and men respond when masculinity is questioned or compromised. Such actions must be viewed through an intersectional framework, as indicated in the introduction to this book. Men who are poor, racial minority, or nonheterosexual, among other inequalities, incur more challenges and possess fewer resources to emulate the hegemonic ideal of masculinity. In contrast to the "boys will be boys" leeway often extended to white boys (see Bird, reading no. 2), Ann Ferguson's "Getting in Trouble" (reading no. 17) explores school punishment among African American boys, who, even when quite young, are viewed as older, menacing figures. Prefiguring recent conversations about shootings of unarmed young black men, Ferguson investigates how the interaction of race and gender guides school perceptions that black boys are troublesome (see also Wilkins, reading no. 22). Boys respond to this stigmatization by crafting strategies of resistance. Such resistance, such as getting into physical fights, grasps at a raw and ephemeral power linked to masculinity, but ironically reinforces the original stereotypes.

The next reading (no. 18), "Epic Glory and Manhood Acts in Fantasy Role-Playing," introduces a group whose masculinity is compromised for a very different reason. James S. Martin and his coauthors study white college men who battle in live-action role-playing games. Although these "nerdy" young men may seem to embody a weaker, less popular, "subordinate" masculine position, the authors show how "manhood acts" (see Schrock and Schwalbe, reading no. 3) within these fantasy battles reassert masculine dominance. This reading indicates that even within marginalized subcultures, men work to demonstrate power over other men and subordinate women. In "I Kick It to Both, but Not in the Street" (reading no. 19), Miguel Muñoz-Laboy and his colleagues explore masculinity among another marginalized group: bisexual Latino men. Weaving spatial dimensions into expressions of sexuality, racial-ethnic identity, and masculinity, the authors show how these men strategize self-presentations in different contexts to defray the potential stigma of nonheterosexual (and therefore subordinate) masculinity.

Finally, reading no. 20, "Economic Shifts, Consumption of Sex, and Compensatory Masculinity in Japan," an original contribution by Kumiko Nemoto, moves the conversation on masculine strategies beyond an American context. Nemoto explores how the Japanese hegemonic model of the bread-winning "salaryman" has been disrupted by economic and family restructuring. This has prompted men to recuperate manly status through other scripts of manhood, a process Nemoto labels "compensatory masculinity" following Schrock and Schwalbe (reading no. 3). Some of these newer strategies of manhood appear to have progressive potential, but others, especially an alarming increase in the hypersexualization of women, tend toward more toxic outcomes. As we find in these readings and other masculinity scholarship, men and boys tend to react to a feeling or position of powerlessness by attempting to reclaim this power through masculinity.

Questions to Ponder

1. In what ways do the Japanese context and patterns outlined by Nemoto appear similar to and different from processes in the United States, either presently or historically? How do ideals and practices of masculinity tend to differ across local, regional, and national contexts?

2. Can you think of other ways masculinity might be threatened, and other ways men (and women) might respond to such threats? Think about how this might occur in "micro" processes such as interpersonal relationships or peer cultures, as well as "macro" processes such as globalization or economic restructuring.

3. How do certain domains of geographical or symbolic space influence masculinity? How might spaces such as fraternities, locker rooms, or online gaming help produce dangerous expressions of masculinity?

4. Ann Ferguson's chapter describes how schools perceive even young African American boys as troublesome, and also how the boys respond. What connections might be drawn between educational and criminal justice systems in the experiences of young African American men?

5. How does being a "nerd" influence masculinity (as in reading no. 18 by Martin et al.)? Boys perceived this way are the subjects of ridicule and bullying, but for adults the term is often used positively. How might "nerds" embody subordinated, hegemonic, hybrid, and compensatory forms of masculinity? What are some ways that "nerdy" men who are seen as less traditionally manly might assert their masculinity?

Key Concepts

Anti-effeminacy
Compensatory masculinity

Nerd masculinity
Performances of masculinity

Sports as homosocial masculine
space

CHAPTER 16

The Sanctity of Sunday Football

Why Men Love Sports

Douglas Hartmann

The American male's obsession with sports seems to suggest that the love affair is a natural expression of masculinity. But sociologists have found that, conversely, sports teach men how to be manly, and studying sports reveals much about masculinity in contemporary America.

My father, a no-nonsense grade school principal, had little time for small talk, contemplation, or leisure—with one major exception: sports. He spent Sunday afternoons watching football games on television, passed summer evenings listening to Jack Buck announce St. Louis Cardinals baseball games, and took me to every sporting event in town. He coached all the youth sports his children played, and spent hours calculating team statistics, diagramming new plays, and crafting locker room pep talks. Though never a great athlete, his high school varsity letters were displayed in his basement work area; just about the only surefire way to drag dad out of the house after a long day at work was to play "a little catch." Sports were one of the few topics he ever joked about with other men.

My father's fascination with sports was not unique. Though women are increasingly visible throughout the sporting world, more men than women play sports, watch sports and care about sports. Is it any wonder that corporate advertising campaigns, drinking establishments, and movements such as the Promise Keepers all use sports to appeal to men? Or that sports figures so prominently in many books and movies dealing with men and masculinity in America? Nevertheless, there is surprisingly little serious reflection about why this is the case. When asked why so many men are so obsessed with sports, most people—regardless of their gender or their attitudes about sports—say something to the effect that men are naturally physical and competitive, and that sports simply provide an outlet for these inherently masculine traits.

To sociologists, however, men love playing, watching, and talking sports because modern, Western sports—dominated as they are by men and by values and behaviors that are traditionally regarded as masculine—provide a unique place for men to think about and develop their masculinity, to make themselves men, or at least one specific kind of man.

Where Boys Become Men

Ask sports enthusiasts why they participate in sports and you are likely to get a wide variety of answers. "Because it is fun and exciting," some respond. Others say it is because they need the exercise and want to stay physically fit. Still others talk about sports providing them a way to relax and unwind, or about the thrill of competition—these responses are especially common for that large percentage

SOURCE: Hartmann, D. (2003). The Sanctity of Sunday Football: Why Men Love Sports. *Contexts*, 2(4), 13–21. Reproduced with permission from the ASA.

195

of sports lovers whose "participation" mainly takes the form of being a fan or watching sports on television. These are important parts of sports' value, but they do not really explain why men are, on average, more likely to be involved in sports than women.

For many men, the love of sports goes back to childhood. Sports provided them, as young boys and teens, with a reason to get together, to engage with other boys (and men), and in doing so to begin defining what separates boys from girls: how to act like men. Barrie Thorne's study of grammar school playgrounds illustrates the phenomenon. Thorne finds that pre-adolescent boys and girls use recreation on the schoolyard to divide themselves along gender lines. How they play—for example, running around or quiet games—Thorne suggests, distinguishes male and female child behavior. As they get older, kids become more aware of these distinctions and increasingly use sex-segregated athletics to discuss and act out gender differences. Gary Alan Fine, in *With the Boys,* describes how much of the learning that happens in Little League baseball involves being tough and aggressive and dealing with injuries and other setbacks; and in off-the-field conversations young ballplayers learn about sex and about what it means to be a man as opposed to a "dork," a "sissy" or a "fag."

When Michael Messner interviewed retired athletes and asked them how they initially got involved with sports, they told him it had little to do with any immediate or natural attraction to athletics and was really based upon connecting to other boys and men. "The most important thing was just being out there with the rest of the guys—being friends," said one. Sports, according to Messner, "was something 'fun' to do with fathers, older brothers, uncles and eventually with same-aged peers."

Girls start playing sports for similar reasons, and children of both genders join in other activities, such as choir or community service, for social purposes, too. (Many boys and girls start to drop out of sports at about ages 9 or 10—when the sports they play become increasingly competitive and require them to think of themselves primarily as athletes.) What is distinctive about the experience of boys and young men in sports, however, is that the sporting world is organized and run primarily by men, and that athletic activities require attitudes and behaviors that are typically understood to be masculine.

Of course, not all boys play sports, and boyhood and adolescent experiences in sports are not uniformly positive. A great deal of the sociological research in this area focuses on the downside of youth sports participation. Study after study confirms what most soccer moms and dads already know: boys' athletics tend to be more physical and aggressive and put more emphasis on winning, being tough in the face of adversity, and dealing with injuries and pain. Donald Sabo, for example, has written extensively about the pain and violence, both physical and psychological, experienced by many boys who compete in athletics. And Harry Edwards has long argued that over-investing in sports can divert poor and minority youth from more promising avenues of upward mobility. But, despite the harsh realities, sports remains one of the few socially approved settings in which boys and men, and fathers and sons, can express themselves and bond with each other.

Sport as a Masculine Enterprise

Once boys and girls separate in physical play, it does not take long for gendered styles of play to emerge. Study after study confirms what most soccer moms and dads already know: boys' athletics tend to be more physical and aggressive and put more emphasis on winning, being tough in the face of adversity, and dealing with injuries and pain. Even in elementary school, Thorne finds boys take up far more of the physical space of the playground with their activities than girls, who tend to play (and talk about their play) in smaller spaces and clusters.

People debate whether there is a physiological component to these differences, but two points are clear. First, parents, coaches, and peers routinely encourage such intensity among boys in youth sports. More than a few single mothers bring their boys to the teams I coach out of concern that their sons are insufficiently tough or physical because they lack a male influence. Messner writes about how he learned—against his inclinations—to throw a ball overhand with his elbow tucked in because his father did not want him to "throw like a girl." Stories about overly competitive, physically abusive coaches may be overplayed in the American media, but in many ways they are the inevitable consequence of the emphases many parents express.

Second, the behaviors and attitudes valued in men's and boys' athletics are not just about sports, but about masculinity more generally. The inherent connection of sports to the body, physical activity and material results, the emphasis on the merit of competing and winning, the attention to rules, sportsmanship and team play, on the one hand, and gamesmanship, outcomes and risk, on the other, are not just the defining aspects of male youth sport culture, but conform to what many men (and women) believe is the essence and value of masculinity. Female reporters, homosexual athletes, and men who challenge the dominant culture of men's sports—especially in the sacred space of the locker room—quickly learn that sports are not just dominated by men but also dominated by thinking and habits understood to be masculine (in opposition to the more nurturing values of compromise, cooperation, sympathy, understanding, and sharing typically associated with femininity). If the military is the quintessential institution of Western masculinity, then sports is surely a close second.

The notion that sports is a masculine enterprise is closely connected with the development of modern Western sports. As historians have detailed, middle- and upper-class men used sports in the 19th and early-20th centuries to present and protect their particular notions of masculinity in both schools and popular culture (the classic literary expression being *Tom Brown's School Days,* a 19th-century English story of boarding school boys' maturation through hard-nosed sports). The media is a critical part of perpetuating sports' masculine ethos today, because most adults participate in sports as spectators and consumers. Not only are female athletes and women's sports downplayed by most sports coverage, but the media accentuates the masculinity of male athletes. For example, Hall of Fame pitcher Nolan Ryan's media coverage, according to a study by Nick Trujillo, consistently described him in terms of the stereotypical American man: powerful, hardworking, family patriarch, a cowboy and a symbol of heterosexual virility. Such images not only define an athlete's personal qualities but legitimate a particular vision of masculinity.

The authority of the masculine ethos is underlined by the fact that so many female athletes believe they can receive no higher compliment than to be told they "play like a man." Many feminists cringe at the irony of such sentiments. But they also realize that, while the explosion of women in sports has challenged their male dominance (2.5 million girls and young women participated in interscholastic sport in 2003, up from 300,000 in 1972—before Title IX's federal mandate for gender equality), women's sports have essentially been based upon the same single-minded, hyper-competitive masculine model. Not surprisingly, they are witnessing the emergence of the same kinds of problems—cheating, physical and emotional stress, homophobia, eating disorders—that have long plagued men's sports.

Sports and Maintaining Masculinity

As the men Messner interviewed became more committed to being athletes, they began to construct identities and relationships that conformed to—and thus perpetuated—sport's masculine values. Athletes are so bound up with being men that when, in his initial interviews, Messner inadvertently referred to them as "ex-athletes," his interviewees responded as if he were taking away their identities, their very manhood. A professional baseball player expressed a similar sentiment when I asked how he dealt with his time on the disabled list last summer because of a serious arm injury: "I'd throw wiffle balls left-handed to my eight-year-old son—and I had to get him out! Just so I could feel like a man again."

Of course, few men participate in sports with the intensity of professional athletes. Those who cannot move up the competitive ladder can still participate in other ways—in recreational sports, in coaching, and perhaps, most of all, in attending sporting events, watching sports on television, and buying athletic gear and apparel. Indeed, it is in being a fan (derived from *fanatic*) that the male slant of sports is clearest. While women often follow sports, their interest tends to be driven by social ends, such as being with family or friends. Male spectators are far more likely to watch events by themselves, follow sports closely, and be affected by the outcomes of games and the performance of their favored teams and athletes. The basic explanation is similar to the one developed out of sports activity studies: Just as playing sports provides many boys and young men with a space to become men, watching sports serves many men as a way to reinforce, rework, and maintain their masculinity—in these cases, through vicarious identification with masculine pursuits and idealized men. Writing of his obsession with 1950s football star Frank Gifford in *A Fan's Notes,* novelist Fredrick Exley explained: "Where I could not, with syntax, give shape to my fantasies, Gifford could with his superb timing, his uncanny faking, give shape to his." "I cheered for him with inordinate enthusiasm," Exley wrote, because he helped me find "my place in the competitive world of men . . . each time I heard the roar of the crowd, it roared in my ears as much for me as for him."

It was no accident that Exley chose to write about football. With its explicit appropriation of the rhetoric and tactics of combat, the sport supplanted baseball as the most popular spectator sport in the United States in the 1970s. Football's primary ideological salience, according to Messner, "lies in its ability . . . to symbolically link men of diverse ages and socioeconomic backgrounds. . . . Interacting with other men and interacting with them in this male-dominated space . . . [is] a way to assert and confirm one's own maleness. . . ." Being with other men allows males to affirm their masculine identity. Listen to today's sports talk radio. These programs are not only sophomorically masculine, many of them serve as little men's communities unto themselves: Tiger fan Jack; Mike from Modesto; Jay the Packer's guy—even teams' announcers have unique personalities and identities, fostering the impression that this is an actual club where all the guys know each other.

The salience of sports as a medium to validate masculinity may be best illustrated when it is taken away. Journalist Susan Faludi reported on what happened when the original Cleveland Browns football team left town to become the Baltimore Ravens. The mostly working-class men who occupied the section of seats in Cleveland called the "Dawg Pound" talked about the team's departure with an overwhelming sense of loss and powerlessness. As it often is for former athletes, it was as if they'd had their manhood taken from them. In tearful media interviews, John "Big Dawg" Thompson compared the team's departure to witnessing his best friend die in the hospital.

Sports as "Contested Terrain"

Critics of sports' heavy masculinity (most scholars doing work in this area are critics) have focused on its neglect or even exclusion of women. The way that golf outings perpetuate the privileges men enjoy in the corporate world is a frequent example. Others have gone so far as to suggest that the powerful appeal of sports for men arises because sports provide them at least symbolic superiority in a world in which men's real authority is in decline. As columnist and former professional basketball player Mariah Burton Nelson put it in the deliberately provocative title of her popular 1994 book, "The stronger women get, the more men love football."

In recent years, sociologists of sports have also begun to identify tensions within the masculine culture of athletics. Looking at Great Britain's soccer stars, for example, Garry Whannel has studied how the hedonism of the "new lad lifestyle" (as represented by players like David Beckham) rubs up against the disciplined masculinity traditionalists perceive to be necessary for international football success. Messner, for his part, has shown how "high status" men (white and from middle-class backgrounds) and "low status" men differently understood themselves as athletes. The former tended to transfer what they learned in sports about being men to pursuing success in other spheres, such as education and career. Men from lower status backgrounds saw sports as their only hope for success as a man—an accomplishment that the higher status men looked down upon as a narrow, atavistic type of masculinity. Expanding from this, some scholars have demonstrated that in popular culture the masculinity of African-American athletes is often exaggerated and linked to racial stereotypes about violence, risk and threat. Basketball star Dennis Rodman, for example, gained notoriety by playing on his persona as a "bad" ball player. While problematic in many respects, these images of black masculinity can also provide African-American men with unique opportunities for personal advancement and broader political visibility (as I have suggested in my work on the 1968 black Olympics protest movement).

Such research has led many scholars to see sports not only as a place where mainstream masculine culture is perpetuated, but also a place where it is challenged and possibly changed. These issues have played out clearly in the debates over the implementation of Title IX legislation for women's equal access to sports. While still hotly contested (as evidenced by the recent controversy surrounding the all-male Augusta National Golf Club, as well as speculation that the legislation may be challenged in court by the Bush administration), Title IX has transformed men's relationship to sports, to women, and even to masculinity itself. Sports' most vital social function with respect to masculinity is to provide a separate space for men to discuss—often indirectly, through evaluations of favorite players or controversial incidents—what it is to be a real man. And that space is increasingly shared with women.

Some scholars envision new, more humane or even feminine sports—marked less by an emphasis on winning, record-setting and spectatorship, and more by open participation, enjoyment and fitness. Cross-cultural studies of sports show that these are real possibilities, that sports are not "naturally" and inherently masculine as Americans have long assumed. Sexism and homophobia, for example, have never been a real problem in Chinese sports, anthropologist Susan Brownell explains, because sports emerged there as a low-status activity that more powerful men felt no special compulsion to control or participate in. As a consequence, it is widely believed that a skilled female practitioner of kung fu should be able to defeat stronger but less-skilled men. At the same time, Brownell points out, the current proliferation of Western, Olympic-style sports in China seems to be contributing to the redefinition of gender roles there nearer the pattern of Western sports and masculinity.

Playing Deeply

In a famous paper on cockfighting in Bali, American anthropologist Clifford Geertz used the term "deep play" to capture the way fans make sense of such competitions as the cockfight, cricket or American football. As passionate and articulate as they may be, these enthusiasts generally do not attempt to justify their pursuits. Instead, they downplay the significance of sports as separate from the serious concerns of real life. We can learn a great deal from such play, Geertz said, if we think about it as an "art form" which helps us figure out who people really are and what they really care about. Similarly, American men who love sports may not be able to fully articulate and understand how it is part of their being men, but their passion for sports can certainly help us understand them and their masculinity.

This peculiar, "deep play" understanding of sports makes it difficult for most men to recognize or confront the costs and consequences that may come with their sports obsessions. But in many ways isn't this true of masculine culture in general? It makes male advantages and masculine values appear so normal and "natural" that they can hardly be questioned. Therein may lie the key to the puzzle connecting men and the seemingly innocent world of sports: they fit together so tightly, so seamlessly that they achieve their effects—learning to be a man, male bonding, male authority and the like—without seeming to be doing anything more than tossing a ball or watching a Sunday afternoon game.

References

Birrell, Susan and Cheryl L. Cole, eds. *Women, Sport and Culture*. Champaign, IL: Human Kinetics, 1994. A collection of feminist critiques of sport that includes several influential contributions on men and masculinity.

Brownell, Susan. *Training the Body for China: Sports in the Moral Order of the People's Republic*. Chicago: University of Chicago Press, 1995. The chapters on sex, gender, and the body offer a fascinating cross-cultural contrast, and provide an introduction to sports in the nation that will host the 2008 Olympics.

Burstyn, Varda. *The Rites of Men: Manhood, Politics and the Culture of Sport*. Toronto: University of Toronto Press, 1999. The most comprehensive treatment of the social, cultural, and historical forces that account for the relationship between men and sports in modern society.

Fine, Gary Alan. *With the Boys: Little League Baseball and Preadolescent Culture*. Chicago: University of Chicago Press, 1987. A pioneering field study from a noted sociologist of culture.

Kelley, Robin D. G. "Playing for Keeps: Pleasure and Profit on the Postindustrial Playground." In *The House that Race Built*. ed. Wahneema Lubiano. New York: Pantheon, 1997. An ethnographically informed treatment of the opportunities basketball presents to inner-city African-American men produced by the country's preeminent historian of black popular culture.

Klein, Alan M. *Little Big Men: Bodybuilding Subculture and Gender Construction*. Albany, NY: State University of New York Press, 1993. A vivid ethnography of competitive body builders on the West Coast that draws upon Robert Connell's seminal critique of the intersection of men's bodies, identities and sexualities in masculine culture.

Messner, Michael. *Taking the Field: Women, Men, and Sports*. Minneapolis, MN: University of Minnesota Press, 2002. The latest book from the leading scholar in the field. It exposes the ways in which men and women together use sports to define gender differences.

Pronger, Brian. *The Arena of Masculinity: Sports, Homosexuality and the Meaning of Sex*. London: St. Martin's Press, 1990. Pronger explores the problematic connections between gender and sexuality in sport, highlighting its libidinal dimensions.

CHAPTER 17

Getting in Trouble

Ann A. Ferguson

Well you asked me
what my definition
of a homie is
a friend till the end
which starts off
when you kids
little "gargechos" that are always into something
doing something bad
acting like they did nothing
Well here's a little story
bout a homie named Frankie
had another little homie
that was down for hankie pinkie
sorta like Spankie and Alfalfa
little rascals
doing what they do and getting away without a hassle
like going to the schoolyard
forging late pass to their class
cutting in lunchlines
leaving other students last
or strolling to the movies
to see a Rated R
when moms dropped them off
thought ET would be the star
still there was an issue
that just could not be ignored
taking tapes and forty-fives
from the local record stores
being good kids
to them was nothing but baloney
cos this is what you do when its you and your homies.

—LIGHTER SHADE OF BROWN, "HOMIES"

SOURCE: Ferguson, A. A. (2001). Getting in Trouble. In *Bad Boys: Public Schools in the Making of Black Masculinity.* University of Michigan Press. Reproduced with permission from the University of Michigan Press.

Horace has that drained look in his eyes that is always there when he first emerges from the classroom at the end of the day. He moves as if there is just enough energy left to get him through the door and out of school. I see the identical look of stunned exhaustion on the faces of teachers, but I am not surprised to find the aftermath of a hard workday on adult faces. It is unexpected, unsettling to recognize that same slow, defeated posture on a twelve-year-old boy.

Outside the classroom, Horace catches sight of the crowded hallway and his expression lightens. The corridor is choked with kids and adults moving eagerly toward the exits. Everyone, young and old, is in a rush to be outside, to get on with life. He breaks into a run, tossing his backpack playfully in the direction of another kid. I see his body shake loose as he bolts into the toilets in chase of another boy. Now there are shrieks, yells, roars coming from that room into which I, a female adult, cannot follow.

I tutor Horace in an after-school program once a week. He is one of the boys identified as a "troublemaker" by the school. His name had appeared on every list of the school adults whom I had asked to identify boys "getting in trouble" for me to interview. This is the boy described by one of the teachers as "on the fast track to the penitentiary," whose name had become the norm among school adults against which other children could be ranked in terms of their tractability.

Horace shakes off a day in which there have been few rewards, intense surveillance, and the virtual eradication of all that he brings to school. He has been marginalized to ranks and spaces that are full of disgrace. What lessons does Horace learn about self and school as he journeys from classroom to Punishing Room to Jailhouse? How does he fashion selfhood within this context? What is the connection between this self-fashioning and getting in trouble?

In this chapter, we examine masculinity as a nexus of identification and self-fashioning during the school day, a ritualized source of articulating power, of making a name for oneself, of getting respect under conditions where the officially sanctioned paths to success are recognized as blocked. Masculinity, however, exists in a dynamic and structuring relationship with other coordinates of social identity: race and class. Therefore, in the discussion that follows I will elaborate on how gender acts are always and already modulated through race at the constitutive embodied level as well as that of the imaginary and representational.

Schoolwork

School is a workplace. This seems obvious for the adults who work there, from custodians and cafeteria workers to teachers and administrators. But school is also a workplace for children. Certainly what children do in school is characterized as "work" by both adults and kids.

I found many examples in the discipline records of the relationship between "work" and "trouble." Children are described as "working hard" or as "refusing to work." One teacher had scribbled on the referral form, "He has refused to do any work today," as the reason a boy was sent to the Punishing Room. In another case, the charge was that "he won't do the work, won't read, won't write, sits and refuses." Some children are characterized as "good workers," while others defy the conditions of work, go on strike openly or use slowdown tactics through procrastination and escape avoidance. The work of school is compulsory labor: children must, by law, attend school. They have no control over the materials they work with, what they produce, the nature of the rewards for their exertions and performance.

I was interested in how the boys that I interviewed felt about schoolwork so I asked them to describe the school day. Both Schoolboys and Troublemakers characterized it as boring, uneventful, dull, a stretch of time in which you did nothing interesting. The following comment was a fairly typical answer: "Nothing happens—you go to classes and do your work."

When I asked Eddie what was his least favorite part of the day, his answer was, "My teachers. Homework and classwork, yeah, class. When you have to sit there and write and do nothing but listen." Even Ricky, described as an "ideal" student by the teacher, was lukewarm, indifferent about schoolwork. Math was "the worst" and P.E. was his favorite part of the day because it was "fun." Claude, one of a group of boys most marginalized by the school who was described by the principal as a "thug," seemed most alienated from schoolwork. He flatly told me, "School, I don't like school. Really, it's boring. No way. There isn't a single thing about school for me."

In their descriptions, both Troublemakers and Schoolboys presented a timetable of their movement from one set of tasks to another, from one space in school to another. They recalled the mechanics of work: getting books out, writing, listening to the teacher, reading aloud. But they generally found it difficult to come up with the substance of what they actually learned in classrooms, what or who they read or wrote about, for example. This is not surprising since the routine is indeed what the school emphasizes through sheer repetition as the most noteworthy aspect of the school day. Being in the right place at the right time and the physical acts of going about the tasks called for when you are there is the fundamental knowledge about work impressed on the children. The kids recognize this. They have registered that the timetable, the form, not the content of the curriculum, is the significant element in their education.

My own experience as a participant observer in a classroom corroborated the description of the school day as one that was tedious, interminable, and deadening of any imaginative impulse or insight. My field notes, soon after I began observing in the sixth-grade room, record one afternoon when I found myself caught up in a collective effort to break out of the passive mold and do something active to keep myself awake. This spontaneous activity made clear to me that even the children who were most successful in the class had their own methods for helping to pass the time.

I catch the eye of Chris who I notice has made a clever paper gizmo that opens and closes in his hand displaying a little message which he flashes at me. I smile in acknowledgement of receipt. Chris is a white boy who is bussed in to the school. He is a good student, quiet and cooperative who tackles his work with the dedicated fortitude of someone who wants to get it done as quickly as possible so that he can get on with something else. This something else is often a book from the class library which he escapes into. The gizmo, which I learn later is called a "cootie catcher," looks simple enough so I begin to construct one with paper from my notebook as silently and surreptitiously as possible. I have to tear out a sheet of paper without making a loud crackling noise and call attention to myself. Carefully. Chris watches me encouragingly shaking his head as I make a wrong move and guiding me by partly undoing his own creation. As I signal back to him, my work completed, I notice that a few other kids in the room also have cootie catchers. They know what I am doing. We signal back and forth. It is a moment of thrilling complicity. I remember that we are supposed to be sitting listening to other children reading aloud about the Egyptians from the social science textbook. I have not registered a word in the last few minutes. Others are passing time differently. One girl is braiding the hair of one of the girls at her table; some children are openly daydreaming. Surely the teacher is aware of all these activities which she would certainly have stopped instantly earlier in the day. It seems that everybody knows that we are just passing time, waiting for the bell to ring. We are all tired, drowsy, bored, and ready to go home.

When the teacher signals that it is okay to pass time this way, that she will turn a blind eye, even conforming kids fool around. This play at work does not disrupt the routine; rather, it helps to make it more tolerable.

Note passing also helps to make the minutes go faster. It is about the need to communicate with others across a space in which communication is technically only allowed through the adult. Some children pass notes surreptitiously, discreetly. Occasionally a child decides to make the note passing public in order to make things happen by engineering the discovery of a note that will cause adult consternation and "finger" another kid. So Lonnie was banished to the Jailhouse for an entire day when he passed a scrap of paper with a penis drawn on it to a friend who looked at the contents and reacted in a way to draw attention to the communication.

Nothing, however, is as finely practiced an art as getting out of work at the same time as appearing to do it. This usually involves slowing down the pace of task completion to one that would make a snail seem a speedster. Horace's teacher would often complain about his inability to follow instructions promptly; pointing out to me how long it took him to move from one task to another. Long after he has been told to get his book out and turn to a particular page, his head is still in his desk as he ostensibly searches for the book. Once it is out, he stares fixedly into space while the teacher asks him to turn to the page: "Everybody else already has it open in front of them. We're waiting."

One of the few periods of the day that the boys say they look forward to is recess. In contrast to Class time, this is the interlude when kids have some control, though still limited and highly surveilled, over what they do and with whom, This is a moment when you can play games, socialize with friends, run around, shout, laugh, eat.

Frequently, I noticed that Troublemakers engineered subversion as a way of exercising some command over the pattern of work and play during the day. Sometimes this involved prolonging recess through a trip to the Punishing Room. I saw this played out several times in a scenario where Boy Number One would be sent by the teacher to the Punishing Room, where he would tell a story that implicated Boy Number Two, and possibly Three and Four, in an action that happened during recess. So Boy Number One would be sent back to the classroom to bring the others in to tell their story. Trips up and down the hallway, peeking into rooms, making faces in passing, extended the length of time away from class. This was a con-game that worked from time to time.

A variation on this theme was using misbehavior to prolong an outing, So Horace and Lamond, who had behaved like model students on the field trip, on the way home ran ahead of the group in the last few blocks, scaled the school fence rather than going through the gate, and got sent to the office.

While schoolwork was described as boring and hard, getting in trouble was described as "easy" by the Troublemakers. Claude explained to me that it was "easier than staying good" for him. Within the field of power of school, trouble is the condition of being a child, while conformity takes work: "Somebody gets spotted and they just pick out that person," was how he described it to me with a shrug. Like the other Troublemakers, he grounded his conclusion in his observation that troublesome behavior was not all that unusual an occurrence for a kid in school. Another of the boys told me,

> Everybody gets in trouble sometimes. Laura [a white girl in the class who is a very good worker], even she gets in trouble sometimes. Everybody does. [Pauses to reflect for a moment.] Maybe Marsha and Simone [two other white girls], they barely get in trouble.

Under tedious, routinized conditions of work and learning, activities that risk trouble, even trouble itself, function to spice up the workday and make time go faster through creative attempts to make things happen and disrupt the routine.

However, for African American children the conditions of schooling are not simply tedious; they are also replete with symbolical forms of violence. Troublemakers are conscious of the fact that school adults have labeled them as problems, social and educational misfits; that what they bring from home and neighbourhood—family structure and history, forms of verbal and nonverbal expression, neighborhood lore and experiences—has little or even deficit value. The convergence of the routine with the harsh exclusionary ambience of school calls forth a more intensive mode of identity work. My concern now is to home in on this work through an examination of the relationship between trouble and masculinity; of the specific circular relationship between risky, rule-breaking behavior, getting in trouble, and the experience of being and becoming male. Making a name for yourself through identity work and self-performance, even if the consequence is punishment, becomes a highly charged necessity given the conditions of school for the Troublemakers.

Making a Name for Yourself: Transgressive Acts and Gender Performance

Though girls as well as boys infringe the rules, the overwhelming majority of violations in every single category, from misbehavior to obscenity, are by males. In a disturbing tautology, transgressive behavior is that which constitutes masculinity. Consequently, African American males in the very act of identification, of signifying masculinity, are likely to be breaking rules.

I use the concept of sex/gender not to denote the existence of a stable, unitary category that reflects the presence of fundamental, natural biological difference, but as a socially constructed category whose form and meaning varies culturally and historically. We come to know ourselves and to recognize others as of a different sex through an overdetermined complex process inherent in every sphere of social life at the ideological and discursive level, through social structures and institutional arrangements, as well as through the micropolitics of social interactions. We take sex difference for granted, as a natural form of difference as we look for it, recognize it, celebrate it; this very repetition of the "fact" of difference produces and confirms its existence. Indeed, assuming sex/gender difference and identifying as one or the other gender is a precursor of being culturally recognizable as "human."

While all these modes of constituting gender as difference were palpable in the kids' world, in the following analysis of sex/gender as a heightened and highly charged resource for self-fashioning and making a name for oneself, the phenomenological approach developed by ethnomethodologists and by poststructuralist feminist Judith Butler is the most productive one to build on. Here gender is conceptualized as something we do in a performance that is both individually and socially meaningful. We signal our gender identification through an ongoing performance of normative acts that are ritually specific, drawing on well-worked-over, sociohistorical scripts and easily recognizable scenarios.[1]

Butler's emphasis on the coerced and coercive nature of these performances is especially useful. Her work points out that the enactment of sex difference is neither voluntary nor arbitrary in form but is a compulsory requirement of social life. Gender acts follow sociohistorical scripts that are policed through the exercise of repression and taboo. The consequences of an inadequate or bad performance are significant, ranging from ostracism and stigmatization to imprisonment and death. What I want to emphasize in the discussion that follows are the rewards that attach to this playing out of roles; for males, the enactment of masculinity is also a thoroughly embodied display of physical and social power.

Identification as masculine through gender acts, within this framework, is not simply a matter of imitation or modeling, but is better understood as a highly strategic attachment to a social category that has political effects. This attachment involves narratives of the self and of Other, constructed within and through fantasy and imagination, as well as through repetitious, referential acts. The performance signals the individual as socially connected, embedded in a collective membership that always references relations of power.

African American boys at Rosa Parks School use three key constitutive strategies of masculinity in the embrace of the masculine "we" as a mode of self-expression. These strategies speak to and about power. The first is that of heterosexual power, always marked as male. Alain's graffiti become the centerpiece of this discussion. The second involves classroom performance that engage and disrupt the normal direction of the flow of power. The third strategy involves practices of "fighting." All three invoke a "process of iterability, a regularized and constrained repetition of norms," in doing gender;

constitute masculinity as a natural, essential corporeal style; and involve imaginary, fantasmatic identifications.[2]

These three strategies often lead to trouble, but by engaging them a boy can also make a name for himself as a real boy, the Good Bad Boy of a national fantasy. All three illustrate and underline the way that normative male practices take on a different, more sinister inflection when carried out by African American boys. Race makes a significant difference both in the form of the performance as well as its meaning for the audience of adult authority figures and children for whom it is played.

Heterosexual Power: Alain's Graffiti

One group of transgressions specifically involves behavior that expresses sexual curiosity and attraction. These offenses are designated as "personal violations" and given more serious punishment. Inscribed in these interactions are social meanings about relations of power between the sexes as well as assumptions about male and female difference at the level of the physical and biological as well as the representational. It is assumed that females are sexually passive, unlikely to be initiators of sexual passes, while males are naturally active sexual actors with strong sexual drives. Another assumption is that the feminine is a contaminated, stigmatizing category in the sex/gender hierarchy.

Typically, personal violations involved physical touching of a heterosexual nature where males were the "perpetrators" and females the "victims." A few examples from the school files remind us of some of the "normal" displays of sexual interest at this age.

- Boy was cited with "chasing a girl down the hall" [punishment: two days in the Jailhouse].
- Boy pulled a female classmate's pants down during recess [punishment: one and a half days in the Jailhouse].
- Boy got in trouble for "touching girl on private parts. She did not like" [punishment: a day in the Jailhouse].
- Boy was cited for "forcing girl's hand between his legs" [punishment: two and a half days in the Jailhouse].

In one highly revealing case, a male was cast as the "victim" when he was verbally assaulted by another boy who called him a girl. The teacher described the "insult" and her response to it on the referral form in these words:

During the lesson, Jonas called Ahmed a girl and said he wasn't staying after school for detention because "S" [another boy] had done the same thing. Since that didn't make it ok for anyone to speak this way I am requesting an hour of detention for Jonas. I have no knowledge of "S" saying so in my presence.

This form of insult is not unusual. When boys want to show supreme contempt for another boy they call him a girl or liken his behavior to female behavior. What is more troubling is that adults capitulate in this stigmatization. The female teacher takes for granted that a comment in which a boy is called a girl is a symbolic attack, sufficiently derogatory to merit punishment. All the participants in the classroom exchange witness the uncritical acknowledgement of adult authority to a gender or female debasement.

Of course, this is not news to them. Boys and girls understand the meaning of being male and being female in the field of power; the binary opposition of male/female is always one that expresses a norm, maleness, and its constitutive outside, femaleness. In a conversation with a group of boys, one of them asserted and then was supported by others that "a boy can be a girl, but a girl can never be a boy." Boys can be teased, controlled, punished by being accused of being "a girl." A boy faces the degradation of "being sissified," being unmanned, transferred to the degraded category of female. Girls can be teased about being a tomboy. But this is not the same. To take on qualities of being male is the access to and performance of power. So females must now fashion themselves in terms of male qualities to partake of that power. Enactments of masculinity signal value, superiority, power.

Let us return to Alain, the eleven-year-old boy who while cooling off and writing lines as a punishment in the antechamber of the Punishing Room, writes on the table in front of him: "Write 20 times. I will stop fucking 10 cent teachers and this five cent class. Fuck you. Ho! Ho! Yes Baby." Alain's message can be read in a number of ways. The most obvious way is the one of the school. A child has broken several rules in one fell swoop and must be punished: he has written on school property (punishable); he has used an obscenity (punishable); he has committed an especially defiant and disrespectful act because he is already in the Punishing Room and therefore knows his message is likely to be read (punishable). Alain is sent home both as a signal to him and to the other witnesses as well as to the students and adults who will hear it through the school grapevine that he cannot get away with such flagrant misbehavior.

An alternative reading looks at the content of the message itself and the form that Alain's anger takes at being sent to the Punishing Room. Alain's anger is being vented against his teacher and the school itself, expressing his rejection, his disidentification with school that he devalues as monetarily virtually worthless. His message expresses his anger through an assertion of sexual power—to fuck or not to fuck—one sure way that a male can conjure up the fantasmatic as well as the physical specter of domination over a female of any age. His assertion of this power mocks the authority of the teacher to give him orders to write lines. His use of "baby" reverses the relations of power, teacher to pupil, adult to child; Alain allies himself through and with power as the school/teacher becomes "female," positioned as a sex object, as powerless, passive, infantilized. He positions himself as powerful through identification with and as the embodiment of male power as he disidentifies with school. At this moment, Alain is not just a child, a young boy, but taking the position of "male" as a strategic resource for enacting power, for being powerful. At the same time, this positioning draws the admiring, titillated attention of his peers.

These moments of sex trouble exemplify some of the aspects of the performance of sex/gender difference that is naturalized through what is deemed punishable as well as punishment practices. Judging from the discipline records, girls do not commit sexual violations. It is as if by their very nature they are incapable. To be female is to be powerless, victimizable, chased down the hallway, an object to be acted upon with force, whose hand can be seized and placed between male legs. To be female is also to be sexually passive, coy, the "chaste" rather than the chaser, in relation to male sexual aggressiveness. In reality, I observed girls who chased boys and who interacted with them physically. Girls, in fact, did "pants" boys, but these acts went unreported by the boys. For them to report and therefore risk appearing to be victimized by a girl publicly would be a humiliating outcome that would only undermine their masculinity. In the production of natural difference, boys' performances work as they confirm that they are active pursuers, highly sexualized actors who must be punished to learn to keep their burgeoning sexuality under control. There is a reward for the behavior even if it may be punished as a violation. In the case of African American boys, sex trouble is treated as egregious conduct.

African American males have historically been constructed as hypersexualized within the national imagination. Compounding this is the process of the adultification of their behavior. Intimations of sexuality on their part, especially when directed toward girls who are bused in—white girls from middle-class families—are dealt with as grave transgressions with serious consequences.

Power Reversals: Class Acts

Performance is a routine part of classroom work. Students are called upon to perform in classes by teachers to show off their prowess or demonstrate their ineptitude or lack of preparation. They are required to read passages aloud, for example, before a highly critical audience of their peers. This display is teacher initiated and reflects the official curricula; they are command performances with well-scripted roles, predictable in the outcome of who has and gets respect, who is in control, who succeeds, who fails.

Another kind of performance is the spontaneous outbreaks initiated by the pupils generally defined under the category of "disruption" by the school. These encompass a variety of actions that punctuate and disrupt the order of the day. During the school year about two-thirds of these violations were initiated by boys and a third by girls. Here are some examples from the discipline files of girls being "disruptive":

- Disruptive in class—laughing, provoking others to join her. Purposely writing wrong answers, being very sassy, demanding everyone's attention.
- Constantly talking; interrupting; crumpling paper after paper; loud.

Some examples of boys' disruption:
- Constant noise, indian whoops, face hiccups, rapping.
- Chanting during quiet time—didn't clean up during art [punishment: detention].
- Joking, shouting out, uncooperative, disruptive during lesson.

From the perspective of kids, what the school characterizes as "disruption" on the referral slips is often a form of performance of the self: comedy, drama, melodrama become moments for self-expression and display. Disruption adds some lively spice to the school day; it injects laughter, drama, excitement, a delicious unpredictability to the classroom routine through spontaneous, improvisational outbursts that add flavor to the bland events.

In spite of its improvisational appearance, most performance is highly ritualized with its own script, timing, and roles. Teachers as well as students engage in the ritual and play their parts. Some kids are regular star performers. Other kids are audience. However, when a substitute is in charge of the class and the risk of being marked as a trouble maker is minimal, even the most timid kids "act up." These rituals circulate important extracurricular knowledge about relations of power.

These dramatic moments are sites for the presentation of a potent masculine presence in the classroom. The Good Bad Boy of our expectations engages power, takes risks, makes the class laugh, and the teacher smile. Performances mark boundaries of "essential difference—risk taking, brinkmanship. The open and public defiance of the "teacher in order to get a laugh, make things happen, take center stage, be admired, is a resource for doing masculinity.

These acts are especially meaningful for those children who have already been marginalized as outside of the community of "good," hardworking students. For the boys already labeled as troublemakers, taking control of the spotlight and turning it on oneself so that one can shine, highlights, for a change, one's strengths and talents. Already caught in the limelight, these kids put on a stirring performance.

Reggie, one of the Troublemakers, prides himself on being witty and sharp, a talented performer. He aspires to two careers: one is becoming a Supreme Court justice, the other an actor. He had recently played the role of Caliban in the school production of *The Tempest* that he described excitedly to me:

I always try to get the main character in the story 'cause I might turn out to be an actor because I'm really good at acting and I've already did some acting. Shakespeare! See I got a good part. I was Caliban. I had to wear black suit. Black pants and top. Caliban was a beast! In the little picture that we saw, he looks like the . . . the . . . [searching for image] the beast of Notre Dame. The one that rings the bells like *fing! fing! fing!*

Here is one official school activity where Reggie gets to show off something that he is "good at." He is also proud to point out that this is not just a role in any play, but one in a play by Shakespeare. Here his own reward, which is not just doing something that he is good at, but doing it publicly so that he can receive the attention and respect of adults and peers, coincides with the school's educational agenda of creating an interest in Shakespeare among children.

Reggie also plays for an audience in the classroom, where he gets in trouble for disruption. He describes one of the moments for me embellished with a comic imitation of the teacher's female voice and his own swaggering demeanor as he tells the story:

> The teacher says [he mimics a high-pitched fussy voice], "You not the teacher of this class." And then I say [adopts a sprightly cheeky tone], "Oh, yes I am." Then she say, "No, you're not, and if you got a problem, you can just leave." I say, "Okay" and leave.

This performance, like others I witnessed, are strategies for positioning oneself in the center of the room in a face-off with the teacher, the most powerful person up to that moment. Fundamental to the performance is engagement with power; authority is teased, challenged, even occasionally toppled from its secure heights for brief moments. Children-generated theatrics allow the teasing challenge of adult power that can expose its chinks and weaknesses. The staged moments heighten tension, test limits, vent emotions, perform acts of courage. For Reggie to have capitulated to the teacher's ultimatum would have been to lose what he perceives as the edge in the struggle. In addition, he has won his escape from the classroom.

Horace describes his challenge to the teacher's authority in a summer school math class:

> Just before the end of the period he wrote some of our names on the board and said, "Whoever taught these students when they were young must have been dumb." So I said, "Oh, I didn't remember that was you teaching me in the first grade." Everyone in the room cracked up. I was laughing so hard, I was on the floor. He sent me to the office.

Horace is engaging the teacher in a verbal exchange with a comeback to an insult rather than just passively taking it. In this riposte, Horace not only makes his peers laugh at the teacher, but he also defuses the insult through a quick reversal. The audience in the room, raised on TV sitcom repartee and canned laughter, is hard to impress, so the wisecrack, the rejoinder, must be swift and sharp. Not everyone can get a laugh at the teacher's expense, and to be topped by the teacher would be humiliating; success brings acknowledgment, confirmation, applause from one's peers. For Horace, this is a success story, a moment of gratification in a day that brings few his way.

The tone of the engagement with power and the identity of the actor is highly consequential in terms of whether a performance is overlooked by the teacher or becomes the object of punishment. In a study of a Texas high school, Foley documents similar speech performances.[3] He describes how both teacher and students collaborate to devise classroom rituals and "games" to help pass the time given the context of routinized, alienating classroom work. He observes that upper-middle-class male Anglo students derail boring lessons by manipulating teachers through subtle "making out" games without getting in trouble. In contrast, low-income male Hispanic students, who were more likely to challenge teachers openly in these games, were punished. Foley concluded that one of the important lessons learned by all participants in these ritual games was that the subtle manipulation of authority was a much more effective way of getting your way than openly confronting power.

Style becomes a decisive factor in who gets in trouble. I am reminded of comments made by one of the student specialists at Rosa Parks who explained the high rate of black kids getting in trouble by remarking on their different style of rule breaking: "The white kids are sneaky, black kids are more open."

So why are the black kids "more open" in their confrontations with power? Why not be really "smart" and adopt a style of masculinity that allows them to engage in these rituals that spice the school day and help pass time, but carry less risk of trouble because it is within certain mutually understood limits?

These rituals are not merely a way to pass time, but are also a site for constituting a gendered racial subjectivity. For African American boys, the performance of masculinity invokes cultural conventions of speech performance that draws on a black repertoire. Verbal performance is an important medium for black males to establish a reputation, make a name for yourself, and achieve status.[4] Smitherman points out that black talk in general is

> a functional dynamic that is simultaneously a mechanism for learning about life and the world and a vehicle for achieving group recognition. Even in what appears to be only casual conversation, whoever speaks is highly conscious of the fact that his personality is on exhibit and his status at stake.[5]

Oral performance has a special significance in black culture for the expression of masculinity. Harper points out that verbal performance functions as an identifying marker for masculinity only when it is delivered in the vernacular and that "a too-evident facility in white idiom, can quickly identify one as a white-identified uncle Tom who must also be therefore weak, effeminate, and probably a fag."[6] Though the speech performances that I witnessed were not always delivered in the strict vernacular, the nonverbal, bodily component accompanying it was always delivered in a manner that was the flashy, boldly flamboyant popular style essential to a good performance. The body language and spoken idiom openly engage power in a provocative competitive way. To be indirect, "sly," would not be performing masculinity.

This nonstandard mode of self-representation epitomizes the very form the school seeks to exclude and eradicate. It is a masculine enactment of defiance played in a black key that is bound for punishment. Moreover, the process of adultification translates the encounter from a simple verbal clash with an impertinent child into one interpreted as an intimidating threat.

Though few white girls in the school were referred to the office for disruptive behavior, a significant number of African American girls staged performances, talked back to teachers, challenged authority, and were punished. But there was a difference with the cultural framing of their enactments and those of the boys. The bottom line of Horace's story was that "everyone in the room cracked up." He engaged authority through a self-produced public spectacle with an eye for an audience that is at home with the cultural icon of the Good Bad Boy as well as the "real black man." Boys expect to get attention. Girls vie for attention too, but it is perceived as illegitimate behavior. As the teacher described it in the referral form, the girl is "demanding attention." The prevailing cultural framework denies her the rights for dramatic public display.

Male and female classroom performance is different in another respect. Girls are not rewarded with the same kind of applause or recognition by peers or by teachers. Their performance is sidelined; it is not given center stage. Teachers are more likely to "turn a blind eye" to such a display rather than call attention to it, for girls are seen as individuals who operate in cliques at most and are unlikely to foment insurrection in the room. Neither the moral nor the pragmatic principle prods teachers to take action. The behavior is not taken seriously; it is rated as "sassy" rather than symptomatic of a more dangerous disorder. In some classrooms, in fact, risk taking and "feistiness" on the part of girls is subtly encouraged given the prevailing belief that what they need is to become more visible, more assertive in the classroom. The notion is that signs of self-assertion on their part should be encouraged rather than squelched.

Disruptive acts have a complex, multifaceted set of meanings for the male Troublemakers themselves. Performance as an expression of black masculinity is a production of a powerful subjectivity to be reckoned with, to be applauded; respect and ovation are in a context where none is forthcoming. The boys' anger and frustration as well as fear motivate the challenge to authority. Troublemakers act and speak out as stigmatized outsiders.

Ritual Performances of Masculinity: Fighting

Each year a substantial number of kids at Rosa Parks get into trouble for fighting. It is the most frequent offense for which they are referred to the Punishing Room. Significantly, the vast majority of the offenders are African American males.[7]

The school has an official position on fighting: it is the wrong way to handle any situation, at any time, no matter what. Schools have good reasons for banning fights: kids can get hurt and when fights happen they sully the atmosphere of order, making the school seem like a place of danger, of violence.

The prescribed routine for schoolchildren to handle situations that might turn into a fight is to tell an adult who is then supposed to take care of the problem. This routine ignores the unofficial masculine code that if someone hits you, you should solve the problem yourself rather than showing weakness and calling an adult to intervene. However, it is expected that girls with a problem will seek out an adult for assistance. Girls are assumed to be physically weaker, less aggressive, more vulnerable, more needy of self-protection; they must attach themselves to adult (or male) power to survive. This normative gender distinction, in how to handle both problems of a sexual nature and physical aggression, operates as a "proof" of a physical and dispositional gender nature rather than behavior produced through discourses and practices that constitute sex difference.

Referrals of males to the Punishing Room, therefore, are cases where the unofficial masculine code for problem resolution has prevailed. Telling an adult is anathema to these youth. According to their own codes, the act of "telling" is dangerous for a number of reasons. The most practical of these sees it as a statement to the "whole world" that you are unable to deal with a situation on your own—to take care of yourself—an admission that can have disastrous ramifications when adult authority is absent. This is evident from the stance of a Troublemaker who questions the practical application of the official code by invoking knowledge of the proper male response when one is "attacked" that is shared with the male student specialist charged with enforcing the regulation: "I said, 'Mr. B., if somebody came up and hit you, what would you do?' 'Well,' he says, 'We're not talking about me right now, see.' That's the kind of attitude they have. It's all like on you."

Another reason mentioned by boys for not relying on a teacher to take care of a fight situation is that adults are not seen as having any real power to effectively change the relations among kids:

> If someone keep messing with you, like if someone just keep on and you tell them to leave you alone, then you tell the teacher. The teacher can't do anything about it because, see, she can't hide you or nothing. Only thing she can do is tell them to stop. But then he keep on doing it. You have no choice but to hit 'em. You already told him once to stop.

This belief extends to a distrust of authority figures by these young offenders. The assumption that all the children see authority figures such as teachers, police, psychologists as acting on their behalf and trust they will act fairly may be true of middle- and upper-class children brought up to expect protection from authority figures in society. This is not the case with many of the children at the school. Their mistrust of authority is rooted in the historical and locally grounded knowledge of power relations that come from living in a largely black and impoverished neighborhood.

Fighting becomes, therefore, a powerful spectacle through which to explore trouble as a site for the construction of manhood. The practice takes place along a continuum that ranges from play— spontaneous outbreaks of pummeling and wrestling in fun, ritualistic play that shows off "cool" moves seen on video games, on TV, or in movies—to serious, angry socking, punching, fistfighting. A description of some of these activities and an analysis of what they mean provides the opportunity for us to delve under the surface of the ritualized, discrete acts that make up a socially recognizable fight event into the psychic, emotional, sensuous aspects of gender performativity. The circular, interactive flow between fantasmatic images, internal psychological processes, and physical acts suggest the dynamics of attachment of masculine identification.

Fighting is one of the social practices that add tension, drama, and spice to the routine of the school day. Pushing, grabbing, shoving, kicking, karate chopping, wrestling, fistfighting engage the body and the mind. Fighting is about play and games, about anger, and pain, about hurt feelings, about "messing around." To the spectator, a fight can look like serious combat, yet when the combatants are separated by an adult, they claim, "We were only playing." In fact, a single fight event can move along the continuum from play to serious blows in a matter of seconds. As one of the boys explained, "You get hurt and you lose your temper."

Fighting is typically treated as synonymous with "aggression" or "violence," terms that already encode the moral, definitional frame that obscures the contradictory ways that the practice, in all its manifestations, is used in our society. We, as good citizens, can distance ourselves from aggressive and violent behavior. "Violence" as discourse constructs "fighting" as pathological, symptomatic of asocial, dangerous tendencies, even though the practice of "fighting" and the discourses that constitute this practice as "normal," are in fact taken for granted as ritualized resources for "doing" masculinity in the contemporary United States.

The word *fighting* encompasses the "normal" as well as the pathological. It allows the range of meanings that the children, specifically the boys whom I interviewed and observed, as well as some of the girls, bring to the practice. One experience that it is open to is the sensuous, highly charged embodied experience before, during, and after fighting; the elating experience of "losing oneself" that I heard described in fight stories.

War Stories

I began thinking about fights soon after I started interviews with the Troublemakers and heard "fight stories." Unlike the impoverished and reluctantly cold accounts of the school day, these stories were vivid, elaborate descriptions of bodies, mental states, and turbulent emotional feelings. They were stirring, memorable moments in the tedious school routine.

Horace described a fight with an older boy who had kept picking on him. He told me about the incident as he was explaining how he had broken a finger one day when we were trading "broken bones" stories.

When I broke this finger right here it really hurted. I hit somebody in the face. It was Charles. I hit him in the face. You know the cafeteria and how you walk down to go to the cafeteria. Right there. That's where it happened. Charles picked me up and put me on the wall, slapped me on the wall, and dropped me. It hurt. It hurt bad. I got mad because he used to be messing with me for a long time so I just swung as hard as I could, closed my eyes, and just *pow*, hit him in the face. But I did like a roundhouse swing instead of doing it straight and it got the index finger of my right hand. So it was right there, started right here, and all around this part [he is showing me the back of his hand] it hurt. It was swollen. Oooh! It was like this! But Charles, he got hurt too. The next day I came to school I had a cast on my finger and he had a bandage on his ear. It was kinda funny, we just looked at each other and smiled.

The thing that most surprised and intrigued me about Horace's story was that he specifically recalled seeing Charles the next day and that they had looked at each other and smiled. Was this a glance of recognition, of humor, of recollection of something pleasing, of all those things? The memory of the exchanged smile derailed my initial assumption that fighting was purely instrumental. This original formulation said that boys fight because they have to fight in order to protect themselves from getting beaten up on the playground. Fighting from this instrumental perspective is a purely survival practice. Boys do fight to stave off the need to fight in the future; to stop the harassment from other boys on the playground and in the streets. However, this explains only a small group of boys who live in certain environments; it relegates fighting to the realm of the poor, the deviant, the delinquent, the pathological. This position fails to address these physical clashes as the central normative practice in the preparation of bodies, of mental stances, of self-reference for manhood and as the most effective form of conflict resolution in the realm of popular culture and international relations.

As I explored the meaning of fighting I began to wonder how I, as female, had come to be shaped so fighting was not a part of my own corporeal or mental repertoire. A conversation with my brother reminded me of a long forgotten self that could fight, physically, ruthlessly, inflict hurt, cause tears. "We were always fighting," he recalled. "You used to beat me up." Memories of these encounters came back. I am standing with a tuft of my brother's hair in my hand, furious tears in my eyes. Full of hate for him. Kicking, scratching, socking, feeling no pain. Where had this physical power gone? I became "ladylike" repressing my anger, limiting my physical contact to shows of affection, fearful. I wondered about the meaning of being female in a society in which to be female is to be always conscious of men's physical power and to consciously chart one's everyday routines to avoid becoming a victim of this power, but to never learn the bodily and mental pleasure of fighting back.

Bodily Preparations: Pain and Pleasure

Fighting is first and foremost a bodily practice. I think about fighting and physical closeness as I stand observing the playground at recess noticing a group of three boys, bodies entangled, arms and legs flailing. In another area, two boys are standing locked closely in a wrestling embrace. Children seem to gravitate toward physical contact with each other. For boys, a close, enraptured body contact is only legitimate when they are positioned as in a fight. It is shocking that this bodily closeness between boys would be frowned on, discouraged if it were read as affection. Even boys who never get in trouble for "fighting" can be seen engaging each other through the posturing and miming, the grappling of playfight encounters.

This play can lead to "real" fights. The thin line between play and anger is crossed as bodies become vulnerable, hurt, and tempers are lost. One of the white boys in the school who was in trouble for fighting describes the progression this way:

> Well we were messing with each other and when it went too far, he started hitting me and then I hit him back and then it just got into a fight. It was sorta like a game between me, him and Thomas. How I would get on Thomas's back an—he's a big guy—and Stephen would try to hit me and I would want a hit him back. So when Thomas left it sorta continued and I forgot which one of us wanted to stop—but one of us wanted to stop and the other one wouldn't.

Pain is an integral part of fighting. Sometimes it is the reason for lashing out in anger. This description by Wendell also captures the loss of self-control experienced at the moment of the fight:

> Sometimes it starts by capping or by somebody slams you down or somebody throws a bullet at you. You know what a bullet is, don't you? [He chuckles delightedly because I think of a bullet from a gun.] The bullet I am talking about is a football! You throw it with all your might and it hits somebody. It just very fast and they call it bullets. You off-guard and they throw it at your head, and bullets they throw with all their might so it hurts. Then that sorta gets you all pissed

off. Then what happens is, you kinda like, "Why you threw it?" "Cause I wanted to. Like, so?" "So you not going to do that to me." Then: "So you going to do something about it?" Real smart. "Yeah!" And then you tap the person on the shoulder and your mind goes black and then *shweeeee* [a noise and hand signal that demonstrates the evaporation of thought] you go at it. And you don't stop until the teacher comes and stops it.

Fighting is a mechanism for preparing masculinized bodies through the playful exercise of bodily moves and postures and the routinized rehearsal of sequences and chains of stances of readiness, attack, and defense. Here it is crucial to emphasize that while many boys in the school never ever engage in an actual physical fight with another boy or girl during school hours, the majority engage in some form of body enactments of fantasized "fight" scenarios. They have observed boys and men on TV, in the movies, in video games, on the street, in the playground adopting these stances.

These drills simultaneously prepare and cultivate the mental states in which corporeal styles are grounded. So for instance, boys are initiated into the protocol of enduring physical pain and mental anguish—"like a man"—through early and small infusions of the toxic substance itself in play fights. The practice of fighting is the site for a hot-wiring together of physical pain and pleasure, as components of masculinity as play and bodily hurt inevitably coincide.

Consequently, it also engages powerful emotions. Lindsey described the feelings he experienced prior to getting into a fight:

Sometimes it's play. And sometimes it's real. But that's only sometimes, because they can just suddenly make you angry and then, it's like they take control of your mind. Like they manipulate your mind if you angry. Little by little you just lose it and you get in a temper.

One of the white boys in the school who had gotten in trouble for fighting described his thoughts and feelings preceding a fight and the moment of "just going black" in a loss of self:

My mind would probably be going through how I would do this. If I would stop it now or if I would follow through with it. But once the fight actually happens I sort of go black and just fight 'em.

One of the questions that I asked all the boys about fighting came out of my own ignorance. My query was posed in terms of identity work around the winning and losing of fights. Did you ever win a fight? Did you ever lose a fight? How did you feel when you lost? How did you feel when you won? I found the answers slippery, unexpected, contradictory. I had anticipated that winning would be described in proud and boastful ways, as success stories. But there seemed to be a surprising reluctance to embellish victory. I learned that I was missing the point by posing the question the way I had in terms of winning and losing. Trey enlightened me when he explained that what was at stake was not winning or losing per se but in learning about the self:

I won a lot of fights. You know you won when they start crying and stuff or when they stop and leave. I lost fights. Then you feel a little okay. At least you lost. I mean like you ain't goin' win every fight. At least you fought back instead of just standing there and letting them hit you.

Another boy expressed the function that fighting played in establishing yourself as being a particular kind of respectable person:

It's probably like dumb, but if somebody wants to fight me, I mean, I don't care even if I know I can't beat 'em. I won't stop if they don't stop. I mean I'm not scared to fight anybody. I'm not a coward. I don't let anybody punk me around. If you let people punk you around, other peoples want to punk you around.

Standing and proving yourself today can be insurance against future harassment in the yard as you make a name for yourself through readiness to fight: "Like if somebody put their hands on you, then you have to, you have to hit them back. Because otherwise you going be beat up on for the rest of your life."

Gender Practice and Identification

Fighting acts reproduce notions of essentially different gendered natures and the forms in which this "difference" is grounded. Though class makes some difference in when, how, and under what conditions it takes place, fighting is the hegemonic representation of masculinity. Inscribed in the male body—whether individual males fight or not, abjure fighting or not—is the potential for this unleashing of physical power. By the same token, fighting for girls is considered an aberration, something to be explained.

Girls do get in fights at school. Boys asserted that girls can fight, even that "sometimes they get in fights easier. Because they got more attitude." Indeed, girls do make a name for themselves this way. One of the girls at Rosa Parks was in trouble several times during the school year for fighting. Most of her scraps were with the· boys who liked to tease her because she was very tall for her age. This, however, was not assumed to be reflective of her "femaleness" but of her individuality. Mr. Sobers, for example, when I asked him about her, made a point of this singularity rather than explaining her in terms of race, class, or gender: "Oh, Stephanie is just Stephanie."

Fighting is not a means of "doing gender" for girls. They do not use physical clashes as a way to relate to each other in play. Girls did not practice cool moves or engage in play fights with each other. They used other strategies for making the day go by, such as the chain of stories about other children, the "he said, she said," which can build up to a more physical confrontation.[8] More often it leads to injured feelings, the isolation and ostracism of individuals, and the regrouping of friendships. On the playground at Rosa Parks, girls were more likely to interact physically with boys than with other girls. They often initiated encounters with boys to play chase games by pushing, prodding, hitting, or bumping into them.

Through male fighting we can see how gender difference is grounded in a compulsory and violently enforced heterosexuality. The interaction involves the convergence of the desire for physical and emotional closeness with another, the anxiety over presenting a convincing performance of a declarative act of identification, and the risk of ostracism or punishment. Boys from an early age learn that affectionate public physical contact such as an embrace with those who are seen as most like oneself, other males, is taboo. For them, a physical embrace, the close intertwining of bodies is culturally permissible only in the act of the rituals of the fight.[9] Thus the fulfillment of desire for physical intimacy, for body contact, can most safely be accomplished publicly through the apparent or actual infliction and experience of bodily pain. A desire for closeness, for identification with a reflection of oneself can be achieved through an act that beckons and embraces using apparently threatening and hostile gestures.

Most men don't have to actually fight; they can participate in the inscription of power on male bodies through watching. Fighting acts are a major form of entertainment in our society. From popular cultural figures on television, screen, in video games, boxing and wrestling matches, the use of fists and agile feet deeply encode the hegemonic representation of masculinity. Even as the pantheon of cultural superheroes real and fantasy, such as Mike Tyson, Dennis Rodman, Schwarzenegger's "Terminator" and Stallone's "Rambo," are supplemented by cultural representations of the "New Man" who is a more fitting partner for the stronger images of the liberated woman—Kevin Costner's Robin Hood or Keaton's Batman, for instance—these more "sensitive" heroes are also still skilled and courageous physical fighters. They become "real men" because they can, when inevitably called upon to do so, physically vanquish the villain and save the female "victim."

The presence of spectators is a key element. The performance of fighting in settings such as the playground, the boxing ring, the movie theater, the sports arena is not only rousing entertainment for an audience, but a reinscription of an abstract masculine power. This performance is affirmed by ardent spectators, mostly men but some women, who consume the ritualistic enactment of raw, body power. Video games are an excellent example of how even males who avoid physical aggressive behavior in their own personal life symbolically perform a violent masculinity in order to play the game at all.[10]

For Troublemakers, who are already sidelined as academic failures, one route to making a name for yourself, for expressing "normalcy," competency, and humanity, is through this identification with physical power. Once again, a sense of anger and frustration born of marginalization in school intensifies the nature of these performances.

Race makes a difference in how physical power is constituted and perceived. African American boys draw on a specific repertoire of racial images as well as the lived experience and popular knowledge from the world outside the school. Most of the black boys live in an environment where being mentally and physically prepared to stand up for oneself through words and deeds is crucial. However, there is another reason specifically grounded in the history and evolution of race relations in the United States. Up to the 1960s, physical violence wielded by whites in the form of individuals, mobs, or the state was the instrument used to police the racial order; demonstrations of male privilege or assertions of rights on the part of black men was the cause for brutal retaliation. The prevailing wisdom in black communities was that in order to survive males had to be carefully taught to mask any show of power in confrontations with whites. With the emergence of Black Power as an ideology and a practice, the right of black men to stand up for their manhood and their racial pride through physical force was asserted. This was the right to have the physical privileges of white men. This "right" is inculcated into young black males in family and community, many of whom are taught, "Don't let anyone take advantage of you. If someone hits you, you hit them back." First blows are not always physical, but sometimes symbolic; racial epithets are violent attacks. A physical response is especially likely on the part of the Troublemakers, who have a heightened racial consciousness.

Simultaneously, this manifestation of physicality is the very material presence that the school seeks to exclude: black males are already seen as embodying the violence and aggression that will drive away "desirable" families and their children. Fighting on the part of black boys is more visible as a problem, so it is viewed with extreme concern and responded to more swiftly and harshly. Once again, the process of adultification of black male behavior frames the act as symptomatic of dangerous tendencies. The Troublemakers, who have already been labeled bound for jail, have little to lose and everything to gain in using this form of rule breaking as a way of making a name for themselves, gaining recognition through performances of masculinity.

Notes

1. Judith Butler, "Performative Acts and Gender Constitution: An Essay in Phenomenology and Feminist Theory," *Theatre Journal* 40, no. 4 (1988).

2. Judith Buder, *Bodies That Matter: On the Discursive Limits of "Sex"* (New York: Routledge, 1993), 95.

3. Douglas E. Foley, *Learning Capitalist Culture: Deep in the Heart of Texas* (Philadelphia: University of Pennsylvania, 1990).

4. Geneva Smitherman, *Talkin and Testifyin: Language of Black America* (Detroit: J Wayne State University Press, 1977); Lawrence Levine, *Black Culture and Black Consciousness: Afro-American Folk Thought from Slavery to Freedom* (New York: Oxford University Press, 1977); Philip Brian Harper, *Are We Not Men? Masculine Anxiety and the Problem of African-American Identity* (New York: Oxford University Press, 1996); Keith Gilyard, *Voices of the Self: A Study of Language Competence* (Detroit: Wayne State University Press, 1991).

5. Smitherman, *Talkin and Testifyin*, 80.

6. Harper, *Are We Not Men?* 11.

7. One quarter of the 1,252 referrals to the Punishing Room were for fighting; four-fifths of the incidents involved boys, nine out of ten of whom were African Americans. All except three of the girls who were in fights were black.

8. For a full discussion of this strategy see Marjorie Harness Goodwin, *He Said—She-Said: Talk as a Social Organization among Black Children* (Bloomington: Indiana University Press, 1990).

9. In the U.S. context, we see passionate public embraces between males in certain high-contact team sports such as football, basketball, and soccer in moments of great emotion. It is less likely to be witnessed in sports such as tennis or golf where team camaraderie cannot develop or where the masculinity of the participants is not so indubitably demonstrated.

10. R. W. Connell, "Teaching the Boys: New Research on Masculinity and Gender Strategies for Schools," *Teachers College Record* 98, no. 2 (1996).

CHAPTER 18

Epic Glory and Manhood Acts in Fantasy Role-Playing

Dagorhir as a Case Study

James S. Martin, Christian A. Vaccaro,
D. Alex Heckert, and Robert Heasley

Introduction

Every Sunday, in a quad of a northeastern college, nearly 20 men, in their early to late 20s, battle as knights and warriors. The men equip themselves with various swords, shields, and armors crafted from old furniture scraps, wood, and plastic pipes, which are wrapped in foam and cloth. They use their "weapons" to engage in a simulated game revolving around archaic military combat. While their foam weapons are not crafted with the purpose of injuring anyone, participants simulate death cries when struck by their opponents. The winner cries out in victory, proclaiming his glory to an imaginary king, clan, tribe, or army. Once the battle is complete, the losers rise from the place of the simulated death and the battle starts again. As this happens, other college students watch this turn of events from a distance. One mutters to another as commentary of the events they just observed, "What a bunch of nerds."

Dagorhir Outdoor Improvisational Battle Games (shortened as Dagorhir) combines both history and fantasy, allowing players to interact as historical or fictional characters. The activity of Dagorhir is very similar to what outsiders call Live Action Role Playing or LARPing, but members of this group reject the term for a number of reasons.[1] Some of the actions in Dagorhir may involve fantastic acts such as "defeating an invading group of orcs [monsters]" by simulating combat with foam swords and arrows known as "boffers." In addition, participants regularly engage in conversations as historical characters with manners, language, and dress that reflect the culture of the period. Participants also dress according to a genre that is characteristic of the game, such as in a knight's armor or Victorian/ Tudor dress of historical England. Importantly, these participants follow rules for interaction which are agreed upon by individual group members and reflect rules established by a national network of organizations that span nationally and internationally. Larger Dagorhir events, which are called battles, are generally held in a restricted social space, primarily in a rented outdoor field. Small Dagorhir events and practices, however, are generally held at public venues.

The Dagorhir organization was founded in 1977 by Brian Wiese and was later popularized by others in the early 1980s (Tresca, 2011). Wiese's intention was to simulate, through the use of foam

SOURCE: Martin, J. S., Vaccaro, C. A, Heckert, D. A., and Heasley, R. (2015). Epic Glory and Manhood Acts in Fantasy Role-Playing: Dagorhir as a Case Study. *Journal of Men's Studies*, 23(3), 293–314. Reproduced with permission.

weapons and armor, fantasy themed battles. Dagorhir can be considered a form of fantasy play because of its chronological inconsistency between time and space in scenarios as well as use of characters that askew historical fact and physical reality. For example, events include a mix of historical, fantasy, and mythological themes and characters much like the fantasy role-playing board game Dungeons & Dragons (Fine, 1983). In some ways, Dagorhir can also be likened to children's games such as Athenians and Spartans, Cowboys and Indians, and war play but is far more complex in its organization, rules, and stories and also involves mainly adolescents and adults.

The focus of this particular study is on several groups of Dagorhir players in the Northeastern United States and, in particular, a nearly all-male group of players that practice on the college quad of Public North East University (PNEU). These groups are labeled by many outsiders as "nerds." Similarly, many insiders also identify as such. For instance, a member of a Dagorhir organization named Arin[2] said, "We're a dorky, nerdy, geeky bunch at heart. It's what makes us run around in our fantasy world and hit people with foam." In this context, both through external labeling and self-identification, Dagorhir can be categorized as a nerd group. Central to our focus on this group is the common depiction of their subordinate status as men, which make them ideal to further sociological understanding of how definitions of manhood get constructed and enacted within low-status groups.

Review of Literature

Nerds and Nerd Groups

To date, the sociological research on nerds as a social group has been sparse. The focus of extant literature has generally painted nerds as outcasts and examined the negative consequences of this label (Rentzsch, Schutz, & Schroder-Abe, 2011). Nugent (2008) identified four common characteristics of people labeled as nerds: emotional withdrawal, disinterest in traditional physical sport, emphasis on logic, and social exclusion. Awkward interactions, interest in extreme intellectual and/or esoteric topics, and stigmatized body types (glasses, obese, slovenly dress) are also often used by others as symbolic identifiers for nerd status. Those who become labeled as nerds may try to limit social interaction, which may provide explanation for the view that nerds experience social isolation (Evans & Eder, 1993). Related to this, research on nerds tends to be conflated with those who are bullied and isolated within the social context of schools (Brady, 2014; Suitor & Carter, 1999). For example, Bishop et al. (2004) found that students labeled as "nerds" are individuals who tended to be more studious in their academic pursuits and were less institutionally valued than individual students who engaged in group athletics. While it is typical to focus on the negative consequences and isolation of individuals labeled as nerds, it is important to explore the possibility that nerd status is also part of group association.

Extant research on nerd groups tends to focus on group interactions that either help discard the negative label or reframe it into a positive one. For instance, Kinney (1993) demonstrated how group interaction helped shed stigmatized labels, such as "nerd," and allowed members to become less socially awkward. Other groups help redefine nerd-like behavior as masculine and cool, departing from the stereotypical tough guy mind-set and appearance (Cooper, 2000; Wilson, 2002). Other research demonstrates how nerd groups create alternative subcultures whereby nonconformity can be revered, as in the case of teenage groups refusing to smoke as a way to act "cool" (Plumridge, Fitzgerald, & Abel, 2002). Others suggest that groups allow for "nerd" labels to be transformed into something more positive (Ciciora, 2009). Although this research examines how groups help, in some way or another, to transform the stigma of the nerd identity, it neglects a focus on the gendered aspects of these processes including exploring the possibility that they may, intentionally or unintentionally, reproduce inequality regimes (Acker, 2006).

Manhood and Nerds

For many years, the sociological literature on men as gendered beings has focused its attention on masculinity as a "configuration of gender practices" and the notion that there are "multiple masculinities" with some fitting the hegemonic ideal and others subordinate to this status (Connell, 2005). In this line, research on nerd masculinity has emerged as a particular configuration of practices that conform to elements of both hegemonic and subordinate masculinity (Cooper, 2000; Kendall, 1999). For instance, Kendall's (1999) research on nerd masculinity demonstrates how aspects of hypermasculinity such as an intense focus on work skills and disregard for social skills are combined with elements of femininity such as disinterest and lack of talent in sports. Kendall (1999) suggested that elements of nerd masculinity increasingly link to the hegemonic ideal because of the trend of computer professionals occupying high-level positions within the employment structure.

Although the multiple masculinities perspective has helped adjust the research focus away from masculinity as monolithic and static gender role and toward acknowledging the power and privilege behind the status, it has paid too much attention on creating typologies of men and not enough on the commonalities between them (Schrock & Schwalbe, 2009). This is particularly true when it comes to the social practices and processes that simultaneously signify belonging to the gender category of manhood while subordinating others. Schrock and Schwalbe (2009) have forwarded the "manhood acts" perspective, which delineates common processes that males use to signify themselves as real men. Manhood acts consist of social interactions that elicit deference, resist exploitation from others, and assert control over others, self, and environment. These techniques are strategically used in social interactions to both subordinate others and signify manhood. Because the nerd subculture is largely male, but considered subordinate, this context provides an opportunity to explore if and how nerds act in ways that dominate others through their actions. Sociological exploration of male nerds from the manhood acts perspective (Schrock & Schwalbe, 2009) has yet to be researched and can likely contribute to our more general understanding of men as gendered beings.

Self-Enhancement, Glorified-Self, and Manhood Acts

Much of the underlying processes related to the manhood acts perspective can be cast under the principle of self-enhancement. Self-enhancement is a psychological principle whereby individuals favor positive stimuli that augment self-conceptions and protect against negative evaluations of the self (Sedikides, 1993). One particular, and extreme, form of self-enhancement is identified by Adler and Adler (1989) as the "glorified-self." The glorified-self is an aggrandized version of selfhood resulting from internalization of fame. Adler and Adler (1989) found in their research on university basketball players that glorified-selfhood was a consequence of complex group interactions between teammates, coaches, media, and fans that at times inhibited, but ultimately enhanced the self toward internalization of a revered celebrity status. Important to this study, Adler and Adler's (1989) research demonstrated that self-enhancement can be conceptualized beyond a cognitive strategy to also include identification of generic processes of complex group interactions that result in self-enhancement over time. Relatedly, gender scholars have long noted that manhood is a revered social status imbued with power, privilege, and prestige (Acker, 2006; Connell, 1987). In particular, Connell (2005) noted that hegemonic masculine status is "the most honored" form of manhood (p. 849). And the manhood acts perspective delineates some generic processes of self-enhancement that, as we will demonstrate, link to a glorified version of gendered selfhood.

The objective of our study of men who participate in Dagorhir was to utilize the manhood acts perspective as a framework for better understanding how subordinate men enhance their sense of selfhood. In addition, we use the manhood acts perspective to understand if such self-enhancement strategies contribute to the reproduction of inequality and gender stratification within this subcultural setting.

Settings and Methods

Data for this study derive from 10 months of fieldwork and 18 direct interviews of Dagorhir players.[3] During the study, the first author observed 30 practice sessions of a Dagorhir group, which held practice in the quads of PNEU. The first author also observed three larger gatherings of multiple chapters of Dagorhir and two discussion sessions of Dagorhir events.

Each of the 18 interviews lasted approximately 1 hr. The purposes of the interviews were to gather information from members about their participation in Dagorhir, the subcultural aspects of the group, and how members identify with the Dagorhir group. Interviewing men about their identities and, in particular, masculinity can be perceived as a threat to their credibility and lead to defensiveness and/or shutting down. Thus, the first author approached questions about how Dagorhir membership may also link to manhood through indirect questioning[4] during interviews (Schwalbe & Wolkomir, 2001). During practices and events, the first author also questioned participants about how they handle themselves when harassed by outsiders.

The Dagorhir PNEU college chapter was founded in 2004 and named "The Oaks." Participants were mostly men (15 of 18 members), and all members were White. At the time the Oaks was founded, Dagorhir was already established nationwide, with hundreds of active chapters. The Oaks chapter was founded by three men and two of the chapter founders, Ryuji and Strider (their Dagorhir character-names), were still active members at the time of the study.

In addition to interviewing members of PNEU, the first author also observed, created field notes, and informally interviewed participants at three regional Dagorhir battles: "Battle of Grand Summit" in September 2011, "Winter Invasion" in February 2012, and "Fires of Purgatory" in April 2012. Aside from "The Oaks," other chapters such as the "Triumvirate Phalanx" and the "Orc Monsters" participated in these events. It was at these events where multiple chapters met, battled, and socialized. Because each of the battles consisted of over one hundred members and a day's worth of activity, the first author captured many conversations about Dagorhir and viewed, firsthand, the unfolding of events. The first author also "lurked" on Dagorhir-themed Internet forums and discussions to get a clear understanding of mythology and of the culture of Dagorhir as a whole (Hine, 2000).

Qualitative Analytical Methods

Analysis proceeded inductively using a modified form of grounded theory (Charmaz, 2006; Glaser & Strauss, 1967) to derive emergent themes within the data. Upon review of the field notes and interviews, we found Dagorhir members identified with the term *nerd* and came to learn that the nerd label was viewed by group members as relating to a deep investment in a task or hobby such as Dagorhir. What we came to understand during our early analysis of data was that gender identity played a far greater role within group interactions than originally anticipated.[5] Realizing that Dagorhir's focus on battle and conquest incorporated an abundance of opportunities to signify a masculine self, we were broadsided by our own oversight of the key focus on manhood. After all, war, battle, and violent conquest are part and parcel of gender hegemony, which was the main focus of the practice and simulated combat in the group. We came to see that participation had the effect of valorizing, in Arin's words, "a dorky, nerdy, geeky bunch" of male participants into real men.

Beyond the act of fighting, complementary themes within the data emerged, including heavy drinking, a focus on real and fantasized pain, and a conquest for producing a glorified version of the self (Adler & Adler, 1989). As these themes coalesced, we began to see how they also related to gendered signification.

The first author's self-identification as a fellow "nerd" was also important to our analysis. Because of this identity, the authors had access to the unique orientation, language, and understanding of "nerd" topics that made them more readily available for sociological analysis. It also helped in gaining access to the group and facilitated sympathetic understanding (Blumer, 1969) of the members within the Dagorhir organization. At times, however, the orientation of the first author as a nerd/researcher blinded him to some phenomena, but this myopia was reduced by continually sharing ideas, data, themes, and initial analyses with the other authors who do not self-identify as nerds. This procedure acted as a check and balance against blindness and bias to the other themes within the data.

Gendered Participation in Dagorhir

The enumeration of members in Dagorhir practices and events suggests that it is a masculine arena. For instance, more than 80% of members in the PNEU chapter were men, and this ratio was reflective of other chapters as well. Photographs taken during and after events were generally helpful in documenting the gender composition of membership, which clearly demonstrated that there were many more men than women. Almost every Dagorhir group, or "tribe," takes photos during events. For instance, the group photo of the tribe "Triumvirate Phalanx" at the Battle of Grand Summit documented only one woman member among their 44 person army (97% male). The count of the "Orc Monsters" tribe revealed that of the 23 members, 19 of them were men (82%). Other tribes, such as the "Fantasia," had a greater proportion of women members, but photos suggested that the group was comprised of about 10 women compared with 20 men (66%). By combining photographic data with official participant counts at the Battle of Grand Summit, we estimate that of the 378 participants, between 78% and 85% were men. Photographs and field jottings suggest that roughly 40 women participated in battle and an additional 40 women were documented in costume and gear that was inconsistent with battle role-playing.[6] We were unable to get as accurate of estimates for ratios of men and women during the Winter Invasion and Fires of Purgatory battles, but the first author found no indicators that gender composition significantly deviated from the other events.

Similar percentages indicating the overwhelming participation by men are consistent in publicly available data found on Dagorhir-themed websites. Photographs from the website of the Triumvirate Phalanx demonstrate that approximately 85% of participants in affiliated clubs in the North Eastern United States were men (n-male = 189 of N = 220). However, website data are also not comprehensive, as many more participants take part in events than what the websites suggest. Nonetheless, we conjecture that members who are featured on websites likely comprise the group core and reflect the overall gender composition of its members.

Participant counts were complicated by a gendered division of labor whereby only some members of each tribe took part in the "battle" portion of the events while others did not. Although "battle" was viewed by participants as the central activity, many women opted out of it in favor of other types of labors such as taking care of the tribe's encampments. Women who participated in battle often dressed and acted as men. In fact, similar to girl high school basketball players who act like boys (Pascoe, 2011) some women go to great lengths to transform themselves into convincing male characters in Dagorhir battles. This made it complicated to accurately quantify the gender population during Dagorhir events, which were often chaotic and disorganized, but in many ways reinforce our claim that Dagorhir is a male-centric arena.

Gendered Opportunities and Participation in Dagorhir

While the data generally confirm that males comprise a majority of participants, the occupants of leadership positions in Dagorhir also suggest a preference for men. For instance, during the Fires of Purgatory battle, men comprised the majority of participants involved in administrative tasks for the events, such as treasurers, marshals, and referees. Similarly, during the Battle of Grand Summit, two of the three Fantasia tribe members who acted as garrisons for the encampment were men, including a young male college student and a man in his late 30s. In the Triumvirate Phalanx tribe, the leaders of this group including "Caesar," secretary, treasurer, head minister, and field marshal were all men. In addition, the "heralds," which is the name for the referees in this type of event, were all men. At PNEU, the three founding members and the historical executive committee of the Oaks tribe were men who were revered by other members as the most meritorious warriors within the group. The gender composition of leadership within the Oaks changed from an all-male leadership team recently, just prior to the initiation of the research, with the selection of women as president and treasurer. Yet, it should be noted that the group's decision to select women as executives was based on their previous experience doing campus administrative work rather than their credentials as warriors. In fact, only one woman in the chapter was regarded by others as an experienced "warrior." In sum, men generally benefit from the leadership structure because advancement into these positions is usually contingent upon the ability to fight well in battle, in which women—as we will demonstrate—are typically denied opportunity.

While not every participant in Dagorhir can be a leader, all members can select from a multitude of characters from fantasy fiction and historical stories to emulate in battle. These "super-human" characters include orcs, elves, dwarfs, halflings, and many others in the cavalcade of Dagorhir characters. While it is permissible for group participants to present themselves as a myriad of characters, the universe of character traits among Dagorhir members at PNEU was limited and more often related to manhood than womanhood. For instance, a person mimicking an elf character might try to convey a super-human ability for rational action, a trait of manhood (Connell, 2005), by presenting a sense of calmness in their fighting tactics (Vaccaro, Schrock, & McCabe, 2011). Similarly, characters often must conform to medieval or medieval-fantasy lore, which entails a gendered environment where women are generally constructed as a weaker sex. Participants most commonly selected medieval characters, including knights, paladins, squires, wizards, and barbarians; women warrior types were nearly absent from this spectrum of characters.

Another often used character was the Orc. Orcs, which are part of the Orc Monster tribe, relate to masculinity in a strikingly straightforward manner. They are—by definition—all male. Similarly, they are described as "thuggish, muscular, green, boar faced men" (Tolkien, 1954). These characters are said to be assembled by a wizard from the corpses of dead elves in "flesh pits" (Tolkien, 1954). Participants who adopt the Orc character mythologize their motivation in battles as guided by a desire to pillage, destroy, and participate in other forms of domination which connect them closely to manhood acts (Schrock & Schwalbe, 2009). Participants who enacted Orc characters fought with clubs and carried them in ways meant to convey that the weapons are both primitive and require a great deal of strength to hold. Orc characters were often observed charging into the mock battles without a plan or strategy, which conveyed their reckless abandon. Some participants painted their bodies green and wore costumes that looked like a hide of a boar. Sometimes the Orc characters kept pieces of others' armor, plastic gold, and event entry badges as trophies of their "kill." These trinkets were worn around the neck to designate that they had killed or dominated many other characters. When interviewed,[7] Orc characters acted aggressively and assertively, including yelling obscenities in an attempt to be intimidating, exemplifying manhood acts (Schrock & Schwalbe, 2009).

Other groups, such as the knights, adhere to chivalry, a code of ethics originally used by male warrior aristocrats (Saul, 2011). The members mythologize their knight characters as being granted social power by God and as a result, their demonstration of chivalry simultaneously signifies them as privileged men. In fact, characters that designated themselves as the "good guy" implied a chivalrous code of the ethics. For instance, Ryuji, a founding member of PNEU Dagorhir group, stated that he follows the Japanese code of Bushido chivalry to be "a better man" both inside and outside Dagorhir. While the main goal is to stay in character and is not perceived as purposefully intended to exclude or demean women, character roles and rules tended to value traditional masculinity at the exclusion of women and qualities associated with femininity.

It is important to note that there are neither rules barring women from battle nor are there any rules barring all-women Dagorhir groups. In fact, there are character groups in fantasy works of fiction that are both gender neutral and all female, which would imply that at least some Dagorhir tribes would reflect this diversity. Despite the availability of female and gender neutral character types, we did not record an instance of an all-female tribe either at PNEU or larger regional gatherings. One reason for this might be there is not a significant population of women (or men) who wish to enact all-female characters as part of their participation. More likely, as we assume, the omission of all-female tribes indicates that masculine characters are most highly valued among Dagorhir members.

Costumes in Dagorhir also venerated manhood. First and foremost, costumes helped create a more believable experience that participants were a part of a medieval or fantasy world. Men were most likely to dress in elaborate costumes that signified their warrior status. Similarly, to signify belonging to the warrior class of members, women often dressed as men. We counted at least 11 women dressed as men during battles and practices. Women, costumed as men, at times bound their chest, adorned themselves with war paint, and were garbed in bulky clothing to give the appearance that they were men or young boys. The suggested intent for women to dress as masculine characters reflected a general desire expressed in interviews to be taken seriously as warriors. Conversely, men rarely switched their gender. In fact, only one man was observed donning a woman's wig and mincing around the battlefield in an attempt to distract other male participants in a mocking fashion.

Most women warrior participants in Dagorhir adopted characters that employed archery as their primary combat skill, which turned out to be a feminized weapon within the group culture. For instance, five of eight women on the "Cavalier's" official website are pictured with a bow and arrow with the other three women unarmed. However, none of the 22 men in the tribe were photographed holding a bow and arrows. This is interesting considering the prevailing assumptions about archery skills, which include having strong upper-body strength and possessing a flat chest that facilitates aiming and firing arrows effortlessly. These assumptions have traditionally devalued women's bodies in comparison with men's. To counter these assumptions, many women archers would note the legend of Amazonian female warriors who would "'pinch out' or 'cauterize'" the right breast to compensate (Wilde, 1999). Despite their veneration of Amazonian resolve, women archers were often observed using a rule within the game titled the "suicide option" when their battle line was routed, which signified that they are no longer a fair target in game-play. The rationale given to the first author for the use of the "suicide option" is that the archer's bow and arrows are expensive and easily broken, and this helps save equipment. Yet, because women were often encouraged to become archers and were taught to use the "suicide option," it might also function to avoid breaching norms that proscribe women and men from sharing symbolic space as equals in "battle." This seemed to relate to broader cultural debates about women in combat roles (Boykin, 2013). We found that breaking other equipment was less of a concern. In fact, the first author observed multiple instances of participants bragging about breaking swords, clubs, daggers, spears, and flails during battle, which seemed to signify manhood.

During an informal interview, a female member of PNEU, named Homunculus, talked about the female archer stereotype, "[they are] the girlfriend who gets dragged [into participating] and if she fights at all, she's going to do archery instead of like actually fighting." Homunculus noted that there are differences in the types of participation of women, with some joining battles reluctantly and others joining willingly. It is likely that, for women, being relegated to the position of an archer is a form of group boundary maintenance (Schwalbe & Mason-Schrock, 1996) that reflects a devaluing of women members.

Other non-combat roles within a tribe, such as a scribe or members of the band, are regularly performed by women, and these roles were often devalued. For instance, one woman scribe said in a deflated tone, "I just take pictures for the website. I do not actually fight. I just call myself the scribe to fit in." The first author observed four women performing these lower status roles as opposed to only one man playing the drums and another man acting as a "servant" to the "Emperor of the Triumvirate." These roles themselves do not always have gendered connotations, yet the activity and its value seemed to be reserved for lower status members.

As the descriptions above suggest, participation in Dagorhir is a gendered phenomenon. Men comprise the majority of members overall as well as members in leadership positions in Dagorhir, which we suggest is a reflection of the higher regard given to them within the group. Similarly, opportunities available to enhance one's status within the group, such as selecting a character type and using weaponry, also seemed to prefer men and exclude women. We have demonstrated thus far that these two phenomena are not exclusive of one another but, instead, reflect the support for the signification of manhood as the most honored gender in Dagorhir (Connell, 2005).

Gendered Behavior in Dagorhir: Epic Glory

We have established that Dagorhir is both designed and played out in the context of this research as being structured with opportunities for increasing the status among male members. Here, we argue that Dagorhir is also an organization that, above all else, exalts behaviors that glorify the self. This is exhibited through playing off of the ample use of the word "epic" among Dagorhir members to describe acts that present oneself as heroic or legendary within the group. We call this type of glorification "epic glory." Importantly, asserting epic glory allows participants to associate their actions with revered warriors of historical and mythical lore, and positions them as dominants. Because the arena of Dagorhir favors men, the stories and characters that were epically glorified also tended most often to signify manhood. We demonstrate that opportunities to glorify the self are inherent in the training, fighting, and "dying" in Dagorhir activity. Importantly, threats to glory come from onlookers and hecklers. Obstacles to glory largely affect women participants and reproduce gender inequality.

Epic Glory in Training

Much like men in the sport of mixed martial arts (Vaccaro et al., 2011), it is unusual for new members to have, without a great deal of practice, the ideal kinesthetic and perceptual skill needed to be immediately competent at sparring and fighting. New members rarely have held a Dagorhir sword or weapon prior to joining a group, much less used one in a mock battle. Most new members, therefore, do not have the correct physical self-awareness to fight effectively with a boffer (foam weapon). This fact is quickly made evident to many of the new members as they have no idea when and where to block or strike during sparring, and therefore typically find themselves on the receiving end of a boffer and quickly put out of the game.

Learning the skill to be a competent player in Dagorhir also includes rituals that can enhance one's epic glory. For instance, the PNEU tribe required that "newbies" defeat every member in one-on-one combat before they were allowed to establish a character of their own choosing. The first author observed a newer member, a 16-year-old boy who had been introduced to Dagorhir by his father and named by the group "Random Character Number 42," as he underwent this rite of passage. His given name, "Random Character Number 42," signified that he had yet to earn enough status in the group to be given a "real" character-name. In fact, many new members are given humorous character-names that reflect their low status such as "Dinky Pooter," "Scruffy," "Shithouse," and, in the case of one woman who wanted to be called Tisk, "Tits." Random Character Number 42 lost more than 40 times before he managed to achieve the stated goal. His final competitor was Ryuji, the most skilled member of the group, who did not hold back his attacks. After 10 unsuccessful attempts, bruised and exhausted, the new member mustered up his last amount of strength and managed to "pierce" Ryuji in his gut. Ryuji then fell to the ground in a glorious manner. As Ryuji lay on the ground, someone started the celebration for Number 42 by playing the song, "You're the Best Around," by Joe Esposito on their iPad. The group members began to cheer loudly for Number 42, then picked him up and carried him on their shoulders. After his ordeal, Number 42 would be allowed to create his own name and construct his character for the next battle. Thus, new members move from giving deference to eliciting deference; in terms of the manhood acts perspective.

Along with teaching and practicing choreographed drills and sparring, other physical fitness activities are built in the training regimes such as calisthenics and running. For instance, the "Spartan" tribe made it a requirement for members to pass a physical test to participate in battles, which included 20 push-ups and a mile run in full battle gear. Members stated that physical training prior to a battle helped them "level up," which characterized their activity as helping them become better warriors. This also drew parallels of themselves to the manly warriors found in video games. While physical training alone is not necessarily a masculine activity, the exercises observed in this study were imbued with historical and fictional meanings of war that linked them to masculinity. It was common to see veteran members of tribes acting similar to a military drill instructor, yelling overtop of members to work harder and toughen up.

Despite the emphasis on training and physical fitness, observation suggested that such training was not necessary for participation in battles as each event typically lasted around 10 minutes and required a nominal amount of physical activity. In fact, many of the participants were not in peak physical health; some were overweight and others underweight, but few appeared to have difficulty participating. So why was physical training prior to an event important to members? It was because the interaction offered an opportunity for participants to glorify their chosen character. "Peet the Goblin" expressed the notion that his tribe's physical training provided the opportunity to "just yell at each other for five or so minutes to get ready to go." Here Peet is suggesting that the training and concomitant yelling and military-like drills help participants prepare to think, feel, and identify their actions in military—and hyper-masculine—terms.

Another way that tribe members earned greater status was by being ritually beaten by group members with their boffers. Peet also discussed his advancement in the organization through this ritual:

[We have a] little initiation . . . we take . . . a three-foot sword or club or something like that and for a given amount of time we will beat on you to make you tougher . . . It's a cool ceremony. It's very powerful. I mean very testosterone manly sort of thing. Even just being an outsider and watching it, you get moved by it. Your heart rate will jump. And you will want to join in because it's very primal. I love it. It's so cool.

These interactions suggest that getting into character requires putting on a front of toughness found in the epic glory of training, which links to signifying manhood (Schrock & Schwalbe, 2009). It also resonates with joining other groups that "enact manhood" through initiation ceremonies such as fraternities and gangs.

Epic Glory in Fighting

Because Dagorhir is a fighting activity, battle exposure was a means to epically glorify the self. Fifteen of the 17 people in the Oaks tribe interviewed expressed that their main interest for joining Dagorhir was for the chance of fighting in battles. Conversely, only 9 members expressed a direct interest in enacting fantasy and historical aspects in Dagorhir. Fighting was a main interest because it provided an opportunity to act gloriously. In fact, the founder, Bryan Weise, claimed to have designed the game "to capture that spirit of adventure that could only come from wielding a sword or bow."

In essence, if you are feared and respected on the battlefield, you are epically glorious. Victor, a knight, puts this succinctly:

> You know if you are beating ninety percent of the people that you fight it's a pretty good sign that you're darn good. Especially large groups of new kids will flock to those guys . . . when someone is winning and winning and winning they sort of take on a minor celebrity status.

Gobbler, a member of the PNEU chapter, suggests that in addition to winning the retelling of the epic events is important. He said, "Through their exploits on the battlefield, winning . . . and other things that people talk about. If people talk about your exploits, everybody will know who you are." In addition, epic-glorified status can be conferred by fighting well-known "celebrity" members. Monk Forthwind says of this, "If somebody sparred with 'Bird of Prey' and won, that person would be known as the man who beat 'Bird of Prey.'" In short, the more you fight, the more you win, and the more you defeat well-known fighters the more epic glory you will gain within the Dagorhir community.

Yet, fighting alone is not enough; how you fight is also important in gaining epic glory. This included adopting the values of Dagorhir, dressing like a Dagorhir member, and creating a Dagorhir identity in addition to fighting. In fact, fighting without giving proper respect to the tribe in this manner is somewhat taboo. Dangerous Brother, a female fighter, refers to people who neglect these other aspects as "stick jocks," which held negative connotations within the Dagorhir community. Therefore, fighting is a part of glory, but had to be affirmed by participating in other epic Dagorhir activities. Monk Forthwind talks about how gaining epic glory includes things beyond fighting:

> If you got good skills, fight against seasoned warriors, and you can talk about it, glory is a real bonding experience. . . . Yes, glory is about friendship . . . It's what binds us together. We all share in each other's glory.

Glory in Death

Observation of battles suggests that newer participants tend not to win very often and this can, at first, be seen as a barrier to the rewards of epic glory. More often than not, most new warriors tended to be first "causalities" during the battles. It was even common during the pre-battle events that the veteran warriors would practice their winning techniques on their lesser experienced peers. For instance, Assassin Creed said, "I want to be popular, but I can't seem to win. I am just a new member." On its face, this suggests that veteran members only have access to the reward of epic glory and surfaces an important question: Why would new members continue to fight in Dagorhir if they were generally the first to be defeated in battle? It is because new members learn that winning the battle is not the only measure of success.

As a way to make losing an entertaining part of Dagorhir battles, members learn that pretending to die in a dramatic way is glorious. This type of epic glory is called by participants an "Epic Death." As one member explained, "(It is) called Epic Death because it comes from the word Epic Fail. The death is so horrible that you cannot help but watch it." Observation of epic deaths during battles included people screaming in pain, imitating that their arm was severed, or pretending that the impact from a foam weapon caused the victim to fly off their feet. When a participant loses in Dagorhir, they are not simply out of the game, but a part of the process of creating a glorious battle scene. New warriors quickly learn that acting out an epically dramatized death is an important and fun part of the battle activity and the character building process. The Dagorhir official webpage illustrates that fighting gloriously, whether living through the battle or epically dying in the fight, confers immortality:

Will you listen to the bards sing tales of valor? Or will songs of your valor inspire enduring legends down through the ages? King Arthur and his Knights of the Round Table stood bravely, earning immortality in legend, literature and song. Will you?

In this way, all members are offered opportunity to bolster their characters regardless of who is the actual victor. One motivation for participants to act out an "epic death" is the reward of "regeneration." If noticed by a herald, the "dead victim" can be granted the opportunity to come "back to life" and fight again in the same battle. In addition, participants are also motivated in part by the chance that other participants will notice and valorize their dramatic death after the battle has completed.

Threats to Glory: Onlookers and Hecklers

Dagorhir is most widely associated with general culture as an organization filled with "nerds and geeks . . . playing make-believe" (DeMeglio, 2010). During private events, this status does not pose a problem because it is insulated from outsiders and there is a shared acceptance of the behavior from insiders. However, spectators at PNEU Dagorhir events often gathered during practices held at the college quad including those who occasionally heckled Dagorhir members and caused intermittent interruptions. As such, hecklers were considered a threat to the epic glory of Dagorhir members. The chapter integrated this ongoing threat of harassment by policing it (Schwalbe & Mason-Schrock, 1996).

Most outsiders to Dagorhir do not intentionally harass members, but are piqued by their unusual public behavior and dress. It was a regular occurrence to see a few onlookers give various facial expressions of confusion, interest, or disgust toward the PNEU group. Without prior context, some PNEU students confused Dagorhir as a theatrical practice or performance, while others pointed out that they saw Dagorhir on television or in the movies. Onlookers often had the impression that Dagorhir is a deviant act. As an onlooker turned onetime participant stated, "I would not want to be caught wearing those outfits . . . My friends would call me a nerd." Despite onlookers rarely voicing opinions of Dagorhir members out loud, a minority of onlookers created problems. For instance, a few reportedly stole some of the group's equipment as a prank, and members complained that at times: "We (have) had a bunch of (hecklers) making fun of us because we are just like (those people on TV)." While rare, hecklers constituted a threat that could directly delegitimize Dagorhir's epic glory.

The most common way members handled the uninformed onlookers was to reframe their presence as unimportant to the battle. Peet's account of onlookers reflected the classic technique of neutralization, condemning the condemners (Sykes & Matza, 1957) as he explained, "I really don't care what they are doing. Their lives are boring and mundane." Other members incorporated the presence of non-members into the action as "NPCs" or non-player characters. While unnecessary, these NPCs could help members establish that a setting is inhabited by more than just the actors of the story. By reframing outsiders as unimportant or part of the story as NPCs, Dagorhir members put their action as central and important which helped retain the legitimacy of their epic glory.

Because "the Oaks" group was a public organization, all university students are allowed to pick up a foam sword and battle with other members. Thus, Dagorhir members also used this rule of open membership to their advantage when trying to disarm hecklers or skeptical onlookers. Taylor recalled an event where a few hecklers approached the Oaks. "Ryuji gave one of them a broad sword. He said, 'you try it then!' In turn, Ryuji picked up a sword and began to fight one of the (hecklers). Needless to say, Ryuji kicked his butt." Similar stories of members chasing off thieves or yelling back at drive-by hecklers were commonplace during meetings. For instance, Peet suggests, "(The) people that steal from us . . . we have swords and we will give them a beating." These stories reinforce all three components of manhood acts (Schrock & Schwalbe, 2009); "kicking butt" and "give them a beating" suggest eliciting deference and asserting control in the effort to resist exploitation by menacing hecklers.

Although five separate instances of a person or a group of people briefly verbally harassing members of the PNEU Oaks were observed over the period of the study, no acts of physical harassment toward members were observed. This was consistent with members' testimony that more direct and violent forms of harassment were rare. Yet, stories of warding off violent and serious hecklers served as an important means for coalescing group identity, which was also viewed as an epically glorious act and related to signifying manhood (Schrock & Schwalbe, 2009).

Obstacles to Glory: Gender

While members recognized that more males tend to participate and be attracted to the organization, male members rarely reflected on how gendered performance related to Dagorhir identity. It was seldom during formal interviews that male members of the Oaks would overtly reflect on their participation and character identity in relation to masculine gendered norms. Yet, Dagorhir men expressed their disinterest in and/or a dislike for the idea of enacting feminized characters.

Interviews with female participants tell a different story about gender consciousness. For instance, female participants ($n = 7$) reflected on feminine norms in relation to their participation. Many of these interviews included defensive statements about their gender in relation to their participation. For instance, the female character Dangerous Brother stated,

> [With a raised voice] There are times when guys will go easy on you if they don't recognize you as a really serious female fighter . . . it doesn't bother me, I'm in it for more of a historical aspect . . . I am completely ready to accept the fact that in the past women didn't fight as much as men did . . . plus I am really masculine to begin with so I just don't care.

Here, Dangerous Brother acknowledged the inequalities in participation for men and women, but then focused her desires on historical enactment, excused them as part of the behavior of the period ("In the past women didn't fight"), and deflected the inequality as applying directly to her ("I am really masculine to begin with so I just don't care"). This account demonstrates how gender inequalities are excused or justified as an acceptable part of the group culture (Scott & Lyman, 1968).

Levels of commitment also formed a gendered system of stratification between men, with "serious women" and "non-serious women" participants, further dividing women's interest in the group. For instance, Dangerous Brother stated while laughing sardonically, "There are [women] who just go because their significant other drags them, poor souls." Similarly, Homunculus, another female member, discussed this stratification: "Half are the girlfriend getting dragged along and if she [participates] at all, she's going to be doing archery. The other half is serious female fighters who fight just as brutally as the guys." The implication is that norms of femininity are inconsistent with Dagorhir participation. To be taken "seriously" in Dagorhir, women participants must act "as brutally as the guys." Despite some female fighter's astute abilities in battle, some discussed how they were pigeonholed as "non-serious" vis-à-vis a romantic relationship with a male Dagorhir member. For instance, one female Dagorhir member selected to role-play as an elf with the character-name "Duru" when she began participating in the activity at 17. When she began attending PNEU, she had started to date a male Dagorhir member who had selected the character-name "Harykduru." Coincidentally, her previously selected character-name, "Duru," comprised part of her new boyfriend's character-name, "Haryk-Duru" which one can liken to a woman named Erin dating a man named Aaron. Yet, members of Dagorhir assumed that Duru's name and character were derived from her boyfriend's name Harykduru. Duru said about her experience, "[My boyfriend's role-playing character] was called Harykduru and everyone [also] called him Duru [for short]. So [then] they called me 'Duru's Girlfriend' and I was pissed." Duru was "pissed" because her group did not credit her with her previously chosen character-name, which she developed independently before she met her boyfriend, Harykduru.

Rather than viewing her character-name as a legitimate choice and her as a legitimate and independent participant, they viewed it as a derivation of her boyfriend's name and simultaneously pegged her as a non-serious "girlfriend" participant. She then had to actively resist the pegging of her name as a derivation of her boyfriend's and remind others that she had chosen her name and participated in Dagorhir as "Duru the Elf" long before she met her boyfriend.

Other women not only embraced the themes of masculinity but actually became male characters themselves. Homunculus noted that women's clothing acts as a barrier to participation:

> Guys will actually go easy on you if they don't recognize you as a really serious female fighter. It is kind of frustrating for me to get a serious fight out of someone [male]. The armor I'm designing specifically hides feminine features and accentuates masculine features. So I'm planning on making my shoulders a bit more broad . . . I'm actually binding so I look like a dude. My helmet will be covering my face and my hair is going to be tucked away . . . by the time I am done making my armor and garb, I intend to look like a guy [on the battlefield].

These women are practiced fighters, deserving of epic glory, and yet encounter resistance from members because of their feminine features.

Members of Dagorhir establish a collective storied masculine selfhood, which we dubbed epic glory. While training and fighting were the most available methods of establishing epic glory, new members also had a unique method for gaining epic glory, which is called epic death. Members also incorporated epic glory through the defense against hecklers and onlookers. A consequence of these behaviors is the reproduction of characteristics associated with hegemonic masculinity (Connell, 2005), including gender inequality and the devaluation of women participants within the group.

Conclusion

Men comprise the overwhelming majority of participants in Dagorhir and when viewed through the analytical lens of the manhood acts perspective, it is clear why this is the case. Men are given structural preference in leadership positions, their characters are venerated, and their costumes and weapons are more valued on the battlefield. Women, in contrast, are more typically relegated to subordinate positions within the group, have few character choices, and are expected to follow rules that ultimately defer to men on the battlefield.

Increasing status in Dagorhir involved a type of self-enhancement that we termed "epic glory," which positioned members as social dominants and allowed achievement of manhood. Epic glory was earned through training activities during practices, in battles at Dagorhir events, and through simulating dramatic death scenes. In some contexts, onlookers and hecklers posed a threat to epic glory, but members found ways to reduce the effect of their scrutiny by dismissing the opinions of outsiders or incorporating their presence into their scenes as NPCs. They also constructed and shared stories about how the group bravely defended against particularly egregious harassers and invited onlookers to pick up a boffer and inevitably lose to their better players. Although largely unrecognized by Dagorhir men, opportunities for epic glory were far more elusive for women members. They had fewer choices for developing revered characters and, in battle, were encouraged to use the "suicide option" rather than die an epic death. Women members were largely relegated to subordinate positions within the organization, and it was often assumed that their participation was in support of their male romantic partner. In many ways, for women to gain epic glory, their best choice was to dress, act, and prove that they can fight as men. One question for future research would be if (and whether) women who beat the institutional odds that are against them to regularly achieve "epic glory" are thought of by other participants as more manly, less womanly, or something else?

Our study has many parallels with other research on nerd masculinity (Cooper, 2000; Kendall, 1999), which concluded that the subordinated masculinity of "nerd" has more in common with hegemonic masculinity (Connell, 2005) than we tend to think. Our analysis contributes to the literature by applying the manhood acts perspective (Schrock & Schwalbe, 2009) to the study of nerds. This analytical framework sheds the multiple masculinities perspective proposed by Connell (1995) and instead focuses on the common processes within a predominately male community that have the result of positioning men as dominants and women as subordinates. Through this, we found how men in the context of Dagorhir collectively and interpersonally acted to elevate their status as group members while signifying their manhood in the process. By focusing our analysis on common interaction processes that signify manhood rather than delineating categories of manhood, we feel that the understanding of the gender performances within subordinate groups of men becomes more straightforward and directly demonstrates the commonalities with other masculinity types. Yet, we caution that the use of the manhood acts (Schrock & Schwalbe, 2009) in our study was not intended to imply a contrast or test of the fit of other theoretical models of gender and, in fact, such an analysis would go beyond the data we collected. We would expect that an analysis using alternative theoretical perspectives with similar data would reveal important, but different, insights into the power relations and performances tied to gender inequalities within this and other nerd subcultural groups.

How can a group of subordinate men include a gendered hierarchy among one another, subordinate women within the group, and at times negate harassment or even dominate more culturally honored men? By implementing "epic glory," they simply use a subculturally adapted version of manhood acts, which encompasses eliciting deference, resisting exploitation, and control of self, others, and environment (Schrock & Schwalbe, 2009). An important implication of this research is that manhood acts are not exclusive to stereotypical dominant men; instead, subordinate men can regularly engage in them by echoing the dominant culture. While the men in Dagorhir do not represent all subordinate men our findings are consistent with studies of other groups such as those of gay men (Connell, 1992; Frye, 1983), low-status men in the workplace (Henson & Rogers, 2001), and men of racial or ethnic minority status (Anderson, 1999), all of whom demonstrate hegemonic masculine qualities within subcultural groups.

Our study also demonstrated that within the low-status nerd organization, Dagorhir, manhood acts can be understood as an interpersonally constructed form of self-enhancement. Similar to research by Kinney (1993) that demonstrated how interaction in nerd groups increased confidence levels among members, we too found that Dagorhir's process of epic glory had a self-enhancing effect. In relation to other low-status groups, this form of self-enhancement was very similar to how homeless people engaged in identity work that instilled self-worth (Snow & Anderson, 1987). Yet, our study demonstrates that the means to self-enhancement in Dagorhir were not equally distributed as gender served as a factor in determining opportunities for much of the activities that led to epic glory. Future research may draw on this finding to better understand how organizational and institutional structure influences gender differences in self-enhancement.

In addition, we established early on that participation in Dagorhir events requires the performance of highly physical acts, albeit in brief duration. Thus, group members concerned themselves with kinesthetic and perceptual honing, which counters stereotypical perceptions of nerds as disinterested in physical pursuits (Nugent, 2008). Even a cursory observation of the group's activities establishes that Dagorhir members engage in extensive mock fighting and that such activity is deeply kinesthetic even if members are not in peak physical shape. More importantly, this physical activity is gendered in that it permits greater opportunities for men to participate and more often venerates their actions over those of women. In fact, Dagorhir has many parallels to mainstream sports in this respect (Messner, 2002). Other nerd group activities, such as eSport (electronically played sports) and competitive cosplay (a form of costume fantasy play), incorporate physical activity and training. As such, future researchers may benefit from expanding analytical focus of nerd groups by making more direct connections with the sociology of sports literature.

At first glance, Dagorhir appears unrelated or even opposed to masculinity. Dagorhir is considered a nerd activity and therefore a subordinate one. This article, however, suggests that the Dagorhir members maintain mainstream cultural values (Fine, 1983) about gender that also serve to reproduce a form of hegemonic masculinity that results in gender inequalities (Acker, 2006). As Cooper (2000) has noted, American culture has shifted in recent years, moving toward incorporating what was traditionally considered nerd pursuits as part of mainstream masculinity. Often, cultural shifts and social changes also come with the prognostications that long existing inequality structures will erode and give way to a more equitable society for both men and women. Unfortunately, our study is much less optimistic when it comes to this point. Malaby and Green (2009) concluded from their study of a similar LARPing group that the context is "not far different from traditional arenas of masculine identity performance such as the playing field and job site" (p. 10). We can say that if we look at "nerds" through the lens of manhood acts, we can begin to see that they are, in many ways, no different from any other men—for better or for worse. This also suggests that the performance of the types of manhood acts that emphasize gender inequality and reify hegemonic masculinity within male nerd culture will only change as those acts associated with manhood in the larger culture change.

Notes

1. Many members of the Dagorhir community rejected a comparison with LARPing because of its emphasis on acting in character and differences in equipment. Dagorhir culture tends to emphasize its incorporation of an array of boffer-weapons designed to be used with force in mock battles over acting in character. This type of distancing is very similar to those made with other games such as New England Role-Playing Organization (NERO), Society for Creative Anachronism (SCA), Belagarath Medieval Combat Society (BMCS), and Darkon. We draw a comparison between Dagorhir and LARPing because from an etic perspective both involve character building and fantasy role-playing. We felt that this comparison would be useful to readers because of the greater familiarity with the term *LARPing* and its broad use in mainstream culture.

2. All names used in this article are pseudonyms reflective of the tradition of the Dagorhir fantasy genre.

3. Identifying information such as the names of Dagorhir characters, groups, and events has been changed to protect the confidentiality of participants.

4. Interview questions aimed at tapping masculinity first focused indirectly on group relationships, then worked back to issues of dominance/subordination, and finally (if needed) to men and women.

5. The initial interviews for which this analysis stems was guided by questions aimed to gain sociological insight into the phenomenon of social awkwardness. Rather than deriving interesting findings on social awkwardness, the authors began to see emergent themes relating to masculinity which we then pursued.

6. Participants who engaged in battle role-playing typically were required to wear costume gear with padding and carried "boffer" weapons.

7. When the first author interviewed participants about their experiences directly after engaging in mock battles during Dagorhir events, many would switch between answering questions in their role-playing character identities and "breaking" character to answer questions in their non-role-playing identities. This type of switching on and off character was common among members and most prevalent during events. It was consistent not only with how the members interacted with the first author but also with how they interacted with one another.

References

Acker, J. (2006). Inequality regimes gender, class, and race in organizations. *Gender & Society, 20,* 441–464.

Adler, P. A., & Adler, P. (1989). The glorified self: The aggrandizement and the construction of the self. *Social Psychology Quarterly, 52,* 299–310.

Anderson, E. (1999). *Code of the street: Decency, violence, and the moral life of the inner city.* New York, NY: W. W. Norton & Company.

Bishop, J. H., Bishop, M., Bishop, M., Gelbwasser, L., Green, S., Peterson, E., . . . Zuckerman, A. (2004). Why we harass nerds and freaks: A formal theory of student culture and norms. *Journal of School Health, 74,* 235–251.

Blumer, H. (1969). *Symbolic interactionism: Perspective and method.* Englewood Cliffs, NJ: Prentice Hall.

Boykin, J. (2013, January 26). Women in combat a dangerous experiment. *CNN.* Retrieved from http://www.cnn .com/2013/01/25/opinion/boykin-women-in-combat/

Brady, P. (2014). Jocks, teckers, and nerds: The role of the adolescent peer group in the formation and maintenance of secondary school institutional culture. *Discourse: Studies in the Cultural Politics of Education, 25,* 351–364.

Charmaz, K. (2006). *Constructing grounded theory: A practical guide through qualitative analysis.* Newbury Park, CA: Pine Forge Press.

Ciciora, P. (2009). *Geeks may be chic, but negative nerd stereotype still exists, professor says.* Retrieved from http://www.lis.illinois.edu/articles/2009/03/geeks-may-be-chic-negative nerd-stereotype-still-exists-professor-says

Connell, R. W. (1987). *Gender and power: Society, the person and sexual politics.* Stanford, CA: Stanford University Press.

Connell, R. W. (1992). A very straight gay: Homosexual experience, and the dynamics of gender. *American Sociological Review, 57,* 735–751.

Connell, R. W. (2005). *Masculinities.* Oakland, CA: University of California Press.

Cooper, M. (2000). Being the "go-to guy": Fatherhood, masculinity, and the organization of work in Silicon Valley. *Qualitative Sociology, 23,* 379–405.

DeMeglio, M. (2010, April 13). Nerds and geeks get together for "Lord of the Rings"–style fights this Saturday. *The Brooklyn Paper.* Retrieved from http://www.brooklynpaper.com/ stories/33/16/33_16_mdm_lord_of_ the_rings.html

Evans, C., & Eder, D. (1993). "NO EXIT" processes of social isolation in the middle school. *Journal of Contemporary Ethnography, 22,* 139–170.

Fine, G. (1983). *Shared fantasy: Role-playing games as social worlds.* Chicago, IL: University of Chicago Press.

Frye, M. (1983). *The politics of reality: Essays in feminist theory.* Trumansburg, NY: Crossing Press.

Glaser, B. G., & Strauss, A. L. (1967). *The discovery of grounded theory: Strategies for qualitative research.* Mill Valley, CA: Sociology Press.

Henson, K. D., & Rogers, J. K. (2001). "Why Marcia you've changed!" Male clerical temporary workers doing masculinity in a feminized occupation. *Gender & Society, 15,* 218–238.

Hine, C. (2000). *Virtual ethnography.* London, England: SAGE.

Kendall, L. (1999). "The nerd within": Mass media and the negotiation of identity among computer-using men. *The Journal of Men's Studies, 7,* 353–369.

Kinney, D. (1993). From nerds to normals: The recovery of identity among adolescents from middle school to high school. *Sociology of Education, 66,* 21–40.

Malaby, M., & Green, B. (2009). Playing in the fields of desire: Hegemonic masculinity in live-combat LARPs. *Loading . . ., 3*(4). Retrieved from http://journals.sfu.ca/loading/index.php/ loading/article/view/55/53

Messner, M. (2002). *Taking the field: Women, men, and sport.* Minneapolis, MN: University of Minnesota Press.

Nugent, B. (2008). *American nerd: The story of my people.* New York, NY: Scribner.

Pascoe, C. J. (2011). *Dude, you're a fag: Masculinity and sexuality in high school.* Oakland, CA: University of California Press.

Plumridge, E. W., Fitzgerald, L. J., & Abel, G. M. (2002). Performing coolness: Smoking refusal and adolescent identities. *Health Education Research, 17,* 167–180.

Rentzsch, K., Schutz, A., & Schroder-Abe, M. (2011). Being labeled nerd: Factors that influence the social acceptance of high-achieving students. *Journal of Experimental Education, 79,* 143–168.

Saul, N. (2011). *Chivalry in medieval England.* Cambridge, MA: Harvard University Press.

Schrock, D., & Schwalbe, M. (2009). Men, masculinity, and manhood acts. *Annual Review of Sociology, 35,* 277–295.

Schwalbe, M. L., & Mason-Schrock, D. (1996). Identity work as group process. *Advances in Group Processes, 13,* 113–147.

Schwalbe, M. L., & Wolkomir, M. (2001). Interviewing men. In J. F. Gubrium & J. A. Holstein (Eds.), *Handbook of interview research* (pp. 202–220). Thousand Oaks, CA: SAGE.

Scott, M., & Lyman, S. (1968). Accounts. *American Sociological Review, 33*, 46–62.

Sedikides, C. (1993). Assessment, enhancement, and verification determinants of the self-evaluation process. *Journal of Personality and Social Psychology, 65*, 317–338.

Snow, D. A., & Anderson, L. (1987). Identity work among the homeless: The verbal construction and avowal of personal identities. *American Journal of Sociology, 92*, 1336–1371.

Suitor, J. J., & Carter, R. S. (1999). Jocks, nerds, babes and thugs: A research note on regional differences in adolescent gender norms. *Gender Issues, 17*, 87–101.

Sykes, G., & Matza, D. (1957). Techniques of neutralization: A theory of delinquency. *American Sociological Review, 22*, 644–670.

Tolkien, J. R. R. (1954). *Lord of the rings: Fellowship of the ring.* New York, NY: Del Ray.

Tresca, M. J. (2011). *The evolution of fantasy role-playing games.* Jefferson, NC: McFarland.

Vaccaro, C. A., Schrock, D. P., & McCabe, J. M. (2011). Managing emotional manhood fighting and fostering fear in mixed martial arts. *Social Psychology Quarterly, 74*, 414–437.

Wilde, L. W. (1999). *On the trail of the women warriors: The Amazons in myth and history.* London, UK: Macmillan.

Wilson, B. (2002). The "anti-jock" movement: Reconsidering youth resistance, masculinity, and sport. Culture in the age of the internet. *Sociology of Sports Journal, 19*, 206–223.

CHAPTER 19

"I Kick It to Both, but Not in the Street"

Behaviorally Bisexual Latino Men, Gender, and the Sexual Geography of New York City Metropolitan Area

Miguel Muñoz-Laboy, Nicolette Severson, Jonathan Garcia, Richard G. Parker, and Patrick Wilson

This article explores how behaviorally bisexual Latino men negotiate, modify, and perform their gender within two main spheres of their lives: family home and urban spaces of the city. This examination is of particular interest, as bisexual individuals often face negative perceptions and/or perceived to be rejected from heteronormative and gay environments (Angelides 2001; McLean 2008; Rust 2002; Welzer-Lang 2008). The term "Latino" is used here to refer to an individual of Latin American ancestry. Specifically, this is an individual whose birthplace, or that of his parents or grandparents, was in any territory of Latin America. Traditionally, the term "bisexual" has been used to refer to individuals who are either sexually or emotionally attracted to, or sexually intimate with, members of both sexes (Kinsey et al. 1948; Maguen 1998). This is the definition employed here, although it should be noted that in order for men to take part in the study, they needed to have had sexual contact with a man and a woman in the past six months, excluding those who were emotionally attracted to both sexes but not sexually active.

Urban space can be conceptualized in a number of ways. In one sense, space is defined as the material contents that make it up a backdrop for "the scenery and props for the spate of human action played out before, within, or upon it" (Goffman 1959, 22). Yet space is also a more active, complex entity, one that is constructed by sociocultural forces and takes part in the creation and recreation of every day social dynamics (Lefébvre 1991). Spaces become transformed into "places," permeated with subjective meaning and critical to the formation of social identities and the production of gender (Fullilove and McGrath 2005; Carrillo 2002; Gaissad 2005; Parker 1999; Sanders 1996; Hopkins 2000). The urban landscape presents a condensed sexual geography of the accepted and the transgressive— reflecting the "hierarchies of desire, from the valorized to the stigmatized . . ." (Califia 1994, 205). Furthermore, the organization of space and its distribution of activities may be instrumental in the maintenance of masculine perspectives (Day, Stump, and Carreon 2003; Sanders 1996). As evidenced by the "queering" of city spaces that has made lesbian, gay, bisexual, and transgender (LGBT) lifestyles more visible and accepted in certain designated neighborhoods, streets remain a contested site for the overlap of competing ideologies (Johnston and Longhurst 2010).

SOURCE: Muñoz-Laboy, M., Severson, N., Garcia, J., Parker, R. G., and Wilson, P. (2017). "I Kick It to Both, but Not in the Street: Behaviorally Bisexual Latino Men, Gender, and the Sexual Geography of New York City Metropolitan Area." *Men and Masculinities.* doi:10.1177/1097184X17695036. Reproduced with permission.

In R. W. Connell's foundational work (1987, 1993, 1995), hegemonic masculinity was established as the socially dominant form of idealized masculinity at a given place and time and was useful in revealing the way patriarchal social patterns are reinforced throughout the society. As is often the case with critical conceptual contributions to theory, hegemonic masculinity has been both widely employed and critiqued. Our intention is to use the term carefully. Rather than implying a cohesive lived system, we point to a specific set of idealized attributes valued and reinforced by key social influences. In this way, we use the term as further articulated by Connell and Messerschmidt (2005) in their call for scholars to analyze hegemonic masculinity along lines of local, regional, and global legitimation.

In previous studies, the authors have found that maintaining a heterosexual masculine identity played a crucial role in the ways that behaviorally bisexual Latino men organized their sexual lives, while the pressure to conform to these ideals were found to be sources of stress (Muñoz-Laboy, Garcia, et al. 2015; Muñoz-Laboy and Dodge 2005). In those prior studies, maintaining a masculine public image meant appearing self-reliant, denying physical and mental weaknesses, and distancing from behaviors perceived as feminine, including being discrete or secretive regarding bisexual activity. These traits have been widely connected to dominant masculine norms. Indeed, masculinity has been relationally defined as antifemininity itself, and a "flight from the feminine," homophobia, and overt and exclusive heterosexuality have been noted as key organizing features of hegemonic masculinity (Kimmel 2005; Joseph and Black 2012).

The value of an antifeminine, masculine ideal for behaviorally bisexual Latino men can be seen as reinforced on social, cultural, and institutional levels. In other words, what Connell and Messerschmidt would label "local" (constructed through daily interactions with families and immediate communities) and "regional" (constructed at a society-wide level of culture) legitimation (Connell and Messerschmidt 2005; Messerschmidt 2012). The association between a masculine ideal and heterosexuality may be particularly strong among Latino populations, where institutional and cultural factors combine to promote the primacy of heterosexual masculinity in patterning social relations (Martinez et al. 2011). Previous studies by the authors have found a connection between high family involvement and compartmentalization of bisexual activity and relationships— even when this compartmentalization causes stress—in order to maintain a masculine, heterosexual identity and a connection to the family unit (Muñoz-Laboy, Severson, and Bannan 2014; Muñoz-Laboy 2008).

Meanwhile, sentiments of anti-effeminacy have been established within male LGBT culture itself. Studies within bisexual and gay male populations have widely noted the value placed on masculinity and the negative attitudes toward perceived effeminacy. For example, Latino gay men seeking partners have been found to seek out stereotypically masculine characteristics and to avoid and devalue stereotypically feminine traits (Jeffries 2009). Anti-effeminacy has been linked more generally to negative feelings about same-sex behavior, with a value placed on traditional masculine norms and roles related to higher levels of internalized homonegativity among gay and bisexual men, both in the general population (Szymanski and Carr 2008; Hamilton and Mahalink 2009) and among Latino men specifically (Estrada et al. 2011). Gay and bisexual men who consider themselves effeminate have been shown to experience increased mental distress resulting from more negative experiences with homophobia (Sandfort, Melendez, and Diaz 2007). Indeed, among our participants, a full 18.6 percent reported having been harassed by police for being perceived as either homosexual or effeminate.

It is not clear to the degree to which behaviorally bisexual Latino men wish to maintain a connection to traditional or hegemonic masculinity, their pursuit of a masculine ideal, or whether they see their bisexual behavior in contradiction or not to their notion of masculinity. For while the "transgressive" potential of bisexuality has been celebrated by academics and activists, most simply want to live lives in which they can feel social connection and value and be free of discrimination (Steinman 2011). Thus, this analysis draws on qualitative sexual history interviews conducted as part of a larger study on the health of behaviorally bisexual Latino men. Because the performance of gender expressions continues and is reproduced during one-time in-person interviews (as opposed to long-term, multiple interviews as part of an ethnographic study), we consider this analysis as exploratory, and yet, important because most of our knowledge of Latino bisexual men has been focused on HIV/sexually transmitted infections (STIs) sexual behavior with limited attention to their masculinity. We titled this article, "I kick it to both, but not in the street" based on one of the quotes of our participants because our analysis focuses on the way that Latino bisexual men embody this desired but problematic relationship through their actions in and understandings of different social and physical spaces.

Method

Sampling and Recruitment

A mixed-methods study was conducted consisting of field observations of sexual partnering venues, 148 in-depth interviews on men's sexual histories and self-administered questionnaires. The present analysis focuses on the qualitative data from the sexual history interviews. We used a qualitative quota sampling per geographical zone of the city. We sampled in four zones of predominantly Latino neighborhoods of New York City (New York), Newark, and Jersey City (New Jersey). These were selected based on US census data. To assure a diversified sample, our parameters in each zone were based on venue quota sampling: 25 percent from Latino venues that were not gay/bisexually oriented nor AIDS-related venues (e.g., religious organizations, sports teams, and workers' programs); 25 percent came from venues that we consider sexual venues for men cruising for sex with other men, including public sex spaces such as parks, piers, and Internet sites; 25 percent of the men were recruited through bisexually oriented venues, which included gay night clubs, sex clubs and bars, as well as bisexual groups, online networks and chat rooms; and 25 percent were recruited from clinical sites, such as STI clinics and community health clinics. This form of recruitment allowed the team to interview behaviorally bisexual men who identified as bisexual as well as those who did not.

The selection criteria for participation were being eighteen to sixty years and bisexually active (having had sex with a least one man and one woman) within the last six months (the literature has pointed to six months as a time frame to establish behavioral sexual orientation stability; Stokes, McKirnan, and Burzette 1993). Oral consent scripts were used in the language of their preference due to the sensitive nature of the research topics of this study. After informed consent procedures, participants were formally interviewed in a place of their selection.

Home Sphere

Among our participants, home was defined as the space of interaction with family defined as kinship networks (parents, siblings), cohabitating sexual partners, and/or roommates who were also friends. For some men in our study, home represented a restrictive space that discourages disclosure of a bisexual identity. For example, "Frankie" found a "best friend" in his mother, whom he shared all of his life experiences with. Despite the disapproval of his "macho" father, Frankie explained:

> I tell my mother everything, what I do with guys, what I do with a female. Me and my mom has an open relationship, I can say whatever.

Although "Sebastian" feared how disclosure of his sexual orientation would affect his relationship to his brother, it actually made them closer. Here he explains his brother and sister-in-law's efforts to relate to him:

> His wife and him have gone with me to gay clubs. His wife and him watch "RuPaul's Drag Race," I think, in an effort to [connect].

Participants' accounts of their gendering experiences at their homes seem to be situated between two polar perceptions of acceptability of gender performance at home. One the one hand, many participants expressed categorical statements into what behaviors are feminine or not, masculine or not. On the other hand, the same participants also disregard whether the behaviors were considered feminine or masculine and engaged in family behaviors because that made them "good sons," "good husbands." For example, "Miguel" considered cooking and cleaning to be "feminine things"—but expressed enjoying doing these activities to help support his family. "Alex's" traditional father objected to his son's love of cooking, which his father considered too "feminine," as well as his son's preference for women's deodorant. Alex explains his father's comments and his response:

> . . . like oh that's for faggots, you shouldn't do that. You know like you know I don't take the word offensive but you know he's old school so I don't really pay no mind to him.

Some participants, such as "Gabriel," understood their own shift in gender expectations within the family as a reflection of changing times. Gabriel, who was in his late thirties at the time of the interview, had suffered the deaths of numerous relatives as a child. Yet back then, he explained, being a man was about "ego and machoness," and he didn't show emotion for fear of being perceived as weak. He explains:

> A man supposed to be perceived as strong, you know, don't cry, everything like that. Nowadays, you can let your emotions out and don't be judged by it. Before, they didn't respect that. They looked down at you.

Moreover, participants who had disclosed their sexual identity to family members and friends often used their home spaces to assert this identity in a proud and confident way, despite their family members' reactions. "Martin" knew about his bisexuality from the age of five. Martin faced negative reactions about his bisexuality from numerous family members, including an aunt who kicked him out of the house, accusing him of "turning" her own son gay. Yet Martin maintained a pride in his bisexual identity, asserting that:

> I'm like you know just be comfortable with yourself but it's just so many old-fashioned people out there that make it hard for people . . . It's like me like I don't care no more. Like before I said like my family gets mad at me but like I tell em, I'm goin fight, I believe in fighting for what I believe and I'm bi. Like that's life. You understand?

Urban Sexual Spaces

Outside of the home sphere, participants described a social geography in which multiple environments provided a landscape with which to organize their behaviors and identities. For some men, seeking sex partners was facilitated by the multiplicity of explicit venues to find potential sexual partners in New York City. As "Javier" explained:

> I could go to a straight spot here and if I'm not finding nothing I can always hit up a gay spot right across the street. That's the best of both worlds.

Some respondents compartmentalized their sexual partnering, often keeping transgendered and same-sex partnering physically distant from primary sexual partnerships with cis-women closer to their place of residence (if they were not cohabiting already). For example, "Jose" expressed:

> I try to keep everything away from my neighborhood. You know what I'm sayin, the farther the better . . . So in my neighborhood it seems like you know I'm kinda like, sorta kinda like a tough guy.

"Abram" struggled with the fact that his favorite gay bar, where he met male and women transgender sex partners, was only two blocks from his apartment. He too explained his compartmentalization strategy:

> I make believe I'm going on the train, and real quick, I just go inside of there. Or either I go to the next bar, have a couple of drinks, go smoke a cigarette, and sneak inside.

For the men in our study, public spaces were not the primary site for the meeting of sexual partners or the engagement in sexual activity. Men in our study did report meeting male sex partners in public areas, such as on trains, in parks, and on the street, but this public behavior was largely described as occurring in well-known gay cruising neighborhoods in New York City.

The men in our study carved out spaces or utilized already existing spaces to meet cis-men, transgendered women, transgendered men, and one-night-stand cis-women partners, at a distance from either their primary cis-woman partner or casual dating scene with cis-women. Because of this distancing, it will be expected that their sex took place in public spaces, but that was not the case for this sample, where the vast majority of men reported their sexual experiences either at their homes or the homes of their partners. The participants in the study viewed themselves as men regardless of the spaces that they were in or the strategies they used to navigate non-cis-women partnering.

Protecting Image in Neighborhood of Residence

Concealing bisexuality while navigating the streets of the neighborhood of residence was a consistent theme across our study participant interviews. "The street," referring to the streets in their neighborhood, represented something differently for different sectors of our sample, depending on levels of contact with the criminal justice system, acculturation, and education. For men in the sample in contact with the criminal justice system, that is, men or close family members who had served time in jail or prison or were on probation, "the street" was characterized as "Felipe" expressed:

> The street calls you . . . seduce you. You just want to hang out on the street.

Street culture in the neighborhoods of residence of our participants was not unique with summer street culture described by the men as street selling of legal and illegal goods, camaraderie, men passing their high from drugs (mostly heroin) watching the street, men playing dominoes, people coming in and out of store fronts (on main streets), and so on. Thus, for the men in the sample that had been impacted by the criminal justice system, the street represented a space to meet street family networks. Similarly, the men in the sample were recent migrants and those with low levels of acculturation repeated the street cliché in many countries in Latin America, "women do not belong in the streets . . . that is the domain of men; women belong at home." Thus, within our sample, three sectors of men actively socialized or viewed the street as a space to be respected. For example, "Ernesto" stated that:

> Closet cases be like . . . you gotta act a certain way on the street. You gotta talk a certain way so people don't find out . . .

"Raul" also articulated his sexuality in terms of the boundaries imposed by the street:

> I kick it to both, but not in the street . . . I think, my stuff would have to be indoors . . . (referring to both expressing femininity and sexual-affective behavior towards other men or transgendered partners).

Fear of being outed in the space of the street was consistent across all participants. Fear of being harmed because of being outed was more variable and seems to depend more on the size of the person's street network and the level of crime in the block. Thus, the social costs of being outed as bisexual or as a "not a normal man" were the most common concerns.

The streets where our respondents live were not inherently heteronormative nor queer but rather physical spaces, with high concentrations and flows of individuals, with also multiple coexisting spaces. Very few participants knew other bisexual or gay men in their neighborhood, yet, some met other bisexual and gay men from their neighborhood while socializing in gay neighborhoods or commercial establishments in the city.

Two of the three men in the study reported feeling lonely and/or socially isolated within their neighborhoods. For these men, the street represented an oppressive space, "plagued with discrimination and violence," as "Jesus" stated it. Notably, the self-regulation of one's gender presentation on the street was not limited to men who considered themselves 100 percent of their time closeted at home and in public. In contrast, those who were openly bisexual in their familial/home sphere nevertheless expressed an adherence to the hegemonic masculine tenet of antifemininity. As "Martin," the man who was kicked out of his aunt's house for allegedly influencing her son's sexual orientation, explained,

> I believe in fighting for what I believe and I'm bi . . . I'm comfortable with who I am. And that's not gonna change.

At the same time, he explained that he was raised to be "presentable" and part of this for him meant his performance in the streets:

> I wouldn't wanna walk down the street . . . with like somebody that I'm having sex with and they very, very feminine . . . I don't like that.

Here "Javier" explained gay clubs served as safe spaces for him and other bisexual men:

> I've opened up and I give guys hugs and kisses, and just say hi . . . Outdoors, that's when it changes, I feel like I have to act straight when I'm outside. Inside it's no problem.

"Fernando" talked about his behavior on the streets of his low-income, high-crime neighborhood:

> I spot random homosexuals, but like even they're pretending to be straight . . . I bump into feminine guys, but I'm not really that kind of person. I wouldn't be like holding hands with my boyfriend in the middle of [name removed to protect privacy] Street . . .

Respondents expressed a need for distancing themselves from "feminine" men in their neighborhood of residence and a need to "blend in." "Rodrigo" explained this desire:

> . . . this is New York City, [Name of neighborhood] the land of both straight and gay. So when I walk through these places, I walk through these places as a man. I don't walk through these

places as a straight man, I don't walk as a gay man, I don't walk as a bisexual man, I walk myself as a man. So nobody comes in and asks me any round about question, at least not yet.

"Javier" explained a similar desire to be a "regular man" distancing himself from both femininity and unnecessary displays of masculinity:

I guess I'm just a regular man. I'm not feminine, I'm not overly macho, I'm just a regular man. I walk through the street, I blend in pretty well. Nobody thinks anything.

These instances point to the need of those who engage in same-sex behavior to perform their gender in a way that did not challenge the norms of the dominant culture of the neighborhood of residence. If "nobody thinks anything" on the streets, then the threat of discrimination is successfully minimized. In addition, an identity based on being a "regular man" may have provided the additional benefits of reinforcing an association to masculinity and releasing them from the complications of an identity based upon sexual orientation.

Discussion

For the men in this study, New York City provided a range of contexts in which men alternately negotiated and navigated the macro-pressures of hegemonic masculinity. While home and openly gay (commercial and social) spaces seemed as spaces for flexibility and assertions of gender difference, these seem to be spaces of tolerance, resistance, and at a minimum contributing to minimize the impact of the stigma of nonheterosexuality. What makes some home spaces protective while others were not in the sample remains a question. We hypothesize that matriarchal-led homes, nonadherent to traditional religious values, allowed for more space of sexual and gender expressions. This idea would apply only to the younger men in the sample who are currently living with their parents. However, this would not apply to men in the samples who were heads of households, married (or cohabitating) with a cis-woman, for whom parental matriarchal/patriarchal values might be irrelevant in the organization of their bisexual lives and gender representations. For this group, openness about and acceptance of bisexuality with spouses and family networks may make a difference in homes being protective or oppressive spaces (in which case the self-regulation of the masculine image on the neighborhood streets is central to avoid family rejection).

When homes are perceived to be oppressive spaces against bisexuality, maintaining a traditional masculine image on the street becomes particularly important in transnational communities, such as Latinos in cities like the New York metropolitan area. Living transnational lives implies not only the sending of remittances to families at the sending communities but also frequent migratory flows and constant communication exchanges between the sending and host communities. Because gossip is central to those transnational exchanges, the management of the street masculine identity is central. As "Jesus," one of the interviewees, expressed to us: "[los compañeros son los màs bochincheros] the members [referring to the members of his street gang] are the biggest gossipers." Thus, it is not surprising that anti-femininity values were expressed consistently across all participants.

André Breton (1928) once described streets as "the only region of valid experience" (p. 113). And while perhaps a bit overstated, much of city life is indeed experienced in the streets. By organizing social space and compartmentalizing sexual partnering, geographical boundaries like the streets of neighborhoods of residence—which separate a myriad of distinctions such as outdoors and indoors, public and private, as well as marking the territories of blocks and neighborhoods—men in the study can construct a sense of identity and flexible public images (Malone 2002).

While our data do show nonneighborhood of residence streets and commercial establishments, such as gay bars, to be sites for meeting potential nonheterosexual partners, those spaces were perceived as "alternative," or what others have labeled as queer spaces (Johnston and Longhurst 2010). Our study reinforced the findings that sexual minorities must rotate plural identities to manage stigma in perceived hostile environments (Harper and Schneider 2003; Zea, Reisen, and Diaz 2003). With the street as a central site of compartmentalized behavior for Latino men (Asencio 2002), it is likely that this function of compartmentalization is organized along a public/private, hostile/not-hostile, and high/low neighborhood social capital. Ethnic minority LGBT people may experience a "double" or "triple" minority status that can require juggling their belonging to multiple identity groups. Because some ethnic minorities associate an LGBT identity with assimilation into white culture, they may feel that they must choose between LGBT and ethnic identities (Harper and Schneider 2003) or hide their gay and bisexual identity to avoid stigmatization (Zea, Reisen, and Diaz 2003). Congruent with this line of scholarship, our respondents often reported their behavior and identity as context-specific.

Our study findings suggest the adeptness of a sector of our bisexual population in successfully navigating multiple spaces, juggling context-specific identities and behavior. We may label this as high "sexual acculturation"; drawing on the concept of acculturation, we posit that some men in our sample were able to acculturate to the localized sexual cultural spaces without transgressing the gender sexual rules of public performances. Thus, bisexual men who viewed the world in terms of binaries, heterosexual and nonheterosexual binary, may feel socially isolated and with a higher need to perform a hegemonic masculinity. This is also consistent with other studies, where bisexual individuals often feel left without a place within organized sexual communities and related spaces (Dodge et al. 2012). Because our data collection was conducted between 2009 and 2012, positive historical events that may contribute to the sexual acculturation of bisexual Latino men such as the hyper, mass availability and utilization of Internet apps for dating, the 2015 ruling making legal same-sex marriages in the United States, are not reflected in the accounts of our participants. Further research is needed on the role of sexual acculturation on bisexual Latino men's masculinities.

In summary, our findings suggest that behaviorally bisexual Latino men's relationship to masculinity varied by space, where the main domain of negotiation at home is determining "genuine" identities while the neighborhood streets primarily discipline the participants into enacting hegemonic masculinity. Whether behaviorally bisexual Latino men may self-regulate their gender presentation in public to a higher degree than other groups is outside the scope of this study. However, pervasive street performances of masculinity described by participants did indeed work to strengthen their association to acceptable gender norms, thereby minimizing the threat of stigma and allowing them to "pass" as "regular men." These accounts suggest the persistence of dominant gender scripts and the ever-present threat of discrimination for those who vary from widely accepted gender characteristics.

References

Angelides, Steven. 2001. *A History of Bisexuality*. Chicago, IL: University of Chicago Press.

Asencio, Marysol. 2002. *Sex and Sexuality among New York's Puerto Rican Youth*. Boulder, CO: Lynne Rienner Publications.

Breton, André. 1928. *Nadja*, 113. Paris, France: Librairie Gallimard.

Califia, Pat. 1994. *Public Sex: The Culture of Radical Sex*. London, UK: Routledge.

Carballo-Diéguez, Alex, Curtis Dolezal, Luis Nieves, Francisco Díaz, Carlos Decena, and Ivan Balan. 2004. "Looking for a Tall, Dark, Macho Man . . . Sexual-role Behaviour Variations in Latino Gay and Bisexual Men." *Culture, Health & Sexuality* 6: 159–71.

Carrier, Joseph. 1995. *De Los Otros: Intimacy and Homosexuality among Mexican Men*. New York: Columbia University Press.

Carrillo, Héctor. 2002. *The Night Is Young: Sexuality in Mexico in the Time of AIDS*. Chicago, IL: University of Chicago Press.

Carrillo, Héctor. 2003. "Neither Machos nor Maricones: Masculinity and Emerging Male Homosexual Identities in Mexico." In *Changing Men and Masculinities in Latin America*, edited by Matthew Gutman, 351–69. Durham, NC: Duke University Press.

Connell, Raewyn. 1987. *Gender and Power*. Palo Alto, CA: Stanford University Press.

Connell, Raewyn. 1993. "The Big Picture: Masculinities in Recent World History." *Theory and Society* 22:597–623.

Connell, Raewyn. 1995. *Masculinities*. Berkeley: University of California Press.

Connell, Raewyn, and J. W. Messerschmidt. 2005. "Hegemonic Masculinity: Rethinking the Concept." *Gender & Society* 19:829–59.

Day, Kristen, C. Stump, and D. Carreon. 2003. "Confrontation and Loss of Control: Masculinity and Men's Fear in Public Space." *Journal of Environmental Psychology* 23:311–22.

De, Moya, E. Antonio, and R. Garcia. 1996. "AIDS and the Enigma of Bisexuality in the Dominican Republic." In *Bisexualities and AIDS: International Perspectives*, edited by Peter Aggleton, 119–34. Bristol, PA: Taylor and Francis.

Dodge, Brian, P. W. Schnarrs, M. Reece, O. Martinez, G. Goncalves, D. Malebranche, B. Van Der Pol, R. Nix, and J. D. Fortenberry. 2012. "Individual and Social Factors Related to Mental Health Concerns among Bisexual Men in the Midwestern United States." *Journal of Bisexuality* 12:223–45.

Estrada, F., M. Rigali-Oiler, G. M. Arciniega, and T. J. Tracey. 2011. "Machismo and Mexican American Men: An Empirical Understanding Using a Gay Sample." *Journal of Counseling Psychology* 58:358.

Fox, Ronald. 1996. "Bisexuality in Perspective: A Review of Theory and Research." In *Bisexuality: The Psychology and Politics of an Invisible Minority*, edited by B. Firestein, 3–50. London, UK: Sage.

Fuller, Norma. 2001. "The Social Constitution of Gender Identity among Peruvian Men." *Men and Masculinities* 3:316–31.

Fullilove, Mindy T., and M. M. McGrath. 2005. "Introduction to the Special Issue on Sexuality and Place." *Journal of Sex Research* 42:1–2.

Gaissad, L. 2005. "From Nightlife Conventions to Daytime Hidden Agendas: Dynamics of Urban Sexual Territories in the South of France." *Journal of Sex Research* 42:20–27.

Goffman, Erving. 1959. *The Presentation of Self in Everyday Life*. New York: Doubleday.

Hamilton, C. J., and J. R. Mahalik. 2009. "Minority Stress, Masculinity, and Social Norms Predicting Gay Men's Health Risk Behaviors." *Journal of Counseling Psychology* 56:132–41.

Harper, G. W., and M. Schneider. 2003. "Oppression and Discrimination among Lesbian, Gay, Bisexual, and Transgendered People and Communities: A Challenge for Community Psychology." *American Journal of Community Psychology* 31:243–52.

Hopkins, Jeff. 2000. "Signs of Masculinism in an 'Uneasy' Place: Advertising for 'Big Brothers.'" *Gender, Place and Culture: A Journal of Feminist Geography* 7:31–55.

Jeffries, W. L. 2009. "A Comparative Analysis of Homosexual Behaviors, Sex Role Preferences, and Anal Sex Proclivities in Latino and non-Latino Men." *Archives of Sexual Behavior* 38:765–78.

Johnston, Lynda, and Robyn Longhurst. 2010. *Space, Place and Sex*. Plymouth, UK: Rowman & Littlefield.

Joseph, Lauren, and Pamela Black. 2012. "Who's the Man? Fragile Masculinities, Consumer Masculinities, and the Profiles of Sex Work Clients." *Men and Masculinities* 15:486–506.

Kimmel, Michael S. 2005. *The Gender of Desire: Essays on Male Sexuality*. Albany: SUNY Press.

Kinsey, A. C., W. B. Pomeroy, C. E. Martin, and S. Sloan. 1948. *Sexual Behavior in the Human Male*. Philadelphia, PA: W. B. Saunders.

Lefébvre, Henri. 1991. *The Production of Space*. Oxford, UK: Blackwell Publishing.

Liguori, A. L., M. Gonzàlez-Block, and P. Aggleton. 1996. "Bisexuality and HIV/AIDS in Mexico." In *Bisexualities and AIDS: International Perspectives*, edited by Peter Aggleton, 74–97. Bristol, PA: Taylor and Francis.

Maguen, S. 1998. "Bisexuality." In *Encyclopedia of AIDS: A Social, Political, Cultural, and Scientific Record of the HIV Epidemic*, edited by R. Smith, 96–99. Chicago, IL: Fitzroy Dearborn.

Malone, K. 2002. "Street Life: Youth, Culture and Competing Uses of Public Space." *Environment and Urbanization* 14:157–68.

Martinez, Omar, B. Dodge, M. Reece, P. W. Schnarrs, S. D. Rhodes, G. Goncalves, M. Muñoz-Laboy, D. Malebranche, B. Van Der Pol, R. Nix, G. Kelle, and J. D. Fortenberry. 2011. "Sexual Health and Life Experiences:

Voices from Behaviorally Bisexual Latino Men in the Midwestern USA." *Journal of Culture, Health & Sexuality* 13:1073–89.

McLean, Kristen. 2008. "Inside, Outside, Nowhere: Bisexual Men and Women in the Gay and Lesbian Community." *Journal of Bisexuality* 8:63–80.

Messerschmidt, J. W. 2012. "Engendering Gendered Knowledge: Assessing the Academic Appropriation of Hegemonic Masculinity." *Men and Masculinities* 15:56–76.

Muñoz-Laboy, Miguel. 2008. "Familism and Sexual Regulation among Bisexual Latino Men." *Archives of Sexual Behavior* 37:773–82.

Muñoz-Laboy, Miguel, and B. Dodge. 2005. "Bisexual Practices: Patterns, Meanings, and Implications for HIV/ STI Prevention among Bisexually Active Latino Men and Their Partners." *Journal of Bisexuality* 5:79–101.

Muñoz-Laboy, Miguel, J. Garcia, A. Perry, P. Wilson, and R. Parker. 2015. "Heteronormativity and Sexual Partnering among Bisexual Latino Men." *Archives of Sexual Behavior* 44:895–902.

Muñoz-Laboy, Miguel, N. Severson, and S. Bannan. 2014. "Occupations, Social Vulnerability and HIV/STI Risk: The Case of Bisexual Latino Men in the New York City Metropolitan Area." *Global Public Health* 9:1167–83.

Parker, Richard G. 1991. *Bodies, Pleasures and Passions: Sexual Culture in Contemporary Brazil.* Boston, MA: Beacon Press.

Parker, Richard G. 1996. "Bisexuality and HIV/AIDS in Brazil." In *Bisexualities and AIDS: International Perspectives*, edited by Peter Aggleton, 146–58. Bristol, PA: Taylor and Francis.

Parker, Richard G. 1999. *Beneath the Equator: Cultures of Desire, Male Homosexuality, and Emerging Gay Communities in Brazil.* London, UK: Routledge.

Rust, Paula C. Rodriguez. 2002. "Bisexuality: The State of the Union." *Annual Review of Sex Research* 1:180–240.

Sanders, Joel. 1996. *Stud: Architectures of Masculinity.* New York, NY: Princeton Architectural Press.

Sandfort, T. G., R. M. Melendez, and R. M. Diaz. 2007. "Gender Nonconformity, Homophobia, and Mental Distress in Latino Gay and Bisexual Men." *Journal of Sex Research* 44:181–89.

Schifter, Jacobo. 2000. *Public Sex in a Latin Society.* New York, NY: Haworth Hispanic/Latino Press.

Steinman, Erich. 2011. "Revisiting the Invisibility of (Male) Bisexuality: Grounding (Queer) Theory, Centering Bisexual Absences and Examining Masculinities." *Journal of Bisexuality* 11:399–411.

Stokes, Joseph P., David J. McKirnan, and Rebecca G. Burzette. 1993. "Sexual Behavior, Condom Use, Disclosure of Sexuality, and Stability of Sexual Orientation in Bisexual Men." *The Journal of Sex Research* 30:203–13.

Szymanski, D. M., and E. R. Carr. 2008. "The Roles of Gender Role Conflict and Internalized Heterosexism in Gay and Bisexual Men's Psychological Distress: Testing Two Mediation Models." *Psychology of Men & Masculinity*, 9:40.

Taylor, Clark. 1986. "Mexican Male Homosexual Interaction in Public Contexts." *Journal of Homosexuality* 11:117–36.

Welzer-Lang, Daniel. 2008. "Speaking Out Loud about Bisexuality: Biphobia in the Gay and Lesbian Community." *Journal of Bisexuality* 8:81–95.

Zea, María C., C. A. Reisen, and R. M. Díaz. 2003. "Methodological Issues in Research on Sexual Behavior with Latino Gay and Bisexual Men." *American Journal of Community Psychology* 31:281–91.

CHAPTER 20

Economic Shifts, Consumption of Sex, and Compensatory Masculinity in Japan

Kumiko Nemoto

The postwar model of salaryman manhood, with its emphasis on the ideal worker, lifelong employment and economic protection, and the breadwinning father of the family, has long been dominant in Japan. However, because of Japan's economic decline, the rise of single households, the rapid decline in the social pressure to marry, and the increasing prevalence of a consumption-led or immaterial-economy-led lifestyle, Japanese men's lives have become increasingly stratified depending on their employment status. The expectation remains that the lifelong employed salarymen will be devoted to his company and be a workaholic with little time for himself and his family. The family and work remain the source of such men's masculinity building; however, unmarried men who desire autonomy are increasingly surrounded by consumptive sexual commodities, from paid sex to virtual sex games, that offer them compensatory masculine scripts. These sexual scripts, images, and commodities serve as popular cultural media by which men in different social classes and jobs seek their "patriarchal dividend" or their taken-for-granted privilege that they increasingly cannot obtain in more traditional ways. The gendered sexual scripts of cultural commodities such as anime, games, and paid sex also explicitly reflect the absence of women's socioeconomic power. Even though Japanese women have increasingly attained a higher level of education in Japan, they continue to lack economic power and thus have effected little change in family dynamics.

This paper looks at how Japan's postwar salaryman hegemonic masculinity has been destabilized through various economic shifts and the decline in lifelong employment in Japan, and at the same time, how various forms of consumption of hyper-gendered sex and sexual images are providing men with an alternative way of experiencing compensatory manhood. The consumption of sexual images and paid sex is reifying Japan's prioritization of work over family and personal life and recasting men's interest in marriage, family, and reproduction, which will have an impact on Japan's future.

Postwar Salaryman Masculinity and Japan's Family-Work Regime

Japan's model of hegemonic manhood, embodied by the salaryman or lifetime-employed, dedicated worker, has been a part of the nation's postwar economic development and modernization

SOURCE: Nemoto, K. *Economic Shifts, Consumption of Sex, and Compensatory Masculinity in Japan.* Reproduced with permission.

and was thus shaped by the nationalist gender regime and ideologies. Dasgupta (2000, 193–194) describes the Japanese salaryman as the outcome of Japan's system of heterosexual patriarchal industrial-capitalism:

> Typically he would be middle-class and often university-educated, entering the company upon graduation from university in his early twenties. Once within the organization, he would be expected to display qualities of loyalty, diligence, dedication, self-sacrifice, hard work; qualities which in an earlier era had been associated with another influential discourse of masculinity— the bushido of the samurai. . . . In return for his loyalty and conformity, the salaryman could expect such benefits as lifelong employment security, automatic increases in salary and status linked to length of service, and an overall paternalistic concern for him on the part of the organization. Significantly, his success (or lack of it) would be premised not only on his conduct in the workplace, but also on his ability to conform to the discourse of heterosexual patriarchal family ideology, i.e., to marry at an age deemed suitable, and once married to perform the appropriate gender role benefitting a husband/father/provider.

Japan's contemporary hegemonic masculinity stands at the nexus of the business imperative of the ideal worker and breadwinner of the household, and correspondingly, a model of "emphasized femininity" serves as its complement, represented by the housewife and sole caretaker of the family. Emphasized femininity is a position that accommodates the interests and desires of men, in which women are expected to display sociability, fragility, and compliance with men's desires, as well as acceptance of the traditional arrangements for marriage and child care (Kimmel 2000, 11). The ideology of separate gendered spheres has been at the core of the national welfare and labor regime in Japan. The Japanese government has explicitly promoted the gender-divided family-work regime by providing tax, pension, and health insurance benefits to male-breadwinner-led households, in which women earn less than $10,000 per year, mostly as part-time workers (Gottfried & Hayashi-Kato 1998). Japanese business management, which has strong ties with the major banks and with the state, has traditionally offered lifelong employment and security to workers to uphold this model.

Salarymen are offered these family benefits, as well as lifetime economic security, in exchange for long hours of labor and dedication to the employer. The salary and promotion system in Japanese companies has traditionally been characterized by seniority, in which individual performance is less important than age and years of service, and this type of promotion and pay system has lessened workplace competition and contributed to a sense of mutual equality among workers. Many companies have offered family benefits to their male workers and thereby saved the Japanese government vast welfare costs. This model of lifelong employment is also called a "flexicurity" system, which means that an employer can use its workers "flexibly" to adjust its labor costs in exchange for giving them lifelong jobs. In such cases workers are expected to work extra hours for little or no pay, and if necessary, can even be transferred to different jobs or forced to retire early. Yet under such a system a worker rarely changes his employer in midcareer.

Workers are expected to show the company loyalty and to conform to the age-based community-like corporate culture, in which management power is generally concentrated in the oldest workers. The employees, even at the top levels of management, commonly view the firm as a transcendental entity to obey (Dore 2000, 106). When the Japanese economy was prosperous, Japanese companies assisted the state with its welfare costs by offering lifelong economic security to its workers and even family benefits to their wives and children. Women are expected to dedicate themselves to being the caretakers of the family, thereby also saving the Japanese state welfare expenditures. Thus, the institutional nexus of the business community, the state, and the family has shaped a particular type of hegemonic manhood in Japan.

Hegemonic salaryman manhood is characterized by men's intense dedication to their work and their companies, thus necessitating long working hours on a daily basis. Extreme overwork is common and often costly, depriving men of their autonomy and time with their families. In 2006 over 60 percent of workers in Japan worked more than ten hours daily, and one in three male workers in their twenties, thirties, and forties worked about twelve hours per day, while 40 percent of workers were not compensated for their overtime (Research Institute for Advancement of Living Standards, 2006). In 2013, while full-time workers in Japan were given eighteen vacation days on average per year, they took only nine days off (Ministry of Health, Labour and Welfare, 2014). Incidents of *karoshi* (death by overwork) and *karo-jisatsu* (suicide by overwork) remain common and most instances of both involve men. Those who commit *karo-jisatsu* typically have been working extremely long hours with enormous responsibility, taking no holidays, managing a heavy workload, and enduring pressure to attain difficult goals (Kawanishi 2008). It is estimated that more than ten thousand workers in Japan die annually due to cerebral or cardiac disease caused by work overload (Kawahito 1998).

Meanwhile, under the patriarchal work and family division, Japanese women are expected to focus on the family, and as a result their social and economic status have remained low. Japan ranked 104th in the global gender gap index in 2014. Women's low earning ability and the absence of women in authorial positions are primary shapers of Japan's gender inequality (World Economic Forum 2014). Over 80 percent of employed men work as full-time regular workers, but only 45 percent of women work full-time regular jobs, with the rest employed as temp or part-time workers. Women are absent from middle and upper managerial positions in most Japanese companies. Because there has been a continuing gender gap in terms of economic power and because changes to the male breadwinner paradigm have been so slow, with the Japanese government favoring male-breadwinner households with pensions and lower taxes—regardless of the fact that the number of dual-earner households in Japan already exceeded that of solo-male-earner families by the early 1990s (Gender Equality Cabinet Bureau 2015)—Japanese men and women continue to live with the ideal of the male breadwinner and housewife type of marriage.

Even with the global shift from a patriarchal gender arrangement to egalitarianism, Japan's institutional and ideological shift has been slow. Japanese men continue to locate their self-worth and identity mostly in work (Dasgupta 2009, 90). Among other things, men's long working hours constrain their participation in political engagement and citizenship (LeBlanc 2010, 41). The institution of marriage in Japan has been strongly driven by obligation rather than by the importance of emotional ties and individual happiness (Tipton 2002), and divorce is not the norm (Mathews 2003, 119). There has rarely been an emphasis on communication between husbands and wives (Mathews 2003), and wives develop emotionally intense mother-child relationships that don't involve their husbands (Allison 1994). Mathews observed that many Japanese working men can "find real personal fulfillment in neither work nor family but . . . cannot deviate from the social roles they are obliged to play" (Mathews 2003, 119). Since obligatory roles are emphasized over affection, it is not surprising that Japanese married couples do not have sexual relations very often. One Japanese newspaper reported that more than half of Japanese marriages are "sexless" (Asahi Shinbun 2013).

Under such obligation-based pressures from work and family, alcohol, hostess clubs, and even paid sex have long been among the cultural and consumptive outlets for the salaryman. In order to assert their masculine presence in Japan, "men must drink and get drunk with other women" (Christensen 2015, 12), as "[d]rinking is an act that simultaneously serves to perform, solidify, and maintain masculinity" and allows one to transgress the rigid given roles; not surprisingly, alcohol addiction is a challenging issue in Japan (Christensen 2015, 15). Allison's well-known research on hostess clubs in Japan illustrates that Japanese men use hostess clubs to be successful in business, to feel taken care of or pampered by women, and to build homosocial relations with other men. The hostess women are there to cater to the men via "emphasized femininity"; they "empty" themselves or depersonalize themselves and become "device[s] to enhance the male's self-image"(Allison, 1993, 182). For men who work long hours, hostess clubs and the sex entertainment industry offer an atmosphere of informal relaxation and recreation that simultaneously increases their sense of masculinity.

Late Marriage and Men's Desire for Autonomy in Japan

While the Japanese salaryman continues to dedicate long hours to his company and to being the breadwinner of the family, young men in Japan increasingly seem to desire more individual autonomy, freedom from work and family. Even though the phenomenon of late marriage in Japan often tends to be seen as deriving from educated women's postponement of marriage, educated and employed men are also postponing it. Also, because men's late marriage is often explained by a lack of economic security, the trend toward late marriage among economically secure men has gained little attention. My previous research found that, with marriage as a declining social norm and thus less pressure to marry, even educated men with secure jobs are postponing it, due to a preference for autonomy over the obligations of marriage (Nemoto 2013). Regardless of education, the ratio of unmarried men in all age groups increased between 1995 and 2010 in Japan, and the rate of increase among those in their twenties and thirties was particularly high (Cabinet Office 2015). In terms of education, the number of never-married men with a low level of education doubled from 1985 to 2005. The numbers of never-married men with a high level of education or a middle level of education underwent a moderate increase during the same period (Shirahase 2010).

In the same study of never-married corporate men (Nemoto 2013), there were a few men who showed an explicit lack of interest in the obligatory aspects of marriage. One man I talked with, a 36-year-old worker for a large construction company, usually came home around midnight due to overwork. Even though he wanted to have a traditional marriage to a woman who is devoted to being a housewife, he had a hard time seeing marriage as something he could invest meaningful time and energy in. "I don't know what I want in marriage. I don't really see the advantages of getting married. I have been wondering to myself why I need to marry. Is it because I should pass on my genes? . . . Or is it to provide security as you get old? . . . Well, if I pay, I can eat and have fun without marriage." Another man, Koji, a 32-year-old pharmacist, said, "I think marriage is bondage. It is an invisible constraint. . . . If I marry, I cannot do what I want to do." Koji emphasized the wide variety of sports and hobbies he has enjoyed over the years by delaying marriage (Nemoto 2013, 15). Akio, a 38-year-old worker at an electronics company with an MBA, said he prioritized his job over marriage, and he did not mind being single for the rest of his life as he had a well-paying job, hobbies, and friends. Some men I interviewed had occasional sex with dates they met at casual gatherings, singles parties, or bars. A small number of the unmarried Japanese men that I interviewed emphasized the importance of work and autonomy, but they never mentioned a desire for a relationship, the quality of a marriage, or the marital partner's career. This reflects the fact that Japanese marriages continue to be based on gender-divided obligations, and the man has the decision-making power over the woman as he is the sole or major earner. Most men I talked with (some in their twenties but most in their thirties) expected their marital partner to be a traditional housewife who does all the housework for him. Their views of women and family were monolithically self-centered, anachronistically traditional, and mechanically gender-role-divided. Such views may simply reflect women's lack of power in the corporate hierarchy in Japan.

In this same study of unmarried employed men in Japan, one 37-year-old engineer at a large computer company talked about his long history of enjoying paid sex and the sex entertainment industry in Tokyo, which offers a variety of sexual services. He pointed out that he started using paid sex because of his workaholic life in male-dominated colleges and companies, where he met with very few women. He added that many single employed men in highly male-dominated workplaces, like him, commonly use paid sex services. Even though he said he may marry in the future and had dated a few women, he said he might continue to use the sexual services. Another 32-year-old single engineer said he preferred paid sex to dating since paid sex takes less time and involves no commitment and no responsibilities. His only concern was the high price for paid sex. He occasionally dated women but this never lasted long. He had no desire to marry and form a family. He preferred spending time on work and his hobbies, which including shopping for designer-brand clothes and collecting motorcycles with new designs. He started using paid sex when he was in college; many of his coworkers in the manufacturing company, both married and unmarried, commonly use the services and talk about them openly, so he never questioned his use of them. "It is just so normal for men in Japan to use these services."

The sex entertainment industry in Japan has had a close relationship with Japanese companies; it offers sexual outlets to corporate employees to help with their sexual frustration and isolation, as well as providing a workplace treat or enhancing masculine bonds among workers. In addition, corporate workers sometimes take business clients or partners to sex entertainment venues for the purpose of hospitality. Japan has had in place a Prostitution Prevention Law since 1957 that prohibits sexual intercourse with unspecified persons for money and bans the promotion of organized sexual activity or brothels; many Japanese sex entertainment services get around the law by claiming that they only offer customers opportunities for dates, not outright sexual intercourse. There are various types of paid and commodified sex such as massage parlor, delivery types, call girl, and strip club. Among them, the so-called "soapland" or private bathhouse is one of the most popular services in Japan; in this arrangement, the client and hired worker who bathe together claim that they engage in intercourse on a date, as acquaintances, and therefore their sex is not prostitution (Hongo 2008). Paid sex is therefore easily available to men in Japan (from single men to married men, who are often said to use these services because of their sexless marriages).

While the sex entertainment industry is nothing new in Japan, it is possible that unmarried employed men, whose lifestyles are increasingly singles-oriented and work-centric, increasingly rely on various types of paid sex, and commodified sexual images replace dating and marriage. Overwork, as well as men's aversion to spending too much time on interpersonal relationships, possibly promote men's use of such services as well. Previous generations of Japanese salarymen did not have the option of leading "autonomous" lives, but the social pressure to marry has largely receded in Japan. In addition, men's sex outside of marriage, or infidelity, has long been accepted and this is most likely because Japanese women do not possess economic independence equal to that of men and have few options in the labor market.

Since the 1990s, in addition to the overall decline of social and cultural pressure to marry by a certain age, the decline of the Japanese economy further diminished men's economic stability and their opportunity for lifelong employment. Moreover, because of the aging society and trend toward late marriage in Japan, the number of single households has increased and the market catering to single household consumption has prospered. In other words, several socioeconomic changes since the 1990s have made it increasingly difficult for some groups of men, lacking lifelong, well-paid jobs, to claim traditional manhood as family patriarchs. They compensate by indulging in consumptive images and commodities.

Economic Shifts and Changes in Men's Lives in Japan

The number of single households in Japan more than doubled between 1980 and 2005, and by 2015 they surpassed the number of households with married couples or families. With the surge of single-person households in Japan, Japanese businesses have targeted this market. Not just convenience stores but also department stores devote as much as one-fourth of their floor space to selling bento boxes for lunches and dinners. Various other services are tailored for single workers who have little time: housecleaning services, massage salons, sex dolls, hot spring trips, and restaurants and bars for singles. From relaxation products to paid sex to online sexual images, one can enjoy individual autonomy and interpersonal relationships without committing to marriage and family life.

Anne Allison (2009, 91), employing Hardt and Negri, says that capitalism in the twenty-first century has been shifting from the formerly dominant industrial and agricultural production to an immateriality-driven economy, in which information, communication, affection, and consumption have become the sources and targets of business and labor. The immaterialization-driven lifestyle, combined with increasingly precarious economic conditions for young Japanese, has further promoted Japan's reproduction crisis. Allison (2009) writes:

> . . . the immaterialization of the economy fosters a social relationality based on commodification and privatization. Citizens are now expected to purchase their relations—for companionship, intimacy, care—as private consumers on the marketplace. Not only are those with less money disadvantaged in an era when older forms of social connectedness—family, workplace, community—are eroding, but the format given to sociality in such privatized prosthetics tends to be narcissistically self-referential. One may become deeply attached to a Pokémon, a pet robot, or a customized doll—as is the new trend in Akihabara these days—but the relationship still rebounds to the owner and her needs/desires alone. Herein lies a source of Japan's so-called crisis in social reproduction today. (91)

Indeed, the rise of various consumptive commodities and the normalcy of daily online access relates to alternative masculinities in Japan, including herbivore man and otaku man, who may contest hegemonic salaryman manhood by distancing themselves from patriarchal families and traditional breadwinner masculinities and immersing themselves in consumptive technologies and activities.

The second social change for men has occurred in the form of decreasing lifelong employment and economic security. The marginal men in Japan are increasingly the young men who work in unstable jobs or are entirely withdrawn from work itself. The number of young men without economic security, who are given such labels as "freeter," "NEET," and "hikikomori," has soared in Japan since the 1990s. With the intensification of globalization and competition, many of Japan's companies have increasingly relied, since the 1990s, on young temporary and non-lifetime-employed men and women. The number of non-lifetime-employed workers, including part-time workers and temporary workers, more than doubled between 1990 and 2005 and continues to increase.

There are about 200 million people referred to as "freeter," unmarried part-time or temporary workers who range from 15 to 34 years old (Ministry of Health, Labour, and Welfare 2012). It is estimated that about 60 million young people between the ages of 15 and 34, referred to as "NEET" (Not in Education, Employment or Training), neither work nor go to school. The number of NEET in Japan more than doubled between 1995 and 2012. The term NEET originated with young people in the UK who reject exploitative precarious jobs, but the NEET in Japan are associated with "personal failure, social reclusiveness and even mental illness" (Slater 2008). Also, there are over 60 million "hikikomori" (the term means "withdrawn from society") who spend most of their time at home (Cabinet Office 2013); most of the hikikomori are male. For a man in Japan, being something other than a salaryman, and being economically marginal, makes it difficult to attain a masculine identity and gain adequate social recognition (Slater 2008). Slater points out that not being a salaryman with a college degree or even an economically precarious temporary worker in Japan means being not just a second-class citizen but also a non-citizen of the Japanese corporate world. The social isolation and self-loathing of marginal manhood can lead to terrible outcomes, such as the 25-year-old dispatch worker, Tomohiro Kato, who murdered seven people and injured ten by driving into a crowd with a truck and then stabbing several people in Akihabara, Tokyo, in 2008. Kato's resentment toward his coworkers and society, his social isolation, his otaku manhood, and his overly strict mother were often brought up to account for the alienation and self-loathing which derived from his failure to be a regular lifelong employed worker in Japan.

Since the 1990s, different groups of men have been emerging, both economically and culturally. For example, Takeyama's research focuses on hosts in Japan, the male equivalent of hostesses, who thrive on neoliberal ideology and a belief in entrepreneurship. Hosts sell seductive masculine images to their female clients, and many of them "pity the salaryman with their unreasonable working hours, fixed salary, and lack of career mobility" (Takeyama 2010, 241). In contrast with the salaryman, a host is often a working-class man, with perhaps a high school degree or possibly a high school dropout, who often idealizes the entrepreneurial creativity and freedom of his job and dreams of becoming wealthy and successful, under the ideological influence of neoliberalism and the corporate restructuring of the late 1980s. Japanese host men contest traditional hegemonic masculinity and engage in entrepreneurial subjectivity through self-commodification.

"Herbivore" man refers to a man who is soft, quiet, and perhaps unskilled at communicating with or having relationships with others. These men are known to be feminine in their style and also narcissistic and consumption-oriented in their approach to hairstyles, fashions, hobbies, dieting, body management, and sexual relationships (Charlebois 2013, 95). They contest hegemonic salaryman masculinity in the sense that they prioritize autonomy, stylish appearances, and self-fulfillment and consumption-oriented lifestyles over the salaryman norms of dedication to work and self-sacrifice for the company, or the breadwinner obligations to the family. The retreat from breadwinner and reproductive responsibility represents a departure from patriarchal ideology (Charlebois 2013, 96). Herbivore men often rely on media, including "pornographic magazines, as well as erotic DVDs, websites, and computer games," to fulfill their sexual desires (Charlebois 2013, 96). Yet the corporate man and the herbivore are not entirely oppositional. There are many young, single "herbivore" salarymen who lack communication skills and maintain a consumption-driven lifestyle with expensive outfits and casual sex. Somewhat similar to the "new man" discourse in the UK and the US, the herbivore man is neither egalitarian nor democratic (Charlebois 2013, 99).

Otaku men also distance themselves from the traditional patriarchal family and corporate docility. The term "otaku" became common in early 1980s Japan. There is not a single definition for an otaku man (Lamarre 2011, 166). In the United States, an otaku man is just a serious anime fan, but in Japan the term is often associated with antisocial and potentially dangerous behaviors and some postindustrial sensibilities (Condry 2011, 264). Otaku are represented in Japan as weak, overly sensitive, indulgent, and undisciplined in their interactions with others (Kinsella 1998; Slater 2008); they may be best described as socially inept geeks. But the Japanese public relates the term otaku to such pedophile criminals as Miyazaki Tsutomu, who molested and murdered four girls between the ages of four and seven (Galbraith 2011, 103). Otaku have been often stigmatized in Japan because of their links to child pornography and sexual violence (Galbraith 2011, 103).

On the other hand, others praise the otaku as "a new kind of man," because he "refuses certain forms of disciplinisation and rationalization—especially that of the corporate man and the nuclear family" by playing himself and distancing himself from women (Lamarre 2011, 185). In this sense, otaku masculinity represents the "vulnerability" of those who do not make it in the world of corporate manhood (Condry 2011, 270), or the "sense of shame and failure," or the "dialectical tension between thrill and shame, between self-affirmation and self-negation" (Lamarre 2011, 173), or even the "inept, bumbling . . . object of horror," descriptions that some even apply to the nation of Japan itself (Napier 2011, 174).

One of the otaku man's unique qualities is his inability to engage with women. Otaku men are stereotyped as gaining personal intimacy from their consumption of characters from anime and manga. In fact, the otaku's focus on fictional girls in manga and anime may signify their resistance to dominant manhood or their rejection of real women who often desire men with greater material resources (Galbraith 2011, 87). Otaku men are even seen as having an aversion to "real women" or adult women, and a preference for young women or "lolicon" (Lolita complex). Novelist and critic Honda Toru once suggested that marginal men like "otaku" should turn only to fictional "pure" characters, who are free from socioeconomic concerns, and should disengage from capitalism-based sexual relationships in which men are often materially expected to cater to women (Galbraith 2011, 87). Honda has claimed the men's shift from real women to 2-D characters is "the natural evolution of mankind" (Condry 2011, 269). This indicates marginal men's resentment toward and rejection of the dominant patriarchal model of gender dynamics, but it is also a rejection of one's own social and economic engagement. The otaku's rejection of real women marks their protest against and rejection of the traditional breadwinner obligation and the traditional family, but it is not innovative in terms of equalizing gender relations or realistically challenging salaryman corporate customs. The otaku man may distance himself from his own obligation to the patriarchal arrangement, but at the same time he feverishly and passionately consumes hyper-patriarchal and sexist (submissive) female images. Thus, Lamarre writes, ". . . the otaku's images of women are palatable to the corporate man (and may historically derive from the corporate culture)," and "the otaku does not necessarily present a radical break from received social sexual formations . . ." (2011, 175). Their consumption of digital and media commodities offers common and critical resources for their experiences of compensatory masculinity.

Consumption of Images of Submissive Women and Compensatory Masculinity

The consumption of a wide variety of images of girls and women in DVDs, online, and in games, manga, and anime in Japan allows various groups of Japanese men to consolidate their male identity and maintain a fleeting sense of "control" over women. The use of commodified sexual images may replace traditional men's desires and traditional paths toward marriage and family, especially since the marital norm has been rapidly diminishing and men's economic security has been eroding, even though men continue to be pressured to work long hours. Similar to pornography, the mega industries of commercial sex, comic books and anime, and other sexual images and services serve as sources of sexual commodities for compensatory manhood, regardless of the users' employment status. The pervasion of sex commodities coupled with the immaterialization of Japan's economy could further erode social and cultural pressures on men to marry and start families, and could thus accelerate the increase in autonomous lives in Japan.

The popular images of commodified women in Japan reflect the absence of women's socioeconomic power. One of the major characteristics shared by manga, anime, games, and young female performers is the presence of hyper-feminine female characters, who explicitly cater to male consumers' need to regain virtual masculinity by momentarily acquiring a sense of control and dominance over the female figures. Black (2012, 218) points out that the commodification of virtual femininity is a key feature of otaku culture. The "idol otaku" who dedicates his loyalty to his favorite idol wants hyper-feminine features and an evocative embodiment of "emphasized femininity." Black (2012, 219–220) says the female idols must appear "infantilized and sexualized, endearingly nonthreatening and subservient." He continues:

> The carefully constructed idol persona that appeals to the idol otaku is one that evokes youthful innocence, vulnerability, and meekness, and a lack of remoteness or self-sufficiency. These qualities are endearing in their lack of threat and suggestion that the idol is dependent upon support, encouragement, and indulgence of her fans . . . the kind of femininity prized by otaku

(simultaneously infantilized and sexualized, endearingly nonthreatening and subservient) is unlikely to be satisfactory embodied in any living human being; thus it exists most clearly in media such as animated characters and figurines. The living idol can stage a performance of this femininity, but the virtual idol is *nothing but* such a performance. . . . An idol which exists only as digital data which the fan can own and manipulate holds promises of a more intimate relationship than is possible with a living idol. . . . The appeal of the video game THE iDOLM@STER (and its sequel) by Bandai Namco clearly utilizes the capacity of digital idols to fulfill a desire for control. . . . The game thus caters to fantasies of ownership over idols, reflecting the real-life gendered power relations between male music producers and the disposable, commodified young girls in which they deal.

Through the characters' embodying dependency on and subordination to the fans (men), in addition to their sexually attractive appearance, they symbolically and imaginatively represent "emphasized femininity" to male consumers. In "beautiful girl games," or *kisekae* games, which are recent technologically advanced 3-D games, players have direct access to pornographic materials and enjoy complete mastery over and sexual enjoyment of virtual girls and women (Black 2012, 221). Using the packaged body of a virtual idol and singer with a synthesizer voice called Vocaloid, Yuki Terai, players can alter and trade her face, body, skin, eye color, and genitalia (222). The goal of consuming digital femininity may be to perfect players' privatization of and control over digital femininities and bodies as text (Black 2012, 224). The games are about men's recovery of their power over beautiful and submissive females.

Men's fetishization of young girls is widely known as lolicon (Lolita complex) in Japan. Whether men's fetishization of sexualized images of young girls simply mirrors their anxious display of compensatory masculinity over younger and more powerless women or represents a revolt from traditional gender ideology has been debated. Hinton says that male anxiety about women's sophistication in Japan has led some men to retreat into the fictional world of imaginary young girls in lolicon manga. In these, "the term Lolita represent[s] a mythical shoujo—the opposite of the emancipated woman—undeveloped, cute, childlike, nonthreatening, and obeying the male characters' erotic wishes, providing an imaginary world as an escape from the anxieties of engaging with real *shoujo*" (Hinton 2013, 1593). Furthermore, "these otaku develop . . . an erotic attachment to the idealized (unthreatening) moe characters [erotic and affective feeling for the fictional characters] in manga and anime within a purely virtual world, which provide[s] a space of male sexual fantasy" (1594). Male sexual fantasy in lolicon manga allows men to withdraw from the adult concerns, threats, and responsibilities of the real world. Lolita in Western culture represents a sexually mature teenager, but Japanese men associate the concept with a more nostalgically romanticized and innocent figure (Hinton 2013, 1592), thus alleviating some of the men's anxiety about themselves.

Kinsella (2014) argues that Japan's Lolita complex culture and men's fetishization of young girls relates to the men's being intimidated by these girls, and simultaneously reveals their desire to be liberated by possessing and identifying with them. Kinsella explains that, on the part of adult Japanese men, there has often been a complicated projection of compulsive identification in sexual relations with school girls (called assisted dates or enjo kyosai). Japan's underage girls' prostitution, which is called "syojo baisyun," has been internationally criticized as one of the largest sources of human trafficking in Japan. Similarly, a murky prostitution business including so-called "JK business" (JK means jyoshi kokosei, or high school girls) offers a variety of services from non-sexual dates to compensated dates, including prostitution. Japan's fetishization of school girls is not limited to a particular group of men but has been pervasive throughout the culture; the male clients who pay for this type of commodified sex, targeting high school–age or younger girls, include civil servants and salarymen.

Somewhat similar to Kinsella's explanation of men's ambivalent identification with adolescent girls in Japan, Galbraith (2011, 103) argues that lolicon manga can be transgressive for manhood, because male readers may actually identify not with the men who rape the girls in the manga scripts but with the girls who are the victims of the rapes, thus rejecting the masculine position of control and power. Lolicon can be "a rejection of the need to establish oneself as masculine and an identification with the 'kindness and love'" of the nostalgic and pure image of girls, and "this interpretation reverses the standard understanding of lolicon as an expression of masculinity to one of femininity." Furthermore, "if being a man ceases to promise power, potency and pleasure, it is no longer the privileged subject position" (Galbraith 2011, 103). The man, by identifying with the girls' kindness or femininity, metaphorically criticizes the patriarchal society that oppresses him (Galbraith 2011, 103).

Meanwhile, Kinsella (2014, 162) points out that men's tangled desires to possess these girls is not so straightforward: school girl characters in pornographic Lolita-complex animation "are subject to intimidation, trickery, bondage, and rape by tentacular demon penises, robotic arms, rape machines, and devilish old men." Indeed, "within the male culture of girls, we see an unstable mixture of hostile resentment and a wishful identification with the potential power position and glamour of ascendant girls" (163). The images of school girls or shojo may enable men both to identify with the girls or shojo and also to experience a sense of control and possession over them.

As long as the fetishization of Lolita figures and sexualization of young girls continues, the boundaries among the hegemonic and marginal men who are consumers become blurred, even though the lolicon is typically associated with the otaku men who are commonly understood to be incapable of finding real dates. But salarymen and corporate men, police officers, and politicians have also been known to pay for assisted dating with high school girls. Regardless of the characteristics of the consumer, the popularly circulated materials about girls include images of "disablement through terror, bondage, and dismemberment"; among them are erotic cartoons or ero-manga, in which women are sexually subordinated, coerced, and even killed, and which are thus more explicitly phallic-centered and misogynistic than some of the other materials described above.

Ann Allison (2000) finds that the main theme in this genre of comic books is men's aggression and women's subordination, as well as men's disengagement, distancing, disguising, narcissism, use of the penis as a weapon, and voyeurism, all designed to dominate women. Allison writes:

> The sexual aims that are dominant in ero manga and dominantly male are seeing, possessing, penetrating and hurting. In pursuing these interests men rely heavily on an arsenal of instruments, weapons, and objects that extend their bodily powers and become interchangeable with them. These include baseball bats, tennis rackets, golf clubs, swords, knives, Coke bottles, popsicle sticks, candles, pens, calligraphy brushes, wands, hypodermic needles, periscopes, video cameras, cameras, magnifying glasses, and telescopes (64). . . . A penis acts as a weapon, a hand as a conqueror, eyes as voyeurs. . . . So just as the male body can become polymorphously perverse, so can the world (poly)morphize into a male tool. . . . It is when women are naked that they are subordinated, coerced, and even killed. A naked body is a sign of captivity (hence the importance of the women's expressions of fear, pain, and degradation), as in the endless portrayals of women tied with rope that both semiotically marks their bodies into erotogenic zones and sadistically cuts them into pieces. (67)

The images of women in ero manga in Japan are consumed as an outlet for men's release of the frustration and stress from work over which they have little control, and perhaps as a result of their resentment toward women both for exerting power over them as housewives and mothers and for being economically dependent on them. Allison argues that it is likely that the gender chauvinism and crude masochism in erotic comics in Japan will change only when women increase their socioeconomic power (2000, 78).[1]

In his studies of male consumption of pornography and personal effects on men in the United States, Matthew Ezzell argues that pornography provides male consumers with "a *collective* gain (beliefs in/enactment of male dominance) but exacts an *individual* cost (decreased empathy and intimacy, dependence, anxiety)" (2014, 25). The consumption of pornography is a compensatory manhood act because it enables men to have access to the symbolic experience of male power over women, and can be an outlet for their sexual frustrations, resentment, and powerlessness in daily life. The male consumers of pornography are often "angry, sexually frustrated, and eager to exact some sort of revenge on women" (Kimmel 2008, 186). The men whom Michael Kimmel interviewed spoke of women with contempt. They are "getting back at a world that deprives them of power and control, getting even with those haughty women who deny them sex even while they invite desire, getting back at the bitches and hos who, in the cosmology of Guyland, have all the power" (Kimmel 2008, 188). Pornography also enables men to experience homosociality, and a sense of collective maleness aligned against females (Kimmel 2008). Pornography "delivers the sexual script of patriarchy in which men's sexual aggression is normalized and celebrated" (Ezzell 2014, 28). Similarly, Jensen (2007) writes that the central function of pornography for male consumers is gaining a sense of control. As the sex therapist Marty Klei points out, pornography provides men with feelings of confidence and acceptance, while also offering patriarchal scripts about phallic male bodies conquering the female nature and controlling women who naturally desire men and want sex (Garlick 2010, 609). No matter how these images and narratives compensate men by giving them a virtual sense of manhood, studies also report the negative consequences of pornographic consumption on them. Among his male respondents in his study of the consumption of pornography, Ezzell (2014, 24–25) found that the men tended to replicate sexual acts from pornography in their real relationships, lacked excitement in their real relationships, experienced enhanced anxiety with regard to their own sexual performance, and tended to objectify women.

It is not clear, and it will require further studies, whether regular reliance on such consumptive commodities in Japan as sexual scripts and images in comic books, manga, anime, and games, as well as paid sex, have negative consequences on men similar to those of the consumption of pornography. What remains clear is that the rise of single households, declining men's wages, the rise of consumption-based autonomous lifestyles, the erosion of the social pressure to marry, and the continuing pressure on men to work long hours, are all driving men to further seek out these sexual commodities. Accordingly, commodified sex and consumptive commodities for men's sexual enjoyment could further change the traditional meanings of intimacy, family, and manhood in Japan, and could recast Japanese men's desire for reproduction and the maintenance of the population. These commodified sexual outlets for men may also serve to maintain the traditional gendered regime in Japan, in which men devote themselves to work rather than to family or their personal lives. The normalization of commercial and consumptive mediums for men's sexuality may further promote the decline of marriage and promote the autonomous, work-centered life.

Note

1. The tendency of men to rely on consumption for their sexual outlets is also embedded in child socialization in Japan. Anne Allison finds similarities between the male gaze in children's manga in Japan and corporate workers' use of recreational sex. Boys learn to consume naked females in voyeuristic and fetishistic ways in children's manga, and in doing so they are encouraged to construct their sexuality in similar ways to that of adult workers, all while learning that men's place in society differs from that of women (2000, 48). Allison points out the gendered messages for boy's sexuality in children's manga: "Even as the five-year-old watches *Doraemon* and the twelve-year-old views *Machiko-sensei*, they are likely to be using manga as a diversion in lives that will be increasingly filled with study of . . . the images of naked breasts. . . . These images were also, however, seen as being for males: They are treats that boys digest as they study just as grown men read erotic comic books as they commute to work in the morning or visit a hostess club or a *pinku saron* after work is finished."

References

Allison, Anne. 1994. *Nightwork: Sexuality, Pleasure, and Masculinity in a Tokyo Hostess Club.* Chicago, IL: University of Chicago Press.

———. 2000. *Permitted and Prohibited Desires: Mothers, Comics, and Censorship in Japan.* Berkeley: University of California Press.

———. 2009. "The Cool Brand, Affective Activism and Japanese Youth." *Theory, Culture, & Society* 26 (2–3): 89–111.

Asahi Shinbun. 2013. "Survey: 'Sexless' marriages top 50%." June 28. http://ajw.asahi.com/article/behind_news/social_affairs/AJ201306280055, accessed December 2015.

Black, Daniel. 2012. "The Virtual Idol: Producing and Consuming Digital Femininity." In *Idols and Celebrity in Japanese Media Culture.* Edited by Patrick W. Galbraith and Jason G. Karlin, 209–228. Palgrave Macmillan.

Cabinet Office. 2013. "Jaykunen mugyousya, freeta, and hikikomori." Kodomo Wakamono Hakusyo [White Paper on Children and Youth]. http://www8.cao.go.jp/youth/whitepaper/h25honpen/b1_04_02.html, accessed December 2015.

Cabinet Office. 2015. "Nenreibetsu mikonritsu no suii" [Changes of non-marriage rate by age]. In Syoushika Taisaku [Policy on Declining Birthrate]. http://www8.cao.go.jp/shoushi/shoushika/data/mikonritsu.html, accessed December 1, 2015.

Charlebois, Justin. 2013. "Herbivore Masculinity as an Oppositional Form of Masculinity." *Culture, Society, and Masculinities* 5(1): 89–104.

Christensen, Paul A. 2015. *Japan, Alcoholism and Masculinity: Suffering Sobriety in Tokyo.* London: Lexington Books.

Condry, Ian. 2011. "Love Revolution: Anima, Masculinity, and the Future." In *Recreating Japanese Men*, edited by Sabine Fruhstuck and Anne Walthall, 262–283. Berkeley: University of California Press.

Dasgupta, Romit. 2009. "'The Lost Decade' of the 1990s and Shifting Masculinities in Japan." *Culture, Society & Masculinity* 1: 79–95.

Dore, Ronald. 2000. "Will Global Capitalism be Anglo-Saxon Capitalism? *New Left Review* 6: 101–119.

Ezzell, Matthew B. 2014. "Pornography Makes the Man: The Impact of Pornography as a Component of Gender and Sexual Socialization." In *The Philosophy of Pornography: Contemporary Perspectives*, edited by Lindsay Coleman and Jacob M. Held, 17–34. Lanham: Roman & Littlefield.

Galbraith, Patrick. 2011. "Lolicon: The Reality of 'Virtual Child Pornography' in Japan." *Image & Narrative* 12, 1: 83–119.

Garlick, Steve. 2010. "Taking Control of Sex: Hegemonic Masculinity, Technology, and Internet Pornography." *Men and Masculinities* 12(5): 597–614.

Gender Equality Bureau Cabinet Office. 2015. "White Paper on Gender Equal Society 2015." http://www.gender.go.jp/about_danjo/whitepaper/h27/zentai/html/zuhyo/zuhyo01-02-09.html, accessed December 1.

Gottfried, Heidi, and Hayashi-Kato, Nagisa. 1998. "Gendering Work: Deconstructing the Narrative of the Japanese Economic Miracle." *Work, Employment and Society* 12, 1: 25–46.

Hinton, Perry R. 2013. "Returning in Different Fashion: Culture, Communication, and Changing Representations of Lolita in Japan and West." *International Journal of Communication* 7: 1582–1602.

Honda, Toru. 2005. *Moeru otoko [The Budding Man].* Tokyo: Chikuma Shobo.

Hongo, Jun. 2008. "Law Bends Over Backward to Allow 'Fusoku.' *The Japan Times.* May 27. http://www.japantimes.co.jp/news/2008/05/27/reference/law-bends-over-backward-to-allow-fuzoku/#.Vn-PZ1KrnV2, accessed December 1, 2015.

Jensen, Robert. 2007. *Getting Off: Pornography and the End of Masculinity.* Cambridge: South End Press.

Kawahito, Hiroshi. 1998. *Suicide by Overwork.* Tokyo: Iwanami Shoten.

Kawanishi, Yuko. 2008. "On Karo-Jisatsu (Suicide by Overwork): Why Do Japanese Workers Work Themselves to Death?" *International Journal of Mental Health*, 37 no. 1: 61–74.

Kimmel, Michael. 2000. *The Gendered Society.* New York: Oxford University Press.

Kimmel, Michael. 2008. *Guyland: The Perilous World Where Boys Become Men.* New York: HarperCollins.

Kinsella, Sharon. 2014. *Schoolgirls, Money and Rebellion.* New York: Routledge.

Lamarre, Thomas. 2011. "An Introduction to Otaku Movement." *EnterText* 4.1: 151–187.

LeBlanc, Robin M. 2010. *The Art of the Gut: Manhood, Power, and Ethics in Japanese Politics.* Berkeley: University of California Press.

Mathews, Gordon. 2003. "Can 'a Real Man' Live for His Family? Ikigai and Masculinity in Today's Japan." In *Men and Masculinities in Contemporary Japan: Dislocating the Salaryman Doxa,* edited by James E. Roberson and Nobue Suzuki, 109–125. London: RoutledgeCurzon.

Ministry of Health, Labour, and Welfare. 2012. "Hiseiki koyono jyokyo [Current Status of Irregular Employment]." http://www.mhlw.go.jp/stf/shingi/2r9852000002k8ag-att/2r9852000002k8f7.pdf, accessed December 2015.

Ministry of Health, Labour, and Welfare. 2014. "Syuro jyoken sougo cyosa [Employment conditions research result]." http://www.mhlw.go.jp/toukei/itiran/roudou/jikan/syurou/14/gaiyou01.html, accessed December 1, 2015.

Napier, Susan. 2011. "Where Have All the Salarymen Gone? Masculinity, Masochism, and Technomobility in Densha Otoko." In *Recreating Japanese Men,* edited by Sabine Fruhstuck and Anne Walthall, 154–176. Berkeley: University of California Press.

Nemoto, Kumiko. 2012. "Never Married Employed Men's Gender Beliefs and Ambivalence Toward Matrimony in Japan." *Journal of Family Issues* 34 (12): 1673–1695.

Research Institute for Advancement of Living Standards. Rengou Souken Survey, 2006. http:// rengo-soken.or.jp/report_db/pub/detail.php?uid=39, accessed March 8, 2012.

Shirahase, Sawako. 2010. "Marriage as an Association of Social Class in a Low Fertility Rate Society: Toward a New Theory of Social Stratification." In *Social Class in Contemporary Japan,* edited by Hiroshi Ishida and David H. Slater, 57–83. London: Routledge.

Slater, David H., and Patrick W. Galbraith. 2011. "Re-Narrating Social Class and Masculinity in Neoliberal Japan: An Examination of Media Coverage of the 'Akihabara Incident' of 2008." *Electronic Journal of Contemporary Japanese Studies,* Article 7, September 30, 2011. http://www.japanesestudies.org.uk/articles/2011/SlaterGalbraith.html, accessed December 15, 2015.

Takeyama, Akiko. 2010. "Intimacy for Sale: Masculinity, Entrepreneurship, and Commodity Self in Japan's Neoliberal Situation." *Japanese Studies,* 30(2): 231–246.

Tipton, Elise K. 2002. "Pink Collar Work: The Café Waitress in Early Twentieth-Century Japan." *Intersections: Gender, History and Culture in the Asian Context,* 7 March. http://intersections.anu.edu.au/issue7/tipton.html, accessed December 1, 2011.

World Economic Forum. 2014. Global Gender Gap Index 2014. http://reports.weforum.org/global-gender-gap-report-2014/rankings, accessed December 1, 2015.

PART V
Relationships and Intimacy

Sharon Bird's reading (no. 2) from earlier in this volume, "Welcome to the Men's Club," demonstrated how men use same-sex, or homosocial, bonding to secure dominant expressions of masculinity. The readings in this section build on and move past Bird's study to demarcate the ways that men enter into and nurture relationships with women, children, and other men. In the first reading (no. 21) in this section, we go inside the "hooking up" culture of young men. The chapter is from Michael Kimmel's popular 2008 book *Guyland: The Perilous World Where Boys Become Men.* For his book, Kimmel interviewed hundreds of mostly white college-educated men. "Guyland" is the term Kimmel gives to both a developmental stage in these men's lives, and also the various male-only spaces they occupy, where they are unencumbered by the obligations of adult life. Kimmel finds that these young men engage in hooking up—those sexual interactions between people who are not in a relationship—to deal with insecurities, to avoid the tough work and expectations of relationships, and to impress other men. Hooking up, Kimmel suggests, may prevent men and women from developing a healthy, egalitarian sexuality.

The next reading (no. 22), "Stigma and Status" by Amy C. Wilkins, shifts attention to the intimate lives of black men in college. Adopting an intersectional approach, Wilkins demonstrates that interracial intimate encounters and relationships create tensions among black men, black women, white women, and white men. For instance, black men use "player talk" to characterize themselves as sexually desirable and white women as eager to please black men. This talk further strains relations between black men and black women, while symbolically unsettling traditional hierarchies which white men the exclusive property of white men. However, player talk poses harm by stereotyping all black men as players and athletes. College black men use "intimacy talk" to push beyond the boundaries of player talk and to seek emotional intimacy and authentic connection.

Kathryn Edin and Timothy J. Nelson's "Fight or Flight" (reading no. 23) examines a different population of black men. Edin and Nelson's chapter is a selection from their book *Doing the Best I Can: Fatherhood in the Inner City,* a qualitative study of poor black fathers in Philadelphia and Camden, New Jersey. Contesting stubborn narratives of absent inner-city fathers, the researchers show how challenging circumstances result in unplanned pregnancies, and how mothers and fathers then struggle to establish families. These men have shunned the "traditional package deal"—stable relationships with their partners—in favor of a "new package deal" where they might be able to salvage strong relationships with their children. Yet while many of these men desire committed relationships with their children, the emotional strain is sometime too great for men who are already economically disempowered.

The final readings in this section reveal the complex gender politics in the intimate lives of Asian men. The first reading (no. 24) is Suowei Xiao's "The 'Second-Wife' Phenomenon and the Relational Construction of Class-Coded Masculinities in Contemporary China." Xiao describes how market reforms in China have unsettled family and intimate life, and have resulted in more extramarital relationships. These include men's relationships with "second wives" who are economically dependent on the men. The second-wife phenomenon resembles a tradition of concubinage in China.

Xiao argues that these second wives labor to help their male partners to maintain masculine status in their professional lives. Finally, reading no. 25 is an original contribution to this volume from Allen J. Kim entitled "Beyond Stoic Salarymen." Based on nearly a decade of ethnographic research, Kim explains the rise of "father schools" in Korea. In their diagnosis of contemporary problems in Korean families, Christian Church leaders have placed blame on traditional East Asian masculine ideals of breadwinning and emotional detachment. The antidote are father schools that ask men to reject features of Korean patriarchy and teach them to be emotionally close with their families, thought to be more characteristic of an American masculinity.

Questions to Ponder

1. How do the features of hegemonic masculinity in the "men's club," as Bird described in reading no. 2, compare to the expressions of masculinity in "Guyland," as Kimmel discusses in the first reading of this section? How else does masculinity shape intimate and sexual relations on college campuses today?

2. How does Wilkins complicate the idea that heterosexual success constitutes manhood acts for black men in college?

3. Wilkins argues that for black men there are costs and benefits to engaging in player talk and intimacy talk. How does the strategic use of each compare to the "unisex identity" that Cooper describes in reading no. 12 (on President Obama)?

4. While Edin and Nelson's chapter does not focus on masculinity, per se, the men in this reading construct gendered selves and negotiate gendered relationships. How do the men assert masculinity in their attempts to maintain relationships with their children?

5. Kim's chapter is unique in showing how Western masculinity has a decisive impact on local communities around the globe. Father schools appear to be based on good intentions. But what are the drawbacks in importing hegemonic masculinity as these schools do?

Key Concepts

Hooking up
The new package deal

Player talk and intimacy talk
The salaryman

Second wives

CHAPTER 21

Hooking Up

Sex in Guyland

Michael Kimmel

I know it's different at other schools," Troy patiently tried to explain to me. "I mean, at other schools, people date. You know, a guy asks a girl out, and they go out to a movie or something. You know, like dating? But here at Cornell, nobody dates. We go out in groups to local bars. We go to parties. And then after we're good and drunk, we hook up. Everyone just hooks up."

"Does that mean you have sex?" I ask.

"Hmm," he says, with a half-smile on his face. "Maybe, maybe not. That's sort of the beauty of it, you know? Nobody can really be sure."

My conversation with Troy echoes an overwhelming majority of conversations I have had with young people all across the country. Whether among college students or recent grads living in major metropolitan areas, "hooking up" defines the current form of social and sexual relationships among young adults. The only point Troy is wrong about is his assumption that traditional dating is going on anywhere else. Dating, at least in college, seems to be gone for good.

Instead, the sexual marketplace is organized around groups of same-sex friends who go out together to meet appropriate sexual partners in a casual setting like a bar or a party. Two people run into each other, seemingly at random, and after a few drinks they decide to go back to one or the other's room or apartment, where some sexual interaction occurs. There is no expectation of a further relationship. Hookups can morph into something else: either friends with benefits or a dating relationship. But that requires some additional, and complex, negotiation.

Some of what's going on won't come as that much of a shock; after all, young adulthood since the sixties has been a time of relative sexual freedom and well-documented experimentation. What may be surprising, though, is how many young people accept that hooking up—recreational sex with no strings attached—is the best and most prevalent arrangement available to them. Once, sexual promiscuity co-existed with traditional forms of dating, and young people could maneuver between the two on their way toward serious and committed romantic relationships. Now, hooking up is pretty much all there is; relationships begin and end with sex. Hooking up has become the alpha and omega of young adult romance.

And though hooking up might seem utterly mutual—after all, just who are all those guys hooking up *with*?—what appears on the surface to be mutual turns out to be anything but. Despite enormous changes in the sexual attitudes of young people, the gender politics of campus sex don't seem to have changed very much at all. Sex in Guyland is just that—guys' sex. Women are welcome to act upon their sexual desires, but guys run the scene. Women who decide not to join the party can look forward to going to sleep early and alone tonight—and every night. And women who do join the party run the risk of encountering the same old double standard that no amount of feminist progress seems able to eradicate fully. Though women may accommodate themselves to men's desires—indeed, some feel they have to accommodate themselves to them—the men's rules rule. What this means is that many young women are biding their time, waiting for the guys to grow up and start acting like men.

Yet the hooking-up culture so dominates campus life that many older guys report having a difficult time making a transition to serious adult relationships. They all say that eventually they expect to get married and have families, but they have no road map for getting from drunken sloppy "Did we or didn't we?" sex to mature adult relationships. It turns out that choosing quantity over quality teaches them nothing about long-term commitment. Nor is it meant to. The pursuit of conquests is more about guys proving something to other guys than it is about the women involved.

As a result, most guys drift toward adulthood ill prepared for emotional intimacy better suited to fantasies of being "wedding crashers" (hooking up with women who are attending a friend's wedding) than becoming grooms themselves. They know little more about themselves and their sexuality at 28 than they did at 18, and the more subtle aspects of romance and partnership likewise remain a mystery. They barely know how to date. While the hookup culture might seem like some sort of orgiastic revelry, in truth these guys are missing out. It's not just that they're delaying adulthood—it's that they're entering it misinformed and ill prepared.

Hooking Up

In recent years, scholarly researchers and intrepid journalists have bravely waded in to demarcate the term "hooking up," map its boundaries, and explain its strange terrain. But the definitions are vague and contradictory. One research group refers to it as ". . . a sexual encounter which may or may not include sexual intercourse, usually occurring on only one occasion between two people who are strangers or brief acquaintances." Another study maintains that hooking up ". . . occurs when two people who are casual acquaintances or who have just met that evening at a bar or party agree to engage in some forms of sexual behavior for which there will likely be no future commitment."[1]

Our collaborative research project, The Online College Social Life Survey, found that hooking up covers a multitude of behaviors, including kissing and nongenital touching (34 percent), oral sex, but not intercourse (15 percent), manual stimulation of the genitals (19 percent), and intercourse (35–40 percent). It can mean "going all the way." Or it can mean "everything but." By their senior year, we found that students had averaged nearly seven hookups during their collegiate careers. About one-fourth (24 percent) say they have never hooked up, while slightly more than that (28 percent) have hooked up ten times or more.[2]

As a verb, "to hook up" means to engage in any type of sexual activity with someone you are not in a relationship with. As a noun, a "hookup" can either refer to the sexual encounter or to the person with whom you hook up. Hooking up is used to describe casual sexual encounters on a continuum from "one-night stands" (a hookup that takes place once and once only with someone who may or may not be a stranger) to "sex buddies" (acquaintances who meet regularly for sex but rarely if ever associate otherwise), to "friends with benefits" (friends who do not care to become romantic partners, but may include sex among the activities they enjoy together).

Part of what makes the hookup culture so difficult to define and describe is the simple fact that young men and women experience it in very different ways. They may be playing the same game, but they're often on opposing teams, playing by a different set of rules, and they define "winning," and even "scoring," in totally different ways. Sameness doesn't necessarily mean equality.

Indeed, the current patterns of sociability and sexuality among heterosexuals have actually begun to resemble the patterns that emerged in the mainstream gay male community in the late 1970s and early 1980s, the pre-AIDS era. Sex was de-coupled from romance and love, and made part of friendships that may—or may not—have anything to do with romantic relationships. "Fuck buddies" are the precursors to "friends with benefits." Sex was seen as recreational self-expression, not freighted with the matched baggage of love and relationship. When it comes to scoring, then, gay and straight men have a lot more in common with each other than either group does with women. To put it another way, it is gender, not sexual orientation, that is the key to understanding these campus sexual patterns. If we want to understand the complexities of the hookup culture we must do so with gender in mind.

Deliberate Vagueness

In a sense, hooking up retains certain features of older dating patterns: male domination, female compliance, and double standards. Though hooking up may seem to be mutually desired by both guys and girls, our research indicates that guys initiate sexual behavior most of the time (less than a third of respondents said this was mutual). Hookups are twice as likely to take place in his room as in hers. And, most important, hooking up enhances his reputation whereas it damages hers. Guys who hook up a lot are seen by their peers as studs; women who hook up a lot are seen as sluts who "give it up." According to Duke's study of campus sexual behavior, "Men and women agreed the double standard persists; men gain status through sexual activity while women lose status."

"There is definitely a double standard," says Cheryl, a sophomore at Creighton. "I mean, if I do what my friend Jeff does [hook up with a different girl virtually every weekend], my friends wouldn't talk to me! I mean, that's just gross when a girl does it. But a guy, it's, like, he's like Mr. Man."

"If a guy hooks up with a girl, he sort of broke down her wall of protection," explains Terry, a Stanford junior. "She's the one that let her guard down . . . her job going into the night . . . was to like protect herself, protect her moral character and her moral fiber, and it's like you came in and went after her and she was, like, convinced to let her guard down . . ."

This is a somewhat surprising view of things, given just how much we think everything has changed. It not only echoes the 1950s, but even farther back to the Victorian age. Despite the dramatic changes in sexual behavior spurred by the sexual revolution, sexual experience still means something different for women and men. "It's different from what it used to be when women were supposed to hold out until they got married. There's pressure now on both men and women to lose their virginity," is how one guy put it. "But for a man it's a sign of manhood, and for a woman there's still some loss of value."[3]

The vagueness of the term itself—hooking up—turns out to be a way to protect the reputation of the woman while enhancing that of the man. In addition to that conceptual vagueness after the fact, hookups are also characterized by a certain vagueness before and even during the fact as well. Most hookups share three elements: the appearance of spontaneity, the nearly inevitable use of alcohol, and the absence of any expectation of a relationship.

Planned Spontaneity

In order for hookups to work, they have to appear to be spontaneous. And they do—at least to the guys. One guy told me it's "a sort of one-time, spur-of-the-moment thing. Hookups generally are very unplanned."

"Oh, sure," said Jackson, a 22-year-old senior at Arizona State, "you go to parties on the prowl, looking to hook up. But you never know if it's going to happen. And you certainly don't know who you're gonna hook up with. That takes several drinks."

Yet such spontaneity is nonetheless carefully planned. Guys have elaborate rituals for what has become known as "the girl hunt."[4] There are "pregame" rituals, such as drinking before you go out to bars, since consuming alcohol, a requirement, is also expensive on a limited budget, so it's more cost-effective to begin the buzz before you set out.

There are defined roles for the guys looking to hook up, like the "wing man," the reliable accomplice and confidant. "The wing man is the guy who takes one for the team," says Jake, a sophomore at Notre Dame. "If there are, like, two girls and you're trying to hook up with one of them, your wing man chats up the other one—even if she's, like, awful—so you can have a shot at the one you want. Definitely a trooper."

When guys claim that the hookup is spontaneous, they are referring not to whether the hookup will take place, but with whom they will hook up. Women have a different view of spontaneity. Since they know that hooking up is what the guys want, the girls can't be "spontaneous" about it. They have to think—whether or not, with whom, under what conditions—and plan accordingly, remembering a change of clothes, birth control, and the like. They have to decide how much they can drink, how much they can flirt, and how to avoid any potentially embarrassing or even threatening situations. The guys lounge in comfort of the illusion of alcohol-induced spontaneity; the women are several steps ahead of them.

"Girls, like, before they go out at night, they know whether or not they're going to hook up with somebody," says Jamie, a 21-year-old senior at Arizona State. "It's not spontaneous at all."

Yet the illusion of spontaneity remains important for both guys and girls. It's a way of distancing yourself from your own sexual agency, a way of pretending that sex just happens, all by itself. It helps young people to maintain a certain invulnerability around the whole thing. It's not cool to want something too much. It's better to appear less interested—that way no one will know the extent of your disappointment if your plans don't come to fruition.

The Inevitability of Alcohol

Drinking works in much the same way. Virtually all hooking up is lubricated with copious amounts of alcohol—more alcohol than sex, to tell the truth. "A notable feature of hookups is that they almost always occur when both participants are drinking or drunk," says one study.[5] In our study, men averaged nearly five drinks on their most recent hookup, women nearly 3 drinks. Says one woman:

> Like, drinking alcohol is like a *major* thing with hooking up with people. A lot of the times people won't have one-night stands unless they're drunk. Actually, I can't tell you I know one person who has had a one-night stand without drinking or being drunk, and being, like, "oh, my head hurts. I can't believe I did that."

To say that alcohol clouds one's judgment would be an understatement. Drinking is *supposed* to cloud your judgment. Drinking gives the drinker "beer goggles," which typically expand one's notion of other people's sexual attractiveness. "After like four drinks a person looks a little bit better," explains Samantha, a 21-year-old senior at the University of Virginia. "After six or seven that person looks a lot better than they did. And, well, after ten, that person is the hottest person you've ever seen!" Or, as Jeff puts it, "Everybody looks more attractive when you're drunk."

But intentionally clouding judgment is only part of the story. The other part is to cloud *other people's* judgment. If you were drunk, you don't have to take responsibility for what happens. For guys, this means that if they get shot down they can chalk it up to drunkenness. The same holds true for their sexual performance if they do get lucky enough to go home with someone. In fact, drunkenness provides a convenient excuse for all sorts of potential sexual disasters, from rejection to premature ejaculation to general ineptitude born of inexperience. For a lot of guys, the liquid courage provided by alcohol is the only thing that makes them able to withstand the potential for rejection that any sexual advance entails in the first place.

While both sexes might get to enjoy the lack of responsibility alcohol implies, this turns out to be especially important for the women, who still have their reputations to protect. Being wasted is generally accepted as an excuse. "What did I do last night?" you can legitimately ask your girlfriends. And then everyone laughs. It's still better to be a drunk than a slut. "A hangover," Laura Sessions Stepp writes in her book, *Unhooked*, "is a small price to pay for exoneration."[6]

The Absence of Expectations

One of the key defining features of hooking up is that it's strictly a "no strings attached" endeavor. Young people in college—and this seems to hold true for both women and men—seem generally wary of committed or monogamous relationships. The focus is always on what it costs, rather than what it might provide. And if you consider that half of young adults come from divorced households, their cynicism is neither surprising nor unfounded. "I don't know if I even know any happily married couples," one young woman says. "Most of my friends' parents are divorced, and the ones who aren't are miserable. Where's the appeal in *that*?"

Hooking up is seen as being a lot easier than having a relationship. Students constantly say that having a relationship, actually dating, takes a lot of time, and "like, who has time to date?" asks Greg, a junior at the College of Wooster in Ohio. "I mean, we're all really busy, and we have school, and classes, and jobs, and friends, and all. But, you know," he says with a bit of a wink, "a guy has needs, you know what I mean? Why date if you can just hook up?"

When one older teenager explained her most recent hookup to a *New York Times* reporter, he asked if she thought the relationship might lead to something more. "We might date," she explained. "I don't know. It's just that guys can get so annoying when you start dating them."[7]

"Serial monogamy is exhausting," one young woman tells journalist Stepp. "You put all your emotions into a relationship and then you have to do it all over again." Says another:

Dating is a drain on energy and intellect, and we are overworked, overprogrammed, and over-committed just trying to get into grad school, let alone getting married. It's rare to find someone who would . . . want to put their relationships over their academics/future. I don't even know that relationships are seen as an integrated part of this whole "future" idea. Sometimes, I think they are on their own track that runs parallel and that we feel can be pushed aside or drawn closer at our whim.[8]

Which is a pretty revealing statement since it wasn't so long ago that Doris Lessing remarked that there had never been a man who would jeopardize his career for a love affair—and never been a woman who wouldn't.

Guys seem to agree, but for a different set of reasons. Brian says:

Being in a real relationship just complicates everything. You feel obligated to be all, like, couply. And that gets really boring after a while. When you're friends with benefits, you go over, hook up, then play video games or something. It rocks.[9]

Guys may hook up because they get exactly what they want and don't have to get caught by messy things like emotions. "A lot of guys get into relationships just so they get steady [expletive]," another teen tells journalist Benoit Denizet-Lewis. "But now that it's easy to get sex outside of relationships, guys don't need relationships."[10] "That's all I really want is to hookup," says Justin, a junior at Duke. "I don't want to be all like boyfriend and girlfriend—that would, uh, significantly reduce my chances of hooking up, you know?"

Yet the absence of expectations that supposedly characterizes the hookup seem not to be as true for women. And this is not a simple case of "women want love, men want sex." Rather, it's a case of women being able and willing to acknowledge that there is a lot of ground between anonymous drunken sex and long-term commitment. They might not want to get married, but a phone call the next day might still be nice.

Young women today are more comfortable with their sexuality than any generation in history. There are certainly women who prefer hooking up to relationships. Women also hook up to avoid emotional entanglements that would distract them from their studies, professional ambitions, friendship networks, and other commitments. Or they hook up because they don't think they're ready for a commitment and they just want to hang out and have fun. Yet many also do it because it's the only game in town. If they want to have sexual relationships with men—and by all appearances they certainly do—then this is the field on which they must play. Some women may want more, some may not, but since more is not available either way, they take what they can get. As one young woman explained it to sociologist Kathleen Bogle,

Most of the girls I know are looking for something, you know, someone, even if it's not serious, someone that is there to hang out with and talk to. [Girls want] a feeling of being close to someone and I don't know if it's even that guys don't want that, it's just that they don't care if they have that, it's like "whatever." It could be any other girl any night and you know that's fine with them.[11]

And for the women who do want relationships, hooking up seems to be the only way to find the sort of relationships they say they want. They hope that it will lead somewhere else. Says Annie, 23, who recently graduated from George Washington University, in response to "Why do women hook up?"

Because they want to find love. They want, even though people don't care about consequences, they want to find love. At least girls do. At least I do. I wanted to find love. I wanted to be happy and in love and just have that manly man hold me. They just want to find that. And even if the consequences are bad, it's a lot better going through the consequences and being loved than it is being alone and never loved.

Race and Hooking Up

Hooking up may be a guy thing, but it is also a white guy thing. Of course there are exceptions, but minority students are not hooking up at the same rates as white students. This is partly because minority students on largely white campuses often feel that everything they do is seen not in terms of themselves as individuals but representative of their minority group. "There are so few blacks on campus," says Rashon Ray, a sociologist at Indiana and part of our research team. "If one guy starts acting like a dog, well, word will get around so fast that he'll never get another date." As a result, on some large campuses, black athletes will hook up with white women, but will date black women.

"I know we don't do what the white kids do," said one black male student at Middlebury College in Vermont. "That's right, you don't," said his female companion. "And I don't either. If I even thought about it, my girls would hold me back." Said another black student at Ohio State, "if I started hooking up, I mean, not like with some random white girl, but like with my sisters, oh, God, my friends would be saying I'm, like, 'acting white.'"

As a result, minority students are likely to conform to more conventional dating scripts, especially within their own communities. Our survey found that blacks and Latinos are somewhat less likely to engage in hooking up, and Asian students are far less likely to do so.[12]

Sex as Male Bonding

In some ways hooking up represents the sexual component of young men's more general aversion to adulthood. They don't want girlfriends or serious relationships, in part, because they don't feel themselves ready (they're probably not) and also, in part, because they see relationships as "too much work." Instead they want the benefits of adult relationships, which for them seem to be exclusively sexual, with none of the responsibility that goes along with adult sexuality—the emotional connection, caring, mutuality, and sometimes even the common human decency that mature sexual relationships demand. Simply put, hooking up is the form of relationship guys want with girls.

Yet it's a bit more complicated than simple pleasure-seeking on the part of guys, because as it turns out pleasure isn't the first item on the hookup agenda. In fact, pleasure barely appears on the list at all. If sex were the goal, a guy would have a much better chance of having more (and better) sex if he had a steady girlfriend. Instead, guys hook up to prove something to other guys. The actual experience of sex pales in comparison to the experience of talking about sex.

> When I've just got laid, the first thing I think about—really, I shouldn't be telling you this, but really it's the very first thing, before I've even like "finished"—is that I can't wait to tell my crew who I just did. Like, I say to myself, "Omigod, they're not going to believe that I just did Kristy!"

So says Ted, a 21-year-old junior at Wisconsin:

> Like I just know what will happen. They'll all be high-fiving me and shit. And Kristy? Uh, well, she'll probably ask me not to tell anyone, you know, to protect her reputation and all. But, like, yeah, right. I'm still gonna tell my boys.

Hooking up may have less to do with guys' relationships with women and more to do with guys' relationships with other guys. "It's like the girls you hook up with, they're, like, a way of showing off to other guys," says Jeff, a proud member of a fraternity at the University of Northern Iowa. "I mean, you tell your friends you hooked up with Melissa, and they're like, 'whoa, dude, you are one stud.' So, I'm into Melissa because my guy friends think she is so hot, and now they think more of me because of it. It's totally a guy thing."

He looks a bit sheepish. "Don't get me wrong," he adds, with little affect. "I mean, yeah, Melissa is very nice and blah blah. I like her, yeah. But," he sort of lights up again, "the guys think I totally rule."

Jeff's comments echo those I heard from guys all across the country. Hooking up is not for whatever pleasures one might derive from drunken sex on a given weekend. Hooking up is a way that guys communicate with other guys—it's about homosociality. It's a way that guys compete with each other, establish a pecking order of cool studliness, and attempt to move up in their rankings.

"Oh, definitely," says Adam, a 26-year-old Dartmouth graduate now working in financial services in Boston. "I mean, why do you think it's called 'scoring?' It's like you're scoring with the women, yeah, but you're like scoring on the other guys. Getting over on a girl is the best way of getting your guys' approval."

His friend, Dave, 28, sitting next to him at the bar, is also a Dartmouth grad. He nods. "It's not just like keeping count," he says. "Not a simple tally, you know? It's like 'how many have you had?' Yeah, but it's also 'who did you get?' That's how my guys . . . well, that's how we evaluated you for membership in the worldwide fraternity of guys." They both laugh.

Of course, the awesome insecurity that underlies such juvenile blustering remains unacknowledged, which is interesting since that insecurity is the driving force behind so much of sex in Guyland. The vast majority of college-aged guys are relatively inexperienced sexually. Most of them have had some sex, but not as much as they'd like, and nowhere near as much as they think everyone else has had. Perhaps they've received oral sex, less likely they've performed it, and if they have had intercourse at all it is generally only a handful of times with one partner, two if they're lucky. There are virtually no trustworthy adults willing or able to talk honestly about sex with young people. Talking to their parents is far too awkward. Sex education in schools is often restricted to a quasi-religious preaching of abstinence. Any information that they do manage to cobble together—how it works, what to do, what women like, what they expect—comes almost entirely from their peers, and from pornography. In fact, pornography winds up being the best source of sexual information available to them, and as we've seen pornography is filled with lies.

Yet most guys think that they are alone in their inexperience. They think that other guys are having a lot of sex, all the time, with a huge number of women. And they suspect, but would have no way of knowing, that other guys are a lot better at it than they are. Seen in this light, the hookup culture, at least for guys, is more than a desperate bid simply to keep up. It's a way to keep up, and keep quiet about it—while being rather noisy at the same time.

Hooking Up vs. Good Sex

Mature sexual relationships are complex; good sex takes time to develop. It usually helps to be sober enough to know what is happening. Hooking up may provide quantitative evidence of manly sexual prowess, but it cannot answer the qualitative insecurities that invariably attend sexual relationships. Hooking up may make one feel more like a man when talking with other guys, but it doesn't help—indeed, it may actually hinder—healthy and mutually satisfying sexual relationships with women. And it certainly cannot answer the anxieties that haunt guys when they are alone. Hooking up offers sex without entanglements, but it is attended by so many possibilities for ego devastation, misunderstanding, and crises that it can still become quite entangled. And since there is so much surface interaction in hookup culture, but so little actual connection, most of this stays buried.

With all this hooking up, friends with benefits, and booty calls, guys should feel they have it made. But there is a creeping anxiety that continually haunts guys' sexual activities, particularly these almost-men. They worry that perhaps they're not doing it enough, or well enough, or they're not big enough, or hard enough. Though the *evidence* suggests that men are in the driver's seat when it comes to sex, they *feel* that women have all the power, especially the power to say no.

And these days, those women have a new "power"—the power to compare. Many of the guys I spoke with became suddenly uneasy when the topic of women's sexual expectations came up. They shifted uncomfortably in their seats, looked down at the floor, or stared into their soft drink as if it were an oracle.

Jeff, a sophomore at UC San Diego, said,

Uh, this is the tough part, you know. I mean, well, like, we're supposed to have hooked up a lot, but now so are they, and they, like, talk about it in ways that we guys never would. So, like, you feel like you have to be this fabulous lover and they have to come at least three times, and like, your, you know, your, uh, dick isn't the biggest she's ever seen, and, like, you always feel like you're being measured and coming up a bit . . . [he laughs uncomfortably], short.

"I think guys in your generation were more worried about whether or not you were going to get laid at all," says Drew, a senior at Kansas State. "I'm pretty sure I can hook up when I want, and I have several FWBs and even the occasional booty call. But I worry about whether I'm any good at it. I hear all this stuff from other guys about what they do, and how crazy they get the girl, and I think, whoa, I don't do that."

Guys feel a lot of pressure to hook up, a lot of pressure to score—and to let their friends know about it. And they feel a lot of pressure to be great in bed. In Bogle's study, some students estimated that some of their friends were hooking up twenty-five times every semester. And, they believed that while they thought hooking up meant kissing and other stuff, they thought their friends were actually having intercourse. "It's always the *other* student who, they believed, actually had intercourse every time they hooked up," she writes.[13]

I asked guys all across the country what they think is the percentage of guys on their campus who had sex on any given weekend. The average answer I heard was about 80 percent. That is, they believed that four out of every five guys on campus had sex last weekend. Actually, 80 percent is the percentage of senior men who have *ever* had vaginal intercourse in our college survey. The actual percentage on any given weekend is closer to 5 to 10 percent. This gives one an idea of how pervasive the hooking-up culture is, how distorted the vision of young men by that culture is, and the sorts of pressures a guy might feel as Thursday afternoon hints at the looming weekend. How can he feel like a man if he's close to the only one not getting laid? And if so many women are available, sexually promiscuous, and hooking up as randomly as the men are, what's wrong with him if he's the only one who's unsuccessful?

As it turns out, guys' insecurity is not altogether unfounded. Most hookups are not great sex. In our survey, in their most recent hookups, regardless of what actually took place, only 19 percent of the women reported having an orgasm, as compared to 44 percent of the men. When women received cunnilingus, only about a quarter experience an orgasm, though the men who reported they had performed cunnilingus on their partner reported that she had an orgasm almost 60 percent of the time.

This orgasm gap extends to intercourse as well. Women report an orgasm 34 percent of the time; the men report that the women had an orgasm 58 percent of the time. (The women, not surprisingly, are far better able to tell if the men had orgasms, and reporting rates are virtually identical.)

Many women, it turns out, fake orgasm—and most do so "to make that person feel good, to make them feel like they've done their job." But some women said that they faked it "just really to end it," because they're, "like, bored with it."[14]

"He was, like, trying so hard to make me come," says Trish, a senior at Washington University in St. Louis. "And there was, like, no way it was going to happen. I felt so bad for him. I mean, I had gone down on him and he came already, and he was, like, trying to be a good sport about it, but really . . . So I just faked it, and he felt good and I felt relieved."

Postgraduate Sex in Guyland

Playing the field takes a somewhat different shape after graduation. Though young people still go to bars or parties in groups, and some still drink a lot, fewer are slinking off to empty rooms to hook up. On the whole, post-college-aged people are returning to more traditional dating patterns. Bogle followed recent graduates of two colleges, and found that women and men exchange phone numbers or email addresses, and sometime in the next few days they will contact each other and arrange to go to dinner or something more conventionally social. It turns out that hooking up in college has added a new act in an old drama, but it is hardly a new play.

Of course, the fact that most young people move beyond hooking up still doesn't neutralize its more negative aspects. Though the hookup culture may be the new norm, that still doesn't make it ideal. Even if guys are having sex in order to assuage an understandable insecurity, they are nonetheless using women. And even if women are themselves conscious sexual agents, there remains an undeniable aspect of capitulation in much of their behavior.

"Hookups are very scripted," one woman tells Laura Sessions Stepp. "You're supposed to know what to do and how to do it and how to feel during and afterward. You learn to turn everything off except your body and make yourself emotionally invulnerable."[15]

What kind of sex is this, where a young woman prepares by shutting down and becoming invulnerable? Where a young man thinks more about his friends than about the woman he's having sex with, or even than his own pleasure? Where everyone is so drunk they can barely remember what happened?

Much of what passes for sex in Guyland is not the kind of sex that adults—those with considerably more experience in this arena—would think of as healthy. It sometimes feels as if it doesn't build a relationship but rather is intended to be a temporary stand-in for one. Nor does it seem to be particularly good sex. And the real skills that young people will need as they take on adult sexual relationships rarely feature in the hookup culture. They're not learning how to ask for what they want, or how to listen to their partners, how to keep monogamous sex interesting, how to negotiate pleasure, how to improve their techniques. And while much of adult sexuality is also a learn-as-you-go endeavor, that doesn't mean there isn't plenty of room for advice and counsel.

Yet most adults aren't talking. The more religious among us may have firmly held beliefs that dictate abstinence and tolerate no middle ground, while the more liberal among us may give our adolescent children books that explain the physiological aspects of what they need to know but say nothing of the emotional component inherent in sexuality. But rarely do mature adults actively engage their sons and daughters in the kinds of candid conversations that might actually prove useful to them. Rarely do we talk about a sexuality that can be both passionate and ethical; rarely do we even explain that there is such a thing as ethical sexuality that doesn't promote or even include abstinence as a goal. Instead, the whole subject is so shrouded in embarrassment and discomfort that we generally avoid it, hoping that our kids will figure it out for themselves without too much trouble in the meantime. Lucky for us they often do.

But not always.

Notes

1. Tracy A. Lambert, "Pluralistic Ignorance and Hooking Up" in *Journal of Sex Research* 40(2), May, 2003, p. 129.

2. Our numbers seem to square with other surveys, or, perhaps, run a bit to the conservative side, since we have a large sample of colleges in our pool, and virtually all other surveys were done only at the researchers' university.

3. Laura Sessions Stepp, "Study: Half of All Teens Have Had Oral Sex" in *Washington Post*, September 15, 2005; Sharon Jayson, "Teens Define Sex in New Ways" in *USA Today*, October 18, 2005.

4. See, for example, David Grazian, "The Girl Hunt: Urban Nightlife and the Performance of Masculinity as Collective Activity" in *Symbolic Interaction* 30(2), 2007.

5. Norval Glenn and Elizabeth Marquardt, *Hooking Up, Hanging Out, and Hoping for Mr. Right: College Women on Dating and Mating Today.* New York: Institute for American Values, 2001, p. 15.

6. Laura Sessions Stepp, *Unhooked: How Young Women Pursue Sex, Delay Love and Lose at Both* (New York: Riverhead, 2007), p. 115.

7. Benoit Denizet-Lewis, "Friends, Friends with Benefits and the Benefits of the Local Mall" in *New York Times Magazine*, May 30, 2004, p. 32.

8. Laura Sessions Stepp, *Unhooked*, pp. 40, 174.

9. Ibid., p. 32.

10. Ibid., p. 34

11. Kathleen Bogle, *Hooking Up: Understanding Sex, Dating and Relationships in College and After* (New York: New York University Press. 2008), manuscript, Ch. 6, p. 6, Ch. 4, p. 7.

12. The median number of hookups for white males, juniors and seniors, was 6 (3 for white women). The median for black and Latino males was 4, and for Asians it was zero.

13. Bogle, *Hooking Up*, Ch. 5, p. 20.

14. Paula England, Emily Fitzgibbons Shafer, and Alison Fogarty, "Hooking Up and Forming Romantic Relationships on Today's College Campuses" in *The Gendered Society Reader* (Third Edition), edited by Amy Aronson and Michael Kimmel (New York: Oxford University Press, 2007), manuscript, p. 7.

15. Laura Sessions Stepp, *Unhooked*, p. 243.

CHAPTER 22

Stigma and Status

Interracial Intimacy and Intersectional Identities among Black College Men

Amy C. Wilkins

Introduction

By treating sexuality as performative rather than innate, scholars have untangled the ways men use sexuality to create and challenge masculine identities (e.g., Grazian 2007; Pascoe 2007; Wilkins 2009). Many young men achieve masculinity through the relentless performance of heterosexual success and dominance over women (Pascoe 2007). Most research universalizes heterosexual masculinity as a durable, privileged identity. However, race intersects with gender and heterosexuality to unevenly allocate privilege and power (Collins 2004), complicating the relationship between heterosexuality and masculinity for some men. My study uses in-depth interviews with Black college students to examine the intersections of heterosexuality, masculinity, and race. I focus on Black men's talk about heterosexual interracial relationships, treating this talk as a form of identity work—activity that gives meaning to identities (Schwalbe and Mason-Schrock 1996)—used to claim and signify raced, gendered selves.

Collegiate interracial relationships disrupt racial rules for heterosexual intimacy, making visible underpinning assumptions about race, gender, and sexuality. Predominantly white universities expand opportunities for interracial liaisons, but these opportunities are conditioned in different ways by gender and race (Joyner and Kao 2005). Black college men's greater participation in interracial relationships causes tension between Black college men and Black college women (Childs 2005), while the heightened visibility of Black men's intimate choices on predominantly white campuses increases both peer regulation of their relationships and their significance for men's identities (Ray and Rosow 2009). Research suggests that Black women's anger about interracial relationships stems from their raced and gendered disadvantages in collegiate heterosexual markets (Childs 2005). For Black men, however, interracial relationships present both problems and possibilities. In this article, I examine Black men's talk about relationships with white women. This talk is not explicitly about sexual practices, but it evokes sexual meanings.

More than an arena of private practices, sexuality is a meaning system that is coconstituted with race and gender, used to signify identities, and to allocate social rewards and statuses (Collins 2004; Stein 2008). By examining the ways Black men use talk about heterosexual interracial relationships to

SOURCE: Wilkins, A. C. (2012). Stigma and Status: Interracial Intimacy and Intersectional Identities among Black College Men. *Gender & Society*, 26(2), 165–189. Reproduced with permission.

negotiate their raced gender identities, I focus on the co-construction of race, gender, and sexuality in everyday life, considering these intersections as dynamic rather than a bounded identity.

Theoretical Framework

Following an interactionist view of identities as "strategic social constructions created through interactions, with social and material consequences" (Howard 2000, 371), I focus on the use of talk as a form of identity work used to signify and negotiate identities. People use talk to fashion views of themselves, link themselves to others, and create symbolic boundaries (Schwalbe and Mason-Schrock 1996). Talk is flexible, allowing people to signify and resignify their identities, combine and shift between meanings, and negotiate multiple identity concerns (Howard 2000; Wetherell and Edley 1999). But talk must also negotiate embedded forms of sense-making: Audiences must honor its meanings. Thus, talk is both adaptive and institutional.

Masculinity is a gendered, racialized, sexualized identity constructed and constrained through interactional processes. Gender, race, and sexuality entail interlocking social arrangements from which we take on core identities (West and Zimmerman 1987). For males, being seen as and seeing themselves as masculine is central to the development of a gendered self, differentiates them from women, and "establish[es] eligibility for gender-based privilege" (Schrock and Schwalbe 2009, 287). Men "take on" masculine identities by locating themselves discursively in relationship to conventional masculine expectations (Wetherell and Edley 1999). Men's talk signals credible masculinities to self and others, creates local ideas about masculinity, and creates distinctions among men (Dellinger 2004). Moreover, the intersection of gender with race and sexuality structures both the conditions for masculine identity work and the meaning of masculinity. Race- (and class-)subordinated men are held accountable to different expectations and interpretations of their masculine identities than other men (Wingfield 2008).

Heterosexuality and Young Black Men

Research identifies heterosexuality as central to notions of "real" manhood and thus as an important component of high-status masculinities. Cultural ideas about testosterone-fueled young men who relentlessly chase (hetero)sex, avoid emotional intimacy, and dominate women create heterosexual expectations for young men that can conflict with their lived experiences or preferences. Many young men bridge the gap between expectations and practices by bragging about heterosexual knowledge and practices, talking about women's bodies, anticipating the "girl hunt," and repudiating the "fag" (Grazian 2007; Pascoe 2007). Young men may also situate themselves *against* these expectations. For example, Christian men disdain predatory and promiscuous masculinity, redefining abstinence as masculine and emphasizing the self-control required to avoid heterosexual temptation (Wilkins 2009).

Most research treats heterosexual masculinity as a means of accessing undiluted gendered privilege and power, but heterosexuality does not unequivocally shore up privilege for all men. Gendered sexual discourses associating "normal" heterosexuality with white people and sexual deviance with people of color contribute to inequalities between and among raced men and women (Bederman 1995; Collins 2004). For example, by portraying Black men as rapists who could not stay away from white women, powerful whites justified the need to control Black men through lynching, disenfranchisement, and segregation, and they controlled white women through "protection" (Messerschmidt 2007). For Black men, the intersection of race, masculinity, and heterosexuality entails both masculine privilege and racialized social control of their bodies.

Racialized gender stereotypes are a source of both status and stigma for Black men. The media markets images of Black men as hypersexual, representing Black men as sexually virile "pimps" and "players" able to control women and extract material resources (e.g., get women to buy things for them) without offering commitment (Collins 2004). Because the "player" image caricatures Black men as heterosexually superior and able to control others, it can be a source of masculine status. This same image, however, simultaneously stigmatizes Black men as predatory, promiscuous, uncontrolled, and dangerous, justifying greater institutional control and persistent racial inequality (Ferguson 2000; Pascoe 2007). Black men must position themselves as heterosexual men within the space created by these double-edged images.

Because race reduces Black men's access to other socially valued masculine resources, including status and economic power, the importance of heterosexuality to masculine identity work may increase (Collins 2004; Schrock and Schwalbe 2009). Some research finds that Black men assume the hypersexual image, using it to claim status and respect in the absence of other routes to masculinity (Anderson 1999; Majors and Billson 1992; Staiger 2005). For example, poor urban Black men adopt a "cool pose" in which they gain masculine status, in part, through sexual conquests and the manipulation of women (Majors and Billson 1992). Staiger finds that high school boys also use racialized images of the "pimp" and the "player" to fashion Black masculine identities predicated on their ability to extract resources from girls. By performing as "players," they use heterosexual meanings to position themselves "as in control, rather than being controlled" (2005, 425). Because the player has come to symbolize Black (masculine) authenticity, its appeal extends beyond the urban poor to young middle-class Black men (Ford 2011; Patillo-McCoy 1999). Yet the cool pose has costs: It reinforces sexualized stereotypes of Black men (Staiger 2005), and can derail upward mobility and evoke class disrepute (Majors and Billson 1992).

Differently, some Black men distance themselves from stereotypes of hypersexuality by enacting "respectable" or "decent" Black masculinities in conformance with white expectations (Duneier 1994; Lamont 2002; Wingfield 2007). Historically, Black men have sought eligibility for equal status with white men by aligning themselves with discourses of masculine civility and distinguishing themselves from the stereotype of hypersexuality (Higginbotham 1994). Respectability seems to be particularly important for participation in predominantly white, middle-class institutions. Some Black college men distance themselves from cool pose by emphasizing academics instead of sex (Harper 2004), or by adopting romantic, rather than predatory, orientations toward heterosexuality (Ray and Rosow 2009). Collins (2004) argues, however, that images of Black middle-class respectability portray Black men as weak and effeminate.

Thus, cool pose and respectability each come with benefits and costs: Cool pose bolsters racial authenticity and masculinity, but it can undermine mobility; respectability facilitates mobility but at the expense of Black masculine authenticity—a trait that may be particularly costly for young men for whom high-status masculinity is more tightly linked to heterosexual success. Indeed, Ford (2011) finds that Black university men's "status as upwardly mobile college students may further necessitate the use of certain thuglike . . . signifiers to symbolically maintain semblances of a legitimate black masculine persona that is visibly distinct from that of white men" (2011, 59). Many of the men in her study, however, find these expectations burdensome and inauthentic.

The Study

Data come from 45 in-depth, one- to three-hour interviews conducted with Black undergraduates at two predominantly white universities. I conducted 39 interviews; a research assistant conducted six. Participants were students at one of two large, public universities. Midwestern (all names are pseudonyms) hosts a somewhat higher percentage (5.4 percent) of Black undergraduates than Western (1.4 percent). In different regions (the Midwest and the interior West), these universities are similar to other large, interior public universities with large athletic programs.

I sampled for within-campus heterogeneity among Black students, using initial interviews and informal conversations to map the terrain of Black students, and to develop multiple recruitment strategies. I included members of Black campus organizations and students who avoided those organizations, athletes and non-athletes, members of Black Greek organizations, members of pre-dominantly white Greek organizations, and unaffiliated students. I recruited students who spent time in campus areas associated with Black students and those who did not. Thus, the study intentionally eclipses boundaries between student groups, attempting to include a broad array of campus experiences. Most participants identified themselves as "middle class." However, based on self-reports of parental occupation and home communities, I designated four men and four women as class-disadvantaged. Most others grew up in predominantly white, suburban communities before attending university. All names are pseudonyms.

Aware of my positionality as a white professional woman (the RA was also a white woman), we aimed to increase participants' comfort by establishing common ground through small talk, explaining my interest in learning about racial dynamics from their own vantage, and starting with broad questions that let participants set the interview pace and tone. We also let participants determine where and when the interviews took place. Some chose my office; others chose the campus center or coffee shops. Other factors seemed to be more important in facilitating rapport. First, on both campuses, I received support from Black students who introduced me as an antiracist ally. Second, several participants noted my comfort talking about racial issues, as opposed, I think, to the color-blindness they often confronted in cross-racial communication. Third, because many Black students had grown up in predominantly white communities and trusted (some) white people, whiteness was not an automatic barrier to rapport with all interview participants.

Interviews covered a set of open-ended topics, including schooling, friendship, and dating both before and after the transition to college, but accommodated emerging themes and topics of interest to the participants. In most interviews, we did not ask specifically about interracial relationships. Instead, participants introduced the topic themselves, bringing up interracial relationships when discussing their interactions with other Black students at the university, their dating experiences, experiences with campus organizations, and what it means to be a Black university man or woman.

Following interactionist principles, I treated the interviews as accounts or stories constructed for an audience. Interested in the construction of raced gender identities, I focused on the stories Black students told about each other. Interracial relationships were a central theme in these stories. I then turned to the ways men colluded in and defended themselves against women's stories, asking myself what these particular stories accomplish. I identified two broad frames for interracial relationships. In one, Black men build on the caricature of the player, characterizing interracial relationships as a site of masculine heterosexual accomplishment. In the second, they describe interracial relationships as a site of intimacy. Having identified these distinct ways of talking, I read each interview transcript in its entirety to identify who used each kind of talk, and when, and how men used each kind of talk, attending to contradictions *within* interviews in addition to contradictions between them. I used women's accounts to contextualize the men's, although I am not analyzing their data explicitly in this article. I used a "write to think" process, writing initial analytic drafts that pushed me to deepen and sometimes alter my analysis. Throughout, I compared men's talk about interracial relationships to women's, and compared talk among Black men, looking for similarities and differences between athletes (six) and nonathletes (12), at Midwestern (eight) or Western (10), or between men who identified as heterosexual (15) and those who did not (three). Because men who expressed interest in other men (they do not all identify as "gay") also participated in talk about interracial relationships, I include them in the analysis here. These men's participation in these forms of talk is consistent with my understanding of heterosexuality as a set of meanings that may or may not correspond with people's practices.

Findings

Interracial relationships cause conflict between Black men and Black women on both campuses. Desta, a woman at Western, summarizes, "There's a lot of tension among . . . Black men and Black women on this campus [because of] the stereotype that Black men only talk to [have relationships with] white girls." As Desta indicates, for these students, "interracial" relationships almost always mean relationships between Black men and white women. And when they talk about "Black men," they almost always mean Black athletes. The Black athlete is the dominant cultural symbol of Black manhood on these campuses, but most Black students are not rostered athletes. In this study, six of 18 men are athletes. The invisibility of alternative Black masculinities, however, leads most students to assume that all Black men are athletes, and compels *all* Black college men to negotiate their identities in the athletes' shadow.

The specter of the athlete is both sexually virile and potentially dangerous (Collins 2004). Interracial relationships are central to his lore. Campus stories portray Black athletes endlessly pursued by "snow bunnies" (white women). These stories occlude complexity and variability in Black college men's intimate opportunities and practices. Ten of 18 men in this study report *ever* having had a relationship with a white woman, and six report more than one. Three report preferring Black women. Two are abstinent. Three are primarily interested in men, though none had successfully achieved a relationship (or had much sexual interaction) with one. Athletes describe more interracial opportunities than nonathletes, whom Black students call "regulars." Ekon explains, "White men are looked up higher than regular. But athlete-wise, Black men are looked up higher than white men are." Even some athletes, however, admit their interracial opportunities are not as endless as campus stories make them appear. Nonetheless, campus lore homogenizes Black men and their interracial behavior, painting all Black men in the hypersexual image of the athlete.

I examine Black men's talk about interracial relationships as a form of raced gendered identity work. In the first section, I focus on "player talk"—men's collusion with stories that portray them as "players" relentlessly chased by white women. In the second section, I examine the ways Black men distance themselves from the player by framing interracial relationships as a sign of racial progress and true love. I call this discursive frame "intimacy talk." Although men do not all use player talk and intimacy talk in identical ways, these are not distinct strategies, but instead work together to negotiate Black college masculinity.

Interracial Debates and "Player" Talk

Black men in this study collaborate with other men in talk about interracial relationships regardless of their own practices or preferences, adopting a shared position supporting interracial relationships and opposing Black women's objections. Interracial positions emerge as a predominant feature of raced gender identities in heated intra-racial debates that pit Black men against Black women in classrooms, workshops, and informal confrontations, and on Facebook. In these debates, women blame men's behavior, while men blame women's reactions. Black women, Marcus, a Western football player, explains, are "always stirring up an argument [about]: Why do we have sex with white women and date white women?" These debates foster inter-gender acrimony, and solidify the idea that, as Nick, another Western athlete, says, "all the men" share one perspective on interracial relationships, and "all the women" share another.

By focusing on between-gender differences, debates collapse distinctions *within* raced gender groups, crafting symbolic boundaries that cement the idea that each is a distinct group with shared sets of assumptions, experiences, and concerns. Ekon, the incoming president of the Western Black Student Association, explains the homogenizing effect of these debates: "It's more of an assumption and so then a lot of people fall into the assumption. You know what I mean, it's all talk here and there and then people are like okay and they fall into this assumption . . . and it just becomes reality." The repetitive iteration of gendered views on interracial relationships performs and crystallizes Black masculinity: In this context, endorsing interracial relationships, regardless of actual practice, signals Black manhood. At the same time, gendered debates occlude differences in opportunities, practices, and preferences among Black men.

Debates about interracial relationships create gender boundaries not only because men and women take different sides but because their content crafts shared ideas about what Black men are like. Because this talk draws on cultural images of Black men's heterosexual drive and desirability, and colludes with campus stereotypes about the (exploitative) gender dynamics in interracial relationships, I call this discursive frame "player talk." Player talk bridges discrepancies between men's practices and raced masculine expectations, allowing differently situated Black men to capitalize on the athlete's (presumed) heterosexual success.

Interracial player talk casts Black men as campus lotharios, pursued by relentless white women called "jersey chasers" and "snow bunnies." Craig, an athlete, says, "The amount of white women who are just kind of tossin' themselves at Black athletes is abundant." Nick says, "We could kind of—it sounds kind of bad, we could pick and choose who we want to talk to, and most of us chose white women." Interracial player talk is a form of heterosexual boasting similar to that used by other young men to establish public masculine credentials (e.g., Pascoe 2007), but the subject of interracial sexuality makes its racial content explicit. Talk about "snow bunnies" not only reinforces (to them and others) an image of greater heterosexual opportunities than many men actually have, but also symbolizes the centrality of race to the meaning of these opportunities. As Marcus, laughing, says:

> When I signed my [football] scholarship, I was sayin' I was goin' to go and fuck all these white girls and stuff like that, and . . . like, I'm not gonna lie, bein' young, I thought that havin' sex with white women was also a sense of accomplishment . . . because my whole life I've been told that that's off-limits.

White women's desire for Black men is thus central to this form of talk. Player talk elides variations in the sexual opportunities, practices, and preferences of Black college men by constructing Black men as a uniquely desirable *group*. It emphasizes the universal, rather than individual, attractiveness and sexual superiority of Black men; player talk is usually formulated as "us" rather than "me," as in "*we* could pick and choose." Dominick is also a Western athlete. He says, "I just think white women are attracted to Black men because we're exotic. And we have . . . great natural physiques." Craig asserts, "I know a lot of girls who . . . swear up and down by Black men. They will never date another white man in their life. I guess we're good at having sex, good in bed." Black men's sexual superiority is not, moreover, confined to their bodies. Lance, a high-profile Midwestern student, explains that when Black men are talking to a girl, "he'd be eating her out with his words . . . By the end of it, she's just this pool of nothingness." Men summarize this claim in the expression "Once you go Black, you never go back." In this talk, men draw on cultural ideas about the innate eroticism of Black men, and use them to claim masculine status.

Player talk includes boasting about the things white women will do for Black men. Men only occasionally talked this way to me, but women frequently reported this kind of talk, suggesting that such stories are commonly exchanged among Black students. Yemisi, a leader in the Western BSA, said, "I mean, one of my friends, he was telling me, like, 'I've never had to do my laundry while I was at [university]. And I rarely had to write papers.'" Mei, who runs track at Western, noted, "White girls give the Black guys whatever the hell they want. They always give everything . . . free pussy, free clothes, food." Brenda, a Midwestern student, generalizes that when Black men date white women, "He just wants fuckin'. He just wants to ball her. He doesn't want anybody to challenge him." Here, stories about relationships with *white* women sustain gendered power over *Black* women. To Black women, the message is clear: We don't need you. If you want us, you should cater to our needs.

Some men acknowledged the prevalence of this kind of boasting to me, but often deracialized it, as Dominick does here: "That's any girl. Any girl will do it. You just have to find the right one to do it. . . . But, it's easy to say [that it's about race] when you go to a school that's predominately white." Marcus adds, "[Black women] always say that we always mess with [white women] because they give it up easy. That's part of it. You could say that. But in my lifetime, I've found that all colors and creeds of women can be easy." Vincent, a Midwestern student, makes the same point, "I mean, I messed with everything. . . . The same criteria goes for both races." This deracialized talk claims masculine power over women in another way; by contending that "any girl" will do things for them, these men fortify their desirability, their location in a position of gendered power, and their ability to disregard any woman who doesn't comply with their expectations.

These stories are not just about Black men's relationships with women; they also use gendered ideas to invert racialized hierarchies by depicting white women laboring on behalf of Black men. David, another Western athlete, is explicit: "Some white men hate that African American men are stealing their women." In these stories, crossing racial boundaries confirms Black men's masculinity and upsets racialized hierarchies between white and Black men. At the same time, sexist ideas about women as "property" shore up Black men's right to transgress racial boundaries in the first place.

Player Talk and Campus Position

Black college men do not all participate in player talk in the same ways. As the previous section revealed, athletes boast more often and in more contexts than regulars do, while regular students primarily collude in this talk in community forums. Black men do not have to actively participate in player talk, however, to benefit and lose from the collective meanings it creates. Instead, the repetition of stories about interracial intimacies combines with the content of interracial boasting to conceal differences among Black college men, sustaining stereotypes of Black masculinity as relentlessly heterosexual. This stereotype generates distinct identity opportunities and dilemmas for differently situated men.

Regulars use the image of Black sexuality for their own purposes. Ekon admits to desiring men but has not been intimate with a man or told many people about his interest. He proposes that the image of the hypersexual Black athlete gives him latitude to explore his sexuality: "When people know that you are an athlete, you know, they expect you to date all these girls and do . . . this and that. But when you're not, I mean you . . . [when] you're a regular student you don't have so much pressure on you." Jeffrey, who says he is "waiting for marriage" to have sex, makes a similar claim: "It's interesting because we're stereotyped as very sexual beings . . . I get more respect [for being abstinent] than any kind of criticism." Tim, a member of the Western BSA, uses the homogenized athlete image differently: "My friend . . . a lot of girls hit on him and what he does is he passes them off to me . . . [they ask] 'Oh, do you play sports?' I'm like, 'Yeah, I play basketball.'" Tim gets away with portraying himself as an athlete because of the assumption that all Black men are athletes, and uses this assumption to increase his interracial opportunities. Thus, men enlist the hypersexual stereotype in a range of personal strategies.

These strategies, however, are more complicated than these men propose. They are correct that the stereotype of the hypersexual Black college man is so pervasive that it masks variations in their practices: The success of player talk is evidenced by outsiders' insistence that all Black college men are having endless sex with white women. Contradictorily, the same image constructs a relentless, predatory Black masculine heterosexuality that questions the heterosexuality (and masculinity) of Black men who do not match its narrow expectations. The same women who propose that "all" Black men are having sex with white women also, without any sense of paradox, suggest that non-athlete Black men are gay: "It seems like ok, if you're a Black man you're either an athlete or you're gay," Desta says. "That *is* one of the stigmas," Ekon concedes. "Society has it ingrained that athletes are supposed to be men . . . and if you're not that" then you're gay. Even Tim, a "regular" who described picking up women by successfully posing as an athlete at parties, laments that people insist he's gay. Men's ability to use or deflect the player images thus shifts across contexts and audiences. Regular Black men frame their identities within the rhetorical space of interracial tales that reinforce the idea of relentless Black male heterosexuality—tales that simultaneously enable and constrain their own sexual practices.

Athletes, more likely to participate in interracial relationships, face different opportunities and dilemmas. Player talk deflects attention from the personal frustrations many have finding and sustaining intimacy with women, and thus hides individual worries about heterosexual success. The disjuncture between player talk and talk about relationship troubles is jarring. For example, in the same interview in which he boasted about how "any woman" will do things for him, Dominick lamented, "I've dated girls who told me flat out, 'Hey, I'm using you for this, just to let you know. . . .' They end up doing me wrong, I know that." Like other men's private talk about heterosexual troubles, Dominick's contradictions underscore the use of player talk to do public identity work.

The player image exacerbates athletes' relationship dilemmas. By depicting Black men as a uniquely desirable group, player talk undermines *individual* desirability. Interpreting white women's interest as a fetish, outsiders discount these relationships as "jungle fever"—racialized sexual curiosity but not "real." "Jersey chaser" stories similarly repudiate the authenticity of Black men's relationships. By implying that Black men are desired exclusively because of their (gendered) race, these images deny Black men individual desirability and the possibility of emotional connection. Several Western athletes expressed ambivalence about being desired for their racial otherness. Nick equivocates:

I guess you could say it's flattering . . . like, it's always good to be liked by people, I guess—but I feel like when . . . I think of "groupie," I feel like that's just somebody who's tryin' to get with as many football players as possible type thing. That's not me. I'm not for that.

David regrets,

If I'm walking around with a white woman, a lot of white guys look at me like, "I can't believe that, the only reason she's dating him is because he's an athlete, or because he's Black." And I like to think somebody is dating me—that could be true—but I like to think people date me because I'm me.

These men do not want to be desired *just* because they're athletes; instead, they want women to be interested in them as individuals. Men who have interracial relationships also do not want to be perceived as *only* liking white women. Jackson, a Midwestern football player, laments that other students reduce his relationships to a jungle fever fetish, "[They] say, "He only likes white girls. That's just a dumb thing to say." The manhood that player talk establishes for the group limits the ability of individual Black men to create an unmarked masculinity; instead, they are always desired as *Black athletes*, never just as men.

Black college men benefit from colluding with the racialized image of the player, but the image is homogenizing and limiting, creating tensions for differently situated men. Blackness both bolsters masculine status and jeopardizes it, albeit in different ways for regulars than for athletes. Regulars struggle to be recognized as real Black men within its narrow confines, while athletes struggle to enact unmarked masculinities that extend beyond their racialized bodies.

For both sets of men, the double-edged cultural meanings of Black men's sexuality mean the "player" image slips into predatory stereotypes of Black men. White sororities circulate the image of the Black male rapist in "safety" alerts warning women to avoid potentially dangerous Black men. Black women more subtly link Black men to predatory images, condemning their relationships as exploitative, based only on sex, and motivated by "jungle fever" rather than authentic emotional interest. As Aisha, a woman at Western, says, "Talking to the Black men on this campus, they're like, 'Well, she's easy, she's right there, why not?' Like they don't care for her or like, I don't know. They just don't respect her as much as they should." Thus, Black women turn Black men's player talk back on them, using men's own claims to portray them as sexually uncontrolled.

It's unclear if all Black college men are aware that the predatory image follows them onto campus, but Nick, an athlete, laments that while some white women chase after him, others are afraid to look at him. And Jeffrey, a regular, explains that Black men protect each other from racialized misinterpretations of their behavior: "People make sure you're acting with good sense and not putting yourself into a compromising situation." Lance, a Midwestern regular, explains that Black men also teach each other how to talk about their sexual practices in ways that protect their reputations. He says, "I learned that some things you just don't say as far as explaining [sexual practices]." These comments suggest that many are aware of the pervasiveness of the predatory image—and the problems it entails. Stereotypes of predatory Black masculinity heighten surveillance of Black men, but being viewed as the wrong *kind* of men has additional, more insidious identity consequences for these men. The predatory image conflicts with strategies of respectability used by many middle-class Black men to facilitate participation in white institutions. Thus, player talk can jeopardize mobility strategies premised on masculine heterosexual respectability.

Intimacy Talk

Black college men mitigate the costs of player talk by framing interracial relationships as sites of intimacy, authenticity, and progress. Because this second form of talk emphasizes intimate emotions over sexual practice, I call it "intimacy talk." As with player talk, all of the men in this study used intimacy talk, but not in identical ways. Intimacy talk disassociates Black men from the player image in two ways. First, it draws distinctions among them, casting other Black college men as players. Second, it transforms the meaning of interracial relationships from a site of racialized heterosexual opportunity to a site of racial progress and true love. Thus, in contrast to the boasting in player talk, intimacy talk justifies interracial relationships, connecting interracial intimacy to more broadly held middle-class norms. By resignifying interracial relationships, men also resignify Black college masculinity.

Intimacy talk attributes the image of the player to *other* Black men. Jackson, a Midwestern football player, says, "I've heard people say off the wall shit, like about a white girl, 'You can have sex with them but you can't wife [marry] them.'" Jeffrey, a member of the BSA, says the "Mandingo fantasy" is "an athlete thing." Craig, a Western football player, distinguishes *among* athletes, explaining that some athletes pursue white women indiscriminately, but he does not. Describing a teammate, he says, "All of a sudden he's attracted to white girls, because he's never had a chance to talk to them, a relationship with them, so he's talkin' to all these white girls." These distinctions do two things. First, they sustain, rather than dispute, the image of the player. Second, they censure the player's *racial* motivations, underscoring *racialized* sexuality as the problem. For Jackson, desiring white women is appropriate, but treating them as sexually disposable is not. For Jeffrey and Craig, sex with white women is fine, but desiring white women *because* they're white is not. In both cases, intimacy talk distances the speaker from race-based desire. In contrast, intimacy talk professes a color-blind love for all women. Lance, a prominent student leader at Midwestern, says:

> I've dated so many different races of women within my short life—I'm not sure how that sounds. But you know, a woman is a woman is a woman is a woman. Love is love is love is love. [People who object] always come back to, "Don't you feel a responsibility to who you are?" I'm like, "This *is* who I am. I'm so many nations." . . . The heart wants what the heart wants.

And David, a Western football player, comments:

> I'm a very revolutionary humanist person, and I have very progressive gender roles. I'm not perfect, but I don't believe in living by any standard of the body of demographics or defining roles by your gender or race or anything like that. So for me, I don't see traditional standards of color, I see beauty. I don't contort that with societal influences. I just see beauty, see people for who they are. . . . Beauty to me comes in so many different forms, shapes, sizes, colors.

Intimacy talk portrays interracial relationships in opposition to player talk. It deemphasizes sex, emphasizing instead emotions and authenticity. It replaces crude exploitation with romanticized gender hierarchies in which Black men are motivated by love and beauty. It condemns racial motivations in which "getting white women is a form of accomplishment" and exalts color-blind heterosexuality in which "women are women are women"—and, presumably Black "men are men are men." By thus emphasizing essentialist gender categories, Black men claim their right to (race-neutral, color-blind) masculinity.

Intimacy talk also crafts the meaning of Black college masculinity. First, by portraying interracial relationships as a site of social control, men's participation in (or support for) them becomes evidence of their autonomy and, as Vincent, a Midwestern student, says, "security." Men who won't "wife" white women, Jackson, the Midwestern athlete, explains, "are afraid of what people might think." In intimacy talk, autonomy and self-control signify masculinity. Second, men claim to be "progressive" by depicting interracial relationships as a sign of racial progress. In this formulation, interracial relationships are evidence that Black men are not limited by race, but instead have multicultural, sophisticated tastes. Third, by claiming emotionally authentic motivations, intimacy talk combats "jungle fever" allegations that interracial relationships are inauthentic.

Intimacy talk is strategic. It manages the predatory stigma while justifying interracial practices in a context in which Black men's relationships are always contested and politicized. Even for men who do not have interracial relationships, intimacy talk maintains the *possibility* of interracial relationships as central to the definition of Black masculinity. It stakes out this position not through braggadocio, but by invoking a gentle set of explanations: Intimacy talk transforms Black men's interest in white women from racially motivated, predatory sexuality into authentic (i.e., color-blind), romantic, progressive intimacy. These accounts, in turn, challenge campus understandings of Black masculinity, converting Black men from *bad* men—players—into *good*, that is, respectable, men.

Because all Black college men are figured as predators, they all benefit from the race and gender meanings intimacy talk creates, but not in the same ways. Some men have never been in an interracial relationship. These men do not have to justify their practices but instead have to explain their allegiance with the interests of other Black men. Philip, a queer-identified Western student, says, "I love [interracial relationships] because I think they're honest, I think they're true." To Terry, they are "a sign of [racial] progress." Somewhat ruefully, Ekon, who is more private about his interest in men, admits, "I guess if you love each other, you know, I'm not going to knock love. That just doesn't make sense." Ekon's ruefulness stems from his recognition that he is adopting a masculine position against the Black women with whom he is close. When interracial relationships are framed as authentic and progressive, however, supporting them is logical, recasting this position from a betrayal of Black women to a commonsense call for social progress.

Regardless of whether intimacy talk is personal or more general, Black college men make similar links among interracial intimacy, emotional authenticity, progressiveness, and cosmopolitanism, and use these links to create symbolic boundaries with Black women, who often angrily object to Black men's interracial relationships. Ekon's reluctance notwithstanding, regular men, more than athletes, use intimacy talk to craft distinctions with Black women, perhaps because they have to repudiate feminization. For instance, Tim, who is heterosexual-identified but laments being seen as gay, portrays Black women's objections to interracial relationships as regressive: "It's the twenty-first century! Get over it!" Philip, who is queer-identified and more openly gender transgressive than other men in this study, more gently distinguishes himself from Black women. He explains, "I understand that that's [interracial relationships] a place of pain for [Black women]. I would say, 'Expand your circle. See something greater than just that.'" In these ways, intimacy talk, like player talk, demarcates Black men from Black women. By fashioning Black masculinity as progressive and emotionally authentic, these distinctions stigmatize Black women as regressive, emotionally inappropriate, and unsophisticated. This identity work is enabled by gendered arrangements that accord Black women responsibility for sustaining Black families, and free Black men to pursue their individual desires independent of community concerns (Dalmage 2000).

Nonetheless, men also use intimacy talk to repair their relationships with Black women. Black women are often more sympathetic to intimacy talk than to player talk, as Tiffany reveals: "A lot of the older football players have gotten it," she says, "but the ones coming in are just like, 'Oh, wow!' This is a totally different scene for most of them. So they just kind of like to score the whites." Forthcoming about the strategic uses of intimacy talk, Lance, a Midwestern leader, explains that he "learned there are some things you just don't say" from older Black men students. Intimacy talk allows him to participate in interracial relationships *and* friendships with Black women. Intimacy talk does not always work, however. Aisha, a Western woman, tells me that some men use intimacy talk to "play us like bein' dumb. I feel like they just say that stuff 'cuz it sounds good but I don't know if they really feel it." Thus, women do not always interpret intimacy talk in the ways men hope.

Inasmuch as intimacy talk salvages Black masculinity, it does so at a cost. First, the distinctions men craft sustain the stereotype of the predatory Black man. Second, in claiming that "women are women are women," men discount the ways race and gender meanings organize patterns of attraction. Efforts to distance themselves from the costs of race-based desire, ironically, compress the space for conversations about intimacy that acknowledge race, invalidating the legitimacy of an antiracist discourse based on explicit discussions of racial power. Third, essentialized ideas of "progressive" men sustain the idea that the way to be a good man is to commit to a woman, denying the possibility that some women may too desire sex without emotional intimacy. Thus, intimacy talk, like other strategies of respectability, maintains sexualized distinctions among people of color, and between men and women (White 2001).

Conclusion

Heterosexuality and masculinity are intimately coupled and mutually reinforcing (Connell 1995), but raced gender stereotypes complicate Black men's use of heterosexuality to claim masculinity, according Black masculinity both stigma and status. The double-edged meaning of Black men's sexuality creates complex identity dilemmas for Black college men. While most research on Black men suggests that cool pose and respectability provide distinct strategies for navigating these dilemmas, the men in this study combine both strategies by moving between opposing discursive frames. Player talk and intimacy talk coexist in uneasy tension, working together to achieve and manage Black masculine identities in the context of the university. University status structures and racialized erotic markets reward Black men for enacting heterosexual swagger, and penalize them for relinquishing it, creating incentives for Black men to link themselves to the player image. Player talk occludes variations in Black college men's practices, allowing differently situated Black men to capitalize on the heterosexual status of the athlete. But player talk also comes with costs: It perpetuates narrow ideas about Black masculinity, undermines individual desirability, and reproduces the stereotype of the predator. Intimacy talk buffers men against these costs, mitigating fears that they are threatening, dangerous, or in a relentless quest for white women. Intimacy talk relies on player talk for meaning; it is effective precisely because people think "all Black men are players."

Talk about interracial relationships creates a shared Black masculinity across a range of differences by crafting boundaries between Black men and Black women, aligning Black men's concerns with those of other Black men, and confirming and reworking the meaning of Black masculinity. These strategies, while shared, create diverse opportunities and dilemmas for Black men as they intersect with campus locations, bodies, and personal preferences. Accordingly, men do not benefit equally. Player talk links men to the image of the athlete, and intimacy talk distances them from it, but neither form of talk disrupts the athletes' hegemony as the predominant form of Black masculinity on these campuses. Player and intimacy talk respond *most* to the specific concerns of athletes and less to the concerns of marginalized regular men. While some research on Black college men (e.g., Harper 2004) suggests that nonathletes employ strategies of respectability to differentiate themselves from athletes, I did not find this to be the case. Instead, in both player and intimacy talk, regular Black men align themselves with the perspectives and concerns of athletes, claiming a Black masculinity from which they are otherwise excluded. In doing so, they both manage and reproduce their marginal social identities as nonathlete Black men.

Black college men's identity work manipulates the relationships among race, gender, and sexuality. Player talk uses racialized, gendered ideas about sexuality to claim and fortify Black masculine status, while intimacy talk attempts to transcend racial limits on masculinity by crafting a Black masculinity aligned with broader sexual ideals. The success of their efforts to both use and transcend racialized images is limited, however, as they do not successfully unseat the narrow cultural images of "real" Black men that prompt their identity work in the first place. Regular Black men continue to contend with feminization, while athletes continue to be seen as predators. Investment in masculinity—the need to be seen as real men—itself sustains these racial inequalities between men.

Yet Black men's identity work also disrupts racial boundaries. Intimate boundaries mandating intraracial relationships can be used to maintain race and gender hierarchies (Donovan 2003), but here Black men claim the right to cross these boundaries. Their identity work disrupts race in two ways. First, player talk inverts racial hierarchies, using heterosexuality to claim dominance over white men. In player talk, white women choose Black men because of Black men's physical superiority. By "stealing" white women and extracting labor from them, Black men undercut white men's masculine "right" to control white women's bodies and labor, inverting a historical legacy in which white men could access Black women's bodies and labor with impunity, but maintaining gendered understandings about men's right to women's bodies. In contrast, intimacy talk minimizes the importance of race in Black men's relationships but also essentializes heterosexual femininity: A "woman is a woman is a woman" and "beauty is beauty is beauty." In intimacy talk, heterosexual gender categories justify men's crossing of racial boundaries.

In the case at hand, then, stabilizing gender also stabilizes race, but destabilizing race does *not* destabilize gender. Instead, as I have found in other work, destabilizing one axis of inequality often requires stabilizing another, and thus shifts inequalities without undoing the interlocking structures holding them together. In all of these cases, efforts to transcend the limits of one structure of inequality—to break out of limited race or gender rules—are enabled by the stabilization of another category. Each group justifies breaking some rules by invoking rules in other arenas of their lives. In these examples, intersectional identities provide resources—gender, race, or class meanings—people can use to challenge some of the limits inequality poses in their lives. At the same time, however, the relationship between intersectional categories undercuts these challenges, blunting their transformative potential.

This case thus further underscores the complexity and intractability of intersectional relationships. While previous research has shown how both cool pose and respectability reproduce the structural problems facing Black men, this case shows how men's nuanced, flexible use of both strategies provides small benefits at the cost of supporting the structural conditions that shape identity problems in the first place.

References

Anderson, Elijah. 1999. *Code of the street: Decency, violence, and the moral life of the inner city.* New York: Norton.

Bederman, Gail. 1995. *Manliness and civilization: A cultural history of gender and race in the United States, 1880–1917.* Chicago: University of Chicago Press.

Childs, Erica Chito. 2005. Looking behind the stereotypes of the "angry Black woman": An exploration of Black women's responses to interracial relationships. *Gender & Society* 19:544–61.

Collins, Patricia Hill. 2004. *Black sexual politics: African Americans, gender, and the new racism.* New York: Routledge.

Connell, R. W. 1995. *Masculinities.* Berkeley: University of California Press.

Dalmage, Heather M. 2000. *Tripping on the color line: Black–white multiracial families in a racially divided world.* New Brunswick, NJ: Rutgers University Press.

Dellinger, Kirsten. 2004. Masculinities in "safe" and "embattled" organizations: Accounting for pornographic and feminist magazines. *Gender & Society* 18:545–66.

Donovan, Bryan. 2003. The sexual basis of racial formation: Anti-vice activism and the creation of the twentieth-century color line. *Ethnic and Racial Studies* 26:708–28.

Duneier, Mitchell. 1994. *Slim's table: Race, respectability, and masculinity.* Chicago: University of Chicago Press.

Ferguson, Ann Arnett. 2000. *Bad boys: Public schools in the making of Black masculinity.* Ann Arbor: University of Michigan Press.

Ford, Kristie A. 2011. Doing fake masculinity, being real men: Present and future constructions of self among Black college men. *Symbolic Interaction* 34:38–62.

Grazian, David. 2007. The girl hunt: Urban nightlife and the performance of masculinity as collective activity. *Symbolic Interaction* 30:221–43.

Harper, Shaun R. 2004. The measure of a man: Conceptualizations of masculinity among high-achieving African American male college students. *Berkeley Journal of Sociology* 48:89–107.

Higginbotham, Evelyn Brooks. 1994. *Righteous discontent: The women's movement in the Black Baptist church 1880–1920.* Cambridge: Harvard University Press.

Howard, Judith A. 2000. Social psychology of identities. *Annual Review of Sociology* 26:367–93.

Joyner, Kara, and Grace Kao. 2005. Interracial relationships and the transition to adulthood. *American Sociological Review* 70:563–81.

Lamont, Michèle. 2002. *The dignity of working men: Morality and the boundaries of race, class, and immigration.* Cambridge: Harvard University Press.

Majors, Richard, and Janet Mancini Billson. 1992. *Cool pose: The dilemmas of Black manhood in America.* New York: Touchstone.

Messerschmidt, James. 2007. We must protect our southern women: On whiteness, masculinities, and lynching. In *Race, gender, and punishment: From colonialism to the war on terror,* edited by Mary Bosworth and Jeanne Flavin. Newark: Rutgers University Press.

Pascoe, C. J. 2007. *Dude, you're a fag!: Masculinity and sexuality in high school.* Berkeley: University of California Press.

Patillo-McCoy, Mary. 1999. *Black picket fences: Privilege and peril among the Black middle class.* Chicago: University of Chicago Press.

Ray, Rashawn, and Jason Rosow. 2009. Getting off and getting intimate: How normative institutional arrangements structure Black and white fraternity men's approaches toward women. *Men and Masculinities* 12:1–24.

Schrock, Douglas, and Michael Schwalbe. 2009. Men, masculinity, and manhood acts. *Annual Review of Sociology* 35:277–95.

Schwalbe, Michael, and Douglas Mason-Schrock. 1996. Identity work as group process. *Advances in Group Processes* 13: 113–47.

Staiger, Annegret. 2005. "Hoes can be hoed out, players can be played out, but player is for life": The player phenomenon as a strategy of identity formation. *Symbolic Interaction* 28:407–28.

Stein, Arlene. 2008. Feminism's sexual problem: Comment on Andersen. *Gender & Society* 22:115–19.

West, Candace, and Don H. Zimmerman. 1987. Doing gender. *Gender & Society* 1:125–51.

Wetherell, Margaret, and Nigel Edley. 1999. Negotiating hegemonic masculinity: Imaginary positions and psycho-discursive practices. *Feminism and Psychology* 9:335–56.

White, E. Frances. 2001. *Dark continent of our bodies: Black feminism and the politics of respectability.* Philadelphia: Temple University Press.

Wilkins, Amy C. 2004. Puerto Rican wannabes: Sexual spectacle and the marking of race, class, and gender boundaries. *Gender & Society* 18:103–21.

Wilkins, Amy C. 2008. *Wannabes, goths, and Christians: The boundaries of sex, style, and status.* Chicago: University of Chicago Press.

Wilkins, Amy C. 2009. Masculinity dilemmas: Sexuality and intimacy talk among Christians and goths. *Signs: Journal of Women in Culture and Society* 34:343–68.

Wingfield, Adia Harvey. 2007. The modern mammy and the angry Black man: African American professionals' experiences with gendered racism in the workplace. *Race, Gender, and Class* 14:1–21.

Wingfield, Adia Harvey. 2008. Bringing minority men back in: Comment on Andersen. *Gender & Society* 22:88–92.

CHAPTER 23

Fight or Flight

Kathryn Edin and Timothy J. Nelson

Knowing what inner-city men think fatherhood ought to look like doesn't tell us much about how they live it day to day, or why they don't live it in exactly the way they think they should. This is especially so for those whose lives have taken extraordinarily difficult turns. More than most, Ritchie Weber knows what it is like to hit rock bottom. Just two years ago he was spending nights huddled on the slide in Tacony Park on Torresdale Avenue, a small city park with a playground attached to a baseball diamond, or, when it rained or turned cold, in the storage trailer of the construction company where he worked. Heroin and child support consumed nearly all his earnings—he had to scrounge dumpsters for food, sometimes subsisting on as little as a single doughnut a day—but no matter how bad it got, he never missed a day of work. And he didn't let a week go by without seeing his nine-year-old boy.

Now, though, this thirty-four-year-old white father's life has completely turned around; "I'm living my dream," he says. In fact, just the other day, Ritchie was over in New Jersey with his new girlfriend, Mary, the two of them perusing real estate—just for fun—and fantasizing about the possibility of one day owning a single-family home with two bathrooms and off-street parking. Mary, who he says is his soul mate, makes good money as a nurse at Jefferson Hospital in Center City. Though he's still at the same job he held while homeless—which pays eight dollars per hour—the two plan to pool their resources to secure a rental in the Jersey suburbs. When asked to account for such a dramatic change in his fortunes, Ritchie is ready with an answer. "My son," he says matter-of-factly. "My son is my savior. No matter what I went through, the boy stuck by me. He never got mad at me, everything was always OK, and that is why today I can't do enough for him."

Ritchie never gave up on himself either and credits his perseverance to the "big, close-knit" loving family who enfolded him when he was growing up in Port Richmond, a largely white community just north-east of less reputable Kensington. Ritchie is the youngest of five brothers, their mixed heritage of German, Polish, and French reflecting the neighborhood's long-standing history as a melting pot of Catholic immigrants from all parts of Europe. Though solidly working-class, Port Richmond's slightly larger row houses (sixteen feet wide versus the twelve-foot standard) attracted those whose salaries were a cut above the average Kensingtonian's—plant foremen and skilled craftsmen a bit higher on the pay scale than those who worked the factory floor. When Ritchie was coming of age, the neighborhood was populated by families who took pains to appear respectable, including the ultimate local show of decency: sweeping the sidewalks fronting their homes clean each morning. Ritchie still engages in this ritual and believes it has brought him good luck.

Port Richmond parents also did their best to provide each of their children with thirteen years of Catholic education. Ritchie was sent to Saint Anne's on Lehigh, and then to North Catholic, the

SOURCE: Edin, K., and Nelson, T. J. (2013). Fight or Flight. In *Doing the Best I Can: Fatherhood in the Inner City*. Oakland, CA: University of California Press. Reproduced with permission from the University of California Press.

all-boys school that served the parish, but in tenth grade he "wound up with the wrong crowd" and was expelled.[1] He spent only about a year in public school before dropping out to take a job as an unskilled laborer at a construction site. Never one to set his sights too high, Ritchie says he "ended up" five years later in what he calls a "corner marriage" with Kate, a girl he knew from the local neighborhood set. "We all hung out together," he explains, "and eventually everybody paired off."

However haphazard their origins, corner marriages had formed the bedrock of the Port Richmond community for generations; typically, they had lasted a lifetime, but this was less true in Ritchie's generation. Even the birth of their son, Ritchie Jr., about two years into their marriage couldn't save this volatile union. Just after their son turned two, Ritchie and Kate split for good. Afterward, Ritchie was as faithful to his son as he had always been to his job, visiting nearly every day. But "whenever there was a dispute between me and her, somehow it always got back to where she would keep Ritchie Jr. from me." While Ritchie had gloried in the prospect of fatherhood, the couple's mutual antipathy made enacting the father role very hard. "Kate and I hated each other for a long time. We didn't get along at all. We didn't want nothing to do with one another."

Up to this point in his life, Ritchie had displayed remarkably little ambition—a lack of drive is why he had worked the same job at the same lousy pay for a decade, never really aspiring to anything more. And neither marriage nor parenthood—critical life events that had shifted the trajectories of generations of Port Richmond men—had provided that magic turning point for Ritchie.[2] But suddenly, Kate's attempt to play gatekeeper sparked a steely determination he never knew he had. "She would try to keep him from me, but I was not that type of guy to allow that. I got the police, and I went down there and banged on that door," he recalls. He also says he took Kate to court dozens of times in the early years to ensure his right to visitation.

Still, this wasn't enough to turn Ritchie's life around. In fact, for a brief time, beginning when Ritchie Jr. was five, it seemed as if heroin might win out over Ritchie's paternal commitment. "It was a time in my life when drugs were so important to me that that is all I concerned myself about. I wound up owing five thousand to six thousand dollars in back child support. I wound up to the point where I was living on the street." But even then Ritchie kept stopping by to see his son.

The turning point finally came when a friend tried to convince Ritchie that to conquer his addiction he needed a change of scenery; the friend had a contact in Florida who had agreed to set Ritchie up with a job and an apartment. Initially, Ritchie thought he should grasp at this lifeline, but the thought of leaving his young son instilled a strong conviction that he couldn't simply flee from his problems. "It was the thought of never seeing him again that ripped through me. I remember that night; instinctively I knew that I had to break down and face everything that I caused in order to keep my son in my life." Accordingly, Ritchie started attending AA and NA meetings, determined to reclaim his sobriety. Being homeless while sober was the hardest thing he had done. "I was homeless sober, stone cold sober as a matter of fact. But I was the AA group representative, had keys to two clubhouses. AA was the only place that I had any respect besides my son."

Just as his new resolve and his responsibilities with AA were beginning to resuscitate his self-esteem, Ritchie's boss discovered that he was sleeping in the trailer's storage room and offered him an efficiency apartment he owned in neighboring Harrogate, left vacant because it was located on a run-down street that included two crack houses. With a place of his own, Ritchie was able to petition the court to set a visitation schedule that included overnights. Even though Kate was dead set against it—due to Ritchie's past—Ritchie began taking his son every other weekend when he could afford to feed him—the child support and the payments on his substantial child-support arrears ate into his meager earnings.

Then, about a year ago Ritchie had one other stroke of good luck. Through the matchmaking efforts of his brother and sister-in-law, he reconnected with a woman named Mary, another one of the corner girls from his youth whose marriage had also failed and who was raising her daughter, Kayla, on her own. "We are actually best friends and soul mates before anything," Ritchie says.

He explains the unexpected success of his relationship with Mary in this way: "We know each other from the corner, so it is not like I could be somebody that I am not. I am who I am and she is who she is, and we just really click together." Mary accepts Ritchie as he is and is extraordinarily supportive of his relationship with his son; just last month she purchased a PlayStation for Ritchie Jr.'s birthday but put Ritchie's name on the card instead of her own, knowing he couldn't afford to buy his son the coveted toy.

Every Monday morning Ritchie is up at 5:00 a.m. to finish off a pot of coffee and a cigarette before the thirty-minute walk to the pickup point, where he catches a ride from his boss, an "Italian guy from the old school who is going to push me like the mule that I am." They travel to the day's construction site, where Ritchie and two other laborers "bullwork all day long."[3] For eight hours' hard labor, Ritchie accrues sixty-four dollars in cash; "It's all I know how to do." Then it's the ride back to the office, the walk home, and a quick shower before he's out again to stop by Kate's place on his way to pay a visit to Mary.

Now Ritchie is more than satisfied with his lot: "Life is good. I strive, work, and do everything that I do just for this moment, not for some futuristic thing that is never going to happen to me. If a great big house on the hill comes along, then great. In the meantime I will be happy with what I got. My son says to me, 'Dad I love you,' and that is the most rewarding thing. He makes me be a parent whether I like it or not, just like I make him use his manners whether he likes it or not. We need each other. We are good for each other. We deserve each other."

Even Kate has responded to Ritchie's turnaround, allowing Ritchie Jr. to stay over on some days not on the visitation schedule. This fall he was with Ritchie for a two-week period, while Kate sorted out a "personal problem."[4] Ritchie views this as a particular triumph, which he attributes to his persistence in demanding the right to see his son. "I was always there for that boy. He was my heart and soul. And because I never gave up, because I believed in *me and him*, everybody else finally backed down. I fought for our rights because nobody could fight for him but me."

Just recently, there has been even more good news in Ritchie's life. Mary's six-year-old daughter, Kayla, has asked her mother whether Ritchie would mind if she called him daddy—her own father doesn't visit and she feels the lack of a dad. When Mary came to him with Kayla's request, "Tears came to my eyes," Ritchie says. "Apparently she sees more in me than I do."

Holloway Middleton is not on this upward trajectory, yet he can also recall a time when he thought he was on top of the world, with a steady relationship, a roof over his head, and a night job cleaning office buildings. Through hard work and reliability, Holloway had risen from the minimum wage up to almost nine dollars an hour at the cleaning company, with regular opportunities for overtime at double pay. Not bad, he thought, for a black man without a high school diploma. And he had just moved in with his first real girlfriend, Katrina, whom he had met at a Center City dance club. Katrina was raising her sons, aged eight and ten, in a row house on Gratz Street in North Philadelphia's Nicetown section—a thoroughfare of two-story rows with awnings encased in a rainbow of colored aluminum—a bright spot in the otherwise drab streetscapes of North Philadelphia. She had acquired the home, one among miles of cramped prewar two-bedroom units, from a recently deceased relative.

When Holloway met Katrina, there was no other man in the picture—one of her son's fathers was dead from a bullet and the other from a drug overdose—so Holloway had taken on the role of surrogate dad. With a steady job, a ready-made family, and a decent home over their heads, Holloway felt as though he was living the Nicetown version of the American Dream. "It was like I was the man of the house, bringing in my little pay and stuff like that. It was a family, and she made me feel like I was the boss."

Holloway had grown up just next door to Nicetown in the Fairhill section of the city, the son of a brick mason and stay-at-home mom. His parents provided him with a stable home life, and his father was a good provider. But then Friday night came. "On weekends, man, he used to drink. Ooh man, when he drank my father used to go crazy. Half of the time we had to leave on the weekend. He hit my mom, hit her a lot of times. I mean he used to really give it to her, you know? Sometimes he took it out on us too." Things got so bad that Holloway landed in foster care for a while. Troubles at home were mirrored by troubles at school; Holloway dropped out of high school in the eleventh grade because he simply couldn't keep up with the work. "I was kind of slow. My teachers, they tried to help me, but I just felt bad. You feel bad when you can't do what the other students do." He tried to learn bricklaying from his father, but he failed at that as well.

Desperate to learn a trade, Holloway signed up for Job Corps at seventeen and was sent to a facility in Gary, Indiana. But Job Corps turned out to be more like prison than school. "I had to hang with the guys from Philly, 'cause if I didn't there was no protection for me. People would be like stabbed, beat up real bad." Holloway was thrown out of the program along with another kid after a big brawl between the Philly boys and other boys from another city. He joined the National Guard but quit after just a few weeks. "I got problems with finishing stuff," Holloway admits. "I'm messed up like that."

Finally, at twenty-three he thought he had found his golden ticket—the janitorial job. He had just gotten a raise when he met Katrina. For some time after that things were "perfect." Then, after two years of unprotected sex, Katrina got pregnant. They started talking marriage and Holloway even put down money on an engagement ring. But before he had time to think much more about their future together, the bottom began to fall out.

The first blow was when the company Holloway worked for was bought out by a larger building-maintenance firm. The new management proceeded to fire him and all the longtime employees—those commanding the highest wages. He collected unemployment while looking for another job, keenly feeling the pressure now that a baby was on the way. Then, desperate for cash, he began to seek work through a temporary agency that paid just a little better than the minimum wage. He brought all his earnings home but could see that Katrina was beginning to lose respect for him.

One day Katrina was entertaining friends in the front room while Holloway was back in the kitchen making himself a sandwich out of their sight. What he overheard, he says, cut him like a knife. "How much he make an hour?" one friend asked. "What he give you yesterday?" another insisted. "Fifty dollars," he heard Katrina say in a dismissive tone, followed by derisive laughter from the whole group. Katrina's friends responded, "Come on!" "He can do better than that!" "He's a loser!" Burning with embarrassment and shame, Holloway slinked up the stairs to the bedroom, resolving once again to find a better job. But despite years of solid performance at the cleaning company, and the lack of any obvious impediments like a criminal record or an addiction, he did not succeed.

Soon thereafter tragedy occurred. One night Holloway awoke to the smell of smoke and rushed downstairs to find the row house's kitchen engulfed in flames. He ran back upstairs and shouted for everyone to get out. While Katrina grabbed the boys and, with the help of firefighters, fled out the front second-story window, Holloway escaped out the back door. When they met up in the front of the house, Holloway was relieved to see that everyone was accounted for. Yet something was wrong; Katrina was hysterical, screaming that he had to go back in the house, that there was some-one still inside. Holloway assumed that she had become confused by inhaling the smoke and assured her that everyone was safe. By this time the structure was too far gone for anyone to enter. Paramedics rushed Katrina, Holloway, and the boys to the hospital to treat them for smoke inhalation and burns. But later on firefighters discovered the body of a four-year-old boy—a cousin—who had suffocated in an upstairs closet; Holloway hadn't realized that the child had been sleeping over that night.

In the aftermath of this event, Katrina's family turned against Holloway, whom they blamed for not rescuing the boy. Her kin had never really liked him and the loss of his janitorial job had been further proof of his worthlessness. In their view their young relative's death in the fire was yet another reason to convince Katrina to get rid of Holloway, which she did. Holloway's daughter, Christine, was born soon after. Holloway's father was dead and his mother had moved to New York, so he moved in with his brother, the only member of his immediate family who lived in the area and was not behind bars—a welder who had once worked for the Budd Company and owned a house around the corner.

Six years later Holloway is still showing up at the day-labor agency six days a week at 6:00 a.m. He says he manages to get work only about two-thirds of the time and still makes just over the minimum wage. He makes valiant attempts to stay connected to Christine and comes by to visit almost daily—whenever he has enough left in his paycheck to buy her a treat or to go shopping for something she needs. Katrina initiates contact only when she fears that her daughter is getting out of hand. Recently, she called and told Holloway that the six-year-old had been hanging around some older girls and had run off with them on several occasions, leaving her to search the streets for hours. Alarmed, Holloway gave Christine a stern warning. "So I told her, I said, 'the next time you run off, I'm gonna beat you!'" But Christine had just looked defiantly up at him, put her hands on her hips, and declared, "No, you ain't!"

At first he was taken aback by her insolence, but he has come to view such incidents like these philosophically. "It seems like when you don't have custody of your kids and stuff like that, not being there all the time, they don't really give you that respect." Right now Holloway can't take the child overnight or on weekends because his wages consign him to living with his brother, who was once accused of raping his girlfriend's daughter. Never mind that the charge was later dropped; Katrina won't hear of Christine even entering the brother's home, much less staying there all night. Resigned, Holloway concludes, "I don't blame Christine for her behavior, man. It's just that her mother don't let me be around her enough. If only I could be around her more, like when I get a better paycheck and get a little place of my own, so she could stay over, you know, she wouldn't act that way."

Recently, when Katrina started seeing another man, she told Holloway he couldn't come by the house to visit anymore. What worries Holloway is that Katrina's new boyfriend "seems like he's trying to take my daughter from me." Lately, the only time Holloway sees his daughter is through a chance encounter. In fact, trying to orchestrate such encounters has become a near fixation.

Just the other day, when Holloway had been lurking around in hopes of encountering Christine, he happened to witness the new man buying ice cream for his daughter. The rapport between the two was apparent. Holloway tears up when relating this memory: "I wanted to pull him to the side and say, 'Look man, she's my daughter. You don't really gotta buy her ice cream. You know, I *do* work sometimes. And this guy she's with, he got kids somewhere else. He lost his family, so he gotta take mine." He then shrugs and says, "Well, he has the power to do that because he has a good job. He's like a big shot." Though Holloway, like many other men, rejects the notion that finances are paramount in the fatherhood realm, the power that money affords still figures prominently in his story.

Despite considerable adversity, Holloway is still determined to stay in Christine's life. "My brother, he talking about don't go see my daughter or nothing, leave them alone. But see, I got a problem with that. I don't want to abandon her." "I ain't much," Holloway concludes, "but at least my daughter knows that she has a father."

The Fragile Father

Ritchie and Holloway are both well into their thirties. Neither of them finished high school, which is a large part of why they work manual-labor jobs paying at or just above the legal minimum, have no health insurance or paid vacation, and must rely on others to make ends meet. Ritchie's brother and his girlfriend, Mary, have both taken their turns helping him out with his rent, while Holloway's brother has the good welding job that puts a roof over both their heads. Looking at their situations, we might be tempted to agree with Holloway that these men "ain't much." But there is one attribute that both possess, one that is actually fairly rare in these surroundings, even among men in somewhat better circumstances: they have been able to enjoy uninterrupted relationships with their children, consistently seeing them several times each week.

Neither Ritchie nor Holloway conform to the image of the "dead-beat dad"—a man simply too lazy to try. Indeed, a remarkable degree of commitment and perseverance has been required for each of them to stay involved. Until recently Ritchie had to fight tooth and nail to block Kate's attempts to deny him visitation. He is still thousands of dollars behind on his child support, and paying back the debt plus keeping up with his ongoing support obligation takes up a considerable portion of his income. Holloway has to deal with Katrina's contempt as well as her new boyfriend's money—not to mention Christine's belligerence and disrespect. Perhaps the most profound obstacle, however, is that over time a father's performance scorecard often becomes so littered with disappointment. What kind of father is an addict who sleeps on a slide and has no gift for his son at Christmas? What kind of a dad has such a rotten job that he can't even afford to treat his daughter to ice cream? Sometimes the failures are due to the hard living that many fail to shake when their children are born—take Ritchie for example. At other times, just plain hard luck is the cause—this is Holloway's problem. To persevere in the face of these obstacles, poor inner-city dads who try to stay involved with their children after their relationships with the mother have crumbled must have considerable grit. While men expressed the key quality required in different ways ("responsibility," "prioritizing the kids," "being there," "sacrifice"), this quality is perhaps best expressed by the word "commitment." When the child's mother tries to restrict access, when they don't have ready cash for even an ice cream cone, when their own sense of shame wrought by the lack of a decent paycheck, an addiction, or a felony conviction is telling them that their kids might be better off without them, are they willing to do what they have to do to "make the kids number one," as one father said, or are they going to put fatherhood on hold until some unspecified time when things might get easier?

As partnerships fall by the wayside and children grow older, a father's path often gets steeper and more unpredictable. Despite widespread agreement that paternal commitment ought to be unshakable—a good dad ought to "be there"—our fathers' relationships with their children were remarkably varied. At one extreme are children who see their father face-to-face several times a month. Some of these children live with both parents outside of a marital bond, but others have fathers who manage to build in visits as a regular part of their weekly or biweekly routine, like Ritchie and Holloway—a pattern we call "intensive involvement." Then there are children whose fathers have in-person contact at least once a month, but the contact is not part of a regular routine; we describe this as "moderate involvement." Children whose fathers have had some contact within the past six months, but on a more sporadic and haphazard basis and not always in person, fall in the "somewhat involved" category. Finally, there are children whose fathers are "not involved"—there has been no contact during the past six months.[5]

Among the men we spoke with, the black fathers are somewhat more involved with their children than white fathers are, especially when their children are younger. For those with children under two, all black fathers have been at least somewhat involved with that child in the past six months, and nine in ten report intensive involvement—routine in-person contact with their children several times a month. Intensive involvement characterizes only two-thirds of black fathers with children between two and five, however; just half of children between six and ten; and only a third of children older than ten. In short, though men's rhetoric might indicate otherwise, a father's engagement with his children fades rather markedly over time.[6]

The white fathers we spoke with have had less contact with their children no matter what the children's age. Though nine in ten of white fathers with children under two said they were at least somewhat involved with their child in the past six months, only slightly more than half were intensively involved with their children at this age. These figures don't differ appreciably for white men with two- to five-year-olds, or among those with kids ages six to ten, where just over 40 percent of dads are still intensively involved. But only a quarter of those white fathers with children over ten have in-person contact several times each month.

These figures are roughly consistent with national data, which show very high levels of involvement for young children with a large falloff over time.[7] Survey data also show greater involvement for blacks than whites, when all else is equal.[8] Readers should keep in mind that we are relying on fathers' reports here, which might paint a somewhat more positive picture than what mothers might say.[9] But mothers' estimates of father involvement should not be taken as gospel; some ex-partners would almost certainly underestimate their children's father's involvement because it occurs surreptitiously or through an intermediary. Nonetheless, even based on fathers' own claims, this portrait is far from rosy from a child's point of view. How can we reconcile the gulf between men's ideals with regard to paternal involvement—where commitment triumphs over all—and the reality that they often spend long periods absent from a given child's life?

To explore this conundrum, we asked fathers to identify the barriers that kept them from being as involved as they would like to be with each of their children. Most often, fathers' own limitations and behaviors are the obstacle: the problems that occur when the transition to parenthood fails to turn a young man's troubled trajectory around.[10] While Ritchie is clearly an exception to this rule, men struggling with drug addictions or those for whom prison has become a revolving door often deliberately distance themselves from their offspring, as they are too ashamed to let their children see them in such humiliating circumstances. The "rippin' and runnin'" that typically lead to these problems begin in men's midteens but can extend into their late twenties or early thirties until they are willing and able to "settle down." By then, they've lost precious time with their progeny. The critical point here is that early father–child bonding may be interrupted by a drug or alcohol problem or a prison spell, and this has long-term consequences for fathers who wish to remain connected or reestablish a connection with their children later on.[11]

Barriers due purely to finances usually accrue only to those who are at the very bottom—those working for minimum wage, like Holloway, or at low-end entrepreneurial trades (take Jabir Rose, the neighborhood handyman or David Williams, the guy selling newspapers at the foot of the Ben Franklin Bridge). A father who doesn't even have the wherewithal to treat his child to ice cream or purchase a pair of sneakers will often feel that he has no business coming around. Holloway comes around a little less often than he might for that reason, though it is worth noting that having no "funds" to offer didn't deter Ritchie at all: at one point, Ritchie was so poor that his own son felt compelled to offer him the change from his pocket—which he says was the all-time low in his life.

While it is men's own problems that interfere most often, maintaining contact with one's child is not simply up to the father alone; mothers are capable of throwing up significant barriers too. Of course, his problems and her efforts to keep him away—often called gatekeeping—are often related, but virtually any misbehavior on the father's part can be used by a child's mother as justification for a forced separation. According to Ritchie, Kate has used any number of excuses to try and keep him from his son—his drug use, missed child-support payments, his failure to relent in an argument— while Katrina has had only one excuse to draw on: Holloway's meager financial contributions. It must be said here that gatekeeping is sometimes clearly justified; an ex-partner who is frequently violent or high can pose unacceptable risks for a woman who is trying to shield her child from harm. But such dangers are by no means ubiquitous, and many women who engage in gatekeeping don't, in fact, truly face these risks.

Gatekeeping is often sparked by the denominator problem—the mismatch between what a man feels he ought to provide financially—a sense of obligation that has been sharply curtailed by the "doing the best I can . . . with what is left over" ethos—and the true cost of raising a child. Mothers like Katrina can easily grow tired of having to figure out how to cover the bills, and in the midst of her frustration it can be tempting to conclude that a father like Holloway is not worth bothering with.

Another common precursor to gatekeeping is when the child's mother forges a relationship with a new partner, as Katrina did.[12] Because of the rampant lack of trust between women and men in low-income communities, particularly in the sexual domain, a new paramour can often become jealous when an old lover keeps stopping by.[13] To keep the peace and maintain the new union, mothers may feel that the best course is to try to simulate the nuclear family, isolating old partners while giving the new man the title of daddy, as Mary has done with Ritchie and what Katrina seems to want to do as well. Often, the daddy title is given as a reward for his voluntary contributions to her child, which makes the biological father's meager contributions appear even more paltry by comparison.[14] When a new man comes on the scene and plays daddy, dads' visits can provoke rivalry over the child as well.

Conversely, sometimes a birthday card or a once-in-a-blue-moon visit are the sum total of men's attempts to stay connected, if that, and a lack of involvement seems largely due to an absence of desire. Few men admitted to lack of desire outright; thus our assessment of how frequently lack of interest is a barrier is based on our own judgment drawn from men's larger narratives and behaviors. From that information we determine a lack of interest to be a significant barrier for 7 percent of the father–child relationships we observed. This is no doubt an under-estimate, as men who have lost, or never had, a desire to enact the father role are presumably less likely to engage in a study like ours or are more likely to lie to save face.

We also took stock of those factors that enabled ongoing involvement by fathers. One of the most important is the attitude of the child's mother and the degree to which she regards her child's father as dispensable or replaceable. A man with the good fortune to have a cooperative ex-partner who values the role he can play in his child's life has an enormous advantage; not only does this ease involvement, it also improves the child's attitude toward the father and enhances men's self-regard.

At the moment Ritchie enjoys this advantage; Kate can no longer judge him for his failings because she has developed a "little problem" of her own—in early September Ritchie Jr. called his father, upset that Kate hadn't registered him for school. When Ritchie stopped by to see what was going on, Kate appeared strung out; "it looked like she was high on crack," he says. Alarmed, he announced he was taking the boy until she got herself together. She offered no objection, and he kept Ritchie Jr. for two weeks. This incident must have convinced her of Ritchie's competence, because she has been letting the boy stay over more and more.

Forty-year-old Giovanni, a white father who has been back and forth to prison for much of his adult life, has a shaky relationship with his sixteen-year-old daughter, Nicole, whom he sees only every other month or so. He isn't even sure he deserves the title of father, so he tells her, "Don't call me your dad right now. Talk to me as you would talk to somebody on the street corner." But even this tenuous relationship would not have been possible, he says, without Nicole's mother, who "never bad-mouthed me to my daughter" and allowed her to stay with him on the weekends during a three-year period several years earlier, when he was on the outside and working steadily as a bartender. In contrast, every time twenty-nine-year-old Montay, a black father of a nine-year-old boy who lives with his mother and two younger half siblings in Florida, calls his son on the phone—the boy's mother slams the receiver down on the counter and says, "Hey, it's your deadbeat dad who ain't shit—he's on the phone."

When a breakup causes hard feelings and animosity, the availability of an intermediary can prove invaluable. Debbie is angry that her children's father, forty-five-year-old Bruce, the white father of twins, has taken up with new flame Peggy so quickly after breaking up with her and that his cash contributions to the family are suddenly way down. His longtime boss just retired and closed the construction business, so for now Bruce is subsisting on $205 a month in General Assistance plus proceeds from selling blood. In retaliation Debbie only grudgingly allows him an occasional visit and only when the twins are at her brother's house while she attends evening classes for a nursing degree;

that way, she doesn't have to see him. "But," Bruce gleefully reveals, suddenly animated, "I see them more than she thinks I see them. Between me and you and that tape recorder, I see them maybe twice a week at her brother's house—me and her brother is all right. But if she would ever catch me over there, there would really be a big argument over that."

More commonly, a father's own mother or sister plays this intermediary role. Twenty-one-year-old Kervan, the black father of a one-year-old child, is prohibited from coming by his baby's mother's house by a restraining order.[15] Yet the child's mother is a friend of his own mother—they even go to the same church—and she babysits their child, meaning that Kervan can see his baby at his mother's house without dealing with his baby's mother at all.

Go-betweens mute the animosity and tension that can accompany visitation. In addition, intermediaries sometimes advocate for the father's involvement and work to diminish the mother's resistance. But as children grow older, cooperative mothers or intermediaries become less important, as fathers can forge a relationship with their child directly, without any third party. Marty Holmes's oldest child, Nikka, now lives on her own, which means this forty-year-old African American doesn't have to face his ex-girlfriend Clarissa to maintain contact. Donald, a thirty-seven-year-old African American father of a fourteen-year-old child, has circumvented the efforts of his daughter's mother to keep him out of his child's life by surreptitiously arranging to meet her after school for a quick outing to McDonald's before sending her home on the bus. The daughter's willingness to go along with this scheme is probably due to the connection Donald was able to build with her earlier, when she was young and he was enjoying a period of sobriety before falling off the wagon again, underlining once again the importance of periods of paternal bonding during the child's earlier years.

It should be apparent by now that despite men's best efforts to reject the traditional package deal and establish a direct relationship with their children, their ability to father is still powerfully influenced by their relationships with their children's mothers. When a couple has a child and then splits up, each party's story continues to unfold. Men may get and lose jobs, find new partners, have more children, be evicted from their homes, move to another city, get sick, go to prison for a spell, and then return. Each of these changes has consequences, often profound ones, for their ability to perform the father role. Meanwhile, mothers experience transitions as well, some of which may influence their ability or willingness to facilitate fathers' access to a child. Kate's change of heart toward Ritchie, prompted by both his transformation and her "little problems" is an example. Then there are the children, whose openness and trust may also vary over time—contrast Ritchie's son to Holloway's daughter. To understand shifting levels of father involvement, then, it is not enough simply to examine fathers' characteristics or behaviors. One must also plot the evolution of the mothers' and children's situations and how these correspond to where the fathers are. It is the *alignment* between men's, women's, and children's lives at a given point in time that is the crucial factor.

Rising Above

That there are significant obstacles to nonresident father involvement, particularly among inner-city men without much in the way of education or earnings, should come as a surprise to no one. Yet we came across as many fathers who have prevailed despite these difficulties as have been crushed by them; this is why the stories of Ritchie Weber and Holloway Middleton are so important. How can we understand why some of these father–child relationships remain relatively strong while others atrophy or experience periods of disruption, sometimes for years? One clear prerequisite for achieving the standards men articulate for good fatherhood is the single-minded commitment displayed by Ritchie and Holloway. Like any distribution across a population, our men's commitment to the father role varies; it may even vary from child to child as fathers' maturity and conditions change.

Beyond commitment, though, persistence in the face of mounting barriers to father involvement requires significant emotional muscle. Men must have reserves of self-esteem, optimism, and sheer tenacity to rise above the formidable challenges they face in staying connected to their children. Given their often-difficult pasts and challenging present circumstances, though, many are as deficient in these reserves of inner strength. When one considers that men's families of origin are more often sources of continuing trauma than emotional sustenance, that their own histories are so frequently punctuated with a series of failures—at school, at the workplace, in relationships, in repeated attempts to get clean or stay sober—and that they constantly are made to feel superfluous in a society that rewards attributes that are the opposite of theirs, it is no surprise that the strength to "rise above," both as partners and as parents, is sometimes in short supply.

An often neglected factor in understanding father–child relationships over time is how fathers' psychological resources may be either shored up or diminished by the attitudes and responses of their children, particularly as the kids get older. Ritchie Weber provides the clearest positive example of this dynamic. It was the loving and respectful response of his son, who was always glad to see him even when he was homeless, penniless, and filthy, that gave him the inner strength to turn his life around, and why Ritchie refers to his son as his "savior." This unconditional acceptance is not offered by Holloway's daughter, Christine, who is tendering defiance and disrespect.[16] Christine's attitude is not likely to improve if her mother's gatekeeping continues to reduce him to a shadow lurking around the corner hoping for a chance encounter, or if her mother's new boyfriend—the big shot with the better job—continues to compete for the father role. Here we do not mean to blame the children, as many may have good reason for losing faith in their fathers. It is reasonable for children to ask how long their father will be able to sustain his resolve to stay involved.

Maurice, a thirty-eight-year-old African American father, offers a story about his own childhood that serves as a poignant illustration of the power of children to rob or imbue fathers of the emotional strength to stay involved. When Maurice was sixteen, he stopped going to school and began to hang around with the wrong crowd. Maurice's mother asked his father to come over and set him straight, but Maurice was burning with resentment over his father's spotty presence during his younger years. "I'll never forget this. I told him, I said, 'I don't need you.' He looked at me and said, 'You don't need me?' and I said, 'No, I don't need you.' I was just a sixteen-year-old kid, and he looked at my thirteen-year-old brother, and he asked my brother, 'What about you, do you need me?' My brother said no because he listened to what I was saying. My father left that day, it was in the summer—like July or August, and that was the last time I ever saw my father."

Maurice has three children—a sixteen-year-old son and two daughters, ages fourteen and ten—by one woman. He was out of their lives for many years, first because of a drug addiction and then because of a move to central Pennsylvania, a relocation aimed at facilitating his recovery. He's been back in Philadelphia and "in the picture" with his kids for two years and sees them twice during the week and again on weekends. He is determined to remain involved, but his middle child is beginning to show the same kind of attitude that drove away Maurice's own father. What happened to him is not going to happen to his kids, he says. "They are growing up to be real good kids, and I plan on being there every step of the way, no matter what comes down the pike. My youngest daughter, we got this thing where we are going around to find the perfect water ice. I will pick her up and be like 'We be back, we are going to get our water ice.' And we go out and get our water ice and we talk and everything."

It would be hard to overstate the sense of renewed worth Maurice's relationship with these children has given him. In fact, his unexpected success in resuming his fatherhood role, particularly his ability to deter his teenage son from "going the wrong way," has sparked a desire in Maurice to work with troubled kids. He just resigned from his job as a cook at the Hyatt Hotel and will train for a job as a counselor at an Outward Bound program. "I am looking forward to an exciting job, new adventure, new career. And maybe I can make a difference in some kids' lives."

But Maurice's middle child refuses to come on outings or stay over at his apartment, claiming it is boring and that she would rather be with her friends. Her attitude has sharply curtailed the role he can play—he now can function only as a watchdog. The last time she refused to come over with her siblings, he told her, "OK, you be with your friends and remember I don't want you hanging on the corner in front of no stores, and I don't want to see you out there like that." Still, Maurice refuses to be completely deterred; "I am keeping a close eye on her," he insists.

Our aim here has been to offer insight into some well-known facts: fathers like ours express high hopes at the time that their children are born—nearly all say they plan to stay involved in their children's lives. And in the first year or so, most live out this pledge; but this is easy to do because most are in a romantic relationship with the mother at first—about 80 percent—and half are still with her a year later, when the baby turns one.[17] As parents break up, however, father involvement drops off quite dramatically. In short, when unmarried couples' rough imitation of the old-fashioned package deal is in play, where the mother–father relationship is intact, father involvement is very high—what could be easier? But when men try to enact the new package deal, where it's all about the baby and the mother is peripheral, good intentions are often derailed by complex realities.

We devoted the first part of this chapter to detailing common barriers to father involvement, as well as the factors that facilitate dads' ability to stay involved. These factors are dynamic and multifaceted; at any given time it is the alignment between the father's and the mother's circumstances and attitudes, as well as the child's, that often makes or breaks his ability to be involved. But while understanding these barriers and facilitators may be necessary, it is not sufficient. Some, like Ritchie and Holloway, manage to rise above in the face of tremendous difficulties, while others' good intentions are easily thwarted. We've argued here for the importance of fathers' commitment and their psychological resources—by the latter we mean the emotional mettle to carry on when staying involved becomes difficult and even painful. We've shown that most fathers voice considerable commitment, though this can vary across children and over time, but not all have the emotional strength to persist when things get tough, particularly when two other critical resources, economic and biographical, are also lacking.

Notes

1. Both of these schools have since closed.

2. Sampson and Laub (1993).

3. "Bullwork" is a slang term for hard manual labor.

4. Ritchie suspects that Kate had become addicted to drugs and was trying to regain her sobriety during this time.

5. For patterns of visitation among formerly married fathers, see Cheadle, Amato, and King (2010).

6. This is due in part to a sharp falloff in the percentage of fathers who remain in a romantic relationship with the mother (Edin, Tach, and Mincy 2009). For estimates of levels of father involvement over time by union status using both mothers' and fathers' reports, see McClain and DeMaris (2011).

7. See McClain and DeMaris (2011) for figures over time.

8. See Carlson, McLanahan, and Brooks-Gunn (2005); Lerman and Sorensen (2000); Sorensen and Hill (2004); and Yeung et al. (2001). But our black men are somewhat more connected and our white fathers somewhat less connected than mothers' reports in the Fragile Families survey shows, likely because our white fathers are more disadvantaged than the white portion of the Fragile Families and Child Wellbeing sample.

9. Coley and Morris (2002), McClain and DeMaris (2011), and Mikelson (2008) have all noted the discrepancy in mothers' and fathers' reports of involvement. McClain and DeMaris (2011) estimate that for men with our sample characteristics, the discrepancy ranges from a third of a day to two-thirds of a day per week.

10. A small portion (8 percent) seemed to be hampered not so much by external circumstances but simply by a lack of desire to stay involved.

11. Even fathers' supportiveness during pregnancy exerts a long-term influence on whether fathers remain engaged (Cabrera, Fagan, and Farrie 2008) or stay in a coresidential relationship with their children's mother (Shannon et al. 2009). There is also a long-term link between father residence during early childhood and the quality of the father–child relationship in the fifth grade. Father–child relationship quality is in turn directly linked to children's social adjustment but not to their behavioral problems or peer relationships (Cabrera et al. forthcoming).

12. See Tach, Mincy, and Edin (2010) for data on the falloff in father involvement following the mother forming a new partnership.

13. See Hill (2007) for a discussion of sexual mistrust and infidelity with past partners.

14. Note that Katrina's new man had already lost the connection to his own children from prior relationships. This is not uncommon for low-income, inner-city men who take on the father role for another man's child (Claessens 2007).

15. Edin and Kefalas (2005) find that mothers use restraining orders with surprising frequency to keep fathers away. Sometimes this is because the father poses serious risks to her or the child. At other times, though, retaliation is the main motive.

16. One paper utilizing the Fragile Families and Child Wellbeing Study finds that fathers with temperamentally difficult children are less involved than fathers with easier children (Lewin-Bizan 2006).

17. Center for Research on Child Wellbeing (2007). This figure is based on mothers' reports. Fathers' reports put the figure higher, but fewer of them are interviewed.

References

Cabrera, Natasha, Gina A. Cook, Karen F. McFadden, and Robert Bradley. Forthcoming. "Father Residence and Father–Child Relationship Quality: Peer Relationships and Externalizing Behavioral Problems." Special issue, *Journal of Family Science.*

Cabrera, Natasha, Jay Fagan, and Danielle Farrie. 2008. "Explaining the Long Reach of Father's Prenatal Involvement on Later Paternal Engagement with Children." *Journal of Marriage and Family* 70 (5): 1094–107.

Carlson, Marcia, Sara S. McLanahan, and Jeanne Brooks-Gunn. 2005. "Unmarried but Not Absent: Fathers' Involvement with Children after a Nonmarital Birth." Working Paper 2005–07-FF, Bendheim-Thoman Center for Research on Child Wellbeing, Princeton University, NJ.

Cheadle, Jacob E., Paul R. Amato, and Valarie King. 2010. "Patterns of Nonresident Father Contact." *Demography* 47 (1): 206–25.

Claessens, Amy. 2007. "Gatekeeper Moms and (Un)Involved Dads: What Happens after a Breakup?" In England and Edin 2009, 204–27.

Coley, Rebekah Levine, and Jodi E. Morris. 2002. "Comparing Father and Mother Reports of Father Involvement among Low-Income Minority Families." *Journal of Marriage and Family* 64 (4): 982–97.

Edin, Kathryn, and Maria Kefalas. 2005. *Promises I Can Keep: Why Poor Women Put Motherhood before Marriage.* Berkeley: University of California Press.

Edin, Kathryn, Laura Tach, and Ronald Mincy. 2009. "Claiming Fatherhood: Race and the Dynamics of Paternal Involvement among Unmarried Fathers." *Annals of the American Academy of Political and Social Science* 621 (1): 149–77

Hill, Heather. 2007. "Steppin' Out: Infidelity and Sexual Jealousy among Unmarried Parents." In England and Edin 2009, 104–32.

Lerman, Robert, and Elaine Sorensen. 2000. "Father Involvement with Their Nonmarital Children: Patterns, Determinants, and Effects on their Earnings." *Marriage and Family Review* 29 (2–3): 137–58.

Lewin-Bizan, Selva. 2006. "Identifying the Associations between Child Temperament and Father Involvement: Theoretical Considerations and Empirical Evidence." Working Paper 921, Woodrow Wilson School of Public and International Affairs, Bendheim-Thoman Center for Research on Child Wellbeing, Princeton University, NJ. http://ideas.repec.org/p/pri/crcwel/92i.html.

McClain, Lauren Rinelli, and Alfred DeMaris. 2011. "A Better Deal for Cohabiting Fathers? Union Status Differences in Father Involvement." Working Paper WP11–17–FF, Bendheim-Thoman Center for Research on Child Wellbeing, Princeton University, NJ.

Mikelson, Kelly S. 2008. "He Said, She Said: Comparing Mother and Father Reports of Father Involvement." *Journal of Marriage and Family* 70 (3): 613–24.

Sampson, Robert J., and John H. Laub. 1993. *Crime in the Making: Pathways and Turning Points through Life.* Cambridge, MA: Harvard University Press.

Shannon, Jacqueline D., Natasha J. Cabrera, Catherine Tamis-LeMonda, and Michael E. Lamb. 2009. "Who Stays and Who Leaves? Father Accessibility across Children's First Five Years." *Parenting Science and Practice* 9 (1): 78–100.

Sorensen, Elaine, and Ariel Hill. 2004. "Single Mothers and Their Child Support Receipt: How Well Is Child Support Enforcement Doing?" *Journal of Human Resources* 39 (1): 135–54.

Tach, Laura, Ronald Mincy, and Kathryn Edin. 2010. "Parenting as a 'Package Deal': Relationships, Fertility, and Nonresident Father Involvement among Unmarried Parents." *Demography* 47 (1): 181–204.

Yeung, W. Jean, John F. Sandberg, Pamela E. Davis-Kean, and Sandra L. Hofferth. 2001. "Children's Time with Fathers in Intact Families." *Journal of Marriage and Family* 63 (1): 136–54.

CHAPTER 24

The "Second-Wife" Phenomenon and the Relational Construction of Class-Coded Masculinities in Contemporary China

Suowei Xiao

Introduction

China has a long history of concubinage, an arrangement in which men keep more than one woman as marital partners. Keeping concubines was often reserved as the privilege of autocratic families in traditional Chinese society. In 1950, the Chinese socialist state established monogamy as the only legal form of marriage. The concubine system, seen as the "sin of the feudal society," was condemned and outlawed. In the socialist era, intimate life was under the close scrutiny of the state; divorce rate was low and extramarital affairs were rare in the society at large.

Intimate and family relations have undergone dramatic changes in the past thirty years of China's market reforms launched in 1979. The divorce rate has quadrupled in the past thirty years nationwide. Extramarital affairs have been cited as a major reason for marriage dissolution. Among various forms of male extramarital arrangements, a so-called keep a second wife (*bao er nai/baau yih naaih*) practice, a legally unsanctioned heterosexual relationship that resembles traditional concubinage in certain ways, has become prevalent in many economically developed areas.

"Second wife" (*er nai* in Mandarin and *yih naaih* in Cantonese) currently is a widely used term in contemporary China for a woman involved in a long-term relationship with a married man upon whom she depends economically. Men in these relationships usually purchase or rent separate homes for their second wives and pay their expenses, often unbeknownst to their legal wives.[1] Albeit being legally illegitimate, the phenomenon has emerged in many economically developed cities in China. The Pearl River Delta of Guangdong Province, a region that took advantage of the earliest market reforms and absorbed a large share of foreign investment, is believed to be the hub where the phenomenon first became common. As early as in the late 1980s, Hong Kong and Taiwanese businessmen came to the region for business opportunities and began to take young migrant women workers as second wives (Lang and Smart 2002). In the ensuing decades, the demographics of men keeping second wives came to include professionals from Hong Kong and Taiwan, salaried workers, and truck drivers who work regularly in mainland China. Mainland Chinese men have also adopted this practice. The composition of second wives includes not only

SOURCE: Xiao, S. (2011). The "Second-Wife" Phenomenon and the Relational Construction of Class-Coded Masculinities in Contemporary China. *Men and Masculinities, 14*(5), 607–627. Reproduced with permission.

migrant women but also urban women with higher educational and economic status (Osburg 2008; Shen 2005; Tam 1996; 2005).

The very limited research that has been conducted on this topic does not allow for accurate calculation of the total number of cases. Hong Kong legislative counselors and social workers have estimated that by 1995, about 300,000 Hong Kong men had established second households in different parts of China (Tam 1996). A 2004 survey of Hong Kong truck drivers who regularly crossed the border to transport goods between Hong Kong and the mainland reveals that about 65 percent of the 193 men who responded to the questionnaire kept a mistress in mainland China (Tam, Fung, Kam, and Liong 2009). Although not all but (most possibly) only a small portion of Chinese men have pursued a second wife, the phenomenon has been seen as a major social problem in China. Before the latest revision of China's Marriage Law in 2001, a major public debate took place on whether prohibiting "keeping a second wife" (*bao ernai*) should be literally written into the law.[2]

Most existing research on the second-wife phenomenon seeks to explore why the practice has emerged between men from Hong Kong or Taiwan and mainland Chinese women and has analyzed it in relation to factors of demography, migration, economic disparity, and cultural framing of competing femininities (Lang and Smart 2002; Shen 2005; So 2003; Tam 2005). Some also explore the different stages of mistress-keeping as well as the role media and public discourses play in naturalizing and normalizing the phenomenon (Tam 1996, 2005; Tam, Kam, and Liong 2009). In this article, I examine the phenomenon from the perspective of the relational construction of class and masculinity in contemporary China. I argue that second wives engage in a variety of domestic, emotional, and symbolic work in which they help their men perform as well as reconstruct class-coded forms of masculinity.

In the past thirty years of China's market reform and social restructuring, scholars have witnessed the emergence of new masculine ideologies and practices. Whereas much attention has been focused on elite men (see e.g., Osburg 2008; Zhang 2001; Zheng 2006, 2009), this study adopts a comparative perspective to disentangle how men in different class positions construct masculine worth and honor through which they articulate and negotiate their class identities. I suggest that the conception of class-coded masculinities does not mean that class crosscuts masculinity to put the latter into plural, clear-cut categories. Rather, men in different class positions are affected by the dominant discourse of masculinity. Accordingly, they strategize, consciously and unconsciously, to reconfigure meaningful gendered self within the availability and constraints of their material and cultural resources. Following the insight of Connell and Messerschmidt (2005), I take a relational approach to study the construction of masculinities and highlight the contribution of women's labor in constituting gender and class identities for men in contemporary China.

The data I draw on for analysis is derived from twelve months of ethnographic fieldwork in China with participants in nineteen second-wife arrangements, as well as documentary research on twelve descriptive second-wife cases documented by an undercover newspaper reporter. I embed my analysis of the interplay between gender and class within the context of market reform, globalization, and social restructuring in China over the past three decades.

The Relational Construction of Gender and Class

In their classic piece "Doing Gender," West and Zimmerman (1987) argue that gender is not something one is, but something one *does*. The concept, "doing gender," emphasizes the ways in which gender differences take form through "routine, methodical, and reoccurring" labors associated with femininity and masculinity. Building on West and Zimmerman's interactionist framework, Jane Ward (2007) suggests that an individual's gendered identity may be coproduced by others through interaction. Ward argues that the accomplishment of an individual's gendered identity often occurs through the recognition, validation, affirmation, celebration, and consolidation provided by others in interaction. She emphasizes the laborious practice of doing gender for specific others, which she has termed "gender labor." The concept of gender labor points to the routine emotional, physical, and mental labor that people do to validate, reinforce, and celebrate the gendered expression of others in intimate as well as other kinds of social interaction.

While gender must be understood as something one does, often with important contributions of others in interaction, class should also be perceived as performances that are produced, manifested, and maintained routinely (Bettie 2000; West and Fenstermaker 1995). Scholars have noted that the articulation of class is enabled and conveyed through gendered constructs and practices (Barber 2008; Bettie 2000). Bettie (2000), for example, in her famous study of working-class white and Mexican American school girls, illuminates how the meanings of class are couched in essentialized notions of racial/ethnic and gender identities.

Inspired by Ward's conception of gender labor and scholarly insights of the intertwined nature of gender and class performance, I contend that class is a relational accomplishment with significant contributions of others' labor, mediated through gender. This is particularly the case in contemporary China. As notions of class are understood as associated with the "backward" socialist past and are often muted in public discourse, instructing workers with particular sets of gendered scripts—coded as natural and desirable femininity—to be performed in service settings comes to be especially important in communicating the social status of the privileged customers (Hanser 2005; Otis 2008).

In this article, I examine the relational construction of gender and class in intimate relationships. In the analysis that follows, I will depict how the practice of taking second wives, and more importantly, second wives' deliberate domestic, emotional, and other forms of labor, help men construct meaningful masculinity, thereby enabling workers to negotiate their class disadvantage and assisting businessmen in manifesting their class privilege.

The Reconstruction of Masculinity in Contemporary China

Scholars have noted that the reconstruction of Chinese masculinity has been an active project in the cultural and social arena since the early economic reforms (Brownell 1999; Louie 2002; Zhong 2000). Many male Chinese writers and intellectuals aggressively criticize the earlier socialist regime for strengthening the power and autonomy of women and completely subjecting men to the state, thereby emasculating them. Critics claim that men were psychologically and spiritually castrated by the state (Zhang 2001), which ultimately resulted in a weak national identity and inability to achieve modernity (Brownell 1999).

In the meantime, the dominant ideology of the post-reform masculinity has been centered on men's capacities to make money and generate economic power (Osburg 2008; Zhang 2010). Newly empowered businessmen and entrepreneurs have come to represent a new male ideal of the market era and become highly favored in the marriage market (Farrer 2002; Osburg 2008; Xu 2000). In popular discourse, individual men's economic failure is interpreted as lack of virility; their class struggle is thus understood in terms of masculinity crisis (Yang 2010).

As entrepreneurs, businessmen, and professionals have emerged as the new elite class, their various practices have attracted much social attention. Studies have explored in depth the ways in which the business elites constitute distinctive forms of masculinity, particularly focusing on their consumption of female sexuality as they engage in their frequent visits to bars, nightclubs, and other entertainment venues for networking and business sociability. The performance of "elite masculinity" through the consumption of women serves as important means for group selection and male bonding among the elite businessmen (Osburg 2008; Zheng 2006, 2009). It also indicates business elites' symbolic struggle against the state (Zhang 2001). For instance, Tiantian Zheng (2006, 2009) argues that the process of men engaging with hostesses in nightclubs produces a testament to the ideal of what she calls "cool masculinity," a combination of responsibility, rationality, reliability, and self-control—"masculine traits" that are criteria for group selection, gaining trust, and exchanging favors within business circles. My study extends the scholarship on contemporary Chinese masculinity in a number of aspects. First, while most previous research focuses on the role sexuality plays in constructing masculinity, my work suggests that sexuality is not the only means through which masculinity is manifested. Rather, the ways in which men achieve masculine honor and status encompass various forms of women's labor, including domestic care and emotional support. Further, departing from most previous studies that concentrate on mapping elite masculinity, my work explores how the construction of masculinity varies across class in contemporary China. I argue that similar practices, such as taking mistresses, may express different meanings for elite businessmen and lower-class workers. More importantly, I examine not only how class impacts men's gender identity, but also how men demonstrate and negotiate the meanings of class through gendered constructs in intimate relationships. As I illustrate in the analysis, it is precisely through demonstrating their capacity to attract young, pretty women and "to be served like a king," that business elites constitute their class privilege. In comparison, blue-collar workers and low-end white-collar workers resort to different sets of women's offerings to enhance their gender image and to navigate through class displacement.

Method

Between September 2005 and August 2006 and during the summer of 2007, I conducted nine months of field research in Guangzhou, the capital of Guangdong Province, and three months of fieldwork in Ningbo, a major coastal city in the region of the Yangzi River Delta. Both regions are among China's most economically developed areas where the second-wife phenomenon is prominent. I used mutual friends to meet my respondents in nineteen cases. Although I was not able to interview all the second wives and their partners (it being especially difficult to obtain men's consent to be interviewed), I interviewed sixteen second wives or former second wives and seven men involved in such relationships. In four cases, I interviewed both the men and their second wives. In all of the nineteen cases, I asked each respondent for detailed background information of themselves and their partner. I conducted multiple open-ended interviews with each respondent and engaged in participant observation research with most of them, visiting their home and joining them for social and recreational activities. With their permission, I also interviewed neighbors, friends, and relatives of some respondents.

The relationships I studied in my fieldwork had lasted from eleven months to a few years. The longest-lasting pair had been together for nine years. Second wives in my study include eleven migrant women from rural or inland China who came to coastal cities for job opportunities and eight legal residents of Guangzhou. Their ages ranged from eighteen to thirty-eight years old. None of them had more than a high school education and most of them did not finish junior high school. On the men's part, seventeen were mainland Chinese and two were from Hong Kong. Their ages ranged from the mid-thirties to early sixties. Eleven men owned small-or medium-sized businesses, three were high-end professionals (a general manager, an architect, and a university administrator) and the other five worked for different companies as foreman, salesman, or office staff. Except for five cases, all of these men's two households were in the same city.

To expand the data set for my analysis, I extend my field notes with twelve additional, detailed descriptive cases of Hong Kong blue-collar workers' second-wife arrangements, collected by Tu Qiao, a Hong Kong–based journalist. Tu lived as an undercover reporter for two months in a so-called village of second wives, a migrant workers' neighborhood in Shenzhen where a large number of second wives of Hong Kong container truck drivers and other blue-collar workers lived. She befriended twelve second wives of Hong Kong working-class men and socialized with them on a daily basis.

In her book *Bitter Marriage* (Ku Hun), Tu (2004) documented the experiences of these twelve women in detail without analyzing them systematically. Similar to what I encountered in my fieldwork, she found it more difficult to interview men. However, she succeeded in speaking with four men from the twelve cases and obtained other men's background information from their second wives. In her work, all of the men were manual workers based in Hong Kong—half were container truck drivers who traveled regularly across the Hong Kong Mainland border, while the other six held working-class jobs such as construction worker, retired sailor, and subway booking clerk. Their second wives were all migrant women from inland China, aged from late teens to mid-thirties. The men's two households were all located in two neighboring cities, Shenzhen and Hong Kong.

In the analysis, I use pseudonyms to protect the identity of my informants. Some informants preferred to be called by their English names; in these cases I replace them with fake English names.

Producing Dignity for Workers

To be sure, the workers in this study are better off than the general working-class population in China today. Compared to laid-off SOE employees or rural migrant laborers, workers included here enjoy obvious economic advantage: the mainland workers hold stable, even lower-middle class jobs offering a decent paycheck while the Hong Kong blue-collar workers are able to convert their low wages in Hong Kong to high consumption power in the mainland. Nevertheless, they share the pressure of feeling "left behind" and "emasculated" in a time of rapid social change and increased economic inequality as the dominant ideology of masculinity focuses on the ability to generate money.

Except for one case, workers' second wives are all migrant women. Compared to the second wives of businessmen who are normally younger and prettier, they tend to be older and plain looking on average. They also receive much less allowance or material support from their male partners.[3] In workers' second households, as I illustrate below, second wives engage in convenient, care-laden domestic work and emotional offerings of comfort and assurance for their partner. Through routine yet invisible, therapeutic, and partially decommodified gender labor, they help produce, consolidate, and enhance their men's sense of self-worth and dignity.

Doing Chores, Doing Care

Cai was a forty-year-old salesman, working for a state-owned company in central coastal China where his legal family was located. As part of his job, he had taken on business trips to Guangzhou for ten to fifteen days each month since 2001. In 2002, he set up a second household with Run, a thirty-eight-year-old woman from a small town in Guangxi. Run migrated to Guangzhou for job opportunities after she separated from (and later divorced) her husband. She had to support their ten-year-old son who was then living with her best friend in her hometown.

My first visit to their home was on a December afternoon when Cai had just returned to his hometown. They lived in a one-bedroom apartment in a migrant neighborhood of suburban Guangzhou. Their apartment was about 300 square feet in area, poorly lit and equipped, with plain cement walls and floor. All of the furniture was bought second hand, costing a total of about 600 yuan. The only electric appliance in the apartment was an electronic fan covered by a bath towel. I was, however, very impressed by the cleanliness and tidiness of the apartment. "Homemaking is my strength," Run proudly told me.

As Run recalled, her day typically started at 7 a.m. when Cai was in town. She prepared breakfast for Cai before he left the apartment at around 8 a.m. After he left for work, she made the bed, hand washed the clothes changed the night before, dusted the room, and mopped the floor. If Cai came back for lunch, she would cook at least two dishes and a soup to feed him. If not, she would fix herself a quick lunch, usually with leftovers from the night before. In the afternoon, she took a nap and then joined her neighbors for mahjong or some odd job such as sewing beads onto fashion clothes for the overseas market, for which she earned about 2 yuan an hour. At around 4:30 p.m., she went to the local farmers' market for grocery shopping and prepared dinner. After dinner, while Cai was watching TV, Run washed the dishes and mopped the floor one more time. If Cai looked tired, she would also give him a massage which she learned in the hair salon before the couple met.

As a matter of fact, Cai did the lion's share of domestic chores, cooking and cleaning the house for his legal family, which Run was clearly aware of but disregarded. She explained to me that Cai had more free time in his hometown. More importantly, she enjoyed the "breadwinner–homemaker" style of family life and loved to be needed by him.

In Run's eyes, Cai was a great partner who provided her the stable life that her ex-husband had failed. Cai covered the monthly rent of 350 yuan for their one-bedroom apartment, paid the household expenses, and gave her about 600–800 yuan each month. The couple got along very well. "Being with him makes me feel like fall in love again," Run said, "we are attuned in almost all aspects, including sexual life. I am willing to take care of him."

In all workers' second households I investigated, second wives engage a large amount of domestic care for their partners. Their domestic work provides many benefits for the working men, especially those in traveling occupations. For men like Cai who have limited budgets, it is economically wise to keep a second wife like Run to take care of the household. In stark economic terms, if Cai were to live by himself during his two-week business trip in Guangzhou each month, eating out alone would cost him about 1,000 yuan a month, while paid domestic services such as apartment cleaning and laundry would cost another 200 yuan. That is roughly equivalent to the amount Cai gives to Run (600–800 yuan) plus the living expenses during his stay in Guangzhou (500 yuan). If Cai were to pursue other services that he usually got from Run for free, such as massage, he would have to pay even more to maintain the current quality of life in Guangzhou.

The affordability of second wives' service makes it possible for some working men to set up a second household. More importantly, with the care-laden domestic work, second wives provide priceless emotional meanings of "home." It feels different to have one's food prepared, apartment cleaned, and clothes washed by a loving "family member" rather than a paid servant. The form of payment and the means through which service is delivered mark the emotional and symbolic meanings of particular services (Zelizer 2005). In workers' second-wife arrangements, the domestic work is partially decommodified, coded as a wife's "duty." Furthermore, the chores are done with personalized input by the second wife to feed the man's idiosyncratic needs. For instance, workers' second wives all managed to cook their man's favorite meals. In this manner, the domestic service and care given by second wives reproduces not only working-class men's labor power but also their sense and honor as the "breadwinner."

The Art of Ego-Soothing

Second wives, through their meticulous and sensitive domestic work, honor male status as the economic provider. They also soothe men's egos by engaging in various types of emotion work—"induce or suppress feeling in order to sustain the outward countenance that produces the proper state of mind in others" (Hochschild 1983, 7). By repressing negative feelings (such as disappointment, grievance, and criticism), providing constant support and boosting confidence, second wives validate and consolidate their man's sense of worth.

As one of the victims of the 1990s' economic downturn in Hong Kong, Wang Yao started to work as a subway booking clerk after being laid off from his old company. His new job only paid him $15,000 HK (roughly $1900 US) a month, much lower than the average income in Hong Kong.

As he brought less money to his family, he felt his wife being increasingly disappointed and disengaged with him. During a leisure trip to Shenzhen, he met Ah-Yan, a charming young woman from Hunan Province in a bar. She talked to him in a gentle and loving way, with her soft and enchanting voice "that can calm down a maniac and make him dance," which made him feel like being able to retrieve his sense of masculinity (Tu 2004, 36). He instantly bought her the most expensive drink in the bar and later set up a second household with her in Shenzhen, giving her about 4,000 yuan a month.

Wang Yao's story illuminates the ways in which Hong Kong men negotiate their class and gender identity in a global space. Due to economic discrepancy between Hong Kong and the mainland, their relatively low income by Hong Kong standards, however, can be transferred into higher consumption power that gains them more status in mainland China. Like third-world diasporas in first world countries who often engage in conspicuous consumption in trips to their home countries (Thai 2008), Wang Yao spends extravagantly in the mainland to demonstrate his first world privilege. Furthermore, by engaging in an intimate relationship with a mainland woman who defers to his first-world status as well as masculine superiority, he reconstructs a positive self-image of manliness to cope with feelings of marginalization and emasculation related to his downward mobility.

In a similar manner, many mainland Chinese workers' positive sense of masculinity hinges on their second wife's emotional care. Lao-Wang was a fifty-year-old employee at a state-owned company in Ningbo. He got divorced after his wife discovered his affair with a young migrant woman and vandalized the woman's apartment (which Lao-Wang rent for her). Commenting on his unsuccessful marriage, Lao-Wang said,

> I work every day to earn money. My only hobby is to play mahjong. I just want to socialize with my friends and to relax. But my ex-wife regarded it as gambling and strongly opposed it. She did not allow me to get into bed at night after I returned from the mahjong table. She also compared me with her sister's husband who ran a transportation company, blaming me for not being capable and hard-working enough. I had hoped that home would be a relaxing place for me, but it never was.

Lao-Wang's ex-wife, Fang, expressed a different opinion. Fang, forty-eight, worked as a teller in a small construction company. To her, it was for the benefit of Lao-Wang and their family that she pushed him ahead.

"Unlike my brother in law, he (referring to Lao-Wang) was a man of little ambition," Fang said. "If no one pushes him, he would end up nowhere." Indeed, with her constant urge and support, Lao-Wang had finished a three-year-adult college degree five years before. The degree helped him obtain his current office position, which paid twice as much as his previous job as a taxi driver. To support his career development, Fang sacrificed her own educational and career development prospect and fully devoted herself to the family. She also gave up her personal hobbies such as reading novels and hiking to squeeze time. As a dutiful wife, she was thus very annoyed at Lao-Wang's addiction to mahjong (as he played almost every night and often lost money over it). Admitting that her words were sometimes a bit harsh and disrespectful (such as calling him "idiot" or "loser") when they fought, Fang stressed on her love for him,

> I gave him enough face in public. I just fought with him at home . . . I pointed out his flaws because I cared about him, because he was my husband. I wanted good things for him. Gambling is not a good habit. If I kept silent and let it be, we were not a real family.

Similar to the Hong Kong woman whose husband kept mistresses in the mainland that Siumi Tam (2005) has interviewed, Fang presented herself in a cultural image of legal wife generated within the patriarchal family structure—moral, dutiful housewife with a strong character. Moreover, Fang lived in an era when the economic inequality across household has enlarged dramatically across China. She was stressed out by feeling left behind, especially since a number of people in her social circle (including both of her sisters' family) had already become more affluent. With little access to economic opportunities, she had to depend on Lao-Wang for maintaining her dignity and that of their family in her social circle.

Lao-Wang recognized Fang's sacrifice and good will, which kept him from initiating a divorce. However, Fang's criticism took off another layer of his masculine honor that had already been shied by her brother-in-law's economic prosperity. He thus found his second home more enchanting where no one complained about him; instead, he was adored as a "very good man." Lao-Wang said,

> Xiaomei [his second wife] always welcomed me when I visited her. She cooked meals for me, had faith in me, and never pushed me for anything. She thought I was a very good man and deserved a happier marriage. Even when I told her that I would not divorce my wife and marry her, she still accepted me. I was so moved. I was under a lot of pressure at home, feeling repressed and disrespected. But I was very comfortable and relaxed at this woman's place.

Lao-Wang had originally believed his perfect second household was due to "natural" compatibility between himself and Xiaomei. After he got divorced, he found out that Xiaomei had grieved because he would not marry her and visited her only occasionally. She had painstakingly concealed her inner emotions from him. By repressing her own disappointment and showing constant support and no criticism at all, she made his second household "heaven in a heartless world" and assured him a sense of self-worth as a "very good man."

Workers' second wives whom I have conducted research with are all poorly educated migrant women from rural or inland China. Being a second wife generally secures a better material life compared to laboring in a sweatshop and service floor, which are the typical jobs they are able to find in cities. Furthermore, as I elaborate elsewhere (see Xiao 2009, 2011), albeit stigmatized, the intimate relationship also provides a crucial emotional source of security, connection, and companionship for migrant women who struggle with geographical, social, and emotional displacement in the process of rural to urban migration (Jacka 2006; Pun 2005).

Performing Status for Business Elites

In contemporary China, business elites are the group that has gained the most social status since market reforms. Their consumption power not only enables them to enjoy the best quality goods and services but also raises their social status, as China increasingly becomes a consumerist society. The majority of the fourteen business elites discussed in this article come from working class or even rural family backgrounds. They run small- to medium-sized businesses or work in high-end professional occupations. To be sure, they are not among the most affluent in China today.

Nevertheless, they seek to convert their economic capital to symbolic boundaries that mark their class distinction (Bourdieu 1984; Zhang 2010). The practice of taking a second wife has become an important site for the performance and reproduction of their elite masculinity. Businessmen's second wives perform extensive "symbolic work"—accompanying their partner to social events, monitoring their physical image, and creating positive public perceptions of their relationships. In comparison with workers' second-wife arrangement, which is more privatized and domesticated, the business elites' relationship is semipublic. As workers' second wives help their partners to cope with their besieged masculinity by making them feel worthy and dignified, their counterparts coupled with business elites help their men achieve a sense of being "attractive" and "almighty" in private as well as in public settings.

Making Him Feel Like a King

Compared to workers' second wives, those coupled with business elites conducted much less domestic work. This is in part due to the fact that a majority of (twelve out of fifteen) the business elites in this study established their two households in the same city. The two Hong Kong–based men, a jewelry merchant and an architect, did not go on regular business trips to Guangzhou; instead, they went to the mainland primarily to visit their second wives and for leisure. Businessmen in my study also had dinner with government officials and clients on a regular basis and tended to obtain domestic services from their legal wives as well as paid servants. In addition, second wives of four wealthier businessmen also used paid domestic services for their own household chores. Thus, the economic benefit of second wives' domestic service is minimal in businessmen's arrangements.

Nevertheless, second wives perform occasional domestic labor that conveys to the business elites their status and authority, as the men can always count on their demands being fulfilled. Lucy, second wife of a Hong Kong architect, explained to me that her tactic to stay attractive to her boyfriend was to make him feel significant through tiny things. He typically spent two weekends at her place each month. When he was at her place, Lucy made him the center of her life. She would tentatively ask if he needed anything and then go downstairs to get his favorite snacks, even though she lived on the eighth floor of an apartment building with no elevator.

Jamie, second wife of a Guangzhou care dealer, is a more astonishing example. Jamie normally dined out with friends; she did not get a chance to see her boyfriend every day. But she never made a dinner appointment with friends before he informed her whether he would be available that night, usually around 6 p.m. One night I was having dinner with her and a mutual friend, Beth. Jamie's boyfriend had a dinner appointment with clients. In the middle of our meal, Jamie's cell phone rang. It was from her boyfriend. His dinner appointment was cancelled and he wanted her to cook for him. Jamie, unhappy though, left immediately. Seeing me confused, Beth said calmly, "Don't be shocked! You'll get used to it like I have."

Like workers' second wives, businessmen's mistresses also perform repressive forms of emotion work, deliberately suppressing negative feelings when they interact with their partners. They are, however, more likely to experience verbal abuse. Fei had been with Dong, a local construction contractor in Guangzhou, for three years. Dong purchased a two-bedroom apartment in suburban Guangzhou for her and provided her with an allowance varying from 5,000 to 10,000 yuan a month. Fei was satisfied with his constant financial support and lasting affection for her. Nevertheless, his remarks often hurt her feelings. Once she complained that he was visiting less. He responded, "You bitch! You have been fucked by so many men! Do you still think that you are a virgin? How dare you complain that I am not treating you well enough?" Fei was hurt by his words, but said nothing, partly because she had indeed had a few boyfriends before him. She also excused him for he was stressed out at work and thus easily annoyed. More importantly, she knew that fighting back would worsen the relationship. She said, "Fighting with him will do nothing but to make him more annoyed. He may even turn off the tap (*guan shui hou*, meaning "stop providing"). Why bother?"

Like Fei, many businessmen's second wives reported that their men lost their tempers at them frequently once the relationship has stabilized. During the initial dating or the "honeymoon period" of the relationship (Tam, Kam, & Liong 2009), men tend to be well behaved in controlling their temper. Largely because of their economic dependence, second wives do not feel like having "guts" to fight back. But some second wives have more leverage to deal with emotional abuse. Here's Lucy, who said:

> I can hardly stand his bad temper. He shouts nasty words at me when he is mad about something. At those times, I will fight back if I have money, but if I am really broke, I have to hold my breath, keep silent, and swallow his words. It is really hard.

As a native Guangzhou woman, Lucy was well embedded in social networks that could provide her material and emotional support in difficult times. Although growing up in a single-parent working-class family, she managed to borrow money from her friends occasionally. She also befriended with a group of local women who engaged in a similar relationship. They met regularly to grieve about their mistreatment by their partner and offered each other advice to handle the situation. To a large extent, the local support network enabled her to defend herself in the second-wife arrangement. In comparison, second wives who lacked effective support networks and were more emotionally attached to the men tended to be more tolerant of emotional abuse.

In addition to repressive forms of emotion work such as tolerance for ill treatment and suppressing anger, second wives of business elites also engage in more "expressive" forms of emotional display that workers' second wives do not normally perform, which include produce satisfying conversations. Some women truly enjoyed conversations with their boyfriend, such as Yuan, who coupled with a general manager of a high-tech company, twenty years her senior. She explained,

> Although there is a big difference in age and educational level between us, we share common topics—I really enjoy listening to him talking. He has very rich life experience and knows a whole lot. He enjoys telling me about what happened, what he has seen, etc., and I love everything he tells me.

Others, however, had to stimulate emotions in order to make the conversation delightful. Ying, second wife of a Hong Kong jewelry merchant, regarded answering her boyfriend's phone calls as a most difficult task she had to handle in the relationship. She said, "He calls to talk about his business, which I am not interested in at all. But I have to be the audience for his endless boring speech, pretending to listen attentively and commenting on things he's mentioned as if they were funny."

Through both repressive and expressive forms of emotion work as well as occasional but attentive domestic care, second wives of businessmen seek to make the second household a magic place for their partner, where he can release stress, assert authority, and perform charm. As one male respondent said, "She makes me feel like a king!" Feeling like a "king" is different from the sense of being a "good man" that workers' second wives produce in their men. A king feels entitled to the services others provide and has the status and power to give orders and to be obeyed. In real life, conflicts between the couple happen, such as in occasions when the second wife demands for marriage or the man is caught having affairs with other women. The second household is not always the king's palace. However, on normal days, validating the man's authority and affirming his charm constitute the basic routine of most second wives when they interact with their elite partner.

Gaining Face in Public

In addition to giving their men status in the private realm, second wives of business elites endeavor to present a positive image of the relationship in the presence of others and thereby help the men gain "face" in public. The public face that a couple puts on in front of the man's friends is very important in sustaining the status of the businessmen. For instance, Ying received a very generous stipend of 10,000 yuan each month from her boyfriend, a Hong Kong merchant in his sixties. The "old man" (as she referred to him in our interview) was impotent and never succeeded in consummating their relationship during the year they were together. Ying asked him why he wanted to have a girlfriend if he was unable to have sex. He stated that his friends all had girlfriends, so why couldn't he? He longed to show others that he was a potent, charming, wealthy, and successful man who was still attractive to young women.

To help their male partner maintain honor and status, many second wives of businessmen and entrepreneurs invest deliberate effort in keeping a positive public profile. These women engage in extensive bodily labor (Lan 2003)—working on their appearance and body image to fit their man's vision of a proper mate. Contrary to expectation, not every man wants his second wife to look young or entirely fashionable. For example, two second wives I interviewed—one in her late teens and the other in her early twenties—were often required by their several-decades-older lovers to wear minimal makeup and to dress in expensive formal suits and dresses rather than cheap, fashionable clothes. In this manner, they displayed their body in ways that made them look more mature, so that others would not mistake the couple for grandfather and granddaughter. They also appeared more cultured as well as more respectable, so as to be distinguished from bar girls. In contrast, for second wives in their late twenties and thirties, looking young is a primary task. They exhibit the latest fashions and wear heavy makeup, even resorting to plastic surgery to reduce signs of aging. One woman explained, "If I go out with him without dressing up, others will laugh at him for being with an 'ugly old woman.'"

Another routine activity that the second wives of businessmen engage in is to escort their men to events where the presence of second wives is deemed proper and desirable, such as casual business socializing in nightclubs and other entertainment venues. The second wives of business elites have all accompanied their men to business functions. Her company is even sometimes compulsory.

In the new market-oriented culture, attractive women are often regarded as the most valuable of male trophies, especially in the circle of newly enriched entrepreneurs and businessmen (Osburg 2008). In the routine business sociability among business elites, second wives are presented as a showcase of having face for their partner. In these masculinized social activities, second wives are not simply "positional goods" in that their existence alone compliments the men's status. In addition to putting on appropriate bodily displays, they also manage their behaviors to make their man seem as a modern subject who is desiring and being desired in the eyes of others.

One night, I accompanied Xue to the nightclub her boyfriend Hai owned, where he normally socialized with friends. We joined two of Hai's male friends who both had a female companion in a karaoke booth. While we entertained ourselves playing dice, drinking beer, singing karaoke, and telling jokes in our booth, Hai visited different booths in turn to greet important customers and friends. When he came to our booth, he first initiated a toast with all of us and then sat next to his girlfriend. Xue held his arm tight, leaned her body toward him, swinging gently, and said coquettishly: "You've left me alone for so long." Seeing the couple caressing, one of Hai's friends teased, "Hey man, your lady cannot wait (to make out with you)!" All the men laughed.

To some extent, what Xue did resembles the behavior of bar hostesses as reported in a number of ethnographies of night clubs. Through routinized performances in nightclubs, such as pouring beer, caressing, and flirting, hostesses help male corporate employees project an image of masculine potency and sexual attractiveness (Allison 1994; Osburg 2008; Zheng 2009). Unlike bar hostesses whose affirmation of masculine desirability is commonly understood as a commercial service, temporal, and artificial, second wives' attraction to these men is perceived as more personal and authentic. Under the romantic aura of a private relationship, the quality and performances of a second wife not only indicate a man's economic power, but succeed in conveying his class privilege in social and cultural terms while simultaneously disguising it as a personal quality, that is, his virility and desirability as a romantic partner.

The abovementioned examples of Fei and Xue further reveal a particular social milieu surrounding businessmen's second-wife arrangement. Unlike workers' second-wives arrangements that generally remain as a private means for these working men to reconstruct meaningful gender and class identity, elite men's "face-constructing" occasions accept and even encourage them to present their second wife in public, thereby making the legally unsanctioned intimate relationship open, normalized, and even celebrated. In this manner, the practice of taking a second wife has become a collective way for business elites to manifest their class privilege.

Conclusion

In this article, I demonstrate that gender, rather than an accomplishment made in solitude, is a relational and interactional construction with significant contributions from the effort and labor of others. Second-wife arrangements provide an excellent site to examine the relational aspects of doing gender. Compared with socially legitimate female partners in heterosexual relationships, second wives, due to their economic dependence, sociocultural pressures, and lack of legal protection, take conscious, deliberate, and strategic action in making their men feel masculine and potent both in private and in public spaces. Helping men perform masculinity, in these cases, constitutes an effective strategy for subaltern women in a precarious situation to achieve security for themselves.

Women's labor not only enables men to do gender but also facilitates them to perform class. I contend that class is both a structure that shapes the forms of gender configurations and a performance that is mediated through gender. In the context of contemporary China, men from a lower-class background experience class disadvantage through the deprivation of masculine dignity and honor; by achieving a positive masculine identity, that is, as a respected provider and "man of the house" in alternative intimate relationships, they mute and modify the negative meanings of lacking upward mobility. The new economic elites, in contrast, convert their economic capital to symbolic boundaries of class distinction, which is in large part facilitated by a collective effort in constructing a public image as desiring and desired male subjects.

Connell and Messerschmidt have reminded us that "gender is always relational" as women's practice and identities are "central in many of the processes constructing masculinity" and that our understandings of masculinity "need to incorporate a more holistic understanding of gender hierarchy, recognizing the agency of subordinated groups as much as the power of dominant groups and the mutual conditioning of gender dynamics and other social dynamics" (2005, 848). This article provides a contextualized study that systematically examines women's contribution and agency in the process of constituting masculinities and the dynamic interplay between gender and class. The contemporary Chinese society, with its emphasis on interpersonal relationships and the dramatic reconfigurations of masculinities and class landscape in the past few decades, may have made it easier to examine the relational and interactional aspects of gender. Yet bringing a relational perspective to gender in future studies of masculinities (and femininities) will remedy the problems of the dominant individual-centric approach in gender studies and lead to a more nuanced and holistic understanding of masculinities in a variety of social contexts.

Notes

1. "Yih naaih" was originally a vulgar term used by people in the greater Canton area (including Hong Kong) to refer to concubines in traditional Chinese society. The term has revived in the area as the second households established by Hong Kong, and Taiwanese businessmen have begun to flourish in mainland China since the early economic reform. The use of the term has also been expanded to non-Cantonese-speaking regions in China. In Mandarin, the term is pronounced as "er nai." There is no agreement yet on how the term should be translated in English as it is difficult to find an equivalent word in English. In this article, for the purpose of clarity, I follow the convention of other scholars who have conducted research on this topic (e.g., Lang and Smart 2002; Siumi Maria Tam 1996, 2005) and adopt the translation of "yiih laaih" as "second wife." However, it must be noted that unlike the wife, the "second wife" is legally illegitimate and

unprotected by law. In popular discourse, the term has a negative connotation. My female respondents rarely called themselves "second wife"(*er nai/yih naaih*); instead, they typically referred to themselves as "girlfriend (*nv peng you*)," "lover (*qing ren*)," or even "wife (*lao po*)." Male respondents called their second wife "my girlfriend (*nv peng you*)" or "my woman (*nv ren*)." I reserve the names and terms my informants used when I quote them or describe their own understandings of the arrangement.

2. China's marriage law, from its first establishment in 1950 through its latest revisions in 2001, prohibits a married person from cohabiting with a third party. However, in practice, as long as the couple in the second-wife relationship does not register their relationship as marriage, hold a wedding ceremony, or refer to each other as husband and wife in public, the arrangement is more likely to be considered as an affair rather than bigamy, which is penalized by the criminal code.

3. Second wives of mainland workers generally received between a couple of hundred to less than 1,500 yuan from their male partner each month. The Hong Kong workers gave their second wives a more generous monthly allotment of between 2,000 and 5,000 yuan. The business elites' second wives typically received more than 5,000 yuan of monthly allowance; some businessmen even gave their lovers more than 10,000 yuan a month.

References

Allison, A. 1994. *Nightwork: Sexuality, Pleasure, and Corporate Masculinity in a Tokyo Hostess Club.* Chicago: University of Chicago Press.

Barber, K. 2008. "The Well-Coiffed Man: Class, Race and Heterosexual Masculinity in Hair Salon." *Gender & Society* 22:455–76.

Bettie, J. 2000. "Women without Class: Chicas, Cholas, Trash and the Presence/Absence of Class Identity." *Signs* 26:1–35.

Bourdieu, P. 1986. "The Forms of Capital." In *Handbook of Theory and Research for the Sociology of Education*, edited by J. G. Richardson, 241–58. New York: Greenwood.

Brownell, S. 1999. "Strong Women and Impotent Men: Sports, Gender, and Nationalism in Chinese Public Culture." In *Spaces of Their Own: Women's Public Sphere in Transnational China*, edited by M. M. Yang, 207–31. Minneapolis: University of Minnesota Press.

Connell, R. W., and J. W. Messerschmidt. 2005. "Hegemonic Masculinity: Rethinking the Concept." *Gender & Society* 19:829–59.

Farrer, J. 2002. *Opening Up: Youth Sex Culture and Market Reform in Shanghai.* Chicago: University of Chicago Press.

Hanser, A. 2005. "The Gendered Rice Bowl: The Sexual Politics of Service Work in Urban China." *Gender & Society* 19:581–600.

Hochschild, A. R. 1983. *The Managed Heart: Commercialization of Human Feeling.* Berkeley: University of California Press.

Jacka, T. 2006. *Rural Women in Urban China: Gender, Migration, and Social Change.* Armonk and London: M. E. Sharpe.

Lan, P. 2003. "Working in a Neon Cage: 'Bodily Labor' of Cosmetics Saleswomen in Taiwan." *Feminist Studies* 29:1–25.

Lang, G., and J. Smart. 2002. "Migration and the 'Second Wife' in South China: Toward Cross-Border Polygyny." *International Migration Review* 36:546–69.

Louie, K. 2002. *Theorising Chinese Masculinity: Society and Gender in China.* Cambridge: Cambridge University Press.

Osburg, J. 2008. *Engendering Wealth: China's New Rich and the Rise of an Elite Masculinity.* PhD dissertation, University of Chicago.

Otis, E. M. 2008. "Beyond the Industrial Paradigm: Market-Embedded Labor and the Gender Organization of Global Service Work in China." *American Sociological Review* 73:15–36.

Pun, N. 2005. *Made in China: Women Factory Workers in a Global Workplace.* Durham: Duke University Press.

Shen, H. 2005. "'The First Taiwanese Wives' and 'The Chinese Mistresses': The International Division of Labor in Familial and Intimate Relations across the Taiwan Strait." *Global Networks* 5:419–37.

So, A. Y. 2003. "Cross Border Families: The Role of Social Class and Politics." *Critical Asian Studies* 35:515–34.

Tam, S. M. 1996. "Normalization of 'Second Wives': Gender Contestations in Hong Kong." *Asian Journal of Women's Studies* 2:113–32.

Tam, S. M. 2005. "We-Women and They-Women: Imagining Mistresses across the Hong Kong–China Border." In *Rethinking and Recasting Citizenship: Social Exclusion and Marginality in Chinese Societies*, edited by M. Tam H. Ku and T. Kong, 109–30. Hong Kong: Centre for Social Policy Studies, Hong Kong Polytechnic University.

Tam, S. M., A. Fung, L. Kam, and M. Liong. 2009. "Re-gendering Hong Kong Man in Social, Physical and Discursive Space." In *Mainstreaming Gender in Hong Kong Society*, edited by F. Cheung and E. Holroyd, 335–65. Hong Kong: Chinese University Press.

Thai, H. C. 2008. *For Better or for Worse: Vietnamese International Marriage in the New Global Economy*. New Brunswick: Rutgers University Press.

Tu, Q. 2004. *Bitter Marriage (ku hun, in Chinese)*. Beijing: Zuojia Press.

Ward, J. 2007. "*Femme Labor and the Production of Trans Masculinity*." Paper presented at Conference on Intimate Labors. University of California, Santa Barbara.

West, C., and D. H. Zimmerman. 1987. "Doing Gender." *Gender & Society* 1:125–51.

West, C., and S. Fenstermark. 1995. "Doing Difference." *Gender & Society* 9:8–37.

Xiao, S. 2009. *China's New Concubines? The Contemporary Second-Wife Phenomenon*. PhD dissertation, University of California, Berkeley.

Xiao, S. 2011. "No One Knows What's Gonna Happen Tomorrow": Second-Wife Arrangements and the Emotional Displacement of Migrant Women in Contemporary China" (jintian bu zhi mingtian shi: hunwai baoyang yu dagongmei de qinggan kunjing, in Chinese). *Chinese Studies* (zhongguo yanjiu), forthcoming.

Xu, A. 2000. "Mate Selection Criteria: An Analysis of the Changes in 50 Years" (ze'ou biaozhun: wushi nian bianqian jiqi yuanyin fenxi, in Chinese). *Sociological Research (shehuixue yanjiu)* 6:18–30.

Yang, J. 2010. "The Crisis of Masculinity: Class, Gender, and Kindly Power in post-Mao China." *American Ethnologist* 37:550–62.

Zelizer, V. 2005. *The Purchase of Intimacy*. Princeton: Princeton University Press.

Zhang, E. Y. 2001. "Goudui and the State: Constructing Entrepreneurial Masculinity in Two Cosmopolitan Areas in Southwest China." In *Gendered Modernities*, edited by D. Hodgson, 235–266. New York: Palgrave.

Zhang, L. 2010. *In Search of Paradise: Middle Class Living in a Chinese Metropolis*. Ithaca: Cornell University Press.

Zheng, T. 2006. "Cool Masculinity: Male Clients' Sex Consumption and Business Alliance in Urban China's Sex Industry." *Journal of Contemporary China* 46:161–82.

Zheng, T. 2009. Red Lights: *The Lives of Sex Workers in Postsocialist China*. Minneapolis: University of Minnesota Press.

Zhong, X. 2000. *Masculinity Besieged? Issues of Modernity and Male Subjectivity in Chinese Literature of the Late Twentieth Century*. Durham and London: Duke University Press.

CHAPTER 25

Beyond Stoic Salarymen

Inside South Korea's Father School Movement

Allen J. Kim

"Thus far, I lived to just make money. I thought that was enough, diligently making money . . . now I realize that the purpose of a father is give his family love and encouragement through communication and understanding."

—*56-year-old Father School participant*

Introduction

The Chinese character representing fatherhood [父] shared among East Asian cultures is a pictograph of two arms crossed with a whip in each hand, stressing the authoritarian, disciplinary, and instrumental role that fathers traditionally embodied. Shaped by generations of conservative patriarchal ideology in the Confucian tradition, ideas of male superiority, absolute authority, filial piety, and emotional restraint continue to exert influence in contemporary South Korean life. While the Korean father has been traditionally viewed as breadwinner, leader and disciplinarian, the mother is seen as caregiver, housewife, and emotional provider (Park and Cho 1995). In contrast, pervasive paternal images in American popular media portray what scholars describe as the nurturing "new father" ideal that stresses emotional involvement (Coltrane 1996; E. Pleck and Pleck 1997). Such celebrated masculine norms encourage balance between work and family, co-parenting, and focus on intimacy. In South Korea, the masculinity practices and ideals associated with Western men have gained traction. This is evidenced by images of emotionally nurturing and involved men that have emerged alongside the authoritarian and strict Korean father (Kim et al. 2008).

This study concerns how South Korean adult men, participating in a worldwide men's movement called Father School, undergo a schooling process aimed at altering norms apart from distant patriarchal norms of Confucianism and emphasis upon breadwinning. The umbrella term "men's movement" points to a plurality of organizations and groupings that address specific gender challenges facing men (Clatterbaugh 1997; Culbertson 2007). In the US, the evangelical Promise Keepers, mythopoetic movement, and Million Man March, drew widespread media attention and scholarship for their mass mobilizations. Men's movement research focuses on the published writings, political rhetoric, and philosophical stances of group leaders (Magnuson 2007) and Western English-speaking nations. The South Korean–inspired Father School enjoyed rapid growth following the 1997 Asian economic crisis, when many men lost their jobs overnight. With their breadwinning roles threatened,

SOURCE: Kim, A. J. *Beyond Stoic Salarymen: Inside South Korea's Father School Movement.*

many Korean fathers began questioning their identities and family roles, leading them to seek answers through participation in the Father School movement.

Reminiscent of the Promise-Keeper movement, Father School (hereafter FS) is a religiously inspired organization at the forefront of mobilizing immigrant and nonimmigrant fathers to become actively involved in their families. The change from a distant breadwinning patriarch to an expressive dad is the core transformative focus of their seminars reflected in their motto "Lovely Father, Lovely Family!" Leaders take particular issue with Korean men's orientation to Confucian male privilege, extreme patriarchy, stoicism, family violence, and inordinate focus upon work. Instead, the organization champions a new model of masculinity and fatherhood whose moral buttress involves a complex mixture of cultural ideas for promoting a healthy family culture, considered a precondition for a better society. Operating in diverse settings both religious and secular, the most distinctive feature of FS is its emotionally charged "gender boot camp," where distant patriarchy is abandoned in favor of a more contemporary emotionally expressive and nurturing fathering identity (Kim 2014). *The New York Times* has referred to this challenging event as a "12 Step Program for Men" (Laporte 2011). Researchers have only recently begun to examine the experiences of men from non-Western backgrounds and how they negotiate changing cultural gender role norms via men's movements. This study provides an in-depth portrait of seminars and the masculine reconstitution process that unfolds at FS seminars conducted in Seoul, South Korea.

The Crisis of Masculinity and Rise of Father School

The Father School Movement Center, according to one of its publications, "was established in Seoul, South Korea in response to the growing national epidemic of abusive, ineffective, and absentee fathers." The seminal idea for schooling men came from Do Eun-mi (wife of a family minister), who was raised by a distant and abusive father. Father School was developed at Duranno Bible College in Seoul and further refined under the leadership of elder Kim Sung Mook, the organization's current executive director. Notably, the robust growth of Christianity in South Korea is unique, with almost one third of the population considered adherents of the faith according the 2005 South Korean census. Dubbed the "Korean miracle," five of the ten largest mega churches worldwide in 2007 were located in South Korea (*Economist* 2007). From their early days, Father School was influenced by Christian values, economic decline and the popularity of the Promise Keeper men's movement. The nonprofit organization has a presence across 54 countries and has graduated over 250,000 participants in 250 cities, including those in North America. Father School enlists male volunteers (all former participants) who come from all walks of life: Christian clergy, professors, police officers, government officials, and entertainers to facilitate seminars. Seminars are composed of small-group formations where men openly share their intimate experiences as men in families.

Father School leaders take issue with men who are physically and emotionally separated from family life. Korean cultural norms shaped under Confucianism established "an extreme form of patriarchy" in which a husband "exercises complete authority over his wife and children" (Min 1995). According to traditional Korean norms, good fathering was demonstrated by the proper use of power and authority, and focus on work as opposed to caregiving priorities (Kwon and Roy 2007). The locally hegemonic form of masculinity tied to men in urban South Korea has been popularly referred to as the "salaryman." This Japanese-inspired neologism is a term referring to white-collar men who work long hours in office jobs and often go days without seeing their families, thus contributing to "fatherless households" (Dasgupta 2003; Taga 2005). Stemming from men's inordinate focus on breadwinning, Father School functions as a broader "social campaign" whose aim is to "help men recover their identities, return the father to the family, and reunify the family through the father role"

(FS Brochure 2010). According to leaders, the rise and popularity of this unique men's movement followed the IMF (International Monetary Fund) Asian economic crisis in 1997, followed by massive job losses among Korean men and the highest rates of suicide among OECD countries in subsequent years (OECD 2009). Lacking the breadwinner role central to their identities, many men began to question their gender role and contribution to their families. It is in this context that the Father School movement gained traction in South Korea.

Globally Hegemonic Masculinity

Within the masculinities literature several claims are useful for exploring how Asian men reconstitute their masculinity. In a plurality of masculinities, some forms of manhood are more honored than others. Hegemonic masculinity (and fatherhood) is a configuration of masculinity practices associated with major forms of social power. It is defined in relation to subordinates, including the masculinities identified with "other" nonwhite, lower class, and/or non-Western men, and the femininity associated with women (Connell 1995; Heath 2003; Pyke 1996). For example, as an ideal type, hegemonic masculinity in the United States is associated with a white class-privileged professionally successful man who is highly involved with his family, nurturing, and emotionally expressive. This is often called the "New Man" masculinity or "New Fatherhood" (Adams and Coltrane 2008; Hondagneu-Sotelo and Messner 1994). Hegemonic masculinity takes shapes through its juxtaposition with subordinated masculinities, like the hypermasculine, sexist, domineering masculinity attributed to some men of color and working-class men (Heath 2003; Pyke 1996), as well as non-Western men (Thai 2008).

While scholars examine the negotiation of masculinity in the context of migration and transnational families (Dreby 2006; Hondagneu-Sotelo and Messner 1994; Montes 2013; Thai 2008), few study the specific effects of the global omnipresence of Western masculinity on local, non-Western masculinities in crisis (Connell and Messerschmidt 2005). Indeed, the masculine practices of Western elites are acquiring prominence as the form of masculinity perceived most developmentally advanced and superior to all others (Connell and Wood, 2005; Kimmel 2003).

The emerging global hegemony of Western masculinity is evident in post-colonial feminist research on the increasing number of marriages between non-Western women and white Western men. This research finds that women in Asia, Latin America, the Caribbean, and Eastern Europe who seek romantic relationships with white Western men, or profess such a desire, draw on a globally circulating notion of Western masculinity that depicts Euro-American men as romantic, emotionally expressive, financially stable, gender-progressive, modern-day "knights in shining armor." By contrast, non-Western men are relationally constructed as domineering, financially unstable, emotionally stunted, gender traditionalists (Schaeffer-Grabiel 2004). Furthermore, notions of masculinity are dynamic and shaped by social location and influenced by local, regional, and global practices (Connell and Messerschmitt 2005) and relationships. This is particularly relevant in light of the colonial legacy of the United States and its more than 65-year military occupation of South Korea.

With these dynamics in mind, this study explores the goal of masculine reconstitution taking place at Father School seminars. In doing so, this study seeks to illustrate the local incorporation of a globally hegemonic masculinity and fatherhood and the rejection and denigration of ethnic, national, and class identities around which the previously ascendant regional masculinities are contoured. The author has followed the organization for nine years across the United States and South Korea. The following analysis comes from previously published research and data collection on FS seminars in South Korea. I examine data from five FS conferences involving 25 weekend meetings in and around Seoul from July 2010 to April 2012. The field notes cover 15 guest speaker presentations, 15 video presentations, small-group discussions and approximately 90 public readings of men's letters to family members, 22 by wives to their husbands, and 8 by children read to their father. Father School instructs men to share their feelings and reflections in the letters, including good and painful memories, regrets, and love for family members. I also gathered 145 hand-written letters from participants, consisting of 50 letters to men's fathers, 25 letters to wives, 35 "confessional" letters, as well as 20 letters by wives and 15 by children. I also analyzed the FS manual and FS marketing brochures. In the main, I explore what men do and say at FS events.

Father School as "Gender Boot Camp"

In South Korea, Father School is designed as highly structured five-week socializing contexts designed to improve men's behavioral performance as emotionally expressive, caring, and responsible fathers. Men engage in a collective journey to repair broken relationships and broken communication with family members. Schooling men involves small-group accountability formations similar to those of Alcoholics Anonymous that focus on personal disclosure, camaraderie, and openness about personal feelings. FS recruitment encompasses marketing outreach through advertising postings at malls, business establishments, churches, newspapers, and word of mouth. However, most recruits come to FS through endorsement by local Korean Christian churches, recommendations by former FS members, and pressure from family members. According to a staff member, "family members and friends play a significant role" in motivating a full half of the participants to sign up for FS.

Three broad processes are central in the Father School masculine reconstitution project. The first process involves a *re-identification* process assisting men to adopt the FS gendered worldview. A process of diagnosing the problems with members' former masculinity is followed by the prognosis or masculine ideal men are encouraged to emulate. Secondly, men are given *performance guidelines* helping men to display the behaviors of a "family builder." In this way, leaders refer to Father School as a "movement of practice" assisting men to train for their new gendered selves. Having completed "homework" assignments assigned by leaders, the final process is the *public examine*, by which men's personal missives written to family members are read and scrutinized before fellow members. Men's life stories are handpicked by organization leaders for emotive effect. In this way, men's personal life histories become the subject of public discussion. The result is an emotional spectacle that dramatizes men's failures and the potential for altering their family lives.

(Re)Identifying Models of Masculinity

Diagnosis: Denigrating Korean Patriarchy

Father School denigrates Korean patriarchy and the breadwinning "salaryman" masculinity characterizing men's lives. Leaders blame the physically and emotionally absent father complex associated with the salaryman, the East Asian masculine ideal of a white-collar, breadwinning, salaried husband and father. The FS literature lists the problematic aspects of the Korean salaryman masculinity as (1) workaholism, (2) alcoholism, (3) sex culture, (4) leisure culture, (5) domestic abuse, and (6) emotionally and physically absent fathers (FS Manual 2010:8). Such challenges are dramatized through video reports highlighting instances of excessive drinking, moral failures and alarming statistics from mainstream newspapers such as the *Korea Times* and *Korea Herald*, that report Korean men spend "no more than 10 minutes in conversation per day," the lowest among East Asian men. Another news report mentioned by a speaker publicly highlights that "only 5% of teenagers share their problems with their dad." Leaders criticize Korean men as being aloof, authoritarian and serving little function apart from breadwinning. The Korean man, according to their manual, "believes that making money is sufficient for his role in the family," has "difficulty controlling his temper," and feels entitled to leisure apart from his family (Father School 2010, 6). Further, the manual charges that the Korean father "does not know how to affirm and encourage his wife and children," and that Korean families are marked by "broken communication," deep emotional wounds, and alienation. Previous Father School members provide testimony of their former life (before Father School).

A member tells his fellow group members, "I was like a king within my house, a strict father difficult to approach." He expressed regret that his "traditional" Korean fathering style created distance with his children. Another member discloses, "I was practically forced to admit that my own selfishness combined with Korean Confucianism was the reason I was unable to get to know my children through conversation." The attribution of blame to conservative Korean parenting by member is noteworthy. The hierarchical relationship within the Korean family system is identified as contributing tension between the father and child. In this way, men's masculine reconstitution involves a criticism of Korean patriarchy passed down the generations. FS leaders reiterate the importance of making peace with their adult fathers. According to the FS manual,

> The most important person responsible for the troubles and pain in one's mind is the father. Unless we learn about the sound influence of a truly good father, the image of a father that we may have resented and disliked remains in our mind and affects our children. (FS Manual 2010:12)

In this way, the FS solution involves repairing members' fathering wounds suffered as children before they begin to repair relationships with their family of procreation. Traditionally domineering Korean fathers are characterized as having left behind a negative legacy for their current families. Leaders require that men write letters to their adult fathers to express their hurt beneath domineering Korean fathers, express forgiveness and love, and commit to becoming dutiful sons and loving fathers into the future. In this way, masculine reconstitution occurs multi-generationally. Men become good fathers just as they learn to become appropriate sons who in confronting their own fathers confront a cultural past.

Prognosis: Benchmarking White American Fathers (and Jesus)

Father School leaders scrutinize the ideals and practices of what they construct as a distinctly Korean father. Given the extreme form of patriarchy that characterizes a traditional Korean father, FS leaders focus on establishing an emotionally intimate, non-authoritarian, co-parenting "new father" ideal (Coltrane 1996; Dermott 2008) in men's lives. To accomplish this, speakers rely on benchmarking the qualities of Western white American fathers along with Christian values and the figure of Jesus. Pervasive images of white American men demonstrative of love are glorified in presentations and in small-group discussions, as they are seen to embody qualities deemed desirable and demonstrative of good fathering. Father School presents this intimate "new father" hegemonic masculine ideal as a "healthy" antidote for Korean masculinity and overbearing patriarchy. Alongside its negative packaging of Korean masculinity, including the reiteration of Orientalist stereotypes of Asian men as unemotional, unloving, and poor communicators (Pyke 2010), Father School portrays white American family men as embodying the "new father" ideal. Father School incorporates images of white men from Promise Keepers materials, popular American Christian publications, and U.S. cinema into their video and slide presentations. While Father School presents Korean men as examples of a problematic masculinity, not one negative image of a white man appears in their materials. In fact, in a conference with five weekly meetings, Father School presented 23 images of white American men, all of whom represented "good" supportive family men in scenes of happy, loving family interactions. Father School presentations employ archetypical scenes of nurturing family situations: a man walking hand-in-hand with his wife, son, and daughter and a man throwing a baseball with his son.

Father School deploys white American iconography not only as a positive model but also in the relational construction of Korean fathers as deficient. One Father School speaker comments, "Instead of being a friendly father, Korean fathers are more likely to buy their children a baseball and bat to play with their friends, instead of playing with them." Some Father School speakers refer to their experiences in the U.S. and the "good" American fathers they met, juxtaposing these accounts with criticism of Korean fathers. For example, one guest speaker shared this observation with conference members:

> When I worked in the United States, I would overhear American fathers planning their weekends with family members and they would always say, "I love you." They look forward to spending time with their family after work! Most Korean dads have work or leisure activities with friends or coworkers as their focus—not the family.

Father School uses ideal images of American men to cast Korean fathers as having not prioritized their families and replacing "money" with "time" as required by their children. While criticizing Korean men for being emotionally restrained, Father School fails to acknowledge financial support and filial piety as examples of love and commitment. Such qualities are presumed normative responsibilities required of men.

As an evangelical-inspired men's movement the new father ideal is championed through the elevation of white Western masculinity and biblical values. Organizational texts explain *father* as a term of familial intimacy highlighted by Romans 8:15: "For you did not receive a spirit that makes you a slave again to fear, but you received the Spirit of Sonship." Jesus is identified as one who "loved, cried, and sought to forgive." At seminars, video clips of white American fathers taken from independent Christian US films such as "Courageous" and "Facing the Giants" reinforce the emotionally intimate and morally upstanding Christian American families. At earlier seminars, video clips of Promise Keeper stadium rallies (from the 1990s) were shown, praising mostly white American men hugging, crying, holding hands in prayer, confessing regrets, and pledging to become better family men. Father School leaders referred to the once popular Promise Keeper as a movement to emulate in South Korea and beyond. In this way, Western men are viewed positively for their collective action, their emotionality, and their commitment to prioritize their families. Father School leaders view men's transformation as part of living out a fundamentally Christian commitment. By establishing an emotionally supportive and communicative family environment, men are viewed as changing society for the better.

Performance Guidelines: "Daddy Homework Assignments"

Changing men involves not only a change in gendered worldview, but also altering men's behaviors. Writing, hugging, crying, changing speech patterns, blessing children, dating family members, singing, doing chores at home, and even washing spouses' feet, exemplify how altering norms of masculinity is an embodied project. Participants are socialized into a regimen of revised discursive and physical behaviors designed to alter their lives as men, sons, husbands, fathers, and organization members. Close adherence to organizational guidelines and activities provides men a purposeful structure enhancing intimacy with family members and promoting warmth, friendship, and emotional bonds at seminars. Several highlights of these activities include:

Letter Writing: Considered the central FS activity, men are given stationery to compose letters to family members. Letter writing allows stoic Korean men to express sentimentality and personal feelings that would otherwise not occur in face-to-face familial interactions. Father School stationery include five thematic letter types: (1) letters to fathers, (2) letters to children, (3) letters to spouses, (4) letters written to spouses and children listing their twenty most beloved traits, and (5) a self-reflection "confessional" letter summarizing men's FS experience. Identified as a form of narrative therapy in psychological and psychiatric practices (Jasper 1999; Payne 2006), letter writing affords FS men the opportunity to be introspective, emotionally expressive, and apologetic, while projecting a revised fathering identity and behavior for the future. In order to address the feelings of "anger and hatred" due to the "collapse of father–son relationships" (FS Manual 2010:4), participants are instructed to handwrite letters to their fathers first, living or deceased, followed by letters to family members. The FS manual provides homework guidelines and examples from previous members to assist in crafting their personal letters. These letters are then collected and mailed by the organization. For men shaped by family systems that emphasize emotional restraint writing functions as the primary vehicle by which men admit fault, seek reconciliation, express love, and communicate a new fathering approach into the future.

New Speech Guidelines: Changing one's speech is an important aspect of behavior modification at Father School. The Korean language is considered a barrier toward developing openness with peers and intimacy toward family members. To remove hierarchical differences among members and sexist references toward wives, men are instructed to disregard specific Confucian speech patterns. At home, linguistic modifications include adopting more egalitarian, democratic, and affectionate language with family. For example, FS takes issue with fathers who address their wives in terms of their domestic roles as opposed to more endearing options. In Korea, a common way to refer to one's wife is jipsaram [house person] or ansaram [inside or domesticated person]. Instead, at FS, men are taught to abandon sexist and disrespectful references in favor of a more egalitarian and nurturing language. Men are taught to refer to their wives as anae [spouse] or saranghaneun anae [beloved wife]. In addition to revised labels, men are asked to be supportive of children during conversation and to expand the scope of their conversations. In the small-group setting, one father shared, "the problem with many Korean fathers is that our culture focuses on one-way conversation and our expectation in three areas: children's academic performance, children's job prestige, and adult children's spouse selection . . . there is not much else to talk about." Leaders discourage normative discussion topics that focus only upon children's academic performance and filial obedience. Instead, fathers are instructed to ask "open-ended questions," prioritize "listening and understanding," express words of love and support, and practice two-way conversations, all considered "healthy" communication protocol.

Hug Bombing: Hugging is considered central to masculine change. In a process I describe as "hug bombing," FS members embrace fellow participants more than 100 times throughout Father School meetings. Mandating Korean men to publicly hug and show affection serves to enhance the practice of physical and emotional intimacy. Leaders consider hugging friends and family members essential for developing a "healthy masculinity" and family culture. Hugging functions as a specialized form of greeting, a sign of support for men's role and identity as fathers, a mark of organizational membership, and as preparation and practice for family intimacy. Members actually learn how to hug one-another. Two FS volunteers stand center stage and model the appropriate FS hug characterized by four elements: a male-to-male hug, verbalizing "I love you," followed by the grasping of both hands, and a respectful bow. For several participants, the hugging culture is a source of comfort. One member disclosed to his surprise,

> . . . Although in the beginning the activity was very awkward, over time I felt that it was good to express warmth and to be comforted and to give support in such a way. It became easier over time to incorporate the hugging culture in my own home.

Importantly, hugging challenges Korean Confucian norms of emotional restraint in social relations by authorizing physical expression and ignoring rigid status differences. Having practiced hugging at FS seminars, leaders ask men to hug family members by using the excuse of "assigned homework" from FS leaders. Over time, expressive hugging becomes routinized such that it is practiced as part of small-group rituals and men's behaviors.

Dates with Family Members: Between conference meetings, FS participants are asked to prepare gifts to bring along their family dates. Men are advised to plan memorable activities filled with "two-way" conversations with an emphasis on listening, understanding and happy memories. Interestingly, the FS manual cites the very popular and only subtly Christian book *The Five Love Languages* by Gary Chapman, an American pastor and marriage and family counselor, and instructs men to:

> ". . . guess your wife's and each of your child's primary love language . . . what might it be? Most people have one or two primary love languages that communicate love to them. The five love languages are: words of affirmation, receiving gifts, acts of service, quality time, and meaningful touch" (FS Manual 2010, 9).

Similarly the FS manual also assigns the following: Plan and set up a romantic date with your wife just between the two of you . . . ask her the following questions:

(a) What could I do to make you feel more loved?

(b) What could I do to make you feel more respected?

(c) What could I do to make you feel more understood?

(d) What could I do to make you more secure?

(e) What attributes would you like me to develop? (FS Manual 2010)

In this way, FS leaders freely draw upon Western sources to encourage a shift from emotional endurance and stoicism to an expressive, therapeutic ethic more common in Western society. Walking at the park, watching a movie, or dining at a restaurant are suggested activities that emphasize the importance of being together in a casual setting. During these dates men are instructed to give and read prepared letters titled "The Twenty Things I Love about My Child/Wife" (FS provided stationery). At home, men are encouraged to help wives with domestic tasks such as "doing the dishes" and "cleaning the home" in addition to being less stubborn and authoritarian. While FS does not specifically advocate gender equality per se, and leaders endorse a Christian (if not Confucian) belief in the importance of men as the spiritual family head, leaders nonetheless instruct men to provide greater equity at home.

Feet-Washing Ceremony: The emotional climax and most tear-laden experience at FS involves men washing the feet of their spouses. This event reenacts the foot-washing ceremony performed by Jesus for his disciples (as recorded in John 13:1–17). It signifies the men's devotion and care for family and the importance of humility. Previous FS meetings have gradually intensified affective bonds and intensive interaction among participants and their families, leading to the final graduation ceremony. The final ceremony provides men the opportunity to profess public vows of change and humility before family and friends. Following an FS potluck meal, wives and children are asked to give a public reading of their own letters written for their fathers. As a guest speaker addresses women about the Father School program, men enter a separate room to receive instruction about washing the feet of their wives. Participants are given the official navy blue and white striped FS T-shirt (modeled after the Promise Keepers) that serves as a symbolical embracement of the

FS worldview and organizational membership. With lights dimmed and hymns playing in the background, men march out with washbasin and cloth towel in hand, and kneel before their seated wives. Each step of the foot-washing ritual is narrated as the FS facilitator explains:

> Men take this washing as an opportunity to be cleansed of the past, and to offer yourselves as men who will serve and love your family. Take the time to hug one another and share your renewed promises to build a healthy family.

While men express private words of regret, love, and commitment to change, wives are seen wiping away tears. In this emotionally heightened atmosphere, FS leaders ask men to raise their hands and pledge to become "loving fathers and men of character worthy of emulation." Having pledged their commitment to the FS worldview and family members, the FS facilitator asks that men collectively raise their fists and shout in unison the oft-repeated FS mantra: "If the Father Thrives, the Family Thrives!" Chanting slogans, singing in unison, and complying with directives from FS leaders appear to be a departure from the intimate nature of small-group settings. However, men easily comply given their shared compulsory military service backgrounds and Confucian values respecting elders.

The Public Examine: "Scrutinizing Men's Private Letters"

The signature activity of Father School is the writing of letters to family and their public reading at seminars. Letters serve as the vehicle by which men demonstrate their love to family members and develop emotional bonds with fellow members. Men's private missives become the basis of public scrutiny and the confessional culture at FS. According to one FS leader, "Writing letters is the most important aspect of the conference to get men to communicate with family members from the heart. [...] For the majority, this will be the first time men have written to family members and shared their feelings and regrets." Father School leaders describe the numerous instances of Korean children never told they were loved until their fathers expressed themselves in their letters. Men first asked to address the negative fatherhood legacy handed down to them by their own patriarchal fathers by recounting difficult memories from childhood and expressing their feelings and forgiveness to their fathers.

One man recounts a painful memory to his once abusive father: "But father, there is something you should apologize to me for. When I was a freshman in college, do you remember the huge fight with mother? I know that Mom was the one to blame; however, it was wrong that you hit her." Disclosing deep emotional and even physical wounds suffered as children is cathartic for members. With microphone in hand, a facilitator calls upon several men to stand front stage to give a public reading of their privately penned letters. Holding back tears, a member shares his lack of heartfelt communication between father and child as he reads, "You were a *typical Korean father* and I barely have any memory of you because you were so busy. You were strict and hot-tempered, and I did not feel love from you growing up. [...] I was always in fear of you." The connection between patriarchy and preoccupation with work is common among the testimonies provided by Korean men. Letter writing allows men to express sentimentality and personal feelings that would otherwise not occur in face-to-face familial interactions. Another man in his 50s, specifically blames Confucianism for his inability to establish a greater emotional connection between father and child. He reads, "I was practically forced to admit that my own selfishness, combined with *Korean Confucianism,* was the reason why I was not able to get to know my own children through conversation. I think if I communicated more with my children we would not have had so much conflict." In letters to their children, men express regret for their emotional absence and abusive authoritarian parenting style, invoking notions of a "typical" and distinctively "Korean" parenting style. While reference to a distinctive Korean masculinity is implied in both the teachings of FS leaders and participants' discussions and letters, several contain direct references to a distinctive "Korean" masculinity, "Korean Confucianism," "Korean ways," etc., to which they attribute negative traits.

Interestingly, several participants invoke notions of the American father as a contrast case to their poor parenting or as a goal to which they aspire. That is, men critique their behavior and troubled family relations using the principles of the "new man" Western ideology that stress emotional intimacy, equitable interactions with family members, displays of affection, as well as the importance of therapeutic self-reflection and transformation. One man writes: "I am like the example of the father who would buy things for my children instead of giving them my time and energy. *Like the American father playing catch with his son,* I want to strengthen bonds with my children by playing and sharing through action and dialogue." In what appears to be a major break from principles of filial piety, a few participants discursively adopt Western individualist values of independence, personal freedom and self-development. As one participant shares with small-group members: "I don't want my children to have the burden to take care of me until old age. Children should live their own separate lives and have the choice to pursue their dreams. I think children need to be independent, similar to how American families raise their children." Individualism and emotionality toward children figured favorably in men's perceptions of Western families.

Father School Critiques: Subtle Resistance to White American Masculinity

Despite criticisms of white Western fathers, participants do not challenge the view of them as friendlier and more emotionally expressive than Korean men. Letters and group conversations never veer from the FS goal of emulating the emotionally expressive and involved fathering associated with American men. Not all newcomers reiterate the FS discourse praising white American masculinity. Some subtly resist the glorification of white Western fathers either by defending the nature of Korean fatherhood or identifying weaker aspects of Western fatherhood. These include perceptions of white American fathers as "privileged" by a less demanding work schedule and as indulging children and lacking family authority. A father in his 50s explains that Korean men must work longer hours than American men. He shares in his small group,

> Korean fathers work the most in the world according to the BBC news. Korean fathers must work to death so we don't lose our job and lose face in front of our families. I think I would be a great father if I could finish early every day like Americans and plan weekend activities with my family. They are very fortunate and lucky.

While FS advises men to accord their children greater independence, and some participants reiterate this as a positive goal, other participants regard the American practice of cutting one's child loose upon adulthood as uncaring. Hence they regard American fathers as selfish, too individualistic, and disengaged. One father in a small-group discussion emphasizes the importance of instrumental ways of showing love, such as financial support. He says:

> The Korean father cares just as much, if not more, than Western men. They just feel that buying and providing is their symbol of love to children. This is because Korea was once a poor country. Life was very difficult . . . Maybe Korean fathers care so much about their children's academic or job outcomes because of the difficulty of Korea's economic past and the difficulty finding a job today. This is not wrong.

An older participant in his late 60s, whose son and grandchildren live in the U.S., also praises Korean fathers' self-sacrifice, instrumental care, and sense of obligation for their children. He shares:

Korean fathers and American fathers have their good points and bad points. In the case of American fathers, after their children grow older they want them to live separate lives. They want to be finished with parenting. Korean fathers will sacrifice eating food so their children can eat and live well, or sacrifice their retirement to put their children through school, or for them to have a wedding. This sacrificial thinking is common.

Perhaps the strongest critique of white Western masculinity is that of a participant who has lived in the U.S. He tells other members of his group that American fathers are "not strict" with their children, have less authority in their families, and are "far too accepting" of their children's bad behavior and selfishness. While he feels that Korean fathers are "too stubborn," Western fathers err on the side of "avoiding" confrontation, adding that "they prefer to be accepted so do not strongly voice their beliefs." In this way, race relations and ethnicity play a part in the way in which masculinity is constructed, expressed and negotiated.

A Cleansing of Cultural Sins

Learning to become a new man and new father is an intensive, emotionally bonding endeavor involving participants, family members, and grassroots volunteers. Becoming a new man resembles rebirth: a cleansing of cultural sins. The process of coming to terms with one's Korean father functions as a therapeutic cleansing that allows men to diagnose the problem of manhood and find a new solution. However, the men do not reject their fathers so much as a particular cultural history deemed as problematic by movement leaders. Men understand the pressure their fathers faced to survive and raise children, and the harm caused by emotional restraint and in some cases, violence within the home. The process of masculine reconstitution is deeply personal as adult children make sense of their past for a new future. Father School men look before and up (to their own fathers) and after and down (to their own children) to reassert a new masculinity that has implications for many different family members. This study makes no claim about participants' masculine transformation beyond those enacted during Father School seminars. Nevertheless, accounts of family members reveal how letters penned by husbands and fathers become treasured artifacts—professions of love, regret, and change—cherished far into the future. Father School provides the script and interactive homework assignments allowing men to become contemporary emotionally engaging men.

In attempting a masculinity makeover, Father School leaders and grass-root participants situate themselves in relation to Western hegemonic masculinity in a conscious attempt to modernize their "doing" of gender (West and Zimmerman 1987). Assimilating the "New Man" ideal of emotional engagement, which leaders associate with American hegemonic masculinity and religious manhood, requires complex ideational work. Father School discourse navigates between two cultural mainstreams (Korea and the US) and two religious traditions (Christianity and Confucianism) to achieve masculine transformation. Yet, by advocating emotional involvement, homo-intimacy, and shift apart from rigid gender roles, leaders oppose certain aspects of hegemonic masculinity. Findings from this article affirm how religious manhood and hegemonic masculinity are not the same—evangelical groups can reject (or in this case benchmark) the latter in subculturally specific ways (Gerber 2015). Global organizations such as Father School strategically construct masculinity in ways that resonate with local circumstances and family arrangements. Importantly, similar to the Promise Keeper and mythopoetic men's movement in the US, Father School fails to link masculinity and family arrangements to larger institutional structures. Leaders do not advocate for social changes such as greater gender equity in the workplace so as to enable shared breadwinning and domestic responsibilities. By blaming salarymen for their long workdays, FS fails to problematize corporate arrangements or mobilize around the need to change broader structural conditions through which local masculinities are constituted. There are thus profound contradictions in FS rhetoric regarding the personal and the political and broader institutional structures.

The complete arc of the FS story has not been told here. Father School in South Korea demonstrates the challenges that the globalization of a Western masculine ideal poses for non-Western men. The transformation of masculine norms to an "involved," "caring," and "emotionally expressive" model is mediated by the parallel incorporation to a global culture that is increasingly Western-dominated. Father School rhetoric suggests the internalization of gendered racism embedded in Orientalist constructions of Asians as stuck in an antiquated gender order marked by Confucian patriarchy and in need of Western redemption and liberation (Mohanty 1986; Ong 1988). As men renegotiate identifications, practices and sensibilities embedded in "old" gender relations, there is obvious concern for how a non-Western organization assists men in conforming to an emerging global hegemonic masculinity. Future research should continue to examine non-Western men's organizations and how Asian men renegotiate their masculinity intergenerationally. Research with non-Western fathers struggling to reconstitute their masculinity and fatherhood in the shadow of racial subordination, and in the case of Korea, colonial legacies, can shine new light on how men on the margins repair their lives to enhance family bonds and a healthy masculinity.

References

Clatterbaugh, Kenneth C. 1997. *Contemporary Perspectives on Masculinity: Men, Women, and Politics in Modern Society*. Westview Pr.

Coltrane, Scott, and Michele Adams. 2008. *Gender and Families*. Gender Lens Series, New York: Rowman & Littlefield.

Coltrane, Scott. 1996. *Family Man: Fatherhood, Housework, and Gender Equity*. New York: Oxford University Press.

Connell, R. W. 1995. *Masculinities*. Cambridge, UK: Polity Press.

Connell, R. W., and James W. Messerschmidt. 2005. "Hegemonic Masculinity: Rethinking the Concept." *Gender & Society* 19:829–59.

Connell, R. W., and Julian Wood. 2005. "Globalization and Business Masculinities." *Men and Masculinities*, 7(4): 347–64.

Culbertson, Phillip. 2007. "Christian Men's Movements." *International Encyclopedia of Men and Masculinities*, 65–67.

Dasgupta, Romit. 2003. "Creating Corporate Warriors: The 'Salaryman' and Masculinity in Japan." *Asian Masculinities: The Meaning and Practice of Manhood in China and Japan*, 118–134.

Dermott, Esther. 2008. *Intimate Fatherhood*. London, England: Routledge.

Dreby, Joanna. 2006. "Honor and Virtue: Mexican Parenting in the Transnational Context." *Gender & Society*, 20 (1): 32–59.

Father School. 2010. *Duranno Father School Marketing Brochure*. Seoul: DFS Headquarter Office.

Gerber, Lynne. 2015. "Grit, Guts, and Vanilla Beans: Godly Masculinity in the Ex-Gay Movement." *Gender & Society*, 29(1), 26–50.

Heath, Melanie. 2003. "Soft-Boiled Masculinity: Renegotiating Gender and Racial Ideologies in the Promise Keepers Movement." *Gender & Society*, 17(3): 423–444.

Hondagneu-Sotelo Pierrette, and Michael A. Messner. 1994. "Gender Displays and Men's Power: The 'New Man' and the Mexican Immigrant Man." In *Theorizing Masculinities*, edited by Harry Brod and Michael Kaufman. Thousand Oaks, CA: Sage.

Jasper, M. A. 1999. "Nurses' Perceptions of the Value of Written Reflection." *Nurse Education Today*, 19(6), 452–463.

Kim, Allen. 2014. "Gender Boot Camp for Korean Immigrant Patriarchs Father School and the New Father Conversion Process." *Sociological Perspectives*, 57(3), 321–342.

Kim, H., J.-M. Hwang, B.-Y. Sun, and D.-K. Kim. 2008. *Research on Men's Paternal Experiences and Their Work-father Role Conflict.* Seoul: Korean Women's Development Institute.

Kimmel, Michael. 2003. "Globalization and its Mal(e) Contents: The Gendered Moral and Political Economy of Terrorism." *International Sociology* 18(3): 603–20.

Kwon, Young In, and Kevin M. Roy. 2007. "Changing Social Expectations for Work and Family Involvement Among Korean Fathers." *Journal of Comparative Family Studies*, 2:285–305.

Laporte, Nicole. 2011. "The Korean Dads' 12-step Program." *New York Times Magazine*, May 6, p. MM22. http:// www.nytimes.com/2011/05/08/magazine/mag- 08here-t.html?_r=0

Magnuson, Eric. 2008. "Rejecting the American Dream: Men Creating Alternative Life Goals." *Journal of Contemporary Ethnography* 37(3): 255–90.

Min, Pyong Gap. 1995. "Korean Americans." In P. G. Min (Ed.), *Asian Americans: Contemporary Trends and Issues* (pp. 199–231). Thousand Oaks, CA: Sage.

Mohanty, Chandra Talpade. 1986. "Under Western Eyes: Feminist Scholarship and Colonial Discourses." *Boundary 2* 12 (3): 333–58.

Montes, Veronica. 2013. "The Role of Emotions in the Construction of Masculinity: Guatemala Migrant Men, Transnational Migration, and Family Relations." *Gender & Society* 27:469–90.

"O Come All Ye Faithful," *The Economist*, November 1, 2007, http://www.economist.com/node/10015239

Ong, Aihwa. 1988. "Colonialism and Modernity: Feminist Representations of Women in Non-Western Societies." *Inscriptions* 3: 79–93.

Organization for Economic Co-operation and Development. 2009. *Health at a Glance: Suicide 2009.* OECD iLibrary. http://www.oecd.org/korea/oecdhealthataglance2009keyfindingsforkorea.htm

Park, Insook Han, and Lee-Jay Cho. 1995. "Confucianism and the Korean Family." *Journal of Comparative Family Studies* 31:117–34.

Payne, M. 2006. *Narrative Therapy.* Sage.

Pleck, Elizabeth, and Joseph Pleck. 1997. "Fatherhood Ideals in the United States: Historical Dimensions." Pp. 33–48 in *The Role of the Father in Child Development*, edited by M. Lamb. 3rd ed. New York: Wiley.

Pyke, Karen. 1996. "Class-based Masculinities: The Interdependence of Gender, Class, and Interpersonal Power." *Gender & Society* 10: 527–549.

Pyke, Karen. 2010. "An Intersectional Approach to Resistance and Complicity: The Case of Racialized Desire Among Asian American Women." *Journal of Intercultural Studies* 31(1), 81–94.

Schaeffer-Grabiel, Felicity. 2004. "Cyberbrides and Global Imaginaries Mexican Women's Turn from the National to the Foreign." *Space and Culture*, 7(1), 33–48.

Taga, Futoshi. 2005. *East Asian Masculinities. Handbook of Studies on Men and Masculinities.*

Thai, Hung Cam. 2008. *For Better or for Worse: Vietnamese International Marriages in the New Global Economy.* New Brunswick, NJ: Rutgers University Press.

West, Candace, and Zimmerman, Don. 1987. "Doing Gender." *Gender & Society*, 1(2), 125–151.

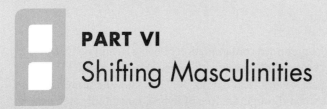

INTRODUCTION

Scholars often repeat that masculinity is "socially constructed," but less often consider the full ramifications of this simple phrase. Because we, as a society, create and sustain masculinity, it is not tethered to biology. Instead, masculinity serves as an idea through which we organize and assign meaning to types of people and types of actions. Biological variations, including bodies and bodily acts, are referenced in this social construction but do not predetermine it. This section introduces research that pushes the boundaries of what we take for granted about masculinity: that it is exclusive to male, heterosexual bodies consistently doing traditionally manly things. The authors explore women who adopt masculinity, heterosexual men who embrace gay self-presentation and feminist principles, and men who have sex with men but still identify as straight. In tracing the borders of masculinity, these readings help us better understand its fundamental components.

Reading no. 26, C. J. Pascoe's "Look at My Masculinity!" focuses on high school girls who "act like boys." Excerpted from a larger in-depth study of masculinity and sexuality in a high school (pseudonym "River High"), this reading follows three groups of girls who present as masculine in various ways. As mentioned in the introduction and section I of this book, a male body helps in projecting masculinity, but it is not essential. The gender bending of these girls troubled the gender order by detaching masculine behavioral norms from biologically male bodies. However, some girls' adoption of masculinity emphasized power, control, and violence, which ironically reinforced masculinity as a mode of dominance.

Kristin Schilt's reading, "Just One of the Guys?" (no. 27), captures another dimension of female masculinity by studying transmen, biological women who transitioned to become men. Schilt uses the unique perspectives of transmen, who have experienced life within both the social category of woman and the social category of man, to expose hidden advantages of masculinity in careers. These respondents report more workplace privileges and comfort as men than as women. Trans identity and experience disrupts the gender binary and also reveals how this binary is a hierarchy that bestows general advantages on men.

The next two readings introduce groups of men who stretch the boundaries of masculinity in different ways. In "Josh Wears Pink Cleats" (reading no. 28), Adi Adams describes an American college soccer team where heterosexual men eschew homophobia and express emotional and physical closeness with other men. Drawing from inclusive masculinity theory (see reading no. 4), the author argues that this evidence indicates a decline of orthodox masculinity as hegemonic, and augurs the growth of egalitarian masculinities. In an interesting contrast, the rural men in Silva's reading, "Bud-Sex" (no. 29), present themselves as traditional, manly men, deriding perceived effeminate behavior (including homosexuality). However, these men regularly engage in sex with other men. Silva shows how the men frame their same-sex contact as masculine, analogous to a form of male bonding. Silva's research explicates the interconnection between sexuality and masculinity, and demonstrates how masculine meanings can be attached to a variety of behaviors. Similar to the findings of Munoz-Laboy (reading no. 19), this work shows that if the presumed contamination of being "feminine" is symbolically avoided, one can still claim to project masculinity, even with same-sex sexual contact.

Finally, "A Very Gay Straight," by Tristan Bridges (reading no. 30), evaluates the seemingly progressive attitudes of contemporary young men through the lens of hybrid masculinity (see reading no. 5). Bridges documents how three groups of heterosexual young men openly support behavior coded as "gay," and even describe facets of their own identities in this way. These findings echo Adams's research among soccer players. However, Bridges renders a very different analysis, arguing that the men use "gay aesthetics" to appear open-minded, while subtly reinforcing their hegemonic position. The appropriation of superficially gay, effeminate, or gender progressive modes of behavior or dress does not necessarily mean that the substance of masculine dominance has fundamentally changed. Instead, enlightened, "sensitive guy" veneers may only mask new configurations of men's power and control.

Questions to Ponder

1. Pascoe and Schilt both examine concepts of female masculinity. Females might do a lot of things considered masculine, such as wearing pants, wearing a short "boy" haircut, or playing sports aggressively. How do different degrees of female adoption of masculinity affect the gender order? Think about how different acts of female masculinity can challenge hegemonic masculinity, and how different acts of female masculinity might actually reinforce it.

2. Adams and Bridges interview respondents who appear to express similarly progressive viewpoints. However, the authors provide very different analyses, one arguing in support of the theory of inclusive masculinity, and the other arguing that these progressive views represent a hybrid masculinity that is only superficially egalitarian. Which perspective do you find more convincing and why? Think about the evidence presented in both articles as well as your own experience.

3. How does the geographical context of Silva's study of rural MSM influence their projection of masculinity? Do you think male expressions of femininity might be more acceptable in urban locations? Do you think female expressions of masculinity might be more acceptable in rural locations? Why or why not?

4. Does hybrid masculinity allow for any positive change? Based on Bridges's analysis, what might this change look like? Or does masculinity just morph from one alignment of domination to the next?

5. What can be done to really move toward positive change in masculinity and greater gender equality? How can men, especially, help this to happen?

Key Concepts

Female masculinity
Hybrid masculinity
Inclusive masculinity

Men who have sex with men
(MSM)
Transgender

CHAPTER 26

Look at My Masculinity!

Girls Who Act Like Boys

C. J. Pascoe

"Girls can be masculine too, you know," Genevieve pointed out to me when I told her I was writing a book on teenage boys and masculinity. Indeed, Genevieve had a point: girls *can* be masculine. At River High several girls identified themselves and were named by other students (both girls and boys) as masculine or as "girls who act like guys." They dressed, talked, and carried themselves in many ways "like guys." None of their peers identified them as actual boys. In other words, these girls weren't trying to "pass" as male, nor did students refer to them as "tomboys," the common way we think of boy-like girls. None of the girls thought of themselves as boys trapped in girls' bodies or identified as transgendered.[1] Several of them, although not all, identified themselves as lesbian.

Most, though not all, of the girls were members of two social groups. I call these two groups the Basketball Girls and the Gay/Straight Alliance (GSA) Girls.[2] The Basketball Girls, athletic, loud, popular, and well liked, were commonly identified by other students as "like boys." The GSA Girls, as their name indicates, were all members of the school's GSA, a club formed to support gay students on campus. They were socially marginalized and less well known and were more likely to describe themselves than to be described by others as masculine. In addition to these two groups of girls, one other girl at River was commonly identified by students as masculine—Jessie Chau. She was not a member of either group and was a senior when the GSA Girls and the Basketball Girls were mostly first-years and sophomores. Like the Basketball Girls she dressed like a boy, was an athlete, and was incredibly popular—serving as both class president and homecoming queen.

By looking at these girls this chapter examines what it means to define masculinity as a set of practices associated with women as well as men. By moving in and out of masculine identifications these girls engaged in what Schippers (2002) calls "gender maneuvering." *Gender maneuvering* refers to the way groups act to manipulate the relations between masculinity and femininity as others commonly understand them. By engaging in public practices that students associated with masculinity (certain clothing styles, certain sexual practices, and interactional dominance), these girls called into question the easy association of masculinity with male bodies. Their gender maneuvering challenges both commonsense and academic understandings of masculinity as the sole domain of men.

These girls engaged in non-normative gender practices in a variety of ways. In their daily interactional practices they engaged in gender resistance, acting in ways most people don't associate with teenage girls. However engaging in non-normative gender practices doesn't always and consistently challenge the gender order. Doing gender in this way opens up issues of gender resistance and reconstruction, illustrating that gender resistance can, but doesn't always, challenge sexism (Gagne and

SOURCE: Pascoe, C. J. (2011). Look at My Masculinity! In *Dude, You're a Fag: Masculinity and Sexuality in High School*. Oakland, CA: University of California Press. Reproduced with permission from the University of California Press.

Tewksbury 1998). Like boys who "inhabit and construct non-hegemonic masculinities," thereby both subverting and reinforcing normative gender relations (Renold 2004, 247), these masculine girls both challenged and reinscribed gender norms. This chapter concludes with thoughts about how to discuss female masculinity and implications for how scholars study both male and female masculinity. While all the girls' practices of gender maneuvering had the potential for challenging the interactional gender order, the GSA Girls' gender practices, with their clear political project, contained the most potential.

Tomboy Pasts

Acting like a boy was not unique to the Basketball Girls, Jessie, and the GSA Girls, nor is it something that occurs only at River High. Many girls and women claim that they were tomboys as children. In *Gender Play*, Barrie Thorne (1993) talks about female students in her college classes who proudly shared stories of childhoods in which they considered themselves tomboys. Similarly, when he asked his undergraduates, "Who was a tomboy as a child?" Michael Messner (2004b) noted that women raised their hands more often than men did when he asked, "Who was a sissy?" In fact, Lyn Mikel Brown (2003) argues that the story of the tomboy girl triumphant over the sissy feminine girl is a common one. Instead of redefining girlhood as tough and powerful, these tomboy stories belittle normative femininity and celebrate masculinity. The girls at River High, both those who were normatively gendered and those who identified as masculine, spoke with pride about tomboy childhoods. Identifying as a tomboy aligns a girl with a romanticized history of masculine identification before she encountered a more restricting femininity.

Several girls who, at the time I spoke with them, identified as normatively feminine shared stories about how they had acted more masculine when they were younger. They illustrate the trajectories of gender identity, in which gender non-normativity may be considered cute in childhood but problematic in adolescence or adulthood. Jenna and Sarah, energetic, thin, attractive white cheerleaders who wore their straight blonde hair up in high bouncy ponytails and frequently pulled out compacts to apply or freshen up already perfectly crafted makeup, rehearsed their lines for an upcoming play as they sat outside drama class. Their talk turned to River High's football team. Sarah announced, "I wanted to play football when I was little! I love football! And my dad totally wanted me to play. But my mom didn't, and I think that's why I didn't get to play. So I became a cheerleader." It seemed as if, in her mind, being a cheerleader was as close to becoming an actual football player as she could get. Like Sarah, other girls often told stories about mothers encouraging them to give up "acting like a boy" as they grew older. During Hoop Skills (the basketball class), Latasha, a petite African American sophomore, said with pride and a bit of regret, "I used to dress like a boy. But I fixed up this year. My ma didn't like it." Her appearance underscored her claim. She now sported large gold hoops, gold jewelry, tight pants, and a tight shirt, with makeup and a gold heart painted on her cheek.

The public face of the tomboy belongs to childhood. This sort of female masculinity in childhood is not only accepted but celebrated (Halberstam 1998). However, this same masculinity in adulthood threatens to destabilize the gender order.

Interestingly, I never heard these sorts of childhood stories from boys. None of them told me they were or knew of boys who used to act more feminine when they were younger. Nor did any of them express sadness about experiences they had missed out on, such as playing with Barbies or dressing up in skirts and heels. The fact that I didn't hear these stories doesn't mean they don't exist. When teaching college classes about masculinity, I've heard stories from my male students about being ruthlessly teased and eventually giving up playing with dolls and Barbies because of this gendered torment. Instead of pride, their stories are tinged with shame. We don't have a cultural narrative, such as that of the tomboy, with which to frame and understand these experiences, so they may be more likely to be silenced.

In high school, female masculinity, once understood as a tomboy identity, translates into a sexual identity. Much as they did with boys, youth at River High associated girls' gender non-normativity with same-sex desire. When I explained to them that I was "writing a chapter on girls who do guy things," Sarah (the aforementioned cheerleader) asked, "Oh, you mean lesbians?" However, the loathing many boys expressed for male same-sex desire didn't appear when boys (or girls) talked about either tomboys or lesbians. James said, "I haven't really heard anybody tease them [lesbians]." In explaining the differential treatment of gay boys and lesbians, students repeatedly asserted that because boys thought that same-sex activity between women was "hot," lesbians were desired, not shunned. When I asked James about this, he told me, "Guys like it for girls. Guys will see two lesbians and they'll be like 'Yeah!' Then when guys see two guys they're like—'Uughh!'" Marco also drew on a discourse of eroticization: "Girls are pretty. They have soft skin, you know? Guys don't. They're hairy. They stink. I can see where a girl would be a lesbian." Ray told me that most guys fantasized about lesbian relationships: "[To] see two hot chicks banging bodies in a bed, that's like every guy's fantasy right there. It's the truth. I've heard it so many times: 'Give me two chicks banging bodies.'" So-called "lesbian" sex is a trope frequently deployed in heterosexual pornography that, far from legitimizing same-sex relationships, titillates and arouses male readers (Jenefsky and Miller 1998). Eroticizing women's same-sex relationships renders them harmless and nonthreatening to the gender order (Rich 1986).

In general, girls who transgress gendered and sexualized expectations don't need to do the same sort of interactional work boys do when they are permanently or temporarily labeled as fags. Unlike gender and sexual non-normativity for boys, which decrease a boy's social status, gender and sexual non-normativity for girls can actually increase their social status. In certain circumstances, such as those in which girls' non-normative gender practices mirror the boys' masculinity processes that I've discussed thus far, such non-normativity can result in popularity. However, as the GSA Girls' gender practices indicate, challenging gender norms, especially when the challenge is framed as a political one in direct opposition to sexism and homophobia, doesn't necessarily result in increased social status for girls.

Rebeca and the Basketball Girls

Not surprisingly, more often than not the Basketball Girls could be found on the basketball court. While in total there were about ten to fifteen of them, Rebeca, Michelle, Tanya, and Tanya's little sister, Sheila, were the girls students talked about when I asked them if they know any "girls who act like guys." They were a racially diverse group (as was the larger crowd)—Rebeca was Latina, Tanya and Sheila were white, Michelle was Filipina. They were all sophomores during the first year of my research, with the exception of Sheila, who was a freshman. The Basketball Girls acted like boys in a variety of ways. Their athleticism and involvement with a male sport instantly aligned them with masculinity (Messner 2002; Theberge 2000). They spat, walked in a limping "gangsta" style, wore boys' clothing, ditched class, and listened to loud hip-hop music, dancing and purposefully singing only the "naughty" lyrics. They performed special handshakes and made fun of me when I didn't execute them correctly. Their energy was never ending. At the homecoming football game, which they all attended, I grew dizzy watching them run up and down the bleachers, screaming, laughing, and pulling each other's long ponytails. They continually shoved each other and wrestled on the top bleachers, every once in a while falling into me, at which point they'd laughingly reprimand each other and profusely apologize to me because I was, in their words, a "grown–up."

The Basketball Girls were instantly recognizable because their attire set them apart from other female students. They wore long hair, typically slicked back into tightly held ponytails that hung long down their backs. They dressed in baggy hip-hop clothes generally indistinguishable from boys' hip-hop clothing, oversize shirts, baggy pants precariously balanced low on their hips and held up with a belt, immaculately clean athletic shoes unlaced with socks rolled up under the tongues so that they stuck out, and large jewelry. While hip-hop culture is often derided for its rampant misogyny, girls and women find ways to appropriate the culture and style in order to express independence and agency (Emerson 2002). This is what the Basketball Girls did in their interactional style, clothing choices, and musical tastes.

None of the Basketball Girls said they self-consciously dressed like boys; instead they said they dressed in baggy clothes for comfort. Michelle said she liked to dress in baggy clothes "'cause it's comfortable. I don't like wearing tight stuff." She told me that other girls dressed in fitted clothing "'cause they want to look cute for people. I really don't care what people think about me, or whatever." She did say other people commented on her unusual clothing choices: "Yeah, they'll always be like, why I dress like this? I'm comfortable. That's what I like."

Rebeca told me that she had dressed this way "my whole life practically." When I asked her why she didn't dress like her girlfriend, Annie, a perky white cheerleader who wore typically feminine, low-slung, tight pants and fitted shirts, Rebeca told me, "It doesn't go right with me. I don't feel the vibe there. I don't like it." On Halloween Rebeca was hanging out at basketball practice with Latasha and Shelly talking about whether they planned to go trick-or-treating that evening. Latasha teased Rebeca, "Are you going as a girl?" They all laughed. Shelley jumped in, saying, "Yeah, I wanna see you in a dress!" Latasha modified this by saying, "No, just tight pants and a tight shirt!" All three continued to laugh at the idea of Rebeca in "female drag."

The Basketball Girls' high-energy antics and proclivity to fights often brought them into conflict with the school's disciplinary rules.

One day at lunch I sat with the Basketball Girls as we watched Tanya's father escort her off the school campus. Casey, a middle-aged blonde security guard, walked up to the Basketball Girls' lunch table shaking her head and saying, "She's back for a day and then she's suspended again." Tanya had shown up late for a class in which the teacher had locked the door to prevent disruptions. Frustrated at being locked out, Tanya started to kick the door loudly and repeatedly. The teacher called security and she was suspended. The rest of the girls were no strangers to fights. At football games their shoving matches were frequently interrupted with pronouncements of which girls they planned to fight, followed by furtive and intense discussions involving mediators between them and groups of girls from a rival school.

Their aggressiveness frequently inspired fear in other students. Ricky said of them, "They're tough! Oh, they're tough! Every time I see them they're like [deep voice], 'Yo man, whatsup!' I'm like [makes a scared face]. I'm used to 'Oh, hi!' [high-pitched female voice]." I asked Ricky if other students gave the girls a hard time. He told me, "I can't imagine that they do, because they're so tough. They have the ambition and the attitude to kick some ass. They [other students] know that if they say anything they're gonna get their ass kicked. So they don't say anything." He was right, I never saw other students fight back against the Basketball Girls, nor did I hear disparaging comments made about them.

None of them had boyfriends. With the exception of Rebeca, who identified as a lesbian, it was unclear whether the others identified as straight or gay. However, they make it clear that boys were not high on their priority list. Michelle said, as we talked on a metal bench outside the locker rooms one afternoon, "I don't really have no time for boyfriends. When I did have one it wasn't fun. I like hanging out with my friends all the time, doing stuff with them. When you're with a boy you don't really have time for them. I don't have time to be with a boy." Regardless, the prevailing view among the student body was that the Basketball Girls were gay. Calvin described them as a "hecka loud" group of girls who "all look like boys, all dress like boys," and are "all gay."

Little five-foot-high Rebeca was, in one student's words, "the leader of the pack." Jose described her by saying, "She kind of looks like a guy but it's a girl." She was well known, well liked, and almost always within earshot. She was a darling girl with a vivacious smile and tangible energy, and she made friends easily. At a football game when I said I was writing "a book on boys," one of her (non–Basketball Girl) friends squealed that "you should interview her! She dresses like a boy and she's a lesbian! She turns straight girls gay!" Indeed, both straight boys and straight girls at River High commented on her attractiveness. Her current girlfriend, Annie, had been straight until she met Rebeca, thus adding to the impression that Rebeca possessed mystical attraction.

Even though she was quite comfortably and publicly "out," Rebeca didn't align herself with the visible group of gay kids at the school, the kids who were active in the GSA. She told me, "I went to it a couple times, but it didn't do anything [for me]. So I really didn't care." Rebeca's experience with the GSA sums up the relations between the Basketball Girls and the GSA Girls. Neither was fully comfortable in the other's social territory. Part of Rebeca's discomfort probably stemmed from the fact that the Basketball Girls resisted politics in general. In high school, it is profoundly uncool to care deeply about most things (save for sports and dating). For instance, the Basketball Girls made light of National Coming Out Day, which fell on the same day as the homecoming football game. As they ran up and down on the bleachers, Annie, Rebeca's cheerleader girlfriend, ran up to Rebeca and yelled, teasing her, "It's National Coming Out Day!" All the girls laughed, including Rebeca, and went on with their rough-housing. This was the only time I heard the girls refer to larger political or social aspects of sexuality.

Rebeca credited her lesbianism with making her more popular. When I asked her if people treated her differently because she dated girls, she said, "I get a lot of nice comments. Like, 'You're a pimp, you have all the girls!' I get a lot of that." I responded, surprised, "So everyone's totally cool with it?" "Yeah, they're like, 'Hey hook me up with some of your girls!'" Rebeca immediately posited boys as her audience, as those who would approve or disapprove of her sexuality. It seems that, as with boys' potential same-sex desire, boys were the ultimate arbiters of what was acceptable and not acceptable at River High. Michelle also told me Rebeca didn't experience homophobia from her classmates. Rather, she told me that both boys and girls were attracted to Rebeca.

At River High when a boy dated a lot or had sex with a lot of girls, he was admiringly called a "pimp." It was a term of honor and respect. At River High, if a girl dated a lot of boys, then she was called a "slut" or a "ho," never a "pimp." Rebeca often recast herself as a "pimp" rather than a "ho." I teased Rebeca at one point by asking her if her nickname was "pimp." She replied defensively and with a smile, "I am pimp!" What follows is an interesting interchange between Rebeca and Ana (one of her non–Basketball Girl friends) on the definitions of *pimp* versus *ho*:

ANA:	You aren't a pimp. Who are you pimpin'?
REBECA:	I'm not a pimp? I'm pimpin' every single girl here. Including you!
ANA:	Oh yeah, right! Including me! Uh uh! Uh uh! No! You ain't pimpin' no one! You think you're pimp. You're a pimp last year. 'Cause you played hecka girls last year. Over the summer. You know how many girls you played over the summer?
REBECA:	Now, that was kind of funny.
ANA:	That was kind of mean! You're an H-O!
REBECA:	No, I can't be a ho. Go look up definition of *ho* in the dictionary.
ANA:	It's gonna tell me it's a gardening tool! (laughs)
C. J.:	Wait, why can't you be a ho?
REBECA:	'Cause I *can't* be!
ANA:	You're not a pimp 'cause you're not.
REBECA:	Okay, Ana.
	(Ana walks away)
REBECA:	I hate her! (smiling and shaking her head)

Rebeca here engaged in a discursive contest over what it meant to be a pimp. She refused a feminized interpretation of her actions in which she had to be a girl; instead she claimed a masculine position as a pimp in sexualized interactions with other girls. She wasn't chasing them. They were chasing her, because she had the virility to incite that sort of desire. Ana, good-naturedly, tried to keep Rebeca in a feminine, penetrated position.

Other Basketball Girls also repositioned themselves as masculine by invoking a "pimp" identity. Michelle, for example, told me about her plans to attend Winter Ball the previous year: "I was going to be like a pimp, and I had like four girls goin' with me." She said she had rented a zoot suit and it was "really cool." Michelle, however, ended up not attending Winter Ball, seemingly because of lack of funds.

In addition to reframing her sexual and romantic practices as "pimp," Rebeca consistently made discursive moves reframing her body as a male one. She posited herself as the center of female desire, saying, "I can't help it if I have girls on my jock!" *Jock* is a slang term for "penis." In a separate incident at lunch Rebeca and her girlfriend, Annie, were playfully shoving each other. Annie put her hands on Rebeca's chest and shoved her back, laughing. Rebeca yelled, "Stop punching my muscle!" and grabbed at her own chest defensively. All the girls laughed. Once again playing the straight person to Rebeca's gender-bending humor, Ana asked, shaking her head, "Why does she call her boobs her muscle?" Rebeca responded, pointing to Annie, "You have boobs, *I* have muscle." In both these instances Rebeca not only aligned herself with masculinity but refashioned her body as a male one, rejecting breasts and replacing them with muscle, rejecting a vagina and replacing it with a "jock." She flirted, in these instances, with embodying maleness by claiming male body parts. In a way she drew on popular understandings of masculinity in which masculinity has to line up with a male body. In the end, though, she never expressed desire to actually be a boy.

Rebeca also participated in a masculinizing process when she engaged in sex talk and rituals of "getting girls." Rebeca's interactions with girls outside her social circle often looked similar to the way masculine boys behaved around girls they found attractive. One day Rebeca stood outside the girls' locker room talking to a couple of boys. A thin, attractive girl walked past wearing snug, low-waisted jeans, a white tank top, and a lacy brown shawl tied tightly around her waist. Rebeca yelled to her, "LET ME SEE YOUR SHAWL!" Rebeca then turned to the boys and said, "I saw a girl wearing one of those the other day, and I thought it was for, like, . . . " She completed the sentence by reaching out as if to grab each side of the sash and pull it toward her, laughing and thrusting her hips as if imitating sex. Both of the boys laughed, as one of them said, "I *bet* you did!" As the girl walked past hesitatingly, Rebeca continued talking, "You look *good* in that shawl." Lyn Mikel Brown (1998) calls this sort of language "ventriloquation" to refer to the ways in which girls adopt boys' points of view. In this instance, Rebeca engaged in masculinizing practices that objectified other girls and thereby enhanced her own social standing with boys. She engaged in ventriloquation in order to appropriate the social power that accompanied masculine identities.

In a sense, however, speaking of the Basketball Girls as masculine or feminine doesn't get at all the aspects of their gendered portrayal. The way they "did gender" also involved racialized meanings. Much like African American boys who identify with hip-hop culture, the Basketball Girls struck a "cool pose" (Majors 2001). Their interactional style, choice of sports, and favorite music and clothing all drew upon those present in hip-hop culture. Like boys identified with hip-hop, they were vaulted to popularity. However, they did not embody the threat of African American maleness. While African American boys in school were seen as threatening to the social order, the Basketball Girls were more likely to be seen as rascals, even though they, self-consciously identified as not-white. Michelle explained this to me by saying that "sometimes white girls act quieter . . . Most white girls are quiet . . . I don't know why that is." She qualified this statement with "But some of the white girls I hang around with, they act loud too, so I don't know." So while she and the rest of the Basketball Girls identified as a variety of races and ethnicities, they did consciously see themselves as different from most white girls.

The Basketball Girls were a high-energy, popular, and engaging group of girls. On the one hand these girls rejected prescriptions of normative femininity, resisting, for instance, heterosexuality, makeup, and dresses. They didn't engage in appropriately feminine sports such as cheerleading, dance, or even soccer. Instead they not only played but were passionate about basketball, a sport associated with men and masculinity (Shakib 2003). In this way it seems that the Basketball Girls were reconstructing what it meant to be a girl. They also engaged in practices that looked a lot like "compulsive heterosexuality." Like sexist and athletic boys, they were at the top of the school social hierarchy, instilling both fear and respect in other students (Connell 1996; Eckert 1989; Eder, Evans, and Parker 1995; D. Epstein 1997; Kehily and Nayak 1997; Martino 1999; Parker 1996). In this sense, their "gender maneuvering" both challenged the gender order and reinscribed it. They challenged the gender order by acting and dressing like boys. They reinscribed the gender order by engaging in many of the dominance practices that constitute adolescent masculinity, such as taking up space, teasing girls, and positioning themselves as sexually powerful.

The Homecoming Queen: Jessie Chau

Clad in wind pants, a T-shirt, and a baseball cap, Jessie Chau sat in Mrs. Mac's advanced placement government class like a boy—positioned sideways, her legs spread wide and her arms splayed across both her desk and the desk behind her. Jessie, a confident, attractive, Chinese American athlete and out lesbian, was River High's homecoming queen and president of the senior class. She was a senior when the Basketball Girls were sophomores, so she might be regarded as a sort of trailblazer for this type of gender maneuvering at River High. She didn't have a group with which to engage in nonnormative gender practices but rather did so on her own—innovating and compromising gender practices at different points in her high school career. Like the Basketball Girls she was popular and well liked. Girls wanted to be her friend, boys wanted to date her. Like the Basketball Girls she dressed in "boy clothes," played sports, and, like Rebeca, identified as a lesbian. Jessie, however, lived these gender and sexual transgressions on her own, without the benefit of a like peer group to support her. Several years older than the Basketball Girls, she had forged this alternative set of gender practices solo.

Boys expressed a combination of confusion and admiration for Jessie. Richard, a conservative white senior, told me,

> She dresses like a man. . . . It's kind of weird. She has always been popular since she was in middle school. It's inevitable for her to be number one. . . . Jessie is a great girl. She's really nice. She's really cool. I just think it's kind of weird that she dresses like a man. She's a softball player and she's hella good. She's a tomboy.

This was one of the few times I heard the word *tomboy* used to describe a girl who acted like a boy at River. Jace explained her popularity by saying, "Most people at River, I mean, guys are going to be like, 'Hey, that's cool!' and she's friends with tons of girls." Like the Basketball Girls Jessie benefited from sexist male fantasies about lesbian sexuality, as Jace indicated with his "Hey, that's cool!" comment. Similarly, because same-sex desire did not threaten girls' gender identity in the way it did boys', Jessie's sexuality and gender transgressions had little effect on her friendships. For instance, when Cathy talked to me about Jessie's sexuality, she said,

> She had a boyfriend her junior year and they broke up. Then people could kind of tell. Because she was real jocky and stuff. People were just like, "I wonder if she is?" She was always with this girl, Sandra. She told me one day "Cathy, I want to tell you something and I don't want you to think differently of me." I was like, "I'm cool with it, I don't care." Some people are a little homophobic. She would sit behind me and play with my hair . . . I don't think it was weird at all that she won. She was the nicest one out there. Being gay had nothing to do with it.

Cathy talked fondly of Jessie and of being touched by Jessie. This fondness couldn't be more different from the at best guarded way straight boys talked about gay boys. While, as Cathy highlighted, Jessie's sexuality certainly made for juicy gossip, such tales did not seem to affect her popularity or likability. If anything, her non-normative gender practices and sexual identity bolstered her popularity among many students.

Jessie self-consciously dressed differently from other girls at River High. Her clothing reflected contemporary "lesbian" styles, mixing both feminine and masculine signs such as baggy pants and fitted shirts (Esterberg 1996). This aesthetic marked her as different from most girls at River High though not necessarily as masculine. She did not share this style with a peer group as the Basketball Girls did. She told me that her friends actively encouraged her to dress more like other girls.

In response to her friends' urgings, Jessie had developed a critique of typical girls' attire. She argued that other girls at River dressed in ways that emphasized their heterosexual availability.

> There's girls at the school who wear shirts that are too provocative. It screams attention. It's just like, what are you trying to get at, you know? I don't want to sit there and try to talk to somebody when their boobs are hanging out at me and I'm just, okay [both of us laugh]. I mean, it's hard not to look when someone's wearing something like that! I mean it's hard to concentrate.

Jessie was most likely both distracted by and critical of such apparel choices. Given that she both was attracted to other girls and was a girl herself, she had a unique criticism of typical girls' clothing. She did not want to be looked at in the same way as these girls, so she specifically bought boys' clothing. "It's just like I don't try to impress anybody. I dress in like a turtleneck and a pair of khakis. And it doesn't look bad. But it doesn't look like I'm dressing like a girl. I don't, most of the clothes I buy aren't girls' clothes. They're boys' clothes. I mean, I'm not ashamed of it."

Unlike other girls, she felt she didn't need to impress or draw attention with her body. Instead, it seemed that she saw her body as functional, active, and agentic, judging by her love of dancing and her passion for sports. Though she lacked a coherent political critique and instead held individual girls responsible for their clothing choices, her own choices left her empowered and confident in the face of a sexist and homophobic social world.

Like the Basketball Girls, Jessie was no stranger to fights. She and her friend Nel spoke fondly of the previous year's CAPA, during which there had been several fights. Jessie seemed to think they were great fun, talking about how she was cheering for Nel during one of the fights. Nel bragged about starting a fight, saying "it was cool" because she knew that "Jessie had my back." Jessie's on again/off again rival was Rebeca. For a while those two couldn't stand each other, in no small part because they were "talkin' to," or flirting with, the same girl, Jana, Rebeca's ex-girlfriend. Jessie explained, "Jana tried to get at me and Rebeca got pissed off." All three of them attended a dance early in the school year, soon after Jana tried to "get at" Jessie. Jessie told me, "I was just walking out and Rebeca said I was an ugly bitch or something. My friend hears her and slaps her. I just like, 'Oh my God.'" The fight didn't escalate because, as Jessie explained, "You know, I could have beat her ass a long time ago. But I didn't, out of respect for [their] relationship. You're my friend and I don't want to start anything. I try my hardest to be nice to her." Jessie laughed at Rebeca's attempt to apologize later: "She knows I'd beat the shit out of her if anything happens. Honestly, she's up to my hip. She's really short and she looks like this little boy." Like the Basketball Girls Jessie saw herself as tough and ready to fight. She and Rebeca never did come to blows, but both spoke often about the possibility of a fight between the two of them.

One of the reasons Jessie didn't like Rebeca was that she saw Rebeca as "flaunting" her sexuality: "They flaunt it all the time at school. I don't need to flaunt my stuff to prove a point. I don't understand what their point is. They're in a relationship and they're together. I just think that they try to show it off too much." The vehemence with which she said this revealed some of Jessie's coping strategies around being gay in high school. While she dressed and acted in many ways like a boy, she balanced this with a sort of "don't ask, don't tell" approach to her sexuality. In large part, this approach reflected her own ambivalence about her non-normative gender practices and her lesbian identity.

During homecoming, which is, like many school rituals, a time of intensified gender and sexual norms, Jessie's non-normative gender and sexual identity caused quite a stir among the student body. When chosen as homecoming queen, Jessie told me that her clothing choices were a subject of gossip. Students saw her non-gender-normative clothing choices as contradicting the traditional requirements of homecoming queen.

> The funny thing is that I get so much trash talked about me as far as homecoming goes: "Oh, like, she's gotta wear a dress." All girls that made it put on their little tight clothes. "I'm trying to get votes," you know? Me, I come in my pajamas, I don't care! I think the reason why I got votes is because I didn't fake it. I think that I was original and I was nice to people and I was myself. I'm a big, like, comedian person. I like to make people laugh. I like to talk and hang out and have a good time.

Jessie both resisted normative definitions of femininity and engaged in them in her varying bodily comportments, clothing choices, and romantic relationships. Like the Basketball Girls she was an athlete, though she drew on the "cool pose" to a more limited extent than they did, and she remained somewhat of a liminal figure, moving in and out of masculine and feminine bodily comportments. Also like Rebeca, she was engaging, beautiful, and charming, all traits that allowed her some leeway in a non-normative gendered presentation of self. She engaged, though to a lesser extent than the Basketball Girls, in sexist practices. She also, I think, exhibited quite a bit of bravery as she bucked many school norms of gender and sexuality to serve as an out-gay homecoming queen.

The Gay/Straight Alliance Girls

Where the Basketball Girls and Jessie espoused a sort of hip-hop ethos, the girls in GSA displayed a more "goth," alternative, or "punk" ethos. The GSA Girls, Genevieve, Lacy, Riley, and T-Rex, often dressed in black clothing with rainbow accents, Doc Martin shoes, or army fatigues. Three of them sported multicolored hair that often changed hue. Riley, a self-described "riot grrl," favored bright pink or blonde short hair accented with barrettes, whereas Genevieve and Lacy tended toward deeper browns, burgundies, and reds for their long dark hair. Tall and imposing, T-Rex wore baggy "skater" clothes, had long blonde hair, and often wore contacts with stars on them. T-Rex was the guardian of the group, describing herself as "their bodyguard." Lacy dressed more traditionally feminine, often wearing long flowing dresses and occasionally wearing baggy cut-off jean shorts and old T-shirts. Genevieve wore button-down shirts and a daily changing variety of ties. Like the Basketball Girls, the GSA Girls were almost always together in and out of school. They were an emotionally intense group of girls, deeply committed to social justice and equality.

They were all active members of the school's GSA. GSAs are school clubs that are increasingly popping up throughout the country. They function as "safe zones" for students where they can be free from gender and sexuality-based teasing and taunts. The meetings consisted of planning political and social activities such as the Day of Silence, movie nights, get-togethers with other GSAs, and the Gay Prom. As many as seventeen kids came to the biweekly GSA meetings, and about five to ten attended regularly. The GSA Girls and Ricky formed the core of the GSA. Students who attended the GSA were a racially diverse group. While many of the members of the GSA did not identify as gay, lesbian, bisexual, or transgendered, T-Rex was the only straight-identified girl in the GSA Girls group.

The students and administration at River High were antagonistic to the existence of the GSA. The girls were keenly aware of this antagonism, experiencing both violence and lack of acknowledgment from school authorities and other students.

GSA meetings served as a place to both challenge norms and explore possibilities for social change. It also gave these youth a place to be with other kids like themselves and to plan a social life outside school.

For Genevieve, Lacy's girlfriend, the GSA was a safe space at school where she could be with people like her. When I asked her, "What does it feel like for you to be in a GSA meeting?" she answered:

> It's really weird, being with people that are like me and then being around people that aren't like me. A lot of times I forget that everybody, that there's a lot of people that aren't gay. I go to GSA and it's normal to me. Then it's like, wow, there's a guy and a girl. That's weird. I see it every day, I don't care, I'm like, whatever, but if I think about it it's different and I feel different, that's the only time I think about it.

But the students often felt that this space was under threat due to both administrative negligence and peer harassment. For instance, students expressed fears of being disrupted or attacked by other students. Genevieve said that she believed that a homophobic student would probably disrupt one of their meetings. During a GSA meeting, Natalia, a white bisexual girl with multicolored hair and baggy pants, shared a nightmare that she had had the previous week. She told the GSA she had dreamt that a bunch of "jocks" had come into a meeting and started "shooting up the place." The other students laughed, but some also commented that they wouldn't be surprised if that happened. The GSA meetings were a safe place and a space that was constantly under threat.

Even in the context of these homophobic experiences, Genevieve described her school experiences before coming to River High as even more homophobic. She had lived with her mother in Minnesota and her father in Arkansas before moving in with her grandmother in California. "In Arkansas, whenever people would find out that I was gay, I couldn't walk down the hall without someone being like, 'faggot,' 'fuckin' dyke,' or whatever." She tried to start a club at her previous high school because "they didn't have any sort of support group or club, but they said no." Before living in Arkansas she had attended school in Minnesota, where students were less vitriolic but generally unsupportive because the town was "hard-core Christian." While she repeatedly noted the homophobia at River High, she said that the presence of the GSA made a big difference. She described being surprised when she came to River High and found out that "wow, there's a GSA. What's a GSA?" She hastened to tell me that the students at River High "don't like the GSA."

Though other students at River High didn't readily describe the GSA Girls as "girls who act like boys," the GSA Girls themselves often described their own gender practices as masculine. Genevieve dressed masculine, although in a different way than the Basketball Girls.

Genevieve's clothes were form fitting, but they were also masculine. She routinely wore button-down shirts with pants and ties. She identified these ties as masculine. In the hallway one day she ran up to me and grabbed her tie, excitedly bouncing up and down as she exclaimed, "Look at my masculinity!" then added a little strut as if for emphasis. She did have large breasts, which seemed a bit at odds with the boy's clothes she wore. She said that she wore the ties because she thought "they're very cute. I feel masculine. I feel bigger and better." Genevieve combined masculine and feminine gender markers in her appearance, wearing typically masculine attire—jeans, button-down shirts, and ties—while making sure they accentuated her curves.

Genevieve also refused to wear makeup, a key signifier of femininity, and put down girls who did wear it:

> I hate it when girls can't leave their house without putting makeup on. I hate that! I went out of my house without makeup on. Just like I feel like wearing a tie. But some girls are like, "I can't leave the house without makeup." Three hours later they're finally coming out.

Genevieve discursively worked to recast herself as masculine by attributing a phallus to herself (much like Rebeca's claiming a "jock"). She described the boys at River High by saying, "They can suck my cock. They're rude. I'm serious. I just don't like them." By claiming a phallus Genevieve symbolically regendered her body. Importantly, Genevieve claimed a penetrative phallus, she exercised dominance through a sexualized discourse in which she framed herself as a powerful penetrator and the boys as feminized receivers. She turned their language upon themselves by reappropriating it defiantly.

Genevieve, Lacy, and Riley self-consciously played with gender at ritualized school events such as the prom and Winter Ball. For the GSA Girls, these events were not a time for the enactment of normative gender codes but rather a time to challenge gendered norms. Instead of joking about and superficially dismissing feminine dress, the GSA Girls talked about the gendered meanings of clothing. As a result, they invented gender-blending outfits featuring masculine and feminine markers.

Genevieve and Lacy both claimed masculine and feminine attributes in their clothing styles, interactional styles, and interests. While, with her long flowing skirts, Lacy appeared normatively feminine, at times at least she proudly talked about ways she saw herself as masculine. One day, when we were sitting in the drama class room, Lacy told me, "My car is my manhood. Ask anyone. Guys talk about dick size. I'll talk about my car." She told me that Genevieve teased her about her car obsession: "You're such a butch guy. It's just a car." Like the Basketball Girls, the GSA Girls lightheartedly teased each other about gender maneuvering.

The GSA Girls talked with ease about relationships among a butch-femme aesthetic, romantic relationships, and gendered oppression. Romantic relationships were a frequent topic of conversation during GSA meetings. Talking about their relationships in this club provided both a forum for personal advice and a place to talk about these relationships in terms of larger meanings about masculinity and femininity. For instance, during one GSA meeting Ally said, "I think no matter who you date there is always one who is more masculine and one who is more feminine." Riley responded,

I totally don't think that is true! Gender roles suck! When I was dating Jenny sometimes I wanted to wear pants and walk on the outside of the sidewalk. She wouldn't let me. It's weird dating in gender roles if you are not particularly in one. I would wear something and she would be like, "You look too butch. Take that off."

Talking analytically about "gender roles" was something that really only happened among the GSA Girls and during GSA meetings. This sort of political engagement and social criticism probably elaborated the GSA Girls' vocabulary about complex issues of gender, identity, and sexuality.

The GSA Girls also challenged this casual, daily homophobia at institutional events. The school's resistance to expressions of non-normative feminine identities was made clear when National Coming Out Day fell on the same day as homecoming, a day when the school celebrates heterosexual pairings through the Homecoming Assembly and football game (resulting in the GSA Girls' joking references to National Homecoming Out Day). Several of the students from GSA had been busy creating special shirts that read "Nobody Knows I'm a Lesbian" or "Nobody Knows I'm Gay" for National Coming Out Day. They wore them proudly to the Homecoming Rally, which, just like the Mr. Cougar Rally, consisted of the six homecoming princesses competing in skits to be voted as that year's homecoming queen. These shirts were planned to contrast sharply with the celebration of heterosexuality that was the Homecoming Rally. As with Mr. Cougar, the weeks leading up to the Homecoming Rally, game, and election were filled with student competitions, spirit days, and votes for homecoming princesses and queens.

The final skit of the Homecoming Rally, entitled "All for You," starred Jessica and Angelica, two Latina seniors. Clad in tight jeans and black tank tops, the two princesses began dancing to a popular dance song by Janet Jackson. Their dance moves consisted of repeatedly gyrating their hips in sexually suggestive dance moves. During the song that followed, seven girls, including Jessica and Angelica, each grabbed a boy as Janet Jackson sang, "How many nights I've laid in bed excited over you / I've closed my eyes and thought of us a hundred different ways / I've gotten there so many times I wonder how 'bout you . . . If I was your girl / Oh the things I'd do to you / I'd make you call out my name . . ." The girls walked up behind the boys and ran their hands down the front of the boys' bodies. Then they turned the boys around and made them kneel in front of them so that the boys were face to face with the girls' crotches. The girls took the boys' heads in two hands and moved them around as the girls wiggled their hips in the boys' faces. The dance ended with the boys getting up and the group posing together with Jessica and Angelica lying down in front with one leg jutting into the air, crotches exposed. This slat followed two other skits featuring homecoming princesses performing similar, only slightly less sexually explicit, dances.

After the Homecoming Rally and its celebration of girls' heterosexual availability, Lacy, Genevieve, and Riley ran up to me wearing all black with rainbow pins and belts. Given the GSA's preparations leading up to National Coming Out Day, I was wondering why they weren't wearing their special gay pride T-shirts. I didn't have time to ask where their shirts were as they tumbled over each other, indignantly explaining to me what had happened. Lacy angrily unbuttoned her sweater revealing her black and white "Nobody Knows I'm a Lesbian" T-shirt, and said, "Mr. Hobart came up to me and said I have to cover this shirt up. I couldn't wear it!" Riley and Lacy, equally resentful, cried, "He made me take mine off too!" Riley unfolded the shirt she had painted in rainbow colors. Neither of them was wearing a gay pride shirt anymore. Lacy, incensed, cried, "And look what they can do up there! All grinding against each other and stuff! And I can't wear this shirt!"

By engaging in a variety of gender practices that challenged sexism and homophobia, the GSA Girls actively reconstructed gender. Instead of giving in to a binary gender system and identifying as either male or female, they drew upon a variety of gender markers. They purposefully wore gender-bending clothing. They saw themselves as agents of social change as they challenged school norms about gender and sexuality. Similarly they self-consciously rejected strict gender roles in dating relationships, moving in and out of feminine and masculine identifications. Their anger at inequality and injustice was a powerful tool that they expressed through politicized gender maneuvering.

Embodying Masculinity

The non-normative gender activities in which these girls engaged may be considered a form of what Geertz calls "deep play" (1973). Their gender practices reveal larger tensions around gendered inequality, sexualized power, and contemporary American notions of youth. This sort of cross-gendered dressing and behavior is a way of challenging currently held notions of masculinity and femininity as well as challenging the idea that youth are passive recipients of socialization rather than active creators of their own social worlds (Thorne 1993). The Basketball Girls, Jessie, and the GSA Girls were recognized by others as masculine because of the way they "did gender" (West and Zimmerman 1991); their clothes, their lingo, the way they held themselves, their romantic relationships. However, none of them fell into the category of "boy." Rather their gender displays drew on tropes and practices of masculinity in such a way that these girls were categorized as masculine by themselves and others. In this way they destabilized, to a certain extent, the sex/gender binary and the easy association of masculinity with boys and femininity with girls. The girls' gender transgressions opened up spaces for social change. As Judith Butler (1993) points out, "doing gender" differently can both reinscribe and challenge the gender order by destabilizing gender norms. This sort of activity challenges the naturalness of the categories of masculinity and femininity by destabilizing the association of these identities with specific bodies.

The Basketball Girls, Jessie, and the GSA Girls all engaged in gender resistance, but they did it in different ways. The Basketball Girls' and Jessie's doing of gender both resisted and reinscribed gender norms; the GSA Girls' doing of gender more consistently challenged an unequal gender order in which femininity, to a large extent, was defined by submission and masculinity by dominance. Their different gendered and sexualized practices show that a politicized understanding of gender is central to challenging the gender order.

While all of these girls were aligned with masculinity, they were aligned differently. The Basketball Girls were seen by others as masculine; in fact, other students usually held them up as an example of girls who "acted like boys." The GSA Girls were only occasionally cited by other students as masculine, though they self-consciously discussed themselves as masculine. For the most part the Basketball Girls and Jessie firmly rejected fully feminine identifications—stopping short of changing their names or self-referential pronouns. The GSA Girls occupied a more self-consciously ambiguous gendered position, alternately purposely rejecting and embracing markers of femininity and masculinity. Several axes of comparison between the two groups—clothing, dominance, rejection of femininity, and sexuality—provide new ways to think about relationships between masculinity, femininity, sexuality and bodies.

Both Rebeca and Genevieve routinely denaturalized the sexualized receptivity of a female body by claiming a phallus and positioning themselves as sexualized penetrators rather than receivers of sexual activity. Rebeca repeatedly disavowed a feminine body by saying that she had girls on her "jock" and arguing that she had "muscles" instead of breasts. She also made sure that her girlfriend did have "boobs" and not muscles. Genevieve also claimed a phallus, bat she did so only to insult boys she saw as homophobic or sexist. She actually sounded like boys in the River High weight room who talked in lewd terms about their sexual adventures with girls. Genevieve used masculine, penetrative insults ironically (if they had come from a boy she probably would have considered them homophobic or sexist) and turned them back upon the boys much as gay activists have reappropriated the word *queer* in their rhetoric.

A close examination of the girls who challenged gender conventions in interaction and personal style demonstrates that theorists of masculinity need to take seriously the idea of female masculinity because it illustrates masculinity as practices enacted by both male and female bodies instead of as the domain of men. However, to look at girls who "act like boys" only as a challenge to a binary gender system is to miss the complex and contradictory ways gendered and sexualized power operates. A variety of masculinity practices enacted by these girls seemed to combat the equation of male bodies and masculinity on several fronts. The Basketball Girls and Jessie garnered students' respect, notice, and admiration for bucking gender expectations. However, their gender practices sometimes came at the cost of dignity for normatively gendered girls as they engaged in dominance practices of fighting and objectifying girls that sometimes looked like boys' masculinity practices. The GSA Girls provided a coherent and sustained critique of the relationship between gender oppression and homophobia through their activism and gendered practices. That said, they didn't have the social power of the Basketball Girls and Jessie to call attention to this political critique of gender and sexual norms at River High. So it seems that, taken as a whole, their varieties of gender maneuvering all called attention, in the world of River High, to the fact that masculinity cannot be easily equated solely with male bodies.

Notes

1. Though after my research ended, toward the end of her senior year Riley started to identify as transgendered.

2. While they recognized themselves as distinct groups, they did not have a label for themselves, nor did others. The majority of youth at River High did not use group labels, with the exception of the term *jocks*, to describe others in their school. For a more thorough discussion of the importance of the category of "jock" in high school, see Pascoe (2003).

References

Brown, Lyn Mikel. 1998. "Voice and Ventriloquation in Girls' Development." In *Standpoints and Differences: Essays in the Practice of Feminist Psychology*, edited by Karen Henwood, Christine Griffin, and Ann Phoenix, 91–114. Thousand Oaks, CA: Sage Publications.

Brown, Lyn Mikel. 2003. *Girlfighting: Betrayal and Rejection among Girls*. New York: New York University Press.

Butler, Judith. 1993. *Bodies That Matter: On the Discursive Limits of "Sex."* New York: Routledge.

Connell, R. W. 1996. "Teaching the Boys: New Research on Masculinity and Gender Strategies for Schools." *Teachers College Record* 98: 206–35.

Eckert, Penelope. 1989. *Jocks and Burnouts: Social Categories and Identities in the High School*. New York: Teachers College Press.

Eder, Donna, Catherine Colleen Evans, and Stephen Parker. 1995. *School Talk: Gender and Adolescent Culture*. New Brunswick, NJ: Rutgers University Press.

Epstein, Debbie. 1997. "'Boyz' Own Stories: Masculinities and Sexualities in Schools." *Gender & Education* 9: 105–15.

Esterberg, Kristin G. 1996. "'A Certain Swagger When I Walk': Performing Lesbian Identity." In *Queer Theory/Sociology*, edited by Steven Seidman, 259–79. Cambridge: Blackwell.

Gagne, Patricia, and Richard Tewksbury. 1998. "Conformity Pressures and Gender Resistance among Transgendered Individuals." *Social Problems* 45: 81–101.

Geertz, Clifford. 1973. *The Interpretation of Cultures*. New York: Basic Books.

Halberstam, Judith. 1998. *Female Masculinity*. Durham, NC: Duke University Press.

Jenefsky, Cindy, and Diane Helene Miller. 1998. "Phallic Intrusion: Girl-Girl Sex in Penthouse." *Women's Studies International Forum* 21: 375–85.

Kehily, Mary Jane, and Anoop Nayak. 1997. "Lads and Laughter: Humour and the Production of Heterosexual Masculinities." *Gender & Education*: 69–87.

Majors, Richard. 2001. "Cool Pose: Black Masculinity and Sports." In *The Masculinities Reader*, edited by Stephen Whitehead and Frank Barrett, 208–17. Cambridge: Polity Press.

Martino, Wayne. 1999. "'Cool Boys,' 'Party Animals,' 'Squids,' and 'Poofters': Interrogating the Dynamics and Politics of Adolescent Masculinities in School." *British Journal of Sociology of Education* 20: 239–63.

Messner, Michael. 2002. *Taking the Field: Women, Men and Sports*. Minneapolis, MN: University of Minnesota Press.

Messner, Michael. 2004. "On Patriarchs and Losers: Rethinking Men's Interests." Paper presented at the Berkeley Journal of Sociology Conference: Rethinking Gender, University of California Berkeley, March.

Parker, Andrew. 1996. "The Construction of Masculinity within Boys' Physical Education." *Gender & Education* 8: 141–57.

Pascoe, C. J. 2003. "Multiple Masculinities? Teenage Boys Talk about Jocks and Gender." *American Behavioral Scientist* 46: 1423–38.

Renold, Emma. 2000. "'Coming Out': Gender, (Hetero)Sexuality and the Primary School." *Gender & Education* 16: 247–66.

Rich, Adrienne. 1986. "Compulsory Heterosexuality and Lesbian Existence." In *Blood, Bread and Poetry*, 23–74. New York: W.W. Norton.

Schippers, Mimi. 2002. *Rockin' out of the Box*. New Brunswick, NJ: Rutgers University Press.

Shakib, Sohailia. 2003. "Female Basketball Participation: Negotiating the Conflation of Peer Status and Gender Status from Childhood through Puberty." *American Behavioral Scientist* 46: 1405–22.

Theberge, Nancy. 2000. *Higher Goals: Women's Ice Hockey and the Politics of Gender*. Albany: State University of New York Press.

Thorne, Barrie. 1993. *Gender Play: Boys and Girls in School*. New Brunswick, NJ: Rutgers University Press.

West, Candace, and Don Zimmerman. 1991. "Doing Gender." In *The Social Construction of Gender*, edited by Judith Lorber 102–21. Newbury Park, CA: Sage Publications.

CHAPTER 27

Just One of the Guys?

How Transmen Make Gender Visible at Work

Kristen Schilt

Theories of gendered organizations argue that cultural beliefs about gender difference embedded in workplace structures and interactions create and reproduce workplace disparities that disadvantage women and advantage men (Acker 1990; Martin 2003; Williams 1995).

The workplace experiences of female-to-male transsexuals (FTMs), or transmen, offer an opportunity to examine these disparities between men and women at work from a new perspective. Many FTMs enter the workforce as women and, after transition, begin working as men.[1] As men, they have the same skills, education, and abilities they had as women; however, how this "human capital" is perceived often varies drastically once they become men at work. This shift in gender attribution gives them the potential to develop an "outsider-within" perspective (Collins 1986) on men's advantages in the workplace. FTMs can find themselves benefiting from the "patriarchal dividend" (Connell 1995, 79)—the advantages men in general gain from the subordination of women—after they transition. However, not being "born into it" gives them the potential to be cognizant of being awarded respect, authority, and prestige they did not have working as women. In addition, the experiences of transmen who fall outside of the hegemonic construction of masculinity, such as FTMs of color, short FTMs, and young FTMs, illuminate how the interplay of gender, race, age, and bodily characteristics can constrain access to gendered workplace advantages for some men (Connell 1995).

In this article, I document the workplace experiences of two groups of FTMs, those who openly transition and remain in the same jobs (open FTMs) and those who find new jobs posttransition as "just men" (stealth FTMs).[2] I argue that the positive and negative changes they experience when they become men can illuminate how gender discrimination and gender advantage are created and maintained through workplace interactions. These experiences also illustrate that masculinity is not a fixed character type that automatically commands privilege but rather that the relationships between competing hegemonic and marginalized masculinities give men differing abilities to access gendered workplace advantages (Connell 1995).

Theories of Workplace Gender Discrimination

Sociological research on the workplace reveals a complex relationship between the gender of an employee and that employee's opportunities for advancement in both authority and pay. While

SOURCE: Schilt, K. (2006). Just One of the Guys? How Transmen Make Gender Visible at Work. *Gender & Society, 20*(4), 465–490. Reproduced with permission.

white-collar men and women with equal qualifications can begin their careers in similar positions in the workplace, men tend to advance faster, creating a gendered promotion gap (Padavic and Reskin 2002; Valian 1999). When women are able to advance, they often find themselves barred from attaining access to the highest echelons of the company by the invisible barrier of the "glass ceiling" (Valian 1999). Even in the so-called women's professions, such as nursing and teaching, men outpace women in advancement to positions of authority (Williams 1995). Similar patterns exist among blue-collar professions, as women often are denied sufficient training for advancement in manual trades, passed over for promotion, or subjected to extreme forms of sexual, racial, and gender harassment that result in women's attrition (Byrd 1999; Miller 1997; Yoder and Aniakudo 1997). These studies are part of the large body of scholarly research on gender and work finding that white- and blue-collar workplaces are characterized by gender segregation, with women concentrated in lower-paying jobs with little room for advancement.

The cultural reproduction of these interactional practices that create and maintain gendered workplace disparities often can be rendered more visible, and therefore more able to be challenged, when examined through the perspective of marginalized others (Collins 1986; Martin 1994, 2003; Yoder and Aniakudo 1997). As Yoder and Aniakudo note, "marginalized others offer a unique perspective on the events occurring within a setting because they perceive activities from the vantages of both nearness (being within) and detachment (being outsiders)" (1997, 325–26). This importance of drawing on the experiences of marginalized others derives from Patricia Hill Collins's theoretical development of the "outsider-within" (1986,1990). Looking historically at the experience of Black women, Collins (1986) argues that they often have become insiders to white society by virtue of being forced, first by slavery and later by racially bounded labor markets, into domestic work for white families. The insider status that results from being immersed in the daily lives of white families carries the ability to demystify power relations by making evident how white society relies on racism and sexism, rather than superior ability or intellect, to gain advantage; however, Black women are not able to become total insiders due to being visibly marked as different. Being a marginalized insider creates a unique perspective, what Collins calls "the outsider-within," that allows them to see "the contradictions between the dominant group's actions and ideologies" (Collins 1990, 12), thus giving a new angle on how the processes of oppression operate. Applying this perspective to the workplace, scholars have documented the production and reproduction of gendered and racialized workplace disparities through the "outsider-within" perspective of Black women police officers (Martin 1994) and Black women firefighters (Yoder and Aniakudo 1997).

In this article, I posit that FTMs' change in gender attribution, from women to men, can provide them with an outsider-within perspective on gendered workplace disparities. Unlike the Black women discussed by Collins, FTMs usually are not visibly marked by their outsider status, as continued use of testosterone typically allows for the development of a masculine social identity indistinguishable from "bio men."[3] However, while both stealth and open FTMs can become social insiders at work, their experience working as women prior to transition means they maintain an internalized sense of being outsiders to the gender schemas that advantage men. This internalized insider/outsider position allows some transmen to see clearly the advantages associated with being men at work while still maintaining a critical view to how this advantage operates and is reproduced and how it disadvantages women. I demonstrate that many of the respondents find themselves receiving more authority, respect, and reward when they gain social identities as men, even though their human capital does not change. This shift in treatment suggests that gender inequality in the workplace is not continually reproduced only because women make different education and workplace choices than men but rather because coworkers and employers often rely on gender stereotypes to evaluate men's and women's achievements and skills.

Method

I conducted in-depth interviews with 29 FTMs in the Southern California area from 2003 to 2005. My criteria for selection were that respondents were assigned female at birth and were currently living and working as men or open transmen. These selection criteria did exclude female-bodied individuals who identified as men but had not publicly come out as men at work and FTMs who had not held any jobs as men since their transition, as they would not be able to comment about changes in their social interactions that were specific to the workplace. My sample is made up of 18 open FTMs and 11 stealth FTMs.

At the onset of my research, I was unaware of how I would be received as a non-transgender person doing research on transgender workplace experiences, as well as a woman interviewing men. I went into the study being extremely open about my research agenda and my political affiliations with feminist and transgender politics. I carried my openness about my intentions into my interviews, making clear at the beginning that I was happy to answer questions about my research intentions, the ultimate goal of my research, and personal questions about myself. Through this openness, and the acknowledgment that I was there to learn rather than to be an academic "expert," I feel that I gained a rapport with my respondents that bridged the "outsider/insider" divide (Merton 1972).

In reporting the demographics of my respondents, I have opted to use pseudonyms and general categories of industry to avoid identifying my respondents. Respondents ranged in age from 20 to 48. Rather than attempting to identify when they began their gender transition, a start date often hard to pinpoint as many FTMs feel they have been personally transitioning since childhood or adolescence, I recorded how many years they had been working as men (meaning they were either hired as men or had openly transitioned from female to male and remained in the same job). The average time of working as a man was seven years. Regarding race and ethnicity, the sample was predominantly white (17), with 3 Asians, 1 African American, 3 Latinos, 3 mixed-race individuals, 1 Armenian American, and 1 Italian American. Responses about sexual identity fell into four main categories, heterosexual (9), bisexual (8), queer (6), and gay (3). The remaining 3 respondents identified their sexual identity as celibate/asexual, "dating women," and pansexual. Finally, in terms of region, the sample included a mixture of FTMs living in urban and suburban areas.

The experience of my respondents represents a part of the Southern California FTM community from 2003 to 2005. As Rubin (2003) has demonstrated, however, FTM communities vary greatly from city to city, meaning these findings may not be representative of the experiences of transmen in Austin, San Francisco, or Atlanta. In addition, California passed statewide gender identity protection for employees in 2003, meaning that the men in my study live in an environment in which they cannot legally be fired for being transgender (although most of my respondents said they would not wish to be a test case for this new law). This legal protection means that California transmen might have very different workplace experiences than men in states without gender identity protection. Finally, anecdotal evidence suggests that there are a large number of transgender individuals who transition and then sever all ties with the transgender community, something known as being "deep stealth." This lack of connection to the transgender community means they are excluded from research on transmen but that their experiences with the workplace may be very different than those of men who are still connected, even slightly, to the FTM community.

Transmen as Outsiders-Within at Work

In undergoing a physical gender transition, transmen move from being socially gendered as women to being socially gendered as men (Dozier 2005). This shift in gender attribution gives them the potential to develop an "outsider-within" perspective (Collins 1986) on the sources of men's advantages in the workplace. In other words, while they may find themselves, as men, benefiting from the "patriarchal dividend" (Connell 1995, 79), not being "born into it" can make visible how gendered workplace disparities are created and maintained through interactions. Many of the respondents note that they can see clearly, once they become "just one of the guys," that men succeed in the workplace at higher rates than women because of gender stereotypes that privilege masculinity, not because they have greater skill or ability. For transmen who do see how these cultural beliefs about gender create gendered workplace disparities, there is an accompanying sense that these experiences are visible to them only because of the unique perspective they gain from undergoing a change in gender attribution. Exemplifying this, Preston reports about his views on gender differences at work posttransition: "I swear they let the guys get away with so much stuff! Lazy ass bastards get away with so much stuff and the women who are working hard, they just get ignored. . . . I am really aware of it. And that is one of the reasons that I feel like I have become much more of a feminist since transition. I am just so aware of the difference that my experience has shown me." Carl makes a similar point, discussing his awareness of blatant gender discrimination at a hardware/home construction store where he worked immediately after his transition: "Girls couldn't get their forklift license or it would take them forever. They wouldn't make as much money. It was so pathetic. I would have never seen it if I was a regular guy. I would have just not seen it. . . . I can see things differently because of my perspective. So in some ways I am a lot like a guy because I transitioned younger but still, you can't take away how I was raised for 18 years." These comments illustrate how the outsider-within perspective of many FTMs can translate into a critical perspective on men's advantages at work. The idea that a "regular guy," here meaning a bio man, would not be able to see how women were passed over in favor of men makes clear that for some FTMs, there is an ability to see how gender stereotypes can advantage men at work.

The kinds of occupations FTMs held prior to transition also play a role in whether they develop this outsider-within perspective at work. Transmen working in blue-collar jobs—jobs that are predominantly staffed by men—felt their experiences working in these jobs as females varied greatly from their experiences working as men. This held true even for those transmen who worked as females in blue-collar jobs in their early teens, showing that age of transition does not always determine the ability to see gender discrimination at work. FTMs working in the "women's professions" also saw a great shift in their treatment once they began working as men. FTMs who transitioned in their late teens and worked in marginal "teenage" jobs, such as fast food, however, often reported little sense of change posttransition, as they felt that most employees were doing the same jobs regardless of gender. As a gendered division of labor often does exist in fast food jobs (Leidner 1993), it may be that these respondents worked in atypical settings, or that they were assigned "men's jobs" because of their masculine appearance.

Transmen in higher professional jobs, too, reported less change in their experiences posttransition, as many of them felt that their workplaces guarded against gender-biased treatment as part of an ethic of professionalism. The experience of these professional respondents obviously runs counter to the large body of scholarly research that documents gender inequality in fields such as academia (Valian 1999), law firms (Pierce 1995), and corporations (Martin 1992). Not having an outsider-within perspective, then, may be unique to these particular transmen, not the result of working in a professional occupation.

Transition and Workplace Gender Advantages[4]

A large body of evidence shows that the performance of workers is evaluated differently depending on gender. Men, particularly white men, are viewed as more competent than women workers (Olian,

Schwab, and Haberfeld 1988; Valian 1999). When men succeed, their success is seen as stemming from their abilities while women's success often is attributed to luck (Valian 1999). Men are rewarded more than women for offering ideas and opinions and for taking on leadership roles in group settings (Butler and Geis 1990; Valian 1999). Based on these findings, it would be expected that stealth transmen would see a positive difference in their workplace experience once they have made the transition from female to male, as they enter new jobs as just one of the guys. Open FTMs, on the other hand, might find themselves denied access to these privileges, as they remain in the same jobs in which they were hired as women. Challenging these expectations, two-thirds of my respondents, both open and stealth, report receiving some type of posttransition advantage at work. These advantages fell into four main categories: gaining competency and authority, gaining respect and recognition for hard work, gaining "body privilege," and gaining economic opportunities and status.

Authority and Competency

Illustrating the authority gap that exists between men and women workers (Elliott and Smith 2004; Padavic and Reskin 2002), several of my interviewees reported receiving more respect for their thoughts and opinions posttransition. For example, Henry, who is stealth in a professional workplace, says of his experiences, "I'm right a lot more now. . . . Even with folks I am out to [as a transsexual], there is a sense that I know what I am talking about." Roger, who openly transitioned in a retail environment in the 1980s, discussed customers' assumptions that as a man, he knew more than his boss, who was a woman: "People would come in and they would go straight to me. They would pass her and go straight to me because obviously, as a male, I knew [sarcasm]. And so we would play mind games with them. . . . They would come up and ask me a question, and then I would go over to her and ask her the same question, she would tell me the answer, and I would go back to the customer and tell the customer the answer." Revealing how entrenched these stereotypes about masculinity and authority are, Roger added that none of the customers ever recognized the sarcasm behind his actions. Demonstrating how white men's opinions are seen to carry more authority, Trevor discusses how, posttransition, his ideas are now taken more seriously in group situations—often to the detriment of his women coworkers: "In a professional workshop or a conference kind of setting, a woman would make a comment or an observation and be overlooked and be dissed essentially. I would raise my hand and make the same point in a way that I am trying to reinforce her and it would be like [directed at me], 'That's an excellent point!' I saw this shit in undergrad. So it is not like this was a surprise to me. But it was disconcerting to have happen to me." These last two quotes exemplify the outsider-within experience: Both men are aware of having more authority simply because of being men, an authority that happens at the expense of women coworkers.

Looking at the issue of authority in the women's professions, Paul, who openly transitioned in the field of secondary education, reports a sense of having increased authority as one of the few men in his work environment:

> I did notice [at] some of the meetings I'm required to attend, like school district or parent involvement [meetings], you have lots of women there. And now I feel like there are [many times], mysteriously enough, when I'm picked [to speak]. . . . I think, well, why me, when nobody else has to go to the microphone and talk about their stuff? That I did notice and that [had] never happened before. I mean there was this meeting . . . a little while ago about domestic violence where I appeared to be the only male person between these 30, 40 women and, of course, then everybody wants to hear from me.

Rather than being alienated by his gender tokenism, as women often are in predominantly male workplaces (Byrd 1999), he is asked to express his opinions and is valued for being the "male" voice at the meetings, a common situation for men in "women's professions" (Williams 1995). The lack of interest paid to him as a woman in the same job demonstrates how women in predominantly female workspaces can encourage their coworkers who are men to take more authority and space in these careers, a situation that can lead to the promotion of men in women's professions (Williams 1995).

Transmen also report a positive change in the evaluation of their abilities and competencies after transition. Thomas, an attorney, relates an episode in which an attorney who worked for an associated law firm commended his boss for firing Susan, here a pseudonym for his female name, because she was incompetent—adding that the "new guy" [i.e., Thomas] was "just delightful." The attorney did not realize that Susan and "the new guy" were the same person with the same abilities, education, and experience. This anecdote is a glaring example of how men are evaluated as more competent than women even when they do the same job in careers that are stereotyped requiring "masculine" skills such as rationality (Pierce 1995; Valian 1999). Stephen, who is stealth in a predominantly male customer service job, reports, "For some reason just because [the men I work with] assume I have a dick, [they assume] I am going to get the job done right, where, you know, they have to second guess that when you're a woman. They look at [women] like well, you can't handle this because you know, you don't have the same mentality that we [men] do, so there's this sense of panic . . . and if you are a guy, it's just like, oh, you can handle it." Showing how perceptions of behavior can change with transition, Trevor reports, "I think my ideas are taken more seriously [as a man]. I had good leadership skills leaving college and um . . . I think that those work well for me now. . . . Because I'm male, they work better for me. I was 'assertive' before. Now I'm 'take charge.'" Again, while his behavior has not changed, his shift in gender attribution translates into a different kind of evaluation. As a man, being assertive is consistent with gendered expectations for men, meaning his same leadership skills have more worth in the workplace because of his transition. His experience underscores how women who take on leadership roles are evaluated negatively, particularly if their leadership style is perceived as assertive, while men are rewarded for being aggressive leaders (Butler and Geis 1990; Valian 1999).[5]

Stephen, who was a female forklift operator, described the resistance women operators faced from men when it came to safety precautions for loading pallets:

[The men] would spot each other, which meant that they would have two guys that would close down the aisle . . . so that no one could go on that aisle while you know you were up there [with your forklift and load] . . . and they wouldn't spot you if you were a female. If you were a guy . . . they got the red vests and the safety cones out and it's like you know—the only thing they didn't have were those little flashlights for the jets. It would be like God or somebody responding. I would actually have to go around and gather all the dykes from receiving to come out and help and spot me. And I can't tell you how many times I nearly ran over a kid. It was maddening and it was always because [of] gender.

Thus, respondents described situations of being ignored, passed over, purposefully put in harm's way, and assumed to be incompetent when they were working as women. However, these same individuals, as men, find themselves with more authority and with their ideas, abilities, and attributes evaluated more positively in the workforce.

Respect and Recognition

Related to authority and competency is the issue of how much reward workers get for their workplace contributions. According to the transmen I interviewed, an increase in recognition for hard work was one of the positive changes associated with working as a man. Looking at these stories of gaining reward and respect, Preston, who transitioned openly and remained at his blue-collar job, reports that as a female crew supervisor, she was frequently short staffed and unable to access necessary resources yet expected to still carry out the job competently. However, after his transition, he suddenly found himself receiving all the support and materials he required:

> I was not asked to do anything different [after transition]. But the work I did do was made easier for me. [Before transition] there [were] periods of time when I would be told, "Well, I don't have anyone to send over there with you." We were one or two people short of a crew or the trucks weren't available. Or they would send me people who weren't trained. And it got to the point where it was like, why do I have to fight about this? If you don't want your freight, you don't get your freight. And, I swear it was like from one day to the next of me transitioning [to male], I need this, this is what I want and [snaps his fingers]. I have not had to fight about anything.

He adds about his experience, "The last three [performance] reviews that I have had have been the absolute highest that I have ever had. New management team. Me not doing anything different than I ever had. I even went part-time." This comment shows that even though he openly transitioned and remained in the same job, he ultimately finds himself rewarded for doing less work and having to fight less for getting what he needs to effectively do his job. In addition, as a man, he received more positive reviews for his work, demonstrating how men and women can be evaluated differently when doing the same work.

As with authority and competence, this sense of gaining recognition for hard work was particularly noticeable for transmen who had worked as women in blue-collar occupations in which they were the gender minority. [...]

Another form of reward that some transmen report receiving posttransition is a type of bodily respect in the form of being freed from unwanted sexual advances or inquiries about sexuality. As Brian recounts about his experience of working as a waitress, that customer service involved "having my boobs grabbed, being called 'honey' and 'babe.'" He noted that as a man, he no longer has to worry about these types of experiences. Jason reported being constantly harassed by men bosses for sexual favors in the past. He added, "When I transitioned . . . it was like a relief! [laughs] . . . I swear to God! I am not saying I was beautiful or sexy but I was always attracting something." He felt that becoming a man meant more personal space and less sexual harassment. Finally, Stephen and Henry reported being "obvious dykes," here meaning visibly masculine women, and added that in blue-collar jobs, they encountered sexualized comments, as well as invasive personal questions about sexuality, from men uncomfortable with their gender presentation, experiences they no longer face posttransition. Transitioning for stealth FTMs can bring with it physical autonomy and respect, as men workers, in general, encounter less touching, groping, and sexualized comments at work than women. Open FTMs, however, are not as able to access this type of privilege, as coworkers often ask invasive questions about their genitals and sexual practices.

Economic Gains

As the last two sections have shown, FTMs can find themselves gaining in authority, respect, and reward in the workplace posttransition. Several FTMs who are stealth also reported a sense that transition had brought with it economic opportunities that would not have been available to them as women, particularly as masculine women.

Carl, who owns his own company, asserts that he could not have followed the same career trajectory if he had not transitioned:

> I have this company that I built, and I have people following me; they trust me, they believe in me, they respect me. There is no way I could have done that as a woman. And I will tell you that

as just a fact. That when it comes to business and work, higher levels of management, it is different being a man. I have been on both sides [as a man and a woman], younger obviously, but I will tell you, man, I could have never done what I did [as a female]. You can take the same personality and it wouldn't have happened. I would have never made it.

Wayne also recounts negative workplace experiences in the years prior to his transition due to being extremely ambiguous or "gender blending" (Devor 1987) in his appearance. Working at a restaurant in his early teens, he had the following experience:

> The woman who hired me said, "I will hire you only on the condition that you don't ever come in the front because you make the people uncomfortable." 'Cause we had to wear like these uniforms or something and when I would put the uniform on, she would say, "That makes you look like a guy." But she knew I was not a guy because of my name that she had on the application. She said, "You make the customers uncomfortable." And a couple of times it got really busy, and I would have to come in the front or whatever, and I remember one time she found out about it and she said, "I don't care how busy it gets, you don't get to come up front." She said I'd make people lose their appetite.

Once he began hormones and gained a social identity as a man, he found that his work and school experiences became much more positive. He went on to earn a doctoral degree and become a successful professional, an economic opportunity he did not think would be available had he remained highly gender ambiguous.

In my sample, the transmen who openly transitioned faced a different situation in terms of economic gains. While there is an "urban legend" that FTMs immediately are awarded some kind of "male privilege" post-transition (Dozier 2005), I did not find that in my interviews. Reflecting this common belief, however, Trevor and Jake both recount that women colleagues told them, when learning of their transition plans, that they would probably be promoted because they were becoming white men. While both men discounted these comments, both were promoted relatively soon after their transitions. Rather than seeing this as evidence of male privilege, both respondents felt that their promotions were related to their job performance, which, to make clear, is not a point I am questioning. Yet these promotions show that while these two men are not benefiting undeservedly from transition, they also are not disadvantaged. Thus, among the men I interviewed, it is common for both stealth and open FTMs to find their abilities and skills more valued posttransition, showing that human capital can be valued differently depending on the gender of the employee.

Barriers to Workplace Gender Advantages

Having examined the accounts of transmen who feel that they received increased authority, reward, and recognition from becoming men at work, I will now discuss some of the limitations to accessing workplace gender advantages. About one-third of my sample felt that they did not receive any gender advantage from transition. FTMs who had only recently begun transition or who had transitioned without using hormones ("no ho") all reported seeing little change in their workplace treatment. This group of respondents felt that they were still seen as women by most of their coworkers, evidenced by continual slippage into feminine pronouns, and thus were not treated in accordance with other men in the workplace. Other transmen in this group felt they lacked authority because they were young or looked extremely young after transition. This youthful appearance often is an effect of the beginning stages of transition. FTMs usually begin to pass as men before they start taking testosterone. Successful passing is done via appearance cues, such as hairstyles, clothes, and mannerisms. However, without facial hair or visible stubble, FTMs often are taken to be young boys, a mistake that intensifies with the onset of hormone therapy and the development of peach fuzz that marks the beginning of facial hair growth. Reflecting on how this youthful appearance, which can last several years depending on the effects of hormone therapy, affected his work experience immediately after transition, Thomas reports, "I went from looking 30 to looking 13. People thought I was a new lawyer so I would get treated like I didn't know what was going on." Other FTMs recount being asked if they were interns, or if they were visiting a parent at their workplace, all comments that underscore a lack of authority. This lack of authority associated with looking youthful, however, is a time-bounded effect, as most FTMs on hormones eventually "age into" their male appearance, suggesting that many of these transmen may have the ability to access some gender advantages at some point in their careers.

Body structure was another characteristic some FTMs felt limited their access to increased authority and prestige at work. While testosterone creates an appearance indistinguishable from bio men for many transmen, it does not increase height. Being more than 6 feet tall is part of the cultural construction for successful, hegemonic masculinity. However, several men I interviewed were between 5' 1" and 5' 5", something they felt put them at a disadvantage in relation to other men in their workplaces. Winston, who managed a professional work staff who knew him only as a man, felt that his authority was harder to establish at work because he was short. Being smaller than all of his male employees meant that he was always being looked down on, even when giving orders. Kelly, who worked in special education, felt his height affected the jobs he was assigned: "Some of the boys, especially if they are really aggressive, they do much better with males that are bigger than they are. So I work with the little kids because I am short. I don't get as good of results if I work with [older kids]; a lot of times they are taller than I am." Being a short man, he felt it was harder to establish authority with older boys. These experiences demonstrate the importance of bringing the body back into discussions of masculinity and gender advantage, as being short can constrain men's benefits from the "patriarchal dividend" (Connell 1995).

In addition to height, race/ethnicity can negatively affect FTMs' workplace experiences posttransition. My data suggest that the experiences of FTMs of color is markedly different than that of their white counterparts, as they are becoming not just men but Black men, Latino men, or Asian men, categories that carry their own stereotypes. Christopher felt that he was denied any gender advantage at work not only because he was shorter than all of his men colleagues but also because he was viewed as passive, a stereotype of Asian men (Espiritu 1997). "To the wide world of America, I look like a passive Asian guy. That is what they think when they see me. Oh Asian? Oh passive. . . . People have this impression that Asian guys aren't macho and therefore they aren't really male. Or they are not as male as [a white guy]." Keith articulated how his social interactions changed with his change in gender attribution in this way: "I went from being an obnoxious Black woman to a scary Black man." He felt that he has to be careful expressing anger and frustration at work (and outside of work) because now that he is a Black man, his anger is viewed as more threatening by whites. Reflecting stereotypes that conflate African Americans with criminals, he also notes that in his law enforcement classes, he was continually asked to play the suspect in training exercises. Aaron, one of the only racial minorities at his workplace, also felt that looking like a Black man negatively affected his workplace interactions. He told stories about supervisors repeatedly telling him he was threatening. When he expressed frustration during a staff meeting about a new policy, he was written up for rolling his eyes in an "aggressive" manner. The choice of words such as "threatening" and "aggressive," words often used to describe Black men (Ferguson 2000), suggests that racial identity and stereotypes about Black men were playing a role in his workplace treatment. Examining how race/ethnicity and appearance intersect with gender, then, illustrates that masculinity is not a fixed construct that automatically generated privilege (Connell 1995), but that white, tall men often see greater returns from the patriarchal dividend than short men, young men and men of color.

Conclusion

Sociological studies have documented that the workplace is not a gender-neutral site that equitably rewards workers based on their individual merits (Acker 1990; Martin 2003; Valian 1999; Williams 1995); rather "it is a central site for the creation and reproduction of gender differences and gender inequality" (Williams 1995, 15). Men receive greater workplace advantages than women because of cultural beliefs that associate masculinity with authority, prestige, and instrumentality (Martin 2003; Padavic and Reskin 2002; Rhode 1997; Williams 1995)—characteristics often used to describe ideal "leaders" and "managers" (Valian 1999). Stereotypes about femininity as expressive and emotional, on the other hand, disadvantage women, as they are assumed to be less capable and less likely to succeed than men with equal (or often lesser) qualifications (Valian 1999). These cultural beliefs about gender difference are embedded in workplace structures.

In this article, I have suggested that the "outsider-within" (Collins 1986) perspective of many FTMs can offer a more complex understanding of invisible interactional processes that help maintain gendered workplace disparities. Transmen are in the unique position of having been socially gendered as both women and men (Dozier 2005). Their workplace experiences, then, can make the underpinnings of gender discrimination visible, as well as illuminate the sources of men's workplace advantages. When FTMs undergo a change in gender attribution, their workplace treatment often varies greatly—even when they continue to interact with coworkers who knew them previously as women. Some posttransition FTMs, both stealth and open, find that their coworkers, employers, and customers attribute more authority, respect, and prestige to them. Their experiences make glaringly visible the process through which gender inequality is actively created in informal workplace interactions. These informal workplace interactions, in turn, produce and reproduce structural disadvantages for women, such as the glass ceiling (Valian 1999), and structural advantages for men, such as the glass escalator (Williams 1995).

However, as I have suggested, not all of my respondents gain authority and prestige with transition. FTMs who are white and tall received far more benefits posttransition than short FTMs or FTMs of color. This demonstrates that while hegemonic masculinity is defined against femininity, it is also measured against subordinated forms of masculinity (Connell 1995; Messner 1997).

The experiences of this small group of transmen offer a challenge to rationalizations of workplace inequality. The study provides counterevidence for human capital theories: FTMs who find themselves receiving the benefits associated with being men at work have the same skills and abilities they had as women workers. These skills and abilities, however, are suddenly viewed more positively due to this change in gender attribution. FTMs who may have been labeled "bossy" as women become "go-getting" men who seem more qualified for managerial positions. While FTMs may not benefit at equal levels to bio men, many of them do find themselves receiving an advantage to women in the workplace they did not have prior to transition. This study also challenges gender socialization theories that account for inequality in the workplace. Although all of my respondents were subjected to gender socialization as girls, this background did not impede their success as men. Instead, by undergoing a change in gender attribution, transmen can find that the same behavior, attitudes, or abilities they had as females bring them more reward as men. This shift in treatment suggests that gender inequality in the workplace is not continually reproduced only because women make different education and workplace choices than men but rather because coworkers and employers often rely on gender stereotypes to evaluate men and women's achievements and skills.

This critical eye, or "outsider-within" (Collins 1986) perspective, has implications for social change in the workplace. For gender equity at work to be achieved, men must take an active role in challenging the subordination of women (Acker 1990; Martin 2003; Rhode 1997; Valian 1999; Williams 1995). However, bio men often cannot see how women are disadvantaged due to their structural privilege

(Rhode 1997; Valian 1999). Even when they are aware that men as a group benefit from assumptions about masculinity, men typically still "credit their successes to their competence" (Valian 1999, 284) rather than to gender stereotypes. For many transmen, seeing how they stand to benefit at work to the detriment of women workers creates a sense of increased responsibility to challenge the gender discrimination they can see so clearly. This challenge can take many different forms. For some, it is speaking out when men make derogatory comments about women. For others, it means speaking out about gender discrimination at work or challenging supervisors to promote women who are equally qualified as men. These challenges demonstrate that some transmen are able, at times, to translate their position as social insiders into an educational role, thus working to give women more reward and recognition at these specific work sites. The success of these strategies illustrates that men have the power to challenge workplace gender discrimination and suggests that bio men can learn gender equity strategies from the outsider-within at work.

Notes

1. Throughout this article, I endeavor to use the terms "women" and "men" rather than "male" and "female" to avoid reifying biological categories. It is important to note, though, that while my respondents were all born with female bodies, many of them never identified as women but rather thought of themselves as always men, or as "not women." During their time as female workers, however, they did have social identities as women, as coworkers and employers often were unaware of their personal gender identities. It is this social identity that I am referencing when I refer to them as "working as women," as I am discussing their social interactions in the workplace. In referring to their specific work experiences, however, I use "female" to demonstrate their understanding of their work history. I also do continue to use "female to male" when describing the physical transition process, as this is the most common term employed in the transgender community.

2. I use "stealth," a transgender community term, if the respondent's previous life as female was not known at work. It is important to note that this term is not analogous with "being in the closet," because stealth female-to-male transsexuals (FTMs) do not have "secret" lives as women outside of working as men. It is used to describe two different workplace choices, not offer a value judgment about these choices.

3. "Bio" man is a term used by my respondents to mean individuals who are biologically male and live socially as men throughout their lives. It is juxtaposed with "transman" or "FTM."

4. A note on pronoun usage: This article draws from my respondents' experiences working as both women and men. While they now live as men, I use feminine pronouns to refer to their female work histories.

5. This change in how behavior is evaluated can also be negative. Some transmen felt that assertive communication styles they actively fostered to empower themselves as lesbians and feminists had to be unlearned after transition. Because they were suddenly given more space to speak as men, they felt they had to censor themselves or they would be seen as "bossy white men" who talked over women and people of color. These findings are similar to those reported by Dozier (2005).

References

Acker, Joan. 1990. Hierarchies; jobs, bodies: A theory of gendered organizations. *Gender & Society* 4:139–58.

Butler, D., and F. L. Geis. 1990. Nonverbal affect responses to male and female leaders: Implications for leadership evaluation. *Journal of Personality and Social Psychology* 58:48–59.

Byrd, Barbara. 1999. Women in carpentry apprenticeship: A case study. *Labor Studies Journal* 24 (3): 3–22.

Calasanti, Toni M., and Kathleen F. Slevin. 2001. *Gender, social inequalities, and aging.* Walnut Creek, CA: Alta Mira Press.

Collins, Patricia Hill. 1986. Learning from the outsider within: The sociological significance of Black feminist thought. *Social Problems* 33 (6): S14–S31.

—1990. *Black feminist thought.* New York: Routledge.

Connell, Robert. 1995. *Masculinities.* Berkeley: University of California Press.

Crenshaw, Kimberle. 1989. Demarginalizing the intersection of race and sex: A Black feminist critique of antidiscrimination doctrine, feminist theory, and antiracist politics. *University of Chicago Legal Forum* 1989:139–67.

Devor, Holly. 1987. Gender blending females: Women and sometimes men. *American Behavioral Scientist* 31 (1): 12–40.

Dozier, Raine. 2005. Beards, breasts, and bodies: Doing sex in a gendered world. *Gender & Society* 19:297–316.

Elliott, James R., and Ryan A. Smith. 2004. Race, gender, and workplace power. *American Sociological Review* 69:365–86.

Espiritu, Yen. 1997. *Asian American women and men.* Thousand Oaks, CA: Sage.

Ferguson, Ann Arnett. 2000. *Bad boys: Public schools in the making of Black masculinity.* Ann Arbor: University of Michigan Press.

Leidner, Robin. 1993. *Fast food, fast talk: Service work and the routinization of everyday life.* Berkeley: University of California Press.

Martin, Patricia Yancy. 1992. Gender, interaction, and inequality in organizations. In *Gender, interaction, and inequality*, edited by Cecelia L. Ridgeway. New York: Springer-Verlag.

—2003. "Said and done" versus "saying and doing": Gendering practices, practicing gender at work. *Gender & Society* 17:342–66.

Martin, Susan. 1994. "Outsiders-within" the station house: The impact of race and gender on Black women police officers. *Social Problems* 41:383–400.

Merton, Robert. 1972. Insiders and outsiders: A chapter in the sociology of knowledge. *American Journal of Sociology* 78 (1): 9–47.

Messner, Michael. 1997. *The politics of masculinities: Men in movements.* Thousand Oaks, CA: Sage.

Miller, Laura. 1997. Not just weapons of the weak: Gender harassment as a form of protest for army men. *Social Psychology Quarterly* 60 (1): 32–51.

Olian, J. D., D. P. Schwab, and Y. Haberfeld. 1988. The impact of applicant gender compared to qualifications on hiring recommendations: A met-analysis of experimental studies. *Organizational Behavior and Human Decision Processes* 41:180–95.

Padavic, Irene, and Barbara Reskin. 2002. *Women and men at work.* 2d ed. Thousand Oaks, CA: Pine Forge Press.

Pierce, Jennifer. 1995. *Gender trials: Emotional lives in contemporary law firms.* Berkeley: University of California Press.

Reskin, Barbara, and Heidi Hartmann. 1986. *Women's work, men's work: Sex segregation on the job.* Washington, DC: National Academic Press.

Reskin, Barbara, and Patricia Roos. 1990. *Job queues, gender queues.* Philadelphia: Temple University Press.

Rhode, Deborah L. 1997. *Speaking of sex: The denial of gender inequality.* Cambridge, MA: Harvard University Press.

Rubin, Henry. 2003. *Self-made men: Identity and embodiment among transsexual men.* Nashville, TN: Vanderbilt University Press.

Valian, Virginia. 1999. *Why so slow? The advancement of women.* Cambridge, MA: MIT Press.

West, Candace, and Don Zimmerman. 1987. Doing gender. *Gender & Society* 1:13–37.

Williams, Christine. 1995. *Still a man's world: Men who do "women's" work.* Berkeley: University of California Press.

Yoder, Janice, and Patricia Aniakudo. 1997. Outsider within the firehouse: Subordination and difference in the social interactions of African American women firefighters. *Gender & Society* 11:324–41.

CHAPTER 28

"Josh Wears Pink Cleats"

Inclusive Masculinity on the Soccer Field

Adi Adams

Soccer occupies a prominent position in the global sporting hierarchy. Heavily imbued with notions of hegemonic masculinity (Harris, 2009), it is a physical culture that centers on the domination of other men and the subordination of women (Clayton, 2005; Parker, 2001). In the United States, however, soccer's lesser-than status means that it is not as much at the center of athletic masculinity as other competitive sports. Anderson (2005) suggests that this permits men in the sport to express more inclusive attitudes than American football or basketball players. But, despite the fact that soccer is characterized by more fluid gender roles in the United States (Messner, 2009), it still retains the structure of an invasion sport, and players are increasingly masculinized the higher they progress.

Considering that rapidly decreasing homophobia among young men in the United States (Kozloski, 2010) is generating more inclusive forms of heterosexual masculinity (Anderson, 2009), this makes an investigation of competitive university soccer timely. This research, therefore, analyzes notions of gendered identity within the cultural context of a men's college soccer team in the American Northeast. Using participant observation, informal conversations and semistructured in-depth interviews, this ethnography provides an insight into the lives of these men. By cross-referencing what they say with what they do, I critically explore the construction of gendered identities and show a deviation from hegemonic (orthodox) masculinity in sport.

Men and Sport

The ways in which gendered identities are constructed and reconstructed through sport has garnered much research interest over the years (c.f. Anderson, 2005; Coad, 2008; Messner, 1992, 2002). For boys in early childhood, demonstrating competence in sport has often been considered the dominant characteristic of individual identity (Parker, 1996; Renold, 1997). However, the close link between sporting competence and individual identity is also reflected in men's adult lives. Sport has often been described as the last bastion of traditional male values (Hawes, 2001; Jacobson, 2002; Kimmel, 1987; Messner, 1987). Organized, competitive team sport provides men an opportunity for doing gender in the most culturally esteemed way. This orthodox form of masculinity traditionally relies on the public demonstration of violence, aggression, and physical prowess, alongside a violent rejection of femininity and homosexuality. The institution of sport has, therefore, played a pivotal role in the (re)construction of conservative forms of masculinity among boys and men in Western cultures (Messner, 1992).

SOURCE: Adams, A. (2011). "Josh Wears Pink Cleats": Inclusive Masculinity on the Soccer Field. *Journal of Homosexuality,* *58*(5), 579–596. Reproduced with permission.

In a society that conflates sexuality with gender expression (specifically femininity with homosexuality), organized competitive team sports traditionally serve as a defense against this feminizing process. Indeed, as a mechanism of masculinization, sport has traditionally (and erroneously) been thought capable of "making" boys heterosexual (Anderson, 2009). Thus, in the early twentieth century, when it was feared that boys were becoming weak, soft, and homosexual, sports developed great cultural esteem as a valuable tool in the "heterosexualization" of boys and men.

This mythical quality of sport is theorized, by both Messner (2002) and Anderson (2009), to have helped secure sport's value in American culture. They argue that sports taught boys and men (gay and straight) to repress fear, deny pain, conceal "feminine" and (homo)sexual desires and behaviors (Anderson, 2009), while simultaneously committing acts of violence against oneself and others (Messner, 1992). On these sporting battlegrounds, men came to know the meaning of manhood by defining themselves in opposition to femininity, homosexuality, and anything associated with these concepts (Britton & Williams, 1995; Burstyn, 1999; Burton-Nelson, 1994). Sports were, therefore, effective in fostering a narrow range of highly conservative and orthodox behaviors and attitudes. As Clayton and Harris (2009) suggest, "through processes of excluding, removing and concealing 'suspect' masculinities, sport reproduces hegemonic norms and values" (p. 143).

Messner (2009) suggests that sport remains a powerful institution for the conservative expression of gender, one capable of keeping adults who are resistant to wider social change in privileged positions. Messner (1987) points to sport's ability to link men of varying social and economic circumstances when done successfully. High-achieving sportsmen are, for example, given greater cultural prestige. This reinforces the importance for men to demonstrate their domination of others. Being successful at sport also places men at the focus of women's (hetero)sexual attention, improving their "masculine status" among peers (Clayton, 2005; Clayton & Harris, 2004; Parker, 2001). Conversely, failing to live up to culturally exalted constructions of masculinity result in physical and discursive subordination, both on the field and among peers in school (Pascoe, 2005). Such gender norms have, however, been subject to rapid reformulation in recent times (Anderson, 2009; McCormack, 2011b; Weeks, 2007).

Metrosexual and Inclusive Masculinities

Highlighting the displacement of older, more orthodox masculinities and changing gender norms in western cultures, Simpson (1994) writes "what is being made over is masculinity itself." Simpson's notion of a "makeover" culture is exemplified through his concept of metrosexuality. Originally, the term referenced male narcissism: a heterosexual city executive who wore designer clothes. But this image has moved into sporting men as well. Clayton and Harris (2009) describe how, through the media, the "metrosexual" man, "said to indulge in daily routines that might previously have been labeled effeminate, such as grooming and dressing for style" (p. 134), has become more acceptable in the culture of sport. This is something colleagues and I previously found among young men on a football team in England (Adams, Anderson, & McCormack, 2010). In addition to this, we also found players positively engaged with one another, emotionally and physically, in ways that would once have been considered highly deviant (c.f. Curry, 1991).

We also found that being aggressive on the football field did not equate to orthodox masculinity off the field. Thus, I highlight the importance of distinguishing between purported metrosexual athletes' on-the-field behaviors and their off-the-field behaviors and attitudes in assessing their forms of masculinity as representations of progressive social change. To clarify, the seemingly superficial fashion-focused metrosexual masculinity outlined by Coad (2008) is not tantamount to what Anderson (2005) calls inclusive masculinity, a liberal pro-feminist masculine form of greater attitudinal substance that is constructed in opposition to hegemonic orthodox masculinity and, among other inclusive characteristics, is grounded in a rejection of patriarchy, sexism, homophobia, and femphobia. Of course, this is not to say that metrosexuals cannot be inclusive; rather it is to say that "metro" and "inclusive" are not the same interchangeable concept.

The metrosexual label has frequently invoked discussions about men's contemporary gender and sexuality—often deconstructing essentialist notions of both in the process. This has helped problematize orthodox masculinity and mobilize fresh inclusive perspectives on gender relations and masculine and feminine identities (McNair, 2002). Indeed, as a marker of progressive social change, Berila and Choudhuri (2005) assert that the embodiment of gay masculinities (i.e., routines more traditionally associated with femininity) by heterosexual, middle class men may suggest more positive attitudes toward gay masculinities.

As a result of the declines in homophobia in recent years (Loftus, 2001), men are rapidly reconfiguring their own notions of masculinity. Despite overt homophobia and femphobia being the leitmotif among sportsmen in the 1980s and 1990s (Anderson, 2000; Messner, 1992; Pronger, 1990), contemporary research points to the growing esteem attributed to progressive attitudes and behaviors among men in team sports today (Anderson, 2009, 2011; Harris & Clayton, 2007; Price & Parker, 2003; Pringle & Markula, 2005). This is especially true of young men. These are men who are guided by public figures such as English soccer star David Beckham; these are men who have not been culturally stamped with the homophobia their fathers were as youths (Anderson, 2009). Indeed, there is a growing body of literature in which young men today are described as rejecting orthodox or hegemonic tenets of masculinity: the homophobia, misogyny, femphobia, emotional stoicism, and aggressive acts of physical violence that are characteristic of it (Anderson & McGuire, 2010; McCormack & Anderson, 2010a, 2010b; McNair, 2002; Stotzer, 2009; Schrack-Walters, O'Donnell, & Wardlow, 2009; Southall, Nagel, Anderson, Polite, & Southall, 2009).

Elsewhere, Southall, Nagel, et al. (2009) found that, in a survey of competitive team sport athletes in the American South, just 22% expressed reservations about having a gay male on their team. And, among the White male respondents, that number was only 14% (Southall, Anderson, Southall, Nagel, & Polite, 2011). These changes toward inclusivity are also shown to be occurring among boys in secondary- and sixth-form educational settings (McCormack, 2011a, 2011b; McCormack & Anderson, 2010b). It is framed by this changing cultural, social, institutional, and political landscape that I engage in this ethnographic research.

Methods

In this ethnographic research, I use participant observation and in-depth interviews of 21 self-identified heterosexual men, aged 18–22 years, on a soccer team from a large, liberal university located in the American Northeast. Before arriving at the university, the head coach put me in touch with some of his players via a popular online social networking site to promote my socialization into the group of players.

The players are a fairly homogenous group of men. Most are from middle class backgrounds, and there are only three players of color on this team. Also, most of the participants were raised in urban or suburban areas, with only a few coming from rural areas. The campus of this college is situated in the middle of a major city in the American North East.

After securing signed consent forms from these players and their coaches (none refused), I socialized and trained with the team for a period of 10 days (during their soccer season). Data concerning their attitudes to homosexuality and bisexuality were simultaneously obtained from in-depth interviews as well as participant observations. Casual conversations also provided a more "real" sense of participant's views and understandings of masculinities and sexualities compared to formal (private) interviews—which can result in participants telling the interviewer what they think they want to hear

(Gratton & Jones, 2004). Even though this was not covert research, all note taking was conducted by recall immediately after casual conversations to reduce the visibility of researcher presence (Spradley, 1970). This enabled players to quickly forget that I was conducting research, and I was, therefore, able to examine their attitudes concerning masculinities and sexualities in multiple social settings.

Results

Decreased Homophobia

While decades of sport/gender scholarship has described the institution of sport (particularly contact sport) as highly homophobic (c.f. Kimmel, 1987; Messner, 1987; Pronger, 1990), the findings I present here contrast this outdated and often universally ascribed perspective. I found no intellectualization or overt performances of homophobia during my time observing, socializing with, and interviewing these men. Furthermore, the men on this team do masculinity in markedly different ways to that presented by previous research.

Participant observations and in-depth interviews show an extensive degree of social contact (and friendships) with gay men, friendships with feminine men they suspect to be gay (without homophobic judgment), and pro-homosexual attitudes. Highlighting this, one participant, Donny, told me, "I did a persuasive speech for a debate class. I did mine on gay marriage. I was quite persuasive," he jokes, "I totally believe in it. And gay adoption, too. Saying they shouldn't be allowed to is just stupid."

Furthermore, while eating dinner with a group of eight soccer players, they discussed sex, gender, and homosexuality. I asked them who had gay or bisexual friends. "My best friend from home is gay," Derrick said. "Yeah, one of mine is too," Mike added. "He told me last summer. I think he thought there'd be some big reaction. I was like dude, chill. You're my boy."

Two other players joined us later in the evening. I asked them the same question. "No. I can't think of any gay friends," Robert told me, but Jordan added, "I've got lots of gay friends. My uncle is gay, too." Furthermore, many of the players told me that their high schools were accepting places, perhaps influencing them into inclusive attitudes before entering their current school.

A couple of days later, I was eating with players in the college food halls. There were always clusters of students there, so I spent a lot of time sitting in there, talking to new players as others left. Sitting with Gary, Will, and Mike, Mason joined us. He is described as one of the team's biggest fans, and is extremely camp in his mannerism. When Mason left, one of the players told me, "We think Mason is gay," as if to ask me whether I agreed with them. "How would you feel if he came out to you?" I asked. "It wouldn't be an issue, we just think he is anyhow," Greg said. "Yeah," Will added, "It's just when he hangs out with us and we get drunk at parties he sometimes gets really mad when we hook up with girls or pretty much cock-blocks us [prevents them from hooking up] by saying stuff to the girls to annoy them." "I asked him once [if he was gay]," Mike added, "and he said, no." "What do the other guys on the team think?" I asked. "Most of us still think he is," Gary responded, "It's funny that he doesn't just come out."

Tied to my other conversations in the food hall and at other locations, the above exchanges demonstrate three things: First, that there is a level of intellectual acceptance of homosexuality among these three men (and in general among the team). Second, that while their attitudes to homosexuality may have improved with decreasing cultural homophobia, they still retain cultural stereotypes of homosexuality. That is, they still perceive that because Mason is feminine and does not interact well with heterosexual girls, he is more likely to be gay. Finally, these exchanges highlight that they are not afraid to talk about their social experiences and relationships with gay or effeminate men in front of their peers. There is, for example, no guilt-by-association that Anderson (2000) found when he came out as a gay coach in 1994.

Emotional Bonding

One evening the entire team went to see the movie *I Love You, Man* (De Line et al., 2009). A same-sex romantic comedy, the movie focuses on the lead character's lack of male friends. Peter attempts to go on man-dates to find new friends, which end in comic failure because of his lack of knowledge about being a man. During one scene, he finds out that his man-date was gay, when the date kisses him. This kiss is not met with cries of "Gross!" from any of the players on the team or anyone in the audience. Peter eventually bonds with another man called Sydney, and at the end of the movie, the two declare their platonic love to each other.

I discussed the movie with the players after and observed no negative backlash from them. Jay and Luke laughed loudly in remembering some of the scenes, and then Jay leaned across to me, "We're so like that!" He then leaned back into Luke, to show his intimacy. Jay told me that they hang out in each other's rooms and have "pillow talk" late into the night, mirroring the platonic relationship at the heart of the on-screen "bro-mance." Jay added:

> I think you'd find we're a lot like Peter and Sydney. We bond over all kinds of things, we talk about sex all the time, and we talk about silly and stupid things, too. Sure, we play videogames together, and maybe that's more traditional, but we are also there for each other. Like the other night, after Luke broke up with his girlfriend, we just talked for hours . . . That's what you do for a friend—you have to be there for them, regardless of whether that seems "gay" or not.

This is not to say that these men are fully liberated from orthodox masculinity. Some of the men are more conservative in their emotional expression. For example, two of the men indicated that they did not have the type of friendship that Peter and Sydney did in the movie. When I told Cameron (an avid cricket fan) about the rise of emotional bonding among young heterosexual university-aged men in England (Anderson, 2009), he joked, "That's why you girls [meaning the English] never win the Ashes [a biennial cricket tournament between England and Australia]." Still, Cameron told me that he was physically and emotionally close with his friends. "You got to love them," he said, I just don't tend to share as much of the mushy stuff as they do. Maybe I will someday though."

Physical Tactility

Anderson (2005, 2009) suggests that not only are heterosexual men who ascribe to inclusive masculinity more open to sharing their emotions of fear, pain, and rejection, but they are also increasingly likely to support each other with acts of physical tactility that, traditionally, would homosexualize them. I found that the men I observe and interview in this research express affection and tenderness verbally, too, and that they support it with demonstrative acts of physical tactility (see also McCormack & Anderson, 2010b).

For example, on my first day with the team, we were loading a van to head to a practice match. Men piled onto the van, each passing the team captain, Craig, who stood on the sidewalk briefly hugging some the players as they entered. One player passed by without acknowledging him. The team captain stood, his arms spread wide, as he exclaimed to the passing athlete, "What, no hug today?" "Sorry Craig," the athlete said, stepping back to hug his friend before jumping back into the van. Further demonstrating the physical tactility among these men, once in the van, they sat with their arms over each other's shoulders, some sitting with their legs on each other's laps. A late arrival even had to sit on someone's lap. In interviews, the men tell me that, on long coach trips, they regularly fall asleep with their heads on each other's shoulders. "It's way more comfortable than having my head smacking against the window!" Travis told me.

When we arrived at the locker room, one of the players, Cameron, approached me to explain that he has just returned to the team this semester. He had been away because his brother had been diagnosed with cancer. He asked if it was still okay for him to be involved in the research, saying that he was not really part of the team anymore since he had been away. Hearing this, a teammate shouted, "Cameron, you're still part of the team emotionally." Another player was leaving the locker room as this occurred. "Yeah Cam, you'll always be part of the team," he hugged Cameron from behind, holding his arms over Cameron's shoulders, "We'll always love you, man."

These men support each other with other acts of physical tactility, too. For example, these men pat each other on the back and wrap their arms around each other's necks and heads with regular frequency. They occasionally placed an arm around another man's waist, too. Brief hugs (in addition to the more orthodox back slaps) were often given out of celebration or consolation when a player won or lost in soccer, but also sometimes when greeting each other.

Although this emotionally and physically tactile behavior contrasts what older literature says about heterosexual men (Field, 1999; Plummer, 1999), it aligns with a pattern of inclusive masculinity reported in other research settings. In Britain, where cultural homohysteria is considerably less, McCormack and Anderson (2010b) show that, for some men, homosocial tactility is a normal operation of heterosexual friendship (see also McCormack, 2011a). In fact, in some parts of England, once two "mates" have progressed their friendship to a certain level, they often (and not always when drunk) kiss their mate on the lips as a way to express friendship (Anderson, Adams, & Rivers, 2010).

Josh Wears Pink Cleats

As well as demonstrating emotional closeness and physical tactility, these men also value more material aspects of masculinity; aspects associated with metrosexuality. They are well styled and groomed, as they demonstrate a broader range of clothing styles. This contrasts older research on athletes' clothing choices.

My findings on this U.S. college soccer team suggest a subversion of the rigid boundaries of gendered assessment that exists among male team sport athletes today. These men wore a whole variety of patterns and colors of underwear without ridicule and without their bond to the other men on their team being threatened. I watched one of the players, Josh, rooting around his gym bag. Eventually, he pulled out a new pair of soccer cleats (boots). They were a shockingly bright pink, a color traditionally coded as feminine since the 1920s (Paoletti, 1987) and a color that has been documented to induce negative responses when worn by boys (Kane, 2006). But, upon unveiling his new shoes to the team, rather than being censured for them as girly, feminine, or gay, one of his teammates called out, "Wow, those are fucking sweet!" Mark shouted to his friend, "Yo, Tom! Check out Josh's pink cleats!"

A number of men expressed the positive opinion that Josh's pink cleats were "wicked cool." Josh smiled broadly, tied up his bright pink cleats and jogged out to join the rest of the team. While jogging a warm up, he said to me, "I thought people might make a bigger deal out of them, because pink is meant to be girly, but it seems that most of the guys love them!" I asked Josh if he had been worried that friends would think he was gay for wearing pink cleats. But this was not Josh's concern. Instead, his main concern was that people might think he was "getting too flashy" and that if he didn't perform well on the field then they might contribute to him getting singled out for criticism. This, too, did not occur. After playing a match in the shoes, I asked Jayson about how he felt concerning Josh's wearing them. "It's not like he'll play better or worse just because he's wearing pink. When you're playing it's not something you think about."

Because of the gendered association of pink with girls and femininity, and by cultural conflation with sissies and homosexuality, it is noteworthy that on this team none of the players raised any suspicion that Josh was gay because he was wearing pink cleats. His teammate, Luke, said:

They're like "wow" aren't they?! Just right in your face. You can tell that Coach isn't delighted with them though. He probably thinks it's a sign of arrogance. I don't think Coach is outraged by them, though . . . It's like that with the older coaches and players—they probably just think it [wearing pink cleats] shouldn't be happening in soccer.

Danny added:

You know, other coaches will try to use that against Josh. They'll say, "Look at him in his pink boots, who does he think he is? Make sure you give him a good kicking." But for us it doesn't mean he's flashy or arrogant or gay. It's just everyone is different and that's Josh's style.

There is some evidence to suggest that inclusive attitudes toward wearing nontraditional sporting equipment (i.e., pink cleats) is relatively new. While none of the men on this team complained about Josh's cleats, Will (a fifth-year senior) said that when he was a freshman (four years ago), "I got called out for wearing someone else's socks once." He explained, "My sister got them for Valentine's Day; and they were pink and white with big hearts on them. They said, 'I'm too sexy for my socks.' For something as stupid as that, I had an older teammate on my case."

Discussion

Previous literature highlights how men's sport has long-served to reinforce heterosexuality and reinforce acceptable conceptions of masculinity (Anderson, 2005; Griffin, 1998; Lenyskj, 1991; Messner, 1992). As an institutional space where women, gay men, and less-masculinized straight men have been formally or informally excluded from participation and oftentimes harassed, contact teamsports have historically been a valued tool in socially constructing boys and men to learn that "real men" were not weak, soft, emotionally intimate with other men, effeminate, or homosexual. Thus, a key component of being a man was to actively distance oneself from femininity and homosexuality. This extended to the regulation of one's clothing choices and styles as well.

On, and confined to, the soccer field, I find some orthodox expressions of masculinity, much like colleagues and I previously found among U.K. college-based soccer players (Adams, Anderson, & McCormack, 2010). Players often take great physical risks with their bodies, express aggression toward opposition players, and use warrior narratives ostensibly to promote their performance. However, off the field, I categorize all of the men on this U.S. college soccer team as representing what Anderson (2009) calls inclusive versions of masculinity. In varying levels, they displayed physical tactility and emotional bonding in the form of hugging and talking about emotional issues with their male friends. There was no judgment for relating to each other in ways that gender literature associates more with the social mechanisms through which women bond (c.f. Diamond, 2002; Griffin, 2002; Reis, 1998; Salas & Ketzenberger, 2004; Thompson, 2006). While all of the men exhibit these behaviors some of the time, they do so to varying degrees. Yet, even when some of the men do not judge a situation appropriate to hug, cry, or emotionally relate to their male friends, none intellectually stigmatize or homosexualize those who do. Furthermore, these men were well styled and groomed, and they were accepting of a broad range of clothing styles within their team—this even extended to the wearing of pink cleats.

Although pink remains a cultural symbol of femininity in contemporary Western cultures—something traditionally avoided by boys and men (Kane, 2006; Pomerleau, Bolduc, Malcuit, and Cossette, 1990)—Josh isn't the only one who wears pink cleats. The colored soccer boot phenomenon perhaps found its definitive moment in 2008, when 20-year-old Arsenal fringe player, Nicklas Bendtner, donned a pair of bright pink cleats, the same brand and style as Josh. "I love my pink boots," he told *The Sun* (a British tabloid), "I've wanted to play in that colour ever since I was young . . . think it's an outstanding colour and looks amazing" (Irwin, 2008). He later told the *Guardian* newspaper, "People made a big fuss because pink is meant to be a girl's colour. They were outraged because they said it shouldn't happen in sport. Well, we are all different. I have my own opinion about what is a man and what is not a man" (Taylor, 2009).

It is in this context that this research highlights pink cleats as a symbol of changing gender relations among youth, compared to those just a decade older. For example, there is strong evidence that generational differences exist in the reactions to pink cleats. In a reaction to Bendtner's pink boots, 35-year-old former Arsenal player, Ray Parlour, said, "Why would you want to wear a pair of pink boots?" Parlour commented on a national radio show, "Straight away you look a bit arrogant or flash . . . Not being funny but if I was marking someone with pink boots I'd definitely want to kick him hard." Similarly, in February 2010, 31-year-old Queens Park Rangers' youth-team coach, Marc Bircham (who was famous for his blue and white striped hair as a player), reportedly banned his players from wearing pink cleats as a precaution against becoming too flash. Later that same month, Manchester United was reported to have issued a ban on all its youth players from wearing anything other than black cleats, an attempt to curb arrogance and flashiness (Ronay, 2010). Furthermore, in the United Kingdom in 2008, one of British football's legendary hard men, Ron "Chopper" Harris, now in his sixties, commented that "Pink is a woman's colour . . . If I'd worn pink boots in those days, people would have thought I was a funny person" (Davies, 2008). While pink cleats are described as flashy, arrogant, and girly, there are also clear undertones of homophobia in the stigmatization of pink, something that can be traced to the conflation of femininity with homosexuality in western cultures. Accordingly, the stigmatization of pink can be read as an attempt by these older men to police other men's deviation from traditional scripts of heteromasculinity.

Among youth today, however, the meaning behind pink is changing. But it is not that pink has become masculinized; instead, it is that men are proud to associate with its feminine associations. These players either do not think they will be homosexualized for wearing pink or they do not care if people erroneously assume they are gay. Not only is this revealed in this research, but this change is evident among the under 14s boys I coach in England. My athletes regularly wear pink. Pink is just one of a variety of other popular colors and shades—white, red, yellow, green, silver, blue, and combinations of these. Another way of viewing this generational divide is to compare the experiences of two British soccer players over the past two decades. This, therefore, represents a generational shift.

The transformation from deviant gendered practice to metrosexual, is made salient by the example of English soccer icon David Beckham who, in 1998, was pilloried in the British tabloids for wearing a sarong. The intention was to emasculate him in much the same way English soccer player Graeme Le Saux was homosexualized by his teammates and opponents for the way he dressed a decade earlier (Le Saux, 2008). But the tabloids were ineffective in sustaining this emasculation campaign. The public was not interested in demonizing Beckham's gender nonconformity. Accordingly, Clayton and Harris (2009) suggest that, "In the decade that followed, emasculation turned to detestation, back to emasculation and to acclamation and imitation, in what appeared to be the dawn of a transformation of male footballing identity" (p. 132). Beckham's performance of a new incarnation of metrosexual masculinity contrasted the strong traditional sense of working-class masculinity that threads its way through Le Saux's experiences and is deeply associated with modern football culture in the United Kingdom (c.f. Parker, 2001; Roderick, 2006). After the earlier efforts of the media to subvert Beckham's "doing" a divergent form of masculinity and to reemphasize hegemonic forms (what Clayton & Harris, 2009, call "retrosexuality," p. 136), they changed tack—this is exemplified by the *Sun's* discussion of David Beckham as "the perfect role model for every generation . . . a glamorous, handsome fashion icon" (Clayton & Harris, 2009).

Evidencing the transformation of a gendered practice/symbol from deviant to accepted, the wearing of pink cleats in this research provides a powerful example of how young men today are, over time, challenging and reconstructing established gender norms and orthodoxy. Here, I suggest that the mostly indifferent reaction to, and among others the joyous acknowledgement of, Josh's pink cleats demonstrates an expansion of the rigid boundaries of acceptable gender performance. Wearing pink cleats is an acceptable way of doing gender on this team.

The stigmatization of the color pink, by older sporting men, symbolically highlights the shifting generational difference in masculinity making. Pink cleats stand as a marker of a more inclusive masculinity, one in which heterosexual men bond over emotions and brotherhood, not homophobia. Thus, with this research, I add to the canon of work that shows that inclusive attitudes and behaviors are increasingly becoming an acceptable part of the contemporary college athletes' performance of masculinity. When it comes to fashion and grooming, it seems that many of yesteryear's gender-deviant acts are today's trends. Furthermore, their metro-inclusive behaviors (hugging, holding, and emotionally bonding) aren't even noticed. Because this gendered difference is neither policed nor congratulated, it suggests that, for these young men, what was once profane has become mundane.

References

Adams, A., Anderson, E., & McCormack, M. (2010). Establishing and challenging masculinity: The influence of gendered discourses in organized sport. *Journal of Language and Social Psychology*, 29, 278–300.

Anderson, E. (2000). *Trailblazing: America's first openly gay high school coach.* Fountain Valley, CA: Identity Press.

Anderson, E. (2005). *In the game: Gay athletes and the cult of masculinity.* Albany, NY: SUNY Press.

Anderson, E. (2009). *Inclusive masculinity: The changing nature of masculinities.* New York, NY: Routledge.

Anderson, E. (2011). Updating the outcome: Gay athletes, straight teams, and coming out at the end of the decade. *Gender & Society*, 25(2).

Anderson, E., Adams, A., & Rivers, I. (2010). "I kiss them because I love them": The emergence of heterosexual men kissing in British Institutes of Education. *Archives of Sexual Behavior.* doi: 10.1007/s10508–010–9678–0.

Anderson, E., & McGuire, R. (2010). Inclusive masculinity theory and the gendered politics of men's rugby. *Journal of Gender Studies*, 19, 249–261.

Berila, B., & Choudhuri, D. (2005). Metrosexuality the middle class way: Exploring race, class and gender in Queer Eye for the Straight Guy. *Genders OnLine Journal*, 42. Retrieved from http://www.genders.org

Braun, V., & Clarke, V. (2006). Using thematic analysis in psychology. *Qualitative Research in Psychology*, 3, 77–101.

Britton, D. M., & Williams, C. L. (1995). Don't ask, don't tell, don't pursue: Military policy and the construction of heterosexual masculinity. *Journal of Homosexuality*, 30, 1–21.

Burstyn, V. (1999). *The rites of men: Manhood, politics and the culture of sport.* Toronto, ON, Canada: University of Toronto Press.

Burton Nelson, M. (1994). *The stronger women get, the more men love football: Sexism and the American culture of sports.* New York, NY: Harcourt Brace.

Clayton, B. (2005). Tales from the pitch: An ethnography of male collegiate football masculinities. Unpublished PhD thesis, Brunel University.

Clayton, B., & Harris, J. (2004). Footballers' wives: The role of the soccer player's partner in the construction of idealised masculinity. *Soccer and Society*, 5, 317–355.

Clayton, B., & Harris, J. (2009). Sport and metrosexual identity: Sports media and emergent sexualities. In J. Harris & A. Parker (Eds.), *Sport and social identities* (pp. 132–149). Basingstoke, UK: Palgrave Macmillan.

Coad, D. (2008). *The metrosexual: Gender, sexuality and sport.* New York, NY: SUNY Press.

Curry, T. (1991). Fraternal bonding in the locker room: A profeminist analysis of talk about competition and women. *Sociology of Sport Journal*, 8, 119–135.

Davies, S. (2008, November 29). Pink's for women, says soccer hard man Chopper Harris. *Daily Mail online.* Retrieved from http://www.dailymail.co.uk/sport/football/article-1090585/Pink-8217-s-women-says-soccer-hard-man-Chopper-Harris.html

De Line, D., Hamburg, J. (Producers), & Hamburg, J. (Director). (2009). *I love you, man* [Motion Picture]. United States: De Line Pictures.

Diamond, L., M. (2002). "Having a girlfriend without knowing it": Intimate friendships among adolescent sexual-minority women. *Journal of Lesbian Studies*, 6, 5–16.

Field, T. (1999). American adolescents touch each other less and are more aggressive toward their peers as compared with French adolescents. *Adolescence, 34*(136), 754–758.

Glaser, B. G., & Strauss, A. L. (1967). *The discovery of grounded theory: Strategies for qualitative research.* New York, NY: Aldine de Guyter.

Gratton, C., & Jones, I. (2004). *Research methods for sports studies.* London, UK: Routledge.

Griffin, P. (1998). *Strong women, deep closets: Lesbians and homophobia in sport.* Champaign, IL: Human Kinetics.

Griffin, P. (2002). Girls' friendships and the formation of sexual identities. In A. Coyle & C. Kitzinger (Eds.), *Lesbian and gay psychology: New perspectives* (pp. 45–62). Malden, MA: Blackwell.

Harris, J. (2009). Shaping up to the men: (Re)creating identities in women's football. In J. Harris & A. Parker (Eds.), *Sport and social identities* (pp. 70–89). Basingstoke, UK: Palgrave Macmillan.

Harris, J., & Clayton, B. (2007). The first metrosexual rugby star: Rugby union, masculinity, and celebrity in contemporary Wales. *Sociology of Sport Journal, 24,* 145–164.

Hawes, K. (2001). H—The scarlet letter of sports: More people in athletics say it's time to start talking openly about homophobia. *NCAA News, 38*(21), 13–14.

Irwin, M. (2008, November 27). I dreamt of playing in pink! *The Sun.* Retrieved from http://www.thesun.co.uk/sol/homepage/sport/football/article1975997.ece

Jacobson, J. (2002, November 1). The loneliest athletes. *Chronicle of Higher Education,* pp. 33–34.

Kane, E. W. (2006). "No way my boys are going to be like that": Parents' responses to children's gender nonconformity. *Gender & Society, 20,* 149–176.

Kimmel, M. (1987). *Changing men: New directions in research on men and masculinities.* Newbury Park, CA: Sage.

Kozloski, M. (2010). Homosexual moral acceptance and social tolerance: Are the effects of education changing? *Journal of Homosexuality, 57*(10), 1370–1383.

Lenyskj, H. (1991). Combating homophobia in sport and physical education. *Sociology of Sport Journal, 8,* 61–69.

LeSaux, G. (2008). *Left field: A footballer apart.* London, UK: HarperSport.

Loftus, J. (2001). America's liberalization in attitudes toward homosexuality, 1973 to 1998. *American Sociological Review, 66,* 762–782.

McCormack, M. (2011a). The declining significance of homohysteria for male students in three sixth forms in the south of England. *British Educational Research Journal, 37*(2), 337–353.

McCormack, M. (2011b). *The declining significance of homophobia: How teenage boys are redefining masculinity and heterosexuality.* New York, NY: Oxford University Press.

McCormack, M., & Anderson, E. (2010a). The re-production of homosexually-themed discourse in educationally-based organised sport. *Culture, Health & Society, 12,* 913–927.

McCormack, M., & Anderson, E. (2010b). "It's just not acceptable any more": The erosion of homophobia and the softening of masculinity at an English sixth form. *Sociology, 44,* 843–859.

McNair, B. (2002). *Striptease culture: Sex, media and the democratization of desire.* London, UK: Routledge.

Messner, M. A. (1987). The life of a man's seasons: Male identity in the life-course of the jock. In M. Kimmel (Ed.), *Changing men: New directions in research on men and masculinity* (pp. 53–67). Beverley Hills, CA: Sage.

Messner, M. A. (1992). *Power at play: Sports and the problem of masculinity.* Boston, MA: Beacon Press.

Messner, M. A. (2002). *Taking the field: Women, men, and sports.* Minneapolis, MN: University of Minneapolis Press.

Messner, M. A. (2009). *It's all for the kids: Gender, families, and youth sports.* Berkeley, CA: University of California Press.

Paoletti, J. B. (1987). Clothing and gender in America: Children's fashions, 1890–1920. *Signs, 13,* 136–143.

Parker, A. (1996). The construction of masculinity within boys' physical education. *Gender and Education, 8*(2), 141–157.

Parker, A. (2001). Soccer, servitude and sub-cultural identity: Football traineeship and masculine construction. *Soccer and Society, 2,* 59–80.

Pascoe, C. J. (2005). "Dude, you're a fag": Adolescent masculinity and the fag discourse. *Sexualities, 8*(3), 329–346.

Plummer, D. (1999). *One of the boys: Masculinity, homophobia and modern manhood.* New York, NY: Harrington Park Press.

Pomerleau, A., Bolduc, D., Malcuit, G., & Cossette, L. (1990). Pink or blue: Environmental gender stereotypes in the first two years of life. *Sex Roles*, 22(5–6), 359–367.

Price, M., & Parker, A. (2003). Sport, sexuality and the gender order: Amateur rugby union, gay men, and social exclusion. *Sociology of Sport Journal*, 20, 108–126.

Pringle, R., & Markula, P. (2005). No pain is sane after all: A Foucauldian analysis of masculinities and men's experiences in rugby. *Sociology of Sport Journal*, 22, 472–497.

Pronger, B. (1990). *The arena of masculinity: Sports, homosexuality, and the meaning of sex.* New York, NY: St. Martin's Press.

Reis, H. T. (1998). Gender differences in intimacy and related behaviors: Context and process. In D. L. Canary & K. Dindia (Eds.), *Sex differences and similarities in communication* (pp. 203–231). Mahwah, NJ: Erlbaum.

Renold, E. (1997). "All they've got on their brains is football": Sport, masculinity and the gendered practices of playground relations. *Sport, Education and Society*, 2, 5–23.

Roderick, M. (2006). *The work of professional football: A labour of love.* London, UK: Routledge.

Ronay, B. (2010, February 22). Sir Alex Ferguson sticks the boot in on football's flashy young stars. *Guardian.* Retrieved from http://www.guardian.co.uk/football/2010/feb/22/manchester-united-premierleague

Salas, D., & Ketzenberger, K. E. (2004). Associations of sex and type of relationship on intimacy. *Psychological Reports*, 94(3c), 1322–1324.

Schrack-Walters, A., O'Donnell, K. A., & Wardlow, D. L. (2009). Deconstructing the myth of the monolithic male athlete: A qualitative study of men's participation in athletics. *Sex Roles*, 60(1–2), 81–99.

Simpson, M. (1994, November 15). Here come the mirror men. *The Independent*, 2.

Southall, R., Anderson, E., Southall, C., Nagel, M., & Polite, F. (2011). An investigation of ethnicity as a variable related to US male college athletes' sexual-orientation behaviors and attitudes. *Ethnic and Racial Studies*, 34, 293–313.

Southall, R., Nagel, M., Anderson, E., Polite, F., & Southall, C. (2009). An investigation of male college athletes' attitudes toward sexual orientation [Special issue]. *Journal of Issues in Intercollegiate Athletics*, Special Issue, 62–77.

Spradley, J. P. (1970). *You owe yourself and drunk: An ethnography of urban nomads.* Boston, MA: Little & Brown.

Stotzer, R. L. (2009). Straight allies: Supportive attitudes toward lesbians, gay men, and bisexuals in a college sample. *Sex Roles*, 60(1–2), 67–80.

Taylor, D. (2009, October 31). Nicklas Bendtner ignores doubters to concentrate on his Arsenal masterplan. *Guardian.* Retrieved from http://www.guardian.co.uk/football/2009/oct/31/nicklas-bendtner-interview-arsenal-tottenham

Thompson, E. M. (2006). Girl friend or girlfriend? *Journal of Bisexuality*, 6(3), 47–67.

Weeks, J. (2007). *The world we have won.* London, UK: Routledge.

Wright, T. C., Aron, A., McLaughlin-Volpe, T., & Ropp, S. A. (1997). The extended contact effect. *Journal of Personality and Social Psychology*, 73(1), 73–90.

CHAPTER 29

Bud-Sex

Constructing Normative Masculinity Among Rural Straight Men That Have Sex With Men

Tony Silva

Mainstream understandings of heterosexuality emphasize that straight men's attractions, behaviors, and desires should be oriented exclusively toward women, and yet research indicates that some straight-identified men have sex with other men. There are multiple reasons why some men who have sex with men (MSM) identify as straight, including internalized heterosexism, participation in other-sex marriage and childrearing, and enjoyment of straight privilege and culture (Ward 2015). Few interview-based studies of straight MSM exist, and previous studies focus on urban, military, or prison contexts. Additionally, there is a widespread urban focus in sexualities and gender literatures (Halberstam 2005), which obscures the role of geography in the construction, maintenance, perception, and experience of gender and sexuality. As Connell and Messerschmidt (2005) explain, researchers should examine masculinities that differ by place; few have done so with rurality (exceptions include Morris 2008). By using interviews, this study is one of the first to examine how straight MSM themselves understand their own genders and sexualities, and how rurality affects these perceptions.

How do rural, white, straight MSM understand their gender? Through complex interpretive processes, participants reworked non-normative sexual practices usually antithetical to rural masculinities to actually construct normative masculinity. Participants selected male sexual partners on the basis of masculinity, race, and sexual identity. Most chose other masculine, white, and straight or secretly bisexual men for secretive sex without romantic involvement. By choosing these partners and having this type of sex, the participants normalized and authenticated their sexual encounters as straight and normatively masculine. The married men framed sex with men as less threatening to their marriages than extramarital sex with women, helping to preserve a part of their lives that most described as central to their straightness.

Rather than referring to participants as MSM, a public health term, I describe them as guys who engage in bud-sex. I use "bud-sex" when referring to the participants' sexual activities and "MSM" when referring to broader populations of straight men that have sex with men.[1] Similar sexual practices carry different meanings across populations and contexts, including among different groups of MSM. Ward (2015) examines dude-sex, a type of male–male sex that white, masculine, straight men in urban or military contexts frame as a way to bond and build masculinity with other, similar "bros." Carrillo and Hoffman (2016) refer to their primarily urban participants as heteroflexible,

SOURCE: Silva, T. (2017). Bud-Sex: Constructing Normative Masculinity Among Rural Straight Men That Have Sex With Men. *Gender & Society, 31*(1), 51–73. Reproduced with permission.

given that they were exclusively or primarily attracted to women. While the participants in this study share overlap with those groups, they also frame their same-sex sex in subtly different ways: not as an opportunity to bond with urban "bros," and only sometimes—but not always—as a novel sexual pursuit, given that they had sexual attractions all across the spectrum. Instead, as Silva (forthcoming) explores, the participants reinforced their straightness through unconventional interpretations of same-sex sex: as "helpin' a buddy out," relieving "urges," acting on sexual desires for men without sexual attractions to them, relieving general sexual needs, and/or a way to act on sexual attractions. "Bud-sex" captures these interpretations, as well as how the participants had sex and with whom they partnered. The specific type of sex the participants had with other men—bud-sex—cemented their rural masculinity and heterosexuality, and distinguishes them from other MSM.

The results demonstrate the flexibility of male heterosexuality and the centrality of heterosexuality to normative rural masculinity. First, the participants interpret same-sex sex as compatible with heterosexuality. While there is a framework to describe women's sexual flexibility—"sexual fluidity" (Diamond 2009)—there is no such framework for men. Straight men's sexual flexibility is often described as indicative of lessening homophobia (e.g., Anderson's 2008 study of young men), when it also demonstrates that male heterosexuality is fundamentally flexible across the life course. Second, heterosexual identification is key to constructing normative rural masculinity. While the participants' sexual practices did not align with mainstream definitions of heterosexuality, their identification with straightness—and their interpretations of their sexual practices that reinforced it—bolstered their normative rural masculinity. Given that normative masculinity is critical for social acceptance in rural areas, identification with heterosexuality to bolster normative masculinity was especially important. The findings reinforce the centrality of place for how individuals identify and express their sexuality and gender.

The Social Construction of Sexuality

Cultural norms about what sexual practices are acceptable, their significance, their relation to identity, and even what practices are considered sexual are all socially constructed (Foucault 1978). Gender performance and sexual practice, rather than biological sex or attractions, were key for understanding sexuality in the late nineteenth and early twentieth centuries. At that time, many conventionally masculine men who penetrated men, before heterosexuality was introduced as an identity, were considered "normal" (Chauncey 1994). This continued in some rural areas into the mid-1900s, where same-sex sex involving "normal" men was common, albeit often intentionally ignored (Boag 2003; Howard 1999; Johnson 2013).

Despite increasing acceptance of same-sex sexuality, hegemonic masculinity remains distinctly heterosexual (Connell 1987). The relationship between heterosexuality and normative masculinity remains, even as overt homophobia has lessened in many contexts (Anderson 2008; Bridges 2014; Connell 2005; Dean 2014; McCormack 2013). Heteronormativity is entrenched within U.S. institutions and is strongly related to normative masculinity, which affects men's sexual identification, practices, and interpretations. This article draws on Connell's (1987, 2005) framework explaining gender as a social structure, composed of hierarchically organized masculinities that together legitimate inequalities between men and women and among men. It also reflects that masculinity is an ongoing interpersonal process through which actions inconsistent with hegemonic masculinity are policed by others, and often suppressed in homosocial spaces (Bird 1996). Incorporating these theoretical elements, "normative masculinity" in this article refers to gender practices that eschew femininity and reinforce white, straight, male, and masculine (i.e., nonfeminine) dominance. Because rural spaces in different regions (e.g., rural Alabama vs. rural Québec) are distinct and will consequently develop unique masculinities in those spaces, this article specifically examines normative masculinity in

U.S.-based rural regions in the Midwest and Pacific Northwest—areas that share social conservatism and demographic white majorities (Bump 2014; United States Census Bureau 2016).

Intersections of Rural Masculinities and Sexualities

Research about the intersections between rural masculinities and sexualities points to the importance of normative rural masculinity for social tolerance, normality, and safety, though historically this may have varied (Johnson 2013). Bridges (2014) finds that some young, straight, white men expand socially acceptable masculine performances by drawing upon "sexual aesthetics" relating to tastes, behaviors, or ideologies appropriated from gay cultures, albeit in ways that reinforce inequalities related to sexualities and gender. Although seemingly more sensitive expressions of masculinity are available to some privileged men in or near urban areas, this is not something most rural men do. Nor do most change the "style" of masculinity (Messner 1993), for example by investing an increasing amount of time and money into personal appearance (Barber 2016). Most rural men do not have socially viable alternatives to conventional expressions of masculinity, and the masculinity they construct reflects the rigid expectations of many rural men today (Courtenay 2006). Thus, due to differing social contexts, masculinities in rural areas are distinct from those in urban locations.

"Rural masculinity" refers to masculinity as it is "constructed within what rural social scientists would recognize as rural spaces and sites" (Campbell and Bell 2000, 540). Rural masculinities differ based on local context as well as intersections of social identities, and central to many of them are physical labor and toughness (Morris 2008; Kazyak 2012). The strong link between heterosexuality and masculinity is especially evident in rural areas, which are often more conservative than urban locales (Bump 2014). Rural men are likelier than urban men to engage in unsafe behaviors, and intersections with non-normative sexualities can exacerbate these dangers (Courtenay 2006). For rural men with marginalized sexualities, normative rural masculinity is particularly important because it provides them a degree of social acceptance (Boulden 2001; Fellows 2001). Many rural gay men even distance themselves from feminine gay men and point out their similarities with (purportedly masculine) straight men (Annes and Redlin 2012). Relatedly, in her interview study of rural Midwestern gays and lesbians, Kazyak (2012) found that gay men had little flexibility in gender practices; they either performed conventional rural masculinities or were rejected by their community. Research on rural queer youth (Gray 2009) and rural trans men (Abelson 2014) indicates that challenging gender norms often leads to fear of physical harm, encouraging gender normativity.

Methods

I posted advertisements in several men-for-men casual encounters sections of Craigslist, which is organized regionally. Unlike most other apps/websites, Craigslist is widely used, anonymous, free, and frequented by individuals with a variety of sexual identities. I also included project information on Grindr, an app catering to gay and bisexual men, which recruited two participants. Of the approximately 100 men that inquired about participation, 19 agreed to participate: 15 over the phone and four in person. This study utilizes phone/in-person semistructured interviews.

All the participants live in Missouri, Illinois, Oregon, Washington, or Idaho; these rural spaces share similarities by virtue of their social conservatism and predominantly white populations (Bump 2014; United States Census Bureau 2016). All but two participants currently live in, or were raised in, a rural area. Thirteen currently live in a rural area, and 15 were raised in rural areas. By rural, I refer to an area with fewer than 25,000 residents. The only two exceptions were participants who were raised in urban areas but currently live in what I term semirural areas: cities with 25,000–60,000 residents in isolated areas of the Pacific Northwest. All the participants are white, challenging the perception of straight MSM as urban blacks on the "down low" (Ward 2015). They are skewed toward older ages with the majority over 50: 20s (1), 30s (3), 40s (1), 50s (6), 60s (6), and 70s (2). The participants have a variety of educational and occupational backgrounds, but most are middle class. One reported a doctorate as his highest degree, five a master's, three a bachelor's, five an associate's, two some college, and three high school. The sample has considerable diversity in sexual attraction. Further, although all tell others they identify as straight, 17 actually identify as straight or some variation thereof, one as gay, and one as bisexual. Thus, while all are secretive about their same-sex sex, only two are "closeted" in terms of sexual identity, as only two identify as gay or bisexual but tell others they identify as straight.

Constructing Bud-Sex

"Strictly Masculine": Average, Rural, Masculine Guys

All 19 participants described themselves as masculine, and they did so in terms of their actions: mannerisms, behaviors, communication styles, hobbies, and skills. Through these descriptions, all framed themselves as normal, masculine men. Given the association of femininity with same-sex sexuality, subcultures of gay men may embrace or reject femininity (Hennen 2008). The men in this study, however, uniformly described themselves as masculine, thus distancing themselves from the purported relationship between same-sex sexuality and femininity.

The men's gender self-descriptions largely conform to conventional understandings of masculinity. Brad (48) is a "T-shirt and Levi kind of guy" who is "straight-acting [and] masculine." Jon (39) is "pretty much masculine" because "I'm a . . . straight guy that likes to hunt, fish, camp, and I raise cattle for a living." Jack (52) shared similar sentiments: "The things I do, interests, all masculine. I like to shoot, I like to hunt. . . ." Cain (50) explained, "My demeanor may be more gentleman-like than . . . the rugged cowboy type," but described himself as having "a type A personality" with the potential to "be kind of aggressive." Similarly, David (74) is an "alpha male" who enjoys shooting and fishing. Richard (75) described himself "as masculine as John Wayne; I'm definitely not feminine in any way, shape, or form." Kevin (69) noted, "I've always done blue-collar type work, I live in a rural area, I'm a farmer." Will (52) leans "a lot toward masculine," because "I can clean a deer. . . . I can catch some fish. . . . and I'm a very good handyman," while Billy (59) enjoys "trudgin' in the wilderness, cuttin' firewood and throwin' logs." Will and Billy both conflated masculinity with heterosexuality, describing themselves as individuals no one would suspect to be attracted to men. Pat (69) similarly blurred the lines between masculinity and heterosexuality, and used rural tropes to describe himself:

> [V]ery masculine. 15 year collection of *Playboy* magazines, I don't think gay people subscribe to *Playboy*. Fantasize about women, oh yes. . . . Drive a pickup . . . I like guns, I'm not good at hunting, but I like to go up in the woods and sit there and drink my half pint of Jack Daniels and act like I am hunting. I'd say very masculine. I like baseball.

Marcus (38) similarly noted, "I portray myself as very masculine. I wear jeans and boots and camouflage hats and sleeveless T-shirts, drive a truck, and like to shoot stuff." Reuben (28) also noted rural hobbies: "I exercise, I play sports, I take part [in] what you'd call stereotypical masculine activities. I go hunting every now and then . . . things that a quote unquote manly-man would do."

The participants' rural locations played a large role in their self-descriptions as masculine. Eleven described themselves using elements of rurality, such as hobbies (hunting, fishing, shooting, cutting firewood), occupations (farming, ranching), ways of dressing (camo, T-shirts, and Levi jeans), or images of rugged rurality (John Wayne). Another used rural tropes (rugged cowboys) as a comparison to his own masculinity. Central to the men's self-understanding is their rural background; they perform a rural masculinity, which they seek to reaffirm through their same-sex sexual encounters.

"Guys Like Me": Partnering with Other Masculine, White, Non-Gay Men

The participants overwhelmingly preferred to have sex with men like themselves: masculine, white, and not gay—straight or secretly bisexual. This is a key element of bud-sex. Partnering with other men similarly privileged on several intersecting axes—gender, race, and sexual identity— allowed the participants to normalize and authenticate their sexual experiences as normatively masculine. The socially constructed (and problematic) relationship between normativity and male masculinity, whiteness, and straightness shapes sexual desires such that individuals with these characteristics are often perceived as desirable sexual partners. By having sex with these *types of men*, the participants were able to construct and reinforce normative masculinity—*despite having sex with men*. Alignment with normative masculinity is especially important for men in rural areas, where it is a virtual prerequisite for social acceptance (Abelson 2014; Annes and Redlin 2012; Boulden 2001; Fellows 1998; Kazyak 2012).

Seventeen participants—all of those who identify as straight—stated that they prefer masculine male sexual partners, and each explained that the majority of their male sexual partners are masculine. Masculinity in sexual partners helped construct and validate their own normative masculinity. The straight participants often equated masculinity with non-gayness (heterosexuality or secretive bisexuality) or normality. As Cain said, "I'm really not drawn to what I would consider really effeminate faggot type[s]," but he does "like the masculine looking guy who maybe is more bi." Similarly, Matt (60) explained, "If they're too flamboyant they just turn me off," and Jack noted, "Femininity in a man is a turn off." Ryan (60) explained, "I'm not comfortable around femme" and "masculinity is what attracts me," while David shared that "Femme guys don't do anything for me at all, in fact actually I don't care for 'em." Jon shared, "I don't really like flamin' queers." Mike (50) similarly said, "I don't want the effeminate ones, I want the manly guys. . . . If I wanted someone that acts girlish, I got a wife at home." Jeff (38) prefers masculinity because "I guess I perceive men who are feminine want to hang out . . . have companionship, and make it last two or three hours."

The four participants who reported exclusive sexual attractions to women also stated a preference for normatively masculine male sexual partners, revealing the social origins of their attractions. As Marcus explained,

> A guy that I would consider more like me, that gets blowjobs from guys every once in a while, doesn't do it every day. I know that there are a lot of guys out there that are like me . . . they're manly guys, and doing manly stuff, and just happen to have oral sex with men every once in a while [chuckles]. So, that's why I kinda prefer those types of guys. . . . It [also] seems that . . . more masculine guys wouldn't harass me, I guess, hound me all the time, send me 1000 emails, "Hey, you want to get together today . . . hey, what about now." And there's a thought in my head that a more feminine or gay guy would want me to come around more.

Like Jeff, Marcus finds normative straight, masculine men like himself better sex partners than feminine and/or gay men. Echoing Mike, Richard stated, "Given a choice I prefer masculine; I don't want a substitute woman," and Joe (63) shared, "Feminine guys don't interest me at all." Preferences for masculine men both validate the participants' own normative masculinity and reveal the socially constructed nature of sexual desires.

Similarly, the vast majority of the past and present male sexual partners of 16 participants—all except Reuben, Tom (59), and Mark—are white. For most of the straight participants, racial sameness was a strategy to align themselves with normativity and, in so doing, to construct normative masculinity. Thus, whiteness is central to bud-sex, which reinforces the participants' straightness and normative rural masculinity. Twelve participants stated that they prefer white male sexual partners, and four others explained their mostly white sexual history as happenstance. When explaining why he prefers white men, Kevin noted, "I guess because I'm white and, I guess you'd say more normal for me to be with white guys." Marcus and Richard reported exclusive sexual attractions to women, and yet they too noted preferences for white men, indicating that attractions are not the only determinant of sexual partnering and reinforcing the social influence of sexual desires. Although Richard reported, "It's not about the person, I'm only interested in the dick," he also stated, "White would be my choice." Joe shared, "The closer to white you get, Hispanic's OK, but the further from me you get, if you get to the black side, I'm just not in." Jeff also explained racial preferences as stemming from desiring men like himself: "Probably because I am sexually attracted to myself. . . ." David echoed, "I would lean primarily towards white guys that are more or less like me." By choosing men like themselves—other white men—the participants normalized their encounters as straight and normatively masculine.

Of the 17 straight participants, nine reported preferences for straight or bisexual men and 13 noted that a majority of their sexual partners are straight, bisexual, and/or married to a woman. Their partners' not-gay sexual identities—straight or secretly bisexual—are an important component of the men's normative masculinity. The narratives of the four men with predominately straight or bisexual sexual partners who did not state a preference reveal numerous reasons: (1) They did not want to sound prejudicial; (2) rurality makes it difficult to find sexual partners, so they are at times open to gay men; (3) mostly engaging with straight or bisexual men makes meeting with gay men less threatening; and (4) their partners' masculinity and the discreet, nonromantic nature of the encounter makes them comfortable enough to occasionally hook up with gay men. Many of the straight participants who noted preferences for straight or bisexual men did so because of perceived greater compatibility and greater confidence in discreetness. As Jeff stated, he is "basically seeking the same" kind of guy as himself. Marcus explained his preferences as a cultural fit:

> Straight guys, I think I identify with them more because that's kinda, like [how] I feel myself. And bi guys, the same way. We can talk about women, there [have] been times where we've watched hetero porn, before we got started or whatever, so I kinda prefer that. [And] because I'm not attracted, it's very off-putting when somebody acts gay, and I feel like a lot of gay guys, just kinda put off that gay vibe, I'll call it, I guess, and that's very off-putting to me.

Marcus feels more comfortable with straight or bisexual men because he dislikes a "gay vibe," reinforcing how social factors such as culture affect sexual desires. Similarly, Tom noted choosing a bisexual man as his ideal male sexual partner because he would "kinda be closer in tune to what I am." Joe would also choose a bisexual man "because he would be of the same mind that I am. He would understand what I'm feeling, and would respond probably similarly. So we could engage with common knowledge." Jack noted, "He would be in the same boat as me. He would be straight, preferably married or definitely partnered up with a female, with one thing on his mind, getting his rocks off with me . . . they're not gonna out me." Similarly, Cain said he would not hook up with gay men, explaining, "No, I'm not out, and so, someone who is out, I'm sometimes a little bit hesitant about what they may say to others."

That a majority of 13 straight participants' male sexual partners are straight or secretly bisexual, despite bountiful opportunities for sex with gay and openly bisexual men on Craigslist, indicates that partnering with non-gay men is a strategy to reaffirm their own normatively masculine sense of self. It also reflects that the sexual meanings attributed to encounters are socially produced; while many gay men are also masculine and enjoy romance-free sex, most of the participants view straight or secretly bisexual partners as more desirable because of the link between normativity and non-gayness. Given the centrality of heterosexuality to normative rural masculinity, the participants were able to align themselves closer to both by selecting straight and secretly bisexual male sexual partners. While most expressed frustration about the difficulty of finding sexual partners in rural areas, they nonetheless mostly chose men who are masculine, white, and straight or secretly bisexual, underscoring the importance of these characteristics for their normative masculinity and bud-sex.

Secretive and Nonromantic: Ingredients for Bud-Sex

Consistent with other research about straight MSM (Humphreys 1970; Reynolds 2015; Ward 2015), the participants preferred secretive, nonromantic same-sex sex, key ingredients of bud-sex. They did not necessarily prefer one-time meet-ups, however; their histories with "regular" male sexual partners indicate they appreciate the benefits of a sexual friendship. All 19 participants described the need for sexual encounters to be secretive, and this secrecy was tied to rurality. Rurality had both its advantages and drawbacks. On one hand, vast expanses of unpopulated land meant participants could easily find places to have secretive sex. On the other, community interconnectedness necessitated increased caution. As Pat said, "[I]n a small town everyone knows more about your business than you do. . . . I suppose in the city you don't have to be discreet. But here in [a] small rural area, yes, you've gotta be discreet." By meeting men who understood the need for secrecy—most of them straight or secretly bisexual—the participants were able to maintain their public identities. The absence of romance reframed encounters as normatively masculine and compatible with straightness. Even while avoiding romantic attachments, 13 participants currently have regulars, three others had regulars in the past, and two others would like one or are open to it. While most are open to one-time hookups, most also prefer regulars. By doing so, they reinforce their masculinity by seeking consistent partners on the same page about what sex between straight guys should constitute. This is especially important in rural areas, given that each attempt to find a new sexual partner opens the participants to potential discovery in a small pool of acquaintances.

While relationships with regulars were free of romance and deep emotional ties, they were not necessarily devoid of feeling; participants enjoyed regulars for multiple reasons: convenience, comfort, sexual compatibility, or even friendship. Jack explained that with his regular "we connected on Craigslist . . . [and] became good friends, in addition to havin' sex . . . we just made a connection. . . . But there was no love at all." Thus, bud-sex is predicated on rejecting romantic attachment and deep emotional ties, but not all emotion.

The participants enjoyed a wide range of sex acts, but few framed penetrating/being penetrated as tied to masculinity or straightness; these interpretations reaffirmed their own straightness and normative masculinity, regardless of sexual practices. Eleven both penetrated others and were penetrated in oral and/or anal sex, often with the same person, while eight either mostly penetrated or were penetrated. Of those who had anal sex more than a handful of times, five were mostly tops, four mostly bottoms, and two versatile.[2] Only three of the straight participants, plus Reuben (who identified as bisexual), tied sex positions to masculinity or straightness, yet none questioned their own masculinity or straightness, and none of the straight participants viewed the men they penetrated (if any) as not masculine because of that penetration. As Mark (61) noted, "I see it [being penetrated] as a very masculine thing. No one knows how to please a man better than another man." Likewise, David shared, "It's a mutual sexual satisfaction, however you get it. I don't feel any less of a man if I'm bent over and he's in me, at all. I just don't." Sex acts were overwhelmingly driven by personal preferences and physical abilities (e.g., erectile dysfunction). By rejecting stereotypical associations between masculinity and straightness, on the one hand, and sex acts involving penetrating or being penetrated, on the other, the participants reaffirmed both their straightness and normative rural masculinity.

It was not *what* the participants did sexually, but *how* they did it, that affected their perceptions of their masculinity. By maintaining secretive and romance-free same-sex sex, and interpreting sexual acts as unrelated to masculinity or straightness, they were able to act on desires in a normatively masculine way and reaffirm their normatively masculine sense of self. Collectively, these interpretations and preferences help define the type of sex they had: bud-sex.

No Big Deal: Extramarital Same-Sex Sex

For the 17 straight participants, a key aspect of their straightness was marriage and/or child rearing. Each currently married man indicated a desire to stay married. As they explained, sex with men either does not constitute cheating or is less threatening to their marriage than extramarital sex with women, because it is devoid of deep emotional ties. Sex with women is far more threatening to marriage, as this breaks vows and/or has the potential to involve emotional attachment. Similarly, Cain shared, "I'm not cheating on my wife. I don't have the intention of leaving her." Kevin echoed this: "Meetin' up with women would be cheating on my wife. And when I meet up with guys, I justify it by sayin' 'well it's only fun between me and the other guy, it's not like I have another woman . . .' I'm sure she or other people would argue [with] that, but that's just the way I feel."

For the currently married straight men, their perceptions of their extramarital same-sex sex bolster their normative masculinity: sex with men is simply a way for them to fulfill sexual desires without affecting any other part of their lives. Four framed sex with men as not cheating in part because they no longer had sex with their wives. As Pat said, sex with men is not cheating "because part of marriage is sex, and my marriage has no sex." Perceptions of extramarital same-sex sex as insignificant are tied to rurality: rural areas have a stronger focus on other-sex marriages than urban locales, where cohabitation and nonmonogamous relationships are often more visible (Chetty and Hendren 2015; Leonhardt and Quealy 2015). Thus, by framing same-sex extramarital sex as insignificant, the men interpret their sexual practices in ways that make them compatible with the marriages that are central to their heterosexuality and normative rural masculinity.

Aging: Not Ready to Give Up Sex

Age affected the participants' interpretations of their sexuality and gender, both because of generational dynamics and aging itself. Fourteen participants are 50 or older and internalized heteronormativity and strict masculine norms during some of the most difficult decades to express sexual or gender non-normativity (Seidman 2002). This, combined with the lack of visibility of non-normative sexualities and gender expressions in most rural areas in the 1950s–1980s, shaped the participants' relationship with masculinity and straightness. As Kevin shared, "I grew up in an area where that [being gay/bisexual] wasn't an option, in a time and area both," and Jack noted, "Back in the day when I was growing up, it was absolutely not accepted."

Additionally, sex with men helped nine participants bolster their masculinity, despite the fact that they or their wives were experiencing age-related bodily changes that made sex more difficult. Seven explained that sex became uncomfortable or undesirable for their wives, and sex with men helped relieve sexual desires. As Ryan shared, "As physically there's been changes to our bodies and it's even painful for my wife to have sex, I have no problem taking care of myself with another guy." Similarly, David explained, "I'm not getting sex at home, and I want sex," and "older men are a lot more receptive to sex, they're more enthusiastic," because "senior women have kinda lost their desire to do much of anything." Two others began having sex with men because of erectile dysfunction, which limited their ability to penetrate. As Tom described, "I'm a straight guy that has ED and doesn't want to give up havin' sex." Turning to sex with men or increasing the relative frequency of sex with men was a way for each to maintain their sex lives and masculinity despite bodily changes related to aging. The centrality of sex to masculinity has been noted in other contexts, as well (e.g., Loe 2001).

Conclusion

The results demonstrate that some rural straight men who have same-sex sex construct normative masculinity through their choice of sexual partners on the axes of masculinity, race, and sexual identity, as well as through the type of sex they prefer. By having sex mostly with other privileged men—conventionally masculine, white, and not gay—and by enjoying secretive and romance-free same-sex sex, the participants framed their encounters as straight and normatively masculine. Through complex interpretive processes, they reframed same-sex sex, usually antithetical to rural masculinities, such that it actually helped them construct normative rural masculinity. The type of same-sex sex they have is distinguishable from that of other groups of MSM: bud-sex captures their unique sexual interpretations (Silva, forthcoming), as well as their partnering preferences and the type of sex they have, and it helps construct their normative masculinity and straightness. The concept of bud-sex helps clarify that similar sex practices have different meanings across contexts and populations. Non-normative sexual practices—same-sex sex—can actually be used to reinforce normative masculinity and straightness. The results also demonstrate the flexibility of male heterosexuality over the life course, and the importance of heterosexuality to rural masculinity. Given the centrality of heterosexuality to normative masculinity in rural areas, the participants' identification with straightness—bolstered by their interpretations of their sexual practices—reinforced their normative rural masculinity. Because normative masculinity is critical for social acceptance in rural areas, identification with heterosexuality to bolster normative masculinity was especially important. This study is one of the first to use the narratives of straight MSM themselves to explore how they understand their masculinity. It is also the first to examine this population in rural areas, reinforcing the centrality of place for how individuals perceive and experience gender and sexuality. More broadly, this study is part of a growing scholarship that points to masculinities that differ by time period, race, class, and location (Pascoe and Bridges 2016).

The participants' narratives illustrate historical shifts to the relationship between gender and sexuality. In the late nineteenth and early twentieth centuries, many masculine men penetrated feminine men without feeling as though their masculinity or sexual identity was threatened; this is because gender and sexual practice (i.e., penetrating or being penetrated) was an organizing element for how sexuality was understood, and the concept of sexual identity was not yet widely used (Chauncey 1994). Today, the biological sex of sexual partners is the organizing element for sexuality, and for men there is a widespread perception that femininity is tied to same-sex sexuality. Thus, today, men that engage in bud-sex distance themselves from femininity and normalize their sexual encounters as masculine by partnering with other normatively masculine men.

The social implications of straight masculinities open to same-sex sex are complex. On one hand, diversity within expressions of heterosexuality and masculinities demonstrate that normativity can be unintentionally challenged from within dominant identities. On the other, the participants' masculinity reinforces inequality. All 19 participants in this study maintain straight privilege by publicly identifying as straight and keeping secret their same-sex encounters. All of the straight men avoid effeminate men, and several disparaged male effeminacy, contributing to the widespread devaluation of femininities. Moreover, 13 were married and had extramarital sex without their wife's knowledge, underscoring their male entitlement and unwillingness to consider ethical nonmonogamy. The participants enjoy marginalized sexual practices, but they are unwilling to challenge heterosexism or other forms of domination, maintaining numerous systems of inequality.

Notes

1. The participants did not use any particular phrasing to describe their sex, necessitating a new term. I use "MSM" to refer to broader populations of men that have sex with men that have sex with men, given that can describe them.

2. "Top" means penetrating in anal sex, whereas "bottom" refers to being penetrated; "versatile" means both topping and bottoming.

References

Abelson, Miriam J. 2014. *Men in context: Transmasculinities and transgender experiences in three US regions.* Ph.D. diss., University of Oregon, Eugene, OR.

Adam, Barry. 2000. Love and sex in constructing identity among men who have sex with men. *International Journal of Sexuality and Gender Studies* 5 (4): 325–39.

Anderson, Eric. 2008. "Being masculine is not about who you sleep with . . . ": Heterosexual athletes contesting masculinity and the one-time rule of homosexuality. *Sex Roles* 58 (1–2): 104–15.

Annes, Alexis, and Meredith Redlin. 2012. The careful balance of gender and sexuality: Rural gay men, the heterosexual matrix, and "effeminophobia." *Journal of Homosexuality* 59 (2): 256–88.

Barber, Kristen. 2016. *Styling masculinity: Gender, class, and inequality in the men's grooming industry.* New Brunswick, NJ: Rutgers University Press.

Barnshaw, John, and Lynn Letukas. 2010. The low down on the down low: Origins, risk identification and intervention. *Health Sociology Review* 19 (4): 478–90.

Bird, Sharon. 1996. Welcome to the men's club: Homosociality and the maintenance of hegemonic masculinity. *Gender & Society* 10 (2): 120–32.

Boag, Peter. 2003. *Same-sex affairs: Constructing and controlling homosexuality in the Pacific Northwest.* Berkeley: University of California Press.

Boulden, Walter. 2001. Gay men living in a rural environment. *Journal of Gay and Lesbian Social Services* 12 (3/4): 63–75.

Bridges, Tristan. 2014. A very "gay" straight? Hybrid masculinities, sexual aesthetics, and the changing relationship between masculinity and homophobia. *Gender & Society* 28 (1): 58–82.

Britton, Dana. 1990. Homophobia and homosociality: An analysis of boundary maintenance. *Sociological Quarterly* 31 (3): 423–39.

Bump, Philip. 2014. There really are two Americas. An urban one and a rural one. *The Washington Post,* 21 April.

Campbell, Hugh, and Michael Bell. 2000. The question of rural masculinities. *Rural Sociology* 65 (4): 532–46.

Cantú, Lionel, Jr. 2009. *The sexuality of migration: Border crossings and Mexican immigrant men.* New York: NYU Press.

Carrillo, Héctor, and Jorge Fontdevila. 2014. Border crossings and shifting sexualities among Mexican gay immigrant men: Beyond monolithic conceptions. *Sexualities* 17 (8): 919–38.

Carrillo, Héctor, and Amanda Hoffman. 2016. From MSM to heteroflexibilities: Non-exclusive straight male identities and their implications for HIV prevention and health promotion. *Global Public Health* 11 (7–8): 923–36.

Chauncey, George. 1994. *Gay New York: Gender, urban culture, and the making of the gay male world 1890–1940.* New York: Basic Books.

Chetty, Raj, and Nathaniel Hendren. 2015. *The impacts of neighborhoods on intergenerational mobility: Childhood exposure effects and county-level estimates.* Cambridge, MA: The Equality of Opportunity Project.

Connell, R. W. 1987. *Gender and power: Society, the person, and sexual politics.* Palo Alto, CA: Stanford University Press.

Connell, R. W. 2005. *Masculinities,* 2nd ed. Berkeley: University of California Press.

Connell, R. W., and James Messerschmidt. 2005. Hegemonic masculinity: Rethinking the concept. *Gender & Society* 19 (6): 829–59.

Courtenay, Will. 2006. Rural men's health: Situating risk in the negotiation of masculinity. In *Country boys: Masculinity and rural life,* edited by Hugh Campbell, Michael M. Bell, and Margaret Finney. University Park, PA: Pennsylvania State University Press.

Dean, James. 2014. *Straights: Heterosexuality in post-closeted culture.* New York: New York University Press.

Desmond, Matthew. 2006. Becoming a firefighter. *Ethnography* 7 (4): 387–421.

Diamond, Lisa. 2009. *Sexual fluidity: Understanding women's love and desire.* Cambridge, MA: Harvard University Press.

Diefendorf, Sarah. 2015. After the wedding night: Sexual abstinence and masculinities over the life course. *Gender & Society* 29 (5): 647–69.

Fellows, Will. 2001. *Farm boys: Lives of gay men from the rural Midwest.* Madison: University of Wisconsin Press.

Flood, Michael. 2008. Men, sex, and homosociality: How bonds between men shape their sexual relations with women. *Men and Masculinities* 10 (3): 339–59.

Foucault, Michel. 1978. *The history of sexuality: An introduction, volume 1.* New York: Vintage Books.

Gray, Mary. 2009. *Out in the country: Youth, media, and queer visibility in rural America.* New York: New York University Press.

Halberstam, Judith. 2005. *In a queer time and place: Transgender bodies, subcultural lives.* New York: New York University Press.

Hennen, Peter. 2008. *Fairies, bears, and leathermen: Men in community queering the masculine.* Chicago: University of Chicago Press.

Leonhardt, David, and Kevin Quealy. 2015. *How your hometown affects your chances of marriage. The New York Times,* May 15.

Howard, John. 1999. *Men like that: A Southern queer history.* Chicago: University of Chicago Press.

Humphreys, Laud. 1970. Tearoom trade: Impersonal sex in public places. *Transaction* 7 (3): 10–25.

Johnson, Colin. 2013. *Just queer folks: Gender and sexuality in rural America.* Philadelphia, PA: Temple University Press.

Kazyak, Emily. 2012. Midwest or lesbian? Gender, rurality, and sexuality. *Gender & Society* 26 (6): 825–48.

Katz, Jonathan. 1995. *The invention of heterosexuality.* New York: Dutton.

Kimmel, Michael. 1994. Masculinity as homophobia. In *Theorizing masculinities,* edited by Harry Brod and Michael Kaufman. Thousand Oaks, CA: Sage.

Kitzinger, Celia, and Sue Wilkinson. 1995. Transitions from heterosexuality to lesbianism: The discursive production of lesbian identities. *Developmental Psychology* 31 (1): 95–104.

Loe, Meika. 2001. Fixing broken masculinity: Viagra as a technology for the production of gender and sexuality. *Sexuality and Culture* 5 (3): 97–125.

McCormack, Mark. 2013. *The declining significance of homophobia.* Oxford: Oxford University Press.

Messner, Michael. 1993. "Changing men" and feminist politics in the United States. *Theory and Society* 22 (5): 723–37.

Morris, Edward. 2008. "Rednecks," "rutters," and 'rithmetic: Social class, masculinity, and schooling in a rural context. *Gender & Society* 22 (6): 728–51.

Pascoe, C. J. 2011. *Dude, you're a fag: Masculinity and sexuality in high school,* 2nd ed. Berkeley: University of California Press.

Pascoe, C. J., and Tristan Bridges, eds. 2016. *Exploring masculinities: Identity, inequality, continuity, and change.* New York: Oxford University Press.

Plummer, Ken. 1996. Symbolic interactionism and the forms of homosexuality. In *Queer theory/sociology,* edited by Steven Seidman. Cambridge, MA: Blackwell.

Reback, Cathy, and Sherry Larkins. 2010. Maintaining a heterosexual identity: Sexual meanings among a sample of heterosexually identified men who have sex with men. *Archives of Sexual Behavior* 39 (3): 766–73.

Reynolds, Chelsea. 2015. "I am super straight and I prefer you be too": Constructions of heterosexual masculinity in online personal ads for "straight" men seeking sex with men. *Journal of Communication Inquiry* 39 (3): 213–31.

Robinson, Brandon, and David Moskowitz. 2013. The eroticism of Internet cruising as a self-contained behavior: A multivariate analysis of men seeking men demographics and getting off online. *Culture, Health & Sexuality* 15 (5): 555–69.

Robinson, Brandon, and Salvador Vidal-Ortiz. 2013. Displacing the dominant "down low" discourse: Deviance, same-sex desire, and Craigslist.org. *Deviant Behavior* 34 (3): 224–41.

Rust, Paula. 1992. The politics of sexual identity: Sexual attraction and behavior among lesbian and bisexual women. *Social Problems* 39 (4): 366–86.

Sedgwick, Eve. 1990. *Epistemology of the closet.* Berkeley: University of California Press.

Seidman, Steven. 2002. *Beyond the closet: The transformation of gay and lesbian life.* London: Routledge.

Silva, Tony. Forthcoming. "Helpin' a buddy out": Perceptions of identity and behavior among rural straight men that have sex with each other. *Sexualities.*

Simon, William, and John Gagnon. 1986. Sexual scripts: Permanence and change. *Archives of Sexual Behavior* 15 (2): 97–120.

Stein, Arlene. 1989. Three models of sexuality: Drives, identities, and practices. *Sociological Theory* 7 (1): 1–13.

United States Census Bureau. 2016. Annual estimates of the resident population by sex, age, race alone or in combination, and Hispanic origin for the United States and states: April 1, 2010 to July 1, 2015. Washington, DC: United States Census Bureau, Population Division. http://factfinder.census.gov/faces/table-services/jsf/pages/productview.xhtml? src=bkmk#.

Ward, Jane. 2015. *Not gay: Sex between straight white men.* New York: New York University Press.

CHAPTER 30

A Very "Gay" Straight?

Hybrid Masculinities, Sexual Aesthetics, and the Changing Relationship Between Masculinity and Homophobia

Tristan Bridges

This article explores the gender and sexual dynamics of three groups of men—with varying commitments to feminist ideals (from anti- to pro-) and levels of interest in gender and sexual inequality (from highly concerned to apathetic)—to investigate heterosexual men's relationships with gender, sexuality, and inequality, and the potential for change embedded within a peculiar practice. Heterosexual men in each group defined aspects of themselves as "gay." But they did so in a way that allowed them to retain a "masculine" distance from homosexuality. The practice initially appears to be the mirror image of Connell's (1992) research on gay men classifying themselves as "a very straight gay." Rather than gay men co-opting elements of "straight" culture and style, I discuss straight men borrowing elements of "gay" culture and discursively framing themselves as "gay." Compared with Connell's (1992) "straight gay" men, however, the men in this study engage in this practice for different reasons and with distinct consequences. They rely on "gay aesthetics" to construct *hybrid masculinities* (Demetriou 2001; Messner 1993) that work to distance them in subtly different ways from stigmatizing stereotypes of masculinity.

While scholarship discusses homophobia as a fundamental element of contemporary masculine identities (Connell 1992; Herek 1986; Kimmel 1994; Lehne 1976; Pascoe 2007), the practices of the men I studied—straight men who identify with some "gay" cultural styles—appear to challenge this relationship. I theorize "sexual aesthetics" to make sense of this apparent contradiction. "Sexual aesthetics" refer to cultural and stylistic distinctions used to delineate boundaries between gay and straight cultures and individuals. The ways in which heterosexual men in each group deploy gay aesthetics reveal group-specific meanings and consequences. Broadly speaking, straight men's reliance on aspects of gay culture illustrates some of the ways that sexual prejudice, inequality, and the relationship between masculinity and homophobia are better understood as transforming than disappearing. Similar to other analyses of contemporary hybrid masculine practices, these men's behavior conceals privileges associated with white, heterosexual masculinity.

SOURCE: Bridges, T. (2014). A Very "Gay" Straight? Hybrid Masculinities, Sexual Aesthetics, and the Changing Relationship between Masculinity and Homophobia. *Gender & Society, 28*(1), 58–82. Reproduced with permission.

Hybrid Masculinities

Hybrid masculinities refer to gender projects that incorporate "bits and pieces" (Demetriou 2001) of marginalized and subordinated masculinities and, at times, femininities. "Hybrid" is used in the social sciences and humanities to address processes and practices of cultural integration or mixing (Burke 2009). Hybridity is a useful framework to address scholarship on contemporary transformations in masculine practices, performances, and politics (e.g., Anderson 2009; Arxer 2011; Barber 2008; Bridges 2010; Demetriou 2001; Heath 2003; Messerschmidt 2010; Messner 1993, 2007; Pascoe 2007; Schippers 2000; Ward 2008; Wilkins 2009). The fact that masculinities are changing is nothing new, but the incorporation of elements coded as "feminine" (Messerschmidt 2010; Messner 1993), "gay" (Bridges 2010; Demetriou 2001), or "Black" (Hughey 2012; Ward 2008) into white, heterosexual masculine identities and performances may be. Messner's (1993) analysis of high-profile men crying in public or new norms surrounding involvement among fathers is one example.

A central issue in research on hybrid masculinities is whether they challenge and/or perpetuate systems of inequality. There are three streams of research that address this question: One questions the extent of hybridization (e.g., Connell and Messerschmidt 2005); a second considers hybridization as pervasive and as illustrating a unilateral move toward greater gender and sexual equality (e.g., Anderson 2009; McCormack 2012); and a third—agreeing that hybridization is significant—argues that it perpetuates inequalities in new and "softer" ways (e.g., Demetriou 2001; Messner 1993).

Connell and Messerschmidt, briefly addressing hybrid masculinities, acknowledge that "specific masculine practices may be appropriated into other masculinities" (Connell and Messerschmidt 2005, 845). Yet, they are not convinced that hybrid masculine forms represent anything beyond local subcultural variation. Others have been less dismissive. For example, Anderson's (2009) theory of "inclusive masculinity" argues that contemporary transformations in men's behaviors and beliefs are pervasive and undermine gender and sexual hierarchies and inequality. While many stress an intimate connection between masculinity and homophobia (Kimmel 1994; Pascoe 2007), Anderson proposes that this connection exists only in social contexts with high levels of "homohysteria,"[1] a condition that, he argues, does not characterize contemporary Western societies (see also McCormack 2012). Anderson frames contemporary masculinities as characterized by increasing levels of "inclusivity" and equality.

The bulk of the literature agrees with Anderson that hybrid masculinities are widespread, but departs from him when analyzing their meanings and consequences. As Messner argues, hybrid masculinities represent highly significant (but exaggerated) shifts in the cultural and personal styles . . . but these changes do not necessarily contribute to the undermining of conventional structures of men's power. Although "softer" and more "sensitive" styles of masculinity are developing among some privileged groups of men, this does not necessarily contribute to the emancipation of women; in fact, quite the contrary may be true (Messner 1993, 725).

More recently, Messner (2007) theorized a culturally ascendant hybrid masculinity combining "toughness" with "tenderness" in ways that work to obscure power and inequality. Similarly, Demetriou (2001) addresses the appropriation of elements of subordinated and marginalized "Others" by white heterosexual men that ultimately work to recuperate white, heterosexual, masculine privilege. Focusing on the incorporation of gay male culture, Demetriou illustrates how hybrid masculinities can be understood as contemporary expressions of existing forms of inequality. "New, hybrid configurations of gender practice . . . enable [heterosexual men] to reproduce their dominance . . . in historically novel ways" (Demetriou 2001, 351). Like Messner, Demetriou theorizes hybrid masculinities as blurring gender differences and boundaries, but presenting no real challenges to inequality.

Sexual Aesthetics

The literature on hybrid masculinities focuses on the assimilation of aspects of cultures and performances associated with various marginalized and subordinated "Others." A significant strand in this research deals with the incorporation of "gay" cultural styles to enact masculine gender identities (e.g., Anderson 2009; Bridges 2010; Demetriou 2001; McCormack 2012; Pascoe 2007; Wilkins 2009). Theorizing the "aesthetic" elements of sexualities enables a more thorough analysis of the consequences of their incorporation into hybrid masculine identities and practices.

Connell's (1992) work on gay men who identify as "a very straight gay" is a useful illustration. Connell found that gay men's use of "straight" had less to do with cultural subversion and more to do with safety and gender identification. Gay men who incorporate elements of "straight" masculinity are a powerful illustration of the co-construction of gender and sexuality (e.g., Hennen 2005; Ocampo 2012; Ward 2008).

Ward's research on "dude sex"—white, heterosexual-identified men seeking sex with other heterosexual-identified men—highlights the aesthetic elements of sexuality as gendered and racialized as well. Ward theorizes "queer and straight as cultural spheres that people choose to inhabit in large part because they experience a cultural and political fit" (Ward 2008, 431). Similar to Connell's participants, the men in Ward's (2008) study rely on what I call "straight aesthetics" to craft identities as straight men. Sexual aesthetics play a central role in claims to cultural affiliations with both gay and straight culture, but affiliations with sexual cultures also involve more than simply claiming ownership of the "appropriate" aesthetics.

Sexualities are communicated and adopted to define one's self and others based on a wide array of sexual aesthetics. Sexual aesthetics refer to cultural and stylistic distinctions utilized to delineate symbolic boundaries between gay and straight cultures and individuals.

A variety of things can "count" as sexual aesthetics: interests, material objects, styles of bodily comportment, language, opinions, clothing, and behaviors.

Like hybrid masculinities, there is a dual potential embedded within sexual aesthetics to challenge and/or reproduce inequality. Whether this potential is realized is an empirical question. While capable of being used to subvert gender and sexual boundaries and inequality, this shift can also work to obscure inequality in new ways by relying on an aesthetic discourse that (implicitly) disregards its existence.

Data and Methods

I selected groups of men for this study based on two axes of variation: their gender-political affiliations and the level of reflexivity with which they consider gender-political concerns. The three groups vary on both axes[2]: fathers' rights activists, pro-feminist men, and a group without formal gender-political affiliation—bar regulars. The majority of the men in my sample are white (56 of 63) and all but two identify as heterosexual (61 of 63).

Men Can Parent Too is a fathers' rights activist organization attempting to raise awareness about and protest what they perceive as gender inequality in divorce and custody proceedings. Ask any member if gender inequality exists and he will give you an answer similar to Dave, a 35-year-old lawyer who volunteers his time providing information and support to divorcing fathers: "Men and women are not equal. It's really as simple as that. Women get more than men. They get more from men in their marriages just like they get more when those marriages break up. Inequality exists. Men are getting screwed."

Guys for Gender Justice is a pro-feminist group of men who meet regularly to discuss gender and sexual inequality, raise money for nonprofit organizations dealing with violence against women, and volunteer for feminist organizations and causes. Ask a member about the existence of gender inequality, and he will likely tell you something akin to Dan, a 25-year-old graphic designer: "Women have been getting the shaft for millennia. . . . Men don't get how they are actually a part of it. Women and men are unequal and we all have a part to play to fix it."

The Border Boys are a group of bar regulars at a small, privately owned restaurant and bar. Their weekly meetings are less structured than the other two groups, though no less frequent. They are also less reflexive about gender and inequality, but gender, sexuality, and inequality are popular topics of conversation. Ask one of The Border Boys whether gender inequality exists and he might give you an answer like Jeffrey's, a 29-year-old restaurant employee still uncertain of his life ambitions: "I don't know. . . . Actually, let me qualify that: I don't care. If men and women are unequal, they are, and if not, they're not. Everybody has to deal with the shit they are dealt."

Each of the groups kept regular meeting times. I observed participants both in and out of their meeting settings. I informally interviewed men throughout the study, but formal, in-depth, semi-structured interviews were conducted at the conclusion of my study as well.

A Very "Gay" Straight?

Dan is a member of Guys for Gender Justice, a group he says meets for two purposes:

> We . . . talk about how guys are a part of inequality and how we can change that. . . . We try to, like, volunteer our time and stuff to other groups . . . You know, that are for gender equality. . . . So, basically, we say we're feminist in two ways: how we think and how we act.

I asked whether the majority of the members of his organization identified as heterosexual. "They're straight . . . they're all straight," Dan told me. Jokingly, he continued, "And it's funny, 'cause we're all involved in this totally *gay* thing, but we're all straight . . . you know?" When I asked whether Dan also identified as straight, his response was interesting: "Yeah, I'm straight. I've always been straight. . . . But actually, I'm also pretty gay in *how* I'm straight."

Identifying Gay Aesthetics

When I began my study of Men Can Parent Too, Dave—the group organizer—and I talked in his office at a small law firm about the group and my research. I told him I was interested in studying men who were attempting to figure out "how to be a man." Dave immediately responded that I'd "want to meet" Luke. Luke was getting a divorce because he had recently come out as gay. He came to the group after recently separating from his wife and concerned that he would lose access to his children.

When Luke first talked with me about deciding to come out, he discussed the realization of how it might affect his relationship with his children (because of both his wife's feelings about homosexuality and Luke's struggle to obtain steady employment). He had some difficult, but interesting, things to say. I asked whether he always knew he was gay: "Well, I *was* always gay, but also not . . . I mean, I was gay even when I was straight . . . I always had, you know, certain things about me that made me realize . . . you know, little things, but important still." When asked about the "little things," Luke illustrates his understanding of the nuances of gay aesthetics:

> I mean, I didn't play with dolls or anything . . . though I might have if my mother let me [laughs] . . . I mean, I like fish more than steak, you know? I don't like cars or driving. I actually prefer to bike or walk. Just little things like that. I prefer to go to museums over action movies. I'd rather watch the Food Network than something like "The Man Show." I'm just gay!

Here, Luke relies on gay aesthetics to identify the seeds of belonging to gay culture long before adopting a gay identity. Specific features of life narratives are an important piece of gay identities; having the "right" sexual aesthetics is often part of framing oneself as *authentically* gay. Interestingly, the gay aesthetics Luke discusses are also markers of class status (e.g., Halperin 2012; Valocchi 1999). Straight participants in this study also framed middle- and upper-class tastes as "gay."

At Guys for Gender Justice meetings, men often discussed having been mistaken for gay. Shane shared one experience:

> People sometimes think I'm gay. . . . They just think I, like, might be or something. . . . I take it as an opportunity to help gay people. . . . I'll usually say something like, "Because I'm stylish? Or because I'm nice to people?. . . What? Because I'm healthy and care about my clothes and the way I look?" You know? Like, "Oh, because I have good taste in music?"

Shane's point here illustrates one way he resists heterosexism: by strategically reframing the implications of being called "gay." Rather than as an insult, Shane reinterprets the "insult" as a compliment by guessing at why he might be taken for gay and claiming those traits as his own. While attempting to neutralize differences, however, Shane's comments simultaneously reinforce symbolic boundaries separating gay from straight by (re)classifying those tastes and behaviors as gay.

A separate way that gay aesthetics were identified was through the use of "gaydar"—a portmanteau combining "gay" and "radar." "Gaydar" was discussed by men in all three groups to suggest that an individual was particularly well attuned to gay aesthetics, or to more forcefully argue that gay men are easily identified. Henry, one of The Border Boys, illustrates one use:

> I just have good gaydar. . . . I'm not gay, but I know the signs. . . . I have gay friends. . . . Actually, some gay guys I know think I have better gaydar than them. . . . I'm in the know, that's all I'm saying.

Henry's use here was similar to the ways that "gaydar" was employed by men in Guys for Gender Justice as well. "Gaydar" was used most frequently by the pro-feminist men. Andrew, a young economics professor at a community college, said:

> My gaydar is pretty sensitive. . . . It's not that I'm, like, always on the lookout or whatever, but my gaydar picks it up [cups his hand above his head, imitating a satellite dish]. I think when you're involved in a group like [Guys for Gender Justice], you're just thinking about more than your average man on the street. Gaydar's part of that.

While Henry's and Andrew's uses of gaydar are fairly innocent, both participate in the reification of sexual differences. Beyond that, they demonstrate some of the ways these men framed themselves as *different from* and often *better than* "most men" by claiming a better cultural (and sometimes political) "fit" (Ward 2008) with gay culture, illustrated by their knowledge of and comfort with gay aesthetics.

On the Elements of Gay Aesthetics

In an interview with Richard (The Border Boys), he told me: "I'm emotional, man. I cry at movies. I cry when my friends hurt my feelings. . . . That's what you need to know. I'm not your average man . . . all masculine and all that. . . . And if that makes me gay then fuck it, I'm gay . . . but, of course, I'm not *gaaaay.*" When pressed to explain, Richard delineated some of the elements that make up gay aesthetics:

Well, of course, it's gay if you go like this [cocks his wrists] and if you're all pansy or whatever. It's gay to talk like this [affects his voice]. But, it's also gay if you're, like, into how you look too much. . . . It's gay if you're all emotional . . . like if you cry or . . . or even if you care too much about your friends. That's gay! It's gay to read, or . . . like, if you like novels rather than books. That's fucking gay. It's also gay to be into gay rights . . . or even women's rights. That's totally gay! Basically, being kinda gay could be a lot of things. . . . For me . . . I'm gay in like how I'm not all into bein' manly.

As Richard explains, gay aesthetics are composed of diverse elements. For the purposes of this article, I discuss three: (1) Sexual aesthetics can be *tastes*, as Richard characterizes concern with appearance or interest in certain kinds of literature as gay; (2) sexual aesthetics can be *behavioral*, such as Richard's mention of bodily comportment and speech patterns; (3) sexual aesthetics can be *ideological*, as Richard identifies support for certain issues as gay.

Tastes

Similar to Luke's analysis of his preferences for museums, seafood, and certain kinds of television programs, straight men in each group identified some of their own tastes as gay. Ralph, a member of Men Can Parent Too, made similar comments:

Ralph:	The guys I work with are just not the same kinda guy as me. . . . All of 'em . . . want action. . . . I'm just trying to be a dad and make a paycheck. . . . I actually am not all into this action . . . You know . . . like, an action kinda mindset . . . I don't drink beer. . . . I really don't like it. I mainly drink wine. But, I'm gay like that and it doesn't bug me.
Interviewer:	What do you mean?
Ralph:	Oh, no . . . no, no, no. I'm not a fag or something like that. I just mean I'm into kinda gay stuff like that, you know? I mean, you've been over to my house. I'm a neat freak. It's just how I am.

Only men in The Border Boys and Men Can Parent Too used the word "fag." Ralph's use strategically distances himself from homosexuality, illustrating how men can utilize gay aesthetics while simultaneously promoting gender and sexual inequality. Thus, Ralph's reliance on gay aesthetics to discursively distance himself from a stereotype of masculinity is not necessarily indicative of a weakening relationship between masculinity and homophobia or sexual prejudice (e.g., Anderson 2009). Rather, it illustrates the ways that hybrid masculine practices can perpetuate inequality in new ways (Demetriou 2001; Messner 1993).

All three groups talked about various tastes as gay as a way of creating some symbolic distance between themselves and "other men." Only men in Guys for Gender Justice, however, also attempted to garner status as politically progressive by employing gay aesthetics. Many members of Guys for Gender Justice excitedly shared experiences of being "confused for gay." Indeed, at several group meetings, this kind of storytelling often turned into a contest. The youngest member of the group, Peter, explained:

People always think I'm gay . . . always! . . . People meet me and they just don't know what to do with me. They see what I wear and . . . and they see how I talk. . . . Maybe I'm just too nice. Maybe that's the problem. I always tell people that I constantly have to come out . . . . I come out as straight every time I meet someone new . . . I mean, I was in the closet and I didn't even know it. That's me, though . . . [pursing his lips] I like to sprinkle some gay on my straight.

Peter's comments frame his appearance and demeanor as gay. Like Ralph, Peter uses gay aesthetics to discursively situate himself as a hybrid masculinity. The practice allows both men to distance themselves from stereotypes of masculinity. But, unlike Ralph, Peter also attempts to frame himself as politically progressive. Peter proudly flaunts being "mistaken for gay," and later matter-of-factly stated, "It's basically impossible to be homophobic if people think you're gay." In the process, however, Peter implicitly neutralizes power relations that make "the closet" a meaningful metaphor. The closet is born from social oppression, requiring individuals to conceal their identities (Seidman 2002). Peter's use casually disguises heterosexual privilege and implicitly deflates claims to sexual inequality made by truly gay individuals. While much less overt than Ralph's use of the word "fag," Peter's discursive performance more indirectly constructs his own straight identity through a disavowal of gay identity.

Similarly, and somewhat ironically, Travis, a member of The Border Boys, identified himself as gay because of his interest in women:

> I'm into hanging out with women . . . I'm not a man's man or whatever. I'm more of a woman's man. I like art, jazz, and . . . I hate to say it this way, but I just actually think I'm a lot better than [The Border Boys]. . . . Sure, some of that is gay . . . but I mean . . . sometimes I feel like I really get along with gay men. . . . We just have a lot of things in common, with one *really* big difference.

Travis defines himself as distinct from The Border Boys. This was a common practice among all of The Border Boys, though not all of them sought to illustrate the ways they perceived themselves to be different with gay aesthetics. It is also significant that while Travis never said "fag" (as Ralph did), he is similarly careful to disavow gay identity by explaining the "*really* big difference" between *having* gay tastes and *being* gay.

These men are all participating in an essentialist discourse that reestablishes boundaries between gay and straight individuals and cultures. While all of the men are interested in framing themselves as different from "most men," some of them (particularly those in Guys for Gender Justice) also use gay aesthetics to frame themselves as politically tolerant. Thus, as Gary (Guys for Gender Justice) said, "If people thinking you're gay doesn't bug you, it's a good sign that you're on the right side." Yet, as Peter illustrates, men in Guys for Gender Justice also "outed" themselves as straight in various ways.

This illustrates something important about the straight men's use of gay aesthetics in this study—the practice was not associated with an understanding of sexual aesthetics as part of systems of power and inequality.

Behaviors

A second dimension of gay aesthetics is behavioral—inscribing sexual meaning to individuals' actions. For instance, Doug, a therapist and member of Guys for Gender Justice, explained to the group, "You can't hide your sexuality . . . You can try, but it comes out. Gay guys are more flamboyant and they can't hold it in. . . . It's science." Doug's comment illustrates how beliefs about gay aesthetics come to be more than just beliefs. In fact, there is a history of people looking for behavioral "tells" of gay identity such that many individuals carefully control presentations of self to guard against inadvertently disclosing their latent desires. The behavioral dimensions of gay aesthetics are typically signifiers of gender as well, illustrating the co-construction of gender and sexuality (Pascoe 2007; Schippers 2000; Ward 2008). Gender transgressive behavior was understood as a gay aesthetic among all three groups, though only members of Guys for Gender Justice and The Border Boys discussed some of their own behaviors as gay.

Henry (The Border Boys) claimed the behavioral dimension of gay aesthetics: "That's just me. I'm not gay . . . but I've got flair, dude." Affecting his voice, he continued, "I've got tons of flair and I don't care." Laughing, Jeffrey rejoined, "This is my fucking voice, man. It's the way I talk." Jeffrey has a higher-pitched voice and enunciates. They laughed at themselves as fitting what they consider behavioral cues associated with homosexuality despite identifying as straight. While neither Henry nor Jeffrey used the phrase "mistaken for gay," this is part of the same discourse. They participate in promoting stereotypes of effeminacy as a natural part of being a gay man by identifying with aspects of these qualities.

Behavioral gay aesthetics were much more common among members of Guys for Gender Justice. A conversation between these two illustrates this dynamic:

Peter: I mean . . . I don't know. I walk, sit, and talk funny. I just do. Actually, I get a lot of shit for it. I'm just more . . . you know. I'm ladylike . . . but it's like, get over yourself.

Gary: I actually get that at school. I had a group of students ask me if I was gay. I asked, "And why would you think that?" They said that it was because . . . how I speak or wave my hands around . . . I was like, "What?" I teach English, you know? I'm being emphatic!

Peter: Exactly . . . but who cares? I like the attention . . .

Gary: I don't mind either. If the way I speak makes you think I'm gay, think away. . . . Some of the greatest writers of all times were gay. . . .

Peter and Gary are conscious of the ways they believe their behavior is interpreted and "don't mind." Indeed, many of the men in Guys for Gender Justice discussed identification with gay aesthetics as a reason for joining the group.

Ideologies

A third dimension of gay aesthetics is ideological. Ideological stances taken by individuals can be marked with sexual meaning. Feminism was the most frequently discussed ideology with sexual connotations. Situating masculinity and feminism as opposed causes men's engagements with feminism to be understood as emasculating (Bridges 2010). The men in this study were acutely aware of this fact. For instance, when Dan (Guys for Gender Justice) says, "They're straight . . . they're all straight. And it's funny, 'cause we're all involved in this totally gay thing," he is referring to feminism. Similarly, and noted above, Richard (The Border Boys) states, "It's . . . gay to be into gay rights . . . or even women's rights. That's totally gay!"

Of all the groups, only Guys for Gender Justice utilized ideological positions to identify aspects of themselves as gay. This highlights an important distinction between the groups. All three relied on gay aesthetics to distance themselves from what they understood as stigmatizing stereotypes of masculinity. But only the pro-feminist men also relied on gay aesthetics to situate themselves as authentically politically progressive. Indeed, they seemed to be attempting to discursively "queer" themselves to demonstrate their feminist convictions.

Saul (Guys for Gender Justice) epitomizes this position. When we met, he was wearing a T-shirt with "Feminist chicks dig me!" on the front and an AIDS awareness ribbon on his bag.

I initially got involved with a sexual violence resource center as a volunteer. . . . All the ladies I worked with there . . . they all totally thought I was gay. . . . It's funny how people think you're gay if you, like, are for gay marriage. . . . Apparently even being against sexual violence is gay. . . . It's like clothes. . . . I don't wear straight guy clothes and I don't have straight guy politics . . . and to be perfectly honest, that's one of a few reasons I'm different from most guys. I'm better.

Nearly every member of Guys for Gender Justice mentioned something about how their involvement with feminism related to their gender and sexual identities, framing their affiliation with gay issues as a mark of distinction. By subjectively framing themselves as having a variety of gay aesthetics, they discursively attempted to "prove" this.

On Motivations and Consequences

Thomas, a member of The Border Boys, is openly gay, Black, and though he was present fewer nights a week than the others, he was central to the group when he joined them at the bar. He spoke directly about straight men's interest in an affiliation with gay men and how he believes this has changed:

> When I was in college, having a friend who was gay, even if people just thought he was gay, meant you were gay . . . like, having a gay friend [now] is totally in. . . . If you've got a gay friend . . . you aren't a piece of shit. People think gay people are really discriminating too, I think . . . If you hang out with a gay person, you must be really "down" or whatever.

Thomas's assertion seems to have been correct, but much more so for men in The Border Boys and Guys for Gender Justice than those in Men Can Parent Too.

Many members of Guys for Gender Justice felt that heterosexuality was somewhat dull and meaningless, and voiced a desire to distance themselves from stereotypes of masculinity. This seemed to be a primary motivation for relying on gay aesthetics. Jacob (Guys for Gender Justice) put it this way:

> Being straight is lame. There's just nothing exciting about saying, "Mom, Dad . . . I turned out just like you expected." . . . There was a time when I actually really wanted to be gay . . . not to, like, get with guys or whatever . . . but just 'cause . . . gay people are just more fun. Straight men are probably the most boring, cardboard people ever. So, I certainly do stuff that makes people question if I'm gay or not, 'cause I might not be gay, but I'm not going to be a robot.

Jacob explains some of the reasons that he "queers" his performance of masculinity. It's a contradictory practice, and all of the men in this study either smiled or laughed when I asked them to talk more about calling aspects of themselves gay. They did so in ways that implied the answer was self-evident, at least to them.

Similarly, Doug (Guys for Gender Justice) said, "Guys . . . hold that . . . straight guys are pretty boring for the most part. That's part of the reason I joined this group. . . . They might be straight, but they fooled me when I first met 'em." Doug and Jacob not only distance themselves from "most men," but also use gay aesthetics to forge hybrid masculinities that are experienced as more exciting than the options they perceive themselves as having access to as young, straight, white men.

Like Jacob and Doug, almost all of the men presented themselves as unique from other men, as Bob's (Men Can Parent Too) comments illustrate as we talked in the office of a restaurant he manages:

> Being a regular guy is, like, being a regular dad . . . it's not good enough. . . . If you want to go through your whole life playing by all the rules, you're gonna be a kinda "Who cares?" kinda guy. Most guys just wanna prove they're, like, tough guys or something. I'm not like that . . . I mean, in some ways I think my marriage ended 'cause I'm just not an average guy.

Men in each group echoed Bob's expressing an urge to distance himself from "regular guys." Yet, what qualified as a "regular guy" was subtly different among the three groups. For instance, Bob relied on gay aesthetics as a mechanism symbolically creating some discursive space between himself and "tough guys." Bob later said,

> It's gay that I'm all into my family. I get teased [by some of my employees] for havin' pictures of my kids all up in my office. They say, "That's gay!" and all that. And I'm like, "Okay, I'm gay, then." You know? If yer not a dickwad, you get called gay. . . . I'll just be like, "I'd rather be gay than a dick."

Bob is not attempting to distance himself from *all* heterosexual men here—just *those* heterosexual men (the "dickwads"). It's a discursive strategy allowing him to create some rhetorical space in which he frames his own masculinity as not the "real problem."

The men in this study utilized gay aesthetics to fill the perceived emptiness of straight masculinities—but they maintained a heterosexual identity and thus continued to benefit from the privileges associated with heterosexuality. This finding corroborates Seidman's claim that gender and sexual inequality are alive and well, but something significant has changed: "the formation of a self-conscious, deliberate public culture of heterosexuality" (Seidman 2002, 115). Thus, while perhaps insensitive, Peter's comment "I come out as straight every time I meet someone new" is indicative of this transformation. This change, however, does not necessarily indicate that inequality no longer exists or that masculinity's relationship with homophobia is disappearing. Rather, it is part of a hybridization of masculinity that works in ways that obscure contemporary inequality (e.g., Demetriou 2001; Messner 1993; Messerschmidt 2010).

Straight men's use of gay aesthetics may illustrate that stereotypes of homosexuality are not viewed negatively by all straight men. Yet, this simple change is not sufficient evidence of a unilateral move toward greater gender and sexual equality (e.g., Anderson 2009; McCormack 2012). Rather, these findings corroborate other research on contemporary hybrid masculine forms (Demetriou 2001; Messerschmidt 2010; Messner 1993, 2007), suggesting that they are pervasive and work to obscure (rather than weaken) existing systems of power and inequality. Thus, as Demetriou writes, "Hybridization in the realm of representation and in concrete, everyday practices make [new iterations of inequality] appear less oppressive and more egalitarian" (Demetriou 2001, 355).

First, the belief in the pre-social nature of gay aesthetics is part of an essentialist discourse that identifies and fortifies symbolic sexual boundaries between gay and straight aesthetics, and solidifies social boundaries between gay and straight individuals. These men's identity work could contribute to disrupting gendered sexual boundaries by illustrating our collective capacity to "play" with gender and sexual aesthetics. Yet, in practice, these men's behaviors are best understood as reinvigorating symbolic sexual boundaries and recuperating gender and sexual privilege in historically novel ways.

Second, these men—seemingly unintentionally—capitalize on symbolic sexual boundaries to distance themselves from specific configurations of hegemonic masculinity, but not necessarily the associated privileges. The effect is to disguise gender and sexual privilege by crafting hybrid masculinities with gay aesthetics. By framing themselves as gay, they obscure the ways they benefit from being young, mostly white, heterosexual men.

Third, straight men's reliance on gay aesthetics to enrich their heterosexual gender identities implicitly softens more authentic claims to sexual inequality. As Doug put it, "Face it, gay guys are just more colorful. . . . They're just more fun." The men in Guys for Gender Justice were motivated to engage in this practice out of more than a desire to distance themselves from stigmatized masculinities (i.e., to prove feminist authenticity). But, comments like Doug's were common among this group and illustrate that the practice is also a hybrid masculine strategy associated with cultural miscegenation and its associated problems and critiques.

For the men in this study, heterosexuality lacked the luster of an identity forged in a struggle for equal rights and recognition. However, while they symbolically invert the sexual hierarchy for aesthetics (i.e., gay is more desirable that straight), they simultaneously maintain heteronormative hierarchies for sexual acts, desires, and orientations. By casually framing being gay only as fun and exciting, this practice allows these men to ignore the persistence of extreme sexual inequality and the hardships that actual gay men face every day.

Conclusion

Hybrid masculinities illustrate the flexibility of contemporary masculinities (perhaps particularly young, white, straight masculinities), and straight men's reliance on gay aesthetics is one kind of hybridization. These "gay straight" men might appear to blur the boundaries between gay and straight through assimilating a variety of gay aesthetics. Yet, this move toward "inclusivity" (Anderson 2009) can be interpreted in more than one way and does not necessarily indicate declining levels of gender and sexual inequality. Research and theory suggest a more nuanced interpretation of the motivations behind and consequences of these kinds of practices. Straight men who identify aspects of themselves as gay in this study draw on varied resources to simultaneously assert heterosexual masculine identities, to distance themselves from stigmatizing stereotypes of masculinity, and—for some—to communicate authentic allegiance with groups to which they claim no formal membership.

Consistent with other research implying that hybridization may be a social practice more available to socially privileged groups of men (e.g., young, straight, and white), this research also implies that the existence of hybrid masculinities does not inherently imply that social inequalities are diminishing. Rather, as Messner (1993, 2007), Demetriou (2001), and Messerschmidt (2010) all argue, this research supports the notion that hybrid masculinities are perpetuating inequality in new (and less easily identifiable) ways. Using Messner's (1993) language, these practices are illustrative of a transformation in the "style but not substance" of contemporary gender and sexual inequality.

Notes

1. "Homohysteria" is a measure of popular awareness of gay identity, disapproval of homosexuality, and the extent to which homophobia is fundamental to masculine identification.

2. Messner (1997) situates fathers' rights groups and pro-feminist groups of men at the poles of men's gender-political activism in the United States.

References

Anders, John. 1999. *Willa Cather's sexual aesthetics and the male homosexual literary tradition.* Lincoln: University of Nebraska Press.

Anderson, Eric. 2009. *Inclusive masculinity.* New York: Routledge.

Arxer, Steven L. 2011. Hybrid masculine power: Reconceptualizing the relationship between homosociality and hegemonic masculinity. *Humanity & Society* 35:390–422.

Attwood, Feona. 2007. No money shot? Commerce, pornography and new sex taste cultures. *Sexualities* 10:441–56.

Barber, Kristen. 2008. The well-coiffed man: Class, race, and heterosexual masculinity in the hair salon. *Gender & Society* 22:455–76.

Blumer, Herbert. 1954. What is wrong with social theory? *American Sociological Review* 19:3–10.

Bridges, Tristan. 2010. Men just weren't made to do this: Performances of drag at "Walk a Mile in Her Shoes" marches. *Gender & Society* 24:5–30.

Burke, Peter. 2009. *Cultural hybridity.* Malden, MA: Polity Press.

Butler, Judith. 1990. *Gender trouble.* New York: Routledge.

Connell, Raewyn W. 1992. A very straight gay. *American Sociological Review* 57:735–51.

Connell, Raewyn W., and James Messerschmidt. 2005. Hegemonic masculinity: Rethinking the concept. *Gender & Society* 19:829–59.

Demetriou, Demetrakis. 2001. Connell's concept of hegemonic masculinity: A critique. *Theory and Society* 30:337–61.

Deutsch, Francine. 2007. Undoing gender. *Gender & Society* 21:106–27.

Gates, Eugene. 1988. The female voice. *Journal of Aesthetic Education* 22:59–68.

Halperin, David. 2012. *How to be gay.* Cambridge, MA: Harvard University Press.

Heath, Melanie. 2003. Soft-boiled masculinity: Renegotiating gender and racial ideologies in the Promise Keepers movement. *Gender & Society* 17:423–44.

Hennen, Peter. 2005. Bear bodies, bear masculinity. *Gender & Society* 19:25–43.

Herek, Gregory. 1986. On heterosexual masculinity. *American Behavioral Scientist* 29:563–77.

hooks, bell. 1992. Eating the other. In *Black looks: Race and representation.* Boston: South End Press.

Hughey, Matthew. 2012. *White bound.* Stanford, CA: Stanford University Press.

Kimmel, Michael. 1994. Masculinity as homophobia. In *Theorizing masculinities*, edited by Harry Brod and Michael Kaufman. Thousand Oaks, CA: Sage.

Lehne, Gregory. 1976. Homophobia among Men. In *The forty-nine percent majority*, edited by Deborah David and Robert Brannon. Reading, MA: Addison-Wesley.

McCormack, Mark. 2012. *The declining significance of homophobia.* New York: Oxford University Press.

Messerschmidt, James. 2010. *Hegemonic masculinities and camouflaged politics.* Boulder, CO: Paradigm.

Messner, Michael. 1993. "Changing men" and feminist politics in the United States. *Theory and Society* 22:723–37.

Messner, Michael. 1997. *Politics of masculinities.* New York: Alta Mira.

Messner, Michael. 2007. The masculinity of the Governator. *Gender & Society* 21: 461–80.

Ocampo, Anthony. 2012. Making masculinity: Negotiations of gender presentation among Latino gay men. *Latino Studies* 10:448–72.

Pascoe, CJ. 2007. *Dude, you're a fag.* Berkeley: University of California Press.

Pfeil, Fred. 1995. *White guys.* New York: Verso Books.

Russell, Bertrand. 1937. The superior virtue of the oppressed. *The Nation* 26: 731–32.

Savran, David. 1998. *Taking it like a man.* Princeton, NJ: Princeton University Press.

Schippers, Mimi. 2000. The social organization of sexuality and gender in alternative hard rock. *Gender & Society* 14:747–64.

Seidman, Steven. 1996. Introduction. In *Queer theory/sociology*, edited by Steven Seidman. Oxford, UK: Blackwell.

Seidman, Steven. 2002. *Beyond the closet.* New York: Routledge.

Small, Mario Luis. 2009. How many cases do I need? *Ethnography* 10:5–38.

Stein, Arlene, and Ken Plummer. 1994. "I can't even think straight": "Queer" theory and the missing sexual revolution in sociology. *Sociological Theory* 12:178–87.

Strauss, Anselm, and Juliet Corbin. 1998. *The basics of qualitative research.* New York: Routledge.

Valocchi, Steve. 1999. The class-inflected nature of gay identity. *Social Problems* 46:207–24.

Ward, Jane. 2008. Dude-sex: White masculinities and "authentic" heterosexuality among dudes who have sex with dudes. *Sexualities* 11:414–34.

Wilkins, Amy. 2004. Puerto Rican wannabes. *Gender & Society* 18:103–21.

Wilkins, Amy. 2009. Masculinity dilemmas. *Signs* 34:343–68.

PART VII

Violence and Resistance

The final section of this volume returns to a core theme of the opening section: the importance of understanding how power structures masculinity and gendered practices. Specifically, these readings focus on how masculine power is expressed through violence, and efforts to curb gender-based violence. As Raewyn Connell writes in reading no. 1, while hegemony is marked more by the "claim to authority" than "direct violence," hegemony is backed by the threat and use of violence.

The first reading (no. 31) by Christian A. Vaccaro and his colleagues, "Managing Emotional Manhood," takes us into the brutal world of mixed martial arts (MMA). This combat sport has become a popular participant and fan activity in the last two decades, especially since the establishment of the Ultimate Fighting Championship (UFC) in the early 1990s. Given the violence and potential for injury in the sport, the researchers found that men who participate in amateur MMA work deliberately to manage fear: to control their own fear so they could participate in the sport, and to foster fear in their opponents. The authors suggest that this form of emotional management constitutes a manhood act (see reading no. 3).

The second reading (no. 32), Christina M. Alcalde's "Masculinities in Motion," analyzes the link between men's weakening institutional power and male violence against women. Alcalde interviewed Latino men who had assaulted their female partners and were required by courts to take part in a batterer intervention program. Her interviews revealed that the men's migration to the United States led to anxiety and feelings of a loss of power. For instance, the men, as undocumented immigrants, were in a precarious position in the workforce. Alcalde found that these men turned to using violence against their partners inside the home in response to a sense of powerlessness in public. Alcalde's chapter raises important questions about the troubling causes and consequences of gender-based violence in multiply marginalized communities.

Our volume concludes with three exciting new contributions, all of which address men's efforts to address violence against women. The first of these readings, "Reaching Out and Digging In" by Juliana Carlson (reading no. 33), documents the global reach of this work, which the World Health Organization has called an international epidemic. Carlson summarizes key findings from her research with several colleagues on the goals and challenges in engaging men in the work to prevent gender-based violence around the world, in organizations such as MenEngage and HeforShe. While Carlson offers an aerial view of important gender-based violence prevention efforts, Max A. Greenberg's chapter, "The Former Lives of Anti-Sexist Men" (reading no. 34), takes us into the lives of four men who have done this work. (Greenberg's reading builds on his work with Michael A. Messner and Tal Peretz in the book *Some Men: Feminist Allies and the Movement to End Violence Against Women*.) Greenberg's use of life history narratives reveals the particular "sensitizing experiences" that encourage these men to take up work against gender-based violence. There is Robert, a white man in his 40s who was exposed to domestic violence as a child and eventually came to work full-time with an anti-violence organization; JJ, a young black man and father who viewed anti-violence work as a way of modeling a healthier masculinity for youth; Jose, a Mexican immigrant who saw capitalism as a barrier to social justice work; and Randy, an accomplished high school student who was inspired to join an anti-violence club after hearing a guest speaker in his health class.

Last is reading no. 35, "College Men, Hypermasculinity, and Sexual Violence" by Richard Mora and Mary Christianakis. The authors first discuss how homosocial spaces such as fraternities and men's sports teams promote hypermasculine behavior and harmful behaviors against women (and other men). They next turn to Mora's own involvement with an anti–sexual assault group, Oxy Men Against Rape (OMAR), at the authors' home institution of Occidental College. The mission of OMAR was to "educate and mobilize men to create cultures free of all forms of sexual violence." The authors share the pledges the OMAR members took to fighting sexual violence, and discuss challenges to sustaining a group like OMAR on college campuses.

Questions to Ponder

1. While Vaccaro and his coauthors examined a unique population of mixed martial arts fighters, they develop a concept—emotional manhood—that could be applied to many settings. Think of other high-stakes situations where men (and women) are required to control their fear and the fear of others.

2. As with a number of readings in this volume, Alcalde demonstrates that men see violence as a legitimate response to social turmoil. However, unlike more privileged men, the Latino men in her study were institutionally disempowered, and most closely embodied a "marginalized" masculinity in Connell's typology. How can a model of hegemonic masculinity help to explain differences in the violence perpetrated privileged and disadvantaged men? And the consequences that violence has for partners, children, and communities?

3. Carlson describes the challenges in recruiting men to participate in gender-based violence work. One concern is male privilege. Organizations have tried to use welcoming messages to recruit men—and even "tiptoe" around sensitive topics—but at the same time try not to "collude" with male privilege. How can organizations recruit men into this work while also contesting male privilege? (Note that Mora and Christianakis also identify male privilege as one challenge to sustaining anti-rape groups on college campuses.)

4. The four men in Greenberg's study, who come from diverse backgrounds, take part in counter-hegemonic projects, or work that actively contests the practices of hegemonic masculinity. How do we reconcile these projects with manhood acts?

5. The readings by Carlson, Greenberg, and Mora and Christianakis document the challenges in starting and supporting long-term efforts to involve men in work against gender-based violence. What can be done to support this kind of work? And can you think of other challenges to engaging men in this work?

Key Concepts

Counter-hegemonic projects   Gender-based violence   Migration
Emotional manhood   Hypermasculinity

Reference

Messner, Michael A., Max A. Greenberg, and Tal Peretz. 2015. *Some Men: Feminist Allies and the Movement to End Violence Against Women*. New York: Oxford University Press.

CHAPTER 31

Managing Emotional Manhood

Fighting and Fostering Fear in Mixed Martial Arts

Christian A. Vaccaro, Douglas P. Schrock, and Janice M. McCabe

While fighters in the locker room prepared for combat in the cage, two men from the previous fight staggered in. Juan[1]—the victor—had shiny contusions under both eyes and made it to a folding chair where he sat staring into space. As two paramedics tried to keep him conscious, he cracked a smile with swollen lips and tried unsuccessfully to communicate meaningfully. As the paramedics carried Juan off on a stretcher, Mike—his opponent—leaned against a wall and talked with his trainer. As blood flowed from his nose and mouth, Mike began to sob. His trainer handed him a towel, which he brought to his face with shaking hands. When asked if he was upset about Juan, he pulled away the bloodied towel and said, "I don't like losing."

Juan and Mike's post-fight experiences highlight what competitors of mixed martial arts (MMA) most often say they fear: injury and losing. Competitions generally occur in a locked cage and fighters wear thin, open-fingered gloves and are allowed to punch, kick, wrestle, and use martial arts techniques. Fights are broken into rounds and end when one fighter submits or "taps out" due to pain or exhaustion, is rendered unconscious, is deemed physically unable to continue by a referee, or time runs out. Preparing for these fights entails not only perfecting "guillotine chokes" and "superman punches," it also involves fighting fear.

Although MMA fighters' emotion management may appear unique, it reflects a long-lived cultural mandate that "real men" control their fear and other emotions (Kimmel 1996). Peers (Fine 1987), parents (McGuffey 2008), and coaches (Messner 1992) often ostracize boys who express fear, pain, empathy, and sadness. Boys learn that they are supposed to exhibit emotional restraint and "quiet control" (Messner 2009:96). But how do men control their emotions, and what does this have to with gender identity?

Scholars of emotion management—the process through which people suppress or evoke emotions (Hochschild 1979)—are particularly well suited to address this question. A sizable literature on gender and emotion work has developed. The dominant approach has been to neglect men and focus exclusively on how women do emotion work as subordinates at work or home (e.g., DeVault 1999; Elliott and Umberson 2008). Although less common, research on gender and emotion work has brought men into analyses in two primary ways: (a) quantitative studies compare men and women's frequency of various types of emotion management (e.g., Erickson 2005; Lively 2008), and (b) qualitative studies compare men and women's emotion management strategies in work settings, often showing how it reproduces hierarchies of status and power (e.g., Lois 2003; Pierce 1995). While contributing greatly to emotions and gender scholarship, these lines of research neglect how such emotion management

SOURCE: Vaccaro, C. A., Schrock, D. P., and McCabe, J. M. (2011). Managing Emotional Manhood: Fighting and Fostering Fear in Mixed Martial Arts. *Social Psychology Quarterly, 74*, 414–437. Reproduced with permission from the ASA.

is implicated in the active construction of identity. Our study contributes to the aforementioned research by showing how men's emotion management can constitute gendered "identity work" (Snow and Anderson 1987).

To emphasize the gendered and processional aspects of this emotional identity work, we refer to the MMA fighters' emotion *management as managing emotional manhood.* We define managing emotional manhood as emotion work that signifies a masculine self. Importantly, by the "masculine self" we are not referring to a psychological entity, how men view themselves, or the self-concept. Rather, we take the dramaturgical view that the masculine self is a virtual reality, a self that is imputed to actors based on the information given or given off (Goffman 1959). Schwalbe (2005) defines such identity work as a "manhood act" and emphasizes that signifying control is fundamental. Manhood here is not a static concept, but a malleable image that is constructed for public consumption. While there are many ways that males can put on a convincing manhood act (see Schrock and Schwalbe's [2009] review), in this study we emphasize that controlling and transforming one's own or others' emotions—especially fear—is key.[2] Emotions here are not simply added to or subtracted from one's presumed manhood (as if manhood exists as a thing rather than a social construction); they are expressions that signify what kind of man one is.

Theoretical Background

Emotion management involves suppressing or evoking particular emotions so as to resonate with culturally defined feeling rules (Hochschild 1979). Emotion work may be accomplished individually, as when a college student personally tries to control his or her anxiety when sitting down to take an exam (Albas and Albas 1988), or when a person vents anger when sitting down to pray (Sharp 2010). Emotion work can be also accomplished interpersonally (Cahill and Eggleston 1994; Francis 1994). Interpersonal emotion management may involve one person trying to control the emotions of others in a unidirectional fashion, such as when a leader of a therapeutic group tries to heal the emotional wounds of the widowed, divorced, or seekers of true selves (Francis 1997; Thoits 1996). It can also be "reciprocal," as when paralegals suppress each other's boss-and-client-induced stress in ways that maintain inequality (Lively 2000:33).

Social psychologists' perception that men are less skilled at and less likely to manage their emotions than are women can be traced back to the origins of the sociology of emotions. Hochschild (1983: 165) argued that men are "less likely [than women] to develop their capacity for managing emotion," largely because women are socialized into and more likely to occupy positions that require the presumably more common kind of "emotion work that affirms, enhances, and celebrates the well-being and status of others." Gendered feeling rules that implore men not to express shame, pain, love, or fear (see e.g., Cancian and Gordon 1988; Stearns and Stearns 1986) further create the impression that men's emotional lives are muted. It would seem, however, that keeping so many emotions under control would require much work.

Scholars of gender and emotion have begun to paint a more complex and nuanced picture of men's emotional lives. Recent survey research suggests that women and men do not significantly differ with regard to their overall experience and expression of emotion, although women generally report more negative emotions (Lively and Powell 2006; Simon and Nath 2004; but see Simon and Barrett 2010). Research also suggests that men less frequently engage in emotion management to suppress anger and irritation at work (Erickson and Ritter 2001) and home (Erickson 2005) and that men are more likely than women to efficiently transform one emotion into another (Lively 2008).

Qualitative researchers are better positioned to advance a processual approach (Snow 1999), but studies of gendered emotion work generally focus on how *women's* emotion work involves "feeding egos and tending wounds" (Bartky 1995) as they navigate life in subordinate positions. However, a growing body of ethnographic research suggests that men bring to work a biography of emotional socialization that shapes how they manage and express emotions in "masculine" ways (Lewis 2005; Lois 2003; Martin 1999; Pierce 1995). For example, Lois (2003:182–83) characterized male rescue workers as developing a "masculine emotional line" by interpreting their work as exciting and maintaining emotional control when things go bad. Similarly, Pierce (1995:59, 135) labels male lawyers' "intimidation and strategic friendliness" as exemplifying "a masculine style of emotional labor." While such research importantly views men's emotion work as gendered, by labeling such work *masculine* (or not), it undertheorizes how such emotion work is implicated in the construction of gender identity.

An alternative way to view men's emotion management—whether that of lawyers, rescuers, or MMA fighters—is as identity work. Identity work refers to how people dramaturgically signify an identity (Snow and Anderson 1987). While people accomplish identity work individually or collectively and can use language, physical gestures, and fashion to signify selves (Schwalbe and Mason-Schrock 1996), it is also an "emotional process" (Fields, Copp, and Kleinman 2006: 164). Wilkins (2008) shows how campus Christians use conversion stories, group singing, and introspection to evoke happiness, which the group defined as a "compulsory" signifier of Christian identity. Although this research integrates emotion and identity work approaches, it neglects to focus on gender. In contrast, we analyze MMA fighters' emotion management as central to their gendered identity work.

It is important to acknowledge that organizational cultures can be structured so as to emphasize or de-emphasize gender (e.g., Acker 1990). While MMA fighting may seem unique, it is like other sports in which men participate in that it orients participants and audiences to view participating as a test of manhood (e.g., Messner 1992). A key way that MMA bolsters its "gendered organizational frame" (Martin 2005) is by marketing a hypermasculine image. For instance, promoters dubbed the MMA Ultimate Fighting Championship as "The Most Controversial Event of the Decade" in which there are "no rules" and "two men enter, one man leaves" (Snowden 2008). The sport not only creates the conditions under which fighters experience and manage fear, it—in combination with the larger culture—also primes people to view fighters' management of fear (as well as their violence) through the lens of gender.

By managing their own fear and evoking it in others, MMA fighters thus present themselves in ways that are commonly interpreted by others as indicative of manhood. We term this process *managing emotional manhood* to emphasize its processual nature and how such emotion management is important for signifying a masculine self or putting on a manhood act. Importantly, our interactionist approach makes us less interested in trying to unearth fighters' motivations for managing fear—such as whether it increases their chances of winning or because it validates their sense of being "real men"—than we are in understanding the processes through which they accomplish such emotion work and its social meanings. Overall, examining how fighters manage emotional manhood builds on the aforementioned research by deepening our understanding of men's emotion work and bringing together two lines of research that have thus far been isolated from each another: studies of gendered emotion management and studies of emotional identity work.

Setting and Method

Data for this study derive from 24 months of fieldwork and 121 interviews. The first author gained access to a local MMA gym after calling the owner, Bruce, mentioning a long-time friendship with a professional fighter who had once been Bruce's training partner, and talking about his research interests. The ethnographer observed and openly jotted notes at about 100 evening practices at Steel Hangar Gym, which was located in a small industrial park on the outskirts of a midsized southeastern city. During practices, the fighters helped each other learn new techniques, worked out with punching bags and other equipment, and sparred with each other. When taking breaks, some of the men sat beside the first author to ask about his research and talk about their training and upcoming fight. He also traveled with the fighters to 10 competitions, where he observed the weigh-in the day before the fight, pre- and post-fight locker room interactions, the fights themselves, and the evening after-parties. While he jotted notes at these events, he also openly made audio and video recordings. He used his notes and recordings when writing full fieldnotes as soon as possible after each observation.

The first author conducted 24 formal 45- to 75-minute interviews with 15 local and 9 regional fighters and 97 brief 5- to 15-minute short interviews at competitions with 64 fighters and 15 trainers, promoters, and officials (some fighters were interviewed multiple times). During the longer interviews, the fighters were asked about their backgrounds, how they got involved in MMA, how they prepared emotionally and physically for fights, how they dealt with injuries, and their competition experiences. The brief interviews focused on fight preparation and experiences. While the formal interviews allotted more time to delve into a wider range of experiences, the brief interviews—conducted either during weigh-ins or soon after a fight—were surprisingly revealing, perhaps due to the intense emotionality surrounding competitions. Of the interviewees, 70 percent were white, 16 percent were black, 11 percent were Hispanic, and 3 percent were Asian. They ranged in age from 19 to 40 (average = 26.5). The majority (18 out of 25) of local interviewees had earned degrees from a community college or university.[3] All interviews were recorded and transcribed.

As the first author began fieldwork, he shared copies of fieldnotes, and the coauthors became intrigued by fighters' allusions to fear. This initial interest sensitized us to pay attention to how fear permeated the field and also led us to create interview questions aimed to better understand (a) what fighters worried about and (b) how they managed it. These questions also guided the coding of fieldnotes and interview transcripts, which led to creating typologies of what they most feared (injury and losing) and how they managed their fear (scripting, framing, and othering).

The Fears of Fighting

Underneath their bravado, Mixed Martial Arts fighters harbored fear. During interviews, at the local gym, and in locker rooms before competitions, the fighters often alluded to their fears by talking about "nerves," being "nervous," "worries," "pre-fight jitters," and "butterflies." For example, just before their fights, Ted said, "Oh, I'm nervous as hell!" and Buster said, "I was nervous. I was in the back about to throw up." Shortly after winning a fight, Robin said, "I was extremely nervous going into this." After losing fights, the men often blamed their poor performances on fear. For example, Ted explained, "It must have been nerves or something," and Garrett said, "I sort of felt like I kind of panicked and bitched-out a little bit." As Garrett implied, uncontrollable fear was like being momentarily inhabited by womanhood, which is probably why fighters usually—but not always—avoided saying "I'm afraid/scared/fearful." Saying they were nervous or worried was arguably less damaging to their manhood acts.

MMA fighters most commonly talked about fearing injury and losing. Fighters understood how painful injuries were and that serious ones could end their fighting careers, or worse. There have been two well-publicized deaths of fighters resulting from brain injuries sustained in North American MMA fights since 2007. Although interviewees agreed that, as Rocky put it, "in most cases you're going to come out of it [and] you're going to live," death lurked in the shadows of the cage. When asked what he worried about before his fights, for example, Kenneth said, "You are wondering if they are thinking of this incredible move that is really going to kill you." Dominic said, "This sport is not golf; you can't get hurt or killed playing golf." The possibility of death elevated MMA's manhood quotient.

Fighters more frequently discussed worrying about injuries they could live through. Dean worried about "getting choked out or . . . getting hurt." Lou said "I can get my arm broken [or] my nose broken, I can just get pounded." Jimmy said, "I was apprehensive about getting hurt." Such fears were not unfounded. Local fighters suffered dislocated ribs and concussions, Louis tore his ACL, Rocky broke his foot and seriously injured his back, Lou broke his wrist and finger, and Dominic's retina became detached from his eye twice. Because injuries were common, fighters could not easily escape the specter of pain.

In addition to fearing injury, cage fighters also feared losing. Casey feared looking "like a chump in front of all these people . . . if you get knocked out at your first fight in three seconds, then that's all they will remember." Mike said, "You really don't want to let your family or teammates down," and Kenneth said, "The name of the [MMA] school is kind of riding on you. You have to represent for your school." Minutes after Dean lost a fight, he said, "I feel like shit! I came out in front of my hometown and I got tapped out in like under a minute." Buster said "the feeling of losing is the worst feeling in the world, especially when you sell 100 tickets and you have a lot of your friends and family there." Echoing others, these men suggested that they feared losing because it made them feel embarrassed and ashamed—emotions that are antithetical to cultural definitions of manhood.

In a micropolitical fashion (Clark 1990), audience members often undermined losers' manhood acts by publicly shaming them. When Armand tapped out after being caught in a chokehold, his friends stood up and one yelled "Pussy!" before they all walked out in disgust. Three men who owned an MMA clothing business sat near the cage during another competition and enthusiastically chanted "Bitches get stitches, pussies get fucked!" at the losers of each fight. Drawing on the larger culture of sexism thus helped the audience shame losers in an emasculating fashion.

It was not uncommon for fighters to withdraw from competitions, presumably due to uncontrollable fear. Promoters said that fighters often backed out at the last minute, which required them to scramble to fill holes in the fight card. For each of the regional competitions observed, one or two men listed on the program did not participate. The first author observed one fighter who looked at his competitor during weigh-ins, said he forfeited the fight, and walked out. It was more common for dropouts to blame injury or sickness, even if they had passed prefight medical exams. Although none of the local fighters admitted that fear led them to back out of a fight, they believed others—including Armand—"chickened out." Armand claimed the police detained him for violating probation, but others said privately that they did not buy it.

Cage fighters had much to fear. Injuries were inevitable and threatened to end their careers. Losing was also difficult to stomach, although it also seems unavoidable. Being controlled by fear, shame, or pain, however, would have undermined their manhood act, as expressing such emotions contradicted feeling rules culturally bound to manhood. But if the men could fight off their fears and foster it in their opponents, they might be victorious men.

Fighting Fear

Fighters often said that feeling fear itself was not the problem as long as they kept it under control. As Taylor put it, "Fear is an okay thing as long as you can manage it." This belief let them off the hook if they felt some fear but also oriented them toward controlling it. As we will show, their emotion work often involved transforming fear into confidence, which is more consistent with cultural ideals of manhood. One reason that feeling but managing fear is "okay" is that keeping one's poise in a dangerous situation constitutes one of our culture's most honored characteristics of manhood: bravery (see e.g., Connell 1995). As Rudyard Kipling (1976:163–64) put it in a poem often memorized by schoolboys: "If you can keep your head when all about you are losing theirs and blaming it on you . . . you'll be a Man, my son!" To avoid losing their heads, as well as their masculine status, cage fighters managed emotional manhood through scripting, framing, and othering.

Scripting

To the untrained observer, cage fighting appears to be chaotic violence. Competitors themselves understood that fights are relatively unpredictable because, as Kenneth put it, "Think of all the things you need to worry about in MMA: take-downs, knees, kicks, and elbows." To evoke a sense of control and minimize fear, fighters developed game plans. We refer to the individual as well as the collective creation, embodiment, and review of the game plan as *scripting* because such work involved planning out and rehearsing combat. MMA fighters' scripting constituted managing emotional manhood to the extent it suppressed emotions that did *not* and evoked emotions that *did* resonate with cultural ideals of manhood.

When asked how they dealt with emotions before competitions, fighters frequently brought up their game plans. Isaac responded, "I need to have a game plan and stick to that. I don't want to fight too much out of emotion." Troy said, "I would do a lot of visualization of the event [so] I was emotionally prepared." John replied, "I just think about what I want to do. What is this guy going to try to do? If I know he's a southpaw, what do I have to do to avoid that hook?" After Blake mentioned that "fear and nerves work together to make you more tired and gets your heart rate going" and was asked how he "avoided feeling that way," he responded:

Just think about my training. Our game plan is always to hit it on the mat whenever possible . . . and work towards first position. Within that there are always plans that are somewhat different. Like . . . I want to go out there and shoot or crunch up and throw and try to stay on top. Just because I feel like that sets the pace . . . and that fighter is going to feel like you have them totally dominated.

While the inherent unpredictability of fights could evoke various fears, going over one's game plan enabled the men to suppress their fear and put on a more convincing manhood act.

More experienced fighters seemed better able to put together game plans for themselves as well as others, perhaps because they were more attuned to one's strengths and weaknesses. One veteran trainer/fighter said, "If you're a great grappler then don't stay on your feet . . . when you're training a guy, you got to start gauging where that person performs the best." Another veteran, Kenneth, said of a local fighter: "I know that his strength is his athleticism, his height, his range, and his explosiveness. Those things I kept telling him [to use to his advantage]."

Developing game plans also involved researching their opponents. Rocky said,

Me and Dominic get together and we do extensive research . . . we go to BattleBase.net—the most complete database of fighters thus far—and look at what his record is. I look at what his [fight] style is. I look at how he's won his fights. I look at how he's lost his fights. And I implement that into a strict training regimen. If I'm fighting the kick boxer who wins all his fights by knock outs, you're going to be damn sure I'm practicing my striking . . . But if I know I'm fighting a wrestler, I'm going to be working on my kick-down defenses and my knock-out punches.

Fighters regularly searched for videos and information about opponents on YouTube, MySpace, Facebook, and other Internet sites for MMA fighters and fans, such as MMAUniverse.com and Sherdog.com. In addition, if gym members had previously seen a fight involving a future opponent of a local member, they shared what they remembered. Overall, such intelligence gathering and sharing helped fighters to script game plans that bolstered confidence and manhood.

Although such scripting minimized fear as fighters prepared for competitions, fighters believed that to be successful they needed to instill the script into "bodily memory" (McCaughey 1998:290). As fight night neared, said Kenneth, "You should already have your game-plan . . . *in you* right now. You don't have time to be thinking about that kind of stuff during a fight." To get the plan "in you," Allan echoed others when he said: "I practice to the point to where it becomes natural, where you can just do it naturally in the fight situation." When asked how he dealt with his emotions as he prepared for a fight, Ed referenced embodying the script, "It is all about putting yourself in the situation over and over again, so that nothing is new to you. [T]hat's what separates the good fighters from the mediocre fighters: [Good ones] don't panic, they are comfortable." Embodying the script thus helped manage emotional manhood by evoking confidence.

Embodying the script also helped fighters inject some bravado into their manhood acts. For example, one evening Scotty strutted around the gym and loudly proclaimed that he was going to win his upcoming fight. The first author approached him and asked, "So, you feel pretty confident about your fight?" Scotty replied, "Yeah, I am going to choke him out. I can feel it . . . I've been taking necks everywhere I go. So I will probably get him up against the cage and give him a little." Demonstrating the script, he then threw a flurry of punches followed by a high knee before declaring, "Take him to the ground and finish it!" Scotty later explained that because his opponent was a "striker" (boxer), he planned to knee him in the face, wrestle him to the ground, and strangle him until he loses consciousness.

Fighters also said that scripting helped them keep their fear under control during the emotionally intense minutes before their fights commenced. In the locker room, fighters often warmed up by hitting pads as their trainers went over their game plans. For example, after saying, "I was real nervous, I was sweating" before a recent fight and being asked if anything helped, Dustin said: "I had my coach and he was holding pads as well as telling me the game plan." Some fighters suggested that bringing their scripts into the cage helped them keep their worries under control before the first bell rang. After being asked if he was "experiencing fear or any type of emotions" when he recently entered the cage, Garrett said, "I sort of remember just being chill when I was in there. I had my game plan and I was going to try to implement it."

Framing

MMA fighters also used framing to do emotion work that signified masculine selves. Following Goffman (1974), we define a frame as a definition that answers the question, "What is going on here?" Framing shapes how one not only thinks about a situation but also how one feels. Fighters' emotional framing most often involved defining cage fights as (a) just another day in the gym, (b) business, and (c) a valuable experience. They used these strategies individually and interpersonally, although they generally hid them from members of the local gym who did not compete in competitions.

Framing a fight as just another day in the gym boosted confidence and mitigated fear by defining competitions as banal. Although the audience, announcers, ring girls, medical professionals, and steel cage made competitions objectively different than training, fighters often equated fights with every-day training. Lou said that he kept "calm and composed" by thinking "in my mind that [the fight] is a sparring match. [I] think of it as another day in the gym." When asked how they dealt with their emotions prior to a competition, Scotty said, "Just be natural and do the same things that I do in the gym"; Felix answered, "I basically want the mindset that I have in practice"; and Nick said he "stay[s] cool because it's just like every other day in training." Such framing thus managed emotional man-hood by mitigating fear.

Unlike scripting, framing fights as "just another day in the gym" was not part of the culture of the local gym. Because many men trained but did not participate in competitions, MMA fighters pre-served their status as more dominant men by maintaining a public distinction between training and competition. Backstage, however, MMA competitors learned about this emotion management strategy from veteran fighters and trainers. When asked about how he helps fighters control their pre-fight emotions, for example, Dominic said:

> A lot of those conversations happen behind closed doors. [Or] at three in the morning. You get a phone call from a fighter and he is like, "I don't know that I can do this." And you have to be like, "Yes, you can. You do this every day in the gym."

Whereas fighters often presented themselves as invincible in the gym, they expressed more vulnerability backstage. In these hidden moments, more experienced fighters often engaged in interpersonal emotion work to ease their fears. Although such emotional support is culturally coded as "feminine," new fighters used what they learned to enact emotional manhood.

In addition to defining the fight as another day in the gym, fighters also managed fear by framing the fight as business. For example, Victor said, "Before a fight you are always a little nervous . . . but when you step into the cage . . . you just go and do your job. It is like an everyday office guy." Steven said that when he goes into the cage, he "must remain a sportsman about it and understand that it's a profession." Larry said, "A true professional in this sport approaches this as a business . . . I got to put this dude down and get my money so I can put food on the table." When asked how he dealt with his pre-fight emotions minutes after he won his first fight, Forest said, "I had to turn into a professional . . . I wanted to be calm." Although newcomers sometimes used this strategy, the more experienced fighters most often invoked the rhetoric of professionalism and business, probably because they could more credibly claim it.

Cage fighters' framing of fighting as a business endeavor was commonplace at the gym, perhaps because it reinforced the status differences between competitive fighters and those they occasionally derided (in interviews) as "hobbyists." In addition to overtly referencing professionalism in the gym, fighters alluded to it by talking about prize money. One of the more successful fighters, Rocky, for example, bragged one evening that he never accepted a fight for less than $1,000 and talked about being on the verge of gaining sponsors who would help him double his pot. Although competitive fighters often evoked the business metaphor, none turned a profit.

In contradiction to framing the fight as "just another day in the gym," the fighters also mitigated fear by framing the fight as a valuable experience. Newcomers more often used this strategy than veterans. When asked what helped him deal with emotions before a recent fight, Steven said, "I just kind of looked at it as there's no pressure on me . . . it's an opportunity, obviously, to get some experience and [I should] just go out and enjoy it." Isaac managed emotional manhood by framing a fight in the wider context of his biography:

> When I showed up . . . all those doubts crept into my mind. Doubts like, "Why in the hell am I doing this?" There is obviously a risk of having your face punched in . . . "Why am I doing this to myself? Why do I put myself in this position?" So for me what works is just to sit back . . . and say, "I'm doing something that is so important to me. And it is something that I want to do so badly. And that this is something that I am going to remember for a long time. That is why this is making me this nervous."

In this example, Issac explains how he manages his fear by framing a fight as one of his life's most cherished moments. Doing so swept his doubts under the rug, enabling him to more convincingly display emotional manhood.

While losing matches could make fighters fear that they were no longer cut out for the cage, framing their losses as valuable learning experiences often eased their fears and gave them enough confidence to continue. Nick said, for example, that a recent "loss taught me a lot of things about being inside the cage, a lot about being calm and my nerves and just how to compose myself in the cage. So this time coming in I am ready for it." Dean emphasized that even if one loses, one gains: "And all my lessons learned from losing are the kind of lessons that stick." Fighters seemed to have learned this strategy of viewing losses as learning experiences from other fighters. For example, Steven explained how a famous fighter made sense of losing before proceeding to similarly frame his own recent loss:

> He said that [his loss] was the best thing that ever happened to him. . . . When you are able to gain more from a loss, in some cases it can become a win. And mentally, I think it does more for your psyche. [H]aving suffered [a] loss . . . the next fight that you have, your mental preparation will probably be a little bit more crisp and sharp. . . . The reinforcement is, "This is one to learn from. Don't let this same thing happen again."

Framing losing as lessons thus helped fighters with various levels of experience keep their fear in check and maintain commitment to cage fighting, both of which signified manhood.

Framing fights as another day in the gym, a business opportunity, and a valuable experience helped MMA fighters manage emotional manhood by keeping their fear under control. In addition, by framing fighting as business, they also drew on cultural ideals of manhood (Connell 1995).

Othering

Fighters also mitigated fear and bolstered confidence and pride by defining themselves as superior to their opponents. Such "othering" (see e.g., Schwalbe et al. 2000)—whether it involved creating powerful virtual selves ("implicit othering") or defining their opponents as inferior ("oppressive othering")—made them feel like victory was within reach. As we will show, both the meanings of such othering and its emotional impact helped fighters signify credible masculine selves.

Managing emotional manhood via othering was often an interpersonal process and generally involved more experienced gym members easing the less experienced members' fears. "If I say, 'Oh, I feel uncomfortable with this,'" Donovan said that his trainer tells him, "'You got great hands [and] can take this guy down [and] submit him.'" Henry said of his trainers, "They're building me up, telling me I got all the ability in the world [and] I'll win." Tanner said his fears were eased when "my teammate told me that there is no way in the world that this guy is going to be as tough as the guys you're training with." Felix explained that his trainer gave him the "usual pep talk" before a recent fight: "'You've trained better than this guy. You're a better fighter.'" Trainers and gym mates thus painted fighters as superior to their opponents, which mitigated fear and bolstered their confidence and pride as dominant men.

Interviews with trainers revealed that such othering was intended to manage men's pre-fight jitters. When asked how he kept his fighters from "getting nervous," one trainer said: "I was telling Colby before this fight, 'This guy is not even in your league. He shouldn't even be fighting you.'" Another trainer, Kenneth, said that he takes into account what he knows about the fighters' habits and training when crafting an emotionally uplifting message:

> I was really pumping Rocky up because I know that's what he needs. He is just a testosterone-laden guy. I am like, "You are going to out athleticism this guy, you are so much stronger," and I got him to be really aggressive . . . and feel really confident.

With Scotty, however, Kenneth took a different strategy:

> We didn't bring in enough yuppies for him to beat up on. His training partners were all people who he could probably never beat in a fight. . . . And so with that he has developed this mindset

where he is very comfortable being on his back, being in a bad position, being beat up. With him you just want to tell him that, "You know what, Scotty, you know what you are doing, you can finish people. You do it all the time."

These excerpts demonstrate how trainers incorporate their perceptions of each fighter's "mindset" and training into their interpersonal emotion management strategies. Such implicit othering was intended, as Kenneth put it, to make fighters "confident." Transforming fear into confidence was crucial in enabling fighters to put on a credible manhood act.

Fighters individually used creative variations of these othering strategies to quell their fears and emotionally prepare themselves for battle. A few drew on cultural products such as films and racial stereotypes. When asked how he kept his fear in check, Cecil, an African American fighter, said:

Right before my fight, I go ahead and do my pre-fight ritual. [Guys from] my gym call me "King Kong" because of my grappling style and [so] I awaken that inner gorilla . . . I rock back and forth and I have visions of a gorilla coming out of a cage, [like] when King Kong comes out of the cage and he pounds his chest powerfully just as lightning strikes. I hear the thunder and [see] lightning hitting the ground when I roar. You hear my roar and you look at my eyes. And I am ready to go into the cage.

Like medical students envisioning themselves as healers in order to mitigate their fear of disgust (Smith and Kleinman 1989), Cecil quelled fear and bolstered confidence by viewing himself as an animalistic monster. He thus drew on a film to symbolically align himself with dehumanizing stereotypes of violent African American men (see Collins 2004), which ironically helped him emotionally signify that he was a "real man."

Fighters' othering used not only Hollywood scripts, but also video games as resources. After Rocky asserted that he does not fear the cage, he was asked how he managed that. He said:

I pretty much think of it as a video game. He has a little energy bar and a stamina bar above his head and every time I hit him that bar goes down. I try to think about the fact that every second that I don't hit him that energy bar may be going back up. I think of myself the same way, except I pretend that my energy bar never goes down. It's just like I am in invincible mode.

Similar to medical students who manage emotions by, for example, "dehumanizing" a patient as a "broken toaster" (Smith and Kleinman 1989:61), Rocky muted fear by constructing his opponent as well as himself as pixelated pugilists. His othering also conveyed masculine dominance by representing his virtual self as so "invincible" that "nothing can hurt me."

In addition to defining themselves as physically superior to their opponents, fighters also regulated emotions by constructing themselves as mentally superior. Rocky explained his thoughts before the fight, "I'm not intimidated . . . I'm just as strong mentally as I am physically," and Allan said, "I think, 'My will is a little bit stronger than yours.'" When asked how he dealt with his emotions before a fight, a veteran fighter said:

The specific thing that I always tell myself is that I am way smarter than the other guy. And that may or may not be true obviously, but that's the thought I have because everybody trains their asses off for a fight . . . For me, I am going to say—while I am looking across [the cage]—that, "I know you trained hard, but I trained better. I trained smarter. I know more of what I am doing than you do. I am going to be able to think faster than you and be able to deal with any situation you put me in better than you."

Similar to other fighters, he boosted his confidence by constructing a powerful virtual self as intellectually superior to his opponent. As he implied, however, the emotion work strategy's success at mitigating fear was contingent on denying the fact that "it may not be true." Suspending disbelief likely helped him as well as others manage emotional manhood.

Instead of focusing on their own mental or physical acuity, some fighters painted opponents as, emotionally speaking, insufficiently masculine. When Dominic was asked how he dealt with his nerves before entering the cage, he said,

> I like thinking about the fact that whatever the other guy is doing, you're going to beat him anyway. If the guy needs to cry like a girl in order to fight, you are still going to beat him. If he needs his parents in the stands to support him, you are still going to beat him.

Drawing on the larger culture, Dominic thus constructed competitors as fearful girls who depended on others ("parents") for emotional support.

Before fighters left the locker room and entered the arena, trainers often engaged in othering to emotionally prepare them. Before one fight Emil ran in place backstage, fixing his eyes on the ground, and his trainer leaned in and in a dramatic tone said, "You got more heart." Emil nodded once and continued to run in place, before the trainer leaned in again and said a little more loudly, "You're the best." The trainer then peeked out at the audience momentarily before moving just inches from Emil's face, saying in a serious tone and with widened eyes, "All these people came to see you." The trainer then glanced toward Emil's opponent warming up a few feet away and said, "He is not going to steal it from you." Emil began rhythmically nodding his head and banging his fists together. As music began and the announcer dramatically introduced Emil, he left the locker room and made his way to the cage.

Nationalism and implicit racism were also occasionally used in such othering, which bolstered confidence as fighters headed to the cage. In the locker room before one contest, Larry and his trainer—both of whom were white and U.S. citizens—were waiting as Larry's opponent—a Peruvian national—entered the cage. Larry's trainer then told him that he had requested a "special song" be played for his own entrance. As Bruce Springsteen's "Born in the USA" began to play loudly over the sound system, the crowd erupted.[4] Larry glanced at his trainer and cracked a smile, pounded his fists together, and confidently growled, "I'm taking this fucker to school" as they entered the arena.

Fostering Fear

Another way fighters managed emotional manhood was by fostering fear in their opponents. Inducing fear in other men essentially signified that they themselves were so powerful that they could turn other men, emotionally speaking, into women. Such emotional micropolitics not only raised one's own status (Clark 1990) but also signified masculine selves—that is, it conveyed that they were in control of not only their own but also their opponents' feelings.

Competitions provided many opportunities for the men to try to evoke fear in their opponents. The day before a match, fighters saw each other during weigh-ins and meetings with promoters and officials. Fighters sometimes strategically presented themselves backstage in hope of intimidating opponents; they walked around "trying to be a badass," as one fighter put it. Local fighters sometimes donned new hairstyles at competitions that bolstered their tough image, such as getting a Mohawk, dying their hair outlandish colors, or shaving it off. Interviewees sometimes strategically displayed their physique and, if given a chance, added some verbal innuendo intended to evoke fear. After discussing how he managed his own fear, for example, Taylor said, "Not everybody is built like me.

I've had guys that have just seen me and backed out of a fight before." Asked to expound, he described what happened at a tough man contest:

> I'm walking around with my shirt off . . . And another guy walks up to me and he says, "Hey what weight class are you fighting in?" And I said, "I'm fighting a light weight." And he looks at me and he's like, "Man, there is no way you're a light weight." And since then I ain't never seen that guy again. He was obviously in my weight class [and] was like, "Shit." And the next thing you know, all the promoters were talking, "We just lost a fighter." (mutual laughter) Intimidation is a huge, huge, huge portion of it.

Here Taylor suggests that he evoked fear in his opponent by going shirtless and displaying his considerable muscularity. Telling his opponent that he was fighting "*a* light weight" instead of "*in* the light weight division" may have also been effective.

The weigh-in ritual was a key moment in which fighters attempted to intimidate each other. It generally began with fighters being called up for quick medical checkups. During this time, the room was filled with chatter and laughter as fighters, trainers, and promoters from different cities mingled. When it was time for fighters to weigh in, however, fighters and trainers coalesced into gym-based groups and—except for the announcer calling up opponents—the room was silent. When called, fighters walked up to the center of the stage, wearing nothing but boxers, and stepped on a scale. After their weight was announced, they flexed their muscles and briefly posed for pictures. Once each opponent did this, the two men posed together for "stare down" photos, in which they stood eye-to-eye in fighting stances. When asked how he tried to intimidate his opponent during the pre-fight ritual, Forrest said:

> You never let them know that you're scared of them. So you always look them dead in the eye. Never back down, never do anything to make it look like you're nervous. You know, just pretend like you're—act like you're confident the whole time.

Keeping one's own fear under control was thus key to instilling fear in opponents. Fighters typically put on one of three intimidating personas during the stare down: (a) the arrogantly confident "High School Quarterback," (b) the barely controllable angry "Wide-Eyed Madman," or (c) the unflappable "Bored Russian." The most overt attempts to induce fear were the "madmen," who often invaded opponents' personal space and made bodily contact.

On the day of the fight, fighters usually had opportunities to intimidate each other backstage, as they often shared a locker room or had backstage areas that were connected. For example, Dustin said, "The way the locker rooms were set up, I could see [my opponent] watching me when I was warming up." Dustin said he looked at his trainer and said loudly, "Are you ready for me to knock this mother fucker out? I'm going to fuck him up!" He added, "I could just tell he didn't want to fight me . . . he was worried about it." When Garrett similarly saw his opponent checking him out in the locker room, he whacked the punching mitts his trainer was holding with particular vigor, hoping to intimidate his opponent. Managing emotional manhood thus involved using the body and language in an attempt to control others' emotions.

Many fighters said they tried to intimidate opponents when entering the cage. Most often fighters said that they attempted to do this in a subtle fashion. When asked if they tried to intimidate opponents once in the ring, Tommy said, "I try to look at his face when the referee is talking to us"; another said, "I give my opponent a little stare-down and intimidate him"; and Ayden said, "I just come out and let him know that I'm not afraid. I size him up and give a little stare." Fighters' demeanor was thus part of their dramaturgical arsenal.

African American fighters sometimes presented themselves in ways that resonated with racial stereotypes, hoping to evoke fear in opponents. Dion would enter the ring doing "the gorilla stomp, just to intimidate my opponent . . . and get the crowd going." At one event he was observed running into the cage and jumping vertically about four feet into the air before stomping down on the middle of the mat with both feet, shaking the whole cage and creating a loud noise that reverberated through the arena. He then charged at his opponent, who was required to remain in his corner, and repeated the gorilla stomp, coming down a mere foot from his competitor as he yelled in unison with the roaring crowd. Immediately after this fight, the loser was asked how he felt before the opening bell: "I was terrified." Taylor, another African American, fashioned himself in stereotypical gang attire, wearing dark glasses and a doo-rag, and sometimes a black t-shirt with "Danger" printed on the front, and generally entered the arena to a song that started with gun shots. When asked about his presentation, Taylor, a college-educated information technology professional, responded:

> That's all Hollywood. I'm not a gangster. Do I sound like a gangster? . . . I kind of put all that into a persona. . . . If me coming out to some music or wearing something on my face, or glasses will put a little ounce of doubt in this guy's head, make him think, "Hey, man, this is a bad mother fucker right here," it's only to my benefit.

While Dion's and Taylor's performance constituted "passion work" (Smith 2008) because it could generate crowd excitement, it also managed emotional manhood by evoking fear in their opponents. This worked in part because the cultural stereotypes of African American men orient others to view them as dangerously animalistic and criminal (Collins 2004).

Conclusion

Mixed martial arts competitors feared injury and losing and needed to manage these emotions to put on a convincing manhood act. Through scripting game plans; framing the fight as another day in the gym, business, or a valuable experience; and othering opponents as inferior, fighters usually kept their fear under enough control to enter the cage. They accomplished such emotion management personally and interpersonally and not only suppressed fear but evoked confidence. Fighters also engaged in a kind of micropolitical emotion management, seeking to instill fear in opponents by strategically using language and their bodies to enact intimidating personas.

Whereas most scholarship on gendered emotion work focuses on how women manage emotions at work and home in ways that reinforce their subordination (e.g., DeVault 1999; Elliott and Umberson 2008), we show how men do emotion work aimed at facilitating domination. We also show, however, that fighters' experience shaped how they managed emotions and that despite their best efforts, their fears often came true. The most experienced fighters more credibly used some strategies (e.g., the rhetoric of professionalism) than did newcomers, and as more "privileged emotion managers" (Orzechowicz 2008), they were better able to quell or transform their fear. Similar to leaders of support groups (Francis 1997; Thoits 1996), experienced fighters more often acted as emotional guides who not only managed newcomers' fear but taught them strategies that they could use individually or on other fighters—that is, they passed down some "emotional capital" (Cahill 1999) to the next generation of cage fighters. More generally, although all fighters' emotion work aimed to manage their fears of losing and pain, because fighters inevitably lose and are injured, the sport created the conditions under which their emotion work was in some ways "doomed to fail" (Copp 1998). While such failure could lead some fighters to quit, our analysis shows how many used some of the same emotion work strategies (scripting and framing) to quell fears that they were not cut out for the sport, bolstering commitment to the cage despite repeated beatings.

Our study also contributes to sociological social psychology by developing the notion of "managing emotional manhood" in order to bring together insights from research on emotions and gender and research on emotions and identity work. In doing so, we promote an interactionist approach that views emotion, identity, and gender as intertwined social processes. Because people are held accountable to present appropriately gendered self-presentations (West and Zimmerman 1987), their emotion management is often geared toward signifying gender identity. One implication of this is that emotion scholars should move beyond considering gendered feeling rules as "masculine" or "feminine," as if these concepts have some objective status (see Bem's [1993] critique). Instead, we advocate viewing such rules as part of an "identity code" (Schwalbe and Mason-Schrock 1996) that defines what acts—emotional or otherwise—are commonly interpreted as signifying one is a real "man" or "woman." As our study suggests, controlling one's own fear while fostering it in others is key to the identity code of manhood.

Understanding that emotion management may constitute gendered identity work may enrich our understanding of qualitative and quantitative research that has found sex differences in emotion work. In her structural equation analysis, for example, Lively (2008:927) finds that men efficiently transition from one emotion to another whereas women making similar transitions generally "move through more intervening emotions." She suggests that these differences may be due to how men and women's brains differently process emotions, social structure, or "subculture variation" in how women and men feel and manage emotions (Lively 2008:929). Consistent with our approach, another possibility may be that men do emotion work more efficiently because expressing many emotions, especially those indicating vulnerability, is inconsistent with signifying masculine selves (and vice versa for women). Erickson and Ritter (2001:160) find that men are more likely than women to experience agitation at work but less likely to manage it, suggesting it might be due to "power and status" or the different types of jobs men and women typically hold. We might add that because anger is one of the few emotional expressions that is consistent with the identity code for "being a man," men may feel freer to express irritation at work (and vice versa for women). Ethnographic research comparing how men and women differently manage emotions at work suggest that gender socialization leads women to engage in feminine and men to engage in masculine styles of emotion management, which preserves status distinctions (Lewis 2005; Lois 2003; Martin 1999; Pierce 1995). Our analysis would suggest that such differences may exist because men and women's emotion work are part of their differently gendered identity work projects. Thus, while socialization, status hierarchies, and working conditions may indeed shape emotion work, our approach would emphasize that people still put their agency to use to regulate emotions so as to signify their gendered identities.

More broadly, our analysis shows how culture is implicated in gendered emotion work. In addition to providing the identity categories and codes that enable us to interpret an emotional display as signifying the gender identity, we can also see how culture is a "tool kit" (Swidler 1986) of resources that can be used to accomplish gendered emotion work. More specifically, our analysis shows how fighters mitigated fear and cultivated confidence by using cultural ideals of men as rational, business-minded, and physically intimidating (Connell 1995). In addition, the men sometimes drew on stereotypes of women as dependent and overemotional and of men of color as animal-like and criminal (Collins 2004) to manage emotions. Furthermore, fighters' emotion work helps reproduce the cultural ideals that men should feel confident and fearless in the quest to dominate others. Of course, MMA fighters have a larger audience than do most others who do so. Because MMA is the fastest growing professional sport in contemporary society (Snowden 2008), such gendered emotion work (as well as their violence) also constitutes a cultural product consumed by the masses.

Our study also demonstrates the value of adopting a social psychological approach to emotions for gender scholars of men and masculinity. Although research and theory on men and masculinity often suggests men are supposed to be emotionally inexpressive (Connell 1995; Sattel 1976), social psychology can deepen our understanding of why that is the case (feeling rules/identity codes), the processes through which men regulate emotions (emotion management), and how such regulation signifies a virtual masculine self (identity work). Furthermore, whereas it has been said that men and other dominant groups attempt to evoke fear in subordinates to better control them (e.g., Schwalbe et al. 2000), our study suggests that controlling one's own fear may also be important for maintaining one's power or at least deriving compensatory benefits from those who control distribution systems.

Notes

1. All names are pseudonyms.

2. In developing an identity work approach to studying men, Schrock and Schwalbe (2009) point out that although Connell (1995) critiqued sex role theory and legitimated the study of men as gendered beings, scholars often reify masculinity as a thing or trait rather than a social practice, problematically equate anything that people with male bodies do as masculinity (essentializing) and ignore power and control in their attempts to uncover new "types" of masculinities. They developed the notion of manhood acts as an antidote to such problems.

3. On the SPQ website, we have provided an appendix listing all fighters interviewed along with their age, race, education, win/loss record, what type of interview they participated in, and if they were observed at the local gym and/or in regional competitions.

4. Although the lyrics of this song are critical of the United States, it was used here (as well as in most public events where it is played) in a nationalist fashion.

References

Acker, Joan. 1990. "Hierarchies, Jobs, Bodies: A Theory of Gendered Organizations." *Gender and Society* 4:139–58.

Albas, Cheryl and Daniel Albas. 1988. "Emotion Work and Emotion Rules: The Case of Exams." *Qualitative Sociology* 11:259–74.

Bartky, Sandra. 1995. "Feeding Egos and Tending Wounds: Deference and Disaffection in Women's Emotional Labor." *In Power, Dignity and Social Structure: Readings in Multicultural Social Theory*, edited by M. Rogers. New York: McGraw-Hill.

Bem, Sandra L. 1993. *The Lenses of Gender: Transforming the Debate on Sexual Inequality.* New Haven, CT: Yale University Press.

Blumer, Herbert. 1969. *Symbolic Interactionism: Perspective and Method.* Englewood Cliffs, NJ: Prentice Hall.

Cahill, Spencer E. 1999. "Emotional Capital and Professional Socialization: The Case of Mortuary Science Students (and Me)." *Social Psychology Quarterly* 62:101–16.

Cahill, Spencer E. and Robin Eggleston. 1994. "Managing Emotions in Public: The Case of Wheelchair Users." *Social Psychology Quarterly* 57:300–12.

Cancian, Francesca M. and Steven F. Gordon. 1988. "Changing Emotion Norms in Marriage: Love and Anger in U.S. Women's Magazines Since 1900." *Gender and Society* 2:308–42.

Clark, Candace. 1990. "Emotions and Micropolitics in Everyday Life: Some Patterns and Paradoxes of Place." Pp. 305–33 in *Research Agendas in the Sociology of Emotions*, edited by T. Kemper. Albany, NY: State University of New York Press.

Collins, Patricia H. 2004. *Black Sexual Politics: African Americans, Gender, and the New Racism.* New York: Routledge.

Connell, Robert W. 1995. *Masculinities.* Sydney: Allen and Unwin.

Copp, Martha. 1998. "When Emotion Work Is Doomed to Fail: Ideological and Structural Constraints on Emotion Management." *Symbolic Interaction* 21:299–328.

DeVault, Marjorie L. 1999. "Comfort and Struggle: Emotion Work in Family Life." *Annals of the American Academy of Political and Social Science* 561:52–63.

Elliott, Sinikka and Debra Umberson. 2008. "The Performance of Desire: Gender and Sexual Negotiation in Long-Term Marriages." *Journal of Marriage and Family* 70:391–406.

Erickson, Rebecca J. 2005. "Why Emotion Work Matters: Sex, Gender, and the Division of Household Labor." *Journal of Marriage and Family* 67:337–51.

Erickson, Rebecca J. and Christian Ritter. 2001. "Emotion Labor, Burnout, and Inauthenticity: Does Gender Matter?" *Social Psychology Quarterly* 64:143–62.

Fields, Jessica, Martha Copp and Sherryl Kleinman. 2006. "Symbolic Interactionism, Inequality, and Emotions." Pp. 155– 78 in *Handbook of the Sociology of Emotions*, edited by J. E. Stets and J. H. Turner. New York: Springer.

Fine, Gary A. 1987. *With the Boys: Little League Baseball and Preadolescent Culture*. Chicago: University of Chicago Press.

Francis, Linda E. 1994. "Laughter, the Best Mediation: Humor as Emotion Management in Interaction. *Symbolic Interaction* 17:147–63.

Francis, Linda E. 1997. "Ideology and Interpersonal Emotion Management: Redefining Identity in Two Support Groups." *Social Psychology Quarterly* 60:153–171.

Goffman, Erving. 1959. *The Presentation of Self in Everyday Life*. New York: Doubleday.

Goffman, Erving. 1968. *Interaction Ritual: Essays on Face-to-Face Behavior*. New York: Doubleday.

Goffman, Erving. 1974. *Frame Analysis*. New York: Harper.

Hochschild, Arlie R. 1979. "Emotion Work, Feeling Rules, and Social-Structure." *American Journal of Sociology* 85:551–75.

Hochschild, Arlie R. 1983. *The Managed Heart*. Berkeley: University of California Press.

Kimmel, Michael. 1996. *Manhood in America: A Cultural History*. New York: The Free Press.

Kipling, Rudyard. 1976. "If." Pp. 163–64 in *The Forty-Nine Percent Majority: The Male Sex Role*, edited by D. S. David and R. Brannon. New York: Random House.

Lewis, Patricia. 2005. "Suppression or Expression: An Exploration of Emotion Management in a Special Care Baby Unit." *Work, Employment & Society* 19:565–81.

Lively, Kathryn J. 2000. "Reciprocal Emotion Management: Working Together to Maintain Stratification in Private Law Firms." *Work and Occupations* 27:32–63.

Lively, Kathryn J. 2008. "Emotional Segues and the Management of Emotion by Women and Men." *Social Forces* 87:911–36.

Lively, Kathryn J. and Brian Powell. 2006. "Emotional Expression at Work and at Home: Domain, Status, or Individual Characteristics?" *Social Psychology Quarterly* 69:17–38.

Lois, Jennifer. 2003. *Heroic Efforts: The Emotion Culture of Search and Rescue Volunteers*. New York: New York University Press.

Martin, Patricia Y. 2005. *Rape Work: Victims, Gender & Emotions in Organization & Community Context*. New York: Routledge.

Martin, Susan E. 1999. "Police Force or Police Service? Gender and Emotional Labor." *Annals of the American Academy of Political and Social Science* 561:111–26.

McCaughey, Martha. 1998. "The Fighting Spirit: Women's Self-Defense Training and the Discourse of Sexed Embodiment." *Gender and Society* 12:277–300.

McGuffey, C. Shawn. 2008. "Saving Masculinity: Gender Reaffirmation, Sexuality, Race and Parental Responses to Male Child Sexual Abuse." *Social Problems* 55:216–37.

Messner, Michael. 1992. *Power at Play: Sports and the Problem of Masculinity*. Boston: Beacon Press.

Messner, Michael. 2009. *It's All for the Kids: Gender, Families, and Youth Sports*. Berkeley: University of California Press.

Orzechowicz, David. 2008. "Privileged Emotion Managers: The Case of Actors." *Social Psychology Quarterly* 71:143–56.

Pierce, Jennifer. 1995. *Gender Trials: Emotional Lives of Contemporary Law Firms*. Berkeley: University of California Press.

Sattel, Jack. W. 1976. "The Inexpressive Male: Tragedy or Sexual Politics?" *Social Problems* 23:469–77.

Schrock, Douglas P. and Michael Schwalbe. 2009. "Men, Masculinity, and Manhood Acts." *Annual Review of Sociology* 35:277–95.

Schwalbe, Michael. 2005. "Identity Stakes, Manhood Acts, and the Dynamics of Accountability." Pp. 65–81 in *Studies in Symbolic Interaction*, edited by N. Denzin. New York: Elsevier.

Schwalbe, Michael, Sandra Godwin, Daphne Holden, Douglas Schrock, Shealy Thompson, and Michele Wolkomir. 2000. "Generic Processes in the Reproduction of Inequality: An Interactionist Analysis." *Social Forces* 79:419–52.

Schwalbe, Michael L. and Douglas Mason-Schrock. 1996. "Identity Work as Group Process." Pp. 113–47 in *Advances in Group Processes*, edited by B. Markovsky, M. Lovaglia, and R. Simon. Greenwich, CT: JAI Press.

Scully, Diana. 1990. *Understanding Sexual Violence: A Study of Convicted Rapists.* New York: HarperCollins Academic.

Sharp, Shane. 2010. "Does Prayer Help Manage Emotions?" *Social Psychology Quarterly* 73:417–37.

Simon, Robin W. and Anne E. Barrett. 2010. "Nonmarital Romantic Relationships and Mental Health in Early Adulthood: Does the Association Differ for Women and Men?" *Journal of Health and Social Behavior* 51:168–82.

Simon, Robin W. and Leda E. Nath. 2004. "Gender and Emotion in the United States: Do Men and Women Differ in Self-Reports of Feelings and Expressive Behavior?" *American Journal of Sociology* 109:1137–76.

Smith, Allen and Sherryl Kleinman. 1989. "Managing Emotions in Medical School: Students' Contact with the Living and the Dead." *Social Psychology Quarterly* 52:56–69.

Smith, R. Tyson 2008. "Passion Work: The Joint Production of Emotional Labor in Professional Wrestling." *Social Psychology Quarterly* 71:157–76.

Snow, David A. 1999. "Assessing the Ways in which Qualitative/Ethnographic Research Contributes to Social Psychology." *Social Psychology Quarterly* 62:97–100.

Snow, David A. and Leon Anderson. 1987. "Identity Work among the Homeless: The Verbal Construction and Avowal of Personal Identities." *American Journal of Sociology* 92:1336–71.

Snowden, Jonathan. 2008. *Total MMA: Inside Ultimate Fighting.* Ontario: ECW Press.

Stearns, Carol and Peter Stearns. 1986. *Anger: The Struggle for Emotional Control in America's History.* Chicago: University of Chicago Press.

Swidler, Ann. 1986. "Culture in Action: Symbols and Strategies." *American Sociological Review* 51:273–86.

Thoits, Peggy A. 1996. "Managing the Emotions of Others." *Symbolic Interaction* 19:85–109.

West, Candace, and Donald H. Zimmerman. 1987. "Doing Gender." *Gender & Society* 1:125–51.

Wilkins, Amy. 2008. "Happier than Non-Christians: Collective Emotions and Symbolic Boundaries among Evangelical Christians." *Social Psychology Quarterly* 71:281–301.

CHAPTER 32

Masculinities in Motion

Latino Men and Violence in Kentucky

M. Cristina Alcalde

When I asked Miguel, a thirty-year-old man from Mexico, who was two sessions away from completing a court-mandated batterer intervention program whether he thought men's violence against women was more widespread in Mexico or the United States, he responded that there was more violence in Mexico. According to Miguel, "in the U.S. when the woman knows that the law here protects her, she is the one who becomes abusive . . . and here the police listens more to the woman than to the man." When I asked Ramón, a twenty-six-year-old man from Guatemala to tell me about his relationship with his wife, he explained he had never been physically violent toward her although they regularly argued. As he described how he helped around the house, he explained that although his guy friends teased him about it, "I'm not *maricón* [gay], but I do help my partner when she's sick. I cook." Like Miguel and Ramón, other men I interviewed referred to the use of violence and to messages they received from their peers as they discussed what it means to be a Latino man in Kentucky.

This article examines how men construct masculinity in response to the following three interrelated factors: migration, women's behaviors, and peer pressure. These factors do not determine men's use of violence, yet situating them within men's lives allows us to better understand men's on-the-ground experiences as well as possible connections between men and violence. First, and most broadly, migration brings men increased work opportunities and earning power in comparison to their lives in their communities of origin. Perhaps somewhat paradoxically, migration also renders men especially vulnerable to discrimination, exploitation, and deportation (in the case of undocumented migrants). Second, Latina women's behavior—particularly how they relate to their intimate partner—may change in the United States as a result of women's increased independence from men, and some men consider these changes to be a threat to their masculinity. Third, adult male peer socialization and peer pressure reinforce toughness, dominance, and even violence as necessary expressions of masculinity in a setting in which men may feel there are few other ways of affirming their manhood and in which they may have limited social and familial support networks.[1]

My research contributes to recent literature on migrant men's negotiation of familiar notions of masculinity within new settings (Donaldson et al. 2009). More specifically, it contributes to an emerging group of studies that examine the destabilization of masculinity and its connections to men's use of violence against women (Carrington and Scott 2008; Hautzinger 2003, 2004, 2007, 34; Hondagneu-Soteo and Messner 1994; Schuler, Hashemi, and Badal 1998; Staudt 2008; Wa Mungai and Pease 2009). I suggest the factors I examine contribute to (in the case of migration and women's behaviors)

SOURCE: Alcalde, C. M. (2010). Masculinities in Motion: Latino Men and Violence in Kentucky. *Men and Masculinities, 14,* 450–469. Reproduced with permission.

and reflect (in the case of peer pressure) the destabilization of masculinity in men's lives. Although men do not always respond to such destabilization through violence (see Walker 2005), men rely on violence to assert threatened masculinities in many settings.

Building on the literature on destabilized masculinities and men and migration, I propose that rather than being viewed simply as a reflection of men's desire to dominate and control women (Yllo 2004), the violence some of the men I interviewed used can be more accurately understood as symptomatic of men's perception that they are losing power within broader, sometimes unfamiliar systems of oppression outside the home. More importantly, men perceive that they are losing power just as women are gaining power both within and outside the home in the new host community. In dealing with the destabilization of masculinity that results from broader social, political, and economic sources outside the home, men may use violence against their intimate partner because their partners are easier targets than these more abstract sources, as a way to attempt to regain a sense of control over their lives.

My attention to men's exploitation and real or perceived powerlessness within the context of migration to and settlement in the United States does not mean that men's violence is justified or that men do not want to control women.[2] However, examining contributing factors within a broader oppressive setting provides a more complete picture of Latino men's experiences in the United States. It also underscores the importance placed on force and interpersonal violence as a signifier of masculinity in the absence of access to other forms of masculine power for some Latino men and in the absence of broader forms of protest directly against the social and economic discrimination and vulnerability men may face in their host communities.

Getting to Perspectives on Men's Violence

Men's perspectives on their violence and nonviolence against women are a relatively recent topic of feminist research (Anderson and Umberson 2001, 359). Little anthropological research has been conducted on men who are abusive and even less on nonviolent forms of masculinity. More specifically, research on Latino masculinities in the United States is scant and only rarely results in full-length monographs (but see Cantú 2009; Mirandé 1997). At the same time, men's violence against women is a global problem. My focus on Latino men should not suggest that Latinos are somehow more violent than men within other broad identity categories.

In approaching men's lives I take seriously Moore's point that "a single subject can no longer be equated with a single individual" (1994, 55) and understand men's and women's identities as relational, fluid, and situational (Glissant 1989). Consequently, my references to men's use of violence do not imply that I advocate an understanding of these or any other men as unidimensional persons whose identities can be summarized through such labels as "batterer" or "abuser." My interest in men's violence is grounded in the belief that masculinity is multidimensional, varied, and malleable. Men's violence against women is only one of many resources available to men in the construction of masculinity (Messerschmidt 1993). There are many dimensions to men's lives and identities. This article focuses only on a select few among a specific group of men.

Data for this article come from interviews conducted with twenty Latino men in 2007 and 2008 in Louisville and Lexington, Kentucky's two largest cities. I contacted participants through a Latino men's community group, the facilitator for the only batterer intervention program in Spanish in one of the two cities, and through a bilingual therapist. Interviews addressed a range of topics, from childhood experiences to intimate relationships as adults to crossing the border and discrimination in the host community. Interviews were semistructured and open-ended and lasted between forty minutes and two and a half hours. I interviewed each person one time, in Spanish. In a few cases, the interview consisted of a combination of Spanish and English (Spanglish) to reflect the interviewee's preference.

Most interviews took place either in an office in a Latino community center where the batterer intervention program met or in an office in a nonprofit organization at which a Latino men's community group met. In interviewing both men in a batterer intervention program and men in a Latino men's community group that sought to educate others about the importance of not using violence, my goal was to include a diverse group of men.

The majority of the participants was Mexican or of Mexican descent, but three men were from Central America (one from Honduras and two from Guatemala) and one man was from South America (Chile). Most men (75 percent) were undocumented. Two men were born in the United States and had U.S. citizenship, while three others were legal permanent residents. Participants' ages ranged from twenty-one to sixty-nine. Nine men were in their twenties, four in their thirties, another four in their forties, and three in their sixties. Educational background ranged from some elementary school to graduation from college and professional graduate school. Men had been in the United States anywhere from three to forty years. The majority of men had been in the country between five and ten years.

Batterer intervention programs for court-referred men arrested for assaulting their partner generally last between three and six months. The program from which I recruited men lasted 28 weeks. Like other batterer intervention programs, it consisted of weekly meetings. Each meeting lasted one and a half hours. Meetings were aimed at getting men to take responsibility for their behaviors, examine the attitudes that support abusive behaviors, and change their attitudes and behaviors. Participants paid an initial evaluation fee of $50 before being allowed in the program. Each week, participants paid $25 at the beginning of the meeting. Generally, men in these programs tend to be in their late twenties and early thirties and to be underemployed (Gondolf 2002, 94), and this was also the case for men I interviewed.

Men in the community group were concerned primarily with outreach to the local Latino community about gender equality, health issues, and immigration. The group held monthly meetings. Made up of a small group of committed men and women allies, the group was primarily made up of middle-class, professional men and women who are in the United States legally.

While my choice of these two main groups may at first glance suggest a neat division between documented/professional/nonviolence and undocumented/low-skill labor/violence, in reality no such division exists. This trend has more to do with the low number of men interviewed, the availability of groups through which to interview men, the increased resources professional men have to deal with domestic violence, and the relative newness of the Latino men's group. Although the Latino men's group wanted to attract Latinos of all backgrounds as members, my interviews with members of the group took place during the group's first year when it was still working on expanding its membership base. In part, the predominantly professional membership of the group reflected undocumented, poorer Latino men's longer working hours and sometimes lack of transportation, which left little time to dedicate to these types of community groups.

Latinos in the United States and in Kentucky

At 15 percent of the national population, Latinos are the largest and fastest growing minority group in the United States (U.S. Bureau of the Census 2006). By 2050, Latinos are expected to make up one-fourth of the U.S. population. While many Latinos have been in the United States for several generations, migration continues to be a significant force in the lives of many other Latinos. More than half of all Latinos are first-generation immigrants and an additional one-fifth of Latinos are children of first-generation immigrants (Mariscal 2005).

The U.S. West and Southwest boast the greatest concentration of Latinos, yet the South has experienced a significant increase in Latino immigration over the last two decades. Today, six of the top ten growth states for Latinos are in the U.S. South (Barcus 2007, 92), yet few studies of Latinos in the region exist and even fewer of Latinos in Kentucky. Latinos have moved to the South for varying reasons, but among work-related ones, the availability of jobs in meat processing, carpet manufacturing, tobacco, oil extraction, as well as horse, fruit, poultry, and dairy farms stands out (Barcus 2007, 91). Employment opportunities within the manufacturing and agriculture industries have generally shrunk in the United States. However, in the South, jobs in these industries increased from 1970 to 2000 as companies moved to the region to avoid higher wages and stronger environmental regulations in other parts of the country (Shefner and Kirkpatrick 2009, xxv).

Kentucky's non-Latino population is roughly 90 percent white and 8 percent African American (U.S. Bureau of the Census 2008). These percentages are above the national average for whites and below the national average for African Americans. Latinos do not constitute a single race, nationality, or culture, but as a group their presence defies the black–white binary that has historically characterized life in the South, including in Kentucky. This binary may be reflective of a local white population that has not yet developed definitive attitudes toward Latinos as Latinos. Instead, local whites may treat Latinos as part a larger nonwhite group, or persons of color, precisely because of the relatively recent influx of significant numbers of Latinos and because Latinos are dispersed rather than concentrated in one city or rural town.

Between 1990 and 2000, the growth rate of Kentucky's Latino population ranked eighth in the United States (National Council of La Raza n.d.). The majority of the state's Latino population is of Mexican origin and close to 60 percent of Latinos in Kentucky are men (Shultz 2008). Between 1990 and 2006, Kentucky's Latino population increased by 300 percent, marking a significant change in the population of a state characterized by out-migration much more than in-migration (Shultz 2008).

As a state on the border of the north–south divide, Kentucky, and particularly Louisville, prides itself on being open to northern and western influence. This does not mean, however, that there is no anti-immigrant sentiment or that Latinos are impervious to the south's more infamous history of racism. There is widespread evidence that low-income Latinos "are encountering widespread hostility, discrimination and exploitation" in the South (Southern Poverty Law Center 2009, 4). More generally, in the United States, "half of second-generation Latin youths and up to two-thirds of Mexican Americans report having suffered discrimination" (Portes 2009, 18). Discrimination against new immigrants and second-generation Latinos underscores the pervasiveness of anti-Latino sentiments and the need to consider discrimination as a significant issue for Latino men.

In spite of the hostility some immigrants experience, many others find much to praise about their new home and, according to recent studies, many Latinos are planning on making Kentucky their home in the long term (Barcus 2007, 100). Long-term residency in Kentucky reflects not only increased work opportunities but also Latinos' knowledge of the increasing difficulty and dangers persons, particularly those who are undocumented, may face when attempting to re-enter the United States, if and when they visit their home community. In other words, increased border security has had "the ironic effect of encouraging rather than discouraging permanent settlement in the United States" (Rich and Miranda 2005, 198).

Although men find more opportunities to earn enough money to support a family in the United States than in Mexico, in Fayette county (which includes Lexington) Latinos generally earn below-poverty wages (Rich and Miranda 2005, 202). Earnings among the undocumented men I interviewed ranged from roughly $1,000 a month for a restaurant cook to $2,000 a month for a construction worker. As elsewhere in the country, in Kentucky, most undocumented Latinos "have no insurance, no job security, no legal recourse in case of job discrimination or exploitation, little chance of accessing social services available to U.S. citizens, and no chance of someday recapturing their contributions to the Social Security system" (Rich and Miranda 2005, 202).

In the United States, approximately 26 percent of women report being abused by their intimate partner (Tjaden and Thoennes 2000). In Kentucky, the average is higher, with approximately 37 percent of adult women having been abused by an intimate partner (Fritsch et al. 2005). There are no studies specifically on Latinas' or Latinos' experiences of domestic violence in the state. Additionally, nationally there is almost "a complete absence of treatment outcome studies for Latino men who undergo court-mandated therapy as a result of their conviction for domestic violence" (Welland and Ribner 2008, 22). This article addresses the gap in studies on Latino men and their attitudes toward and uses of violence.

Migration: Increased Work Opportunities, Increased Vulnerability

Among the men I interviewed both in the batterer intervention program and in the Latino men's community group, migration played a significant role in destabilizing men's feelings of power and shaping emerging feelings of powerlessness and vulnerability. On one hand, men came to the United States in search of better work opportunities for themselves and a better future for their families. On the other hand, finding work commonly meant that they encountered long and strenuous workdays, unscrupulous bosses, and social discrimination.

As noted by Connell, actively "grappling with a situation, and constructing ways of living in it, is central to the making of gender" (1995, 114). Although migration studies have traditionally focused on men, they have rarely examined men as gendered beings (Donaldson et al. 2009). For some Latino men in the United States, the making and performance of masculinity in the context of migration involves prioritizing physical labor as a signifier of masculine power. In San Francisco, Mexican and Central American day laborers feel vulnerable because of the hostility, exploitation, and discrimination they encounter on street corners as they wait for work, on the job, and in running everyday errands. In this context, men increasingly rely on their work to maintain self-esteem and to define themselves as "real" men who are tough, hard-working, and able to provide for their families (Walter, Bourgois, and Loinaz 2004). Men place significant value on their ability to work as a way to "resist their structural vulnerability in a historically evolved low-wage labor migration system that denies them citizens' rights" (Walter, Bourgois, and Loinaz 2004, 1162).

My interviews with men in Lexington and Louisville similarly underscore the centrality of work, particularly physical labor, to men's sense of masculine power within a migration context. However, even as men placed heightened importance on their identities as workers, they understood that this source of masculinity is precarious because they can be laid off at any moment. One man explained that although he was trained as a veterinarian, his undocumented status only allowed him to find work as a construction worker. He viewed his work in the United States as below his professional qualifications but felt proud of it because it allowed him to continue to be the breadwinner in the family. In responding to my question of how, if in any way, Latino and U.S. non-Latino men are different, several men stated with pride that Latinos worked more and harder than non-Latino American men. As one man put it, "there are Americans who think like Latinos and Latinos that think like Americans." More common responses were that "some Americans don't work as hard as Mexicans." Or, as another man explained,

> Since they are in their country, they don't really care [about work]. Since we are not from here we are more careful in our work, we try to follow the rules here more. And for them, how does it affect them? If they lose the job, tomorrow they get another one. And for us, even if it doesn't go well on the job, or they say this or that to you, well we have to put up with it, there are times you have to put up with it for the family.

Work became an especially significant source of value and pride in a setting that denies undocumented Latino men rights and a sense of security afforded to U.S. men on the basis of citizenship. At the same time, men understood that their undocumented status made them vulnerable to intimidation and exploitation and that this increased vulnerability made it easier for them to lose a very important source of value: their job. Many men and women are vulnerable to job loss in the current economy, yet undocumented workers are especially vulnerable. Undocumented men face additional obstacles to providing for their families as compared to men who are U.S. citizens because of the precariousness of jobs for undocumented workers.

The undocumented men I interviewed are among the approximately eleven million undocumented migrants in the United States, most of whom are from Latin America. Together with other undocumented workers, the men I interviewed make up about 5 percent of the U.S. labor force (Hincapié 2009, 94). Far from their country of origin and extended families, men who had recently migrated to the United States felt isolated due to their lack of English skills, their long workdays, difficulties in transportation, and their undocumented status. Being undocumented prevented men from visiting their communities of origin as well as from becoming full participants in their host communities. Several men felt anxious about the possibility of being pulled over because they were driving—a necessary task to get to and from work—without a license. They stated that they believed police could pull them over simply because they looked Latino.

Men emphasized that they had heard stories of others being discriminated but had not really felt discrimination personally. Antonio's response to whether he had been discriminated against in Kentucky was typical in this respect: "Well, you know we Latinos are discriminated. I haven't experienced it, but I've seen it." Antonio had been in the United States, and in Kentucky, for approximately six years. He was in the batterer intervention program when we met. In part, some men's hesitance to discuss discrimination in personal terms may have resulted from their desire to appear tough in front of me—a Latina woman.

Although men generally stated that they did not feel personally discriminated against because of their undocumented status, I found that the longer men lived in Kentucky, the more likely they were to bring up discrimination as something they had personally experienced. This may be because the longer someone is in Kentucky, the more likely it is that his undocumented status—if he is undocumented—will prevent his upward mobility as he is passed up for promotions and raises. I also found that professional Latino men in the States legally were more likely than undocumented men in low-skill labor jobs to bring up discrimination during interviews. In part, this may be because undocumented men live more isolated from the local community precisely because of their legal status and therefore have fewer opportunities to experience social discrimination directly. Undocumented men may have felt more hesitant to bring up discrimination because they wished to avoid unwanted attention to their presence in the United States.

When I asked Alberto, a sixty-seven-year-old business leader in the Latino community and a member of the Latino men's community group, if he had ever experienced discrimination in Kentucky, he replied that "the doors do not open for the person of color like us, even if we were Chinese, African, it's the same thing. The gringo here doesn't help us, first he helps the other gringo . . . and that's discrimination." Antonio, whom I met in the batterer intervention program, agreed that it was not so much because he was Latino than because he was a person of color that he could be discriminated against. Alberto and Antonio, although they have divergent views on how men and women should behave, both point to a broader white–nonwhite binary in Kentucky that affects Latino men's sense of self and power. Given the environment of potential and real discrimination outside the home, some men place increased importance on their ability to exert power within the home. As the following sections underscore, some men perceive women's behaviors toward them as something that threatens and destabilizes their sense of masculinity.

Women's Behaviors

Femininities and masculinities vary throughout Latin America and from one country, city, village, and family to the next. Nonetheless, according to dominant Latin American discourses, men should be powerful, independent, and in control of women in the family. In recognizing diverse forms of masculinity in the lives of the men I interviewed, Connell's (1987) differentiation between hegemonic and subordinate masculinities is useful because it underscores the differential access men have to power according to their social position. The hegemonic Latin American construction of masculinity is one of dominance over women. This model facilitates discrimination against men who do not satisfy the ideal of the dominant, heterosexual man as well as against women who challenge this form of masculinity. Although violence is not inherent to hegemonic masculinity, it is widely taught and practiced as a way to control women. Through violence, men conform to, and perform, the forms of masculinity and power expected of them (see Anderson and Umberson 2001; Kimmel 2008). Although men in marginalized social positions may not have access to power in the same ways or amounts as more privileged men, within the home violence against women may serve as a signifier of masculine power across social positions.

Migration resulted in better work opportunities but also in an overall sense of powerlessness, vulnerability, and frustration among the men I interviewed. Within this broader context of increased opportunities coupled with increased vulnerability, men referred to feelings of diminished power at home. Overall, men in the batterer intervention program insisted on being dominant within the family even as women's entrance into the workforce, monetary contributions to the household, and increased social freedom challenged men's views of themselves as heads of household.

In their work with Latino men in a batterer intervention program, Hancock and Siu (2009) found that

> The most common source of marital conflict reported by the men was the shift in gender roles that resulted from migration as their wives became involved in the workplace and contributed to family finances. Wives who never drove a car or worked outside the home in the pre-migration marriage gained new freedoms in the host culture that were troubling to the men. Even men whose wives did not work outside the home expressed fear that their wives might acquire notions of increased freedom and independence. (129)

Similarly, for some of the men I interviewed, changes in gender relations caused conflicts within the home. Some men responded by doing something they knew they could not do in their jobs because they would be fired: they used violence to assert their power. In this sense, Staudt's (2008, 46) point (originally made in reference to domestic violence on the United States–Mexico border) that although it is the "global political-economic octopus" that is responsible for their low wages and exploitation, men more commonly direct their rage against their partners because their partners are easier targets rings true for some of the men I interviewed.

According to Parrado et al. (2005), working class Mexican couples who have recently migrated to the United States commonly hold on to, and even exaggerate, traditional gender role expectations as a way to cope in an unfamiliar setting. Even as women find increased opportunities for independence in part as a result of migration, for men the "patriarchal definition of the male head-of-household as primary provider develops exaggerated importance . . . because of the hardships and danger they undergo in order to fulfill that masculine script" (Walter, Bourgois, and Loinaz 2004, 1163).

As Miguel complained to me during an interview, and as I noted earlier, "in the U.S., when the woman knows that the law here protects her, she is the one who becomes abusive." For Miguel, women's increased work opportunities in the United States results in a reversal of roles. This perceived change in roles is troubling to Miguel because men are no longer able to exert power over their partners in the same way as before. For Miguel, women become abusive in the United States because they ignore or even challenge some men's insistence on maintaining and even exaggerating gendered expectations common in their communities of origin. In my research, Latin American men identified divergent gender ideologies between their country of origin and the United States and between themselves and their partner as a source of conflict.

Although the majority of the men I interviewed lived with their partners, there were two cases in which men's partners remained in Mexico. In one of these cases, the man explained that although he sent money to his wife and children in Mexico regularly he had not seen them in two years. Far from his wife and family, he explained he had "gone astray" in the United States and become involved with an American woman. He had not told his wife about his new relationship and hoped that once he returned to Mexico, she would forgive him—if she ever found out about the relationship. His use of violence in his U.S. relationship led to his referral to the batterer intervention program. During the interview, he insisted that he had not had any similar problems with his wife in Mexico. Whether or not that was actually the case and if he romanticized the more traditional gender roles he had become accustomed to with his wife is unclear. Overall, however, many of the men in the batterer intervention program called upon traditional gender roles as they sought to adapt to their new environment.

Interviews with men reveal two important points related to men's perception of women's behaviors. First, men generally viewed Latina and American women as fundamentally different from one another. Second, it was when men believed that their Latina partners were taking on the negative characteristics they attributed to American women that a conflict—which the men in the batterer intervention program attempted to solve through violence—erupted. The following are some men's answers to my question on if and how they considered Latina and American women to be different or similar to one another:

Alberto: "Well, I think that American women, in my opinion, behave like any man. They like to go to bars like men. They like to do everything a single man likes to do. And the Latina woman, no, the Latina woman likes to stay home, the domestic life, she likes to behave well."
Alfredo: "American women are more liberal, they can do whatever they want."
Miguel: "I think Hispanic women think the man is the boss, and American women don't think that way."
Manuel: "The Latina woman is more reserved [shy], she has more values."
David: "Latinas do what they are supposed to do at home."

Although these answers are not representative of all Latino men's views, among the men I interviewed in the batterer intervention program they were common.[3] The theme of American women behaving "like a man" and being "wild" came up repeatedly. Men brought up the Americanization of Latina women as justification for men's attempts to exert greater control over their partner, sometimes through violence.

When I asked men to describe their ideal partner, men offered a range of responses, from the hierarchy-laden "someone who looks after me and cooks for me when I get home from work" to the more egalitarian "someone who values friendship and the balance between giving and taking." However, the most common characteristic men in the batterer intervention group attributed to the ideal partner was the more vague "someone who understands me." Men complained that women began to behave like American women the longer they were in the United States. What men perceived to be their partner's Americanization caused problems in their relationship because, according to the men, women could not *understand* men's needs once they began to behave like American women, and thus failed to meet men's expectations.

In her work with transnational Mexican families on both sides of the border, Hirsch (1999) found that men perceive women to have more power in the United States than in Mexico because in the United States a man cannot hit his wife without police interference and because women work outside the home more. As the previous paragraphs suggest, some men I interviewed in Kentucky also believed this. Significantly, women's increased work opportunities and accompanying increased independence do not necessarily translate into higher rates of women leaving abusive men. In the United States, less than half of Latinas who experience intimate violence seek one or more types of institutional help, compared to two-thirds of non-Latina white women who experience intimate violence

(Moracco et al. 2005, 340). Lower rates of reporting may be due to several reasons. In the case of undocumented Latinas, these reasons may include fear of deportation and fear of being separated from their children. In some cases, however, a woman may stop herself from calling the police to allow her partner to exert power over her. In allowing her partner to feel in control, she shows him that she has "not forgotten what she learned as a girl about how to get along *por las buenas* (by being nice)" and that despite their migration she still holds the same place she did in their community of origin in relation to him (Hirsch 1999, 1343).

Changes in women's behaviors, and more broadly in the dynamics within the marital relationship, are due only in part to migration. Attitudes toward marriage and gender roles also vary by generation, with the older generation emphasizing the more hierarchical *respeto* (respect) and the younger generation preferring the more egalitarian *confianza* (trust) model of marriage (Hirsch 1999). A companionate marriage built on *confianza*, however, "has more to say about the emotional intimacy couples can achieve through talking than it does about who gets the last word" (Hirsch 1999, 1340). Although I found both the *respeto* and the *confianza* marriage model among the men I interviewed, there was no clear division generationally. Additionally, having a companionate marriage model ideologically does not necessarily mean that the marriage is egalitarian in practice (Hirsch 1999). It also cannot guarantee that men will not at some point use violence to have the final word.

Peer Pressure

Previous studies suggest that men who use violence against women do so when their masculinity is threatened (Anderson and Umberson 2001; Dobash and Dobash 1992). Men may define acceptable and unacceptable ways for a woman to relate to a man in part according to the messages they receive from their male peers. Several of the men in the batterer intervention program described using violence against women as a way to enforce the power and privilege they had been socialized to expect not only as children but also as adults by other men. Women's behavior that men perceived as threatening to their masculine identity included talking back, telling men about women's legal rights as a way to reject men's violence, refusing to cook, and leaving the house without asking men for permission or telling them where they were going.

As noted in Ramón's response at the beginning of this article, his friends teased him that he was gay, and therefore not behaving in typically masculine ways, because he helped his wife when she was sick. Like Ramón, other men relied in part on peer pressure to evaluate their partner's as well as their own behavior. Men also looked to their male peers to assess the desirability and acceptance of using violence to enforce masculine dominance and privilege in specific situations.

In describing his relationship with his wife and the onset of violence in their relationship, Antonio tells me that "I changed a lot because of her. Because she would go to parties, with her girl friends, with her guy friends. And a lot of the guys would tell me, 'Look, you give her too much freedom.'" Antonio identifies external sources—his wife and his guy friends—as the reasons for *his* violence. More importantly, he echoes what he tells me his friends tell him: that his partner's behavior is unacceptable and that he has to do something about it. Similarly, in describing the violent episode that led to his arrest and participation in the batterer intervention program, Juan explains that "What happened is that I went to a party and a friend offered me a beer. I told him, 'No, I don't drink anymore' [but he said], 'Just one' and since the party was nice I accepted, and then another, and another, and another." Like Antonio, Juan blames mostly external factors for his violence rather than take full responsibility for his behavior. Juan went on to say that his wife reprimanded him when she saw he was drunk after he came home from the party. He pushed her because he told her "Don't yell at me, I don't like that" yet she did not stop yelling at him. In Juan's description of events, it is the guy friend who pushed him to drink, the wife who talked in a way she should not, and, later, the police officer who showed up when he should not have that led to his arrest. Like other men in the batterer intervention program, he initially placed blame primarily on others.

Several men described male coworkers and friends who advised them or others to not allow women too much freedom. What male peers had said would often come up as men described episodes in which they had been violent toward their partner, as a way of explaining—or perhaps justifying—their actions. Men looked after one another by policing women's behaviors so that these did not threaten the superior status men expected vis-à-vis women. As one man explained, when he saw a friend's partner out late at night without her husband he advised his friend that "you have to control her." He went on to say he would expect his friends to similarly advise him, if they ever saw he could not control his wife. He then quickly added that his wife knew how to behave and would not be out late at night partying without him.

Peer pressure reinforced hegemonic forms of masculinity, which sometimes included the use of violence and kept alternative ways of being a man hidden. For some men, talking about their marital problems in more than a superficial way with their male peers threatened to make the men revealing marital problems vulnerable to insults of being weak by exposing ways of behaving that deviated from hegemonic forms of masculinity. About half way through several interviews with men from the batterer intervention program, with the door firmly closed and as each man became more comfortable answering questions about his life, each man commented that he did not have anyone else to *really* speak with about marital issues. Two men went on to apologize to me for speaking so much. For these men, the need to appear tough prevented them from opening up and dealing with emotionally charged marital issues in constructive ways with their male peers.

Another area in which hegemonic forms of masculinity made men reluctant to reveal alternative form of masculinity was in relation to their sexuality. For example, for the two men in the study who identified as gay—both professionals not involved in the batterer program—peer pressure to conform to dominant, heterosexual forms of masculinity prevented them from disclosing their sexual orientation to their male coworkers. As Kimmel (2000) has emphasized and these and other men know, homophobia is a key component of hegemonic masculinity.

Implications for Interventions

Men's perception that familiar forms of masculinity are being threatened and their responses to this destabilization of masculinity are partly informed by men's experiences of migration, changing gender roles, and peer pressure. Beyond underscoring the need for more scholarly attention to the destabilization of masculinities as connected to men's use of violence, the research presented here may also have implications for batterer intervention program design.

Three-fourths of Latinos who have entered the United States "since 1990 are unable to speak English well" (Welland and Ribner 2008, 39), and some of those Latinos are at some point referred to batterer intervention programs. However, Spanish-language programs are extremely limited. As recently emphasized by Hancock and Siu (2009) and Welland and Ribner (2008), culturally sensitive batterer intervention programs are central to reaching Latinos. In Lexington, Kentucky, there is only one such batterer intervention program, and the provider who facilitates it cannot meet the demand for his services. The scarcity of batterer intervention programs in Spanish not only in Kentucky but also elsewhere in the United States underscores the need to develop and offer more culturally sensitive, Spanish-language programs. Yet, given findings that question the effectiveness of batterer intervention programs (Gondolf 2002), it is clear that simply creating more programs may not be sufficient.

In designing culturally sensitive programs for Latinos, incorporating and discussing the role of migration, gender role changes, and peer socialization and pressure in men's behaviors may lead to the creation of an atmosphere that is more conducive to men engaging with and being receptive to program content. Although in the program men I interviewed participated in migration, changing gender roles, and peer socialization all came up repeatedly during discussions, as far as I could observe there were no sessions dedicated specifically to dealing with these issues. Given men's feelings of vulnerability and the peer pressure to conform to gender stereotypes they may experience, it is equally important that programs avoid oversimplifying "Latin American" and "Latino" cultures, ideologies, and practices in their search for culturally sensitive materials. Discussing diversity among Latino masculinities may help validate alternative masculinities and allow men such as those I interviewed to feel safe expressing their feelings of vulnerability in a male group setting.

Conclusions

Connections among masculinity, violence, and nonviolence in Latino men's lives are varied. On one hand, given the centrality of hegemonic forms of masculinity that emphasize men's power and privilege in relation to women and to some other men, "to deny the existence of a cult of 'exaggerated masculinity' in Latin America would be inappropriate, when there is so much evidence of male domination and/or mistreatment of women" precisely as a result of dominant constructions of masculinity (Chant and Craske 2003, 16). On the other hand, the practices and beliefs of men who do not use violence, and especially of those who purposefully seek to educate others about the importance of not using violence, challenge the popular view of "a biologically fixed master pattern of masculinity" that is inherently violent and of the inevitability of violence as an expression of masculinity (Connell 2000, 22).

Men I interviewed, both those who used violence against women and those who did not, brought up several factors that influenced their views of what it meant to be a man and the desirability and acceptability of using violence against women. This article has explored three of these. The first and broadest of these is migration to the United States. Men identified migration as a source of both increased work opportunities and increased feelings of vulnerability and powerlessness. In many ways, migration destabilizes expected forms of masculinity as men adapt to the host community and men felt some of the changes associated with migration to be emasculating. Some men used violence against women in the home to attempt to regain power they could not claim in public as a result of the exploitation and discrimination they faced. Thus, although women were not responsible for the discrimination men experienced, women proved to be easier targets on which to vent men's feelings of vulnerability and frustration and exert control. The second is women's increased freedom as a result of migration. Within a broader context in which men already felt their ability to exert power threatened due to social discrimination, men perceived women's behaviors to be potentially emasculating because they challenged men's "right" to control a wife or partner.

The third factor is peer pressure, which men most commonly described as promoting the control of women through violence, if necessary. Peer pressure and socialization are more commonly discussed in relation to young boys and adolescents. Interviews with adult men in the batterer intervention program underscore the need for further analysis of the role of adult male socialization in men's use of violence against women. This may be an especially important area to study in the case of immigrants who may not count on family support networks in their new community.

The knowledge we gain from examining migrant Latino men's beliefs and practices about being a man and the use of violence against women in the context of multiple identities and roles in their lives brings us one step closer to closing gaps in our understanding of domestic violence and of Latino experiences in the United States. It suggests that some men use violence against women as a strategy to attempt to regain power and control in an increasingly uncontrollable setting that destabilizes their masculinity and that interventions would benefit from more fully incorporating specific factors that inform men's perception that their gendered identity is being destabilized.

Notes

1. In spite of its variation, one thing we know for certain about violence against women is that it is generally men who commit it. Yet, as Connell reminds us, "though most killers are men, most men do not kill or even commit assault" (2000, 22) and connections between masculinity and violence are far from natural. In focusing on three factors, this article suggests that rather than pinpoint single causes of men's violence against women, a more productive approach to conceptualizing connections between masculinity and men's use of violence is to contextualize and analyze multiple contributing factors within the broader systems of power and oppression in which they occur (Heise 1998).

2. In examining men's violence against women in a working-class neighborhood in Mexico city, for example, Gutmann (1996) concludes that men who use violence feel that "they are losing control over their wives" (213).

3. Less common answers included "Latinas lie more than American women" (by a man who believed his wife had been unfaithful to him) and "there are no differences."

References

Anderson, Kristin, and Debra Umberson. 2001. Gendering violence: Masculinity and power in men's accounts of domestic violence. *Gender and Society* 15:358–80.

Barcus, Holly. 2007. New destinations for Hispanic migrants: An analysis of rural Kentucky. In *Latinos in the New South: Transformations of Place*, ed. H. A. Smith and O. J. Furuseth. Burlington: Ashgate Publishing.

Cantú, Lionel. 2009. *The sexuality of migration: Border crossings and Mexican immigrant men.* New York: New York University Press.

Carrington, Kerry, and John Scott. 2008. Masculinity, rurality, and violence. *British Journal of Criminology* 48:641–66.

Chant, Sylvia, with Nikki Craske. 2003. *Gender in Latin America.* New Brunswick: Rutgers University Press.

Connell, R. W. 1987. *Gender and power.* Stanford: Stanford University Press.

Connell, R. W. 1995. *Masculinities.* Berkeley: University of California.

Connell, R. W. 2000. Arms and the man: Using the new research on masculinity to understand violence and promote peace in the contemporary world. In *Male roles, masculinities, and violence: A culture of peace perspective*, ed. I. Breines, R. W. Connell, and I. Eide. Paris: UNESCO Publishing.

Dobash, Russell, and Rebecca Emerson Dobash. 1992. *Women, violence, and social change.* New York: Routledge.

Donaldson, Mike, Raymond Hibbins, Richard Howson, and Bob Pease, eds. 2009. *Migrant men: Critical studies of masculinities and the migration experience.* New York: Routledge.

Fritsch, Travis A., Sergey S. Tarima, Glyn G. Caldwell, and Shannon Beaven. 2005. Population-based surveillance of intimate partner violence against Kentucky women: A comparison of state and national definitions and findings. Frankfort: Kentucky Epidemiological Notes and Reports 2–6.

Glissant, Édouard. 1989. *Caribbean discourse: Selected essays.* Translated by Michael Dash. Charlottesville: University Press of Virginia.

Gondolf, Edward. 2002. *Batterer intervention systems: Issues, outcomes, and recommendations.* Thousand Oaks: Sage.

Gutmann, Matthew C. 1996. *The meanings of Macho: Being a man in Mexico City.* Berkeley: University of California Press.

Hancock, Tina, and Karla Siu. 2009. A culturally sensitive intervention with domestically violent Latino immigrant men. *Journal of Family Violence* 24:123–32.

Hautzinger, Sarah. 2003. Researching men's violence: Personal reflections on ethnographic data. *Men and Masculinities* 6:93–106.

Hautzinger, Sarah. 2004. "Here the crock does not crow for he is not the lord of the land": Machismo, insecurity, and male violence in Brazil. In *Cultural shaping of violence: International perspectives*, ed. M. Anderson. Indiana: Purdue University Press.

Hautzinger, Sarah. 2007. *Violence in the city of women: Police and batterers in Bahia, Brazil.* Berkeley: University of California Press.

Heise, Lori. 1998. Violence against women: An integrated, ecological framework. *Violence Against Women* 4:262–90.

Hincapié, Marielena. 2009. Aqui Estamos y No Nos Vamos: Unintended consequences of current U.S. immigration law. In *Global connections, local receptions: New Latino immigration to the Southeastern United States,* ed. F. Ansley and J. Shefner. Knoxville: The University of Tennessee Press.

Hirsch, Jennifer. 1999. En el Norte la Mujer Manda: Gender, generation, and geography in a Mexican transnational community. *American Behavioral Scientist* 42:1332–49.

Hondagneu-Soteo, Pierrette, and Michael Messner. 1994. Gender displays and men's power: The 'New Man' and the Mexican immigrant man. In *Theorizing masculinities,* ed. H. Brod and M. Kaufman. Thousand Oaks: Sage.

Kimmel, Michael. 2000. Masculinity as homophobia. In *Reconstructing gender: A multicultural anthology,* ed. E. Disch. Boston: McGraw-Hill.

Kimmel, Michael. 2008. *Guyland: The perilous world where boys become men.* New York: Harper.

Mariscal, Jorge. 2005. Homeland security, militarism, and the future of Latinos and Latinas in the United States. *Radical History Review* 93:39–52.

Messerschmidt, James. 1993. *Masculinities and crime: Critique and reconceptualization of theory.* Lanham: Roman and Littlefield.

Mirandé, Alfredo. 1997. *Hombres y Machos: Masculinity and Latino culture.* Boulder: Westview Press.

Moore, Henrietta. 1994. *A passion for difference: Essays in anthropology and gender.* Oxford: Polity Press.

Moracco, Kathryn, Alison Hilton, Kathryn Hodges, and Pamela Frasier. 2005. Knowledge and attitudes about intimate partner violence among immigrant Latinos in rural North Carolina. *Violence Against Women* 11:340.

National Council on La Raza. n.d. State fact sheet: Kentucky. www.nclr.org/files/33190_file_ KY_final.pdf Accessed: October 18, 2009.

Parrado, Emilio A., Chenoa A. Flippen, and Chris Metzger McQuiston. 2005. Migration and relationship power among Mexican women. *Demography* 42:347–72.

Portes, Alejandro. 2009. The New Latin nation: Immigration and the Hispanic population of the United States. In *Global connections, local receptions: New Latino immigration to the southeastern United States,* ed. F. Ansley and J. Shefner. Knoxville: The University of Tennessee Press.

Rich, Brian L., and Marta Miranda. 2005. The sociopolitical dynamics of Mexican immigration in Lexington, Kentucky, 1997 to 2002: An ambivalent community responds. In *New destinations: Mexican immigration in the United States,* ed. V. Zúñiga and R. Hernández León. New York: Russell Sage Foundation Publications.

Schuler, Sidney Ruth, Syed M. Hashemi, and Shamsul Huda Badal. 1998. Men's violence against women in rural Bangladesh: Undermined or exacerbated by microcredit programmes? *Development in Practice* 8:148–57.

Shefner, Jon, and Katie Kirkpatrick. 2009. Globalization and the new destination immigrant. In *Global connections and local receptions: New Latino immigration to the Southeastern US,* ed. Fran Ansley and Jon Shefner. Knoxville: University of Tennessee Press.

Shultz, Benjamin J. 2008. Inside the gilded cage: The lives of Latino immigrant males in rural Central Kentucky. *Southeastern Geographer* 48:201–18.

Southern Poverty Law Center. 2009. *Under siege: Life for low-income Latinos in the South.* Montgomery: Southern Poverty Law Center.

Staudt, Kathleen. 2008. *Violence and activism at the border: Gender, fear, and everyday life in Ciudad Juarez.* Austin: University of Texas Press.

Tjaden, Patricia, and Nancy Thoennes. 2000. *Extent, nature, and consequences of intimate partner violence: A research report.* Washington, DC: National Institute of Justice and the Centers for Disease Control and Prevention.

U.S. Bureau of the Census. 2006. *Statistical abstract of the United States.* Washington, DC: U.S. Department of Commerce.

Wa Mungai, Ndungi, and Bob Pease. 2009. Rethinking masculinities in the African Diaspora. In *Migrant men: Critical studies of masculinities and the migration experience,* ed. M. Donaldson, R. Hibbins, R. Howson, and R. Pease. New York: Routledge.

Walker, Liz. 2005. Men behaving differently: South African men since 1994. *Culture, Health & Sexuality* 7:225–38.

Walter, Nicholas, Philippe Bourgois, and H. Margarita Loinaz. 2004. Masculinity and undocumented labor migration: Injured Latino day laborers in San Francisco. *Social Science and Medicine* 59:1159–68.

Welland, Christaura, and Neil Ribner. 2008. *Healing from violence: Latino men's journey to a new masculinity.* New York: Springer.

Yllo, Kersti. 2004. Through a feminist lens: Gender, diversity, and violence. *In Controversies in family violence*, ed. R. Gelles, D. Loseke, and M. Cavanaugh. Thousand Oaks: Sage.

CHAPTER 33

Reaching Out and Digging In

A Global Perspective on Engaging Men in Gender-Based Violence Prevention

Juliana Carlson

Men's role in the perpetration and prevention of gender-based violence is a central issue. Discourse ranges from male gender norms that promote men's use of violence to male notions of accountability as anti-gender-based violence activists to women's organizations. Australian pro-feminist sociologist Michael Flood (2011) makes it even clearer, stating "we have no choice but to address men and masculinities if we want to stop violence against women" (p. 359). One place these discourses converge is the study and practice of engaging men in preventing gender-based violence before it starts. Across the globe, organizations and governments alike are taking strategic strides to develop and implement approaches to (1) engage men to see gender-based violence, and more broadly gender equity, as a men's issue, and (2) activate men to take a role in preventing gender-based violence.

Throughout this chapter, I will be using the term gender-based violence, rather than violence against women; this is a conscious and political choice. Gender-based violence is defined by the United Nations as "a wide range of human rights violations, including sexual abuse of children, rape, domestic violence, sexual assault and harassment, trafficking of women and girls and several harmful traditional practices" (http://www.unfpa.org/gender/violence.htm). Operationalizing violence perpetrated disproportionately against women and girls as *gender-based* brings concepts familiar to the study of masculinities, such as gender identity and gender norms, to the forefront. At the same time, constructing violence against women and girls as gender-based violence also brings to the vanguard the value of gender equity, which is central to the operationalization of gender-based violence prevention.

To increase and diversify the strategies to end the global epidemic of violence against women, efforts to engage boys and men in primary prevention of gender-based violence has surged over the last 15 years. Hundreds of organizations in individual countries and international bodies across the globe have mobilized to actively engage boys and men in stopping gender-based violence. The United Nations and the World Health Organization have spearheaded much of the political and financial support of these primary prevention efforts.

With the awareness of the structural, economic, and political nature of gender-based violence, prevention approaches have simultaneously pursued systemic social and policy change to address gender inequality and gender-based violence. These new individual and community level tactics place more

SOURCE: Carlson, J. *Reaching Out and Digging In: A Global Perspective on Engaging Men in Gender-Based Violence Prevention.*

concerted attention on primary prevention. These new tactics also grow from the understanding that in order to end violence against women and girls, men and boys must identify and enact their role in primary prevention. This differs fundamentally from the approach of men's engagement as perpetrators of violence in what are called "batterer intervention programs" (BIP). BIPs are designed to intervene with men currently using violence. However, generational transmission of patterns of violence mean that even if individuals choose to stop being violent, the impact of the previous use of violence ripples out past their victims to the children and other individuals in their lives. Primary prevention is therefore essential. International and regional efforts to develop the organizational capacity to implement primary prevention strategies to engage men and boys have also emerged. Although the emphasis to engage men and boys grows, the evidence of what works and, equally important, how it works, is growing; but it is still limited.

This chapter provides a global snapshot of organizational level efforts to engage men and boys in gender-based violence prevention (Carlson et al. 2015; Casey et al. 2014; Storer et al. 2015). This collection of studies provides perspectives from a small sample of organizational representatives involved in the day-to-day work of engaging men and boys within organizations from multiple countries around the globe. I begin with the conceptualization of gender-based violence within the larger social structure and some of the current approaches to engage men in the primary prevention of gender-based violence.

Gender-Based Violence in Context

Gender-based violence—which is all forms of violence perpetrated due to gender inequality and traditional gender norms—is recognized as one of the greatest social problems in our global society. Violence against women is a "global public health problem of epidemic proportions" (WHO, 2013). Gender-based violence operationalizes violence, which is predominantly perpetrated by men and boys against women and girls, as a gendered phenomenon. This means that social norms of masculinity and femininity help produce violence. Constructing gender-based violence as a gendered phenomenon identifies both the prevalent victims (i.e., women and girls) and the disproportionate perpetrators (i.e. men and boys) in the phenomena (Reed et al. 2010).

Gender-based violence perpetrated by men is a global epidemic. Data from the International Men and Gender Equality Survey (IMAGES), one of the most comprehensive and global studies on men's report on violence, fatherhood, and gender equity, shows that up to 46 percent of men report having used physical intimate partner violence (Levtov et al. 2014). Sexual violence is also relevant to the discussion. IMAGES data show that men who perpetrate physical violence are significantly more likely to report sexual violence perpetration (Heilman et al. 2014). Findings from the IMAGES show that rates of sexual violence perpetration were between 4% and 25% (Heilman et al. 2014). Additionally, between 6–59% of women surveyed in a World Health Organization study of 10 low- and middle-income countries reported sexual violence sometime in their lives (WHO, 2010).

In addition, the framework of gender-based violence, rather than violence against women, highlights that men (both cisgender and transgender male) can be uniquely susceptible to violence for reasons related to gender. For example, sodomy may be used in conflict areas as a type of violence and torture to try and "emasculate" enemy forces (Carpenter 2006; Sivakumaran 2007). Viewing violence against men through a gender lens enables us to unpack the connections to complex social and gender norms. At the same time, the study of men as victims of violence—intimate partner, sexual violence in conflict areas and outside conflict areas—is a hotly debated area of research, particularly in the U.S. where some researchers have followed a trend of using scales and theoretical frameworks which ignore gender (for a lengthy discussion see Reed et al. 2010). Researchers who study violence using a gender-based violence framework argue that a gender lens must be included in all aspects of this discourse.

This gender lens application is also needed to situate gender-based violence not only as a relational act. Gender-based violence occurs and must be understood within the larger structural context of economic, health, political, and social gender inequity (Peacock & Barker 2014). For example, in 2013, child marriage—girls being married before the age of 18—was allowed with parental consent in 93 countries (World Policy Analysis Centre 2013). Female genital mutilation is common legal practice in Africa, Middle East and Asia, often performed by women elders under the social norm of male sexual satisfaction, impacting 200 million girls and women alive today (World Health Organization [WHO] 2016). Women's pay inequality continues to be an issue in low- and middle-income countries, as well as high-income countries such as the United States, with limited policies to address the issue. The social and political context of gender inequality perpetuates gender-based violence, showing that the personal is political.

Engaging Men and Boys to Prevent Gender-Based Violence

To address gender-based violence as an interpersonal and structural phenomenon, national and international bodies, such as the United Nations and WHO, have identified and promoted prevention strategies that work across multiple levels in the social ecology. The social ecological framework typically includes four nested systems: individual, relationship, community, and societal. Each of these systems must be considered as interconnected and interrelated dynamics. The argument for the social ecological framework to gender-based violence prevention rests on the belief that by considering only one of these four systems would be to miss out on an important part of the bigger picture. Preventionists—practitioners and researchers who focus on prevention—use the social ecological framework as the foundation for a multilevel (i.e. simultaneously across all four systems) prevention strategies. One commonly adopted multilevel approach to prevention is the Spectrum of Prevention, which outlines six levels: (1) influencing policy and legislation, (2) changing organizational practices, (3) fostering coalitions and networks, (4) educating providers, (5) promoting community education, and (6) strengthening individual knowledge and skills (Cohen and Swift 1999). Implementation of strategies across all these levels in tandem is required to effectively prevent gender-based violence. Applied to engaging men and boys in preventing gender-based violence prevention, multilevel social ecological approaches like the Spectrum of Prevention aim to identify strategies that will comprehensively engage men (Flood 2011).

Another prevention framework used to conceptualize efforts to engage men in gender-based violence prevention is the public health model. The public health model organizes prevention into three main approaches: primary, secondary, and tertiary prevention. The Center for Disease Control and Prevention (CDC) defines the three approaches clearly in their violence prevention literature (for example, see CDC 2004). Primary prevention approaches take place before violence has occurred to prevent initial perpetration or victimization. Secondary prevention is defined as immediate responses after violence has occurred to deal with the short-term consequences of violence. Tertiary prevention is defined as long-term responses after violence has occurred to deal with the lasting consequences of violence and treatment. Gender-based violence primary prevention within a public health framework seeks to stop violence before it starts (Chamberlain 2008).

Aim and Overview

In this chapter, I provide an overview of the qualitative research project conducted by a US-based research collaboration I am a part of (Carlson et al. 2015; Casey et al. 2014; Storer et al. 2015). This overview aims to shed light on one set of data cataloging the organizational level efforts to engage men and boys to prevent gender-based violence before it starts. These three studies provide a unique look at organizational representatives' perspectives on (1) strategies to engage men initially, and principles for deepening their engagement, (2) challenges and tensions in the work, and (3) how "primary prevention" is conceptualized in organizational practice. Following the overview of those studies, I will provide a short discussion on four questions: How have things changed since the time of these studies? What does the evidence base and theoretical frameworks used in the efforts to engage men and boys tell us about the work? How can organizations help hold male anti-gender-based violence activists accountable? Who should be engaged: men or the community?

How to Engage Men and Boys: Strategies and Principles

After my colleagues and I conducted interviews across the globe, we noticed that the actions of anti-violence organizations fell into two categories: "strategies as initial engagement" and "principles for deepening men's engagement" (Carlson et al. 2015). This conceptualization reflects the overall finding that the process of engaging men is not singular. Organizations develop "strategies"—specific actions and approaches—to invite men initially to participate, and different "principles"—actions and approaches—for facilitating and nurturing men's ongoing engagement.

Strategies to Reach Out

All the organizational representatives discussed the importance of reaching men through recruitment or initial engagement efforts (Carlson et al. 2015). These recruitment or initial engagement effort strategies were the practical techniques organizations used to enlist men and boys' participation in gender-based violence prevention, strategies were used to engage men in particular programmatic efforts and also in the more overarching personal orientation of seeing gender-based violence prevention as within their purview and responsibility as human beings. Together this makes up the category of strategies to reach out or initially engage. Clearly, these strategies are vitally important because if organizations fail to engage men in initial conversations, then they might not have another opportunity. Therefore, understanding organizations' conceptualization of and experience implementing initial engagement strategies is critical. The strategies emerged as five main themes: the who (enlist ambassadors), what (concrete opportunities), where (accessible entry points), why (men's reasons for becoming engaged) and how (intentional invitation) of initial engagement strategies.

The who. Twenty-seven percent of the organizational representatives identified that their organization used ambassadors as a strategy to initiate engagement (Carlson et al. 2015). The role of the ambassador to engage men in violence prevention efforts is to represent the mission of the organization—ending gender-based violence—to members of their communities and social networks. Ambassadors therefore can act as links in the community to the organization, and avoid the potential "outsider" status that organizational workers might have. These ambassadors were men who played different roles, such as sports figures, community leaders or members. Although a common strategy across many regions, including Asia, Australia, Europe, and North America, the ambassador approach was not a globally endorsed strategy.

The what and the where. Organizational representatives from the project also defined the "what" of engaging men and boys in ending gender-based violence as concrete opportunities. In other words, men and boys needed to be invited to join something tangible, such as a type of social action, event or program. Asking men and boys to become engaged requires offering them something concrete to engage with. Along with the importance of providing men and boys with a defined activity or behavior, organizational representatives stated that finding locations to meet and engage men and boys proved an important strategy (Carlson et al. 2015). Across the geographic regions, the representatives (48%) identified how determining the "accessible entry points" to reach out to men and boys was critical (pp. 1413–1414). The locations types varied and were shaped by the cultural and social context. For some organizations the market place where men might gather to sell goods were locations where they might easily reach out to men. For others it was sports venues such as rugby matches.

The why. Although my colleagues and I point out that the interview guide questions did not include organizations' perspectives on why men and boys were becoming engaged, several organizations discussed their interpretation of these reasons alongside of their organizational strategies (Carlson et al. 2015). Understanding why men and boys become engaged emerged in several organizational representatives' (21%) interviews, which may speak to one of the underlying strategies of engaging men and boys: understand why they may want to be involved and use that in your engagement.

The how. The strategy of "intentional invitation" emerged as the main way organizational representatives identified how they sought out men and boys' participation in gender-based violence prevention efforts (Carlson et al. 2015, p. 1414). Endorsed by nearly half of the representatives (41%), intentional invitations were not without regional specificity. Representatives in Europe or South America did not report this strategy.

To summarize, the five themes that were used globally in gender-based violence prevention can be understood as: the who (enlist ambassadors), what (concrete opportunities), where (accessible entry points), why (men's reasons for becoming engaged), and how (intentional invitation) of initial engagement strategies. However, it is clear that some of these strategies are regionally bound, and considering the need for cultural relevance within the discourse of gender justice, human rights, and gender-based violence, these general understandings and the exceptions are equally important to consider.

Strategies to Dig In

In addition to strategies to reaching out, organizations constructed "principles for deepening men's engagement" (Carlson et al. 2015), what I call here: strategies to dig in. As discussed above, engaging men in gender-based violence prevention doesn't end with reaching the men or even with raising men's awareness that gender-based violence is an issue, and that they have a role in ending that violence in their daily lives. Instead, participants described that organizations seek to develop men's engagement in sustainable and deep ways. Indeed, some organizational representatives stated that this deep engagement of men and boys in prevention was a fundamental requirement to end gender-based violence.

My colleagues and I describe four principles for deepening men and boys' engagement that emerged from the organizational representatives' perspectives. The principles were "(a) rooted in the community, (b) relationships and power first, (c) hopefulness about men, and (d) beyond workshops" (p. 1416). A brief overview of each of these principles demonstrates organizational representatives' underlying beliefs and values that they bring to the work of engaging men and boys.

The principle *rooted in the community* points to the organizational representatives' belief that to deepen men's engagement the work must be tailored to the particular community or communities where the work is happening (Carlson et al. 2015). In practice, organizations chose culturally and historically relevant organizing strategies. For example, one organizational representative from Asia talked about using marches in a country where other social justice movements had used that organizing strategy. Another organizational representative shared strategies to use dance and music, which was a common community strategy for bringing people together, as a way to open doors in villages in Africa. Both of these examples illustrate organizational representatives' responsiveness to being culturally aware of where they were working and incorporating the knowledge from that awareness to build a deeper engagement of male-identified individuals within that community.

Organizational representatives also identified the principle of placing *relationships and power first*, instead of directly drawing attention to male violence (Carlson et al. 2015). The rationale behind this strategy of beginning conversations/engagement of men with the topic of relationships and power stemmed in part from the desire to connect with men based on experience they have had. All people can relate to experiences of power within relationships (e.g. employee/boss, child/parent, student/child); therefore organizational representatives suggested starting conversations with men's understanding and experience of relationships and power might disarm men, and lead to less defensiveness. This soft pedal approach could appear as a way of not holding men accountable for their own violence and their complacency in gender-based violence. However, organizational representatives spoke about the importance of reaching men through avenues that didn't collude with negative gender norms but also didn't push men away before a conversation could begin.

Similarly, the third principle, *hopefulness about men*, communicated an overall belief that to successfully sustain the engagement of male-identified individuals organizations' approach must be a hopeful one (Carlson et al. 2015). Moreover:

> This hopefulness about men and boys ranged from their general "goodness" to their ability to change, to being inspired and mobilized for change in larger systems, such as their workplaces, communities, and society-wide, in the face of the gender-based violence that men perpetrate. (Carlson et al. 2015, p. 1427)

Organizational representatives contrasted a hopeful approach to approaches that tend to blame and disdain men. Although being hopeful about men emerged as a theme, 31% of the representatives from all the regions but South America identified it as a principle of engagement.

The final principle for deepening men's engagement was *moving beyond workshops*. Some organizational representatives saw the need for a shift away from the prevalent approach of hosting workshops as a strategy to engage men. Although this was not a principle endorsed by many organizational representatives, or across regional differences, the overall sentiment was strongly held and therefore was included in the findings (Carlson et al. 2015).

These principles echo sentiments from other engaging men scholarship. Approaching men from a place of hopefulness, for example, resonates across the last decade of scholarship. In what has been described as a "pro-feminist" rationale, activists and scholars argue that men have a positive role to play (Flood 2011), and that men's engagement should include positive messages (Barker & Peacock 2014; Berkowitz 2004; Flood 2006). This is particularly relevant as it may be challenging to sustain men's engagement in anti-violence work overtime (Funk 2008).

"Tensions" Within the Work

Organizational level participants also explored the challenges found within the work (Casey et al. 2013). Specifically, the participants identified five core challenges: "(1) negotiating issues of gender, (2) intersectionality, (3) sustainability, (4) legitimacy, and (5) ideological inclusivity" (Casey et al. 2013, p. 234). Although all challenges are relevant to the future of the efforts to engage men and boys in gender-based violence prevention, I will focus on negotiating issues of gender and intersectionality for this chapter.

Casey et al. (2013) describe that 86% of the participants identified that issues related to gender shaped their organization's approach to engaging men. The two main subthemes—male privilege and men only spaces—illustrate some of the ways organizations experience these tensions. Male privilege is understood as the way in which men as individuals and as a group benefit—directly and indirectly—from the social norm of male superiority in interpersonal, social, and economic ways. Organizational representatives (62%) described that they lived in tension between inviting men to participate using welcoming messages while simultaneously not colluding with male privilege. While the desire to speak directly to men about their participation in accepting violence against women, and their male privilege existed for participants, they also described having to "tiptoe" around these issues in the name of trying to engage them in prevention efforts (Casey et al. 2013, p. 236).

In addition to the way male privilege impacted their approach to engage men, organizational representatives in Casey et al. (2103) also described how their work in general challenged structural forces and social norms that caused broader push back. Casey et al. describes how "program representatives identified institutionalized male power within governmental, media, criminal justice, religious, tribal, and other community institutions as a significant barrier" (p. 236). The structural nature of male privilege therefore shapes organizations' access to funding, recognition, and membership, all critical elements in organizational development within communities.

These challenges speak to the tensions implicit in the work of engaging boys and men in gender-based violence, that includes asking them to acknowledge their direct and indirect experiences of privilege and the oppression of women. Therefore the imperative that organizations engage men in critical analysis of the cost of male privilege dovetails with the need to develop approaches that are culturally relevant and meet men where they are.

Primary Prevention: Is It?

Although my colleagues and I framed our research using a primary prevention framework, we found that in organizational practice, primary prevention is not a fixed idea (Storer et al. 2015). Organizational representatives reported a much less tidy conceptualization of primary prevention than the defined public health model of stopping violence before it begins. If the reader will recall, the public health model of prevention constructs prevention as three unique types: primary (i.e. stopping violence before it starts), secondary (i.e. intervening after initial incidents of violence), and tertiary (i.e. responding to long-term effects). In contrast, Storer et al. (2015) found that organizations' prevention conceptualizations included

> (a) preventing new incidents of abuse; (b) generating individual and community awareness and providing education about violence against women; (c) fostering individual competencies and skill building among non-indicated community members; (d) redefining masculinity at the individual, community, and societal levels; and (e) advocating for long-term institutional and social change such as promoting gender equality, human rights, and healthy relationships. (p. 9)

Although each of these conceptualizations is unique, the overarching lack of agreement reveals that how organizational representatives across global geographic regions conceptualize primary prevention in practice does not fit neatly into the public health conceptualization. Storer et al. (2015) point out that there appears to be a disconnect between "Western public health frameworks," that include the delineation of primary, secondary, and tertiary prevention, and the "blended approaches and broader organizational definitions of primary prevention" (p. 15). Storer et al. defines this as a "translational gap" that is important to consider as we define particular organizational work with men and boys as primary prevention.

Meditations: Looking Forward

What Has Changed?

Organizational level strategies to engage men and boys in preventing gender-based violence continue to grow and develop. Evidence from the field indicates an increased investment in time, funding, and effort toward this particular type of prevention approach. Kimball et al. (2013) found that of the 165 organizational participants in a survey about programs that engage men and boys to end gender-based violence, approximately 45% had been doing so for eight years or more. A clear indicator of this growth is the increase in organizations' members from 400 in 2013 to 700 of MenEngage (2015), the global membership-based coalition of organizations who aim to engage men and boys to end gender-based violence. Another piece of global evidence of the proliferation of the strategy is UN Women global initiative HeForShe, launched in October 2014 (HeForShe 2016). HeForShe seeks to enlist the support of men in promoting gender equality, via signing a statement that affirms gender equality as a basic human right (HeForShe 2016). As an individual pledge for men and a call to action for governmental leaders and nation states alike, HeForShe aims to strengthen the overall umbrella approach of engaging men and boys in gender equity work, which gender-based violence preventions fall under.

As the number of organizations and initiatives engaging men and boys continues to grow, further inquiry could provide the field with critical knowledge to inform future and potential corrective developments in organizational approaches, structure, funding, and frameworks. For example, in the last five years particularly, more attention has been paid to several issues, including the use of empirical knowledge of the effectiveness of primary prevention strategies, the question of men's accountability as "allies," and whether the approaches/interventions being used for individual and community level engagement of men are gender transformative. In addition, some have called for global efforts to be particularly mindful of the limitations and yet the propensity for organizations to work only at the individual and group level, when social level change action must take place across the social ecological system (Peacock & Barker, 2014). These issues are contemplated briefly here.

Theoretical Lens, Evidence-Based Practice, and Efforts to Engage Men and Boys

With the increased call for evidence-based programs tested using rigorous methods such as randomized controlled trials, questions regarding organizations use of these programs as part of their strategies to get men to dig into their gender equitable attitudes and behaviors should be included. This impacts local organizations. It may make certain organizations more poised for successfully receiving funding, which could lead these organizations to expand while other organizations may shrink. My colleagues and I found that funding was one of the issues that impacted organizations. This is something to consider: how do small community-based, innovative initiatives emerge when funders want programs tested using expensive, long-lasting randomized controlled trials?

Along with the evaluation of the evidence of an intervention's effectiveness, another important consideration is the theoretical framework of those programs. It is not enough that organizations engage men, and use evidence-based or promising interventions to do so. The guiding theoretical and conceptual framework of these interventions is of the utmost importance as the ultimate goal is gender equity. Barker and colleagues (2007) found in their review of programs to engage men and boys that gender sensitive and gender transformative interventions showed more effectiveness at attitudinal and behavior change than gender neutral or exploitative. More recently, Dworkin and her colleagues (2013) reviewed gender transformative interventions aimed at preventing HIV and gender-based violence through working with men. An example of a gender transformative intervention is the program *SASA!* the community mobilizing approach of preventing violence against women and HIV developed by Raising Voices, a non-governmental organization in Kampala, Uganda (Abramsky et al. 2014). In their review, Dworkin et al. (2013) reported that the evidence suggested that these gender transformative interventions were effective at changing gender norms and decreasing gender-based violence behaviors.

Organizations Can Promote Men's Accountability as Allies

Despite the well-intentioned efforts of organizations, the recent focus on men's activism against gender-based violence can also become problematic. Several issues are important to discuss. Defining the social problem as men's perpetration of gender-based violence alone potentially ignores the reality that relationship violence is nested and perpetuated within the larger systems of gender inequity and injustice. Further, caution must be used when we promote men's activism in the recent past and future without full recognition and affirmation of women and girls' critical, ground-breaking, risk-taking activism for centuries across the globe. Macomber (2015) describes five suggestions for organizations "to implement practices that support men's involvement without reinforcing existing gender inequalities" (p. 23). The suggestions are: "(a) require newcomers to receive training and education work before stepping into leadership roles, (b) cap men's speaking fees, (c) link men's organizations to women's organizations and groups, (d) institutionalize a process to address issues of privilege internally, and (e) reconceptualize accountability to include an emphasis on building gender equity" (Macomber, 2015, p. 23). These ideas are a good starting place for organizations whose work has engaged men over many years, and those organizations who are just beginning to. Depending on a gender-based violence prevention organization's level of engagement with men, including having men who are staff, volunteers, and key participants, more comprehensive and critical assessment of men's accountability within the organization may need to take place. Macomber's suggestions, particularly institutionalizing a process to address issues of privilege internally, and reconceptualizing accountability to include an emphasis on building gender equity, could provide a foundation for these organizational level assessments.

Engaging Men or Engaging the Community?

Along with the theoretical frameworks used, and the conceptualization of men's activism, there is a related challenge about whether the target for prevention strategies to prevent gender-based violence should be uniquely focused on increasing men's involvement or should they instead have a community involvement or mobilization approach. Although the purpose of our global research was to understand the organizational work of engaging men and boys in violence prevention, some organizational representatives identified a tension was between putting emphasis on particular content and strategies to engage men and framing the issue of gender-based violence as a community issue (Carlson et al. p. 1419). The distinction, and subsequent concern, stems from the inherent separation of men and women when organizations frame their efforts as working in isolation from women and the community in general. An increased awareness of these concerns has prompted closer attention to prevention efforts that engage both men and women (Ellsberg et al. 2014).

Conclusion

Organizations, be they small NGOs or large nation states, are increasing their commitment to systematic efforts aimed at ending gender-based violence. Initiatives that intentionally include men and boys are a vital part of a comprehensive community approach. The future of strategies to engage men and boys to take part in the local and global efforts to end gender-based violence will be directly shaped by the ongoing development of theoretical and evidence-based initiatives, across the social ecological landscape. Several challenges must be faced. The choice of theoretical framework for gender-based violence prevention has critical implications (Reed et al., 2010). Whether organizational approaches are gender transformative, gender sensitive or gender neutral, will influence all aspects of the work, including the long-term impact. Alongside the need for investment in theory building, it will be essential to strengthen the evidence base for the interventions aimed at ending gender-based violence (Ellsberg et al. 2014) and promoting gender equity. To broaden the impact of gender-based violence prevention, careful attention must be paid to assessing the effectiveness of community mobilization and structural level change. Clearly, change will not take place if gender-based violence remains a "women's issue." Organizations' comprehensive prevention approaches, therefore, must include strategies that reach out to men and boys as part of the community, and invite men to critically analyze and dig into analyzing the social causes of gender-based violence, and participate in dismantling systems of oppression.

References

Abramsky, Tanya, Karen Devries, Ligia Kiss, Janet Nakuti, Nambusi Kyegombe, Elizabeth Starmann, Bonnie Cundill et al. 2014. "Findings from the SASA! Study: A cluster randomized controlled trial to assess the impact of a community mobilization intervention to prevent violence against women and reduce HIV risk in Kampala, Uganda." *BMC Medicine* 12(1):1.

Barker, Gary Thomas, Christine Ricardo, and Marcos Nascimento. 2007. *Engaging Men and Boys in Changing Gender-Based Inequity in Health: Evidence From Programme Interventions.* http://vawnet.org/summary.php?doc_id=1459&find_type=web_desc_GC

Berkowitz, Alan D. 2004. "Working With Men to Prevent Violence Against Women: An Overview (Part One)." http://www.vawnet.org/applied-research-papers/print-document.php? doc_id=413

Black, Michele C., Kathleen C. Basile, Matthew J. Breiding, Sharon G. Smith, Mikel L. Walters, Melissa T. Merrick, and M. R. Stevens. 2011. "National Intimate Partner and Sexual Violence Survey." http://www.vawnet.org/research/NISVS/

Carlson, Juliana, Erin Casey, Jeffrey L. Edleson, Richard M. Tolman, Tova B. Walsh, and Ericka Kimball. 2015. "Strategies to Engage Men and Boys in Violence Prevention: A Global Organizational Perspective." *Violence Against Women*: 1077801215594888

Carpenter, R. Charli. 2006. "Recognizing Gender-Based Violence Against Civilian Men and Boys in Conflict Situations." *Security Dialogue* 37 (1): 83–103.

Casey, Erin A., Juliana Carlson, Cathlyn Fraguela-Rios, Ericka Kimball, Tova B. Neugut, Richard M. Tolman, and Jeffrey L. Edleson. 2013. "Context, Challenges, and Tensions in Global Efforts to Engage Men in the Prevention of Violence Against Women: An Ecological Analysis." *Men and Masculinities* 16, no. 2: 228–251.

Centers for Disease Control and Prevention. 2004. "Sexual Violence Prevention: Beginning the Dialogue." www.cdc.gov/ViolencePrevention/pdf/SVPrevention-a.pdf

Chamberlain, Linda. 2008. "A Prevention Primer for Domestic Violence." VAWnet Applied Research Forum. Retrieved from http://www.vawnet.org/Assoc_Files_VAWnet/AR_ PreventionPrimer.pdf

Cohen, Larry, and Chehimi, Sana. 2010. "The Imperative for Primary Prevention." In *Prevention Is Primary.* Edited by Larry Cohen, Vivan Chavez, & Sana Chehimi. 3-31. San Francisco, CA: Jossey-Bass.

Cohen, Larry, and Susan Swift. 1999. "The Spectrum of Prevention: Developing a Comprehensive Approach to Injury Prevention." *Injury Prevention,* 5(3): 203–207.

Dworkin, Shari L., Sarah Treves-Kagan, and Sheri A. Lippman. 2013. "Gender-Transformative Interventions to Reduce HIV Risks and Violence With Heterosexually-Active Men: A Review of the Global Evidence." *AIDS and Behavior,* 17(9): 2845–2863.

Ellsberg, Mary, Diana J. Arango, Matthew Morton, Floriza Gennari, Sveinung Kiplesund, Manuel Contreras, and Charlotte Watts. 2015. "Prevention of Violence Against Women and Girls: What Does the Evidence Say?." *The Lancet* 385 (9977): 1555–1566.

Flood, Michael. 2006. "Changing Men: Best Practice in Sexual Violence Education." *Women Against Violence,* 18, 26–36.

———. 2011. "Involving Men in Efforts to End Violence Against Women." *Men and Masculinities* 14 (3): 358–377.

HeForShe. 2016. HeForShe. http://www.heforshe.org/en

Heilman, Brian, Luciana Hebert, and Nastasia Paul-Gera. 2014. "The Making of Sexual Violence: How Does a Boy Grow Up to Commit Rape? Evidence From Five IMAGES Countries." Washington, DC: International Center for Research on Women (ICRW). http://www.icrw.org/publications/making-sexual-violence

Jewkes, Rachel, Mzikazi Nduna, Jonathan Levin, Nwabisa Jama, Kristin Dunkle, Adrian Puren, and Nata Duvvury. 2008. "Impact of Stepping Stones on Incidence of HIV and HSV-2 and Sexual Behaviour in Rural South Africa: Cluster Randomised Controlled Trial." *BMJ*, 337: a506.

Jewkes, Rachel, Michael Flood, and James Lang. 2015. "From Work With Men and Boys to Changes of Social Norms and Reduction of Inequities in Gender Relations: A Conceptual Shift in Prevention of Violence Against Women and Girls." *The Lancet*, 385(9977): 1580–1589.

Kimball, Ericka, Jeffrey L. Edleson, Richard M. Tolman, Tova B. Neugut, and Juliana Carlson. 2013. "Global Efforts to Engage Men in Preventing Violence Against Women: An International Survey." *Violence Against Women*, 19(7): 924–939.

Levtov, Ruti G., Gary Barker, Manuel Contreras-Urbina, Brian Heilman, and Ravi Verma. 2014. "Pathways to Gender Equitable Men: Findings From the International Men and Gender Equality Survey in Eight Countries." *Men and Masculinities*, 17:467–501. doi: 10.1177/1097184X14558234

Macomber, Kris. 2015. "'I'm Sure as Hell Not Putting Any Man on a Pedestal': Male Privilege and Accountability in Domestic and Sexual Violence Work." *Journal of Interpersonal Violence*: 0886260515618944.

MMVP. 2015. Mobilizing Men for Violence Prevention. http://www.tacoma.uw.edu/social-work/mobilizing-men-violence-prevention

MenEngage. 2015. Men Engage. http://menengage.org/

Nation, Maury, Cindy Crusto, Abraham Wandersman, Karol L. Kumpfer, Diana Seybolt, Erin Morrissey-Kane, and Katrina Davino. 2003. "What Works in Prevention: Principles of Effective Prevention Programs." *American Psychologist*, 58(6-7): 449–456.

Peacock, Dean, and Gary Barker. 2014. "Working With Men and Boys to Prevent Gender-Based Violence Principles, Lessons Learned, and Ways Forward." *Men and Masculinities*, 17(5): 578–599.

Reed, Elizabeth, Anita Raj, Elizabeth Miller, and Jay G. Silverman. 2010. "Losing the "Gender", in Gender-Based Violence: The Missteps of Research on Dating and Intimate Partner Violence." *Violence Against Women*, 16(3): 348–354.

Sivakumaran, Sandesh. 2007. "Sexual Violence Against Men in Armed Conflict." *European Journal of International Law*, 18(2): 253–276.

Storer, Heather L., Erin A. Casey, Juliana Carlson, Jeffrey L. Edleson, and Richard M. Tolman. 2016. "Primary Prevention Is? A Global Perspective on How Organizations Engaging Men in Preventing Gender-Based Violence Conceptualize and Operationalize Their Work." *Violence Against Women*, 22(2): 249–268.

World Health Organization/London School of Hygiene and Tropical Medicine. 2010. "Preventing Intimate Partner and Sexual Violence Against Women: Taking Action and Generating Evidence." http://www.who.int/reproductivehealth/publications/violence/9789241564007/en/

WHO. 2013. "Global and Regional Estimates of Violence Against Women: Prevalence and Health Effects of Intimate Partner Violence and Non-Partner Sexual Violence." http://www.who.int/reproductivehealth/publications/violence/9789241564625/en/

World Health Organization. 2016. "Female Genital Mutilation." http://www.who.int/mediacentre/factsheets/fs241/en/

World Policy Analysis Centre. 2013. "Changing Children's Chances: New Findings on Child Policy Worldwide." http://www.girlsnotbrides.org/child-marriage-law/

CHAPTER 34

The Former Lives of Anti-Sexist Men

Max A. Greenberg

How do some men come to make challenging hegemonic masculinity part of their identity? While doing research for our book, *Some Men: Feminist Allies and the Movement to End Violence against Women*, Michael Messner, Tal Peretz and I interviewed dozens of men who participated in the feminist anti-violence movement and worked to challenge dominant definitions of manhood. Take, for example, Gilbert Salazar, who was 29 when we interviewed him about his pathway into a position as a Rape Prevention Education Manager. He explained, "I was a boy in the median who, I think had there been other challenges or opportunities, you know, perhaps I could have done violence." Instead, he chose to spend his career focusing on challenging men's violence—why? Gilbert's assessment of his former self was similar to those made by other men doing anti-violence work, many of whom also expressed a belief that their lives could have led down a path to violence. The lives of men like Gilbert, who reconcile manhood acts aligned with hegemony and political work that challenges male domination, provide a unique opportunity to explore shifts in gender performance across time and social context.

There is, for good reasons, a critical analysis of male feminist allies (for example, see Pascoe and Hollander 2015), which has drawn attention to the ways that male feminists can reconstruct masculine power both intentionally and through de facto mechanisms (for example, by earning higher salaries in the field of anti-sexism work or by inflicting sexual harassment in the workplace). The men in this study did acquire some tangible and at times disproportionate benefits from their anti-violence work when compared to their female colleagues. However, such an analysis on its own risks obscuring the things that we can learn from these men.

Hoping to understand how to cultivate healthy masculinities, scholars have studied men's pathways into feminism and other forms of anti-sexist work, finding that men often describe a multi-part reaction: some kind of *sensitizing experience*, an *opportunity* for engagement and a radical spark of *meaning* (Casey & Smith 2010). However, we do not understand how men's pathways into gender justice work matter for their gender identity, informed by intersections of race, sexuality and class. In *Some Men*, my colleagues and I show that men's diverse pathways into anti-violence introduce new ways of making sense of the connections between social location and violence, which we call "organic intersectionality" (Messner, Greenberg and Peretz, 2015). Men's sensitizing experiences, opportunities and radical sparks take dramatically different forms depending on the historical moment in which they become engaged and their social location, as do the meanings they draw from these experiences.

Drawing on focused life history interviews with marginalized men involved in anti-violence feminist work, this chapter provides portraits of the lives of four men who came to see themselves as challenging dominant definitions of masculinity through a diverse array of interactional, emotional, and discursive resources. I analyze engagement with anti-violence feminism as one aspect of men's ongoing "gender projects": the unfolding processes of constructing gender over the course of one's life, in relation to shifting social and historical contexts (Connell & Messerschmidt 2005). From this

SOURCE: Greenberg, M. *The Former Lives of Anti-Sexist Men*.

perspective, one's gender is never settled, but rather constantly shifting in response to life circumstances. For each man, I describe the cultivation of their counter-hegemonic gender project over the course of their lives: their early experiences with masculinity, their engagements with gender politics, and their ongoing experiences with masculinity in their daily lives and work.

Four Men

In our book *Some Men*, Michael Messner, Tal Peretz and I draw on focused life history interviews with 52 men to explore how historical context shaped men's engagement with anti-violence feminism across three generational cohorts. While *Some Men* captures the breadth of men's experiences, in this chapter, I explore the lives of anti-sexist men in depth.

The men discussed in this chapter are part of a cohort of men who came into feminist anti-violence work between the mid-1990s and the early-2010s. The "professional cohort" engaged with feminism through academic departments and nonprofit organizations, as opposed to the grassroots activism that predominated in the 1960s and 1970s (Reger 2012; Markowitz & Tice 2002; Messner, Greenberg & Peretz 2015). This cohort includes an increasingly diverse swath of men for whom feminism was less political, and more diffuse (Reger 2012).

This research is drawn from focused life history interviews conducted with men who have worked with an anti-violence organization in a large city in the United States. All of the men came to the organization between 2002 and 2012, having done no such similar work with other organizations previously. These interviews are drawn from our work on *Some Men* as well as interviews I conducted independently. I focus on these men in particular because they represent diverse pathways into anti-violence work: Robert, a reggae-loving white construction worker; JJ, a religious black teen-father; Jose, a Mexican-American veteran committed to social justice; and Randy, a bisexual Filipino football team captain. Their stories provide vital insight into the ways men incorporate feminist anti-violence into ongoing gender projects.

Robert

Robert, a white man in his early 40s, was tall and broad, and he kept a close-cropped beard. He and his two brothers were raised by a single, working-class mom, "without a dad and not having positive role models for males." His mother worked ten hour days in a factory, being paid less than her male colleagues. Looking back, Robert described his mother through the lens of his current work. "Even though she would never ever qualify herself as a feminist," he observed, "in every way shape and form she acted like a feminist." In conversation, Robert also often described his mother as the "definition of a real man." Robert enjoyed disrupting the taken for granted categories of feminist and "real man."

Like many of our interviewees, Robert had personal experience with male violence. Both he and his mother were exposed to domestic violence at an early age. "Seeing the various oppressions that women were going through, it kind of, on a subconscious level, fed my whole understanding." He also experienced violence outside the home. "I grew up in kind of a rough neighborhood and got beat up a lot." Masculinity clearly shaped his relationship to violence: "My mother was almost raped twice and she told me about this, and I thought, this is screwed up. I've always been very protective I guess, maybe that's not the right term, but feeling protective of women in general. I know that's not the proper attitude to have, but it's just kind of there."

As Robert described it, he responded to his mother's difficult past by becoming protective of women. In his twenties, Robert began training in martial arts, which he viewed in large part as a response to the violence he experienced in his youth. His training provided Robert with a level of masculine status, which he used to build social connections. At one point, during our interview,

Robert looked past me and called out, "Hey, look out. That guy will kick your ass!" A man with slicked back hair, and tattoos on his neck and arms walked over, smiled, and shook Robert's hand. The man was training to be an ultimate fighter and he talked with Robert about starting up a Jujitsu class.

Robert was brought up "basically Atheist, Agnostic," but in his early twenties he underwent a dramatic change. "I guess you'd call it a conversion experience to Christianity," he said. The "pro-humanity, pro-brotherhood message of Reggae" was influential in shaping his worldview. "I would not have even bothered to read the Bible unless Bob Marley talked about the Bible." His conversion also grew out of his admiration for Doctor Martin Luther King. "At a pretty early age I remember hearing about the civil rights movement. I remember seeing it on TV, some of the marches and I was always fascinated with the work that Doctor King was doing." He continued:

[Doctor King] set up his work through a paradigm that was a Christian paradigm of being sacrificial for the good of the community, that sort of thing. That sort of resonated with me . . . that understanding that there's other things that are more important than you, and that we're all connected and that we're a community. If this woman here ends up getting shot on the way home, it's not just her, it's going to affect everyone here.

For Robert, this sense of connection provided ways for him to make sense of violence, especially violence committed by men against women.

Robert grappled with masculinity both politically and personally. "I got my girlfriend pregnant when I wasn't planning on doing so, then we got married and ended up having four sons and all those were unplanned too." While hesitant, he strove to do what his own father hadn't and threw himself headlong into fatherhood: "When I got stuck, literally stuck in the experience, I found it to be a very wonderful thing. And I've probably found no other role in my life more satisfying than that of being a father." He and his wife eventually divorced and he took on steady work as a construction worker, "banging things into the ground all day."

At this point in his story, one would be hard pressed to predict a pathway into anti-violence work. Robert did tai-chi and chi-gong trainings on the side to "promote self-care." But he wanted something more "spiritual." "My then fiancée, and now wife, and I were at some hippy gathering in the park and I signed up for like a newsletter or something. Then they sent out the thing about the violence prevention training and I was like wow, this sounds cool, it's smart, it's what I want to do." Robert worked as a volunteer with an anti-violence organization while completing his master's thesis on alternative approaches to conflict resolution, drawn from indigenous cultural practices and continuing to work construction. When he would get rained out on work sites he would call the volunteer coordinator and ask to do presentations. The training exposed Robert to new questions and new ways of making sense of his experiences: "What are the roots of these issues? Why do people act violently to begin with? It was a very mind opening experience, a very healing experience for me too, because it set a context for the experiences I'd gone through." In this way, the feminist anti-violence training provided resources for Robert to use in re-defining aspects of his biography.

After nearly four years of volunteering, Robert eagerly took a full-time position working with boys and young men. When I asked him if he saw the work as political, he explained, "I hesitate [because] political is almost too shallow of a word. It's political-slash-spiritual connection with what's going on with humanity." At the same time, Robert didn't hesitate to describe himself as a feminist: "I share the same values, it's not like I have to take any of my core beliefs and put them in check." He explains that "It was actually harder for me when I was in construction because it was an all-male environment and often times I would have other construction people say some very offensive, sexist statements, some very offensive racist statements and I would try to confront it in a way that was best and that was more frustrating for me because our values were so different in many ways."

In his work with young men, Robert sees echoes of himself. Most markedly, he sees the limitations that they experience on their humanity:

Why this resonates with guys is not just the fact that they're connected to women, not just the fact that a lot of their sisters and moms have been abused, all that stuff. The thing I'm selling, and how I hook 'em, is you can express your full personality without having to kowtow to these stupid male stereotypes. And once you start saying that message very firmly, very richly and showing them all the different ways that they can express [themselves]. Oh, you like writing rap, that's poetry, you like spoken word, wow that's a beautiful thing. Like sometimes there's a question like, what are the three favorite things you like, and I'm like I'm a pretty big guy, a second degree black belt in jiujitsu, and I'll say one of the most beautiful things in the world to me is flowers. So they'll watch this big dude, who's older, who they know can handle himself saying I like pretty flowers. They go wow, I can do that too? And they start opening up in that safe environment about the full expression of their humanity, their personality, and that is intoxicating to them.

As he explains, Robert sees his work with young men as a way to provide them with new ways to talk, think and act as men. He uses his background with jiujitsu as a symbolic marker in order to show that masculinity and enjoying flowers are not contradictory. He hopes to show young men a lesson that he himself learned through his years of work as a volunteer, that masculinity doesn't need to be constraining.

JJ

I first met JJ, a black man in his early 20s, in the back of Robert's beat-up white two-door sedan. JJ relied on Robert or public transport to get to the various schools and community centers across the city where the program was running. JJ explained that Robert is an important figure in his life. "He's like a mentor slash big brother, slash father, like, he's cool." Watching JJ and Rob together, this overlap of masculine relationships is on display. JJ laughs easily and Robert relishes in the attention.

JJ grew up in the late 1990s in a working-class part of the city, marked by high crime rates and limited resources. He attended church every day with his grandmother, and believes this spiritual and authoritative guidance helped him avoid the widespread violence in his community and graduate from high school. JJ explains: "It's normal, but it's not normal. It's normal that it happens in almost every home, but it's not normal because it's not right." As a teenager, JJ spent most of his time with his family and didn't have many close male friends. Like other young unwed fathers in urban contexts, when JJ found out he was having a child, he was overjoyed at the connection and responsibility that the new role offered (Edin & Nelson, 2013). He believes that part of this responsibility is to help his son become a savvy and respectful young man:

Yeah. Just the other day we're walking going to the restaurant and I opened the door and I said no, wait, let her go first. Just teaching him little things like that, women go first, be a gentleman. The other thing too, one time him and my niece were playing and he hit her and I told him, you not supposed to hit anyone, you don't hit anyone, you don't hit girls, you don't hit no one and he just look at me and I said tell her you're sorry and he's like, sorry. So I'm trying to teach him violence is not the way to resolve your issues or problems.

JJ saw these lessons on how to be a gentleman as a response to the other messages that young men received in his community:

I feel like as a male, as a young male, as a young man, young boy, a teen, you are taught as a baby, as a little guy, don't do that, you a man, don't cry, be tough. So you take that along with you as you grow up so as you grow up and you continue to hear this voice in your head, don't cry, it makes you hard and it makes you, sometimes it makes you violent, sometimes you do things or you get into a rage or you don't really think, so like I said it all starts at the home. What you teaching your child is what they're going to be.

Like many young black men in poor and working class neighborhoods, JJ was well versed in a code of masculine respect. However, he drew on a reformulated code, still focused on respect, but inverted in order to emphasize equality: "I love women so I would never say anything to disrespect anyone because I treat people with respect. You give respect to get respect. I don't believe respect is earned, no, respect is given."

JJ put added weight on his role as a father because he distrusted the institutions that surrounded him: "I feel like no governor, no mayor, no government is going to help me protect my family, give me money to help my family out. I feel like, every man for themselves basically. Everybody has to go out and get it." Faced with untrustworthy institutions, JJ invested in a belief in personal responsibility. JJ explained that *Antwon Fisher* is his favorite movie: "It's so motivating, it's basically telling you there's no excuse, get off your ass, get up and do something." One of his favorite songs is Nas's "I Know I Can," which proclaims "I know I can / Be what I wanna be / If I work hard at it / I'll be where I wanna be." However, JJ's deeply held belief in personal direction and hard work was difficult to achieve in a community with few job opportunities and struggling schools. As a young black man with limited job prospects, trying to be a good father to a son, anti-violence work was not only something that he believed in, but a vital avenue for earning a living.

JJ was first introduced to the organization by chance, when Robert brought a program to his high school health class: "If I wasn't at the school I was at, if I wasn't talking to the certain people I was talking to, no I wouldn't. I probably wouldn't know nothing." The program, he says, resonated with him despite his lack of experience with feminist thinking because it provided skills and connection during a tough time. "When I was going through certain things they was like, 'it's going to be alright,' and I got through it. It was something that I wanted to teach others, other guys and other young males about. Letting them know it's okay, what you're doing is wrong, ask for help." JJ told the facilitator of the program that he was looking for a job and "if you guys have anything open let me know."

After JJ graduated, he enrolled in the required training and soon after began working part-time as "a youth violence counselor . . . I try to prevent as much abuse or violence that I can." When we talked, he was working part time. I asked JJ if he saw this as the first step in a career: "Not necessarily. It could be something that I take with me along the road, but it's not something that I can just settle for because I think that there is much more, another purpose for me, but it's cool to know that I have something to fall back on, someplace I can go and call home basically."

JJ's personal experiences as a young man of color put him in an ideal position to relate to the young people he presented to about healthy masculinity and the "roots of oppression"—both of which are central components of the curriculum he often used.

See, it's the difference between knowing something and being able to relate to it because you have a deeper feeling and emotion about it. When you can relate to something, you know what that person's been through, you know what they're going through. When you know something you just know of it, you have no clue, no deeper emotion about it. I feel like I've been fortunate enough to have been through and get through those things so that I can show other people that I've been gotten through it and it's okay.

In this way, JJ drew on his own biography, alongside the counter-hegemonic logic of the curriculum to connect with young men as best he could:

You had kids that really had issues that just, they didn't want to seem soft or anything like that because they had to be hard. I heard one of the kids ended up being kicked out or got into a gang or something like that. I felt like that was a failure to me . . . I feel like I could have done something.

JJ saw his work with young men as an attempt to model an alternative form of masculinity for young men growing up like him, a role he also enjoyed as a father and in his religious life. It seems likely that he would have chosen to work with young men even if he had not found himself in an anti-violence program and later, if there had not been a position available to him.

Jose

Jose was born in Mexico and spent his teenage years in the U.S. He does not talk much about his time in the military. He carries literal and symbolic scars, along with a distrust of authority and a disciplined teaching style. "I grew up with no dad," he shared, "and at times . . . I understand a lot of these youth don't have a dad, they don't have a mom, or sometimes, they don't have both." Like Robert, Jose grew up with a single mother and felt that this provided him with a way of connecting with many of the young people he worked with. "I try to put space in their brain so they can say, 'Hey, I can make it to college. I don't have to be a dropout. I don't have to end up in jail or be a nobody.' I believe the youth, you can mold them and then they can take it from there. So that's what I do." During one class, a young man described his desire to join the military and Jose made it his goal to change his mind, speaking with the man for long periods before and after every class.

After leaving the military Jose began reading any book he could find about social justice, a passion informed by his ethnic background:

Being Mexican-American, I guess, in a country where race does affect who you are in society and then coming from Mexico and then seeing the inequality that people go through on a day-to-day basis. Inequality, some people having more than others. I mean, we can look outside and somebody's driving a Porsche, and next thing you know you have a homeless man. It's like, the disparity that is filled within a society, right? So I'm all about helping those that have no voice, per se. Or the people that are always being, are always out in the periphery. . . . That's my social justice that I live, so it's just not [about] women, per se.

Jose thinks of himself as a "radical." By the time he was hired to do anti-violence work with young men, he had a sharper awareness of how capitalism fueled injustice, even in the nonprofit sector. "I do feel like those people in power, who have [the] title of director, I don't think that they're really there for the hearts and minds of the youth. I think that they're there to collect a check, do their job, go home." Jose didn't blame individuals, but instead viewed this as part of a wider problem caused by the influence of capitalism on programming. He said:

Capitalism portrays itself to be the ultimate way of fixing things. Capitalism is the money, profit-making machine that is supposed to be there producing and making change and whatnot. Then I feel like, capitalism in society is so out of touch, especially with people who are most vulnerable, especially the youth of inner cities.

He explained that this pushes nonprofits and their workers to emphasize funding over action, putting a "cloud in their brain" and turning allies into competitors. Ultimately, Jose believes that capitalism and social justice are fundamentally at odds: "Social justice cannot fit in a capitalist society, because people are just thinking about the money and not about the change that they need to create."

Jose had been working part time as a tutor and looking for full time employment for a year without much luck. His sister suggested looking at idealist.org, a website which lists nonprofit positions, where he "stumbled on" a job posting: "Something with education, empowerment, and especially working with young men. So right before that I was in tutoring, math tutoring, and I was doing after-school programs. So then I was like, 'Well, it's kind of educational and I always wanted to be a teacher.'" Jose saw the anti-sexist aspects of the job as one piece of a larger effort of empowerment. Sometimes, this led to tensions with his more feminist-oriented colleagues: "I feel like I'm a man who's working with them, they should see me as an ally, a comrade, someone who will have feminist thoughts. However, I'm also a man so I bring my own idea of the thing to it." At the same time, he explained that he had learned a lot through his work and that it had a lasting impact on his life. I interviewed Jose seven months into his time at the organization.

> It has opened my mind to kind of see what life really is about. So where before I would be at a college football game, a soccer game, I see the cheerleaders and I feel like a lot of skin and hungry-like. Oh, that is great, that is just part of the commercial. Now, it makes me question like, really like why are we denigrating women to that point, or like why does the mass media or why do profit-making corporations do commercials, whatever. Why do we need to show so much skin?

In just a short span of time, Jose took up many of the messages about masculinity from anti-violence feminism, even as he pushed for more radical approaches and for more consideration of his perspective as a man. When we talked again a year later, he was similarly conflicted about his anti-violence work.

Randy

Randy, 17 when I interviewed him, was captain of the football team, class president, anti-violence activist on campus, and out as a bisexual. Randy's confidence made it look easy to reconcile these multiple facets of his identity. While he worked against interpersonal violence with a club on campus, he enjoyed putting in solid hits on the football field. I asked Randy if he thought that football was violent.

> That's a good question. I do. But the thing is, there's consent. That's the nature of the sport. You don't go into war and go, "Do you want to play the Xbox with me?" That's actual life and death situations. I think one of the contradictory things about [the organization] is us being football players . . . "I'm going to hurt you, you're going to hurt me, but we're still friends at the end of the game, but I still hate you." That's a fact. Did I hold it against the guy who broke my leg? No. But at the same time, I wish he didn't. That's just a fact.

Randy frames violence in sport as enabled by consent, which distinguishes men's violence against other men on the field from other, non-consensual forms of violence.

Randy traced his interest in understanding violence back to when he came with his family to the US from the Philippines five years before we spoke. His aunt was being verbally abused, maybe more than that: "It was just very uncomfortable, it was a very tense situation. I've never lost weight that much. I lost weight. It was just depressing." This trauma has stuck with him. "I really wanted to understand why. I'm never going to be able to find the answer perfectly, but I think I have a better overview." To some extent, Randy's story illustrates a tension between shifting cultural ideas of family life seen in other immigrant families. He remembers that his father, a solar panel installer, would tell stories about how "him, and his brothers and sisters, were actually beaten by their grandmother to clean and stuff." Looking back, Randy was glad that his parents didn't see violence as a tool.

> It was really cool that my dad didn't believe in that, because my mum didn't believe in it. They never hit us. They only hit, I remember, probably when I cursed. I was playing a video game and I died, and I was oh "F . . . ," you know, and my mum slapped me, and I was like, "What?" That

was scary. Other than that, no. My dad is verbally aggressive though, I'd say. I think he releases it through his voice, which I think is healthier than corporal punishment . . . I'm only going to say my parent's relationship is violent, but when I talk to my mum, I'm just like, "Stand up for yourself sometimes," because I feel like the argument is unequal. She's just, "No, your dad is right." I understand that, because that's the way she grew up, pleasing the husband and stuff like that. She's the wife. I'm just like, "That's pretty . . . " I'm so happy I didn't grow up like that.

Like other children of immigrants, Randy struggled to reconcile how his parents thought about patriarchal gender norms in contrast with his own more equality-focused beliefs. Today, Randy is conflicted about violence, "One of the questions that I was thinking, would the absence of violence be okay? Wouldn't that be kind of weird? . . . I think there's a healthy amount of violence in everyone's life. A little punishment. A little sit at the corner. I just believe that you should do something. I feel like you sugarcoat everything, and then when the kid grows up, it's the real world where not everyone's inclined [not to do] violence."

Despite stresses at home, Randy acclimated well and enjoyed school, in part thanks to a dedicated aunt. "When I was a kid, my aunt would make us read this really big long history books. I would be interested in Hitler and all those really oppressive mofos, and these civil rights movements." While the movements Randy learned about were historical and often distant, he felt that the lessons resonated with him today. He described a 2006 film, *Walkout,* which dramatizes the experiences of a group of Chicano/a youth in Los Angeles in 1986.

They walked out of high school and stuff, and it was this big thing. I was like, "Maybe we should do that, that's so fun. I want to do that." I think that's what led me to [the organization]: the movement. Being part of the movement and leading the movement. I'm kind of like, I'd say, a camera whore. I like the spotlight, that's a plus for me. That was my motivation to lead, I guess, to lead and to act on it.

Randy became involved in an anti-violence club on his campus two years prior, when a presenter visited his health class. "It was weird, because I was the only one who was so interested. I was like, "Do you have anything . . . Do you guys have internships or something?" Yeah, I just got hooked from there." Randy became dedicated to anti-violence work, spending much of his free time working with the club, speaking at public events, etc. But he viewed this work, at least in part, as marketing rather than political activism. "For me, I think my favorite part is education too, just hands down. I don't know, it's kind of like selling stuff. You sell your product, and it's just like you're trying to pull someone in." But the work of the club was not just a product. For Randy, it helped him become more open about being bisexual. "I remember back in the summer [program] we did this healthy sexual day or something like that, healthy sexuality. That was my realization that it was okay. Subsequently, the year later, I came out to my football team, and they were cool with it, they were very supportive actually." Despite this self-confidence and team support, Randy still struggles with how to share this sexual identity with others. "When you asked me my sexual orientation, I was still kind of hesitant, because I feel like it's not something we talk about on an everyday basis, and everybody's secretive about it. It's like the elephant in the room."

When I asked Randy what it meant to be a real man, he explained that "There's no definition of a man any more. I guess, I'm a football player. Is that enough for me to be a man? I don't know. If people look at me in a different way because when I came out and stuff, that's on you, I really don't care." Randy understood, in part informed by lessons learned in the club, that masculinity was not an inherent quality, but a cultural one. When he asked if being a football player was enough, he seemed to be reiterating a question he had asked himself and grown tired of. In this way, Randy drew on the notion that masculinity is socially constructed.

Counter-Hegemonic Projects

I have sought here to provide portraits of the lives of four men, marginalized along lines of class, race and sexuality, who came to see themselves and their actions as challenging dominant definitions of masculinity. Over the course of their lives, from their early experiences with masculinity, to their engagements with gender politics, and their ongoing experiences with masculinity in their daily lives and work, these men developed a counter-hegemonic gender project. For these men, their pathways into feminist anti-violence work was only one aspect of their ongoing projects of engaging, resisting and remixing hegemonic performances of masculinity.

Robert, JJ, Jose, and Randy's stories began like those of many others. All four of the men described being raised by strong women as a key part of their development. At the same time, all of their early years were defined by violence. Robert and Randy's lives were shaped by violent family experiences. JJ and Jose felt the structural violence of racialized poverty and policing. For the men in this study, a strong female role model and experiences of gendered violence contributed to a critical assessment of dominant narratives of masculinity. They saw that a man was not necessary for parenting, and that masculinity could be a source of violence and pain.

It was in response to violence and marginalization that all four men invested in masculine endeavors. Robert honed his martial arts skills. JJ invested his hopes in fatherhood and individualized respect. Jose joined the military. Randy played football. These endeavors were and remain significant aspects of their identities; however the meanings the men attach to them changed as they became more involved in social justice work and anti-violence feminism.

While participation in dominant masculine institutions was a core aspect of their gender projects, access to the ideals of masculinity—breadwinning, status in business and politics, heterosexuality, and so on—were often closed to them. Robert felt the limits of an embodied, working-class masculinity as his construction work and martial arts failed to provide the mental and spiritual life he wanted. JJ struggled to make a living as a black man in an urban neighborhood devastated by unemployment while he worked to be a good role model to his son. Jose believed in the power of military discipline, while disdaining the violence against people of color that often undergirds it. Randy achieved masculine status on the field while navigating anti-bisexual sentiment. In this way, marginalization framed their critical assessment of the contradictions of hegemonic masculinity.

These tensions led them to political engagements. Robert was inspired by MLK's spiritual non-violence. JJ critiqued governmental authorities' responses in urban communities. Jose criticized the failures of capitalism. Randy took leads from the social movements he read about in history books. In this way, they drew on their political engagements to defy the expectations placed on them. This made it possible for them to see anti-sexist work not as a challenge to their personal notion of masculinity, as many men do, but as a challenge to the systematic construction of inequality through hegemonic masculinity.

For all four of these men, engagement with a feminist organization served as a catalyst for an already emerging counter-hegemonic gender project. However, while all of these men incorporated anti-violence feminism into their lives, they also doubt that they will continue to work for feminist nonprofit organizations in the long term. Instead, they hope to use what they have learned to continue their work to challenge dominant ideals of masculinity in work with boys and men. Robert and Jose shared a belief, rooted in social justice, that capitalism undermines their work with young men and hope to participate in work that is less strictly beholden to grant pressure. JJ and Randy shared a view that the future holds something greater for them, which, while it may incorporate what they have learned, is unlikely to be with an organization.

While these particular men developed counter-hegemonic projects shaped by anti-violence feminism, a variety of strategies for subverting, challenging and remixing hegemonic masculinities are likely to be found in the lives of those who work to actively challenge and often engage with the hegemonic gender order. Future research should consider the counter-hegemonic projects of gay, trans, queer and gender fluid individuals. These individuals likely develop distinct counter-hegemonic projects that could provide new ways for men to make sense of the contradictions in masculinity in diverse ways and perhaps to problematize the construction of any consistent definitions of masculinity.

References

Alcalde, M. C. 2010. "Masculinities in Motion: Latino Men and Violence in Kentucky." *Men and Masculinities* 14(4):450–69.

Anderson, E. 1999. *Code of the Street: Decency, Violence, and the Moral Life of the Inner City.* WW Norton & Company.

Casey, E. A. et al. 2013. "Context, Challenges, and Tensions in Global Efforts to Engage Men in the Prevention of Violence Against Women: An Ecological Analysis." *Men and Masculinities* 16(2):228–51.

Casey, E. and T. Smith. 2010. "'How Can I Not?': Men's Pathways to Involvement in Anti-Violence Against Women Work." *Violence Against Women* 16(8):953–73.

Connell, Robert. 1987. *Gender and Power: Society, the Person, and Sexual Politics.* Stanford University Press.

Connell, R. W. 1992. "A Very Straight Gay: Masculinity, Homosexual Experience, and the Dynamics of Gender." *American Sociological Review* 735–51.

Connell, R. W. 2005. *Masculinities.* Berkeley, CA: University of California Press.

Connell, R. W. and J. W. Messerschmidt. 2005. "Hegemonic Masculinity: Rethinking the Concept." *Gender & Society* 19(6):829–59.

Dworkin, S. L., A. M. Hatcher, C. Colvin, and D. Peacock. 2013. "Impact of a Gender-Transformative HIV and Antiviolence Program on Gender Ideologies and Masculinities in Two Rural, South African Communities." *Men and Masculinities* 16(2):181–202.

Edin, Kathryn and Timothy J. Nelson. 2013. *Doing the Best I Can: Fatherhood in the Inner City.* Review Copy edition. Berkeley: University of California Press.

Flood, M. 2011. "Involving Men in Efforts to End Violence Against Women." *Men and Masculinities* 14(3):358–77.

Flood, Michael. 2015. "Work With Men to End Violence Against Women: A Critical Stocktake." *Culture, Health & Sexuality* 17(2):159–76.

Gibbs, Andrew, Cathy Vaughan, and Peter Aggleton. 2015. "Beyond 'Working With Men and Boys': (re)Defining, Challenging and Transforming Masculinities in Sexuality and Health Programmes and Policy." *Culture, Health & Sexuality* 17(sup2):85–95.

Kimmel, Michael. 2015. *Angry White Men: American Masculinity at the End of an Era.* First Edition, First Trade Paper Edition. Nation Books.

Markowitz, L. and K. W. Tice. 2002. "Paradoxes of Professionalization." *Gender & Society* 16(6):941–58.

Messerschmidt, J. W. 2000. *Nine Lives: Adolescent Masculinities, the Body, and Violence.* Boulder, CO: Westview Press.

Messner, M. A. 1992. *Power at Play: Sports and the Problem of Masculinity.* Boston: Beacon Press.

Messner, Michael A., Max A. Greenberg, and Tal Peretz. 2015. *Some Men: Feminist Allies and the Movement to End Violence Against Women.* 1st edition. New York, NY: Oxford University Press.

Murgia, A. and B. Poggio. 2009. "Challenging Hegemonic Masculinities: Men's Stories on Gender Culture in Organizations." *Organization* 16(3):407–23.

Pascoe, C. J. and Jocelyn A. Hollander. 2015. "Good Guys Don't Rape: Gender, Domination, and Mobilizing Rape." *Gender & Society* 0891243215612707.

Peacock, D. and G. Barker. 2014. "Working With Men and Boys to Prevent Gender-Based Violence: Principles, Lessons Learned, and Ways Forward." *Men and Masculinities* 17(5):578–99.

Piccigallo, J. R., T. G. Lilley, and S. L. Miller. 2012. "'It's Cool to Care About Sexual Violence': Men's Experiences With Sexual Assault Prevention." *Men and Masculinities* 15(5):507–25.

Reger, J. 2012. *Everywhere and Nowhere: Contemporary Feminism in the United States.* New York and Oxford: Oxford University Press.

Schrock, Douglas and Michael Schwalbe. 2009. "Men, Masculinity, and Manhood Acts." *Annual Review of Sociology* 35(1):277–95.

Shefer, T. 2014. "Pathways to Gender Equitable Men: Reflections on Findings From the International Men and Gender Equality Survey in the Light of Twenty Years of Gender Change in South Africa." *Men and Masculinities* 17(5):502–9.

CHAPTER 35

College Men, Hypermasculinity, and Sexual Violence

Richard Mora and Mary Christianakis

In 2012 and 2013, college students across the country inspired a nationwide movement to end sexual violence on college campuses and hold schools accountable for not properly handling of sexual assault complaints.[1] Most notably, in 2013, Annie E. Clark and Andrea Pino, students at the University of North Carolina, Chapel Hill, filed a complaint with the U.S. Department of Education's Office of Civil Rights, charging the university with Title IX violations. The following year, Emma Sulkowiscz, a student at Columbia University, carried a mattress with her across campus to protest that the student who allegedly raped her was not expelled. Across the country, college students have directed our attention to the failure of higher education institutions to protect their students from sexual violence—a point made clear by a recent survey of students across 27 campuses, which found that 23.1% of women reported sexual contact involving incapacitation, physical force, or threats of physical force (Cantor et al. 2015).

The college women leading the movement have reminded us that sexual violence *is* a men's issue. Nearly all rapes on campuses involve male rapists preying on women, the vast majority of which are women known to them (Fisher, Cullen, and Turner 2000). What is more, a quarter to more than 50% of college men report having committed sexual assault, with between 6% to 15% acknowledging that they raped or attempted to rape women (Abbey and McAuslan 2004). One survey finds that 16% of college male perpetrators who acknowledged having raped women indicated they participated in gang rapes (Koss 1998), which are more threatening, demeaning, aggressive, and violent than single perpetrator attacks (Gidycz and Koss 1990). The staggering statistics leave no doubt that sexual violence on college campuses is inextricably tied to men.

Sexual violence against women is one way some men go about "doing gender" (West and Zimmerman 1987). Among college men, there is a strong association between sexual violence and both the belief in traditional gender roles and the power and dominance of men (Murnen and Kohlman 2007). These men's gender practices are typically rooted in hypermasculinity, the exaggerated expression of traditional masculine attitudes and behaviors, such as a willingness to fight, enjoyment of risk and danger, and the aggressive and dominating pursuit of sexual intercourse with women (Edwards, Bradshaw, and Hinsz 2014). Men who subscribe to hypermasculine beliefs report more willingness to use force to initiate sexual contact (Schewe, Adam, and Ryan 2009). Additionally, as part of their masculine identities, many men promote rape culture, a culture that blames rape survivors, defends rapists, normalizes men's sexual aggression, and encourages the sexual objectification of women. Consider, for example, the messages on banners members of the Sigma Nu chapter at Old Dominion University hung from the balcony of a house near campus in August of 2015: "Rowdy and Fun! Hope your baby girl is ready for a good time"; "Freshman girl drop off"; " Go ahead and drop mom off too"

SOURCE: Mora, R., and Christianakis, M. *College Men, Hypermasculinity, and Sexual Violence.*

(Fieldstadt 2015). Most college men share masculine attitudes and behaviors that put college women at risk of being sexually assaulted.

On college campuses, there are also men who, spurred by anti-rape activists, have organized anti-rape organizations on their campuses. Similarly, some men are engaged in the White House's rape prevention campaign, *It's On Us*, pledging to, amongst other things, intervene if they observe someone in danger of being sexually assaulted. Among college men, there are those who perpetuate cultures accepting of sexual violence against women, participate in such violence, excuse the violence, and/or work to bring an end to it.

In this chapter, we focus on cultural norms and practices that promote hypermasculinity and sexual violence on college campuses. We pay particular attention to fraternity men and male athletes, who typically have more masculine status on campus than other men (Harris 2010), to highlight how college men participate or are complicit in sexual violence in order to strengthen bonds within their homosocial groupings and to construct their hypermasculine identities. We then discuss the anti-rape efforts of some college men on our campus, Occidental College, and examine both the role college men can play in ending sexual violence and how their actions can reiterate the existing patriarchal gender order.

In the next section we turn to fraternities and male sport teams, two homosocial groups especially rooted in masculinity.

Fraternity Men, Male Athletes, and Sexual Violence

Fraternities and male sport teams are two sociocultural sites on college campuses wherein hypermasculinity is greatly valued and engaging in sexual violence may confer masculine status. These social worlds encourage attitudes and behaviors that are more outwardly hypermasculine, sexist, and misogynistic than the general college male population (Connell 2005). Fraternity men and male athletes bond around negative attitudes about women and are more sexually aggressive than non-athletes and non-fraternity men (Anderson 2005; Boeringer 1999). Also, the use of violence against women is often viewed positively and endorsed (Humphrey and Kahn 2000). Group dynamics in these insular male groups may create social opportunities for men to normalize sexual violence as a masculine practice, which may be easier to take up if the men view themselves as "good guys" and define rape narrowly "as something a *bad* man does, not something that informs all gendered relationships between men and women" (Pascoe and Hollander 2015, 74). When new fraternity members and new team members are socialized by older peers to embrace and normalize a collectively shared culture, such attitudes and behaviors are maintained year after year.

Fraternity houses are sites where fraternity members collectively construct and reiterate their culture, including their views of college women. Fraternity members are more likely to believe both that men should be in charge of relationships and that women want rough sex and to be raped (Boeringer 1999); to use alcohol or drugs to have sex with a woman; to have friends that engage in similar behavior; and believe friends would not disapprove (Boeringer, Shehan, and Akers 1991). These attitudes and behaviors may explain why there is a positive association between the frequency with which college women attend fraternity parties and their likelihood of being sexually assaulted while incapacitated (Krebs et al. 2007). In fact, women associated with fraternities (e.g. little sister organizations) are degraded, sexually objectified, and sexually abused by fraternity men (Stombler 1994). Similarly, sorority women, who typically have more access to fraternity parties, have a greater likelihood of being sexually assaulted than college women as a whole (Minow and Einolf 2009). The masculine practices many fraternity members promulgate make their fraternity houses unsafe for women.

Hypermasculine norms make some fraternity houses more dangerous for college women than others (Sanday 1990). In houses identified as spaces where women run higher risks of being raped, men are more likely to be single, interact with women for the sole purpose of sex, and be athletes (Boswell and Spade 1996). When compared to members of low-risk fraternities and non-fraternity males, the men in high-risk houses subscribe to more sexually aggressive and hostile views when it comes to women (Humphrey and Kahn 2000). In high-risk houses, misogyny and rape culture were more commonly shared attitudes and behaviors; thus, parties held at these houses regularly involved excessive drinking and an environment more accepting of abusing women (Boswell and Spade 1996). Such cultures can thrive in fraternity houses because fraternity members, who may share a sense of privilege due to their affluence, control the space, are usually not supervised, and insist upon secrecy (Martin 2015). In this way, the confidentiality of the brotherhood serves to house and provide protection for those who engage in rape as a practice of fraternal masculinity. Thus, those fraternity members who do not engage in sexual violence are still complicit when they contribute or acquiesce to the maintenance of both hypermasculine norms and physical space that facilitate sexual assault.

Like fraternity members, male athletes often live, and mostly socialize, with one another, developing shared hypermasculine norms. The culture among male athletes often encourages the objectification of women, promotes sexist, misogynistic, homophobic attitudes and behaviors (Anderson 2005), and the expectation of secrecy (Martin 2015). Protecting teammates and maintaining secrecy is considered protecting the integrity of the team. Male athletes in center sports, like football and basketball, which have higher status on campuses and larger budgets, are even more insulated, hypermasculine, sexually active, and sexually aggressive than other male athletes (Gage 2008). These shared attitudes and behaviors can combine with the sense of entitlement that many male athletes feel (Martin 2015), may explain why male athletes account for a disproportionate percentage of assaults on college campuses.

Fraternity members and male athletes are responsible for a significant amount of sexual violence on college campuses. Fraternity men are three times more likely to commit rape than other college men (Loh et al. 2005). Male college athletes account for a disproportionately high percentage of individuals identified as perpetrators in sexual assault complaints (Crosset 2000), and those in physical-contact team sports have even higher rates of rape (Franklin 2004). Moreover, 50% of all gang rapes on college campuses are committed by fraternity members (Martin and Hummer 1989) and 40% by members of male sports teams (O'Sullivan 1991). During gang rapes, rapists display heteronormative, masculine performances for one another at the expense of the victim, who is treated like a prop (Franklin 2004). In homosocial groups with high rates of gang rapes, such as fraternities and sports teams, men share a sense of entitlement, engage one another in misogynistic and homophobic talk, collectively take part in risky behavior, view sex with women as conquests, and watch each other engage in sex with women or openly discuss their sexual encounters (O'Sullivan 1998). While not all fraternity members and male athletes are sexual predators, all fraternity and team members in insular cultures that promote hypermasculinity and sexual violence against women are complicit.

Colleges validate fraternity members and male sports team athletes and their homosocial groups. They recognize the fraternal orders as part of student governance and institutional heritage, relying on their membership and alumni for fundraising (Martin 2015). The restrictive alcohol policies on most campuses lead many students to attend fraternity house parties off campus (Armstrong, Hamilton, and Sweeney 2006). At many of these parties, fraternity men restrict the number of non-member men to ensure a favorable women-to-men ratio, control alcoholic beverages (Hamilton 2007), and accept sexual coercion and aggression (Sanday 1990), all of which may explain why women who attend are at greater risk of being sexually assaulted (Krebs et al. 2007). Separately, male athletes on center team sports often get privileged access to college facilities, sometimes even their own housing (Messner 2015), wherein shared hypermasculine, misogynistic norms may be collectively reiterated. The significant influence team boosters, fraternity members, and fraternity alumni have on academic institutions may influence sexual assault investigations involving fraternity men and male athletes (Martin 2015). As a result, the college men more likely to promote rape culture and participate in sexual violence may be the least likely to be held accountable for their sexual crimes.

College Men Against Rape

In 2013, the anti-rape activism of college women motivated college men to stand up against sexual violence. On our campus, Occidental College, anti-rape efforts were driven by Occidental Sexual Assault Coalition (OSAC), a campus group established in 2007. OSAC members publicly acknowledged "male allies" in attendance at OSAC demonstrations and events. More and more college men at Occidental (Oxy) voiced their support for both survivors and OSAC's calls for the College to expel rapists, provide survivors with the necessary support services, and revise its sexual assault policies based on best practices.

On April 1, 2013, Mora and a male colleague sent out an email directed to "Oxy Men" with the subject, "Oxy Men Against Rape." The email read, in part: "As you know, there has been much discussion about the role men can play to make our campus safe for all students. And, we'd like to discuss both ways in which the faculty can support your efforts and the possibility of establishing a group composed of Oxy men committed to ending sexual assaults at Oxy. Please feel free to bring fellow male allies to the meeting." The email resulted in six meetings during the remaining six weeks of the semester. On a campus with approximately 900 college men at the time, about 40 college men attended the first two meetings; men of distinct racial, ethnic, class, and sexual identities, members of fraternities and non-members, athletes, and non-athletes. Attendance dropped off to 16 to 35 men at the subsequent four meetings.

The first two meetings were moderated by the two professors, who set a tone of respect. The vast majority of men shared that they were woefully uninformed about sexual assault and rape culture. Many indicated that they had given little, to no thought, to these issues prior to OSAC's efforts on campus.

The last four meetings were student-moderated and focused on the establishment of a student club, Oxy Men Against Rape (OMAR). These Oxy men drafted the following working mission statement for the club: "The mission of Occidental Men Against Rape (OMAR) is to educate and mobilize men to create cultures free of all forms of sexual violence." After a unanimous vote in support of the mission statement, they drafted the OMAR Code of Conduct, comprised of a preamble and "rules" that OMAR members would pledge to abide by throughout their membership.

We now present the draft preamble and rules (in italics), situating most within relevant academic literature that helps explain why the drafters considered the pledges necessary. Throughout, we point out how, despite the drafters' good intentions, the actions called for in the pledges can nonetheless uphold inequities, including those that reiterate the current gender order.

As a member of OMAR, I stand with and support the fellow men of OMAR to educate, empower, and mobilize men to create cultures free of all forms of sexual violence. I believe sexual violence is a MEN'S issue, involving men of all ages, socioeconomic, racial, ethnic, and sexual orientation backgrounds. I view men not only as perpetrators or possible offenders but also as empowered survivors and bystanders who can confront abusive peers.

As a member of OMAR, I pledge to abide by the following rules:

I PLEDGE NOT TO COMMIT ANY FORMS OF SEXUAL VIOLENCE.

I will educate myself and others about what active-mutual, verbal consent means, and ALWAYS get active-mutual verbal consent before engaging in any sexual act.

Men tend to view women's friendliness as sexual interest and to view women as more sexually interested than women report being (Abbey 1987). Consequently, for college men to truly know that their sexual partners are freely engaging in sexual activities they must engage in active-mutual verbal consent, free of coercion, threats, or incapacitation. However, many colleges, including Oxy, do not mandate verbal consent, so active-mutual verbal consent is unlikely to become a common practice among their students.

I PLEDGE NOT TO ENGAGE IN VICTIM BLAMING. I will believe survivors. I will educate myself about the many myths surrounding sexual violence, and I will work towards combating those myths.

Refraining from victim blaming is extremely important given what we know about sexual violence on college campuses. Most college rapists know their victims (Fisher, Cullen, and Turner 2000) and survivors who were raped by acquaintances are viewed as more responsible for their victimization than survivors raped by strangers (Monson, Langhinrichsen-Rohling, and Binderup 2000). What is more, rape survivors who had consumed alcohol are blamed more than sober victims (Girard and Senn 2008). Such victims blaming is misguided. Rapists often use alcohol and drugs as weapons and the vast majority of sexual assaults of women on college campuses involve incapacitation by either alcohol or drugs at the time (Krebs et al. 2007). When accused, some rapists even appropriate the language of incapacitation, arguing that since they too consumed alcohol and drugs, they themselves were incapacitated, could not give consent, and were, therefore, sexually victimized by their accusers.

College men are not only more likely to be perpetrators of sexual violence, they endorse rape myths—or false beliefs about rape, rape victims, and rapists that shift blame onto the victims (Burt 1980)—at higher rates than college women (Vonderhaar and Carmody 2015). Fraternity members are more likely to accept rape myths than non-members (Boeringer 1999). Similarly, male athletes are more accepting of traditional gender roles and rape myths than other college men (Boeringer 1999), with those fraternity members in high-risk houses reporting higher rates of rape myth acceptance (Boswell and Spade 1996). Those college men who endorse rape myths are more likely to have hypermasculine attitudes than men who do not (Forbes, Adams-Curtis, and White 2004) and to support traditional gender norms (Angelone, Mitchell, and Lucente 2012). These men are also more likely to be hostile (Suarez and Gadalla 2010) and sexually aggressive (Lonsway and Fitzgerald 1995) toward women. Furthermore, college men who endorse rape myths report a greater willingness to rape if there were no consequences for doing so (Chiroro et al. 2004). Rape myths are part of the rape cultures that perpetuate sexual violence against women.

Challenging rape myths is imperative. The acceptance and endorsement of rape myths negates that rape is a serious crime, justifies the use of sexual aggression against women (Lonsway and Fitzgerald 1995), and makes it hard to hold sexual predators accountable (Bosow and Minieri 2011). Rape myths also contribute to the hostility directed at survivors (Suarez and Gadalla 2010) and discourage rape survivors from reporting. College men can, thus, support anti-rape efforts by actively combating rape myths.

I PLEDGE NOT TO REMAIN SILENT AS A BYSTANDER. If someone on campus (e.g. [fraternity] brother, friend, classmate, or teammate) is abusing another person, I will not look the other way. I will take action, whether talking to him or her myself to urge him or her to seek help, or consulting a friend, professor, or counselor, and I will remain committed to holding him or her accountable.

Research shows that college men are willing to act as bystanders, intervening when they observe others about to engage in sexual violence (Foubert, Godin, and Tatum 2010). Their intervention may be especially needed in spaces controlled by men, such as fraternity parties, where women are repeatedly asked to have a drink and go to private spaces (Armstrong, Hamilton, and Sweeney 2006). The more often women attend these parties the greater the likelihood they will be sexually assaulted while incapacitated (Krebs et al. 2007). Intervention by college men, however, is not a certainty and may be less common in spaces wherein the dominant culture promotes both hypermasculinity and secrecy. Within homosocial groups, men who do not support misogyny and sexual violence may remain silent so as not to endanger their membership and standing (Messner 2015).

It should be noted that the very notion of men intervening as bystanders is problematic. With an emphasis on men, bystander training may reinforce the gender order such that "[m]asculinity becomes the savior of women, rather than something we see as a root cause of violence and inequality, and thus in need of transformation" (Messner 2015, 58). If male college bystanders do not understand how problematic masculinity is, they will likely fail to recognize that men's violence is a "collective privilege" of all men, a privilege that maintains the existing gender order (Connell 2005; Martin 2015). What is more, since bystander training assumes that the college men being trained are good men it may unintentionally ascribe the label of rapists to men of other racial, ethnic, and class backgrounds, thus, promulgating stereotypes (Martin 2015). Focusing on the choices men make may also distract from the institutionalized inequities that make sexual violence possible, for example, the longstanding institutional recognition and support of insulated male peer groups, such as fraternities and athletic teams.

I PLEDGE TO OPPOSE RAPE CULTURE WHEREVER IT IS FOUND IN ALL OF ITS MANIFESTATIONS. I recognize that rape culture is embedded within racism, sexism, heterosexism, cis-genderism and other forms of discrimination. To oppose rape culture is to oppose these other forms of domination as well. I will not use degrading slurs to oppress others. I will work toward understanding how using degrading slurs not only dehumanize others, but dehumanizes myself.

Opposing rape culture does require opposing all forms of inequalities and the views that reify them. There is a strong association between acceptance of rape myths and homophobic, racist, and ageist beliefs (Suarez and Gadalla 2010). Such beliefs partly account for why underrepresented college students—students who are racial and ethnic minorities, LGBT, deaf, and/or hard of hearing—experience higher rates of victimization (Porter and McQuiller-Williams 2011). Consequently, it is imperative that those wanting to bring an end rape recognize that, as Pascoe and Hollander (2015) explain, "changing rape culture involves more than teaching men not to rape or rendering sexual dominance unsexy or unmasculine; it involves rethinking gendered dominance *intersectionally* such that attempts to combat sexual assault do not reinscribe gendered, raced, sexualized, and classed inequalities in more subtle ways" (75–76). Taking such an intersectional approach requires a commitment to reflect on and alter those day-to-day practices that impede social equality.

I PLEDGE TO ACTIVELY QUESTION MY OWN ATTITUDES. I have the courage to look inward. I pledge not to be defensive when something I do or say ends up hurting someone else. I will try hard to understand how my own attitudes, language, and actions might inadvertently perpetuate symbolic or physical violence, and I will work toward changing them. I will not allow my intentions to outweigh the effects of my acts.

College men hold many beliefs that perpetuate rape culture. As mentioned earlier, they endorse rape myths at higher rates than college women (Vonderhaar and Carmody 2015). They are also less empathetic toward potential victims (Katz, Pazienza, Olin, and Rich 2014) and actual victims (Osman 2011), less likely to feel the need to intervene on behalf of women at risk (Banyard and Moynihan 2011), and more apt to blame rape victims rather than rapists (Osman 2011). Additionally, college men are more likely to consider the relationship between perpetrator and victim and the victim's sexual history when determining whether an instance of rape is rape (Monson,

Langhinrichsen-Rohling, and Binderup 2000). College men need to question whether their beliefs and actions perpetuate rape culture and sexual violence.

I PLEDGE TO EDUCATE MYSELF AND LEARN FROM OTHERS. I will proactively seek out trainings, programs, courses, films, books and articles about multicultural masculinities, gender inequality, and the root causes of gender violence. I will educate myself and others about how large social forces affect the conflicts between individuals particularly on Oxy's campus.

Educating college men may make a difference. Research suggests that college men who participate in anti–sexual assault programs may become more empathetic toward victims (Foubert, Godin, and Tatum 2010). Also, male college students who are exposed to sexual assault peer educators and perceive close friends as being against sexual violence express more willingness to prevent rape (Stein 2007). What is unclear is the extent to which college men, including those who have participated in educational programming, actually intervene as bystanders and alter the rape-promoting attitudes and behaviors of peers.

I PLEDGE TO BE AN ALLY. I will be an ally to others who are working to end all forms of sexual violence. I will recognize and support the individuals on this campus who have taken the initiative to create cultures free of sexual violence. I will support the work of OSAC [Oxy Sexual Assault Coalition], Project S.A.F.E. [for a Sexual Assault Free Environment], the CGE [Center for Gender Equity], and OTHER groups on-and-off campus working to create cultures free of sexual violence.

College men who publicly support anti-rape activists on college campus are often identified or self-identify as allies.

I PLEDGE TO BE A MENTOR. I will teach other men about forms of masculinities that do not involve degrading or abusing individuals.

Attitudes and behaviors that support male dominance, the objectification, and sexual aggression toward women are common among college men (Sanday 2004). College men who exhibit hypermasculine norms also exhibit less empathy and more hostility and sexual aggression toward women (Forbes, Adams-Curtis, and White 2004). Sexually assertive men are often praised by male peers (Martin and Hummer 1989). Across the country, many heterosexual college men talk about women and sex, objectify women, hook up sexually with women, and abuse alcohol as part of hypermasculine performances (Harris 2010). Many of them fear being perceived as feminine and value sexual conquest and sexual performance, both of which may earn men masculine status within their homosocial peer groups (Harris 2010). Thus, hypermasculinity needs to be challenged. However, simply substituting hypermasculinity with masculine attitudes and behaviors that reiterate the present gender order will not contest gender inequities or bring about an end to sexual violence.

IN CONCLUSION, I pledge to respectfully learn from my mistakes, and, if necessary, remove myself from this organization and get professional help depending on the severity of the violation. I also understand that if I commit an act of sexual violence (e.g. sexual harassment, sexual battery, sexual assault, and/or rape), I will cease to be a member of this organization, resulting in the loss of any and all rights of membership.

NOTE: Pledges "NOT" are immediately enforceable. Pledges "TO" are understood as a process of constant growth and refinement.

The OMAR pledges are in line with the three sorts of actions Berkowitz (2004) indicates men interested in ending sexual violence should engage in—refrain from using violence against women; work toward reducing such violence; and challenge the social norms that contribute to violence against women. However, by publicly abiding by such pledges, college men may participate in "mobilizing rape," using rape to establish their masculinity and dominance (Pascoe and Hollander 2015). While rapists mobilize the actual act of rape to establish their masculinity and dominance over women and men, pledgers mobilize a public repudiation of rape to proclaim themselves good guys, thus, asserting their "masculinized dominance" over rapists, who lack self-control and the ability to sexually attract women (Ibid., 74). The construction of good guys and bad guys resulting when rape is mobilized reiterates inequalities since it does not challenge inter- and intra-gender hierarchies. What is more, in our stratified society, the construction of the symbolic bad guy is likely to rely on stereotypes of socially marginalized men. Last, pledging does not negate the possibility of men speaking up against rape and also engaging in sexual coercion and rape culture. In fact, it is highly likely that within anti-rape groups comprised of college men, there exist "hybrid masculinities" (Bridges and Pascoe 2014), masculinities that symbolically distance men from hegemonic masculinity while simultaneously upholding existing inequities.

Despite the early enthusiasm and planning, OMAR did not become an established student group. A month after the meetings began, a few of the most active men graduated and no one took the initiative to organize meetings when the fall semester commenced a few months later. Had more Oxy men attended the OMAR meetings perhaps other leaders would have emerged. Institutional interference and resistance at the upper administrative levels, however, may have kept some men, particularly male athletes, away. Just one week before the first OMAR meeting, Carl Botterud, the College Counsel (also an Oxy alumnus and former student athlete), convened a meeting with male athletes at which he spewed rape myths and made disparaging comments about OSAC members. He lied, stating that sexual assault complaints filed by OSAC members and other women were the actions of spurned ex-girlfriends. He went on to dismiss the anti-rape work of two female professors affiliated with OSAC and punctuated his statement with "fuck them"—words with two possible reads, the first being "disregard them" and the second being a more provocative "screw them" or take action against them. Botterud's sexists words, and their corresponding sentiment that women's anti-rape is an attack on men and the hegemonic masculinity they have cultivated across generations, carried the weight of his position as an Oxy administrator.[2] As a result, the male athletes in attendance may have concluded that sexual assault was not a problem on campus and anti-rape efforts like those of men in OMAR were unnecessary. Furthermore, when the activist energy on campus dissipated in the fall, some of the Oxy men who attended OMAR meetings may have disengaged from the issue of sexual violence because they did not view it as directly impacting their daily lives. Lack of institutional support, if not outright obstruction, and male privilege may make male anti-rape groups on college campuses unsustainable.

Conclusion

Thanks to the work of anti-rape activists the issue of sexual assault on college campuses has certainly gone mainstream. On Sunday, February 28th, 2015, at the 88th Academy Awards, Vice President of the United States Joe Biden addressed the matter. He called on viewers to take the *It's On Us* pledge to "change the culture" and bring an end to sexual violence. He then introduced Lady Gaga, who went on to perform "Til It Happens To You," a song she co-wrote for *The Hunting Ground*, an Oscar nominated documentary that examines the mistreatment rape survivors have experienced on college campuses, including Occidental College. Lady Gaga performed while seated at a white piano, surrounded by male and female sexual assault survivors holding hands. After singing the last two verses—Till it happens to you / you won't know how I feel—Lady Gaga joined hands with the survivors and together they raised their hands triumphantly. The performance left some in the audience in tears and received much attention on social media.

In this chapter we have made the case that that kind of cultural change Vice President Biden calls for must include the critical examination of college men's hypermasculinities and the hybrid masculinities that arise when college men mobilize rape. Ending rape culture requires a variety of radical changes at the discursive, psychological, interpersonal, and institutional levels needed. On college campuses, a rethinking is especially needed in insular, homosocial groups, such as fraternities and male athletic teams, which tend to promote hypermasculinity and rape practices, including sexual coercion, sexual aggression, and gang rape.

Going forward, anti-rape activists and scholars alike would benefit from new research on the hypermasculine cultural norms and practices that promote sexual violence on college campuses. Lacking in the literature are close analyses of whether male anti-rape organizations mobilize rape and promote the construction of hybrid masculinities. Similarly, little is known about whether and how the men in male anti-rape organizations interact with fraternity members and male athletes and whether those interactions alter the sociocultural landscape of insular male groups. Last, there is a need for further research examining the role of college administrations in the construction and maintenance of social environments (e.g. clubs, teams, etc.) wherein rape culture and sexual violence are normalized.

Notes

1. "College" is used throughout to refer to both colleges and universities where students can earn a B.A.

2. Weeks later, at a faculty meeting, Carl Botterud was asked about his comments to male athletes. He did not deny having made them and said that he met with male athletes, not in his capacity as General Counsel, but informally as an alumnus. A week later the faculty passed a vote of no confidence against Botterud. Months later, during the fall semester, he resigned.

References

Abbey, Antonia and Pam McAuslan. "A Longitudinal Examination of Male College Students' Perpetration of Sexual Assault." *Journal of Consulting and Clinical Psychology* 72 (2004): 747–756.

Abbey, Antonia. "Misperceptions of Friendly Behavior as Sexual Interest: A Survey of Naturally Occurring Incidents." *Psychology of Women Quarterly* 11 (1987): 173–194.

Anderson, Eric. *In the Game: Gay Athletes and the Cult of Masculinity.* New York: State University of New York Press, 2005.

Angelone, David J., Damon Mitchell, and Lauren Lucente. "Predicting Perceptions of Date Rape: An Examination of Perpetrator Motivation, Relationship Length, and Gender Role Beliefs." *Journal of Interpersonal Violence* (2012): 2582–2602.

Armstrong, Elizabeth A., Laura Hamilton, and Brian Sweeney. "Sexual Assault on Campus: A Multilevel, Integrative Approach to Party Rape." *Social Problems* 53, no. 4 (2006): 483–499.

Banyard, Victoria L. and Mary M. Moynihan. "Variation in Bystander Behavior Related to Sexual and Intimate Partner Violence Prevention: Correlates in a Sample of College Students." *Psychology of Violence* 1, no. 4 (2011): 287–301.

Berkowitz, Alan D. "Working With Men to Prevent Violence Against Women: An Overview (Part One)." *National Resource Center on Domestic Violence* (2004): 1–7.

Boeringer, Scot B. "Associations of Rape-Supportive Attitudes With Fraternal and Athletic Participation." *Violence Against Women* 5, no. 1 (1999): 81–90.

Boeringer, Scot B., Constance L. Shehan, and Ronald L. Akers. "Social Contexts and Social Learning in Sexual Coercion and Aggression: Assessing the Contribution of Fraternity Membership." *Family Relations* 40, no. 1 (1991): 58–64.

Bosow, Susan A., and Alexandra Minieri. "'You Owe Me': Effects of Date Cost, Who Pays, Participant Gender, and Rape Myth Beliefs on Perceptions of Rape." *Journal of Interpersonal Violence* 26, no. 3 (2011): 479–497.

Boswell, A. Ayres and Joan Z. Spade. "Fraternities and Collegiate Rape Culture: Why Are Some Fraternities More Dangerous Places for Women?" *Gender and Society* 10, no. 2 (1996): 133–147.

Bridges, Tristan and C. J. Pascoe. "Hybrid Masculinities: New Directions in the Sociology of Men and Masculinities." *Sociology Compass* 8, no. 3 (2014): 246–58.

Burt, Martha R. "Cultural Myths and Supports for Rape." *Journal of Personality and Social Psychology* 38, no. 2 (1980): 217–230.

Cantor, David, Bonnie Fisher, Reanne Townsend, Hyunshik Lee, Carol Bruce, and Gail Thomas. *AUU Campus Climate Survey on Sexual Assault and Sexual Misconduct.* Washington D.C.: Association of American Universities, 2015.

Chiroro, Patrick, Gerd Bohner, G. Tendayi Viki, and Christopher I. Jarvis. "Rape Myth Acceptance and Rape Proclivity Expected Dominance Versus Expected Arousal as Mediators in Acquaintance-Rape Situations." *Journal of Interpersonal Violence* 19, no. 4 (2004): 427–442.

Connell, Raewyn W. *Masculinities*, 2nd ed. Berkeley: University of California Press, 2005.

Crosset, Todd. "Athletic Affiliation and Violence Against Women: Toward a Structural Prevention Project." In *Masculinities, Gender Relations, and Sport*, edited by Jim McKay, Michael Messner and Donald Sabo, 147–161. Thousand Oaks, CA: Sage, 2000.

Edwards, Sarah R., Kathryn A. Bradshaw, and Verlin B. Hinsz. "Denying Rape but Endorsing Forceful Intercourse: Exploring Differences Among Responders." *Violence and Gender* 1, no. 4 (2014): 188–193.

Fieldstadt, Elisha. "Old Dominion's Frat Suspended During Probe Into Sexually Suggestive Signs." MSNBC (August 24, 2015). http://www.msnbc.com/msnbc/old-dominions-frat-suspended-during-probe-sexually-suggestive-signs

Fisher, Bonnie S., Francis T. Cullen, and Michael G. Turner. *The Sexual Victimization of College Women.* Washington, DC: U.S. Department of Justice, Bureau of Justice Statistics, 2000.

Forbes, Gordon B., Leah E. Adams-Curtis, and Kay B. White. "First- and Second-Generation Measures of Sexism, Rape Myths and Related Beliefs, and Hostility Toward Women: Their Interrelationships and Association With College Students' Experiences With Dating Aggression and Sexual Coercion." *Violence Against Women* 10, no. 3 (2004): 236–261.

Foubert, John D., Eric E. Godin, and Jerry L. Tatum. "In Their Own Words: Sophomore College Men Describe Attitude and Behavior Changes Resulting From a Rape Prevention Program 2 Years After Their Participation." *Journal of Interpersonal Violence* 25, no. 12 (2010): 2237–2257.

Franklin, Karen. "Enacting Masculinity: Antigay Violence and Group Rape as Participatory Theater." *Sexuality Research & Social Policy* 1, no. 2 (2004): 25–40.

Gage, Elizabeth Ann. "Gender Attitudes and Sexual Behaviors Comparing Center and Marginal Athletes and Nonathletes in a Collegiate Setting." *Violence Against Women* 14, no. 9 (2008): 1014–1032.

Gidycz, Christine A., and Mary P. Koss. "A Comparison of Group and Individual Sexual Assault Victims." *Psychology of Women Quarterly* 14, no. 3 (1990): 325–342.

Girard, April L. and Charlene Y. Senn. "The Role of the New 'Date Rape Drugs' in Attributions About Date Rape." *Journal of Interpersonal Violence* 23, no. 1 (2008): 3–20.

Hamilton, Laura. "Trading on Heterosexuality College Women's Gender Strategies and Homophobia." *Gender & Society* 21, no. 2 (2007): 145–172.

Harris III, Frank. "College Men's Meanings of Masculinities and Contextual Influences: Toward a Conceptual Model." *Journal of College Student Development* 51, no. 3 (2010): 297–318.

Humphrey, Stephen E., and Arnold S. Kahn. "Fraternities, Athletic Teams, and Rape: Importance of Identification With a Risky Group." *Journal of Interpersonal Violence* 15, no. 12 (2000): 1313–1322.

Katz, Jennifer, Rena Pazienza, Rachel Olin, and Hillary Rich. "That's What Friends Are For: Bystander Responses to Friends or Strangers at Risk for Party Rape Victimization." *Journal of Interpersonal Violence* 30, no. 16 (2014): 2775–2792.

Koss, Mary P. "Hidden Rape: Sexual Aggression and Victimization in a National Sample of Students in Higher Education." In *Confronting Rape and Sexual Assault (Worlds of Women, No. 3),* edited by Odem, Mary E., and Jody Clay-Warner, 51–69. Wilmington, NC: SR Books/Scholarly Resources Inc., 1998.

Krebs, Christopher P., Christine H. Lindquist, Tara D. Warner, Bonnie S. Fisher, and Sandra L. Martin. *The Campus Sexual Assault (CSA) Study*. Washington, DC: National Institute of Justice, US Department of Justice, 2007.

Loh, Catherine, Christine A. Gidycz, Tracy R. Lobo, and Rohini Luthra. "A Prospective Analysis of Sexual Assault Perpetration Risk Factors Related to Perpetrator Characteristics." *Journal of Interpersonal Violence* 20, no. 10 (2005): 1325–1348.

Lonsway, Kimberly A. and Louise F. Fitzgerald. "Attitudinal Antecedents of Rape Myth Acceptance: A Theoretical and Empirical Reexamination." *Journal of Personality and Social Psychology* 68, no. 4 (1995): 704.

Martin, Patricia Yancey. "The Rape Prone Culture of Academic Contexts: Fraternities and Athletics." *Gender & Society* 30, no. 1 (2015): 30–43.

Martin, Patricia Yancey, and Robert A. Hummer. "Fraternities and Rape on Campus." *Gender & Society* 3, no. 4 (1989): 457–473.

Messner, Michael A. "Bad Men, Good Men, Bystanders: Who Is the Rapist?" *Gender & Society* 30, no. 1 (2015): 57-66.

Minow, Jacqueline Chevalier, and Christopher J. Einolf. "Sorority Participation and Sexual Assault Risk." *Violence Against Women* 15, no. 7 (2009): 835–851.

Monson, Candice M., Jennifer Langhinrichsen-Rohling, and Tisha Binderup. "Does 'No' Really Mean 'No' After You Say 'Yes'?: Attributions About Date and Marital Rape." *Journal of Interpersonal Violence* 15, no. 11 (2000): 1156–1174.

Murnen, Sarah K., and Marla H. Kohlman. "Athletic Participation, Fraternity Membership, and Sexual Aggression Among College Men: A Meta-Analytic Review." *Sex Roles* 57, no. 1–2 (2007): 145–157.

Osman, Suzanne L. "Predicting Rape Empathy Based on Victim, Perpetrator, and Participant Gender, and History of Sexual Aggression." *Sex Roles* 64, no. 7–8 (2011): 506–515.

O'Sullivan, Chris S. "Acquaintance Gang Rape on Campus." In *Acquaintance Rape: The Hidden Crime*, edited by Andrea Parrot and Laurie Bechhofer, 140–156. New York: Wiley, 1991.

——. "Ladykillers: Similarities and Divergences of Masculinities in Gang Rape and Wife Battery." In *Masculinities and Violence*, edited by Lee H. Bowker, 82–110. Thousand Oaks, CA: Sage. 1998.

Pascoe, C. J., and Jocelyn A. Hollander. "Good Guys Don't Rape: Gender, Domination, and Mobilizing Rape." *Gender & Society* 30, no. 1 (2015): 67–79.

Porter, Judy Lee and LaVerne McQuiller-Williams. "Intimate Violence Among Underrepresented Groups on a College Campus." *Journal of Interpersonal Violence* 26, no. 16 (2011): 3210–3224.

Sanday, Peggy Reeves. *Fraternity Gang Rape: Sex, Brotherhood, and Privilege on Campus*. New York: New York University Press, 1990.

——. (2004). "Rape-Prone Versus Rape-Free Campus Cultures." In *Sexualities: Identities, Behaviors, and Society*, edited by Michael S. Kimmel & Rebecca F. Plant, 428–437. New York, NY: Oxford University Press, 2004.

Schewe, Paul A., Najma M. Adam, and Kathryn M. Ryan. "A Qualitative Analysis of the Temptation to Use Force in Sexual Relationships." *Violence and Victims* 24, no. 2 (2009): 219–231.

Stein, Jerrold L. "Peer Educators and Close Friends as Predictors of Male College Students' Willingness to Prevent Rape." *Journal of College Student Development* 48, no. 1 (2007): 75–89.

Stombler, Mindy. "'Buddies' or 'Slutties': The Collective Sexual Reputation of Fraternity Little Sisters." *Gender & Society* 8, no. 3 (1994): 297–323.

Suarez, Eliana, and Tahany M. Gadalla. "Stop Blaming the Victim: A Meta-Analysis on Rape Myths." *Journal of Interpersonal Violence* 25, no. 11 (2010): 2010–2035.

Vonderhaar, Rebecca L., and Dianne Cyr Carmody. "There Are No 'Innocent Victims': The Influence of Just World Beliefs and Prior Victimization on Rape Myth Acceptance." *Journal of Interpersonal Violence* 30, no. 10 (2015): 1615–1632.